One hundred and twenty-five copies of this first
edition are bound in three-quarter leather.

Numbers 1–100 are Sponsors' and Collectors' copies
and numbers 101–125 are presentation copies.

Donors' and Subscribers' copies are fully
bound in skivertex and gold blocked.

PIETERMARITZBURG

1838 – 1988

PIETERMARITZBURG

1838 – 1988

A new portrait
of an African city

Edited by

JOHN LABAND   and
ROBERT HASWELL

 **University of Natal Press**
AND
Shuter & Shooter

Co-published by

University of Natal Press
P.O. Box 375
Pietermaritzburg 3201

and

Shuter & Shooter (Pty) Ltd
Gray's Inn, 230 Church Street
Pietermaritzburg 3201

First edition 1988

ISBN 0 86980 639 4

Set in 10 on 11 pt Century
Printed by The Natal Witness (Pty) Ltd, Pietermaritzburg
3973L

Contents

Acknowledgements *J. Laband and R. Haswell* xiii

Foreword *C. de B. Webb* xv

Introduction *J. Laband and R. Haswell* xvii

Recasting the portrait of Pietermaritzburg
        J. Laband xxiii

CHAPTER ONE

The Setting

The living environment
        M. Brett 2
The physical environment
        O. McGee 6
  Fog or smog?
        O. McGee 10
  Flooding of the Dorpspruit
        W. Bizley 11
  'cloudburst over machibise'
        dikobe wa mogale 11
  Floods
        O. McGee 11

CHAPTER TWO

Before White Settlement

Pietermaritzburg: the first 2 000 000 years
        T. Maggs 14
Before Mgungundlovu: the upper Mngeni and upper
Mkhomazi region in the early nineteenth century
        J. Wright 18

CHAPTER THREE

The Making of the City

Pieter Mauritz Burg: the genesis of a
Voortrekker *hoofdplaats*
        R. Haswell 24

Pieter Mauritz Burg
  R. Haswell   26
The Church of the Vow
  A. Labuschagne   28
Pietermaritzburg and its environs: the early decades of
 white settlement
  B. Ellis   29
The segregated city
  T. Wills   33
Pietermaritzburg's coat of arms   34
The place of the elephants?
  A. Koopman   44

CHAPTER FOUR

The Face of the City

'A bad row of teeth'? Pietermaritzburg's architecture
  M. Hillebrand   48
Of bricks and bonds
  A. Duigan   52
Architecture: the new amidst the old
  H. Fransen   53
The Pietermaritzburg Town Hall
  M. Hillebrand   54
Parks and gardens
  D. McCracken   59
Tales trees tell
  K. Jones   63

CHAPTER FIVE

The Inner and Outer City

Edendale, 1851–1930: farmers to townspeople,
 market to labour reserve
  S. Meintjes   66
Vulindlela
  N. Bromberger   71
Growing up in Loop Street
  B. Spencer   75
Nineteenth-century Loop Street
  S. Spencer   77

Servants in the 1920s and 1930s
W. Bizley 80
Sobantu Village
H. Peel 82
140 years of family ties with Pietermaritzburg
H. W. Ahrens 84

CHAPTER SIX

Capital City

Colonial capital
J. Benyon 86
Government House
T. Frost 88
Colonial capital to provincial centre, 1904–1912
J. Raybould........................... 90
The old Natal Parliament
G. Dominy 93
Royal visitors
R. Gordon 94
Royal visits
W. Bizley 95
Legal centre of Natal
P. Spiller 96
The trial of Langalibalele
W. Guest.............................. 97
Gandhi's admission as an advocate
H. Seedat 99

CHAPTER SEVEN

Maritzburg and the Military

Fort Napier: the imperial base that shaped the City
G. Dominy and H. Paterson 102
The City laager, 1879
P. Thompson.......................... 106
The glitter of the garrison
H. Paterson 108
Regiments in garrison at Fort Napier, 1843–1914
G. Dominy 109
Three camps of World War II
J. Deane 110

The Natal Carbineers and Pietermaritzburg

  M. Coghlan and H. Paterson   114

What's in a name?

  M. Coghlan   117

Sweat and fun

  M. Coghlan   118

CHAPTER EIGHT

Economic Hub of the Midlands

Economic development of the capital city, 1838–1910

  W. Guest   120

The economic depression of the 1860s

  J. Parle   124

The Great Depression and white unemployment

  D. Owen and J. Sellers   129

The Pietermaritzburg market and the transformation of
the Natal Midlands in the colonial period

  J. Lambert   130

Unemployment in Pietermaritzburg, 1986

  N. Bromberger   134

The coming of the railway to Pietermaritzburg

  B. Martin   135

From rickshaws to minibus taxis

  T. Wills   138

Pietermaritzburg and the railway

  W. Bizley   139

African reaction to the beer halls

  P. du Plooy   142

Industrialization, 1838–1987

  C. Torino   144

The Royal Show

  R. Gordon   146

CHAPTER NINE

Educational Capital

Educational capital of white Natal

  S. Vietzen   150

Teacher education

  T. Frost   152

An appraisal of black education in the Pietermaritzburg
   area, 1987
                D. Lawrance   155
         City of libraries
                J. Verbeek   156
The University of Natal and Pietermaritzburg
                J. Sellers   157
The Natal Museum
                B. Stuckenberg   160
The Voortrekker Museum
                I. Pols   163

CHAPTER TEN

City of Diverse Faiths

World religions in Pietermaritzburg
                I. Darby and P. Maxwell   166
         The controversy surrounding Bishop Colenso
                I. Darby   174
         Pietermaritzburg cemeteries
                R. Haswell   176
The Roman Catholic centres
                J. Brain   179

CHAPTER ELEVEN

Health in the City

Grey's Hospital
                A. Rose   182
Mental health in colonial Pietermaritzburg
                G. Fouché   186
         Midlands Hospital
                G. Fouché   188
Edendale Hospital
                D. Robbins   189
         Northdale Hospital
                L. Dwarkapersad   191
Infectious diseases in Pietermaritzburg
                J. Brain   193

CHAPTER TWELVE

Politics and Protest

The Pietermaritzburg voter and parliamentary elections
    P. Thompson 198
Liberals in Pietermaritzburg
    P. Brown 200
Gandhi: the Pietermaritzburg experience
    H. Seedat 201
The *Natal Witness* and 'Open Testimony'
    B. Leverton 202
The freedom of the Press
    R. Steyn 205
Afrikaners in Pietermaritzburg: cultural patterns and
political awareness
    P. Prinsloo 206
Dr E. G. Jansen
    P. Prinsloo 207
Opposing apartheid in the Pietermaritzburg region
    P. Brown and J. Aitchison 209
The University and political protest
    D. Schreiner 212
Mrs E. E. Russell and the role of Pietermaritzburg
women in public life
    P. Merrett 213
'I remember Mr Gandhi'
    R. Haswell 217
Governing Pietermaritzburg
    R. Lawrence 218
'echo sounds in maritzburg'
    M. Mkhize 219
Background to political violence in the Pietermaritzburg
region, 1987–8
    J. Wright 221

CHAPTER THIRTEEN

Arts and Entertainment

The performing arts
    M. Lambert 224
The Christy Minstrels
    M. Lambert 227

Charles Lascelles Grey
  J. Mitchell 230
The Tatham Art Gallery
  L. Ferguson 231
'Sleepy Hollow?'
  G. Candy 234
Afrikaans authors of Pietermaritzburg
  W. Jonckheere 235
'Sinjale'
  D. J. Opperman 236
Alan Paton and Pietermaritzburg
  C. Gardiner 237
Cinema and theatre in the 1920s and 1930s
  W. Bizley 238
The Imperial Hotel
  A. Labuschagne 239
The pubs of Pietermaritzburg
  N. Ogilvie 240

CHAPTER FOURTEEN

Sport and Recreation

The Sporty Hollow!
  R. Haswell 244
Problems of black sport in an apartheid city
  C. Merrett 246
Aurora Cricket Club
  C. Merrett 248
The Comrades Marathon
  M. Coghlan 251
Herman's Delight
  M. Coghlan 252
The Duzi Canoe Marathon
  M. Coghlan 254
Clubs and societies
  A. Rose 257
The Maritzburg Croquet Club
  P. Murgatroyd 259
Motor racing
  W. Bizley 260

CHAPTER FIFTEEN

Building the Future

Architectural conservation: the challenge
      H. Davies 262
Pietermaritzburg red brick: then and now
      A. Duigan 265
Towards a new Pietermaritzburg
      R. Haswell 266

List of Sponsors, Donors and Subscribers 271

List of Contributors 273

Select list of sources 275

Sources of illustrations 279

Index 280

List of maps

Africa, showing position of Pietermaritzburg	xvi
Pietermaritzburg and environs: ecological zones	4
Archaeological sites in and around the City	12, 16, 17
Chiefdoms in the Pietermaritzburg area before 1819	18
Upper Mngeni-Upper Mkhomazi region in the 1830s	19
Plan of Pietermaritzburg by C. Piers and H. Cloete, 1845	22
Plan of Pietermaritzburg by Alex Mair, 1870	34
Pietermaritzburg and its environs, 1988	37
Three camps of World War II	110
Durban–Pietermaritzburg railway, 1880	137
Pietermaritzburg: industrial areas, 1988	146
Map of Pietermaritzburg by D. Seccadanari, 1906	268

Acknowledgements

One of the happiest aspects of the preparation of this book — which began some three years ago — has been the warmth and friendliness shown us by all the people who have become involved. Everyone we have approached in our search for material has responded with enthusiasm for the project, and hospitality and helpfulness towards ourselves. We are indeed grateful for this readiness to assist, for advice and encouragement offered and for the spontaneous generosity with which writers, photographers and copyright-holders have provided material without asking for payment. We hope the sense of helping to create a lasting tribute to our City is as rewarding for all of them as it is for us.

Without the writers there could not have been a book at all, and it is fitting that we should thank them first. Then we must thank the many people who helped us in our search for photographs and illustrations — individuals and organizations are listed on page 279. We are also grateful to the *Natal Witness* for publishing our appeal for photographs and to the people who responded, even though we were not able to use all the pictures that were offered. For permission to include items that had been published elsewhere we are indebted to:

Ad Donker for the poem by dikobe wa mogale;

The family of Mlungise Mhkize for his poem 'echo sounds in maritzburg';

Mr Jock Leyden for the cartoons on pages 40 and 210;

The Editorial Board of *Natalia: the Journal of the Natal Society* for extracts from William Bizley's article, 'Pietermaritzburg: the missing decades', which originally appeared in *Natalia* 17, 1987;

The Ridge Women's Institute for the map of the Alexandra Road motor racing circuit;

Tafelberg Publishers for D.J.Opperman's poem 'Sinjale'.

As the text and illustrations were assembled, we became increasingly grateful to our publishers who brought order and shape to the work. Here we particularly thank Jo-Anne Goodwill for her critical editing and John Sharpe for his design and lay-out. They and their colleagues at Shuter & Shooter and the University of Natal Press have advised and guided us, and given us an abundance of tea and encouragement. The deepest thanks of all are due to Margery Moberly of the University Press. Without her initiatives and direction at every stage our labours would not have come to fruition.

A book such as this is an enormously costly undertaking. We are most grateful for the faith in this project shown by the sponsors, donors and subscribers, and, above all, the City Council of Pietermaritzburg. Their investment has made it possible to offer this book at a lower price than would otherwise have been possible. The publishers join us in thanking the *Natal Witness* for entering into the spirit of the Pietermaritzburg project by offering to print this book at a generous discount.

Our wives and families also deserve our gratitude. They have shown the greatest forbearance during the long period when this book has absorbed so much of our energy and attention.

Finally a word of thanks to the people of Pietermaritzburg — past and present — to whom this book is affectionately dedicated. It has been a rare privilege for us to have had the opportunity to give them back their past and to interpret the present. The future — and all that it holds — is theirs.

JOHN LABAND
ROBERT HASWELL

Orthographic note

Modern orthographic practice has been adopted in the spelling of Zulu names. Thus the familiar Umzinduzi has given way to Msunduze, and Umgeni to Mngeni. Similarly, the modern spelling of place-names has been preferred, so that in text and maps we have Swartkop rather than Zwartkops. As the counties into which the Colony of Natal was divided in the nineteenth century have disappeared, the spelling of their names has not been affected. On the other hand, when the original spelling of a name has become corrupted over the years we have chosen to use the original form: thus we refer to Ortmann, although city street signs give Ohrtmann. In all quotations the spelling used by the original writer has been retained.

Foreword

'The disadvantage of men not knowing the past is that they do not know the present.' So wrote G. K. Chesterton. He might have added that the less people understand of the present the more limited is their ability to think constructively into the future.

It is awareness of that vital continuum between past, present and future that is reflected in this admirable new work on the City of Pietermaritzburg. Planned and edited by an historian and a geographer, the book is more than a nostalgic journey into the past or a self-congratulatory celebration of what the City now offers. Not that these aspects of its being have been neglected! On the contrary, as one turns the pages of the book one gains, very strongly, a sense of the charm of what was, and of the good things that now are. But one also gains more, for through the richly varied contributions which the editors have brought together, the reader is led forward to a deepened understanding of the forces that have made the City what it is, and of the potential that it has as a place for people in the future.

These are the qualities that distinguish this work as a truly worthy contribution to the commemoration of Pietermaritzburg's one hundred and fifty years. The identification of the University of Natal with that contribution is a matter for pride, for it serves as an example of research and learning being put to the service of the community.

The editors, the authors, indeed all who have assisted in the making of this book are to be congratulated on a splendid and most valuable achievement.

C. DE B. WEBB

Vice-Principal
University of Natal, Pietermaritzburg

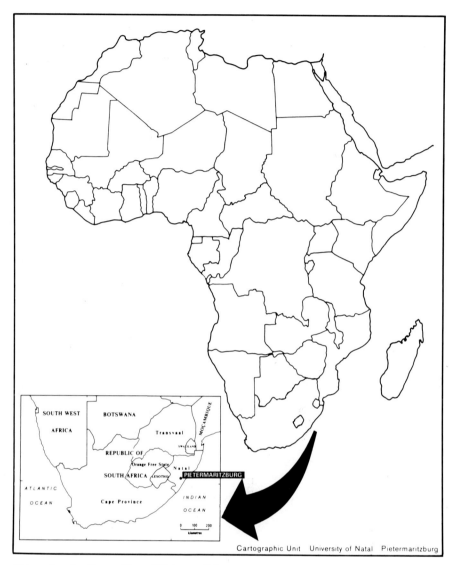

Africa, showing the position of Pietermaritzburg.

Introduction

JOHN LABAND
ROBERT HASWELL

'PIETERMARITZBURG the lovely city', Alan Paton hailed it. So it remains for countless others, whether they too were born and brought up within the same basin of hills, or whether they came to make their homes here only later in their lives. Paton regretted, though, that as a young person he knew little of the realities of the place where he lived; and certainly even less of the thousands of black people on the periphery of the white man's city or beyond those encircling hills, people who were nevertheless an integral part of its being. He was not alone in these derelictions, which so many others still share, and which this book hopes to redress.

The celebration of a sesquicentennial is an apt moment for any society to reflect on its history, on the stage it has reached, and on what it aspires to be. That it could also be a moment for constructing idealized images of its past, for smoothing over the faults of the present and projecting unrealistic hopes for the future, should be resisted. This book sets out, therefore, to present a critical portrait of 150 years of a city in Africa, founded by white settlers very conscious of their European roots, but today the home of peoples of diverse colours, faiths and heritages, all seeking to secure acceptance and opportunities in the place where they make their living. That 1988 is not so much a time of rejoicing, as one of deep divisions and tragic violence within many of the City's communities, underscores the need for a sound appreciation of how such contentions have arisen, and how far they have been moulded by Pietermaritzburg's own past.

When we began to plan this book, it was our intention to cover as wide a field as possible, though we never presumed to aim at absolute completeness. It was obvious from the outset that adequate and recent research was still required into any number of the topics we considered

Three views south-east across central Pietermaritzburg with Table Mountain in the distance, from the end of the 19th century until today: *c.*1895, from below the present suburb of Clarendon[1]. The tower of the first City Hall dominates the cityscape. *c.*1960, from Villiers Drive, Clarendon[2]. Although the centre of the City was then considerably more built up than only a few decades earlier, the tower of the present City Hall had still to be dwarfed by high-rise buildings. 1988, from the air over Clarendon[3]. The City Hall is now quite lost among the towering structures of the modern City.

significant. Besides, some experts were not prepared for political or personal reasons to commit their findings to print, or were prevented in terms of the emergency regulations from doing so. Such constraints mean that our book cannot be as comprehensive as we might have wished. Nor can it be as definitive, for even the most satisfying of contributions only suggests further avenues for exploration; while new perspectives appear as rapidly as the political kaleidoscope shifts or the physical fabric of the City is transformed, and change must inevitably outpace the preparation of the book.

The problem of selection is complicated enough in the preparation of any publication, let alone in one of this complexity and scope. Here it is exacerbated by political considerations. Let the section on sport provide sufficient indication of the difficulties encountered. A great number of sporting activities take place in Pietermaritzburg. Some, like the Comrades Marathon, are of very special significance to the City, and require appropriate coverage. In the interests of balance, though, and because there are already published works on the event, this should not be done at the expense of others less celebrated. Yet only a few, such as the Comrades, have been sufficiently researched to warrant articles in their own right; while merely to list other sports about which we know considerably less would do nothing to further understanding of sport as a whole in Pietermaritzburg. Analysis, nevertheless, in a realm as delicate as that of sport in South Africa today, creates problems of its own. It is as possible, for example, to sing the praises of the City's white sporting greats (and to enthuse over its sporting facilities), as it is to deprecate the fate of those sportsmen who have been discriminated against because of their colour, and to advocate confrontation and sporting boycotts as the best means of remedying the situation. Which approach should the editors adopt? Since, at this stage, ethnocentricism and ideological commitment make any generally acceptable synthesis difficult to achieve, we have settled for a presentation of conflicting approaches, in the hope that by doing so we have facilitated the evolution of an at least more balanced grasp of the problem.

The inevitable but regrettable consequence of our difficulties must be as apparent to the reader as to us: there are gaps we should all have liked to have seen filled; and distortions of perspective we would have preferred to have had corrected. Our hope can only be that our efforts, where they have fallen short, will spur on others to greater endeavours in pursuit of the still elusive goal of a complete and universally acceptable portrait of Pietermaritzburg.

Nor can we pretend that our book has been illustrated exactly as once we envisaged it should. Here too, as with the text, part of the fault lies with the material. While the last few decades of the nineteenth century

The changing face of the Church Street–Commercial Road intersection and environs between 1858 and 1988: By 1858 Church Street was lined by both Voortrekker and British buildings[4]. A portion of the Raadsaal and the Presbyterian Church stand out on the left of the street, while on the right shops give way to a row of Voortrekker houses shaded by oak trees. Syringa trees are in the foreground, and the water furrows on either side of the street can be made out. Note the dress of the people and the means of transport. A view up Church Street in the late 1880s[5]. The Raadsaal and the Presbyterian Church still stand, though the Market Hall now faces the Supreme Court across Commercial Road. By c.1895 the first City Hall was presiding over the intersection across the way from the familiar landmarks of the Presbyterian Church and the Anglo-Zulu War memorial[6]. The second -and taller- City Hall dominates this view taken c.1960[7]. The market Hall to the far left is largely over-shadowed. Today, the Natal Society Library and the City Hall make strikingly different architectural statements[8].

and the first of the twentieth were covered extensively by the photographer, later decades (especially those between the two World Wars) seem to have been relatively ignored. Perhaps this is only apparent, since people have yet to donate their photographs to public collections or to make them otherwise available. The consequence, nevertheless, is that there is not the richness of choice among scenes of later Pietermaritzburg (despite photographs especially commissioned for this book) as there is for the earlier period. The temptation has therefore arisen to over-illustrate the colonial period at the expense of more recent times, and this is aggravated by the extreme difficulty today of finding views of historic buildings and central streetscapes which are not obscured by the unsightly clutter of traffic-lights, neon signs, electric wires, parking meters and all the other equally ugly features of the modern city. Then, for the sake of variety, photographs have been leavened with the far scarcer drawings and paintings of Pietermaritzburg. In any case, space for illustrations in a publication, no matter how lavish, is limited. These considerations have combined to demand strict selection, which has entailed the rejection of literally hundreds of wonderful photographs, as well as numbers of intriguing pictures. In the end only those which make a significant statement of their own, or underline a vital point in the text, have been retained.

Those illustrations ultimately chosen have generally had the additional attribute of containing visual landmarks to help orientate the reader as the scene changes through the years. If there seems to be too much of a concentration on the city centre, this is not simply because it is the best documented part of Pietermaritzburg, but because it is the most readily recognizable, and therefore the most effective window onto a city in the process of transformation. Indeed, it is this sense of change that the pictures are intended to emphasize — changes not only in buildings, vehicles and people's clothes, but in the general aspect of the City as it progresses from a straggling settlement of white pioneers, through self-important decades as a prim colonial capital, until it becomes a teeming modern city whose face is unmistakably African.

The enduring symbol of the City, shown here on a postcard of 1909.

Recasting the portrait of Pietermaritzburg

JOHN LABAND

WRITTEN WORKS on Pietermaritzburg have fallen, until recently, into two broad categories: descriptive guides which seek to attract tourists and capitalist enterprise to the City; and more personal essays which attempt to portray the full sweep of its history. There are considerably more of the former class than the latter, for while there have been dozens of booklets, pamphlets, brochures and chapters in guidebooks devoted to Pietermaritzburg between 1895 and the present, only four full-length histories have appeared from the first in 1898 to the latest in 1981. A feature of almost all these works is that the emphasis is on the growth of the white community, and its achievements and potential, and that scant mention is made of the blacks, coloureds and Indians who are equally part of the City.

J. Forsyth Ingram, in his chapter on Pietermaritzburg in *The Colony of Natal: an Official Illustrated Handbook and Railway Guide* (London, 1895), set the pattern for the purely descriptive guidebook. A brief general description of the City is followed by an account of the history of the settlement under the Boers, and then under the British. Next come sections on municipal and commercial history, the water supply, statistics on population, number of houses, rateable value of property, and building activity. Ingram then describes public buildings and monuments, and educational institutions such as the Natal Museum and Maritzburg College. Benefit societies as well as newspapers are considered, and there is much emphasis on local industrial development, the Agricultural Show and banks. Blacks seem to play no part in this white colonial capital, and Ingram's only reference to them is a passing description of Edendale Mission and approval of the 'loyalty of Natal Christianized Natives'. Clearly, the City was to be presented as an attractive place for whites to live and prosper.

Art in the Park: one of the popular occasions
usually singled out in literature publicizing
the City.

C. W. Francis Harrison (compiler and editor), *Natal: an Illustrated Official Railway Guide and Handbook of General Information* (London, 1903), is just what it purports to be. The chapter on Pietermaritzburg leans heavily on Ingram's earlier work, but has good maps and illustrations, and provides more information on the general attractions and recreational possibilities of the City. There is not even a nod towards the black population in this straightforward description of white Pietermaritzburg just after the Second Anglo-Boer War. *Twentieth Century Impressions of Natal: its People, Commerce, Industries and Resources* (Natal, 1906) is a much more lavish production. Cased in leather, it is filled with photographs, especially of buildings and white notables. Two chapters are devoted entirely to Pietermaritzburg, while others on the judiciary, education and so on, make considerable reference to the City. The first chapter follows what was already the set pattern, though specific institutions like the Natal Society Library and the Botanic Gardens are allowed more space. There is recognition of new developments like the expanding white suburbs and fairly lengthy biographies of the Mayor and his Councillors. The chapter on 'Commercial Pietermaritzburg' consists solely of more biographical sketches —this time of prominent businessmen — and descriptions of their businesses. In this celebration of white commercial enterprise the blacks are quite ignored. They appear in a chapter of their own elsewhere in the book, where the 'Ethnologist' W. A. Squire concludes:

> The future of the Kafir is a very serious problem . . . He is thriftless, thoughtless of the future, lazy and independent, his sole thought being of food and drink for himself. He is a tough nut for the political economist to crack.

The last of this particular genre was A. H. Tatlow (editor), *Natal Province: Descriptive Guide and Official Hand-book* (Durban, 1911). With its chapter describing white Pietermaritzburg's amenities, it adds nothing new.

Yet at that moment a new type of guidebook literature was evolving, which devoted entire booklets and brochures to describing the attractions of Pietermaritzburg. Such a one was the well-illustrated *Pietermaritzburg: Tourist, Residential, Educational and Health Resort. Official Illustrated Guide Book* (Johannesburg, 1912), compiled by the General Manager of the Railways and the Pietermaritzburg Corporation. For a city suffering from the consequences of its loss of status following Union, it is an attempt to attract new white citizens with glowing descriptions of its many advantages. In similar vein is S. Ambler Evans (compiler), *Maritzburg for Business and Pleasure* (1915), which misleadingly describes the City as the business centre of Natal and the 'Riviera of South Africa'!

J. Forsyth Ingram, the first historian to write a
book on Pietermaritzburg.

This type of appeal has persisted. It is very explicit in the illustrated and descriptive brochure *Pietermaritzburg: the Capital of Natal* (Durban, 1929), whose stated aim is to 'place before the visitor the splendid opportunities Pietermaritzburg affords for Holiday, Residential, Educational, Commercial and Industrial purposes'. Naturally, such guides run the danger of becoming boringly bland catalogues of basic information. Such is the Publicity Society's *Pietermaritzburg: the Progressive Capital of Natal* (1934), and its updated successor of 1941. The tradition holds good in publicity booklets up to the present, with essentially the same type of superficial material being brought up to date in an increasingly sophisticated layout. The process can be followed in *City of Flowers and Progressive Capital of Natal South Africa* (1949), which was obviously aimed at Commonwealth immigrants, through *Pietermaritzburg, Capital of Natal: the City of Flowers* (1963), *Pietermaritzburg for the Visitor: City of Beauty and History* (1970), to *Pietermaritzburg: City of Beauty and History* (1984).

The black population plays little part in this type of publication, except as an element in the population statistics. When it is mentioned it is but in two contexts: that of labour or the picturesque. The publicity pamphlet of 1947 refers enticingly to 'a plentiful supply of labour at reasonable rates of pay'; while *The City of Pietermaritzburg* (Johannesburg, 1968), which is a booklet promoting various industries and industrial potential, only describes blacks as being 'close and accessible' to industrial areas. *Your Future Lies in Pietermaritzburg* (1972), a Publicity Association pamphlet on prices and salaries, includes a section on domestic servants and going wages.

A common feature of all this ephemeral literature, which would attract whites to settle in Pietermaritzburg, is its highly complimentary (if not complacent) attitude towards the City. There is never any suggestion that conditions might not be desirable in every way. This is why the article by G. H. Calpin, 'History of Pietermaritzburg', in *Pieter-maritzburg 1838–1938: Centenary Souvenir Hand-Book* (Pieter-maritzburg, 1938) comes as such a refreshing surprise, especially when the occasion of its publication is taken into account. Calpin deplores the isolation, conservatism and economic reversal of the City 'envious of younger and more prosperous neighbours on the Coast'. This note of the recessional was not to be echoed in the future by the Publicity Association, though in 1974 the Natal Midlands Region of the Black Sash put out a pamphlet entitled *This is Your City . . . Pietermaritzburg 1974*. It is quite different from anything else in the field. Through the use of well-researched comparative figures arranged by race on wages, housing, health services, schooling, recreation, cemeteries, and so on, it

4

Prof. Alan F. Hattersley, whose pioneering works on
Pietermaritzburg and the British settlers are now
acknowledged classics. He is shown here with a painting of
the emigrant ship *Haidee*, which brought 216 settlers from
the East Riding of Yorkshire to Natal in October 1850.

shows in stark terms the discrepancies between the opportunities and facilities enjoyed by the different races living in Pietermaritzburg. It is an effective indictment of the effects, in material terms, of the implications of the policy of separate development for the City. One must suppose that it was not a publication which the Publicity Association readily handed out to prospective tourists and industrialists!

The purpose of all the works mentioned here is to describe Pietermaritzburg, and the reader turns to them for specific details about buildings, institutions and personalities of the white City. The lack of the hand of a single historian with a unique vision of the City's essence is evident. Only three historians have devoted entire books to the subject.

The first was J. Forsyth Ingram, with *The Story of an African City* (Maritzburg, 1898). He speculated, probably accurately, that 'but few persons in Maritzburg have ever accorded to the history of the City more than a passing thought'. Yet in attempting to remedy this lapse, Ingram presents a straightforward descriptive account, not very different from his earlier chapter in *The Colony of Natal*. Even so, he does have a theme: the celebration of 'courage, endurance and determination' exercised by 'daring pioneers' in founding a city 'in the wilds of Africa'. It is, moreover, 'the story of men's lives spent bravely and generously in the cause of advancement and civilization'.

This stirring affirmation of the high Victorian sense of the white man's mission was not repeated nearly so vehemently in the next book — after a lapse of forty years — to deal exclusively with Pietermaritzburg. But it was there, nevertheless. Alan F. Hattersley's centenary volume, *Pietermaritzburg Panorama: a Study of One Hundred Years of an African City* (Pietermaritzburg, 1938), is still the best book ever written on the City. A pleasure to read and a mine of information, it is based on thorough research into contemporary books, memoirs, municipal records and newspapers. It follows the development of the City from its foundation by the Voortrekkers, through the colonial era and into the twentieth century. In other words, it is the elegantly constructed story of white Pietermaritzburg, full of fascinating details, excellent vignettes and memorable anecdotes. But if Hattersley is full of sympathy for the trials and triumphs of the settlers, he has barely a mention for the blacks. For this reason, Hattersley's vision is not far removed from Ingram's. Yet his tremendous sense of empathy for the settlers and their achievements, his feelings of nostalgia for their way of life, are a positive force and give life to his second Pietermaritzburg book, *Portrait of a City* (Pietermaritzburg, 1951). Rather than being about the progress of the City itself, which he dealt with in 1938, it is about people, a 'chronicle of the domestic affairs' and the 'solid material achievement' of the 'simple, kindly men and women of the settler type'. In attempting to bring them

Dr Ruth Gordon, whose many popular
writings and talks have done much to
promote a wide awareness and enjoyment of
the City's history.

to life, Hattersley sets out 'to convey some sense of the quiet charm [of] scenes that are gone forever' from a modern Pietermaritzburg. Besides taking a last fond glance at the vanished world of the settlers, he also attempts to lay the ghost of English-Afrikaner conflict by emphasizing the common legacy of the 'fellow-settlers'. The blacks still remain outside the charmed ring held by the colonizing races, and are dismissed with the patronizing reflection (in connection with the creation of Sobantu Village) that 'Pietermaritzburg has done not a little for its Bantu population'.

The elegiac colonial fragrance lingers on in the most recent book on Pietermaritzburg, though it is open to more contemporary concerns. Ruth Gordon, *The Place of the Elephant: a History of Pietermaritzburg* (Pietermaritzburg, 1981), is still essentially a book of white social history, with the emphasis on important settler personalities, distinguished visitors and social gatherings. There is indeed an appreciation of the Indian community, and of Edendale and Sobantu. But the focus is, as it has ever been, on white Pietermaritzburg before Union. Yet if little new ground is broken, then the work is so infused with a passionate love of Pietermaritzburg, a vivid sense of its origins and a faith in its future, that is must stand as a real contribution to the literature.

Increasingly, however, the complexity of modern Pietermaritzburg, and the difficulty a single author encounters in coming to terms with it, has meant that the tendency has been towards composite works by a number of authors. Naturally, there is still room for individual endeavour, but in that case the topic has been confined to an aspect of the wider field. Hattersley blazed the trail with, for example, his *A Hospital Century: Grey's Hospital Pietermaritzburg, 1855–1955* (Cape Town, 1955), and *The Victoria Club, Pietermaritzburg, 1859–1959* (Cape Town, 1959). Ruth Gordon has followed his lead with her full and detailed account of *Natal's Royal Show* (Pietermaritzburg, 1984). Academic writers, like Melanie Hillebrand and J. André Labuschagne, have concentrated on Pietermaritzburg's architecture; while the artist Mat Louwrens, with a text by Ruth Gordon, has portrayed the buildings of the colonial era in *Victorian Pietermaritzburg* (Springfield, 1984). Yet more representative of the recent trend is the booklet edited by Ivor Daniel and Robert Brusse, *Pietermaritzburg* (Pietermaritzburg, 1977), which is a well-illustrated collection of authoritative articles on aspects of the City's architecture and the ways of enjoying it.

This does not mean, however, that the composite approach necessarily results in a new and modern appreciation of the subject. The Ridge Women's Institute's *Annals of the Scottsville Area* (May 1984) is a case in point. Although exhibiting the advantages of a multiple yet integrated venture, it nevertheless is very traditional in its detailed account of the development in the area of clubs, schools, institutions, churches, the aerodrome and so on. In comparison, the Supplement to the *Natal Mercury*, 17 October 1938: *Pietermaritzburg, 1838–1938*, though so much earlier, is more up to date. It is a collection of articles by many contributors on aspects of Pietermaritzburg, with a particular emphasis on social history. Not surprisingly for its period, it has nothing on the black population. More recently, on 2 August 1977, the *Natal Witness* ran a similar supplement: *Pietermaritzburg: Know Your City*. A collection of articles on familiar themes, it at least includes one on 'The City's Three African Townships', so coming partially to terms with the realities of Pietermaritzburg's diversity. Entirely contemporary in its concerns is the booklet *Pietermaritzburg in Profile, 1987*, compiled by members of the Natal Midlands Region of the Black Sash and the Pietermaritzburg Agency for Christian Social Awareness, and edited by V. S. and K. Harris. In this study of housing, employment, public transport, education, health services, law enforcement and sport, the emphasis is on the unequal opportunities and amenities enjoyed by the different races living in a typical apartheid city. The perspective is that of those who are discriminated against, and white local government and institutions are brought under critical review.

Pietermaritzburg in Profile 1987 is indicative of the path writing about Pietermaritzburg is tending to take. The multiplying facets of the City's life — both in the past and the present — which the endeavours of the researchers are exposing, require the attention of experts in multiple specialist domains. Composite authorship thus seems unavoidable in the future, even if it does entail the sacrifice of the personal voice of a Hattersley. At the same time, there is an insistently growing awareness that Pietermaritzburg is not just the City of the white settlers of the nineteenth century and their descendants, but of *all* the people who make their homes here and work for its prosperity. Consequently, the part played by black people in the City's life will increasingly receive the just attention that has been denied it in so many works published in the past.

The present book, inevitably, cannot pretend to present the last word on Pietermaritzburg. If previous works lack balance and comprehensiveness, so must this, despite the spirit in which it was undertaken. As wide an awareness as possible has been brought to it, a consciousness of new avenues of enquiry, a revisionist intention. Yet many rich veins of potential interest and significance remain unexplored, either because they have still to be researched, or because, in the divided and repressive conditions of our time, some specialists are reluctant to share their knowledge. Nevertheless, the net has been flung sufficiently wide for the holes to be obvious, and this is in itself of value. For it is only through discovering what has still to be known, through perceiving what has yet to be modified, that understanding can be extended. If this book achieves only that, if it proves merely a useful tool in the hands of those recasting Pietermaritzburg's portrait in the years to come, then it will have succeeded in its intention.

6

Early morning in Change Lane
in the 1960s.

'Maritzburg from the drift of the Little Bushmans
River [Msunduze]. Fort Napier on the left,' *c.*1850.

Pietermaritzburg
from the Town Hill, *c.*1890.

CHAPTER ONE

The Setting

The living environment

Michael Brett

From my study window, situated a mere 12 km north of the City's edge, I hear the shrill whistle of the reedbuck cut through the darkness of night. Down in the vlei below the house the jackal's eerie call moves on the night breeze, and all is still. Other animals live in the tall grasses of the vlei and the dense bush of the hills, but they are known only from fleeting glimpses on the long road home at night: the bushpig, bushbuck, blue and grey duiker, genet and mongoose.

The yellow light of dawn exposes a party of four oribi on the hillside above the vlei. Down-valley, black eagles and lanner falcons frequent the sheer cliffs of the Mngeni gorge. And on Sundays a fish eagle leaves the motorboat-congested waters of Albert Falls Dam, and circles slowly overhead.

While the variety of wildlife still present on farmland surrounding the City is surprising, few people are aware that wild animals still exist within the City's confines. In the plantations to the west and north of the city centre, bushpig, monkey, bushbuck, duiker, porcupine, genet and mongoose are common.

One of my favourite spots is the Ferncliffe forest above Oak Park. A rough track winds through the trees dividing the forest covering the steep slopes to the left, from the plantation of tall pine trees to the right. On cool, cloudy days the air is enchanted. Thin wisps of cloud cling to the crowns of cabbage trees; cuckoos call.

Eventually the path leads steeply upwards to the crest of the escarpment at Breakfast Rock. Here a large sandstone face projects from the forest wall and offers a commanding view of the entire region. To the left and right the green leafy hues of indigenous forest frame the scene. Below, plantations spread downslope to the suburban gardens of Chase Valley. In the middle distance, the city centre and Scottsville take on pastel shades, while the far distance fades into the grassy savannahs of Thornville and Camperdown. A pair of crowned eagles is often present and their loud *kewee-kewee-kewee* cry and acrobatic flight seem somewhat out of place against a backdrop of suburbia.

Allow your imagination to retract the pieces of civilization. Take away the towering edifice of Grey's Hospital, the city centre, suburbia, the smoking brickworks and the thin, white stripe of concrete that demarcates the N3 highway.

The City from Breakfast Rock, Ferncliffe forest.

Below the misty forest is a flat, grassy valley watered by a meandering river. Tall paperbark acacias *(Acacia sieberana)* are dotted about the valley and in the distance a herd of hartebeest feeds slowly in the direction of the river. In the far distance, where the river rounds a hill and disappears from sight, the hills are clothed in a dense grey-green tangle of scrub. There are no people in the valley below and, except for the hartebeest, no animals domestic or wild can be seen. In the far distance, where land and sky merge, a thin spiral of smoke bears witness to the presence of people.

Many centuries later the Voortrekkers, too, would come to settle in this valley where the interface of three major vegetation types would provide pasture for livestock throughout the year and timber for building.

From the hot, aloe and thornbush valleys of the Mkhondeni the N3 climbs some 540 metres to reach the misty forests and grassy summits of Hilton in less than 20 km. In very few other cities in southern Africa can a resident alter his choice of garden merely by changing suburbs.

The vegetation type most noticeable to the visitor arriving in our City from Durban, is the Valley Bushveld of the Mkhondeni and Mpushini valleys. The best time for studying this fascinating vegetation, undoubtedly, is in summer when the air throbs with a veritable cacophony of insect sounds and the sun beats down relentlessly. Green grass contrasts with the yellow flower balls of the acacia and the fleshy leaves of aloes stand out against a cobalt sky. This is the vegetation most associated with big game country, where a rustle in the leaves could be anything from a mouse to a python. The Valley Bushveld is well-suited to dry valleys receiving a rainfall from 500 to 900 mm annually.

Once the valley of the Mkhondeni has been left behind the vegetation changes to a grassland dominated by Themeda and Hyparrhenia grasses. This vegetation type generally occurs above 600 metres above sea level and forms an open savannah dotted with paperbark acacias. Patches of this vegetation type are still scattered throughout the City, notably in Hayfields, Mkhondeni and Westgate. Rainfall is higher than for the Valley Bushveld and ranges between 650 and 900 mm.

Between the open savannah of the valley and the Ngongoni Veld of the Natal Mistbelt is a vegetation type described by Moll as Moist Transitional Themeda-Hyparrhenia Grassland. Today few areas of this grassland occur naturally as extensive plantations of exotic timber such as wattle, pine and gum have largely replaced it. Remnant forest patches occur on south-facing slopes, the most prominent being Ferncliffe and the Karkloof forests. At one time these extensive forests formed a continuous belt across Natal. Changing climatic conditions forced the forests to retreat to rugged refuges where their demise was hastened by uncontrolled cutting in the last century.

The close juxtaposition of different vegetation types combined with decades of careful tree planting and the inclusion of several streams within the City have made Pietermaritzburg a birdwatcher's haven. The Natal *Bird Atlas* records an impressive list of over 300 birds for the City and I know of some birdwatchers who have sighted 112 species in a single day. Areas of particular interest to birdwatchers include the Darvill Disposal Works where 210 species have been seen, and Ferncliffe and Bisley

Examples of Pietermaritzburg's natural diversity: bushbuck; (4) crowned eagle, (5) subadult; *Cyrthanthus obliquus,* (6) a rare find in this area.

Valley where the bird counts are 120. Maritzburg seems to have attracted, or perhaps nurtured, a large number of very competent amateur ornithologists. The regular activities of the Natal Bird Club, and the very popular courses given by Professor Gordon Maclean, contribute substantially to the interest in bird life.

Up to now I have painted a rosy picture of the City's natural environment and when contrasted with other cities throughout the world we indeed have much of which to be proud. As always, there is room for improvement.

For many years certain aspects of the City's environment were neglected. The inclusion of hundreds of hectares of plantation within the City's confines led to a sense of complacency where protection of other areas was concerned. Many people felt that it was unnecessary to conserve additional land within the City as the plantations already provided enough green space. This widely-held view has resulted in a serious imbalance in open space in Pietermaritzburg. While the upper class suburbs of Montrose and Blackridge have ample open space, the same does not hold true for Pelham, Hayfields and Scottsville. In fact, although several suitable sites exist, Pietermaritzburg has only one nature reserve at present — a small bird sanctuary wedged between two busy roads — while the Natal Parks Board manages the 93 ha Queen Elizabeth Park on the City's north-western edge.

The population of Pietermaritzburg was estimated in 1980 at 160 000 with a density of 1 125 people per square kilometre. This represents an increase in density of 194 per cent in just 34 years. In reality population demand density is far higher as people from far beyond the political boundaries of the City make use of the facilities offered here.

By comparison, Durban's population density is 1 500 per square kilometre and is expected to reach 2 900 within the next 15 years. Nature reserves in Durban total 3 081 ha and an additional 5 214 ha have been recommended for conservation.

While Pietermaritzburg lacks nature reserves at present, several factors favour the City. Its location at the intersection of several major ecological regions, the small size of the City in comparison with Durban, and the close proximity of rugged land of low agricultural value create a far greater potential for active open space than that which exists in any other city in South Africa.

KEY

[Valley Bushveld (23)]

Valley Bushveld (23)

[Paperbark Savanna or Southern Tall Grassveld (65)]

Paperbark Savanna or
Southern Tall Grassveld (65)

[Themeda Hyparrhenia Grassland or Ngongoni Veld (5)]

Themeda Hyparrhenia Grassland or
Ngongoni Veld (5)

( ) : Veld type numbers
after : Acocks J.P.H. : Veld Types of South Africa

Cartographic Unit : University of Natal, Pietermaritzburg.

Fig. 1. Pietermaritzburg's ecological zones.

The City from the Bisley Valley thornveld.

Beginning in 1984 there were signs that environmental awareness was increasing. First the proposal to convert the Darvill Disposal Works into industrial sites was vehemently opposed on ecological grounds. Later in the same year, the election manifesto of a successful candidate in the municipal elections included references to a dassie and leguan, both residents of the constituency.

In the months that followed several important advances were made. Following prolonged negotiation and preparation, a nature trail was opened in Lincoln Meade along a tributary of the Msunduze River.

Other community-motivated projects worth noting were the establishment of a Metropolitan Open Space System (MOSS) committee, and support for the declaration of approximately 150 ha of dense acacia woodland in the upper reaches of Bisley Valley as a conservation area.

What of the future?

Much can still be accomplished, and within the next few years several exciting developments could take place. One proposed scheme is for the development of a system of trails along the fifteen tributaries of the Msunduze which flow through the City. As it is not wise to build too close to a watercourse, streambeds are generally bordered by wide servitudes and lend themselves to the development of nature trails. If the plan reaches fruition, nature trails will radiate out from the city centre like the spokes of a wheel. A circular trail surrounding the City will connect the various steam trails enabling participants to undertake weekend walks of various lengths.

Another proposed project is for the conservation of the Mkhondeni and Msunduze valleys from Ashburton to Camperdown. The plan entails the multiple use of the land in the area delineated into six zones. Each zone takes the present form of land use into consideration and different activities are restricted to individual zones. Agricultural land would be safeguarded, a pioneer farmstead would be reconstructed and special provision would be made for educational groups. Several trails would be laid out but the emphasis would be on self-guided, special interest walks. There would, for example, be an aloe walk and a riverine walk.

In the east, between the Lion Park and Camperdown, the plan calls for the expropriation of some 7 000 ha of rugged, well-wooded country for a nature reserve. Overnight accommodation would be provided for varying requirements, ranging from luxury chalets to bush camps and hostel accommodation. Animals formerly occurring would be re-introduced. There would be room for several hundred zebra and antelope, 35 rhino, 30 giraffe, 70 buffalo and half a dozen hippo.

In the early 1970s a similar proposal was put into operation on the Witwatersrand. Over R3 million was raised for the expropriation of over 13 000 ha. The land was developed into a major nature reserve and today, situated less than 10 km from Johannesburg's southern fringe, it fulfils a vital recreational function.

Durban receives over 600 000 visitors a year from up country, many of whom pass through our City on their way to the coast. The wise management of the surrounding natural environment would not only upgrade our quality of life; it could prove to be a lucrative source of income.

The physical environment

Owen McGee

The geological formations present in the Pietermaritzburg area consist simply of an ancient (1 000 million-year-old), solid, but greatly contorted Basement, and a succession of more recent and much less deformed sedimentary cover rocks overlying the Basement. Intrusions of molten rock here and there penetrated, some 180 million years ago, these formations along fissures, gradually to solidify as dolerite in the form of vertical 'dykes' and horizontal 'sills'.

The Basement is not exposed in the immediate vicinity of the City, being found rather in the valleys to the east of Pietermaritzburg, and particularly in the Valley of the Thousand Hills. The more recent cover rocks resting on the Basement lie horizontally, or may be inclined gently to the west. These rocks may be divided into three groups, the Natal Group, the Karoo Sequence and the most recent deposits, which belong to the Pleistocene Period.

The Natal Group is the lowest rock group and consists of sandstones, formerly rather well-known to local inhabitants as Table Mountain Sandstone, or TMS. This sandstone was originally erosional material deposited over the area by large southward-flowing rivers; after sufficient time and compaction the sediment was transformed into a sandstone plain above the Basement. Long-term subsequent erosion of this plain left many resistant remnants or 'outliers' in the region, the most prominent being Table Mountain itself. 'Conformal' summit levels surmounting the Valley of the Thousand Hills, and including that of Table Mountain, are also very noticeable remnants of this former plain.

Above the Natal Group sandstones are two formations belonging to the Karoo Sequence, i.e. the Dwyka Formation and the Ecca Group.

Two dolerite dykes.

Wall of snuffbox shale in Loop Street, demolished in 1983.

The Dwyka Formation provides evidence of huge continental ice sheets, at least 1 000 m thick, which moved from the north-east over the region about 300 million years ago, planing the underlying surface and depositing glacial sediment referred to as till (which later compacted to tillite). The undulating landscape east of the City is underlain by glacial debris while a veneer of the tillite on a polished glacial pavement is to be found on Table Mountain.

A period of less rigorous climate followed the glacial episode so that the deposits overlying the Dwyka Formation had their origins in rivers flowing from the glacier, and huge river deltas, rather than in ice. This new sedimentary succession (in its compacted form referred to

Fig. 2. Schematic cross-section in the Pietermaritzburg area (not to scale).

(f) = Fault or fracture

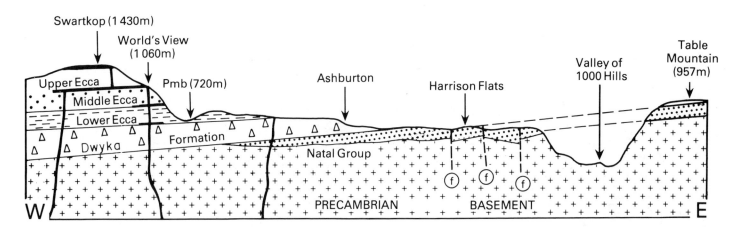

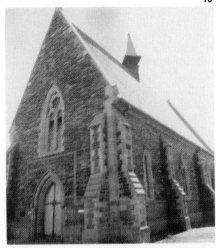

Old St. Peter's Cathedral built of local shale and sandstone.

as the Ecca Group) was deposited on top of the glacial deposits following the melting and gradual withdrawal of the ice around 250 million years ago. Following compaction of the new sedimentary material it consolidated into the well-known horizontally-laminated shales of the Pietermaritzburg area.

The Ecca Group is customarily divided into three formations, the Lower, Middle and Upper Ecca. The Lower Ecca or Pietermaritzburg Formation consists of shales and siltstone. Such material is used in the local manufacture of bricks — an iron oxide content giving the familiar red brick colour to many of the City's buildings. The shales are often exposed in road and railway cuttings as well as in excavations for swimming pools. Not all of the shale is suitable for the construction of crazy paving or buildings, but, should it have been hardened by being in contact with intrusive dolerite dykes or sills, or should it not yet have been weathered, then its hardness is such that it may be used in various ways. The shale foundations and walls of some of the older buildings of the City have been constructed from such hardened shales.

Next above the Lower Ecca are the Middle Ecca ('Vryheid Formation') sandstones and shales. These sometimes occur as outcrops in the area overlooking the City, for example near World's View and in the kranses of Otto's Bluff. Sandstones were quarried at Sweetwaters in earlier days for building-stone while the Cascades near Queen Elizabeth Park are on sandstone beds.

The Upper Ecca (Volksrust Formation) shales and sandstones are generally poorly exposed in the area; they underlie much of the Cedara-Howick region.

The most recent deposits of material in the local area belong to the Pleistocene Period (beginning about 1 million years ago). Alluvium, for example, is found along the flood plain of the Msunduze River; the floodplain is particularly wide in the Edendale area. Former landslides have created hillside scars while associated unconsolidated debris (talus and soil) has created the hummocky terrain in the Queen Elizabeth Park and Country Club area. Such landslides occur when water seeps through the pervious Middle Ecca sandstones to meet the underlying impervious plastic, clayey Lower Ecca shales. The N3 double carriageway in the vicinity of Queen Elizabeth Park has suffered more than once from such slipping. Railway geologists strongly recommended avoiding the area for the reconstruction of

the Natal Main Line and instead the SATS went to the great expense of building the Cedara tunnel at depths where this would not be a problem.

The dolerite sills are most commonly noted in the Ecca Group of shales and sandstones. One resistant sill forms the crown of Swartkop, another that of World's View, while still another provides the raw material for a major quarry near the Greytown road. Loose dolerite boulders (with which many local gardeners must come to terms) are formed by 'spheroidal' weathering. Penetration of air and water, along the cooling or tension joints and crevices of sills of rock, weaken these areas and the continuous weathering leaves rounded residual cores of, often, excellent rockery boulders. Along such joints in the dolerite and adjacent baked or 'indurated' shale, water may percolate to well below the water-table, often to be extracted from boreholes in times of drought.

River erosion by the Msunduze and its tributaries in the Pietermaritzburg area has created the roughly 8 km x 12 km x 300 m basin in which the City is situated. There is a gap to the south-east of the City through which the Msunduze flows to join the Mngeni River. The basin is surrounded by dissected spurs and rounded hills and is one of many such basins in the Natal Midlands. A well-defined sinuous escarpment rises 300 to 400 m above the City on the west and north-west sides; it is situated along the outcrop of Middle Ecca in a region where dolerite sills cap the sandstone and shale. These resistant sills are mainly responsible for the high ground in the area. Erosion in the basin has left a number of ridges between the Msunduze and the Dorpspruit. The spur runs from Fort Napier through the centre of town and tapers off.

The soils occurring in and around Pietermaritzburg owe their distinctive characteristics to an interplay of geological, climatic and topographic factors.

A dolerite quarry.

Taking out shale to put in a swimming-pool in Scottsville.

Pietermaritzburg's rogue storm, 12 February 1978.

On the drier side of town (south and east of the Dorpspruit) three main categories of soil may be recognized: those derived from shale and from dolerite, and alluvial soils.

In soils derived from shale, the topsoil is generally light grey-brown with a loamy texture. It sets very hard when it dries out. The subsoil may be partly weathered shale or impervious clay or a gravelly partly-cemented layer of iron concretions (*ouklip* or *nkubane*). Either too hard or too sticky, the soils are not easy to manage. Mulches may provide temporary help but termites, warmth and humidity soon break these down. The soils are quite fertile, seldom needing more than nitrogen fertilizer for vegetable or flower gardens.

Soils derived from dolerite are usually clayey. They may be dark, chocolate or red coloured, depending on drainage. The dark variety may contain a clay called montmorillonite which, if subjected to extremes of wetting or drying, expands and contracts considerably, often cracking or shifting foundations of houses as well as providing a natural underground pruning action (which may prove fatal) on tree and other plant roots. Such 'black turf' soils may be used by groundsmen in the preparation of cricket pitches. The redder soils are physically better, being well-drained and quite fertile.

Alluvial soils are deep, somewhat silty soils found on the floodplain of the Msunduze and along the banks of its tributaries. They are fertile and easily irrigated.

On the wetter side of town the soil pattern changes considerably. Given the cooler temperatures and higher rainfall, more leaching and weathering of soils have occurred. They are therefore deeper and fairly porous. Topsoils are enriched with humus and hold water well. Fertilizer or manure may be required because the leaching causes chemical infertility. In most cases the soil is acidic so that lime will be needed to counteract this, except where acid-loving plants such as azaleas and hydrangeas are grown.

Numerous factors give Pietermaritzburg its particular weather and climate — its latitude (30°S), altitude (658 m at the City Hall), distance from the sea, and, particularly, the local topography. Fig. 5 gives a summary of the main climatic statistics, taken from various sources.

Variations of rainfall across the area are to be expected, especially in view of the marked change in altitude between the south-east and the north-west of the City. In particular there is a steady increase in the mean annual rainfall total from less than 800 mm in the drier south-east to above 1 100 mm on the wetter north-west. Variations from year to year are also very noticeable (for example 575 mm in 1941 and 1 533 mm in 1917 at the Botanic Gardens), and the available rainfall data do not indicate either a long-term increase or decrease, or wetter and drier cycles.

Most of the rain is associated with the passage of large-scale disturbances such as depressions and cold fronts along the Natal coast which bring to Natal a cool south-west airflow, or with the frequent thunderstorms of spring and summer — either local convectional storms or those which originate in squall lines extending right across the country.

Some 60 per cent of the rain falls with an intensity exceeding about 2 or 3 mm/hour and between 20 per cent and 40 per cent with intensities exceeding 25 mm/hour. Most high intensity rains, of whatever duration, begin between 16h00 and 17h00. About 26 days during the year experience rainfalls greater than 10 mm and thunder will be heard on 60 days a year.

Average monthly rainfalls are given in Fig. 5. The

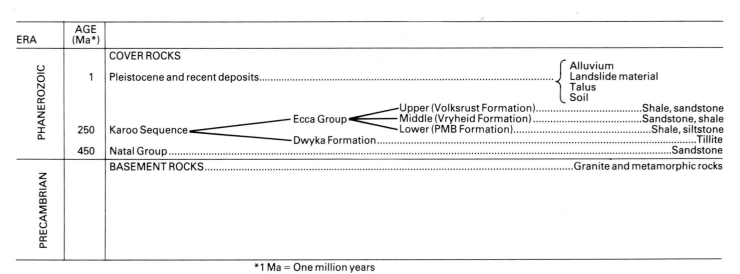

Fig. 3 Geological formations in the Pietermaritzburg area.

most rainfall recorded at the Botanic Gardens in any one month was 468,9 mm in March 1925. On 14 January 1947 a record 246,6 mm was recorded; the next highest was 117,3 mm on 13 January 1915.

Relative humidity (RH) data are seldom collected and are in any case meaningless unless considered against temperature. The RH values in Fig. 5 provide some idea of the fall-off in values as the temperatures increase to midday; the actual amount of water vapour in the air may or may not change over the same period.

If all the water vapour in the air over the City were to condense, the depth of the liquid water would be about 27 mm (37 mm in summer, 13 mm in winter). If the vapour were not continuously replenished, the rainfall would completely dry out the air in about ten days. Only about 10 per cent of the rain comes from locally evaporated water; thus the planting or removal of trees and the presence of dams such as Midmar can have no effect on rainfall, since local rainfall is from water evaporated some ten days previously from areas which could be hundreds if not thousands of kilometres away.

Temperature variations also occur across the City. Suburbs on the cooler north or north-west side owe their lower temperatures in part to higher altitudes and in part to their earlier sunsets each day. More detailed variations are related primarily to the ventilation provided by local air movements. Thus temperatures at the sheltered Botanic Gardens site are lower than those at the exposed Ukulinga Farm site in winter because of earlier sunsets, but are higher in summer because of the comparative lack of ventilation.

Fig. 5 gives temperature data at the Botanic Gardens; the highest temperature ever recorded there was 44,4°C on 18 January 1966, the lowest –5°C on both 2 July and 11 July 1934.

Temperature and humidity combine to produce a 'humiture' figure, or comfort index. Such data have not been mapped across the City but it is certain that it is the

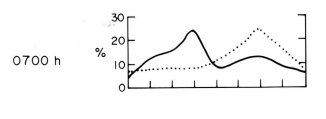

0700 h

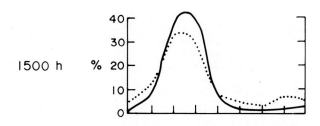

1500 h

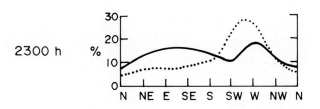

2300 h

—— Summer (Nov., Dec., Jan., Feb.) conditions
······ Winter (May, Jun., Jul., Aug.) conditions

Fig. 4 Seasonal wind direction frequencies in Pietermaritzburg.

Fig. 5 Some climatic statistics

MONTH	RAINFALL[1]			TEMPERATURE (°C)[1]		RELATIVE HUMIDITY[2] (%)		EVAPORATION[3] (mm)
	AVERAGE (mm)	% OF ANNUAL RAINFALL	NO. OF DAYS OF RAIN	AVERAGE MAXIMUM	AVERAGE MINIMUM	MORNING (08h00)	MIDDAY (12h00)	
Jan	163,9	16,7	18	27,4	16,8	76	59	147
Feb	123,9	12,6	15	26,4	17,5	80	59	133
Mar	116,4	11,8	13	25,8	16,2	77	53	140
Apr	69,8	7,1	10	24,4	13,1	87	57	116
May	31,3	3,2	4	20,9	8,9	79	48	105
Jun	9,2	0,9	2	19,9	5,8	64	32	90
Jul	12,7	1,3	3	20,3	5,0	61	36	90
Aug	35,2	3,6	5	21,8	7,1	75	38	115
Sep	59,1	6,0	10	23,1	10,4	65	40	120
Oct	96,2	9,8	15	25,1	12,2	72	60	135
Nov	117,7	12,0	18	25,8	14,4	70	51	132
Dec	148,0	15,0	19	26,8	15,9	78	62	143
Year	983,4		132			74	50	1 466

[1]From Botanic Gardens' data, Pietermaritzburg; daily recordings started 1 January 1907.
[2]University (Bayer and Coutts, 1938).
[3]Simulated values provided by the Department of Agricultural Engineering, University of Natal, Pietermaritzburg. These figures should be multiplied by a factor of 0,85 to give the approximate evaporation from local swimming-pools.

(high) humidity values in the basin rather than high temperatures that produce the feeling of discomfort in the City on many a summer day, especially when ventilation is low and the air is stagnant.

The humiture index may be obtained from temperature (0 °C) and relative humidity (%) data using a specially designed chart. There are probably between 3 and 5 days during the average summer in Pietermaritzburg when out-of-doors humiture values reach or exceed the dangerous 110 mark.

Pietermaritzburg faces wind from four main directions, although not with equal frequencies. (See Fig. 4.)

The main daytime wind in the City is from the east or south-east, a direction up the Msunduze valley. The southeast wind may not be the only local wind controlled in its direction by the delineation of the river valley; other southeast winds are linked to large-scale anticyclones ridging south of the country. They can bring prolonged rainfall to Natal. The south-east wind over Pietermaritzburg is more frequent in summer than in winter and has a greater speed on average in summer.

During the night the wind direction is mainly from the west or north-west, again largely along the Msunduze valley. It is also from the north-west that the unpleasant Berg wind blows. This wind is not related to the direction of any local valley but rather to a large-scale weather situation covering perhaps one-third of the country. Berg winds usually blow between April and September and bring with them temperature rises of perhaps 5 to 10°C. Fortunately when Berg winds die down they are often replaced by far more pleasant conditions, with a cool, cloudy movement of air from the south-west.

Winds from the north-east are more common at the coast than at Pietermaritzburg but they do sometimes penetrate inland. The winds are related to the large anticyclones over the southern Indian Ocean.

FOG OR SMOG?

Owen McGee

Commonly during the early evenings of winter and especially when the sky is clear, when conditions are calm and when humidities are high near the surface, the land cools off rapidly through long-wave outgoing radiation. This cooling is communicated to the adjacent air which then increases in density and slips down sloping ground to form cold air pools in any depression, such as river valleys (locally the Msunduze and its tributaries are ideal sites). With the cooler air now below, and warmer air aloft, a stable stratification known as a temperature inversion is established. Should the cooling continue to the dewpoint temperature, some of the water vapour in the air will condense to form a mist or fog.

The next morning the oblique rays of the rising sun will have difficulty penetrating the air, as will a car's full-beam headlights. This drop in visibility is therefore a natural occurrence and is not caused by 'pollution'. In a natural way, too, the mist or fog will lift by mid-morning, evaporate completely, and the vapour will be ready to start the whole cycle again towards sunset. The stable stratification may persist all day, though in an altered or weakened form.

However, should pollutants be released into the stable air, especially from low-level sources, the visibility may be reduced even further because many of the pollution particles are 'hygroscopic' — that is, they have an affinity for water which results in their growing larger by extracting water vapour from the air. In this way a pall of smoke is added to the air and becomes trapped in the inversion layer.

Thus when the Pietermaritzburg basin is supposedly shrouded in 'smog', part will be anthropogenic (smoke) and part natural (fog) — hence the word 'smog'.

The ratio of smoke to fog over Pietermaritzburg is unknown, but the monthly average smoke levels recorded at the Municipality's six stations leave little room for complacency on the part of householder or industrialist. The only other atmospheric constituent monitored at present is SO_2 — an invisible substance which, when combined with water in the atmosphere, produces an acid.

In addition to these two (the dust and SO_2) there are undoubtedly many other pollutants present in the air. It is probably true that at present the average citizen overreacts, particularly in winter, to the visible inversion layer, and is blissfully unaware of the possibly far more injurious, and virtually unmonitored, invisible pollutants. Bearing in mind local topography, the present level of pollution, and the incompleteness of the pollution picture, one should perhaps firmly endorse the conclusion reached by a CSIR ventilation study: 'all industries subject to smoke control should be situated at least 100 metres above the floor of the Pietermaritzburg Basin and, better still, above the 762 metre (2 500 ft) contour line...' (Liebenberg, 1976).

The Pietermaritzburg basin shrouded in 'smog' on a winter morning: Queen Elizabeth Park in the foreground.

14

William Bizley

In the 1920s and 30s flooding took place with almost every rain-storm. The gutters of the streets parallel to Church Street were primitively shallow, while the transverse gutters were so deep as to be regular sloots, taking rain in a flood down West Street or Chapel Street. The lower part of the town became a great sheet of water; in a Boom Street house you might watch the family ladders floating in the back garden. The Dorpspruit flooded so easily, and caused so much disruption in the Indian areas, that the City Council eventually embarked on what was called the 'Deviation of the Dorpspruit'. This was essentially a straightening exercise, and Mr James MacGibbon, Town Clerk in the 30s, considered it the best single contribution to City life undertaken by the Council.

rain, rain
    with fresh wet grass breath
    heavy deafening rhythmic torrents
    with hooves of thunder
    a wet deluge
        tinkering all over toffee-coloured
        rusted machibise zinc roofs
            leaking carelessly like gossiping mouths
    into brimful dishes, pots and jam tin mugs
        which titter and splash under leaks
    mud walls soft as a fresh chocolate cake
    crumble with slippery sludge
        heavy hearts and crooked roof beams sag
            under this wet deluge
rain, rain
    how i thirst for drought

dikobe wa mogale

Floods

Owen McGee

Sobantu, September 1987.

Possibly the worst storm ever recorded in Pietermaritzburg occurred on Tuesday 14 January 1947. A total of 230 mm of rain fell in the 19 hours between 14h00 on the Tuesday and 21h00 on the Wednesday. At the Purification Works 117 mm fell within one 45-minute period.

Other violent storms were experienced in October 1917, 'King Sol only making his appearance after a week of heavy rain', and in March 1939, but the 1947 storm probably holds the record. Certainly the *Natal Witness* gave its readers a very full twopence worth of detail. The advertisements were appropriate, one appealing for entries to a bathing beauty contest: 'Support Maritzburg's Efforts to Drown Mrs Sleepy Hollow Grundy'.

In September 1987 not a storm but prolonged and heavy rains, producing nearly 400 mm in 36 hours, brought devastating floods to the Msunduze floodplain. The floods were widespread over southern Natal and were labelled the worst in living memory.

At the height of the flood the Camp's Drift Road, West Street, Lindley and the N3 bridges across the Msunduze had to be closed to traffic. The City was therefore virtually cut in two with only the Commercial Road bridge open to traffic. The Edendale Road bridge was partially washed away and reopened three months later.

Houses in low-lying areas of Edendale were washed away, and much of Sobantu Village was inundated by waist-high water. Many of the City's sports facilities which are located on the floodplain were severely damaged. The Sax Young cycle track became a 'duck pond', and the Kershaw Park tennis courts were ruined. The Maritzburg Rugby Sub-Union, which only a week earlier had requested top soil for their four fields, saw their entire complex flooded, and when the water subsided their fields were covered by as much as 20 cm of silt. At the height of the flood the crossbars on the main stadium goalposts were under water, which meant that the water was 3 m deep. The playing fields of Merchiston School were flooded and Longmarket Girls School had to be evacuated.

Floods of this severity are fortunately rare and are invariably associated with low pressure regions in the general circulation pattern. The low which caused the September flood was 'cut-off' from the normal west to east drift of our weather systems. It stalled over the OFS and Natal as a deep and intense system drawing in moisture-laden air from the oceans. What aided this air movement was a high pressure system over the Indian Ocean from which air was being expelled. The resulting 'push-pull' effect produced a strong onshore air flow — with low-level air converging and rising. Heavy cloud, rain and snow was the result.

Flood-producing rains over Natal are rare, requiring as they do the simultaneous occurrence and suitable positioning of a deep and intense inland low and a strong high to the south. Thus not every thunderstorm or heavy rainfall, however severe, should be taken as a potential flood threat.

A flood-devastated home in Edendale, September 1987.

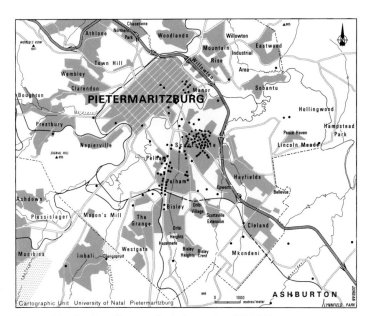

Fig. 1   Distribution of known Early Stone Age (500 000 –
150 000 years ago) sites in Pietermaritzburg.
Further maps on pages 16 and 17 show the distribution of
known Middle and Late Stone Age sites and of Early and
Late Iron Age sites in the same area.

Opposite and pages 14 and 15

Stone Age and Iron Age artefacts found in the Pietermaritzburg
area.

1   Early Stone Age handaxe from White's Road, Pentrich.
2   Fragments of an Early Iron Age pot (6–7th century AD)
    from Alexandra Park.
3   Two worn hoes; part of a cache of Late Iron Age
    implements found at the SOMTA factory.
4   Middle Stone Age spear point from Trelawney Road.
5   Naturally-backed knife from 9 000–12 000 years ago from
    Mason's Mill.
6   Broken bored stone used to weight a digging-stick (Late
    Stone Age) from Willowfountain.
7   Pot-sherd decorated with finger-tip impressions (Late
    Iron Age). From the Botanic Gardens.
8   Fragment of a carved soapstone bowl (Late Iron Age)
    found in Royston Road. The decoration follows a pattern
    frequently used on Zulu wood-carving and pottery of the
    19th century.

12

CHAPTER TWO

Before White Settlement

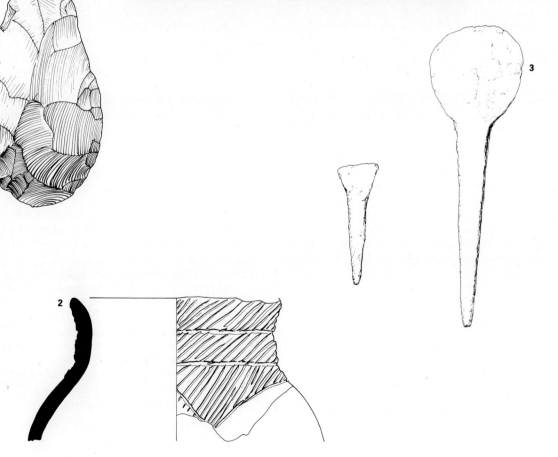

Pietermaritzburg

THE FIRST
2 000 000 YEARS

Tim Maggs

Before Voortrekker Pietermaritzburg there was no urban focus in the area. Indeed, towns and cities as we know them were alien concepts to the pre-colonial peoples of the region. The austerity of a Stone Age hunter-gatherer way of life or of the subsistence farming characteristic of the Iron Age required relatively small-scale and scattered patterns of settlement. Nevertheless, some of the features of the local environment which attracted Voortrekker settlement were also important to the earlier communities who chose to live here.

The present City is situated, by no accident, at the junction of several ecological types — thornveld savannah along the Msunduze and southwards, grasslands to the north and forest patches on the southward slope of the escarpment. Each provided a different set of resources which, because of their proximity to one another, enabled local communities to take advantage of all three. It was thus a particularly favourable area for settlement within the broader context of the Natal Midlands, as is clear from the quantity and variety of archaeological remains that have come to light.

The distribution of the different ecological types would not, however, have remained static over the long period we are examining. Considerable climatic changes took place during this period and these would have affected the vegetation. During cooler periods the savannah would have retreated to lower, hence warmer, limits and vice versa in hotter periods. The forest patches probably expanded when rainfall increased and shrank in drier times.

This earliest period of Pietermaritzburg history can be reconstructed only from the archaeological remains that have been found in and around the City. The story will always be incomplete, for time has destroyed many traces of earlier settlement and others have yet to be found or have been built over. Archaeology enables us to see far back in time and reconstruct some aspects of long forgotten ways of life. But the archaeological traces alone cannot give us the detailed pictures of the past that can be recreated from the well-documented last 150 years.

Even within the Pietermaritzburg area the evidence available to us is very patchy. Many of the ancient items recovered and placed in museum collections are chance finds by members of the public. None is from systematic archaeological research. It is the modern archaeological excavations and reconstructions that have been carried out in other parts of Natal and beyond that can provide some historical 'flesh and blood' to the dry 'bones' of the local artefacts.

The patchy nature of our available data can be seen on the maps where the great majority of finds are in and around Scottsville. This pattern results from the work of one ardent collector, F.H.M. French, who was working in the Borough Engineer's Department when the township of Scottsville was being laid out. He took much trouble to recover and record the location of stone implements that came to light during the development works. His collection was donated to the Natal Museum on his death in 1940. Other areas have not been searched nearly so thoroughly, but it is likely that where similar topography and vegetation are present, for example around Ashburton, similar concentrations of Stone Age material may be present.

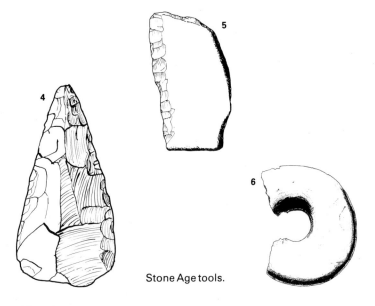

Stone Age tools.

The Stone Age

Pietermaritzburg, the urban centre, was founded in 1838 but archaeological remains show that people have been living in the city area for a quarter or even half a million years, a period some 2 000 times longer than that of the City itself. But we must give some thought to the possibility that there were people here in the even more distant past. Evidence going back two to three million years on our early cultural and biological evolution has all been found on the African continent — the cradle of humanity. Such evidence is preserved only in very exceptional geological circumstances like the limestone caves north of the Vaal (Sterkfontein, Swartkrans, Kromdraai, Makapansgat and Taung) or the ancient lake deposits of the East African rift valleys (Olduvai, Omo, Lake Turkana, etc.). No such sites are known from Natal, nor is there much chance of their being found. This is because the landscape in general, and in Pietermaritzburg as much as anywhere, reflects rapid geological denudation: rivers are rapidly cutting down into their beds and the predominantly sloping landscape is subject to hillwash. Thus the landscape we see today is a relatively young one — no more than 100 000 years old. Consequently the oldest Stone Age artefacts are buried under or incorporated into soils that have been formed since that time. If there were people here a million or more years ago, any remains that they left behind would long ago have eroded away and washed down the Msunduze into the Indian Ocean. The very land surface on which they would have walked, according to the estimates of geologists, was some 15 metres above today's ground surface.

But what likelihood is there that these early ancestors of ours would have inhabited the Natal region at all?

Australopithecus — the first of our ancestors to stand up and walk on two feet — inhabited both eastern and southern Africa from about four million years ago; while the first of our own genus, *Homo habilis*, is recorded from both Sterkfontein in the Transvaal and from Kenya where it is dated around 1,5 to 2 million years ago. These hominids were evidently adapted to a savannah ecology. And since the African savannahs extend through the lower lying parts of Natal, it is probable that the hominids were present in Natal as they were in the Transvaal.

Returning to the material evidence from Pietermaritzburg itself, we find the earliest surviving traces belong to the Acheulian Stone Age industry. Hallmark of the Acheulian is the distinctive but poorly understood 'handaxe' — probably a multi-purpose tool — — that is characteristic of sites dating to the period 600 000 to 150 000 years ago.

The Acheulian industry was developed by our immediately ancestral species *Homo erectus*, who spread throughout the habitable parts of Africa and was the first of our family to emigrate to other continents. Their bones have been found as far east as Java and China, while Acheulian handaxes are found eastwards to India and northwards to southern Britain.

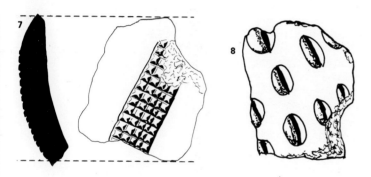

Fragments of Iron Age pots.

Like their Stone Age successors, the Acheulian population lived a hunting and gathering way of life relying entirely on wild plant and animal foods. They would have moved about from place to place, seldom staying for more than a few days at a time. They evidently preferred to live in the open, for their artefacts are seldom found in caves or rock shelters.

Although many of the modern large African mammals were already present, a number of others became extinct in this period. These include *Megantereon*, the last sabre-toothed cat; *Hipparion*, a three-toed horse; *Sivatherium*, a short-necked but antlered relative of the giraffe; and *Hippopotamus gorgops*, a hippo with periscopic eyes. Evidence from Central Africa and Europe shows that the Acheulians could hunt animals as large as elephants.

From the abundance of their artefacts found along river valleys, we conclude that they spent much of their time in these areas. An example can be seen in Fig. 1, which shows sites found on both sides of the Msunduze in the Scottsville and central town areas. Note that the sites are not immediately beside the river but on the slightly higher ground on either side of the valley. This reflects the down cutting of the river and the sideways movements of its meanders during the last 150 000 years or so, which have erased the earlier evidence from the riverside itself. Downstream, and particularly along the Mngeni below Table Mountain, there exist 'terraces', now raised above the river, marking the position of ancient parts of the river-bed. These terraces are frequently covered by sheets of old river pebbles amongst which Acheulian artefacts can be found. Indeed these river pebbles were a major source of suitable stone for the artefact makers.

Acheulian material has also been found further away from the Msunduze valley. Here it is usually from relatively flat areas such as Scottsville-Pelham and the Ashburton ridge or beside smaller streams such as the Slangspruit, Foxhill Spruit and Mkhondeni. Some Acheulian occupation clearly took place on these flatter areas. However, with time, soil creep will have taken place down the steeper slopes carrying any artefacts with it into the small streams. Once into a stream, the artefacts are washed down relatively rapidly, becoming rounded in the process. Such artefacts, often barely recognizable, can be found in the river gravels downstream.

The hunter-gatherer way of life continued through the Middle Stone Age (MSA) which is characterized by a development in stone tool technology. Here the emphasis was on producing long, blade-like flakes of stone, some of which were then trimmed to produce spearheads and scrapers. MSA artefacts are very common over most of Natal below an altitude of 12 000 metres, and the map shows that Pietermaritzburg is no exception. The strong concentration in the Scottsville area again reflects the intensive collecting of Mr French. But the absence of any sites on the higher ground north of the central city is representative of the situation in Natal in general. For a considerable part of the MSA the climate would have been appreciably cooler than today — corresponding to the last glacial period of the northern hemisphere. This climate would probably have made the upland areas of Natal from Hilton up to the Drakensberg relatively unattractive to hunter-gatherers and many of the game animals they hunted.

The MSA people were of our own species, *Homo sapiens*, though not of any racial type surviving today. Their contemporaries in Europe and parts of Asia — the Neanderthals — are currently considered as an anatomically robust adaptation to the glacial conditions of northern climes, not the brutish primitives of cartoon mythology.

The dating of the MSA is still beset by controversy, mainly because existing methods of dating are still relatively ineffective for this period. It may have started any time between 200 000 and 130 000 years ago, and it was replaced at least 35 000 years ago (but possibly as early as 60 000 years ago) by the Late Stone Age (LSA).

The early part of the LSA is still poorly known for Natal, although current research on the Umhlatuzana Shelter, under the N3 freeway midway between Durban and Pietermaritzburg, will provide important new evidence. In Pietermaritzburg itself the evidence consists of several small collections of stone artefacts including a distinctive type known as a naturally-backed knife. These have been dated to the period roughly 15 000 to 7 000 years ago, during which climates worldwide were recovering from the last glacial epoch and becoming similar to today's conditions.

An interesting point about the local spread of these artefacts is that, although far fewer sites have been recorded than for the earlier periods, some sites do occur on the highlands north of the City, and there is even one near the top of Swartkop, the highest local peak. This pattern has been noted elsewhere in the Natal Midlands, and it therefore seems that people at this time were attracted to these cool, sourveld areas despite their being even colder then than now.

During this period several large mammals became extinct in South Africa including *Equus capensis*, a giant zebra; *Pelorovis*, a large, long-horned buffalo; Bond's springbok and antelope species related to the blesbok and hartebeest. Climatic change and man's hunting activities have been suggested as the reasons for some of these extinctions.

The final phase of the Stone Age began about 7 000 years ago and is the most familiar one to us, for its cultural heritage was passed down to the historic Khoisan hunter-gatherers whom the white colonists disparagingly referred to as 'Bushmen'. Their stone tool-kit evolved gradually during this period, and consisted mainly of miniature implements — scrapers, arrowpoints and woodworking tools — that were attached to other materials by the use of adhesives. The bow and arrow was the main hunting weapon and towards the end of the period arrowheads of bone, then steel, used with poison, increasingly replaced stone. The bored stone, made to give more weight to digging sticks, was also a feature of this period.

An increasingly wide range of wild plant and animal foods was exploited during this period. Fish — both marine and freshwater — were caught, sometimes with delicate bone hooks, while shellfish were important along the coast. Among the bones of the occasional large animal we find numerous smaller ones: small buck, dassies, hares and even moles. Bored stones attest to a predilection for underground plant parts — bulbs/corms/roots which are often highly nutritious. Fruit and berries were also much sought after.

This period has left relatively little trace in Pietermaritzburg itself, although rock shelters in the neighbourhood have produced evidence. Best known among the remains are rock paintings, most of which were done in this period. Drakensberg shelters in the Cave sandstone contain the great majority of Natal's rock art, though there are paintings closer afield, for example in the Mngeni valley above Table Mountain and near Shongweni. Indeed, wherever sandstone outcrops have formed suitable rockshelters, paintings may be found.

Khoisan hunter-gatherers continued to occupy the upland portions of Natal, between Hilton and the Drakensberg, down to the coming of white settlers. The Voortrekkers named the escarpment which overlooks Pietermaritzburg 'Boesmansrand', and initially referred to the Msunduze as the 'Boesmansrivier' and the Dorpspruit as the 'Klein Boesmansrivier'.

The most important change in the pre-colonial past was the advent of a new way of life, labelled by archaeologists the Iron Age. Of most significance was not so much knowledge of metals, but rather that of the farming of domestic plants and animals. Food was now produced rather than obtained from the wild. The nomadic hunter-gatherer way of life gave way to sedentary settlement with built homesteads comprising domestic accommodation, food storage structures and stock pens. Pottery, known in simple forms to the last of the Stone Age inhabitants, was now expertly fashioned and well decorated. Such distinctive pottery is a hallmark of this period. Current evidence indicates that this revolution in life style was introduced by new arrivals of Negro physical type indistinguishable from today's black population.

The Iron Age

The Iron Age way of life developed in equatorial Africa, spreading rapidly southwards and reaching the Natal

Fig. 2   Middle Stone Age sites (150 000–30 000 years ago).

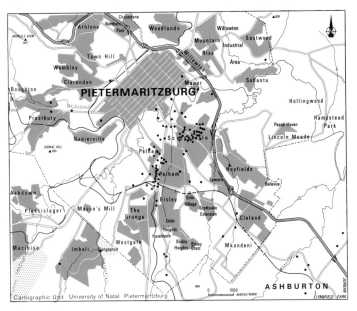

Fig. 3   Late Stone Age sites (30 000 years ago to recent times).

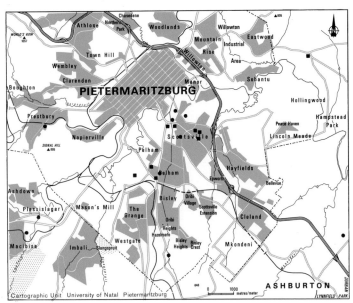

coastal plain around AD250. By AD500 Iron Age villages were established throughout the coastal and savannah areas. Inland, the settlements clung to river valleys, for broad flat areas of good soil beside the rivers were preferred as village sites. These were often large in size and probably housed a few hundred people.

The Pietermaritzburg sites fit into this pattern with one slight exception, which is away from the rivers near the University. Although none has been excavated and dated, the styles of pottery indicate dates between AD500 and 800.

Since Pietermaritzburg is situated at the upper limit of savannah country in the Msunduze valley, these Early Iron Age sites mark their furthest expansion up the valley during this period. In the same way contemporary sites in the Albert Falls area mark the furthest penetration up the Mngeni valley. However, the riverside village locations should not obscure the point that within a few hours' walk from such sites other desirable resources would be available to these communities. In particular the grasslands on the adjacent highlands, for example up towards the Hilton ridge and beyond, would have provided better spring and summer grazing than the sweeter but sparser lowland pastures which in turn have better autumn and winter grazing. Thus, although the permanent settlements remained in the valleys, the surrounding areas would also have been used for a variety of purposes such as grazing, firewood, hunting and collecting wild foods to supplement the products of farming. Each village was relatively self-sufficient, even to the smelting and production of its own iron and steel tools. We can therefore see the beginning of local industry at this time.

The lowland, village pattern of settlement gave way to a more dispersed and upland pattern around AD1000. Reasons for this change are not yet well understood, but it seems that the emphasis was now on smaller and shorter term settlements. These were probably no more than the homestead of a single family group, as was the case with the Nguni-speaking peoples as far back as the earliest written records go, which is to the mid-sixteenth century accounts of shipwrecked Portuguese mariners. One such settlement was built on the shoulder of the spur overlooking the Dorpspruit in the Botanical Gardens. All that remains is a thin scatter of pottery sherds suggesting a family homestead of perhaps only a few years' duration.

The pottery of the last 900 years has relatively little decoration. Many vessels are plain, and what decoration there is usually consists of no more than a few rows of impressions on the rim or neck. An interesting find from Mountain Rise is part of a bowl carved out of soapstone, but both in shape and decoration it is similar to pottery and even wooden vessels made by nineteenth century Zulu craftsmen. It probably dates to shortly before the arrival of white colonists.

Outside the City itself, but in the neighbourhood, are the remains of stone structures which were built during the past few centuries. Earliest of these may be the irregularly-walled areas in naturally defended sites such as one in the Umgeni Valley Nature Reserve. A similar structure at Moor Park near Estcourt, the only one yet excavated, dates to around AD1300. Later in the sequence are numerous circular stone cattle-pens which can be found in many of Natal's grassland areas. Each was the centre of a homestead inhabited by ancestors of today's Nguni-speaking people. Also belonging to this late period are several collections of iron artefacts which have been dug up in recent years. These were no doubt buried by their owners for security but never reclaimed. One such batch of hoes was found at the SOMTA Factory, Plessislaer.

Thus down to the coming of the Voortrekkers, or at least to the Mfecane of a few years earlier, the Pietermaritzburg area had been occupied for 1 300 years by settled black communities of agriculturalists. They evidently avoided the mistbelt sourveld areas from Hilton upcountry, but the savannah areas continued to be attractive throughout this time and from about AD1200 grassland areas with less acid soils also saw Iron Age settlement.

Fig. 4 Early Iron Age sites (AD 250–900).

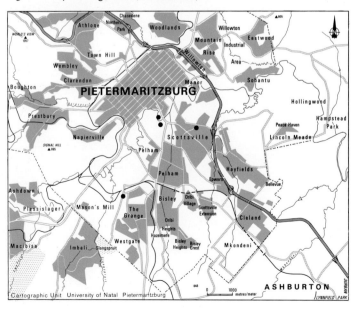

Fig. 5 Late Iron Age sites (AD 1000–1800).

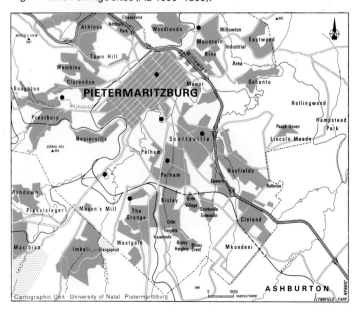

Before Mgungundlovu

THE UPPER MNGENI – UPPER MKHOMAZI REGION IN THE EARLY NINETEENTH CENTURY

John Wright

The intrusion of Boer pastoralists into the region east of the Drakensberg in the late 1830s, the emergence of the Republic of Natalia, and the establishment of Pietermaritzburg as its capital have too often been seen as having occurred in a demographic and political vacuum. Conventional accounts see the Boers as penetrating into a region that had largely been depopulated by war in the 1820s. They describe the dealings from 1837 onward of the Boers with the Zulu kingdom to the north of the Thukela River, and with the British hunter-traders at Port Natal. They pay very little attention to the interaction that took place between Boers and local African communities, or to the prior history of these communities. The aim here is to collate what evidence there is in recorded oral tradition on the history of the region between the upper Mngeni and upper Mkhomazi Rivers to the time of the Boer incursion. The establishment of a Boer-dominated community at Pietermaritzburg can then be set in the context of local history rather than simply in the context of Voortrekker history.

For an unknown period before about 1820 the region under discussion seems to have been dominated by the cluster of Wushe chiefdoms that occupied the Mngeni valley from what is now the Dargle area to beyond Otto's Bluff (kwaKhwela). The valley of the Msunduze where Pietermaritzburg now stands, and the area to the west and south, was occupied by a group of Nqondo chiefdoms. According to some recorded traditions, the section of the Nqondo which lived on the site of the City and in its immediate environs was, *circa* 1820, under a woman chief named Machibise kaMlithwa or kaMlifa: her name survives today as the designation for part of Edendale. To the east and south-east near Table Mountain (emKhambathini) were chiefdoms such as the Njilo, the Nyamvu and the Dlanyawo; in the higher country to the south-west were groups like the Yobeni.

All these chiefdoms, like most of those in central and southern Natal, were small in area and in population. The biggest among them consisted of at most a few thousand people inhabiting an area of a few hundred square kilometres. They were fluid in structure, with homesteads and groups of homesteads not infrequently breaking their allegiance to their chief and moving off to settle under the authority of another chief. The ability of chiefs to deploy force against their subjects was limited,

and their power depended largely on their skills as arbitrators and managers. Though there were clear social and political distinctions between the ruling family and the families that recognized its authority, there were no major discrepancies of wealth. Internal conflicts over succession to the chiefship seem to have been frequent, as do cattle-raids between neighbouring chiefdoms, but wars were generally of low intensity and of brief duration. Contrary to the conventional view of 'Zulu' and related societies as having been primarily pastoralist, the economies of these chiefdoms were based on agriculture, though the husbandry of cattle was regarded socially as more important.

Politically the upper Mngeni–upper Mkhomazi region lay in the shadow of a polity of a rather different order. This was the Thuli paramountcy, which had been established in the coastlands in the later eighteenth century. The Thuli had previously lived in the south-east of what is now Zululand, but had been driven out in the course of conflict between a number of the larger and more militarized states that were beginning to emerge in the region north of the Thukela after the mid-eighteenth century. After their flight southward, the Thuli extended their domination over the region from north of the Mngeni to the Mkhomazi, and inland to about the Camperdown region. Their chiefs ruled what was by far the biggest political unit yet seen south of the Thukela. Though there is no record of the relations that existed between the Thuli and the chiefdoms on its borders, the latter no doubt went about their affairs with a wary eye on their much larger neighbour.

Though all these polities shared a broadly similar language and culture, there were at this time, as there had long been, marked regional variations of both across what are now Natal and Zululand. The people of central and southern Natal spoke variants of the *tekeza* (or Lala) dialect, which was markedly different in some respects from the related dialects spoken by the people who lived across the Thukela to the north. Marriage practices, eating habits, styles of dress, and other cultural features also varied from one locality to another. Standardization

Fig. 6 Approximate location before 1819 of chiefdoms in the Pietermaritzburg area.

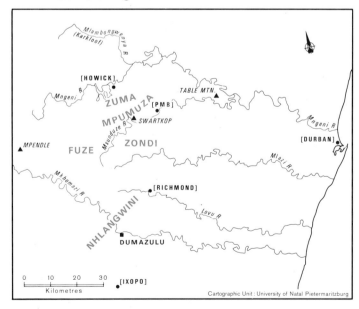

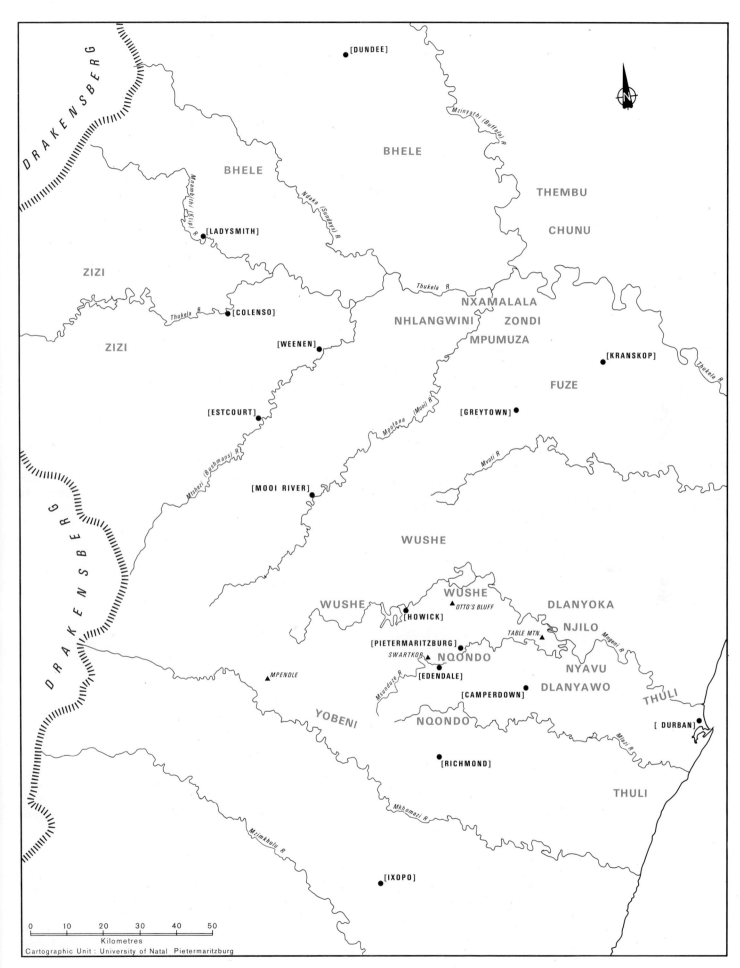

Fig. 7 The Upper Mngeni — Upper Mkhomazi region
in the 1830s.

of language and culture according to what came to be known as the 'Zulu' pattern did not begin until the establishment of Zulu domination of the Phongolo–Mzimkhulu region in the 1820s, but even today clear local differences in dialect and culture still exist in it.

In the last years of the eighteenth century and the early years of the nineteenth the struggle for supremacy among the large states that were emerging north of the Thukela was intensifying. From time to time the southward flight of refugee communities brought these conflicts to the attention of the inhabitants of Natal, but until the late 1810s they remained largely undisturbed by the momentous political events that were taking place in the regions across the river. Then, in about 1819, the victory of the Zulu under Shaka kaSenzangakhona over the Ndwandwe of Zwide kaLanga sent large bodies of refugees spilling across the Mzinyathi (Buffalo) River into northern Natal. The Bhele and Zizi inhabitants of this region fled southwards through the Natal Midlands into East Griqualand and beyond, breaking up or expelling the chiefdoms which they encountered. A year or so later a large group of Thembu fled from the lower Mzinyathi region to escape subjugation to the Zulu, and forced their way through the chiefdoms of the Midlands and southern Natal across the Mzimkhulu. Soon afterwards their former neighbours, the Chunu, followed suit. A short while later, a number of chiefdoms in the northern Midlands, also driven by fear of the Zulu, formed a military alliance, and fled in a body through the already shattered communities to the south.

In the space of two or three years organized community life over most of the area between the Thukela and Mzimkhulu Rivers had been largely destroyed. Most of the chiefdoms that had not joined the exodus to the south had been broken up, and small groups of surviving inhabitants without cattle and often without their former leaders, were hiding out in broken or forested country. Cohesive communities, now under Zulu domination, survived only in the lower Thukela valley and in the northern coastlands. In the hills and valleys of the upper Mngeni–upper Mkhomazi region, pockets of refugees clung on in patches of forest, but all the pre-existing chiefdoms had either been destroyed or had fled to the territories across the Mzimkhulu.

It was not until after the death of Shaka in 1828 and the establishment of a new Zulu regime under Dingane that a few small communities began to re-establish themselves in central and southern Natal. Predominant among them was a group of Nhlangwini under Fodo kaNombewu. These people had originally lived between the lower Bushmans (Mtshezi) and Mooi (Mpofana) Rivers, but had made off during the upheavals of the early 1820s. In the course of nearly a decade of struggling for an existence in southern Natal and East Griqualand they had managed to preserve their cohesion as a group better than most other refugee chiefdoms. By 1830 they had settled on the middle reaches of the Mkhomazi River, and were trading ivory to the British hunter-traders who had been operating from Port Natal (later Durban) since 1824. In the early 1830s they came under the hegemony of the Zulu king Dingane who, to avoid conflict with the British traders at Port Natal, was then withdrawing his garrisons and cattle posts from the coastlands south of the Thukela and, to compensate, was beginning to extend effective Zulu authority over parts of the interior of Natal. In 1835, when Captain Allen Gardiner visited Fodo at his great place, Dumazulu, the Nhlangwini chiefdom numbered several thousand inhabitants.

9

Two much smaller groups which established themselves in the southern Midlands in the early 1830s were a section of Mpumuza under a regent, Yenge kaNontshiza, who acted for the young chief, Nobanda kaNgwane; and a section of the related Nxamalala (or Zuma) under Lugaju kaMatomela. Fear of the Zulu under Dingane had led them to separate from their respective parent chiefdoms, whose territories both lay near the confluence of the Mooi and Thukela Rivers, and to migrate southwards together. After many vicissitudes they found a refuge among the forests of the Swartkop (iMbubu)–Howick (kwaNogxaza) region, where they became tributaries of the Nhlangwini. Also in those years, a section of Fuze under Madlenya kaMahawule was allocated land by Fodo near what is now Boston, after a succession dispute had impelled them to leave the Fuze territory near Greytown. Slightly later arrivals were the Zondi (or Nadi), who moved from near the Mooi–Thukela confluence for reasons which are not recorded. Under their chief, Dlaba KaNomagaga, they were settled by Fodo in the Swartkop region near their genealogically junior relatives, the Mpumuza. A hundred and fifty years later, all four of these groups still have a presence in what was until recently called the Swartkop location.

By the mid-1830s, after a hiatus of ten years or so, a measure of settled existence was returning to the upper Mngeni–upper Mkhomazi region, with a number of small immigrant groups, ever-fearful of the sudden advent of a Zulu army, attempting to re-establish the bases of communal life. To avoid attracting the attention of the Zulu they probably kept few, if any, cattle, and depended for their livelihood on cultivating small patches of crops, gathering wild food plants, and hunting. They paid tribute to Fodo, chief of the Nhlangwini, who in turn recognized the overlordship of the Zulu king Dingane. A surviving tradition records that Fodo paid tribute to the king in pelts and feathers (which were always in demand for the dress of the Zulu armies): this would confirm that there were few cattle to be found in the region.

There is some evidence that further to the east, in the rough country near Table Mountain, small groups of former inhabitants were also re-establishing themselves in the late 1830s. Recorded tradition indicates that among them were families of the Nyamvu and the Njilo people, but it has virtually nothing to say about their history.

This, as far as the evidence goes, was the situation in the southern Midlands when, in the period 1837–9, parties of Voortrekkers came down the Drakensberg into Natal, defeated the Zulu, and proceeded to set up the Republic of Natalia. In the upper Mngeni–upper Mkhomazi region, where the Trekkers placed their capital, small African communities had for some years past been trying to revive something of the life they had known before the upheavals of the 1820s. Suddenly, and dramatically, they were faced with the problems of coping with the demands made of them by a new set of overlords. The story of how they responded still has to be written. New research into the history of the period of Trekker domination in Natal is badly needed; when it comes to be done it will no longer be able to avoid taking as one of its central themes the history of the region's African inhabitants.

Dumazulu, the great place of chief Fodo kaNombewu, was located on the Mkhomazi River some ten kilometres above the present-day Josephine bridge. Allen Gardiner's 'View of Doomazoolu', drawn in 1835, is here contrasted with a photograph taken from approximately the same spot in 1988.

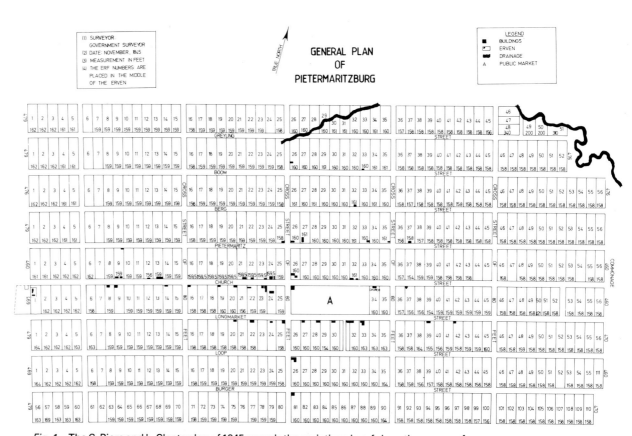

(1) SURVEYOR:
    GOVERNMENT SURVEYOR
(2) DATE: NOVEMBER, 1845
(3) MEASUREMENT IN FEET
(4) THE ERF NUMBERS ARE
    PLACED IN THE MIDDLE
    OF THE ERVEN

GENERAL PLAN
OF
PIETERMARITZBURG

Fig. 1   The C. Piers and L. Cloete plan of 1845 records the variations in erf sizes, the names of
the long streets, the absence of names for the cross streets, and the existence of
some forty buildings — of which three houses still stand (at 333 Boom Street,
Oxenham's Bakery and the Church of the Vow).

Painted from Mountain Rise
in 1844 by L. Cloete,
the fledgling dorp in Pietermaritzburg
was already quite extensive.
No cross streets are apparent.

CHAPTER THREE

The Making of the City

1

Pieter Mauritz Burg

THE GENESIS OF A VOORTREKKER *HOOFDPLAATS*

Robert Haswell

The Voortrekker period of Pietermaritzburg's history, like any other, is eminently worthy of study in its own right. More so because it has received scant attention from ethnocentric historians, with the resultant drawing and subsequent parroting of dubious conclusions. Such harsh judgement is not tempered either by the frustrating incompleteness of the archival record, which makes tentative conclusions the order of the day, or by the fact that the primary sources were written in Nederlands-Afrikaans — the day of the unilingual South African scholar (a contradiction in terms) is surely over. But perhaps above all, the Voortrekker genesis of Pietermaritzburg is important because of the indelible imprint which the choice of site, street and block plan, as well as the choice of street names, etched on the subsequent colonial and provincial capital of Natal.

In November 1837 the Retief party of Voortrekkers descended the Drakensberg into what is now Natal. Retief left the main body of his party in the foothills while he led a small advance party to the Bay of Natal. Their route is unknown, but it seems probable on two counts that Retief himself chose *en route* the site for the *hoofdplaats*.

Firstly, we know from a January 1838 letter written

by Andries Pretorius that the site had already been chosen: 'vier honderd waens was op weg na die kant waar die nuwe stad sou aangelê word die Baai af' (*Het Zuid Afrikaan*, 9 Feb. 1838). Only the Retief advance party had passed through the area by the date of Pretorius's letter. Secondly, the erf size chosen for the *hoofdplaats* matched that of Grahamstown, where Retief had been a prominent builder and citizen, as did all the subsequent dorps established by the Retief party. In the case of Grahamstown, the length of the original erven was determined by the distance from the street to the spruit, which happened to be approximately 150 paces or approximately 450 feet. Fifty paces, or approximately 150 feet, provided sufficient street frontage, so the approximately 450 x 150 foot erf came into being, and was adopted by the Retief party as their dorp *Lebensraum*. This thumbprint is to be found in all the dorps laid out by the Retief party, namely Congella, Weenen, Utrecht and Lydenburg.

One of the primary sources for this period is the diary of Erasmus Smit, the unordained minister who accompanied the Voortrekkers into Natal. A perusal of this diary suggests that although Gert Maritz, *en route* to Port Natal in May 1838, may well have passed through the site chosen for the dorp which was soon to be named partially after him, he played little or no part in the establishment of Pietermaritzburg.

On 21 July 1838 Smith recorded the existence of three small laagers 'een aan Umlaasrivier, een aan Boschmansrand en een aan Stinkhoutsberg' (Schoon, 1897, p.79).

On 23 October 1838 Smit noted that the first, and recently laid out, dorp had been named Pieter Maritz Burg in memory of the two leaders.

In November of the same year, one Gideon Joubert descended 'detweede afsit van het land af, ook genoemd stinkhoud berg ook bosjemans berg' (Jansen, 1938, p. 21), and arrived in the fledgeling dorp. He noted the existence of a sizeable furrow 'vier spit breed en twee spit diep' (Jansen, 1938, p. 22).

According to Smit, more than 100 wagons arrived in Pieter Maritz Burg during January 1839 and not surprisingly, therefore, the Volksraad was prompted to issue the following regulations and instructions to ensure the orderly development of the 'hoofdplaats':

Pietermauritzburg, 15 February 1839.

Regulation en Instructien, Geformeerd door den Raad des Volks, tot bevordering der stand en orde, van bovenstaande Stad en Hoofdplaats.

Art. 1.-Elk afgemeeten erf, zal aan den verzoeker om dezelve, worden toegekend, volgens het lot of nommer, door een ieder te worden getrokken; doch zal het ook in de verkiezing van een ieder gelaten worden, om een geheele blok der erven, 'zynde ieder blok in tien erven verdeeld,' voor hem, met en benevens zoo vele zyner familie of vrienden, 'als er nommers in dezelve zyn,' te doen aanteekenen, 'gez. onder de Suplianten genomen,' hetwelk alzoo toegekend zal worden.

2.-De erven aldus toegekend zynde, zal elk eigenaar verpligt zyn, 'ten einde dezelve te behouden,' te betalen eene somma van Rds. 5, hetzy aan kontante penningen, dan wel met een acceptatie, om binnen den tyd van 12 maanden, te voldoen,-welke betaling strekken zal, tot eene volledige

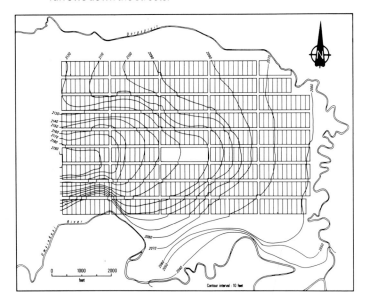

24

The Voortrekker street plan has proved to be indelible, as this 1988 aerial view reveals. Looking east across the City from above Fort Napier, Longmarket Street is in the centre.

By 1848, the date of this Piers sketch, Longmarket Street in particular was lined by rows of Cape Dutch cottages, in compliance with Article 5, and some of the early English buildings, such as the Wesleyan church on Chapel Street, stood out in contrast.

voldoening, aller belasting op dezelve, voor den tyd van vyf jaren.

3.-Doch naardien het wordt vereischt, dat het water, uit de kleine Boschjesmansrivier, opgeleid worde, om tot gedeeltelyke bewatering der stad te strekken; zoo zal ook ieder erf eigenaar verpligt zyn, de belasting in gelyke graden te dragen, tot belooning van dat werk.

4.-Ieder erf eigenaar zal ook gehouden zyn, zyn erf, binnen den tyd van twee maanden te bezaaijen of te beplanten, met kostbare Graan of Planten; alsmede binnen gemelde tyd, dezelve behoorlyk te beveiligen, voor schade, te zeggen, met een sooijen-wal te ommuren, dan wel met palen toeteplanten, doch in goeden order, terwyl na expiratie der gemelde tyd, alle regten, tot schadevergoeding op dezelve, vervalt, volgens Ordonnantie, d.d. 11 February 1839; en de nalatige, mede onderhevig zal zyn, aan boeten en straffen, daartoe expresselyk te zullen worden bepaald.

5.-De woonhuizen zullen, naar aanwyzing van een daartoe gekwalificeerd persoon, in den front moeten wordern gebouwd, en in een gelyke linie.

6.-Het regt van waterleiding, zan zyn, voor ieder erf, by beurten, waarover nadere bepalingen gemaakt zullen worden.

Aldus gedaan en gestatueerd, op Dag, Maand en Jaar als boven.

'Get.' J.S. MARITZ, President.
Op last van den Raad,
JAN GER. BANTJES, Klerk.

Article 1 suggests that individual erven were allocated to applicants by means of a draw, with the proviso that relations and friends could acquire a whole block of ten erven. Article 2 set the price for each erf at five rixdollars, to be paid within twelve months. Yet despite this reference to a lottery and set prices, Theal described the acquisition of erven as follows:

Not one of the farmers had ever heard or read of the successful sale by auction in Rome of land on which a

Carthaginian army was encamped, but they acted as if they were imbued with a similar spirit (Theal, 1964, p. 378).

Articles 3 and 6 dealt with irrigation matters. The former required each owner of an erf to contribute toward the cost of irrigating the dorp with water led from the 'Kleine Bosjeman's River'. The latter stated that each erf owner would have access to the water, and that further regulations would be framed.

Article 4 stipulated that each erf be cultivated and enclosed within two months by a sod wall or wooden palisade.

Article 5 stipulated that dwelling houses should be built in a single line, as would be pointed out by a qualified person, at the front of the erf.

In combination the six articles set the stage for the rapid but regulated growth of the dorp.

In March 1839 Andries Pretorius reported enthusiastically:

... een groote, aangename, water ryk Dorp, Pieter Mauritz Burgh, begint dagelyks deszelfs hoofd boven de omliggende heuwels te verheffen — 300 fraaye erven zyn reeds opgemeten en gedeeltlyk beplant (Graham's Town Journal, 11 April 1839).

Pretorius's description has been discredited as a 'pardonable exaggeration' (Hattersley, 1938, p. 19), a look 'through rose-coloured spectacles' (Nathan, 1937, p. 266) and 'heeltemaal te vleiend' (Liebenberg, 1977, p. 51). However, Commissioner Henry Cloete's 1843 Register of Erven claimed at Pietermaritzburg records that more than 120 erven had indeed been granted by April 1839. If it is borne in mind that every adult male burgher could have claimed an erf in the hoofdplaats, Greyling would have had to lay out several hundred erven as rapidly as he could. Pretorius's description appears therefore to be realistic rather than hyperbolic after all.

A letter of November 1840 which appeared in *De Ware Afrikaan* stated:

> Gy kunt u inderdaad niet verbeelden hoe snel deze Stad bewouwd wordt.

A further indication that the dorp was laid out in rather a hurry is the variation in erf, and therefore block, dimensions. The first British plan revealed that the length of erven ranged from 460 to 479 English feet. If Greyling had used a chain of Rhineland measure which would have enabled him to lay out in Rhineland reet or roods (1 Rhineland foot = 1,03 English feet; one Rhineland rood = 12,36 English feet) the length of an erf should either have been 450 Rhineland feet or 463,5 English feet, or 36 Rhineland roods or 445 English feet. It seems probable then that Greyling paced out the erven in somewhat of a hurry, and this resulted not only in considerable variation in erf lengths, but in most of the erven exceeding the 36 Rhineland roods which I suspect Greyling was aiming at. This suspicion is supported by the Volksraad minutes of 23 February, 1842:

> Voorgeslaan door den Plaatzelyken Llandt dat bevonden is alle de Erfen te Pietr. Ms. Burg volgens Rheinlands maat te groot is (*Notule van die Natalse Volksraad*, 1958, p. 142).

The dorp's eight long streets were named Kerk, Langemark, Burger, Loop, Pieter Mauritz, Berg, Boom and Greyling. Only the two named after persons were not used in pre-English Cape Town and many other Voortrekker dorps, and the others can therefore be identified as the first generation of Afrikaner street names. The cross streets were not named until September 1844. From the upper or western end, with their present names in parentheses,

Outspanning in central Pietermaritzburg in 1854. The gabled stone building is the Church of the Vow.

they read: Rudolph (West); Retief (Chapel); Nel (Commercial); Pretorius (Boshoff); Uys (Retief) and Lombard (East) (*Notule van die Natalse Volksraad*, 1958, p. 238).

One other morphologic feature needs to be noted, and thus complete our review of the dorp's layout, and that is the peripheral location of the Voortrekker cemetery. The early Cape dorps, such as Stellenbosch, Zwartland (Malmesbury), Swellendam, Paarl and Tulbagh have central churches and adjacent churchyards. The Voortrekker dorps on the other hand all have central churches but their cemeteries are located well away on the perimeter of the original layout. Pietermaritzburg therefore, and unlike British settler towns such as Richmond, Howick and Estcourt, does not contain a single churchyard burial ground.

┌─ PIETER MAURITZ BURG

Robert Haswell

It is common knowledge that Pietermaritzburg was named after the two Voortrekker leaders PIETER Retief and Gerrit MARITZ. Yet originally the name was spelt PIETER MAURITZ BURG, and it has been claimed that Pieter and Mauritz were Retief's Christian names.

The handwritten *Minutes of the Natal Volksraad* consistently include the 'u' in Mauritz until October 1843. Bearing in mind that the Minutes were regularly signed by J.S. Maritz, Gerrit's older brother, it is reasonable to conclude that it is not simply a spelling error. Letters written by prominent persons such as Andries Pretorius, the Revd J.J. Freeman and Governor Napier —as well as sketches and an 1850 globe on display in the House of Assembly, Adelaide, South Australia — all refer to Pieter Mauritz Burg.

Was Mauritz Retief's middle name? According to two authors the answer is 'yes'. Dominee Frans Lion Cachet, in his *De Worstelstrijd der Transvalers* (1898), noted: 'Men vindt den naam ook geschreven Pieter-Mauritzburg en ik zelf heb van oude Voortrekkers gehoord dat dit de rechte naam is. Mijn werd verzekerd dat men oorspronklijk alleen Pieter Mauritz Retief wilde vernoemen ...' J.C. Voight, in his *Fifty Years of the History of the Republic in South Africa* (1969), states: '... the place was known as Pieter Mauritzburg, in memory of Pieter Maurits Retief, the fallen leader. In March 1839 Pietermaritzburg was established

as a township, the old name of Pieter Mauritzburg being changed in order to do honour to the memory of Gerrit Maritz as well as that of Retief'.

However, the Volksraad Minutes, which are admittedly incomplete, contain no reference to a name change. Furthermore, Retief did not use Mauritz, or even the initial M in his signature, and neither his birth nor his baptismal certificate record a middle name. Moreoever, the Retief family tree does not contain the name Mauritz.

After all is said and done, is Mauritz simply the older form of Maritz? That is the implication of the use of both spellings by Erasmus Smit, the Voortrekker minister, as well as the 1839 aside by Adulphe Delegorgue 'Mauritz or Maritz'. And yet ...

5

Pieter Mauritzburg den 27 Juny 1839

An extract from the Volksraad Minutes.

Pietermaritzburg in 1845.(6)

Thatching Voortrekker houses in upper Longmarket Street *c.*1845. Fort Napier is in the background and an example of a palisade fence as prescribed in Article 4 can be seen in the foreground. (7)

Understandably, the Voortrekkers appear initially to have erected rudimentary and temporary structures. Late in 1839, Delegorgue described them as crude shanties made of wood and reeds, and plastered with dung (Delegorgue, 1847, p. 194). But the arrival of the Pistorius brothers, who began the manufacture of bricks and tiles in 1840, along with the quarrying of shale by Ortmann, meant that the building materials necessary to erect permanent structures were soon available. Significantly, the Volksraad regulations of February 1839 did not oblige erf owners to build houses within a set period. It should be remembered that the owner's farm, and not his erf in the dorp, was his permanent home. All that was necessary in the dorp was a *tuishuis* — a two-roomed cottage for use during Nagmaal, or quarterly communion services. Such diminutive structures may not have struck the first British

commissioners and surveyors as permanent dwellings and therefore indicative of bona fide occupation. These provisos suggest that one should read between the lines of early British housing documentation.

Furthermore, the early records pertaining to the number and location of houses in the burgeoning dorp are inconsistent. Commissioner Henry Cloete's 1843 *Register of Erven* distinguished between unoccupied, occupied and built-upon erven. His tally of 161 buildings is corroborated by an 1844 listing of houses by street in *De Natalier*. However, in November 1845, surveyors Charles Piers and Lawrence Cloete produced their General Plan, which showed the location of a mere 51 buildings. This discrepancy led certain scholars to contend that as many as 11 buildings existing today appear to be of 1843 vintage (Haswell and Brann, 1983). Thick walls of mudbrick or shale, haylofts, yellowwood floors and/or ceilings, location at street's edge, and the characteristic expansion of the house by the addition of an identical second unit, were submitted, along with historic sketches as corroboratory evidence. Their boldness prompted a detailed, but strictly archival, response which concluded that no more than five buildings — 333 Boom Street, the Church of the Vow, Oxenham's Bakery, Government House and 412 Longmarket Street — date back to 1845 (Labuschagne, 1986). Until such time as further evidence and alternative interpretations appear, the debate is largely academic. Two plans which could well throw considerably more light on the 'oldest houses' question are the Voortrekker-period plan mentioned in the Volksraad Minutes (*Notule van die Natalse Volksraad*, 1958, p. 210) and Hughbert Baker's 1850 plan (*Natal Witness*, 10 Nov., 1851). But, in the final analysis, the existence of a building on an historic plan does not prove that an extant building in the same location is the one shown on the plan. A reliably dated sketch and appropriate building materials may well prove to be more diagnostic.

Despite the fact that Afrikaner hegemony in Pietermaritzburg was short-lived, and that few Voortrekker buildings have survived, the central area of the modern City was indelibly stamped as a dorp. The largely rectangular blocks — approximately 1 500 x 450 feet — were laid out in such a manner that water could be led down the eight long streets, which run basically from west to east. By contrast, the north to south cross streets were almost an afterthought and number only five. Furthermore, only two — Commercial and Boshoff — are through routes to the City's expanding northern and southern suburbs. Thus, that standard modern solution to facilitate cross-town traffic flow, one-way streets, will not materially improve north-south traffic. The City's dorp blocks also encourage jaywalking.

On the positive side, few cities have the legacy of a large central block for public purposes, and there are signs that current plans recognize the focal potential of this 'square', or rather squares. In addition, the central area's deep properties present good opportunities for conservation-minded development. In many instances it should be possible to conserve the historic street-facing buildings by building on the presently often under- or unused midblock area. The historic British reaction to subdivide and create lanes, and an elaboration of this feature, could bequeath an intricate, comparatively tranquil and human-scale pedestrian area to the next generation.

THE CHURCH OF THE VOW

J. Andre Labuschagne

The importance of the Voortrekker Museum in Pietermaritzburg, generally believed to be the Church of the Vow, is almost impossible to overestimate. While the building has undoubtedly effectively served as the Church of the Vow, there is evidence to suggest that it was never meant to be used permanently as a church.

Erf 34 Longmarket Street is the erf on which the first Voortrekker parsonage was built. Known today as the Voortrekker Museum, it was originally built as a house. When in 1947 this view was published a national controversy developed. The acceptance of the building as the Church of the Vow can be attributed to the fact that the existence of the Republic of Natalia was short-lived. Had the Voortrekker Republic developed further, the real church would undoubtedly have been built on Erf 33 Longmarket Street, or the market square, as was the case in the establishment of the vast majority of other Boer urban settlements, where it is by far the outstanding building in the community.

Two academics, Thom and Engelbrecht, were commissioned to research this question independently of one another. They concluded that the building was indeed the Church of the Vow. However, their arguments seem to stem principally from the fear that this relic exemplifying the cultural bond with the past would be disgraced if the building were shown to be built as something other than the church referred to in the Vow. This approach evades the real cultural value of the building. From a cultural geographic point of view the essence of its importance does not lie in the fact that it was once used as a church, but rather that it expresses an essential ingredient of the early Voortrekker dorp, a concept which was firmly entrenched in the Boer immigrant cultural baggage, namely, the position of the building on the front of the erf.

In all probability church services were held in homes until the church was to have been completed. There are references to the effect that Widow Retief's house was used for this purpose, part of which is still believed to be standing on Erf 232 Church Street. According to the wife of the then minister Erasmus Smit, they first used a 'riete kerk gebouw', presumably the one known to have stood in Berg Street. The implementation of one version of the Vow had its first step when, on 13 May 1839, J.J. Burger and J.S. Maritz, representatives of the 'treksraad', wrote requesting that a church be built. While it is reported to have been commenced with soon after this, a Volksraad resolution in September of that year stated that a 'voersoekschrift' was received from the Church Council '... omtrend een huis tot de Kerk...' Pretorius was involved in managing the erection of the building. The reed church is the one probably referred to in the early part of 1839, although it must be noted that the Voortrekkers started collecting subscriptions for the erection of a church at this time.

A problem evidently arose when, on securing the services of Revd Daniel Lindley, they had to build a manse and a church. In March 1840 J.P. Zietsman suggested a definite plan to overcome this difficulty. The decision was to direct the building project to the erection of a parsonage, 50ft. along its frontage, 30ft. wide and 13ft. high and on the 'pastorie grond', after which the church would be completed. These measurements correspond with the existing building. The early Volksraad clearly stated that the building would first be used as a church and then converted to a parsonage when 'een behoorlijke kerk' had been erected. When Cloete registered land claims in 1843 he similarly described the erf as claimed by the Dutch Reformed Church for the erection of the parsonage. In fact, soon after the consecration of this temporary church the Volksraad resolved that a new church be built. This building was thus never intended to be the permanent church and, built as a house, it had, by Volksraad resolution, to be placed on the street line.

According to one old Voortrekker, J.H. Steenkamp, this building was completed in 1841, but in 1843 Registrar Cloete said that it was still in progress. Parts of the building were of questionable standards and soon proved troublesome. The timber roof leaked and was replaced with thatch. A gallery was added to accommodate the growing congregation. Again in 1852 the building was fixed with a new roof and in 1855 the resident minister complained that the building was in a 'state of dilapidation'. On 2 October 1854 deacon J.C. Boshof had suggested that a new building be erected. In correspondence that followed when Dr Faure requested Erf 33 Longmarket Street for this purpose, he argued that it had been reserved by the Volksraad to erect a church and that the building then used as a church was intended to be appropriated for the minister's residence. The contention was supported by T.S. Zietsman who was the Landdrost in 1840. After much public debate it was agreed upon that the church should be granted this erf. The new church was soon commenced and was completed in 1861.

The question still remained what was to be done with the old parsonage since in the meantime another parsonage had been built on Erf 34 Loop Street. Various suggestions were put forward including to use it as a school building, to hire it, and to sell it to overcome debt. It was first sold to V. Brayhirst in 1863 but he went bankrupt and it was then hired to the Government as a school building in 1865. In 1873 David Whitelaw purchased the building with the condition attached that it would not be used as an hotel or canteen. However, subsequent to this sale it is reputed to have been used as a wagonmaker's shop, mineral water factory, tea-room, chemist, blacksmith's shop and a wool shed.

A movement to preserve the building for the descendants of the Voortrekkers was started in 1908 and a commission was appointed by the Church Council for this purpose. A nation-wide collection of funds for the purchasing of the building was undertaken. This was concluded in 1910 and the building was restored at a cost of 505 pounds sterling. The specifications were drawn up by J. Collingwood Tully. The building was opened on 16 December 1912 by General Schalk Burger and in 1938 it was declared a national monument.

The Church of the Vow in the 1880s.

8

The Church of the Vow today.

9

Pietermaritzburg and its environs

THE EARLY DECADES OF WHITE SETTLEMENT

Bev Ellis

At first glance the Trekkers' choice of site for the town may seem a curious one. Admittedly the place was a safe distance from the port, but why choose a treeless, sloping plain nestling in a hollow? Unfortunately we do not know the answer to this question, as the Trekker leaders, in attempting to attract more settlers, exaggerated its potential. But we can follow the course of the environmental history of the area and see what use the settlers made of its vaunted potential and how they, in turn, made their impact on the environment in the first few decades of white settlement. For the sake of convenience, this will be examined in relation to the changes made to the mineral resources and landform, the flora and the fauna.

From the records we have, it seems that the early white settlers made only a few minor changes to the mineral resources and landform of the town and its environs. We know that the Boers affected the natural flow of several rivers and streams, however slightly, by their irrigation schemes. The furrows they led from the Dorpspruit became a feature of the town, while a few local farmers and gardeners were skilled at building furrows and irrigating crops. Boers also quarried stone locally; stone suitable for housing and for the church (the Church of the Vow) probably came from C. Ortmann's shale quarry to the east of the town. The fact that by 1844 more than half of the 132 houses in town were of brick or shale gives us some indication of the demand for building stone and the scale of its exploitation. One enterprising farmer, P. Ferreira of the Karkloof, even mined a small coal outcrop on his farm and it is possible that the wagonload sold on the market in 1842 came from there.

During the next few decades, as the town grew with the arrival of the British settlers, the demand for building stone increased. Men such as Gabriel Eaglestone and Jesse Smith were skilled stonemasons and Eaglestone's best-known work, the Church of St. Peter's, still stands. Up until April 1860 anyone was free to quarry stone in the vicinity of the town, but then the town council resolved that, in future, permission had to be obtained and an annual rent paid for a quarry. Unfortunately all the official records of quarries are very vague, such as that of 1862 which states that quarries were worked 'in several localities chiefly near Pietermaritzburg and for the purpose of building in the City'. We are therefore left in doubt as to the exact dates and the extent of exploitation of old quarries, even ones that are still visible, like that in the Botanic Gardens. All in all, by about 1870 the most obvious signs of human activity on the landform were probably a few quarries close to town and the roads that led to the surrounding towns of Estcourt, Richmond, Greytown and Durban.

When the Trekkers first laagered at the Bushmansrand, the most noticeable features of the indigenous flora would have been the following: while the plain itself was bare, there was a forest to the north-west (the present-day Town Bush Valley area); forests to the west (the Swartkop forests) and, at some distance further inland, the mist-belt forests stretched from the Blinkwater in the north to the Mzimkhulu in the south. The impression of Lieutenant C.J. Gibb in 1843 was that there was 'scarcely any wood about this place ... the little wood where the firewood is procured will all be used up in the course of a few years'. Certainly the greatest demand on the flora around the town in the early 1840s would have been for fuel. It was needed for heating, cooking, and candle- and soap-making. The residents would have obtained fuel from the Town Bush Valley for themselves and for the only fuel-burning industry in town, the brick and tileworks run by the Pistorius family at the foot of Town Hill. From the records of the Raad it is also clear that black people removed large numbers of saplings from this forest, to the concern of the Raad. The fact that Pistorius had to advertise for firewood as early as 1843 suggests that fuel was already becoming more difficult to obtain.

The Swartkop forest and the Karkloof section of the mist-belt forests supplied the timber needed for buildings, wagons, furniture and implements. As a visit to the Voortrekker Museum shows, Boer technology made it possible for them to fell large trees and then work the wood, for they had a variety of handaxes, adzes and saws of different kinds, including the huge *kraansaag* that was taller than a man. A few families supplemented their income by felling particular species, such as yellowwood, sneezewood, stinkwood and ironwood, and selling the timber in town. Wherever this selective exploitation occurred it must have affected the composition of the forests, however slightly.

The arrival of the British settlers and the garrison meant that the demand for firewood increased; not only were there more people in the town but also the British, with their interest in producing for a market economy, established more fuel-burning industries, particularly brickworks. While the garrison's fuel supply seems to have come mainly from Swartkop, residents had several sources available. They could have cut fuel themselves in the Town Bush area or bought it at the market, where it was brought from farms such as Piet Otto's or from the thorn forest at Uys Doorns; they could also have bought it from African women who went from door to door selling bundles of wood cut from the Swartkop forests. By the early 1860s much of the local fuel supply seems to have been exhausted, proving Lieutenant Gibb's prediction correct. Fuel had to be obtained from further away so that by the mid-1870s, when the Capital was using about 555 tons per month, most of it came from the Table Mountain area, about thirty kilometres away. Some enterprising souls even started growing exotic species such as bluegums to sell as fuel to the brickyards.

Like the Boers, the British settlers wanted certain types of timber for buildings, wagons and furniture, so

Fig. 3 A plan of Pietermaritzburg and environs in 1854, showing the lots of Pistorius (bricks and tiles), Ortmann (quarry), Visagie (mill) and the compartmentalized burial ground.

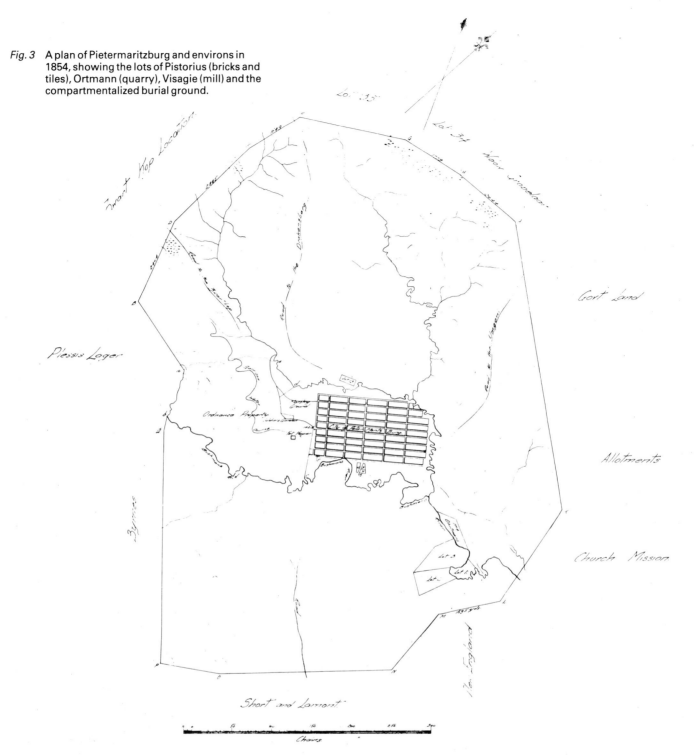

The above Diagram a B.D . . . . 2 b reduced from the original Plans of Messrs Cloete and Piers situate in the County of Petermaritzburg, District of Natal. (Extends Northwards to Lot 35. Lot 34 the widow Grobelaar, Govt. land and Allotments sold by Govt. S. to PlessisLager and Byrnes, E. to the Church Mission Grant, New England and Short and Lamont, and W. to the Zwaartkop Location) represents 28980 Acres of land from which I certify that the following portions have been deducted. Namely.

		Acres	R	P	yds.
Erven in City of Petermaritzburg		824	1	16	
Allotments as follows					
G. J. Rudolf	No. 15			16	22.687
A. Z. Visagie	No. 14			17	24.5
J. C. Boshof	No. 8	2	3	15	
T. Shepstone	No. 2	102	3	2	
T. Shepstone	No. 3	153	3	35	2
P. Ferreira	No. 1	91	0	38	
Wesleyan Burial Ground	No. 10	3	0	16	28
Church of England do.	No. 9	2	2	32	24
Roman Catholic do.	No. 11	1	0	30	
Dutch do.	No. 12	4	1	13	24.5
C. Ohrtmans	No. 4	59	3	35	
Kritzinger	No. 16			13	
Pistorius	No. 13	15	1	29	1.18
		1202	0	31	5.838
Ordinance a,b,c,d,e		1689	3	8	
Total		2891	3	39	5.838
Diagram a.B.D . . . 2.b		28980	0	0	
Alienated in favour of Corporation		26088	0	0	24.422

Leaving as a remainder 26088 Acres 0 roods 0 perches 24.422 yards of land being the extent of the Borough lands of the City of Petermaritzburg which includes the Market place and streets.
Reduced Decr. 1854

(Sgd) Thomas Okes. Govt Surveyor.

they too looked to the mist-belt forests to supply their needs. But whereas there had been only a few Boer part-time sawyers, working mostly in the Karkloof forests with hand-operated tools, the British sawyers spread themselves out through much of the mist-belt forests and set up sawmills which gradually acquired sophisticated machinery. Again, with an eye to producing commodities, the British settlers made full use of the timber resources available to them. In 1865, for example, 29 of the 70 manufactures and works listed for Pietermaritzburg were concerned with timber. These were one sawmill, one cooper, twelve wagonmakers, and fifteen carpenters', joiners', and cabinetmakers' shops, while in the whole Country of Pietermaritzburg there were eight sawmills and twenty pit saws in the Karkloof forests. Whereas the pit saws were still hand-operated, the mills were either water or steam powered, which increased their output enormously.

Timber from these forests, particularly yellowwood, was also exported during the 1850s and 1860s. Wagonloads of timber went over the Berg to the states of the interior, while considerable quantities were also shipped to the Cape. Few residents of Durban could afford to use timber from the Midlands as the high transport costs made it cheaper for them to import timber from America.

Over the years, the authorities took several steps to try to curb the destruction of the indigenous flora. The most important was the proclamation of 1853 that restricted people from removing timber from crown lands without a licence to do so. This proclamation was timed to coincide with the appointment of several resident magistrates and field cornets, for the implementation of the proclamation lay in their hands. To control destruction on the borough lands, the Town Council instituted a licensing system in 1857, but, as it lacked officers to enforce it, the system failed; a special committee of 1863 reported that there was very little timber left, only firewood. In the forests surrounding the town, settler exploitation, coupled with the destruction caused by Africans making clearings for mealie gardens, led to considerable thinning of the forests. This was pointed out in the leader column of the *Natal Witness* as early as 1866. Clearly all attempts at control had failed, and the Colony was paying the price for its shortsighted policy of destroying indigenous flora without replacing it at all. At last, in 1867, the first forest conservator in Natal, James Archbell, was appointed to the Swartkop forests, but Natal still had to wait more than twenty years for a department of forestry.

One of the reasons the Trekkers found Natal attractive was the wealth of game in the area. In the immediate environs of the Bushmansrand there were several species of animals suitable as food for the Boers. On the nearby marshes there were wild duck, snipe and species of widow bird; on the surrounding plains and hillsides there were pheasant and partridge, oribi, duiker and reedbuck. Further afield, one could hunt eland and buffalo in the Noodsberg and buffalo at the Dargle and the Karkloof.

Some Boers hunted particular animals for commercial gain. Using Pietermaritzburg as a market base, they brought in skins, such as buffalo and eland, as well as ivory. While there is no complete record of either the quantity sold or the origin of these commodities, it is

Fort Napier and Pietermaritzburg in 1851.

By the turn of the century only private farms could yield bags such as this.

possible that many of the animals destroyed came from the environment around the town, for these species could all be found there in the early 1840s. Indeed, it was still possible, in 1842, for a man to shoot seventeen elephant in one month in the Karkloof forests! A glance at the prices paid on the market in November 1844 shows the following:

Skins:	Buck	per skin	0 – 2	Rijksdalers
	Eland	per skin	5 – 6	Rijksdalers
	Buffalo	per skin	7 – 11	
	Lion	per skin	11 – 12	Rijksdalers
Ivory:	per pound		0 – 2	Rijksdalers

It is clear that certain species were of far more value to the hunter than others and one therefore presumes that these few species were more heavily exploited: as even an average-sized pair of elephant tusks weighs about 100 pounds, it was obviously far more lucrative to shoot an elephant than a buck.

The Boer leaders in the Raad valued game highly as a food resource and consequently took steps to conserve it. In 1841 the Raad resolved to fine those who killed game unnecessarily or who did not 'use' it properly. (It did not define what it meant by the term 'use'.) This appears to have been the first resolution concerning game preservation made by a Boer state in southern Africa.

When the British settlers arrived, they killed game for much the same reasons as the Boers had. However, because the white population increased dramatically in size in the early 1850s, there was a rapid decline in the populations of certain species of game. The most important animal product for trade was still ivory, but as the last recorded sighting of elephant in the Natal Midlands took place in 1848, when a herd of about 32 was seen 50 kilometres north-west of the Capital, it is clear that ivory sold after that date probably came from the Overberg or from north of the Thukela. Some ivory could have been obtained from hippo, for these were hunted in the Mngeni in the 1850s, but by 1864 they were seen only occasionally in the stretch of river near the Albert Falls. Lion and leopard skins also fetched a good price: while both species were found near the town in the 1840s, by the late 1850s lion had moved away and leopard were seen only in the midst-belt forests.

As the years went by, it became increasingly difficult to find game around Pietermaritzburg for the pot. By the 1860s there are no records of this sort of activity so one

assumes that the bird and buck populations must have been severely reduced. Accounts of hunting for sport give a similar picture. In the 1840s, the officers of Fort Napier found the area a veritable 'paradise' for sportsmen: an afternoon's shooting produced a fine bag. During the next decade, when hunting became fashionable amongst members of the wealthier classes, hunts took place to the south and west of the town and bags included reedbuck, oribi, duiker and paauw. By the late 1860s sportsmen had to travel far further away from the town for the pleasures of the chase. But while game in the environs of the town was thinned out, on the farms of the Dargle and the Karkloof it was still sufficiently plentiful for farmers to hunt regularly for food, and advertisements for farms in the *Natal Witness* commonly included descriptions of the game found on them.

One searches in vain for any records of residents of Pietermaritzburg catching fish from the nearby rivers for sale: it appears that the townspeople did not attempt to make use of this resource. If they wished to eat fish, they either ate dried or pickled fish that had been imported, or occasionally they could buy fresh fish that was brought up from Durban. This was done only in winter because the lack of refrigeration made the transport of fresh fish in the summer heat impossible.

Unlike the Boer administration, the British one made no move to protect game during its first twenty years of control. Eventually it was the sportsmen, led by Charles Barter, who agitated for Natal's first game law, in 1866. The chief concern of this élite group was not an aesthetic appreciation of the fauna of the Colony, but rather that numbers of certain species of game were decreasing and this heralded an end to their sporting pleasure. Hence the main clauses of the law were concerned with the types of animals they liked to shoot. In fact, the protection given was minimal, partly because it prohibited the destruction of a few species during their supposed breeding seasons only, but also because no officers were appointed to implement the law. There was little game left near to the town to be protected: some animals had moved away from the human settlement, others had been destroyed. There was also a marked decrease in the variety of game around the town by 1870 for several species were no longer found there. These included elephant, hippo, buffalo and lion.

The founders of Pietermaritzburg established the town in an area where human beings had utilized natural resources for hundreds of years already. With the arrival of the whites, the nature and scale of human exploitive activities changed, mainly because of superior technology and through production for the market. The most obvious changes in the first few decades concerned the indigenous flora and fauna. The settlers used up much of the woody vegetation near the town and, together with the local black population, were responsible for substantial thinning of the surrounding forests. They also preyed heavily on those species of game that provided food or trade articles, so that game around the town diminished rapidly in both number and variety. Much of the impact made by the whites must have been mirrored in the Swartkop location where some people intensified their exploitation of the forests in response to the presence of a market in the town. When Pietermaritzburg first began to feel the effects of the discovery of diamonds at Kimberley, the early phase of her environmental history ended.

The segregated city

Trevor Wills

In *The Story of an African City*, J. Forsyth Ingram introduces Pietermaritzburg in the 1890s by narrating a journey by train to the Capital from Durban. His description of the Capital, '... nestling under the noble Zwaartkop range of mountains', begins at Foxhill Station, to the south of the City. From the ridge behind Foxhill Station, next to the Richmond Road where it passes the suburb of Westgate, the full extent of modern metropolitan Pietermaritzburg is revealed in one panoramic sweep.

On the northern side of the City, the bright regularity of houses in the Indian residential area of Northdale contrasts with the dark wooded escarpment which partially encircles the City, and with the leafy and affluent suburbs to the north-west of the city centre. The still stark new suburbs to the south-east, such as Hayfields and Bisley, contrast with the well-wooded nucleus of Scottsville. In all these areas the boundary of the City is well defined; one can detect a hard edge where suburbs (or industrial zones) end and farmland or forest begins. This is not true of the western sector of greater Pietermaritzburg, however, where the black residential areas stretch seemingly endlessly up the valley, with the rigidly planned township of Imbali giving way to the more amorphous Edendale. The black commuting belt stretches some thirty kilometres from the heart of the Capital, by which point the density of settlement has thinned considerably and a more traditional landscape pattern is evident. Over half of the metropolitan population of approaching 500 000 is housed within these townships and 'peri-urban' areas.

From this vantage point on Foxhill one can also clearly see that the black, Indian and coloured suburbs of Pietermaritzburg are detached from the core of the City, and the white suburbs flanking it, by strips of open space and/or industrial areas. The form of the City is that of a sliced cake, with some of the 'wedges' removed. This 'apartheid city' form has been maintained for decades by a plethora of laws governing where people may live and move, but has its origins in the founding of the town (or more correctly the 'dorp') by the Voortrekkers, and its subsequent growth as a colonial capital under British rule. The 'colonial' nature of Pietermaritzburg did not disappear with Union. Rather it was enhanced during a period of social engineering which preceded the coming to power of the National Party in 1948, and with it the subsequent imposition of a national urban model based on racial separation.

As the City enters its 150th year, however, Pietermaritzburg stands on the threshold of major changes in form and character. Only once these have been achieved, some will argue, will it truly warrant the title 'African City'. What follows provides a broad overview of the changes in the social geography of the City, looking at where people have lived and worked and why, in the colonial town, the segregated city and the apartheid city; it ends with some speculation about 'post-apartheid' Pietermaritzburg.

The colonial town 1845–1910

The Voortrekker period may well have been of short duration, but the legacy of Trekker town-planning influences Pietermaritzburg to this day. The first Municipal Board of Commissioners, appointed in 1848 and succeeded soon afterwards by an elected Town Council when borough status was accorded the town in 1854, inherited an extensive (if sparsely populated) town of some 460 erven. The borough was also generously endowed with 26 000 acres of townlands, comprising the commonage with which the Voortrekkers invariably surrounded their settlements, and all unalienated erven in the town layout itself.

Although this endowment has been progressively reduced over the years by the sale of townlands, successive town councils have had a considerable say in the nature of development around the City — at times releasing land to raise revenue and prompt development, and even today retaining land as open space.

Whatever the Voortrekkers had intended for Pietermaritzburg, what arose in the latter half of the nineteenth century was a colonial town which echoed in its form and function countless other such towns elsewhere in the British Empire, particularly in Africa.

POPULATION CHANGE: PIETERMARITZBURG 1852–1939

Year	Whites	Asians	Coloureds	Africans	Total
1852[1]	1 508			892	2 400
1860	2 336			1 435	3 771
1863	3 118	78		1 795	4 991
1880	6 008	754		3 309	10 151
1891[2]	9 986	2 545		4 968	17 500
1902[3]	19 521	4 677		10 478	34 676
1911[4]	14 848	6 485	1 196	8 010	30 539
1920	16 925	7 293	1 270	9 067	34 555
1939	21 904	8 775	2 142	12 300	45 121

Notes
1. Coloured persons do not appear to have been enumerated separately until the 1890s and there are no separate figures for them until the first national census — 1911. The Burgess Roll of 1854 adds to the population figures of 1852 by revealing that 50 householders still described themselves as farmers, compared to 26 storekeepers and 21 merchants (plus 7 who preferred to be known simply as 'gentlemen'!).
2. Coloureds were explicitly included with whites.
3. The strain placed on the town's resources by the South African War is shown by the near doubling of population. The total includes the garrison at Fort Napier as well as over 1 500 persons in the 'Burgher Camp'. This influx was temporary as the 1911 figures (first National Census) show.
4. The 1911 National Census listed Pietermaritzburg as the new Union's ninth largest town.
Source: Meineke and Summers (1983)

All the ingredients of the colonial town were present: the military cantonment (in this case the garrison at Fort Napier); the clustering nearby of the civilian élite (at the head of the grid in the vicinity of what was to become Government House); the market square and its surrounding commercial enterprises; the administrative precinct (more grandiose than one would expect of a town of Pietermaritzburg's size, after the Colony became self-governing) — all welded together by a thinly spread population of small tradesmen, craftsmen and artisans. An effective cordon sanitaire separated the colonists from the indigenous population (with the exception of those in

PIETERMARITZBURG'S COAT OF ARMS

The civic coat of arms was registered in the College of Arms, London, on 29 May 1961, and registered in terms of the South African Heraldry Act, 1962, by publication in the Government Gazette on 4 May 1973.

Blazon: Per fesse azure and vert, over all an elephant statant or, tusked argent. Crest: on a wreath or and vert, a sun in splendour bleu celeste charged with five mullets in cross, that in the centre or, the others argent. Mantled vert, doubled or.

Supporters: on each side a black wildebeest proper, each charged on the shoulder with an escutcheon, that on the dexter being a shield of the Union flag of the United Kingdom and that on the sinister being of the old Natalia flag, namely, tierce in pile from sinister to dexter, gules, argent and azure.

Significance: the elephant has reference to the Zulu name for Pietermaritzburg, spelled Umgungunhlovu on the coat-of-arms, and thought to mean 'the abode of the elephant' or the royal capital. The gold star in the centre of the crest alludes to the star of Bethlehem and the discovery of Natal by the Portuguese on Christmas day, 1497. The four silver stars represent the southern cross and indicate Natal's geographical position. The supporters are the black wildebeest (white-tailed gnu) which appear on the coat-of-arms of Natal. The charges on their shoulders allude to Pietermaritzburg having been the capital of a Boer republic and a British colony.

Fig. 4 Alex Mair's 1870 plan.

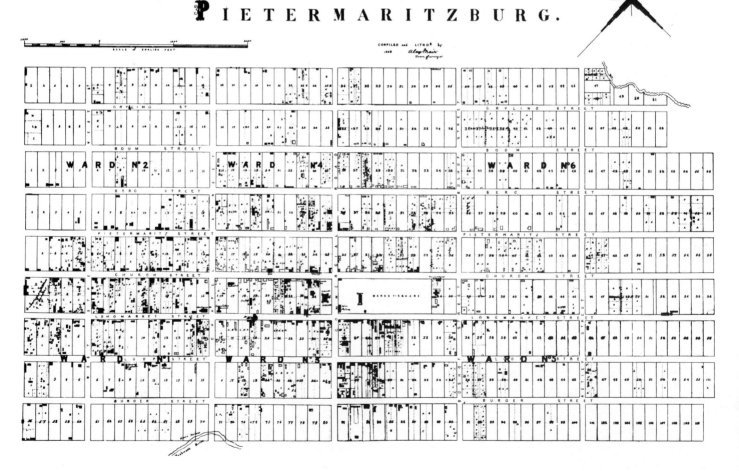

The Knipe Street barracks built to accommodate Indian workers in the late 19th century. (12)

A pavement muthi shop. (13)

An Arabian merchant's store near the intersection of Church Street and Commercial Road. The City Hall tower is dressed to celebrate the relief of Mafeking in May 1900. (14)

domestic employment) who were increasingly drawn towards the town. The black residents were expected to provide their own accommodation on the periphery of the town, although accommodation was typically provided for certain categories of employee, in the form of barracks or compounds.

Borough Surveyor (and cartographer) Alex Mair's 1869 map of Pietermaritzburg reveals just how thinly settled the town was at that time. Indians had begun to arrive in the town from the early 1860s (the table shows that 78 'Asian' settlers were enumerated in 1863). Many of the first Indian settlers were Hindi- or Tamil-speaking Hindus. They were attracted by Pietermaritzburg's large irrigated erven in the lower, largely unoccupied, part of the town layout and later to smallholdings beyond the original nucleus. By the 1890s the lower reaches of Church Street and Longmarket Street had acquired a distinctive Indian flavour, with temples, stores, gabled houses, market gardens and barracks. The 'barrack' became a ubiquitous feature of Indian residential areas and took the form of a row of rooms, usually opening directly onto a veranda on the street side, and onto a yard at the rear with communal ablution facilities. Sometimes the barracks were organized in a rectangle with a central courtyard. It is argued that the 'barrack', as housing type and descriptive term, is a part of what is called the 'colonial third culture', produced by the fusion of British and Indian experiences of British colonialism in India, and exported elsewhere in the Empire. Barracks are very rare in Pietermaritzburg today: now, as then, they tend to house the poorest families in often overcrowded conditions.

In the 1880s an additional Indian component enriched the Pietermaritzburg townscape when Muslim merchants set up shop in increasing numbers, concentrating in the upper Church Street area and in the vicinity of the City Hall. These 'Arabs', as they often liked to be called, to distinguish themselves from their ex-indentured Hindu countrymen, soon captured the dominant share of the 'native' trade.

The cottage character and scale of Pietermaritzburg's small streets: Shepstone Avenue.

35

The City in 1854 compared with an aerial view taken in 1988. Chapel Street can be
clearly seen in both pictures.

Commenting on social segregation in the Capital, A.F. Hattersley wrote:

> Residence in the west end of town in proximity to the ordnance reserve, comparable in Durban to the fashionable Berea, lent distinction to a family. The houses in upper Loop and Longmarket Streets, though in size and construction humble cottages, were mainly occupied by officers of the regiment in garrison or senior officials... Residents erected a barrier of social conventions — newcomers were under suspicion until it was known beyond doubt that they were neither mechanics nor likely to engage in retail trade...

Government House, Macrorie House and a number of fine large red-brick residences (many today sub-divided or sadly neglected) still mirror the past status of this quarter of the City; while in a more modest way the leafy tranquillity of contemporary Shepstone Avenue reflects the atmosphere of an age gone by.

The erosion of the exclusive character of this area began with the arrival of the railway in 1880, and the subsequent erection of a station adjacent to Government House. The departure of the last garrison in 1914 coupled with suburban developments detracted further from this once elite area.

Past histories of Pietermaritzburg share a common failing, in that they have neglected ordinary townsfolk, particularly those who were not white. Ingram's account, for example, does not mention Indians at all, not-withstanding the fact that when his book was published in 1898 there were nearly three thousand Indians resident in the City. Similarly, in Hattersley's histories of the City scant attention is paid to either the Indian or African populations. References to prominent merchants and 'colourful' colonial characters abound, yet of the hundreds of licenced Indian hawkers who carried their baskets of fresh produce from door to door, for example, there is scarcely a mention.

Increasing attention is being paid today to the so-called informal sector, a term used to describe the growing number of usually marginal economic activities resorted to by city-dwellers without any regular, or 'formal' employment. Examples range from hawking through to car-washing, from peddling traditional medicinal remedies to dealing in drugs. Such 'informal sector' activities are not recent phenomena, however, and colonial Pietermaritzburg must have housed many who relied on their wits and ingenuity to get by in the absence of any other employment opportunities.

The Natal Census of 1904 (Colony of Natal) has an extremely detailed breakdown of the occupations of whites, 'Indians and Asians' and 'others', but unfortunately does not give African occupations. From this census we learn that in 1904 there were 284 licensed Indian hawkers, 106 Indian 'dhobies' (laundrymen) and that, of the 415 civil servants enumerated, 414 were white!

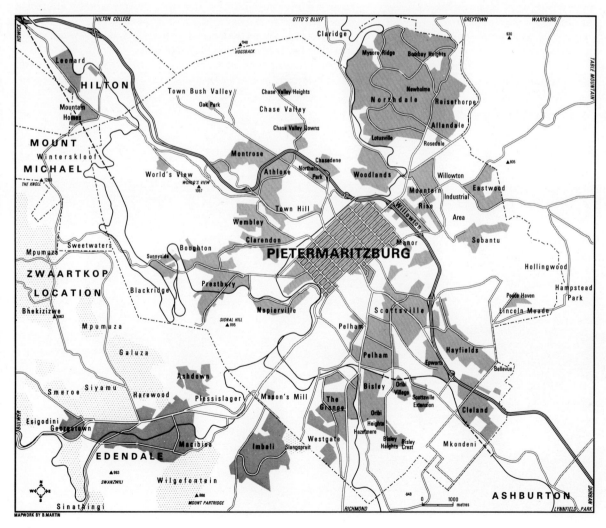

Fig. 5 Pietermaritzburg and environs in 1988.

37

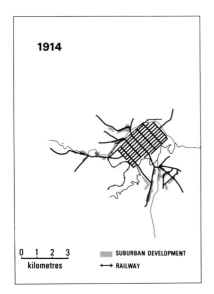

1914

0 1 2 3
kilometres

░░ SUBURBAN DEVELOPMENT
←→ RAILWAY

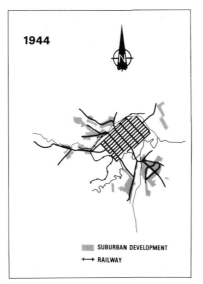

1944

N

░░ SUBURBAN DEVELOPMENT
←→ RAILWAY

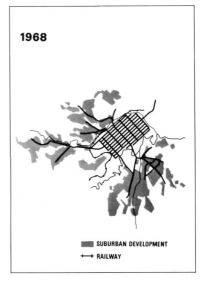

1968

░░ SUBURBAN DEVELOPMENT
←→ RAILWAY

Fig. 6
The growth
of Pietermaritzburg's
suburbs, 1914–1968.

The segregated city 1910–1960

Hattersley wrote, in his *Pietermaritzburg Panorama*, published in 1938 to commemorate the City's first hundred years, that '... little need be said of the post-war years 1918–1938'. Yet it was during the years immediately preceding the First World War and the very period Hattersley referred to, that Pietermaritzburg was transformed by suburban developments and attempts to control a burgeoning 'non-white' population whose plight (along with that of many white families) was exacerbated by long years of economic depression. It was also a period during which national policies on matters such as race and housing impacted on local developments. A not uncommon view of South African

cities is that racial segregation was produced by apartheid, and that the pivotal date in the transformation of such cities was 1948, or the coming to power of the National Party. In fact, racial segregation existed in the very earliest towns in South Africa, and by 1948 most towns were largely segregated (Cape Town being a major exception). Although less segregated than most, Pietermaritzburg became progressively more so from the turn of the century, a process enhanced by the increasing concentration of the City's white population in suburbs flanking the old town core.

The closing years of the nineteenth century had seen an increasing number of substantial 'country residences'

The view down Commercial Road in the 1890s, towards
the still largely uninhabited Scottsville Ridge.

or 'suburban villas' built beyond the confines of the original core of the City, which lay between the Msunduze and the Dorpspruit. The early years of the twentieth century, however, witnessed a more systematic development of suburbs on an entirely different scale, on both private land and townlands.

In 1900, in order to raise funds for a proposed electric tramway system, the City Council resolved to create a new suburb on a tract of land known as Outspan No. 6, which was situated just beyond the Foxhill Stream, straddling one of the routes to Durban. It was anticipated that the proceeds of the sale of land would exceed development costs, realizing funds for the tram scheme, which was itself to be used as a selling point in the development of the suburb. The south-east of the City proved popular, and the original core of Scottsville built up steadily and began to expand in various directions.

Despite the Council's anticipation that the elevated northern side of town would become the Berea of Pietermaritzburg, suburban growth there was slower, and less systematic than in the Scottsville area, with development taking the form in many cases of a gradual subdivision of larger properties. The boom in development in Wembley, Athlone and later Clarendon was to come only after the Second World War.

Some fifty years of 'white' suburban growth is shown in Fig. 6; these areas were almost exclusively occupied by white families despite the lack, until the late 1940s, of legislation enforcing segregation.

Although initially concentrated within the original grid layout of Pietermaritzburg, Indian households soon began to occupy small parcels of land beyond the city centre, often flanking streams where market gardening could take place, for example along the Dorpspruit, or along the fertile (if flood-prone) banks of the Msunduze (particularly in the Camp's Drift/New Scotland area).

The position of Indians at the time of Union in 1910 was that legislative machinery for their compulsory residential segregation existed only in the Transvaal (while Indians were excluded altogether from the OFS and those parts of Northern Natal which had been part of the old South African Republic). The period 1910 to 1946 was marked by strong 'anti-Asiatic' agitation in the Transvaal and Natal, particularly in Durban, and this ill-feeling culminated (after a number of piece-meal attempts to enforce segregation or encourage voluntary segregation) in the 1943 Trading and Occupation of Land (Transvaal and Natal) Restriction Act No. 35/1943 — more commonly known as the 'Pegging Act'. It pegged out the areas occupied by Indians in 1943, and controlled further property transactions between whites and Indians. This Act was followed in 1946 by the Asiatic Land Tenure and Representation Act No. 28/1946 (the 'Ghetto Act') which placed absolute limits on the territory occupied by Indians.

The root cause of the hostility between white and Indian residents was said to have been the alleged 'penetration' of Indians into formerly white residential areas. The government-appointed Indian Penetration Commission heard evidence that between 1927 and 1940, 512 formerly white-owned properties had been acquired by Indians in Durban, whereas during the same period only 16 such cases had been reported for Pietermaritzburg. This demonstrates that well before the introduction of any restrictive measures Pietermaritzburg was, in the minds of its officials in any event, clearly divided along racial lines. Hence municipal housing was designated for specific racial groups long before the Population Registration Act made such racial division mandatory, or the Group Areas Act demanded territorial separation.

Sobantu Village, on the south-eastern outskirts of the City, in 1988.

19

Despite the minor role played by Pietermaritzburg in the penetration debate, anti-Asiatic agitation has a long history in the Capital. In 1885 the Pietermaritzburg Chamber of Commerce unsuccessfully petitioned the Governor requesting that several, and severe, restrictions be placed on Indian traders, and recommending in particular that Indians be allowed to live and trade only in designated areas. This echoed Law No. 3/1885 of the South African Republic (Transvaal) which restricted Indians to 'Asiatic Bazaars'. In 1897 the *Natal Witness* urged that separate locations for Indians be established, whilst in the same year the Mayor of Pietermaritzburg joined his counterparts in Durban and Newcastle in petitioning the Colonial Secretary to stop the acquisition of land by Indians.

It has been generally accepted that the first legislation aimed at segregating Indians in Natal was the 1922 Durban Land Alienation Ordinance No. 14, permitting the Durban City Council to include an 'anti-Asiatic' clause into the title deeds and leases of Borough land. However, there is evidence that Pietermaritzburg had taken the initiative some 24 years earlier. In January of 1898 the Finance Committee recommended to the Town Council that a piece of townlands be '... offered for sale at an upset price of 20 pounds per acre, and that the non-Asiatic clause be inserted'. At the same meeting it was recommended that the lease on a quarry on townlands be offered by public competition '... with the usual non-Asiatic clause'.

Scrutiny of early street directories reveals that until 1905 white and Indian households were widely interspersed in the part of town below Retief Street — the 'recognized Indian area'. From that time onwards, however, the pattern that emerged was one of a mosaic of segregated areas outside the city centre (with exceptions where 'mixed' areas evolved, e.g. Pentrich) and Indian enclaves within the central grid (although on the fringes of these enclaves white, coloured and Indian families occupied the same streets).

In describing the unfolding social geography of the City we have chronicled the movement of the white and Indian residents outwards from the historic core — a phenomenon which accelerated from the 1930s onwards with greatly increased accelerated mobility (thanks to the motor car and public transport). As far as the African population of the City is concerned, however, the story is one of a largely unsuccessful battle to establish a niche near the centre of the town, where jobs were, and are, to be found.

In a letter of January 1848 to the *Natal Witness*, 65 people complained about the continuous and unpunished robbery resulting, they believed, from the influx of 'kaffers'. At the same time Surveyor-General Stanger expressed the view that each town should have a portion of its townlands appropriated for the use of Africans engaged in daily labour. In 1854 it was reported that Africans were squatting on Pietermaritzburg's townlands, and in the following year the Borough Council accepted a motion that a portion of the townlands be set aside for a 'native' village. This motion was vehemently attacked in a letter to the *Natal Chronicle*:

> The burden of proof lies with the Municipality to show that a Kafir village can safely and profitably be laid out on the Town lands. And councillors, perhaps, would do well to

consult ratepayers before they grant any site for that purpose.

In another letter to the same paper the Council's intentions were stated thus:

> They aim not, at least in this instance, at the straightening of city obliquities, but the rearing of a Model Village, where native good manners may find encouragement.

Criticisms of the Council seem to have had an effect, for despite a solitary attempt in 1856 to resuscitate the issue, it was not until August 1875 that a village in Town Bush Valley was proposed. The planned village was to be located beyond the Dorpspruit and the brickfields, and to comprise 200 half-acre plots to be leased or sold freehold. Wide streets were proposed, and sites left for a church and school. However, a number of irate residents protested at the proposed site and the Town Lands Committee was instructed to find an alternative. In fact it was not until separate townships for Africans became enforceable (and fundable) in terms of the 1923 Natives (Urban Areas) Act that the much discussed 'Model Native Village' became a reality. At that stage the major impetus for building such a village came from the Medical Officer of Health who firmly believed that the slum conditions that had developed in peripheral shanty settlements could not otherwise be eradicated.

Before Sobantu was built, municipal housing efforts had been confined to the erection in 1877 of barracks for African employees near the slaughterhouse below the confluence of the Msunduze and the Dorpspruit, the provision in 1890 of barracks for 'togt' workers nearby, and the building of hostels for males and females in 1914 and 1924 respectively.

The apartheid city: Pietermaritzburg today

By the outbreak of the Second World War many of the characteristics of Pietermaritzburg's contemporary social

Fig. 7 A model apartheid city.

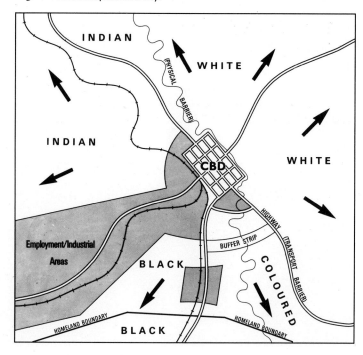

40

geography were in place. The suburbs had largely replaced the central area as the domain of the white élite, and this was particularly true of the new suburban areas blossoming ever higher up the hilly northern edge of the City, on either side of the old transport riders' route to the interior. The central area remained the workplace for the majority of residents of all races (a regular private motor-bus service having linked Edendale and the City many years before the municipal bus service started). The urban African population, with the notable exception of Sobantu Village, was to be found south-west of the centre of town, in the valley of the Msunduze. In contrast, the Indian population distribution pattern was very dissimilar to that today, because, in addition to the large concentration in the central area and in Raisethorpe, there were pockets of Indian settlement all around the City (with the exception of the new northern suburbs). Coloured families were clustered in two major nucleations in the upper Church Street area and in the 'Indian' area below Retief Street, but had also established themselves in areas like Pentrich, Plessislaer and Raisethorpe.

Segregation in Pietermaritzburg, as in other South African cities, had evolved as the natural outcome of the large social distance that had emerged between whites and other racial groupings, and of cultural and ethnic pluralism combined with different levels of technological development. Both imposed and voluntary segregation characterized Pietermaritzburg before 1948, and had contributed to the particular social/racial mosaic that had emerged.

This 'segregation city', however, was not consciously built to a comprehensive social design, and it is this that distinguishes it from the 'apartheid city' of today, which (crudely speaking), reflects a dominant political ideology expressed in concrete form.

Long before the Group Areas Act was passed the principle that Africans were temporary sojourners in the 'white' City had been an integral part of urban planning, and the Native (Urban Areas) Act of 1923 and the

Fig. 8 Pietermaritzburg's Group Areas.

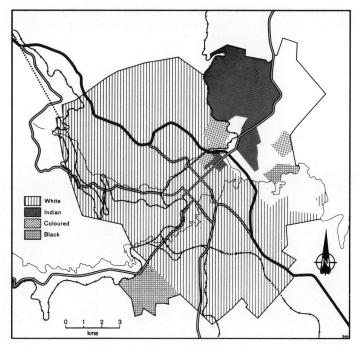

White
Indian
Coloured
Black

0 1 2 3
kms

Amended Act of 1937 effectively kept African residential areas on the distant fringes of the City. The Group Areas Act now aimed not at segregating the other race groups, because this was largely the case in any event, but at separating race groups as defined in the Population Registration Act. In the words of the Minister of the Interior at the time (1950):

> ... now this [the bill] is designed to eliminate friction between races in the Union because we believe, and believe strongly, that points of contact — all unnecessary points of contact — between races must be avoided. Contact brings about heat, and may cause a conflagration.

The removal of 'unnecessary points of contact' was to be achieved by dividing cities up into racially exclusive zones, where only one group would be allowed to live and carry on business. It follows then that if such a system of zoning is to be effective, and at the same time allow access by all to the central business quarters and employment opportunities, then a type of sectoral residential pattern would be most appropriate, with the sectors separated (as required by the Act) by buffer zones. By merging this with the already established policy of keeping Africans on the outskirts of town, or in nearby rural areas, it is possible to postulate an 'ideal apartheid city' form. From 1960 onwards Pietermaritzburg has increasingly come to adopt just such a form. The major exception is that, despite some decentralization, employment opportunities in Pieter-maritzburg remain concentrated in the central area and Willowton (64,7 per cent of the African labour force being employed in those two areas in 1972). Buffer strips have either been created (an example being the strip of land between Imbali and the Grange/Westgate from which African families were moved) or were conveniently to hand (a prime example being the municipal cemetery and the railway servitude which separates the coloured group area of Woodlands and the Indian suburb of Northdale).

The paradox of the apartheid city is that those who can least afford it live furthest from their places of work. In cities throughout the western world one finds a positive gradient in socio-economic status with distance from the city centre. The poor are clustered, often at high density in unsatisfactory housing, in the inner city, while the affluent live at low density in suburban comfort some distance from the heart of the city. This generalization holds true for most white families in our cities, but in the African sectors discriminatory legislation has pushed the centre of gravity of the poor majority (and the more affluent African minority) further and further from the city. The result is an urban African population of commuters—often long distance commuters. The only way in which this seemingly untenable urban structure is maintained is by massive State transport subsidies. Billions of rands are spent paying for this paradox. In Pietermaritzburg, the Group Areas Act quashed any hope of expanding Sobantu *in situ* and African residents of the City were henceforth diverted to the townships of Imbali, Ashdown or Edendale, all south of the City. In the absence of any commuter railway service, commuters have, until recently, had no option but to rely on the bus system (or, in a minority of cases, private transport). Today 'kombi' (minibus) taxis provide a viable alternative for the commuter, and a serious threat to the public transport system.

41

Typical bus terminus scene.

The imposed juxtaposition of high income Indian housing and industry: Mountain Rise and Willowton.

In the furthest reaches of peri-urban Vulindlela, the neighbouring magisterial district, up to three-quarters of the breadwinners commute to the City. As a result of this dependence on public transport, bus termini and their surrounds have become focuses of major importance in the City.

Another paradox of the apartheid city is evident in Mountain Rise, Pietermaritzburg's premier residential area for Indians. Here some of the wealthiest Indian families live in sumptuous houses — in the shadow of Willowton Industrial Area on the edge of the city centre! Their houses and new mosque jostle with the chimney stacks, grain elevators, and smog of the industrial strip. A chronic shortage of land for private development, a direct consequence of the Group Areas Act, prompted the emergence of Mountain Rise as an élite suburb, in a location that in the normal course of events would have attracted far less interest.

POPULATION CHANGE 1951–1985

	1985	1980	1970	1960	1951
Whites	60 161	57 256	47 115	41 221	33 992
Indians	57 006	53 330	35 999	27 758	20 402
Coloureds	13 771	12 774	8 400	5 780	3 904
Africans	61 479	67 364	47 337	64 319	42 052
Total	192 417	190 729	138 851	139 078	100 350
Vulindlela	—	185 099	116 866	27 612	—

Note: Municipal estimates suggest that the census figures for 1985 are underestimates, particularly as far as Indians are concerned.
Source: Republic of South Africa Population Census Report No. 02-85-01.

Although population censuses are notoriously unreliable, it is safe to assume from the latest census figures and growth over the past three decades that the Pietermaritzburg metropolitan area in its 150th year has a population of well over half a million.

In bald terms, the housing position of the City's population can be summarized (as far as supply is concerned) as follows:

Whites: Adequate to over-supply
Indians: Under-supply
Coloureds: Under-supply
Africans: Extreme under-supply of 'formal' housing

These generalizations, however, hide important differences. Based on Group Area zoning at present, there is a more than adequate supply of land for the development of white housing, whereas the shortage of land that can be released for private coloured and Indian housing development has placed an artificial premium on the costs of land and homes in those communities, leading to a widening gap between public and private housing. The result is not only a shortage of housing in absolute terms, but also a poor range of housing opportunities. Purely in terms of area, land may not be a problem as far as the African community is concerned, but serviced land for development that is reasonably near to work opportunities certainly is.

The demand for housing by Africans in Pietermaritzburg is reflected in the proliferation of backyard shacks and informal extensions to houses in Sobantu and Imbali. These *amalawu* or *imijondolo*, as

Sprawling settlement in 1988 in Edendale and beyond into Vulindlela.

22

Looking north across the central city towards some of the verdant and manicured white suburbs of Pietermaritzburg.

they are known, house family members, or lodgers taken in to supplement incomes. In some cases they represent the first stage of an upgrading of the basic house by the occupants, and may be superseded by more elaborate structures later, when the family income permits (this is particularly true in Imbali where there is greater security of tenure).

Backyard dwellings are by no means confined to the African areas, however, and the central Indian and coloured residential zones in particular, contain many examples ranging from converted garages and outbuildings to rudimentary wood and iron shacks. A survey in 1981 enumerated 163 such dwellings, 115 in the coloured group area.

These generalizations made about housing also mask the great range in the quality of the urban environment that has evolved over the past century and a half. Pietermaritzburg can boast of suburbs of great beauty, whose situations and views are seldom rivalled anywhere in South Africa. Examples of such carefully nurtured landscapes are Wembley, Hilton and Winterskloof. These verdant suburbs are in stark contrast to the African residential 'wedge' south of the City, where what little tree cover there was has all but disappeared, depleted by the popularity of wattle and daub construction and the reliance by many residents on open fires for cooking and heating.

The central area of Pietermaritzburg is home to about 23 000 people. Nearly half live in flats of one sort or the other, but the central area does contain tracts of single family housing in sound to excellent condition. Overcrowding reaches a peak, and physical condition a low point, in the comparatively small areas zoned for Indian and for coloured occupation. Here homes compete for space with shops, warehouses, light industry, schools, temples and mosques. For many white households the central area provides cheaper accommodation than the suburbs, or a temporary home. Others, however, are attracted by the historic character of the core of the City and its many fine old red-brick homes on tree-lined streets.

In Westgate houses recently erected for lower income white families stand empty, while across the swath of 'no man's land' Slangspruit bulges at the seams: a triangle of increasingly tightly-packed wattle and daub houses (many of which in turn have rows of lodgers' rooms appended). Sandwiched between Imbali township (built on one half of the farm Slangspruit) and the buffer strip, the Slangspruit community is no stranger to controversy. In the reshuffling of the pieces of the apartheid city, Slangspruit was excised from Pietermaritzburg, but apparently not formally placed under any other body's jurisdiction — an omission that has only recently been rectified, spurred on by the need to upgrade what is one of the poorest areas in the metropolis in physical terms.

As poor as conditions in Slangspruit and similar settlements are, the refuge they provide is undoubtedly better than that enjoyed by the City's 'street people'. Throughout the central area, but particularly in the lower reaches, vacant plots or buildings have become the transitory homes of a growing army of homeless people. Trampled grass, corrugated-cardboard 'mattresses' and the signs of open fires mark the haunts of these people who eke out an existence through begging, or scavenging for food or reusable materials like bottles or paper. Of even greater concern is that recent surveys reported in the popular Press have claimed that up to 300 homeless children roam the City by night.

The post-apartheid city: Pietermaritzburg tomorrow?

Pietermaritzburg has recently become the first city in Africa to attempt to cope with its future by implementing strategic planning procedures developed during the past decade in the United States. This has involved identifying and researching five key issues: housing, employment, the quality of life, human relations and city finances. The research has brought some sobering statistics to light. The population of the borough is expected to top 200 000 by the year 2000, and for the metropolitan area as a whole is likely to exceed 1,2 million (or double the present population). In the borough alone, over 1 000 houses will have to be built each year to keep up with demand, while in the metropolitan area about 65 000 houses will have to be built by the turn of the century. At the same time it is estimated that over 350 000 new jobs must be created in the same period. Clearly new, low-cost ways of creating employment and housing people will need to be found. This must necessarily lead to deregulation and the acceptance of 'informal' employment and housing of a standard more compatible with Pietermaritzburg's increasingly Third World character. As far as the quality of life is concerned, it is often lack of access to amenities that causes hardship, and not necessarily a lack of facilities. For example, the borough of Pietermaritzburg has some 4 000 ha of open space, and taking developed open space alone (i.e. sports

Fig. 9 A post-apartheid city. Repeal of the Group Areas Act would probably result in a move to the central area by blacks, Indians and coloureds, whereas the white suburbs would experience less mixing.

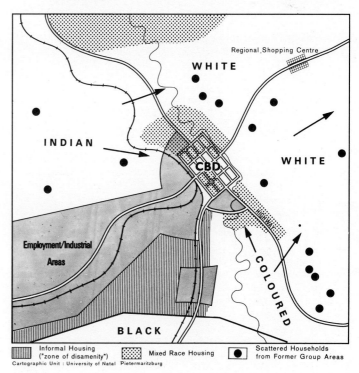

43

THE PLACE OF THE ELEPHANTS?

Adrian Koopman

What have the following words in common: Goobinschlofe, Megoonloof, Umgingiloova, Umkugings Sloave, Umkunkinglove?

They are all variations of 'Umgungundlovu', the name of King Dingane's capital between the two Mfolozi Rivers, which he built immediately after the assassination of his brother Shaka in 1828. The early traders and missionaries in Natal in the 1830s had, of course, no knowledge of Zulu, and the above are five of the sixteen variations of the name that they were responsible for.* It is interesting to see how quickly they developed a knowledge of Zulu. The Revd Owen, for example, who was responsible for 'Umkunkinglove' in an August 1837 letter, had changed this, in a letter dated October 1838, to 'Umgungunhlovu', the form which appears on the City of Pietermaritzburg's coat of arms today.

Dingane's capital was burned by the Zulus after their defeat by the Trekkers at Blood River in December 1838, and for no apparent reason, the name was given to the newly laid-out town of Pietermaritzburg. J. Forsyth Ingram, in his 1898 history of Pietermaritzburg, *The Story of An African City*, suggests that this was a 'natural transition':

> 'Umgungunhlovu', The Kafir name for the city ... was originally applied to Dingaan and his Kraal. By a natural transition it came to signify the seat of Government and Capital of the Colony. [1898: 52]

A statement by a Zulu who was eight years old at the time, recorded in Vol. 4 of *The James Stuart Archive*, is even more vague:

> The name Mgungundhlovu ... was the name of Dingana's great kraal. This was burnt and destroyed by the Boers, so we natives call Pietermaritzburg Mgungundhlovu because the other had been destroyed ... The name ... was given only after Dingana's kraal had been destroyed.

The various spellings of the name became standardized in the last century as 'Umgungunhlovu', in the first half of this century as 'Umgungundhlovu', and the modern spelling is 'Umgungundlovu', although the motto of the civic coat of arms (registered in the College of Arms, London, in 1961) still retains the spelling 'Umgungunhlovu'.

The number of different spellings of 'Umgungundlovu' is matched by the number of interpretations of the name. The following are the various suggestions put forward by historians over the years: 'Enclosure of the Elephant', 'The Place of the Rumbling of the Elephant', 'The Secret Conclave of the King', 'The Secret Plot of the Elephant', 'Lair of the Elephant', 'What is surrounded by elephants', 'The Conqueror of the Elephant'. Small wonder that Pietermaritzburg is popularly known as the 'Place of the Elephant'. An ingenious theory was put forward by James Stuart in his 1925 book *uKulumetule* ('he speaks while being silent'):

> The name Mgungundlovu seems to have derived from *isangung* a bull with horns so bent that they almost meet. Also it is like the tusks of elephants which are curved (*kumbele*) in such a way that if you put them on the ground so they face each other like those of a cow they look like a circle of warriors (*umkhumbi wamabuto*) or a cattle kraal. That is the origin of the name.

Harry Lugg, the well-known Natal historian and Zulu linguist, was obviously impressed by this theory, for in his *Life under a Zulu Shield*, he writes:

> The kraal was designed by placing two curved elephant tusks on the ground to form an oval (*umgungu*) ... It is therefore an abbreviation of *Umgunguwendlovu* or enclosure of the elephant, i.e. the king. Pietermaritzburg, known also by this name, was named after it.

It is clear that most of the proponents of the various interpretations above were aware of the Zulu verb *gunga* 'to surround, enclose', and the Zulu noun *indlovu*, 'an elephant'.

---

*The sixteen variations:

Goobinschlofe	Gungunhlovu	Megoonloof	Mgungundhlovu
Mgungundlovu	Ngungunhlovu	Umgingiloova	Umgunghlovu
Umgungundhlovu	uMgungundlovu	Umgungunhlovu	Umkugings Sloave
Umkungunglovu	Umkunkinglove	Umkunkunglovu	Ungungunhlovu

Lugg and Stuart's theories of *isangung* and *umgungu* are an attempt to explain the presence of the third *u* in 'Umgungundlovu'. Their theories are marred somewhat in that *isangungu* in Zulu is a 'flat-topped basket or earthenware pot (with small mouth) used for beer' (Doke & Vilakazi p. 12), and that *umgungu* does not exist as a separate Zulu word.

The name 'Umgungundlovu' is a compound noun with the first element meaning 'enclosure of', 'encircling', etc., and the second element meaning — apparently — 'elephant'. Perhaps the most common way of forming a compound noun in Zulu is verb + noun. As Zulu verbs end in a vowel and Zulu nouns begin with one, and as Zulu does not permit two vowels to come together, clearly one of them will have to be dropped. So if Zulu wishes to join the verb *dlula* 'to surpass' with *imithi* 'trees' to produce the compound meaning 'giraffe', the result will be either 'indlulamithi' or 'indlulimithi' but not 'indlulaimithi' or 'indlulemithi' or 'indlulumithi', or indeed anything else. (The *in*-at the beginning is the compound noun prefix, as is *um*- in Umgungundlovu. The Zulu word for giraffe is *indlulamithi*.)

Lugg is aware of this: he knows that if one compounds the verb *gunga* with the noun *indlovu*, one must get 'umgungandlovu' or 'umgungindlovu' but not 'umgungundlovu'. Hence his theory of abbreviation from 'umgungu *we* indlovu' ('enclosure *of* the elephant'). But as I have said, *umgungu* does not exist as a word. And compound nouns with the possessive element 'of' do not drop this, as in the Zulu for the elephant's ear plant: *indlebeyendlovu* indlebe 'ear' + ye'of' + ndlovu 'elephant'. This is never abbreviated to 'indlebendlovu'.

So what is the answer? Lugg put his finger on it when he wrote '... of the elephant, i.e. the king'. Since at least Shaka's day, the king has been addressed or referred to by the honorific title of 'Sir Elephant'. But since in Zulu there are noun classes which contain words referring to animals, and others, like class 1(a) which refer *only* to people, it is normal when words referring to animals are used metaphorically for people, for these to be shifted to the personal noun class. Thus Shaka in his praise-poems is addressed as *uNyathi* ('Mr Buffalo', cf. *inyathi* 'buffalo'), *uNgonyama* ('Mr Lion', cf. *ingonyama*, 'lion') and *uMamba* ('Mr Mamba', cf. *imamba*). In the same way does the Zulu king become *uNdlovu*. The mysterious third *u* in 'Umgungundlovu', then, does not belong to the first element of the compound but the second element.

Charles Pettman in his *South African Place Names* has stated:

> Umgungundlovu, the name of the 'great place' built by the monster Dingaan, immediately after his murder of Chaka the terrible, means 'the place of the rumbling of the elephant'.

But despite such rumblings, the name of Dingane's royal capital is much more prosaic — it simply means 'royal capital' — '[the place that] encloses the king'.

The elephant symbol (invariably the Indian variety) adorns both buildings and lamp poles.

fields and parks) there are 5 ha of space for every 1 000 people, which compares very favourably with European countries where a miniumum of 3,2 ha per 1 000 people is regarded as acceptable. If one takes the Indian area of the City, however, the ratio drops to less than 1 ha per 1 000 people, and for the metropolitan area as a whole the position is considerably bleaker. Whatever planning strategies are adopted, there is one inescapable fact: in the future a higher proportion of the City's population will be poor.

Local geographers have recently speculated on the changes that are likely when the Group Areas Act is repealed (Wills, Haswell and Davies, 1987). Their 'post-apartheid' city model suggests that there will be an 'implosion' in the present African residential areas, as people use their new freedom to push for housing closer to employment opportunities (and for most this means the city centre). If such housing is not provided by the public or private sectors, they argue, then the people may take the initiative and extend informal housing, currently only in peripheral collars around South African towns, nearer to the city centre. The city centre is likely to witness the most immediate change, as there are many housing opportunites the Act currently denies to people. A surplus of housing in the present white zones would rapidly be absorbed by people moving in from elsewhere in the City. The historic core of the City attracts some people because it offers the prospect of cheap temporary housing; others are attracted by the existence of homes with historic appeal in the very heart of the City; while others have lived for

generations in the large tracts of modest but sound housing still found in Pietermaritzburg's expansive central grid. All three groups are likely to be found in the city centre of tomorrow, the geographers argue. The central city of tomorrow may then be comprised of enclaves of predominantly white households zealously defending their neighbourhoods against 'invasion', and enclaves of restored, rehabilitated or 'gentrified' housing, all welded together by a matrix of mixed-race housing and non-residential land-uses.

In the long established suburbs, change is likely to be less dramatic as the low incomes of the vast majority of the future City's residents will keep conventional suburban housing out of their reach. New suburban developments constructed after the Group Areas Act goes will in all likelihood be non-racial in character because there is a dire shortage of modest suburban housing in the present Indian and coloured zones. Removing race restrictions would also mean that the protection afforded groups as far as public housing is concerned would also disappear, perhaps to the detriment of the poorer families in the Indian and coloured communities. On the City's fringes informal housing is likely to burgeon as urbanization shows little sign of abating in the near future.

Perhaps on the occasion of the City's bi-centennial some future observer will stand on the Foxhill Ridge, where this account of the changing social geography of Pietermaritzburg began, and reflect on the accuracy of these predictions of change in what will certainly then be an African city.

Fig. 10 Central Pietermaritzburg could well become a mosaic of ethnic, integrated and 'heritage' enclaves if residential segregation laws were repealed.

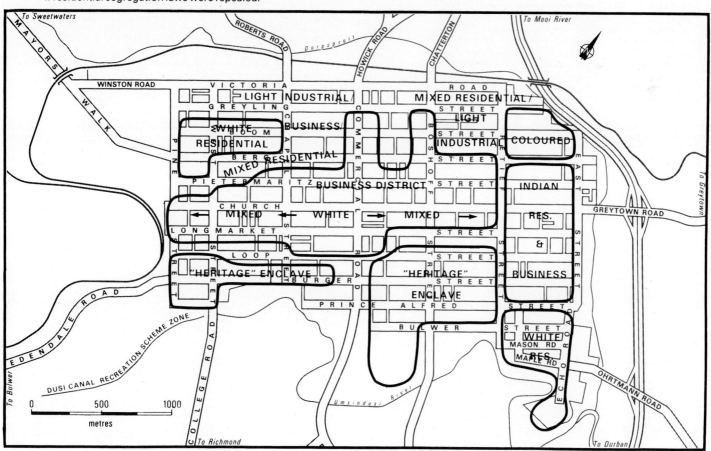

45

1

The YMCA building depicted on a postcard of 1902. A splendid example of late Victorian architecture, it stood on the corner of Longmarket and Buchanan Streets and was shamefully demolished in 1970.

The tower of the first City Hall with the Police Station, now Publicity House, on the right, c.1895.

CHAPTER FOUR

The Face
of the City

'A bad row of teeth'?

PIETERMARITZBURG'S ARCHITECTURE

Melanie Hillebrand

> When the discerning and articulate critic of architecture, who has yet to come, visits us in Natal, his first remark will be that there is no Natal architecture. Occasional efforts, interesting, naive, even scholarly, can be found, but they might have been produced anywhere else. Our public buildings, in Pietermaritzburg and Durban, might be the public buildings of Vancouver or Adelaide.
>
> WALLACE PATON, 1924

> There has been no gradual evolution of later and more civilized forms of architecture from older and more primitive forms... we have simply come upon them suddenly and without warning, and have begun to erect... the selfsame structures that adorn, or otherwise, the cities of London and Birmingham...
>
> C.W. METHVEN, 1898

Discerning critics (and those less discerning) have been visiting Natal for 150 years, but the time has not arrived for the comments of Wallace Paton and Cathcart Methven to be superseded. Natal's Capital City has never been architecturally unique despite its location and the inevitable eccentricities that result from colonial isolation. Numerous visitors have remarked on its pleasant setting, the haphazard range and quality of its structures and the lack of aesthetic town planning which is so characteristic of many nineteenth-century British settlements. Their comments, at best affectionate, usually indicate lack of approval. 'Alongside of Durban,' declares a visitor of 1926, 'Maritzburg cannot claim the adjective "splendid"'. And, at the height of her prosperity and architectural growth, a local journalist in 1898 cuts her down to size, thus:

> Maritzburg naturally is one of the prettiest towns in S. Africa, but artificially it is one of the most hideous. There is a complete absence of symmetry, a total lack of uniformity in colour, and a super-abundance of architectural monstrosities. Our roads are rugged, our footpaths uneven, and wherever it is possible to disfigure or render a place inartistic the opportunity is immediately seized. The Town Hall... always gives one the impression that it was dropped from the skies and just missed striking the kerbstone... The Legislative buildings may not be handsome... but whatever beauty they possess is completely discounted by the fact that on one side they are bordered by diminutive one-storey shanties.

At all stages of its history, even today, Pietermaritzburg's critics express disappointment. Why such criticism, and what, if any, were people's expectations? The comments of Paton and Methven, two of the leading architects of Natal, are revealing. The colonist of 1898 compares his city with those of Britain or 'Home'.

And the provincial architect of 1924 looks with envy at other cities of the Empire. Ambition and homesickness led to the attempted reproduction of familiar environments and structures. The aspirations of a typical Victorian city, no matter how poor, included buildings for every required public function: a town hall in which burgesses could meet and be entertained, a library, a museum, a theatre, schools and colleges, a railway station, a market place and police headquarters, post office, government offices and a prestigious residence for the head of government. Pietermaritzburg was no exception, but was the victim of a series of economic booms and slumps which resulted in the piecemeal collection of these assets. Thus its first public building of merit, Paterson's Courthouse and Post Office (1865), was designed during a period of optimism. A foundation stone was laid, but, with the onset of a disastrous economic depression, no construction work was possible and the building was completed only ten years later. The Courthouse rose in solitary splendour and Pietermaritzburg citizens longed in vain for the means to better the achievements of Durban, its wealthier rival.

Despite its status as the colonial Capital, Pietermaritzburg's private sector was notoriously tight-fisted. The municipality and Government were expected to foot the bill for the grandiose settings in which people of quality could disport themselves. Those who formed the social circles of the Governor, the British garrison, and the intellectual and religious hierarchies of what was, after all, the administrative not commercial, Capital of Natal, lived on fixed salaries. There were no captains of industry, few 'gentlemen' of independent means, and the wealthier professions tended to make Durban their headquarters.

It goes without saying that public buildings were intended as lasting architectural monuments. Most educated Britons had received a classical training and considered the man who could not identify the orders of Greek and Roman architecture to be little more than a savage. Important public buildings were therefore designed to resemble Greek temples or Renaissance palaces. In England, however, a movement, pioneered by church architects, had popularized the non-classical styles, especially Gothic. Medieval styles had been popularized in church architecture to the extent that most Victorians came to assume that Gothic was the only appropriate style for ecclesiastical buildings. Indeed, the majority of church architecture in nineteenth-century South Africa followed these lines. But Gothic only gained respectability for secular works during the 1850s when the Houses of Parliament in London were rebuilt in an elaborate Perpendicular style. The architects and public, faced with such a radical choice, took sides and argued passionately over each major public commission. This state of affairs was referred to as 'The Battle of Styles' and raged uninterrupted until the close of the century.

Natal, cut off from the architectural mainstream, tended to be conservative. Fashionable flights of fantasy were discouraged, at least during the earlier periods. The Courthouse resembles an unpretentious Italian villa. It was followed in 1881 by Dudgeon's elegant Renaissance Town Offices and in 1883 the competition for the new Legislative Assembly Buildings was won by a severely classical design with an imposing Corinthian façade and debating chamber. The next public commission of note was J.S. Brunskill's Police Station (1884), which also toed the line with its rusticated ground floor, heavy balustrades and brick pilasters.

This pattern was broken in 1889 when the municipality chose for its Town Hall, not a Gothic design, but one in the new Free Renaissance style. This was an eclectic mixture of elements based on Flemish Renaissance buildings which combined features from the Middle Ages and classicism. This was indeed an *avant-garde* choice, contemporary with some of Britain's first attempts in the new style. Despite loud protests from local classicists who had hoped to better Durban's old Town Hall, it became popular and set the pattern for architecture in Pietermaritzburg for the next thirty years.

One very practical reason for this was the cheapness and availability of brick which was a feature of the style. The stone required for classical façades had to be imported and was therefore expensive. The municipality had specified brick for the new Town Hall and the warm salmon tones of locally-produced Pietermaritzburg bricks and tiles became the favourite medium of architect William Street-Wilson, head of the firm responsible for this building. His office produced a number of important and influential examples of Free Renaissance architecture in Pietermaritzburg: St. Anne's College, Hilton; the Public Baths, Buchanan Street; Scott's Theatre; the Railway Station; the Bank of Africa Longmarket Street; and, not least, the existing City Hall which was commissioned when the first structure burnt down in 1898. Outraged classicists complained in vain as an even more elaborate collection of turrets, pilasters, gables, and plaster ornament replaced the original design. But other architects soon fulfilled the demand for shops, schools and offices in the new style.

Classicism did not, of course, lose prestige. Loyalty to the Empire was reinforced by the Anglo-Boer War of 1899–1901 and, architecturally, took the form of a bombastic Baroque revival. At the turn of the century, building in Natal was influenced by Baker, Lutyens and Shaw, who had spearheaded this movement in Britain. Important examples in Pietermaritzburg include the Railway Engineer's Office and the new Colonial Buildings.

As far as expression of the grandiose was concerned, this was Pietermaritzburg's swan-song. Edwardian jingoism was suppressed as Natal was subjected to a devastating economic depression following the Anglo-Boer War. Architects and builders were the first to feel its effects. By 1908, 80 per cent of Natal firms had either closed or their owners had emigrated. Financial rescue must have been uppermost in many Natalians' hearts when the electorate were called to vote for or against Union in 1909. Citizens of Pietermaritzburg must have been bitterly disappointed by the outcome, however. Despite its continued status as a provincial capital, Pietermaritzburg's social prestige was destroyed as most senior civil servants were retrenched or removed to the Transvaal. Durban, with its harbour facilities and industry, took over the lead in Natal, socially, economically and architecturally. After 1918, Pietermaritzburg stagnated. Few important public commissions were executed as architects and builders in the City struggled to survive in yet another post-war depression.

The relationship between economic and architectural progress can be seen most clearly when the contribution of the private sector is examined. Private enterprise in Pietermaritzburg tended to cater for the rural community

of the Midlands and for the immediate needs of the inhabitants. As the *Natal Mercury* commented in 1926:

> The principal business places seem to make the handling of agricultural implements their main line. They are run very close, as regards their number and extent, by the motor garages, which one meets at every turning. Both these things are a direct reflex of the fact that Maritzburg is the centre of a vast and rich agricultural district.

It was the intention of public institutions to finance lasting architectural monuments. Current financial difficulties might hinder their attempts, but efforts were usually rewarded with structures that suggested stability and permanency. Private architecture, on the other hand, was at liberty to follow fashion or to ignore it, and is a more obvious reflection of the growth and character of the City. Of such commercial buildings, Paton wrote:

> ... theirs is the history of our commercial growth, our booms and slumps. Business rivalry pulls down and builds up, to be rebuilt in turn. We can honestly claim that each rebuilding marks some advance in beauty and fitness, in strength and stability, in skilful planning. What though our streets resemble more an orchestra tuning up, than a harmonious symphony, or a bad row of teeth, with the perfect incisor flanked by an empty gap and a decaying stump? These may be the faults of youth and growth, of restlessness and individualism.

Ironically, the period of greatest uniformity, not to mention fitness and beauty, was the mid-nineteenth century. Early views of Church Street reveal a preference for classical façades of a Georgian simplicity. As shopowners prospered they began to show a Victorian weakness for architectural excess. Ornate cast-iron verandas were imported from Glasgow and pinned onto the elegant Renaissance fronts, giving Pietermaritzburg streets a trans-Atlantic character. At the time of the late Victorian and Edwardian period, Free Renaissance reigned supreme. Complex arrangements of brick and plaster rose

Loop Street villas.

3

49

Church Street - Pietermaritzburg

above the cast iron and were surmounted by fantastic towers and turrets. Well might the confirmed classicist wince. Yet despite individual aberrations the City retained its pleasantly human scale, and the ubiquitous red brick provided a unifying factor, with the new City Hall forming a climax at the centre of the town.

The origins and development of domestic architecture in Pietermaritzburg followed a similar pattern. The earliest houses built by the Dutch were utilitarian in the extreme. British settler dwellings differed only in their adherence to the vernacular of the English counties. As the century progressed more ambitious red-brick villas became the norm, with deep verandas and steeply pitched roofs. In keeping with the economic conditions described earlier, few palatial dwellings were created. Even the Governor had to make do with a thatched cottage during the early years. And the double-storey residences of the more prestigious areas do not compare even remotely with the grand Edwardian homes of Johannesburg or Cape Town.

The average dwelling was based in most cases on the designs published in builders' manuals popular at the time. There was much use of Free Renaissance details, bow windows, Gothic plaster-work, and ornamental wood or iron verandas. As with commercial architecture, scale, colour and proportion were unpretentious and attractive, this impression being enhanced by the tree-lined streets and well-developed gardens. Alas, the architects of the day did not see things in such a rosy light. The British Arts and Crafts movement, with its insistence on truth to materials, had many followers in South Africa who tried, without success, to educate the public. The widespread practice of speculative building and the use of mass-produced materials imported from Britain and America were frequently criticized. Paton commented:

> Fit and beautiful domestic building — the terms are synonymous — depends on the apt utilisation of local materials, to suit the climate of the country, and the habits of the inhabitants. But what could our poor grandfathers do? They had to build cheaply, and they had to build quickly. We were a commercial and importing community mostly; Natal was described as a forwarding agency in a kafir location. Therefore it was cheaper and quicker, and also good for trade to get our timber and doors and windows and ready-made fretwork for veranda ornaments from Sweden, and corrugated iron from Germany, and cast-iron balconies from Glasgow, and then, with a matchboard lining and perhaps some imported scrim and wallpaper, there was the house. It is still the secret ideal of the building societies and the older and more conservative artisans.

It pained architects to see London suburbia transported to Natal without regard for the climate or locality. According to Methven 'we stew under the corrugated iron

The classical simplicity of central Church Street in the 1880s [4 & 5] compared with the ornateness of the early Edwardian era. [6 & 7]

A turn-of-the-century corner shop, [8] in the Free Renaissance Style.

'An excrescene on a roof behind a covered veranda.' Cape Dutch revival in Scottsville. [9]

A Victorian double-storey veranda house, [10] demolished in 1979.

'A bad row of teeth'? [11]

roofs of houses decorated on the outside with cast iron atrocities, and on the inside with cheap oleography'. A new style of great promise was looming on the horizon, however.

After Union was enacted in May 1910, the novelty of political unity inspired architects nationwide to adopt local rather than imported styles. White settlers had studiously ignored indigenous cultures in Africa. Like British colonists everywhere, the Natalians had tended to be intolerant of all nations except their own. In Natal this intolerance had applied to any coloured races, and to the Dutch whom they despised. Ironically, the 'indigenous' architecture chosen by patriotic architects was the Cape Dutch style, which was introduced to Pietermaritzburg in 1910 by Collingwood Tully who had been invited by the Government to restore the old Church of the Vow.

This humble structure, reputedly built by the Voortrekkers in 1838, was of great emotional importance to the new Union Government and was to be converted into a Voortrekker Museum. Its appearance, never particularly aesthetic, had deteriorated, however. The well-meaning architect organized complete reconstruction with elaborate gables and teak woodwork specially imported from the Cape. To the Arts and Crafts enthusiasts the style was instantly acceptable, with its use of indigenous materials, local associations and picturesque charm. Tully followed his Voortrekker Museum with a Cape Dutch YWCA on the corner of Chapel Street. This structure was an indication of things to come. He abandoned the traditional forms and applied Cape Dutch decorative elements to what is, essentially, a Victorian double-storey veranda house. The speculative builder struck once more. His dubious skills populated Pietermaritzburg during the 1920s and 30s with Cape Dutch houses of all descriptions, very few of them in any way authentic. Wallace Paton, exasperated, asked:

> And are we not tired of the curly gable, planted, willy nilly, on to the four-roomed villa of our suburbs?... At Morgenster or Stellenberg, at Tokai or Constantia, it is fitting and beautiful behind its open pillared stoep. But what is it doing here? — An excrescence on a roof behind a covered veranda.

The Cape Dutch style was the last architectural innovation in Pietermaritzburg before the universal adoption of contemporary modes. It is interesting to note, in conclusion, that some of the earliest examples of the International style in South Africa were built here. Emerging from the depression of the 1930s, Natal, as a whole, was ready to accept modernism as an expression of optimism and progress. The forlorn lack of development before the Second World War was more than compensated for during the 1950s when much redevelopment of an unexpectedly sensitive quality took place in town and in the suburbs. Older inhabitants complained at the time that familiar landmarks were disappearing too rapidly. However, the character of the City must have been sufficiently authentic for Nikolaus Pevsner, the eminent architectural historian, to observe that Pietermaritzburg was one of the best preserved Victorian cities in the world. How different the City appears after the last two decades. Paton's depressing simile of the bad row of teeth has indeed come to pass: isolated Victorian gems exist uneasily in the shadow of anonymous sky-scrapers, and surviving villas are flanked by parking lots and demolition sites. If Pevsner were to visit today, what would his comments be?

OF BRICKS AND BONDS

Alex Duigan

Pietermaritzburg's earliest dwellings were of wattle and daub, but these were soon replaced by small buildings of sun-dried bricks. The walls were built on packed shale foundations with roofs of thatch. While there was an abundance of clay suitable for brick-making, it was only with the arrival of the Pistorius brothers from Grahamstown that the first burned or fired brick was manufactured. The brickyard was located on the western side of the town at the foot of the hill near Chapel Street. Here bricks and roof tiles were manufactured. It was only in later years that Chatterton started his brickworks on the level site north of the town in the area adjoining the present Royal Showgrounds. The shale for foundations and walls was quarried from a site, owned by Ortmann, near Ortmann Road and the N3 Freeway. Several buildings of packed shale still exist today: the oldest double-storey house, located at 333 Boom Street; a single-storey house at 366 Burger Street; old St. Peter's Cathedral; and St. Mary's Chapel at the corner of Burger Street and Commercial Road.

The local clay deposits contained considerable quantities of iron oxide which burned to a clear bright red or deep pink, and this was responsible for the delicate tones of Maritzburg's red brick. With age these bricks weathered, at different rates, to softer salmon hues, thus yielding a tapestry-like quality, especially in the glow of the afternoon sun. Subsequently the introduction of moulded bricks allowed architects and builders of the day greater freedom in detailing façades of the more important buildings.

Traditionally all brickwork is laid to a bond — the bricks in each course are so laid as to interlock in one course and offset in the next so that no vertical joint within the wall is created. In this way bonding gives stability to a wall.

There are various types of bonds, the most common being stretcher bond, followed by headers bond which is generally used on extremely curved walls. Where the radius is sharp the brick is turned on edge to reduce the space between the outer edges of the bricks.

Traditionally English bond (alternating courses of stretchers and headers) and Flemish bond (alternating use of stretchers and headers in each course) were used only on substantial buildings. Both bonds required more bricks, and more skilled craftsmen, than the consequently more common English Garden Wall bond (three courses of stretchers to each course of headers). Not surprisingly Flemish bond is rare in Maritzburg, whereas English bond is to be found in the City Hall, the old YWCA building at 195 Longmarket Street and other important buildings, and English Garden Wall bond is very common.

The variety of moulded brick with sharp arrisses or edges, as well as matching moulded bricks, allied to the presence of talented craftsmen, resulted in the erection of many fine residences and public buildings. Probably the best example is the City Hall, considered by many to be the largest load-bearing brick building in the southern hemisphere, and the relationship, in terms of both style and detail, between this building, Publicity House, the Old Supreme Court and the Old Natal Parliament complex, imparts considerable character to the heart of the City.

There were two forms of moulded or shaped brick: that with a flat weathered surface, such as splayed stretcher or header, generally used in plinth courses or as projecting string courses to parapets and window surrounds; and a rounded surface as in a fluted or reeded brick, used on the header face for the vertical reed mould to corners and door and window reveals of a building. A moulded stretcher face was also used in a plinth course and also at a string course to parapets and window surrounds.

Maritzburg's brick heritage is priceless and virtually irreplaceable. The noted architectural historian Ronald Lewcock wrote:

> ... it was a superb building material... the warm, softly-textured brick, with white painted woodwork trim, transformed the first utilitarian houses...and unified the whole city.

Details of the City Hall brickwork.

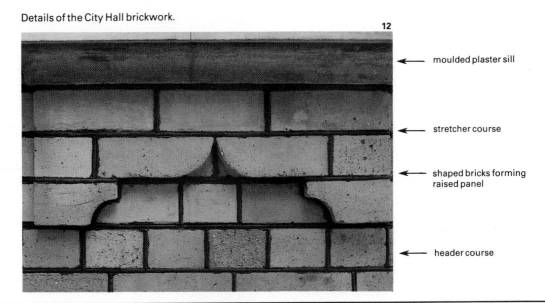

12

← moulded plaster sill

← stretcher course

← shaped bricks forming raised panel

← header course

Architecture

THE NEW AMIDST THE OLD

Hans Fransen

As part of its efforts to make the people of Pietermaritzburg more aware of the quality of its built environment, the Pietermaritzburg Society in 1986 organized a competition in which the participants were asked to name what they thought was the 'ugliest building' in the City. It seemed a fine idea at the time, but if the results proved anything, it was that whatever awareness existed lacked, in most cases, a sound aesthetic basis.

The three 'highest' scorers were all modern buildings: the Capital Towers building in Commercial Road; Natalia; and the Cathedral Church of the Holy Nativity. Their 'ugliness' seemed to be little more than their unashamed modernity. Of the three buildings, perhaps only Capital Towers can be called 'ugly' in that, in scale and texture, it relates badly to its setting. Natalia, with its twin towers, is a decidedly handsome building; though it, too, does not relate to the 'local colour' of its Pietermaritzburg context. Yet its setting, isolated in its own block, hardly calls for this.

The Cathedral is quite simply one of the City's finest buildings of any period. Its red facebrick finish pays its respects to earlier Pietermaritzburg architecture, but with its bold geometric forms and spaces the building represents the best of today, as old St. Peter's did of the nineteenth century. In this way, the old and the new churches complement each other admirably.

Now why is it that a building of such undeniable qualities can be so generally disliked? It is known that as a church, the new cathedral has yet to gain the affection of its congregation that its older counterpart had acquired over the century or more of its existence. The Gothic Revival idea that true devotion is possible only amidst mock-medieval features such as pointed arches, exposed wooden rafters and stained glass still holds good for a large section of older churchgoers. But the respondents to the ugly-building competition did not consist solely of members of the cathedral's congregation, and the building's 'high' rating undoubtedly reflects a generally held feeling that anything in a bold, contemporary style has to be ugly — especially as regards ecclesiastical architecture.

There are, of course, other views on this issue. Few architectural historians would hesitate to rate the best of today's architecture rather higher than most of the eclectic architecture of the nineteenth century. But there is no denying that in a city like Pietermaritzburg the unfortunate, misguided nineteenth century, vainly resisting the new age yet irretrievably cut off from the old, has produced a body of architecture of considerable character, of a *genius loci* greater than that Natalia or Capital Towers has to offer.

The Pietermaritzburg Society owes its initial existence to the nostalgic notions of conservationists. But it now acknowledges that what is old and venerable today was once modern; and that if, by the same token, that which goes up today should one day become venerable too, this will only be by virtue of its once having been good modern work.

If it is accepted that the built environment is, and always has been, a continuum, not a forced co-existence of two basically irreconcilable components: the good old and the bad new, then is there a way in which modern structures can be made to 'fit in' with the old — and should this be attempted?

The concept of new architecture 'matching' older work to create a harmonious totality is a fairly new phenomenon. No matter how homogeneous the architecture of a certain period and locality may have been, builders of different periods usually had no qualms about expressing their different materials, techniques,

An 1850s cottage[13].

The unadorned geometry of the Cathedral of the Holy Nativity. [14]

13

14

THE PIETERMARITZBURG TOWN HALL

Melanie Hillebrand

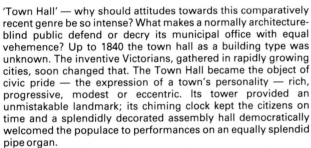

'Town Hall' — why should attitudes towards this comparatively recent genre be so intense? What makes a normally architecture-blind public defend or decry its municipal office with equal vehemence? Up to 1840 the town hall as a building type was unknown. The inventive Victorians, gathered in rapidly growing cities, soon changed that. The Town Hall became the object of civic pride — the expression of a town's personality — rich, progressive, modest or eccentric. Its tower provided an unmistakable landmark; its chiming clock kept the citizens on time and a splendidly decorated assembly hall democratically welcomed the populace to performances on an equally splendid pipe organ.

The Pietermaritzburg Town Council had hankered for such premises since 1855. In September 1860 plans were called for and a foundation stone laid — optimistically as it turned out, as financial difficulties put an end to building operations. The long-suffering officials made do in Dudgeon's elegant (but inadequate) Town Offices (designed 1882) and civic functions were carried out in improvised venues. Only in 1888 did the Councillors discover a way to balance the books. An enterprising bargain with the government of the day provided building materials in return for office accommodation in the new building. A competition was duly advertised and the winner was announced in March 1889: Street-Wilson and Barr's modest Free Renaissance hall and offices. Until that time the conventional choice for civic buildings was neo-Classicism. How did the good citizens of Maritzburg react to the Council's avant-garde choice? Evidence is only found after the disastrous fire of 12 July 1898.

Reports in the daily Press blazed as extravagantly as the conflagration itself:

The elegant first Town Offices[15] with Gray's Inn, now Shuter & Shooter, to the left.

The modest two-storey Free Renaissance first City Hall[16] (1893–98).

The present City Hall[17] soon after its completion in 1903, flanked by the Anglo-Zulu War Memorial to the left, and the Second Anglo-Boer War Memorial to the right.

GREAT FIRE IN THE CITY

TOWN HALL BURNT DOWN

A MUNICIPAL DISASTER

DESCRIPTION OF THE FIRE

A MAGNIFICENT SPECTACLE

... by quarter to eight the north and east sides of the building, from basement to roof were completely under the sway of the fire and five minutes later a portion of the roof fell in. Great volumes of smoke and lurid flame were now rising from that part of the building ... clouds of sparks wafted skywards as the crumbling timbers gave way ... great tongues of fire curled aloft, shooting through the smoking clouds, and lighting up the neighbourhood with a dazzling, almost blinding radiance'. (*Natal Witness*, 16 July 1898)

Almost immediately Street-Wilson was summoned to design a bigger and better version. Now a different set of sparks began to fly. Two hundred and sixty-eight angry citizens unsuccessfully petitioned the Council when the news was made known. They objected to this preferential treatment, to the expense of rebuilding, and not least to the style of the original. Disappointed ratepayers bemoaned the fact that Pietermaritzburg was 'not able to erect anything so graceful, handsome and suitable as Durban Town Hall' (*Natal Witness*, 20 July 1898). It is doubtful, however, that a classical design would have suited the corner site chosen for the building. Many planning problems arose when combining disparate halls, offices and committee rooms into a single block, not to mention the obligatory clock tower which, after all, had no classical precedent. The asymmetrical plan adopted by Street-Wilson and Barr is particularly suitable. The placing of the tower on the corner of Church Street and Commercial Road provides a dynamic focal point. And the appearance of numerous small imitators testifies to the success of the design. Cast-iron and red-brick façades lined the adjacent roads. Presiding over them was Street-Wilson's elaborate tower, once visible from the Town Hill and beyond, now alas obscured by rebuilding and development.

building forms and decorative details even in close proximity to older work. In Pietermaritzburg there is perhaps no better example of this than the old Government House, where the first shale-walled nucleus exists happily side-by-side with extensions differing radically in detail, material (red brick) and scale. To us, this may seem a quaint hotch-potch of elements all possessing the charm of the past, but at the time they represented nothing more or less than modern extensions to an existing building, without any attempt at 'matching'.

In a wider sense, the Pietermaritzburg townscape represents a superimposition of a number of layers, each belonging to a specific period and often population group and each being in its own right fairly homogeneous — a picture made even more complex by the existence of distinctive building types such as shops, school complexes and public buildings. There is no doubt that the City possesses a large body of architecture of both character and charm that should be protected. But for modern developments to 'fit in' with this heritage of the past, it is essential first, that clarity should exist about precisely what the character is that should be respected; and second, that in the process the modern work should not be expected to sacrifice its own, contemporary character.

In his book *The Character of Towns* the British author Ray Worksett has provided a number of models to determine the character of existing urban environments, to which new developments could then try to adhere. He identified factors determining street elevations, such as boundary contours, plot widths, façade rhythms, textures and fenestration, building heights in different areas, and so on. Such models are easier to identify and prescribe in densely built-up and fairly homogeneous European city centres, especially those with a high proportion of historical architecture, than in a city like Pietermaritzburg with its initially wide spacing of buildings allowing different 'characters' to be superimposed upon one another.

The first Pietermaritzburg style is associated with the Voortrekker period, although it persisted well into the British period, probably into the 1860s. It was basically similar to the style employed in Voortrekker towns in the Orange Free State (Bloemfontein, Winburg) and Transvaal (Potchefstroom, Pretoria) and indeed Cape colonial towns of the same period such as Worcester, Graaff-Reinet and Uitenhage. Elongated houses (simple rows of rooms), sometimes with wings or lean-tos at the back, were erected on the street boundary of deep building blocks. Their walls of shale rubble or unburnt brick were plastered inside and out; their roofs were of thatch between simple gables, and a stoep ran in front along the entire length, raised slightly above the street level often between simple end-seats. Though none of these survives unchanged, a dozen or more can still be found, the best group being that in Longmarket Street between Boshoff and Retief Streets.

Gradually houses of a different character started appearing from the 1860s onwards in between the widely spaced houses of this Voortrekker dorp. At first these, too, had plastered walls. They were generally set back from the street, surrounded by their gardens, perhaps reflecting the 'picturesque', romantic desire, especially strong in England, for architecture to merge into nature.

'Collegiate' Gothic Revival: Clark House, Maritzburg College. [18]

The General Post Office and Victoria Club *c.* 1910 on a contemporary postcard. [19] Two International 'Modern Movement' buildings: in Killarney Terrace; [20] and [21] on the corner of Longmarket and West Streets.

The University's Science Block. [22]

A related feature which had started to come into prominence was the veranda, creating a transitional zone between inside and out by breaking down the sheer division between architecture and environment. The veranda style, of course, was also a concession to the sub-tropical climate and occurs in several other parts of the former British colonial Empire. The veranda, in Pietermaritzburg an almost universal feature between 1860 and 1940, was a strongly unifying element, being added to a variety of types of architecture including pre-existing Voortrekker houses.

From the 1870s onwards the plastered finish of soft brick or rubble walls began to be superseded by the excellent locally made salmon-coloured facebrick, which remained the predominant building material until the exhaustion of the local clay deposits in the 1920s and 1930s. This splendid material, which the local architects and builders learnt to use with such exquisite skill and elegance — together with the veranda — is usually identified with the 'typical Pietermaritzburg character' that is so eagerly sought yet remains so difficult to define. For behind the decorative verandas, in wood or, in the then 'ultra-modern' material of cast iron, the architectural forms built of this Maritzburg red brick are as eclectic as the late nineteenth century taste for Revivals and the whimsical mixing of idioms would allow. Forward-projecting wings and bay-windows, sometimes symmetrical but more often asymmetrical, added to the demise of the façade; spiky bargeboard gables, corner turrets and roof ventilators enlivened the roof-line. For commercial buildings, fancy Flemish Renaissance gables and dormers breaking up roof surfaces were in demand. Elsewhere, 'Collegiate' Gothic Revival forms or, for public buildings, the more sedate Italianate column-and-pediment style were preferred. Decorative effects were achieved — apart from 'brookie-lace' or timber fretwork veranda trimmings — by moulded brick details or reliefwork in plaster insets.

Is all of this 'typically Maritzburg'? Somehow all recognizably so, although common denominators are difficult to find. One has only to compare the five important public buildings near the Church Street/Commercial Road intersection to see as many different faces of the City's older architecture. The old Presbyterian Church, plaster-walled with pointed windows and slender steeple, is in the pre-redbrick Gothic Revival style; the old Supreme Court next to it, one of the earliest buildings to use the local red brick, though with bands of different colour, is in a restrained, basically classicist *Rundbogenstil* with round-headed windows repeating the shapes of the recessed arcades; the dignified Greek Revival temple fronts of the Parliament buildings face Longmarket Street; the City Hall across the street, with its *horror vacui* of surface ornament is the very opposite of classicism; while the Colonial Building has a pompous Second Empire treatment.

During Edwardian years, Victorian eclecticism persisted for a while, as did the veranda style, now much simplified with wooden posts or more often prefabricated concrete Doric columns, sometimes seen as late as the 1930s. During the 1920s, the quality of the local red brick diminished, as well as the skill and imagination with which it was used, and its use was often restricted to the lower plinths of walls, the rest being plastered,

until the deposits ran out and the red-brick style ceased, in the 1930s, to characterize local architecture.

It took relatively long for 'modern' architecture to make its appearance in Pietermaritzburg. Even during the 1930s and 1940s work that unashamedly made use of modern techniques and materials, expressing these honestly without eclectic use of features of past styles, remained rare. Bank buildings in Church Street such as Barclays (now First National Bank) and the South African Reserve Bank (now occupied by Boland Bank) are contemporary in the simple geometry of their masses and fenestration, but retain numerous historicizing features: the former its splayed corner 'shop entrance' under pediment and crowned by domed corner turret; the latter with its Italian Renaissance *palazzo* appearance, rustication and columns. Similarly, the new design of the Imperial Hotel in 1935 is still full of eclectic features such as colonnaded balconies, shuttered windows and rustication.

Buildings such as these, no longer belonging to any of the traditional Pietermaritzburg 'styles', nor having made a final break with the past, are familiar landmarks in the City and would cause an outcry if they were to be demolished. Yet do they 'fit into' the traditional townscape any more than, say, the Anglican Cathedral? Busy detailing and eclectic motifs do not in themselves ensure a sympathetic foil to an historical setting.

A more genuinely contemporary style, related to the International 'Modern Movement', now completely free of historical echoes and relying for its aesthetic effect solely on functional design, sleek lines and well proportioned geometric elements, often in white plaster finish, made a very tentative appearance in the late 1930s and 1940s. Two of the earliest and finest examples still stand today: Strathallan, a three-storeyed apartment block in Killarney Terrace, with projecting slabs articulating the floor division and following the agitated outlines of rounded corners and cylindrical bays; and a business block on the corner of Longmarket and West Streets, with similarly rounded corner, projecting slab canopies and a slit bay-window curving back over the flat roof, with porthole windows in the attic. Similar features are found in the University's Science Block.

In much of the City's architecture of the last three decades this international flavour has persisted, though the Gropius-inspired, sparse geometry of white wall surfaces of these pioneering structures often tended to make way for the more weightless look of glazed curtain walls and metal framework structures, as seen at Natalia and the Trust Bank building. It was inevitable that with the acceptance — after a century or more of resistance — of the technological innovations, new materials and design concepts of the international machine age, much intimacy, local character and charm of the past would have to be sacrificed. In Pietermaritzburg this process has as yet had less effect than in cities like Cape Town and Durban. Are there, at this late stage, ways to reverse this process, or at least to minimize its effect?

A number of attempts have been made in the City to create structures that, while not denying their late twentieth century origin, display sensitivity to the character of their older architectural environment. This problem is of course not peculiar to Pietermaritzburg, and some of the best architectural minds in the world have failed to reach any kind of concensus on it. Nor is it likely that many of the participants in our local ugly-building competition would agree on suitable alternatives to the sort of modern buildings they decry.

In near-intact historical townscapes it may be justifiable to erect neutral 'infills' that continue the rhythm in scale and fenestration of the adjoining street elevations, as has been done in war-damaged Middelburg in the Netherlands. Not everyone is happy about such a solution which produces utterly boring structures which are neither genuine period pieces nor good contemporary design, although it does respect the integrity of the older architecture. In any event, Pietermaritzburg, despite its considerable character, does not possess such near-intact townscapes. Let us look at some alternatives as they have been attempted in the City.

The notion that unity of materials would create architectural coherence is a fairly old one, and as the 'white-walled beauty of the Cape' has been translated, with varying degrees of success, into modern design, so too have several architects felt that in the Pietermaritzburg context, red brick would be a prerequisite for architectural harmony. The Municipal Building in Church Street is among the first important examples. As it happens, there are no original red-brick buildings in its immediate vicinity with which to 'fit in'; nor, for that matter does the brick quite match the original local red brick. It is a good building — though somewhat 'sheer' and without links to its setting — but might well have been as successful in a material other than brick. As it now happens, the red brick does establish an effective link with a later building adjoining it: the Supreme Court. Other than the material, neither building contains any formal references to local traditional architecture, the sweeping curves of the walls flanking the Court's parking ramp introduce a rather 'foreign' but nonetheless attractive note in the layout.

The Cathedral of the Holy Nativity, too, makes few concessions to the 'historical character' of the City. It is interesting to reflect why the building, with its sheer cylinder of red brick, nevertheless (in the opinion of many knowledgeable observers, many from elsewhere) works so well and combines so well with old St. Peter's Church facing the street. Perhaps it is precisely because, while standing well back to allow its older neighbour breathing space, it does not try to 'match' the material (shale) and style (Gothic Revival) of St. Peter's. In this way, its unadorned geometry and the even salmon-red of its walls provides the perfect foil for the smaller scale and more ornamented old church with its more broken, darker tones. The wavy brick wall on columns forming 'shop-signs' on the two street fronts are a stroke of genius; they also effectively relate the vast cylinder of the church to its environment, as it were to prepare the visitor for the indeed somewhat overwhelming impact of the building itself.

During the last decade or so the clinical and impersonal character of much of the International Style has led to a reaction, taking on varying forms conveniently labelled 'Post-Modernism'. Though not a style *per se*, this trend, while retaining contemporary techniques and materials, shows attempts to reintroduce stylistic references to earlier local architecture, often in the form of visual

The Municipal Buildings and Natalia. (23)

Sympathetic Post-Modern architecture. (24 & 25)

Architectural 'juxtapositions'. (26)

'Motor Town'. (27)

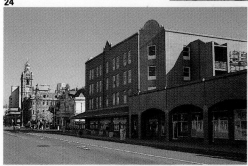

'puns' or reinterpretation in modern materials: never a slavish copying. With its 'local colour', its sense of humour, human scale and its often irregular shapes it is capable of injecting a welcome note of light relief in the modern townscape. In contrast with the bigger centres in this country, Post-Modernism has not yet made much impact on the Pietermaritzburg scene, but one recent building that could be regarded as a local example seems to be well received. It is '69 Boshoff Street', a small shopping precinct which takes its cue from the local Victorian idiom, with verandas, hipped ventilator roofs with ridge lettering, red brick, while most of its details are soundly contemporary.

Yet others might find that such direct references are not essential to a successful coexistence of buildings from different periods. One of the author's favourite 'juxtapositions', bringing out the best in both styles, is the City Hall and the neighbouring Natal Society Library as seen from the new Supreme Court side. It is a fascinating exercise in contrasts, between the fuzzy and fantastical, and the rectilinear and logical (though by no means sterile).

An attractive feature of central Pietermaritzburg is the intimacy and human scale created by the narrow lanes between Church and Longmarket Streets. Their future seems reasonably safe, and the pedestrianization of part of Church Street might complement this feature. But there is no reason why the erection of multi-storey buildings even in this area should necessarily clash with this character. One only has to see how successfully the modern shopping arcade of Shepstone's building blends with the lanes, thus minimizing the scale discrepancy of the building itself.

There is no doubt that the intimacy and charm, and ultimately the quality of life of a city like Pietermaritzburg can be irrevocably eroded by ill-considered modern developments. It is good that inhabitants sensitive to these qualities should try and guard against such influences. But equally important to the quality of life of a city is its harmonious growth, which demands that the present day makes its impact on the city fabric, like any healthy organism constantly renewing itself. The dangers to the city environment and character are not multi-storey office-blocks *per se*, or the bold lines of a new church or court-house (although these admittedly do call for sensitivity to setting, which is not always evident). The culprits are less easy to identify. Most of these are more insidious than the spectacular erection of the occasional stark modern building. They are the gradual stripping of the streetscene of greenery and other forms of 'texture': such as street furniture, gutter bridges, brick or cast-iron garden walls and the like. They are the infiltration into entire areas of drab, characterless workshops, filling-stations and second-hand car lots. Which has done more harm to Pietermaritzburg: Capital Towers or the stretch of Commercial Road between it and the Dorpspruit? Even the controversial red-roofed furniture-store elsewhere in the same street is surely to be preferred to the City's 'Motor Town' nearby? Much irreversible harm has been done even to many of those old buildings which have escaped actual demolition, a process that still continues today, often under the guise of 'restoration'.

The historical charm and character of a city like Pietermaritzburg is indeed a precious asset that calls for sensitivity both in its own preservation and in the

28

Contrasts in style and scale.

planning of that which the present day puts next to it or — often inevitably — in its place. But these are tasks that can only be successfully achieved by complementing the best of the past with the best of today. Only then will the built environment which we hand on to another generation have any chance of receiving the same affection that we rightly bestow on our 'old City'.

58

Parks and gardens

Donal McCracken

Public parks and botanic gardens as we know them today are very much the product of the industrial revolution, the resulting urbanization and the decline in warfare in nineteenth-century Europe. The Millsian movement, looking back to a golden age of a green and pleasant land, fired the early Victorians to recreate the countryside in the town.

Nineteenth-century parks were created initially because of a mixture of Victorian morality and human necessity. The Victorians believed parks and botanic gardens served a dual role: they could educate the populace in matters of nature; and they could create a pleasant environment where a working man could walk with his family. Prolonged debate raged in the 1840s on the question of opening parks on Sundays, one argument being that if parks were not opened the working man would neglect his family and go and drink in a public house. The reality, however, was often different and a common complaint to be heard — even in Pietermaritzburg — was of 'scandalous goings-on amongst the bushes'.

A suburban garden c. 1880.

Private gardens had existed for the wealthy, with notable gaps, since Roman times. The creation of the 'English country garden', which was so faithfully reproduced in Pietermaritzburg, was largely a nineteenth-century invention stimulated by the Victorian plant craze and by the influx into Britain of foreign plants through the Royal Botanic Gardens, Kew, and the Royal Horticultural Society. In British colonial possessions, problems and hardships encountered by early settlers and the common feelings of remoteness and homesickness were partially offset by creating institutions which were familiar to them and reminiscent of home. The most frequent expression of this was laying out parks, botanic gardens and private

The Botanic Gardens, early 1900s.

gardens in the English fashion. Nowhere was this more true than in Pietermaritzburg. In 1911 Robert Russell could write: 'Its dark brown soil, its tile-covered houses, its rose hedges, its trees and its gardens give it the appearance of a large English village'.

In the early years of its existence Pietermaritzburg was anything but attractive. In 1841 Revd Archbell noted, 'Its denuded appearance not merely detracts from its beauty but actually stamps deformity upon its features'. The Voortrekker settlement, however, did have great potential. Though the erven were initially little more than allotments and orchards, their large size afforded the possibility of later elegance and the sluits which fringed the streets offered water for the creation of gardens. Much of the later glory of the Garden City was built on the foundation laid by the Voortrekkers.

Street Planting

The Voortrekkers started the planting of trees in the streets to provide much-needed shade. By 1840 syringa trees, introduced by the missionary Daniel Lindley, had been planted to indicate the layout of the streets. The unsettled years which followed retarded this process and by the early 1850s visitors complained bitterly of the want of shade in the town. The Council gave this matter top priority and by the mid-1850s many streets were lined with oaks, bluegums (allegedly planted as lightning conductors), the occasional weeping willow and large numbers of syringas, which heavily perfumed the air. In 1850 G.H. Mason thought the town had the appearance of 'a vast panorama'. In 1854 Bishop Colenso commented on the town looking 'exceedingly pretty from the number of trees... which rise up in every part of it'.

In the closing decades of the nineteenth century, the covering of sluits for health reasons, kerbing, widening and macadamizing roads, and a scare that syringa fruit could poison children resulted in the destruction of numbers of street trees. Nonetheless by 1900 the attractiveness of tree-lined streets and the propensity of trees to grow in the town was well recognized and a new phase in planting began with jacarandas being planted in less busy streets. These were soon supplemented by Australian chestnuts and increasing numbers of feather palms (*Cocos plumosa*).

Into the twentieth century jacarandas and Australian chestnuts continued to dominate street planting. The street-planting programme was extended to the ever-expanding suburbs, this despite constant problems with trees interfering with drains and street lights. Occasionally different species were planted, such as the red-flowering *Eucalyptus ficifolia*, plane trees, Indian mahogany (*Cedrela toona*), *Grevillea robusta* and *Eugenia eucalyptoides*. In 1938 the Council decided to eliminate vigorous-growing plantation species such as eucalyptus and grevillea. These were replaced by jacarandas, Australian chestnuts and *Spathodea speciosa*.

Only in 1920 were the first indigenous trees planted in a Pietermaritzburg street, these being an avenue of Natal mahogany (*Trichilia emetica*) in Loop Street. This was, however, an isolated gesture and it was not until 1941 that some Cape chestnuts were planted in Golf Road. Today jacarandas and Australian chestnuts are still prominent in the streets of the provincial Capital, though a policy of mixing indigenous trees with exotics has resulted in yellowwoods, rhus, Cape chestnuts and *Dais cotinifolia* being planted by the Parks Department.

Public Parks

While street planting was begun as early as the 1840s, the establishment of a public park for the Capital was delayed until as late as 1863, a full 12 years after Durban had established its Botanic Gardens. The Pietermaritzburg Town Council did allocate 73 hectares for a park in 1850; and in 1857 a number of prominent citizens, including Messrs Akerman, Bergtheil, Ferreira, Leathern, T. Shepstone and Sutherland, combined to form the Pietermaritzburg Botanical and Horticultural Gardens Company with the aim of establishing a public park and swimming baths. The plan was that 200 shares of £5 each would be sold. In addition the Town Council and the colonial Government would be required to give annual grants. The board of nine would be representative of the shareholders, Council and Government. But this unique scheme was stillborn due to official recalcitrance and it was to be six more years before Queen Alexandra Park (83 hectares) was designated south of the town on the right bank of the Msunduze River, and another decade after that before it was properly laid out, by Napoleon Wheeler, the Inspector of Public Works.

In 1880 a plot of ground immediately across the river from Alexandra Park was planted with oaks and Auster Bay pines. This area was first called New Park and fell under the control of the Alexandra curator. Renamed Kershaw Park, it remained very much an appendix of Alexandra. Only in the 1920s was it properly laid out when the river was cleared of debris, and a river walk and a number of tennis courts built.

Four years after New Park was established, a land exchange deprived Alexandra of 13 hectares but allocated 8 hectares adjacent to the townland as Northern Park. At the same time 23 hectares west of the town was designated Albany Park. Northern Park was never developed and in 1880 the land was used to build an asylum. Another piece of townland was selected as compensation for a new park, but it was not until 1926 that what is known today as Settlers Park was developed.

In the 1890s demands were made by the public for additional parks to be established, but these were rejected because suitable land was either privately owned or 'in remote or inaccessible places', a strange conclusion when one considers that the town was surrounded by six large outspans.

The bird sanctuary, established in 1936; the hatcheries; Queen Elizabeth Park, which was leased to the Natal Parks Board in 1959; Lotus Park; Wylie Park; and the 157 playlots the City possesses — all date from the present century. Of these Wylie Park, bequeathed by the Wylie family, is the most interesting horticulturally and has a fine collection of indigenous plants. It is not permitted to be used as a sporting venue.

Alexandra Park has always been the flagship of the City's parks. It served the same role as those parks in Port Elizabeth and Kimberley which were designed for active as well as passive recreation. Alexandra Park's curator often had a salary in excess of that of the curator of the Botanic Gardens. In 1866 the park curator's salary amounted to £120 per annum. He lived in the 'Park house' and was allowed to keep a horse and a cow in the park. His duties were many: in particular, the supervising of fencing, planting, road building, weeding, repairing seats, patrolling and so on. The Council were not always satisfied with the endeavours of these first park superintendents and several were summarily dismissed.

The park in its early years was described as 'beautifully situated and tastefully laid out'. Though it had none of the splendid architecture it was to have, in the 1870s it could boast a wooden pavilion and an ornamental pagoda. At this time the Pietermaritzburg Council was spending twice as much as its Durban counterpart on parks and street planting. In 1879 expenditure of £610 necessitated selling dead wood to recoup a little.

At first the sports facilities in Alexandra Park were very much a means of entertaining the troops, always a problem in a garrison town. Even so the behaviour of soldiers in the park was not always good. The soldiers' practice of throwing cartridge cases onto the Oval was frowned upon by the Council. By 1910 the Alexandra complex of Jubilee pavilion and bandstand (1892), Oval, junior sports ground, cycling track, sports fields and the bath house on the river which had been built in 1865, allowed for many sports: athletics; boating and swimming at the river between Musson's tea-room and Victoria Bridge; bowls, played 'mainly by Scotsmen'; cricket; croquet; cycling; football; Highland games; hockey; polo; and rugby. Though golf was played there from 1894, when a new course was opened nearby in 1902 the game was banned from the park. In 1929 Alexandra Park was described in the *Weekly Advertiser* as the 'Mecca of sport'. Today it also houses the Jan Smuts Stadium.

For passive recreation there were performances twice weekly by the military or police band. There were also the formal flowerbeds of the Mayor's Garden, which was often used for civic occasions and which contained antirrhinums, azaleas, cannas, carnations, chrysanthemums, dahlias, delphiniums and pansies, with avenues of feather palms. Nearby was a conservatory and a rose garden. Access to mains water as early as 1880 greatly assisted the park and especially this garden.

The rest of the park was laid out in attractive tree-lined avenues: the principal species being blackwoods,

35

The City has F. Walton Jameson, Borough Engineer from 1902 to 1909, to thank for the jacarandas lining many streets. [31]

'The English garden' continues to be favoured in the City, [32] although gardening with indigenous plants is becoming increasingly popular. [33]

One of the City's outstanding azalea hedges. [34]

The magnificent plane tree avenue [35] in the Botanic Gardens.

Turn-of-the century postcards showing recreation in Alexandra Park. [36 & 37]

36

37

bluegums, Indian mahogany, loquats, oaks, syringas, wattles and willows. So prolific were the bluegums in the park that in 1918 their seeds were distributed to forestry stations in Natal, Zululand and the Transvaal. In 1920 an avenue of yellowwoods was planted from the main drive to Kershaw Bridge.

In the 1930s unemployed white labour was used at a rate of 3 shillings a day to construct the Percy Taylor rockeries, a massive terraced garden complex. Thanks to F.S. Tatham and Mrs Pope-Ellis, this featured a large number of indigenous plants, in particular aloes and other succulents.

There was no shortage of problems facing the curator of Alexandra Park. On a June night in 1868 the park's four swans disappeared. The theft of plants and general vandalism was not uncommon. By 1877 it was considered necessary to post two policemen in the park on Saturdays, though even the police were on occasion accused of reckless driving in the park. Of special annoyance to many townsfolk were the regular military bugle practices in the park by the bugleboys. Other difficult matters confronting the curator ranged from having to deal with the hostility of footballers to the cricket club, due to the latter's having the monopoly of the use of the Oval on Saturdays, to the unpleasant episode in 1888 concerning the use of a ditch as a 'closet'.

The park's success as a recreational area was due in part to the public transport provided to it from the town centre. In 1892 rickshaws were used to travel to the park. The following year a private horse-drawn omnibus service began and in 1905 the tram service was extended to Alexandra Park and to the Botanic Gardens.

Alexandra Park served as the venue for many official celebrations: there were no fewer than five separate royal functions in the park between 1901 and 1948; and the park has been the venue for many rugby and cricket test matches.

Market Square

Though Market Square remained the site of a market until 1939, it was also a venue for much public entertainment and sport.

Trees had been planted here, but by the late 1850s most of these had been destroyed. In 1858 one correspondent in the *Natal Witness* noted:

> Had proper attention been bestowed upon them when planted, and railings placed round each, we should by this time have had a delightful avenue on either side, and a space in the centre sufficiently shaded to have afforded a retreat for all.

In the ensuing decades acacias, *Grevillea robusta* and syringas were planted, and Prince Alfred planted an oak here in 1860. These trees gave shade to the many people who came to listen to the military band perform there. For many years the lower end of the square was used for sports and general entertainments such as circuses and travelling shows, much to the anger of the wagon drivers. The first rugby match in the town took place here in 1870.

The formal City Gardens in the square date from as late as 1912; two years previously the first children's playground in the City had been laid out in the square.

The Botanic Gardens

Though a botanic garden was proposed in 1867 as a branch of the Durban Botanic Gardens, it was not until 1872 that the Maritzburg Botanic Society was founded with the aim of establishing a gardens. It was a further two years before the 41 hectares to the west of the City on the banks of the Dorpspruit were granted by the Council to the society in trust. The original gardens' plan was drawn up by Samuel Todd, a local nurseryman.

The early years of the Botanic Gardens were not particularly happy ones. There was a large turnover in curators. A small government grant (£350) and an embezzlement fraud in the 1880s further restricted development. However, by the 1880s the Pietermaritzburg Botanic Gardens did serve a useful purpose, very much akin to that of Mr Tidmarsh's Grahamstown Botanic Gardens: the production of fruit trees and of sapling exotic timber trees. The latter helped establish the plantation forestry industry in Natal and acted as a forestry department, a fact which prompted Kew to state that the Pietermaritzburg gardens was in this respect a model for the Empire. Close-growing stands of eucalyptus, wattles, oaks, *Pinus insignis* and *P. pinaster* dwarfed the small area of formal garden with its duck ponds, tea-room and a nursery, which gave plants to public institutions and churches and sold tens of thousands of young plants to the public. Three attractive tree-lined walks were established: the Mayor's Walk outside the Gardens, which was originally made up of oak trees; a hakea walk which survived till 1899; and in 1908 the famous plane avenue was planted.

In the 1890s the curator, G. Mitchell, had begun to rectify matters, clearing some of the stands of exotic trees, laying down shale paths and establishing a rockery. In 1893 an experimental plot of indigenous trees was begun but these were destroyed in a flood two years later and an appeal for indigenous plants to replace them resulted in only two donations. At the beginning of the new century an attempt was made to revive this scheme, and thanks to the efforts of botanists such as T.R. Sim and Medley Wood a collection of indigenous flora was begun. It was unfortunate that R.W. Adlam, the botanist and curator of the gardens fell out in 1889 with the Botanic Society and left, for he would have done much to promote indigenous planting.

Unlike the Durban Botanic Gardens, in the early twentieth century the Maritzburg Gardens went from strength to strength. The Botanic Society was fortunate in having a series of able curators (Messrs Marriott, Newberry, Kidd and Forsythe) trained either by Kew or by the Royal Horticultural Society. The continued afforestation on the hill land and the sale of plants to the public, whilst infuriating nurserymen, ensured in the 1920s a scant but adequate income to develop the Gardens. Special attention was paid to the arboretum and collections of azaleas and camellias. In 1931 the director of Kew stated that except for Kirstenbosch, Pietermaritzburg was the only other botanic gardens in South Africa worthy of the name — 'An ideal botanic garden: the pride of Natal and Kew'.

Sadly, financial restraints led to a progressive decline in the fortune of the Botanic Society and the Gardens from the 1930s onwards. Membership of the botanic society did

Kerri Jones

38

Sheltered under the dappled shade of time, many trees in and around Pietermaritzburg provide a fascinating source of local history.

Listed below are several trees, their situation and a brief outline of the story each one has to tell.

Bird Sanctuary — Several yellowwoods were planted by Field Marshal J.C. Smuts and 'Ouma' in 1939. An acorn of the Royal Oak was flown out from Windsor, nurtured by A.T. Allison (former Mayor of Pietermaritzburg) and planted to commemorate the coronation of King George VI in 1937.

Roberts Road — A magnificent wild fig tree estimated to be well over 100 years old stands proudly in Roberts Road, in the grounds of a block of flats. The tree is said to have been a favourite resting place of the Voortrekkers while making their way up to World's View.

World's View — A number of indigenous trees were planted near World's View (Boesmansrand) to commemorate the symbolic 'Ossewatrek' of 1938. These trees can be seen in Mr R.K. Collins's garden at Hilton.

Parkside — The carefully preserved stump of an *uMkhamba* (thorn tree) can be seen in front of the Administrator's residence. Under this tree the peace treaty between the Boers and the British was signed in 1842.

Voortrekker Museum — A *Cryptomeria* was planted in 1880 by 'Oom' Paul Kruger when he came down to Pietermaritzburg to open the railway line from Durban to Pretoria. The tree has since died but a portion of the bole can be seen in the Voortrekker Museum, while a further section is in Kruger House, Pretoria. An arboretum was planted in 1912 by several dignitaries when the Old Voortrekker Church (Geloftekerk) was restored and converted to a museum. The largest of the remaining trees is a Carob (*Ceratonia siliqua*) planted by Ds. George Pellissier, one of the first ministers of the Old Church.

Garden of Remembrance — Fifty years after the Battle the Somme, a cutting was taken from a tree which survived from the forest of d'Eliville. This tree is now over 6 m high and is thought to be a *Fraxinus angustifolia* (European ash).

Garden of Remembrance — The Delville Wood Cross is made of timber from a remnant of the forest that was obliterated during the Battle of Delville Wood in the First World War. Each year on or about the anniversary of the battle, resin continues to 'weep' from the knotholes of this now famous cross.

Original Standard Bank (Church Street) — Two large oak trees, known as David and Jonathan, were for many years a feature of the Standard Bank in Pietermaritzburg[38].

They sheltered a hansom cab rank, and folklore records that all funeral notices were advertised on Jonathan's broad trunk. The trees were eventually felled (possibly for road widening) and have since been replaced by a further two oak trees donated by Pietermaritzburg's former Mayor, Cllr Pamela Reid.

Two caskets were made from this pair of magnificent oak trees. One is in safe keeping at the new Standard Bank and the second was presented to the Municipality.

King George V Memorial Homes — A *Camelia japonica* planted by His Majesty King George VI during his visit to South Africa can still be seen in front of the homes.

Botanic Gardens — A magnificent avenue of 46 London plane trees was planted by W.E. Marriott (curator of the Botanic Gardens) on 8 November 1908. This was undertaken at the suggestion of Sir Mathew Nathan, last Governor of Natal. At the southern end of the avenue stands a bell-tower. The bell is from the yacht *Lady Enchantress* which took Sir Winston Churchill to Norway at the end of World War II. The Botanic Gardens was officially declared a national monument on 23 June 1983.

---

not exceed 1 000 until 1957. Finally in November 1969 the Natal Botanic Gardens became a satellite of the National Botanic Gardens. Through the exertions of Messrs Peter Law and Brian Tarr the gardens have recovered considerably and today have a healthy blend of indigenous and exotic flora, creating the potential for establishing in Pietermaritzburg the only classical botanic gardens on the African continent.

Private Gardens

From the 1850s Pietermaritzburg was noted for its beautiful private gardens. Visitors to the town often deplored the state of the roads but enthused over the 'green hedges of quintz or pomegranate filled with untrained and unpruned red, white, tea, blush, moss and cabbage roses'; such hedges are sadly lacking today. At the end of the 1880s Dr Mann noted that the town had 'more the aspect of a large garden besprinkled with residencies, than of a town furnished with gardens'.

The nature of the City's gardens has been dictated by two factors: soil type and horticultural fashion. Though the line is not exact, generally speaking the Dorpspruit divides the settlement into sourveld acid soil to the north and sweetveld alkaline soil to the south. The topography of the settlement has produced microclimates which have also led to a diversity in gardening. The type of plants grown in gardens has not changed dramatically over the last 130 years, at least not until recently. 'We want English favourites,' wrote one Victorian lady gardener. These were introduced first by private individuals and later by nurserymen. In 1853 the surveyor-general and noted botanist, Dr Stanger, received from Kew Gardens five varieties of chrysanthemums, four each of dahlia and of roses, three each of camellia, geranium and fuchsia, one rhododendron and a magnolia species, as well as raspberry, fig and oak plants. Two years later, in March 1855, Kew despatched to Bishop Colenso a wardian case of plants containing four more species of camellia, two new dahlias, two franciscea, a gardenia, boehmeria, an assortment of cypresses, cedar and argenia trees, three types of tea and the first known specimens of azalea to be introduced. These were listed as *Azalea georgina*, *A. phoenica* and *A. poistica*. Azalea-growing on an extensive scale dates only from as late as the turn of the century.

By the 1870s gardens were full of violets, honeysuckle, hydrangeas, fleur-de-lis, dahlias, ferns, daturas, roses, sweetpeas, wallflowers, ipomea, petunias, primroses, passion flowers, polyanthus, 'English daisy' and verbenas, this last described as the commonest shrub in a Natal garden. Some enthusiastic gardeners did grow a few indigenous plants and there was a scattering of euphorbia around the town. Which specific indigenous plants were grown is not known: the few surviving references to them are vague, such as 'laburnum-like', 'berg lily', 'Natal lily', 'primrose coloured like petunia' and 'wild asparagus'.

Mention must also be made of the extensive vegetable gardens and orchards in the Victorian town. The Voortrekkers had planted many fruit trees which remained a noted feature of the town until the 1860s. In the latter part of this decade Theophilus Shepstone brought in to the Capital a large number of English fruit trees such as apple and pear, with the result that the variety of fruit species available to the town's inhabitants was considerably greater in 1888 than it is in 1988.

Some of the gardens, such as that adjoining Government House, were formal in design, but most were semi-formal with geometrical flowerbeds, sometimes a summerhouse and a well with an ornamental awning. The covering over of the roadside sluits in the 1880s destroyed much of the charm of the entrances to these gardens, which previously had often had rustic bridges over sluits. Grass lawns were a rarity in the Victorian era, partly because of the difficulty in cutting, partly because of occasional drought and partly because of the fear of snakes.

In the Victorian era as today weeds were a constant problem to the gardener. One writer in 1875 commented in exasperation: 'But the weeds! They are a chronic eyesore, and a grief to every gardener. On path and grass-plot, flowerbed and border, they flaunt and flourish.' Other difficulties to contend with were hail; floods, especially in 1856 and 1868; and drought, which brought with it a terrible dust problem. It has been the perennial problem of drought which has been partly responsible in recent years for an upsurge in interest in growing indigenous plants, a phenomenon which could be further encouraged by the nursery industry. A form of botanical nationalism has also permeated certain gardening circles, producing a pro-indigenous movement as fervent as the Victorian craze for English plants. The result has been a further division in gardening between the indigenous and traditional garden forms. A healthy interest in gardening survives in the City and a number of gardening clubs are active. Since the late 1970s an open garden scheme has permitted the public to visit specially well-kept private gardens and the annual Natal Witness Garden Show held at the end of September during azalea time, in the Royal Agricultural Society's grounds will soon, according to some, rival the Chelsea Flower Show.

The Garden City is appropriately named. Not only does gardening provide much-needed employment in the informal sector of the City's economy but it also gives a dignity and freshness to one of South Africa's most beautiful settlements. Whether it be in the intimate and luscious gardens on the Town Hill, in the more open ones of Scottsville or in the attractive grounds of the University, the mixture of exotic and indigenous flora adds lustre and is a fitting memorial to a century and a half of urban settlement.

Alexandra Park *c.*1866. This footbridge across the Msunduze was replaced by MacFarlane's Bridge in 1899. Scott's Bridge, which connects College Road and West Street, can be seen in the background, as can the Burger Street Prison to the right.

CHAPTER FIVE

The Inner and Outer City

The outer City merges with the inner City: Saturday morning shopping in central Pietermaritzburg.

Edendale 1851–1930

FARMERS TO TOWNSPEOPLE, MARKET TO LABOUR RESERVE

Sheila Meintjes

Edendale is a sprawling black urban area bordering the Pietermaritzburg magisterial district, adjacent to the Swartkop location. Unlike most black urban areas, Edendale has freehold ownership of land. This has given the community a measure of freedom from state-controlled black urban development. The history of Edendale is that of the precarious but tenacious struggle of a mixed community to retain its independence in an increasingly hostile and coercive white South Africa.

In 1851, 100 Christian families of Griqua, Rolong, Sotho, Tlokwa, Hlubi and Swazi origin, some accompanied by non-Christian relatives or retainers, settled on the farm Welverdiend, renamed Edendale, 10 km from the colonial capital of Natal, Pietermaritzburg. They purchased the farm on a share basis with, and under the guidance of, their missionary, James Allison. There, they laid out a village in the Voortrekker grid pattern, and built their houses in the 'European style' — each in important respects pursuing a separate economic existence, but all united by an affiliation to the mission — the church, the school and the community.

Allison and the community had broken with the Wesleyan Missionary Society in 1851, and had moved from the mission they had established at Indaleni in 1847. At Edendale they built their own church and schools, and local preachers stumped the neighbouring homesteads preaching the Gospel that had brought them a new life. Perhaps most significant of all, though, was that the break with the Wesleyans ushered in a new experiment for the Edendale Christian community: that of land ownership.

Land became a new symbol of wealth. Private land ownership was new to Africans in Natal, and its significance at first little understood. Without it, neither the development of capitalist agriculture, nor later, the growth of industry, could take place. At Edendale, farmers and artisans produced for profit, and within a very short time were the major suppliers of vegetables and maize for the Pietermaritzburg market.

Already the community had substantially transformed their lives in adopting Christianity, and moving away from their traditional beliefs and practices. Monogamy replaced polygamy, the plough replaced the hoe, and men applied themselves to cultivation, previously the realm of women. New kinds of socialization awaited boys and girls in the school and in the Church. The sexual division of labour, marriage, notions of the family and property, all found new definition on the mission.

Allison and his wife taught the three R's and skills suitable for artisanal occupations. Men and boys learned building, carpentering and gardening skills, women and girls, sewing and cooking skills requisite to their different stations in life as labouring men and women of colonial society. Indeed, many of the men and women who had moved with Allison to Natal had been brought up in the mission household, where they learned the values of Victorian Christianity.

The 6 120-acre farm was sub-divided into a central village with acre-sized plots and outlying arable fields, as well as large areas of commonage for grazing. Clear rules were established to manage local government, a headman was appointed, with a council of elders, all of whom were subject to the patriarchal authority of Allison. He was not only pastor, father and guardian, but also the legal owner of the farm. His rights were akin to those of a feudal lord in medieval times, or of a chief.

Conflicts between village members were solved in the customary court, *ibandla*, presided over by the headman chosen by the community. Job Kambule, an original convert, who had joined Allison on the Caledon in the 1830s, was the first headman and his successors used a combination of village rules and customary law to settle disputes. Customary law regulated marriage contracts, and lobola continued to be paid by the *kholwa*, the Christian converts, to cement familial connections.

Heterogeneity best described the nature of the village community. Social distinction based on membership of the Church was probably the most significant at first. Even today in Edendale, the *oNonhlevu*, the first converts, hold a special place. Those with property, often members of the Church too, though not invariably, were socially superior to tenants and squatters. Economic success was not uniform, and wealth began to determine social and civic status in the village. Wealth was reflected above all in land but also in wagons, used for trade, and in stock. The well-to-do in Edendale also employed servants. Their existence was little different from that of white colonists.

As for all Natal settlers, the 1850s were years of struggle for the Edendale settlers. They were paying off land, trying out new crops like oats, and venturing into new trading areas to the north and south. Lung-sickness struck their cattle herds in 1854, curtailing ploughing and trade. The struggling mission received the support of Sir George Grey, after whom their village 'Georgetown' was named. By 1858 the farm was at last paid off, and the shareholders were in a position to acquire freehold title. This evoked such dissension that Allison was forced to resign. The landowners believed he had deceived them, and for the rest of his life, Allison was no longer welcome at Edendale.

The community felt a missionary presence was needed at Edendale, both to provide spiritual guidance and to act as intermediary between village interests and the colonial government. They approached the Wesleyan Missionary Society, who though initially cautious, agreed to accept the community, so long as the Society had security of tenure and the secular aspects of the mission station, such as local government and the management of the unallotted portions of the village and farm, were securely established in a Trust.

The Trust held the unallotted portions of the farm, and was responsible for the preservation of the commonage, graveyard, market place, streets, roads and paths. It also protected and controlled the use of timber and the waterways 'for the preservation of the rights of the said several co-tenants...' Three Trustees administered the terms of the Trust, and had the right to claim rates from the landowners. In practice their authority was limited for want of any legal executive force, in spite of the fact that the Trustees were prominent public figures, like the Superintendent of the Wesleyan Society in Natal, the Secretary for Native Affairs, and the Superintendent of Education.

Throughout its history Edendale would suffer for want of borough recognition. This was largely because a shortsighted colonial government refused to see even 'Christian and civilized' Africans as having the capacity to adopt colonial local government. Thus municipal status was refused in 1882, and again as late as 1930, a petition by the Edendale Vigilance Committee and civic guard was turned down. The struggle for municipal status is a central theme of Edendale's modern history.

In the early 1860s the Edendale people began a fresh phase of expansion. This was a period of widespread speculative lending in Natal, to finance trade with the Transvaal and Orange River Sovereignty. Edendale entrepreneurs, eager for profit, took out mortgages to finance their trading ventures. One trading partnership of four entrepreneurs, H. Daniel & Company, borrowed as much as £8 000, with security in the land of eight other leading villagers.

Edendale came to be acknowledged as one of the most advanced Christian communities in the Colony. One visitor described the landed proprietors of Edendale:

> These people have their substantial stone dwellings, and well ploughed fields, with the power of buying or selling at pleasure. They have also erected a church, school-house, and watermill. Every day witnesses the arrival of waggon loads of Edendale produce at the Maritzburg market. It is quite a sight to see the waggons returning, on a summer's evening, packed with the wives and families of these Edendale Caffres; all clad in British manufactured goods, and carrying on their countenances an unmistakeable air of contentment and joyous prosperity.

Ominous signs were on the horizon, however. The speculative bubble in Natal was not based on real productive growth, but merely on mercantile potential. The Boer-Sotho war of 1865 burst the bubble, and trade came to a virtual standstill. For the first time the Edendale community experienced the reality of the vagaries of an international market economy. H. Daniel & Company went under, and their backers were faced with demands for payment or the loss of their land. This meant almost instant ruin and impoverishment, and the prospect of dependence on wage labour at a time when there were few jobs available. Rather than see the destruction of all that had been built up over the past fifteen years, a general

Edendale Mission Station in the 19th century.

meeting of village notables sought to save those on the brink of ruin, and took over £5 000 of the debt.

The ensuing depression affected everyone. The price of maize was very low, and trade so bad that at Edendale, 'wagons have almost nothing to do'. In 1868 the missionary reported:

> With mealies at 3/- per muid less than they cost to grow, and little work for the wagons which are falling to pieces from old age, the people are poorer than they have been for years and though there is plenty of food yet they have but little money to buy clothes with and many of the children go to school almost naked.

Many people began to leave Edendale, some to seek wage employment where they might, and others to hire land from absentee landlords, as at Cedara and Rietvlei. Few sold their land, most people left their properties in the hands of relatives or let them to tenants. Perhaps the most significant development, however, was the purchase of Driefontein, a farm in the Klip River District, 'in order to hide our heads in it', as Johannes Kumalo explained. 'We bought this when we were in a state of poverty.'

At Driefontein a Trust made the land inalienable and racially exclusive. The scheme was a new strategy to cope with the insecurities of colonial life, and prevent the disruption of individual speculation as experienced by the *kholwa* at Edendale. More than forty families moved to Driefontein from Edendale during the last years of the 1860s.

In the 1870s, the Edendale community became more transient. A few Griqua families joined Adam Kok at Kokstad, and new settlements of former Edendale inhabitants were established at Cedara, in the Biggarsberg at Telapi, and on the Umlaas River. It was not only the depression which caused this diaspora, for the second generation was beginning to have their own families, and Edendale was becoming too small to accommodate everyone's productive activity. Village life at Edendale began to lose some of its communal unity, although the *oNonhlevu* did not lose their dominance of social life in the village.

Respectability was the hallmark of social distinction. This involved strict rules of etiquette. Informal visits between friends were frowned upon as they fostered gossip. Women who indulged in this kind of thing were dubbed *uyazula*, or those with a 'long foot'. Instead the villagers met one another in church and at formal tea parties. On special occasions, such as holidays, a family might hold a party at which a sheep was slaughtered, and relatives and close friends would gather to share in the feast. The men would talk, and in later years they might have played cards. Women and children also attended these festivities. The children probably played such games as hide-and-seek. Weddings, christenings and funerals were occasions when the whole village might turn out to attend church. A more select group would later join the family at the party celebrations.

In the 1870s, Lady Barker, wife of the Colonial Secretary, was impressed by the comfort, decency and orderly fashion of life at Edendale. Her descriptions evoke a warmth and vitality amongst the villagers:

> Sitting at the doors of their houses are tidy, comfortable-looking men and women, the former busy plaiting, with deft and rapid movements of their little fingers, neat baskets of reeds and rushes; the latter either eating mealies, shelling them, or crushing them for market. Everywhere are mealies and children.

She described with vividness the cheerful interiors of Edendale homes, which contrast sharply with the conventional sombreness of English Victorian decoration:

> As for the walls, they were the gayest I ever beheld. Originally white-washed, they had been absolutely covered with brilliant designs in vermilion, cobalt and yellow ockre, most correctly and symmetrically drawn in geometrical figures. A many-coloured star within a circle was a favourite pattern. The effect was as dazzling as though a kaleidoscope had been suddenly flung against a wall and its gay shapes fixed on it.

The life-style described by Lady Barker would have been familiar to many rural village dwellers in England, nor would colonial settlers have felt out of place in an Edendale home. It would, however, have been distinctly foreign to any non-Christian African unused to mission or town life.

A natural pride in their own advancement was buttressed by the colonial state's reliance on the Edendale Christians, and other mission communities, for support against recalcitrant chiefs. Whilst the Christians of Edendale, and elsewhere, had considerable grievances about their position in colonial society, there was no question of where their loyalty lay. During the 'Langalibalele rebellion' for instance, one of their most respected members, Elijah Kambule, was killed at Bushman's Neck. The Anglo-Zulu War was the occasion for loyal collaboration with the colonial and British forces and, indeed, for heroism in support of 'the Great White Queen'.

However, neither their respectability nor their collaborative role won for the *kholwa* civil status in colonial society. Like all Africans in the Colony, the *kholwa* were subject to customary law, in spite of their opposition to it. Exemption was possible, but its terms were unpopular, because it allowed only individuals to apply when the *kholwa* wanted group exemption. In the 1890s, under responsible government, applications were anyway reluctantly granted. Discrimination did not deter the loyalty of the *kholwa*, nor of the Edendale community. They served as scouts during the Second Anglo-Boer War, took great risks, yet were unrewarded with even the War Medal. This turned some irrevocably against the administration, though most still believed in trying to negotiate improved social and political status. Collaboration against enemies of the colonial state did not mean that the *kholwa* were content with their lot. Indeed, there is some contradiction in their loyalty, the growing racialism of Natal settler domination and *kholwa* grievance.

In the 1870s, the Edendale community had begun to improve their economic position. The diamond-fields provided opportunities for wage labour and for trade which they were quick to seize. In Natal, the depression continued into the 1870s in spite of widening opportunities for individuals outside the Colony. The Government introduced measures to encourage African cultivators onto the labour market. The hut tax was doubled in 1876, and in the 1880s, pass laws were extensively used to limit the mobility of African stockowners. These measures affected the *kholwa* just as much as any other group.

Petitions and evidence to government commissions show Edendale community notables pushing for recognition of their separateness from the rest of the African community. Many of them sought exemption. This was linked to demands for the franchise. But the colonial state, intent on control over all Africans, suspended exemptions from customary law in 1890, the year the Code of Native Law was promulgated. Urban registration and vagrancy laws were stringently applied, whilst fees for passes were introduced.

Edendale men took the lead in forming the *Funamalungelo* in 1888, the 'Society of those who seek rights', in an effort to press the Government to extend civil rights. This proved of little effect, particularly once the settlers assumed dominance after 1893, so in the early 1900s they formed a broader political movement, the Natal Native Congress. Edendale members were at the forefront of these developments.

Political disabilities were matched by economic restrictions. In the 1880s Crown Land was opened to all for purchase by public auction. Edendale village notables were prominent in taking up land all over Natal. However, because of Pass Law restrictions, their competitive edge diminished. Increasingly, African land-purchasers found it difficult to meet their periodic land repayments.

At Edendale, social problems were beginning to manifest themselves more generally. Missionaries commented on the drinking problem. In the early 1880s drought and crop failure brought a change in the economic fortunes of many of the villagers. There were few wealthy men, and even the headman, Stephanus Mini, was unable to keep up with repayments on land he had purchased in the Polela district.

One trend in response to their difficulties was for landowners to let out their arable land and access to the commonage to Indian and white tenants. Ownership of land still provided a livelihood, but it was now through rents. By the 1900s tenants dominated market production in Edendale. They also tried to dominate village politics, which polarized tenant-landlord relations in the early 1890s. Landlords tenaciously clung to their political overlordship, even as they became poorer.

Changes in the economy were making black artisans redundant, and black trade carriers were losing trade to white competitors and the railways. Rinderpest in 1897 had devastated cattle herds, and in one fell swoop destroyed the carrying trade. This was preceded by drought and a plague of locusts, which had knocked the bottom out of commercial farming. The older generation of *oNonhlevu* who had made a modest living out of these activities found themselves in poverty. People were still able to feed themselves from their gardens, and from the stock they ran on the commonage. But there were few people who could claim to produce all their wants from agriculture or independent artisanal production. It was those with some education who were best able to straddle this change in fortune. Schoolteaching and clerical occupations became the new means of maintaining *oNonhlevu* respectability. But these professions took villagers away, many of them to the Transvaal and the widening opportunities offered by the mining towns. For the poor of Edendale, there was little alternative to migrant labour to the gold-mines.

Even in the 1920s, Edendale held its reputation as a respectable, Christian village. No non-Christian ventured into the village improperly clad. Concertina players did not walk through the streets playing their music, as they did in the hills and dales of the neighbouring Swartkop location. If there were festivities in the village, there was no stamping of feet, *ukusina*, as amongst the 'people outside', instead the more genteel shuffle, *ukutamba*, was associated with dancing at Edendale.

Only in the 1930s and 1940s did Edendale begin to lose its village character, as people from more distant rural areas moved in and the population grew to make it a peri-urban area, under control of Natal's provincial government. Overcrowding and slum conditions which were unknown in the nineteenth century developed. Clearly Edendale was the victim of state refusal to make provision for municipal government amongst constituted black communities.

The history of the Edendale community is a microcosm of the experience of large numbers of African people in South Africa. They were respectable, mission-educated Christians. They had helped to build the colonial town of Pietermaritzburg, both as labourers and as producers. But whilst their labour was greedily accepted by the colonial economy, they were not allowed to participate in the political life of colonial society except as second class citizens. Indeed, when the Edendale people, along with large numbers of African cultivators, became too competitive, legislative measures were introduced to block their advancement.

The story of the Edendale community is that of people striving for a place as profit-making farmers and entrepreneurs in the colonial economy, but whose competitiveness was increasingly seen as a threat to the success of the white colonial gentry. For the colonists, the destiny of all Africans was that of a labouring class. As far as the colonists were concerned, the Edendale Christians, with their education and skills, were to be the vanguard of a disciplined labour force. The history of Edendale shows how the community resisted this definition of its role, and constructed their own cultural world within colonial society.

A Christian wedding at Edendale in the 19th century: Jojo and Nomvuze, Hlalelwa and Payekiwe.

3

70

The people of the City

4. A middle class white family and their servants in the early 1900s. J.T. Henderson, *Hansard* reporter for the Legislative Assembly, in a group before his house in Boom Street.

5. A number of men who had lived in the City since the 1840s, photographed outside Mr Pistorius's Berg Street house in 1908. The range of occupations and status reflects the social structure of colonial Pietermaritzburg.
   Left to right: G. Currey (ironmonger); D.J. Boshoff (farmer); H.J. Panewitz (wagonmaker); J.T. Gutridge (court messenger); H.C. Shepstone (former Secretary for Native Affairs); J.M. Egner (wool merchant); C.W.H. Pistorius (gentleman); J.W. Shepstone (former Judge, Native High Court).

6. In 1988 a group of people, who had been resident in Pietermaritzburg for at least 75 years, was photographed before a turn-of-the-century house in Loop Street. This photograph, and the small number of men in the City's old-age homes, reflect the fact that women generally live longer than men.
   Seated in front: Kathleen Alice Barron, b. Rump, 1907; Lillian M. Crerar, b. Wissing, 1899; Olive Russell, b. 1907; Hilda Olive, b. Loagie, 1908.
   Seated behind: Jess Gutridge, b. Sime, 1895; Beatrice Suttie, b. Turnbull, 1901; Pat Watson, b. Henry, 1913.
   Standing: Nancy Ogilvie, b. St. George, 1898; Cyril Friggens, b. 1905; Ellen Pogel, b. Wilson, 1908; Annie McAlister, b. Peach, 1897; Nellie Deyzel, b. Harrison, 1902; Victor Harrison, b. 1901.

7. In the 1940s the professional and landed English stock of Natal — a party of whom were photographed at the Royal Show in 1949 — were still indistinguishable from their counterparts in the Home Counties.
   Left to right: Priscilla Francis, Phyllis Otto, Mary Richards, Natalie Campbell, Elizabeth Jonsson, Natalie Roberts and Colonel Hugh Richards DSO.

8. Continuities: five generations of an Indian family born and resident in Pietermaritzburg: Elizabeth Surjoopersadh with her eldest daughter, Margaret Poonsamy, her grandson, Raymond, great-grandson, Peter, and great-great-granddaughters Alison (held by Peter) and Alicia.

9. A typical Vulindlela household. Note the large number of women and young children compared to men. This consequence of the multiple structure of households, and the tendency of young mothers to stay with their parents, should be contrasted with the nuclear nature of the usual white household in the City.

9

Vulindlela

Norman Bromberger

When the Revd Stephen Kumalo started his long journey in the pages of *Cry the Beloved Country* from Ixopo to Johannesburg, he travelled by train via Donnybrook and the Mkomaas valley to Elandskop. Then — 'down the long valley of the Umsindusi past Edendale and the black slums to Pietermaritzburg, the lovely city'. Catching his connection to Johannesburg, he left the Msunduze to wind its way south and eastwards past the recently-established African township of Sobantu Village and through farm country to its confluence with the Mngeni in the vicinity of what is now Nagle Dam. The Msunduze rises to the west of Pietermaritzburg and loses its separate identity to the east: both transitions take place in areas historically designated as 'African reserves' — Swartkop Location (now Vulindlela district) to the west; and part of the Inanda Location (now part of Mpumalanga district) to the east. Both areas now have strong economic links with Pietermaritzburg.

The intention here is to discuss Vulindlela, which is more closely linked to Pietermaritzburg and has been more comprehensively surveyed in recent years.

According to the 1985 census, Vulindlela had roughly the same population size (184 658) as the Pietermaritzburg magisterial district (192 417). (In the census Vulindlela includes Edendale and the township of Mpophomeni.) The relative size of the districts tips the other way if we allow for an estimated 20 per cent population undercount in the 'non-urban' part of Vulindlela.

In 1946 roughly 66 per cent of the African population of Pietermaritzburg district lived in those western areas which were to become the Vulindlela district. By 1985 this figure had risen to 80 per cent. The African population had been growing substantially faster in Vulindlela than in the City (taken as the Borough and its townships — Sobantu, Ashdown and Imbali). This 'displaced' urbanization was at least partly the result of State policies aimed at limiting normal urbanization.

The landscape and buildings in Vulindlela[1] are very different from those usually found in an African township. Homes are strung out along the mid-slopes of hills and on flatter land along the roads. The average homestead is not a 'matchbox' but a cluster of two to three dwellings, with thatched rondavels alongside buildings with single- and double-pitched roofs. Older homesteads are set on large sites with substantial cultivated gardens, fruit trees and patches of lawn.

The higher slopes of the hillsides and some higher plateau land are set aside for pastures for some 20 000 cattle. There are areas of consolidated arable fields with contour banks to counter erosion. Clumps of wattle and small areas of residual forest abound. The Msunduze and its tributaries drain the area, winding between the hills and down the central valley to Pietermaritzburg. Where the road climbs from Gezubuso to the next plateau, the

---

[1] In what follows 'Vulindlela' will refer to the area of the old Swartkop Location. Edendale is dealt with elsewhere in this book.

hillside is covered with aloes which glow red among the boulders in winter. From the shoulder of Swartkop there is a view across Henley Dam and beyond it to ridge after ridge of hills. It was not surprising to encounter a young man who looked down the valley from Ngubeni to the townships and said, 'I love this place'.

There are, however, aspects of the environment which do not compare favourably with the urban world. During the summer rains the buses are sometimes unable to travel any distance off the central tarred road and commuters are forced to walk to their destinations through the rain and mud. There are no street lights and at night the darkness is broken only by the flickering of candles. In recent years electricity connections have been installed by some institutions, shops and private individuals. However, the absence of urban-style planning of residential sites has created problems and some electricity suppliers have had to suspend installations until some difficult decisions are made about residential layouts. There is no reticulated water supply system and, while Vulindlela is abundantly endowed with springs, the task of fetching water is often time-consuming and arduous. There is no water-borne sewerage system; as the area has become more urban, most households have converted to drop toilets, but these are unsatisfactory for a number of reasons, including possible pollution of the underground water supply.

The lack of urban services is not necessarily the fault of the authorities. Apparently some residents prefer to do without services if they have to pay for them (or perhaps it is more correct to say if they have to pay the *full* cost). The evidence for this is not entirely clear-cut since alternative township accommodation has not been readily available. However, land in freehold in a substantial part of Edendale has been available for purchase, and water and electricity connections to some of these sites may be had on request. The cost of this has clearly been prohibitive to most, who have chosen the unserviced environment in preference to the serviced one.

There is no reticulated water supply system in Vulindlela, and the fetching of water is a time-consuming and arduous task.

10

72

What one can say about the authorities, however, is that they have been slow to face the reality of unplanned population growth in the area. Some services, such as electricity, become more difficult to install after close residential settlement has developed. In recent years the issue has begun to receive some attention: the Pietermaritzburg transport authorities have accepted the need for a transport plan on a metropolitan basis which will include Vulindlela's future needs; the authorities in Pretoria and Ulundi have commissioned an urban 'structure plan' which will tackle the issues of land-use planning and service provision; and funds have been voted to upgrade springs and install small reservoirs. It is indicative of the historic absence of infrastructural investment in such areas that a water scheme of this type and on the proposed scale is apparently unprecedented and that considerable technical and organizational problems will have to be resolved before the plan can be implemented.

Not surprisingly, the households in the area are rather different from those of urban Pietermaritzburg and probably from those in the African townships as well. For one thing they are generally larger: 8,3 people seems to be the average size and about 10 per cent have more than 12 members. In the townships of Sobantu and Imbali, and the coloured, Indian and white suburbs, the average household has 6 members or fewer.

About half the households have a multiple structure with more than one nuclear unit (though often not full ones) living together. A major cause of this is the frequency of unmarried motherhood and the natural tendency for the often young mothers to stay with parents or siblings in a larger household.

There are of course other causes for the larger average size of households. The processes by which land is allocated play a part, but this matter is under-researched and so will be ignored here. What does seem likely is that a form of economic insurance is involved. In a highly uncertain labour market and in a society where the risk of sickness and death (violent or otherwise) is high, living together decreases the chance that the household will suddenly be left destitute. In a substantial number of Vulindlela's households the average number of employed people is about two, and a not insignificant minority contain more than two. Heads of households are less likely to be unemployed than the adult population in general, but something like 10 per cent have been so in recent years and the presence of other earners makes the household less vulnerable.

Most people in Vulindlela are wage workers, with most of the women in domestic service and most of the men in urban industry, commerce and construction. Incomes derived from agricultural resources are essentially supplementary for the majority of households, being confined to the produce of small gardens. An estimated 12 per cent cultivate fields but average size of field is less than one hectare. Between 25 per cent and 30 per cent own cattle but the average herd size is only slightly over 4 animals. In aggregate 'subsistence' incomes (including collected wood) are an estimated 5 per cent of total money incomes.

In 1984 the percentage of women of working age who were working or looking for work was a little over 45 per cent. Of these, 33 per cent were unemployed, and of those who were employed, 60 per cent were doing domestic-type work. In general, remuneration is lower than that in other jobs. In a survey in Pietermaritzburg in mid-1986 the mean cash wage for full-time live-in domestic servants was R99 per month. However, the recorded range was from R60 to R250 per month. Wages for those who did not live in were similar, though on average a little higher.

The male employment pattern is more varied. Virtually none are in agriculture and mining; although agriculture makes some showing in the northern and western parts of Vulindlela, where a substantial farming and forest plantation belt provides employment for some 7 per cent of employed men and women. However, in Inadi in 1982/3, 30 per cent of employed men were in manufacturing, 18 per cent in construction, 25 per cent in commerce, 20 per cent in government employment outside the area, and 6 per cent worked for local agencies of the KwaZulu Government. This pattern is hardly surprising if we remember the earlier 'border industry' status of Pietermaritzburg and the current availability of 'industrial deconcentration' incentives.

Male occupations are mainly unskilled — at least in the Inadi district studied by Hofmeyr in 1982/3. Forty-two per cent of work was either 'heavy manual' or other unskilled labour, 36 per cent was semi-skilled, 10 per cent skilled (including heavy-duty drivers) and about 12 per cent was professional, supervisory and clerical. In the townships the percentage in this last category is almost certainly higher; it was over 30 per cent in Sobantu in 1986, for instance.

Much is made these days of the 'informal sector'. It is not easy precisely to define this category, but in a general sort of way it is clear enough what is being referred to. The activities, which are intended to generate money incomes, usually take place near the home (though not in the case of taxi drivers, some hawkers and clothes sellers), and are generally small-scale, organized on a self-employment basis and do not involve employment of labour outside the family. They may have an element of illegality, as in the case of liquor retailing and 'tuck shop' operations, where formal licensing requirements are quietly ignored.

With this rough definition of the sector it is possible to report its relative size. In two samples in Vulindlela in 1984 and 1986 between 6 and 7 per cent of men and women who were gainfully occupied could be regarded as 'informal sector' operators. This implies that at this stage the 'informal sector' is not a magic solution to the problem of unemployment, for the number of the unemployed quite dwarfs employment opportunities so far developed in this sector. This is not to say that it may not be capable of expansion; nor does it dismiss the possibility that the reported number of informal operators is severely underestimated. In addition, it does not address the distinct but related question of whether many of the unemployed may not find opportunities for productive work in 'subsistence' activities of one kind or another, such as own home-building, producing food, and collecting water and firewood. However, we have limited our definition of the 'informal sector' to activities undertaken for payment, and excluded production of goods for consumption by the household.

An important cluster of activities is related to the construction and maintenance of dwellings. While some individuals undertake most aspects of building, there is some specialization. Thus some clear sites (and dig

Commuters from Vulindlela have great distances to travel in the poorest of conditions.[11]

Vulindlela homesteads. Notice the combination of thatched rondavels and buildings with single- and double-pitched roofs.[12]

latrines), some make mud blocks and others plaster, thatch or attend to roofing. The maintenance of fences is important because of the livestock; and the need for frequent general repairs follows from the nature of the materials, the often inadequate mastery of the technology, and the economic constraints within which it is applied.

For women, knitting and sewing, involving both repairs and the making of new garments and household linen, are the most important ways of making money outside formal employment. Something like 20 per cent of all persons enumerated in the 1984 Vulindlela survey as being in the informal sector were involved with clothing. In fact, if these activities are regarded as a single cluster, then they involve more people than any other activity. Probably the most serious under-emuneration of informal activities relates to liquor retailing, and a full enumeration in that sector would probably take it to the top of the table.

Wood-trading is also important, as are various forms of hawking. Religion-based activities and the practice of herbalism are as a group on the same sort of scale in the sample as building and hawking. The position of agriculture is a little ambiguous. In the 1984 survey, some 7 out of 71 people in the informal sector were engaged in agriculture-based activities. These people classified themselves as self-employed in this way, but in total some 33 households in a sample of 588 had made what one might term 'agricultural sales'. Twenty of these had sold less than R100 per annum gross value and those with a larger sales value had largely obtained it by the sale of goats. The activities leading to such sales are unlikely to have demanded full-time work by the households concerned. However, if one believes that they belong to the informal sector, and if one guesses that liquor retailing is six or seven times more prevalent than reported, then the percentage of economically-active people involved in the informal sector could well rise from 6 or 7 per cent to 10 or 11 per cent. At this level, though clearly significant, it remains small.

Does the evidence on household incomes in Vulindlela suggest it is just another fragment of the 'poverty-stricken homelands', or can a more optimistic account be given? In mid-1984 and mid-1986 some 1 300 households in 19 separate areas in Vulindlela were asked about household incomes.[2]

Average monthly household incomes for each area varied between R703 per month (Mpushini in Sweetwaters) to R412 per month for the isolated community which nestles below Qanda's Rock in Mafunze in the central-southern part of the district. The mean income[3] in 11 of the areas varied between R400 and R500 per month; in 5 of the areas it was between R500 and R600; and in the 2 areas at the head of the distribution the mean household incomes were between R629 and R703 per month.

The numerical weighting in 1984 of the higher income areas (which lie on the east side closest to Pietermaritzburg) was substantial, and this produced an overall household average income of R543 per month for the seven areas surveyed that year. The corresponding figure for 1986 was just under R500 per month. By mid-1988 these figures will have become, on the assumption of 16 per cent per annum inflation, R731 per month and R673 per month respectively.[4]

Regarding the bottom end of the distribution, it appears that about 20 per cent of households have in recent years received less than the equivalent of R200 per month in 1986 values. In the 1986 survey about 10 per cent of households received less than R100 per month.

It is not easy to move from these figures to an imaginative grasp of the material standard of living which could be financed by (say) R100 per month in 1986. A suggestion made by Leeb and Radford to overcome this gap is as follows:

A loaf of bread a day each for a family of six would cost R100,80 in a 30-day month. If a litre of milk per day for the whole family was added it would bring the cost up to R127,00 per month. Nutritionally, this diet would be totally inadequate and would fail to maintain health.

This is by no means the last word on the reality of what might be termed extreme poverty at the bottom of the income distribution. For one thing, low income households tend to be smaller in size on average than others; secondly, we know that there is often assistance from relatives and the fathers of children born to unmarried members of the household; thirdly, it is almost certainly the case that such households in Vulindlela can gather wild spinaches, collect wood and produce at least some small quantity of food.

However, despite these qualifications, such information as we have about their quantitative scale suggests that the image of extreme poverty conjured up by the above quotation must be accepted. At the same time, it is important to stress that there is an income distribution and that in 1986 in the more western and northern parts of Vulindlela there were roughly as many households with combined incomes over R1 000 per month as there were households with incomes under R100 per month.

Despite the urban character of the economic activities on which the inhabitants of Vulindlela mainly depend for their livelihoods, the local administrative and political systems are 'tribal'. The area is incorporated in KwaZulu, which has a strongly traditional and rural character, and is divided into five chief's wards (or parts of wards). These wards are subdivided into sub-wards within which indunas have authority.

In recent years new political forces have begun to make an impact in the area. The unions have sought to organize workers at the work-place; while political organizations such as the United Democratic Front have found a response among youth, who are conveniently collected together in schools. In the bitter conflicts with 'scabs' in the Sarmcol industrial dispute, in the organization of various urban stay-aways in which the role of bus-drivers is crucial, and in the painful disputes over school boycotts, it seems certain that coercive pressures of varying degrees of intensity have been employed against those who resisted or lacked enthusiasm for the aims and tactics of these new militant forces. It is likely that traditional authorities in Vulindlela would have seen such new forces as usurpatory even had their objections and methods been less controversial.

In 1987–8 this conflict (between Inkatha and UDF-COSATU, as it is commonly described) has engulfed Imbali, Ashdown, Edendale and substantial parts of Vulindlela in a civil war. It is clear that the transitional character of much of this area, between rural and urban, provides bases for competing political forces. It is probable that the existence of substantial unemployment and poor career prospects for many young persons reduces the apparent value of education and makes more attractive life-meanings derived from political identities. But why the conflict should have reached such a level of violent intensity is not easy to say. An extended answer would need at least to look to history and culture, to the sources of widespread violence in rural KwaZulu at present, and to the character of the overall South African political system within which KwaZulu and Vulindlela are confined.

[2] There is no doubt that there are errors in these data but they are consistent and plausible enough to be worth quoting here. Current rates of inflation make a comparision across a two-year period difficult, so the 1984 figures have been adjusted to rough July 1986 purchasing-power equivalents.

[3] Mean (or average) income figures are often correctly regarded with suspicion because the small number of very high incomes at the top of an income distribution can raise the mean well above the level of the bulk of the population. The median is designed to measure 'central tendency' — the median income is such that half the households are above it and half below. For the data that we have been summarizing the medians certainly do lie below the means, indicating that there is some concentration of households at the bottom end of the distributions. Median household incomes for the 1984 sample was R441 per month (mean: R543) and R418 for 1986 (mean: R500).

[4] We must be clear what these conversions mean: they represent amounts which will buy in 1988 what actual incomes bought in 1984 and 1986. They are not predictions of what actual incomes will be in 1988, though it is unlikely that area means will change substantially in 2 to 4 years.

Growing up in Loop Street

Brian Spencer

With my parents and elder brother I lived in house No. 441 Loop Street from 1937, when I was one year old, until 1952. Separated from No. 439 by a shared access to their back gardens, the front elevations of these red-brick houses were identical in reverse. They moved along verandas to gable-ended projecting wings with square bays. Both belonged to Mr Henry Miller who was a conveyancer. He and his wife Agnes lived in No. 439.

In our day the two houses were neat with carefully cleaned white steps. The front gardens were enclosed by post and pipe fences. Along the inside of each front fence was a well trimmed abelia hedge.

One of my earliest recollections is of playing under the may bush in the front garden of No. 443. The bush spilled out onto the pavement. Because of the bush's deep shade I had taken off my sun hat. A passer-by stole it.

Another early recollection is of being scrubbed and dressed in button-through trousers and shirt in preparation for being taken to visit Miss Winnie and Miss Ruby Stacey of Stacey's tobacconist's shop. They lived at 274 Prince Alfred Street. We would have tea with the grown-ups in a room painted avocado green. We found this stifling and when eventually allowed out would run onto the veranda and pull the tail feathers of the cockatiels. Next we would skip into the garden to help the servants saw wood. The Misses Stacey had a wood-burning stove and would use only thorn wood because it burned away to a clean white ash. The firewood was brought to their house from the Mpusheni area on a donkey cart.

Sometimes when we were playing in the back garden of our home we would hear the clicking noise made by the brake ratchets of an approaching ox-wagon. We would run into the street to watch it trundle past laden with pumpkins for sale on the Market Square. Once a swarm of locusts flew over and we banged tin tea trays to frighten them away.

The ice truck used to come down the street. Its cab was round at the front and there was a tall chimney at the back. A man would pick up a block of ice with a caliper, heft it onto his left shoulder which was protected by a folded sack and run into 439. We, on the other hand, were modern, for we had a fridge. By this time our lead ice chest was being used as a store cupboard for wrapping-paper and string where the ice used to go, dusters where the food had been kept and shoe polishing materials in the deep drip drawer on the floor underneath.

Also driving down the street, but not so far as our house, we would see Mr Rupert Holliday in his tall car with folding white canvas top, green body and some kind of chain driven mechanism underneath. Mr Holliday was a big man who always dressed in a dark brown suit and a hat. He was supposed to be bad tempered. There was a story that once, when a young man called to see his daughter, Mr Holliday had chased him away with a double-barrelled shotgun.

Brian Spencer and his brother Derek with their mother at 441 Loop Street about 1939. The family was on its way to a wedding.

My mother's sister and her family lived at 431 Loop Street. My maternal grandparents lived at 326. Grandmother was always baking on her paraffin stove. On the sill of the kitchen window there would be washed currants and raisins drying on wire trays. On the table would be freshly baked rock cakes left out to cool. When we arrived grandmother would knock her hands together to get rid of the flour and urge us to help ourselves to whatever we wanted.

For a while grandfather had a shop on the corner of Loop and Henrietta Streets. We loved it because of the flavoured ice cubes and the ribbons of liquorice we were given. My mother and aunt hated the shop because they had to help out when needed.

Also in Loop Street were Mr and Mrs Rump who were close friends of the family. Mr Rump was caretaker-cum-carpenter at the Natal Museum. They lived in a straight up and down double-storeyed house at the back of it. In front of the house were two squat palms with moss around their roots. We liked the feel of this cool green growth. At the side of the museum was a long narrow garden. We would be left there to play while our mother went shopping. It was a quiet secret place and very special for us. Protecting it from the street was a high wall with a locked gate in the middle. On either side of the gate were two very tall palms. When we tired of playing in the garden we would run into the museum workshop and see how far we could pull the curled, fresh-smelling wood shavings without breaking them.

On the way home we would call at Tommy Nott the chemist. His shop was on the corner of Loop Street and Commercial Road. He had known our great-grandmother, Amelia Spencer, and would tell us how she always wore a widow's cap. What a wonderful shop his was. There were glass cabinets full of bottles and jars and two carboys full of coloured liquid — one blue and the other red. On the wall behind the counter were framed photographs of the Drakensberg. It was said that his assistant, Mr Arbuckle, had once been so ill that straw was put down on the road in front of his house to quieten the noise of passing vehicles.

With all these friends and relations in the street I had a proprietorial feeling about it. It was our street. To me it also seemed like a country street. This was, I suppose, because so many farm people used to live in it. There were the Misses Hodson from Caversham, Miss Comins from Malton and Mrs Parkinson from Shafton Grange in the Karkloof. They all seemed such kind and gentle ladies although I don't remember any of them ever speaking to us. Perhaps it was that they looked so comfortable in their simple home-made clothes. Later Mrs Shaw and Mrs

75

Urquhart lived where the Misses Hodson had been. They were Jacksons from the Fort Nottingham area. They frightened us a little.

Mother didn't always have to go to town to shop. Sometimes the shops would come to her. Mr Wheeler from the Co-op would call with his order book and then a little while later the required groceries would be delivered. The butcher's book had a smell all of its own, damp and bloody. Another person who used to come to the house regularly was the Indian vegetable 'Mary'. Her big brown cane basket creaked as she lifted it off the wound-up cloth on her head. She also had a wooden push-cart on metal wheels. This would be left in the street.

During the Second World War we were taken to see some of my father's staff leave to go up North. The soldiers were mustered in front of the railway station and we slipped through the arch to the side of the main portico just before they were marched onto the platform. Their boots made a threatening noise and I thought they were going to trample right over us. The station was crowded. The troops broke ranks to take leave of their families. A tall soldier was crying, tears dripping off the end of his long nose. The Caledonian Pipe Band and the Carbineer Band were both there. I remember that as the train moved off the man with the big drum was standing on the walk-way between two of the coaches.

It was my task to listen to the lunchtime news and tell my parents if anything important was reported. Sometimes the house would be bleak with grief. This was especially so the day the news came through that Athol Paton had been killed.

One afternoon my grandmother brought a tall man in a blue uniform to the house. He was a cousin from England who was serving in the Royal Navy. From then on he visited us whenever his ship was in Durban. He made my mother a sieve so that she could bake white bread. It was against the law to sieve flour because of wastage of a commodity in short supply. We were sieving one day when there was a knock on the front door. Through the glass panels we could see a blue form and thought it was Fatty Morris the policeman come to arrest us. Hastily we hid everything but it was only mother's cousin who was again on shore leave. It was the Misses Stacey who kept us supplied with organdie through which to sieve the flour, pillars of the church though they were.

There were air raid warnings during the War and the curtains had to be lined with black material. When an alarm sounded my brother and I would run into the street to make sure that no chink of light was showing. After the War the black material was given to the women on our farm and they made doeks out of it.

At night my mother would sit knitting. When we went to bed she would have a new sock on her needles and a packet of liquorice-all-sorts by her side. In the morning there would be no sweets left and another pair of socks ready for the boys at war. Much time and thought went into gathering together and wrapping up food parcels for relatives in England.

There were two canteens in Loop Street where troops could go for refreshment and entertainment. They were on opposite corners of Henrietta Street. Many Maritzburg ladies made a valuable contribution towards winning the War by helping in these canteens.

A very wrinkled old lady used to come and collect money

14

431 Loop Street where the writer's aunt and uncle lived. Like many of the houses in the street it retains much of its original character today.

to buy comforts for the patients at Oribi Hospital. Quite often she didn't feel very well and would ask for a drop of something to keep her going. She did splendid work and I do believe helped many sick and lonely men.

1944 found people working hard for the Dawn of Victory Cavalcade in aid of the Governor-General's National War Fund. Many different functions were organized for months on end. The Fair in Alexandra Park with its trackless trains for touring the grounds in, is what I remember best.

Following hard on Cavalcade's heels was Navy Week which for us was even more exciting as our family participated in this fund raising campaign. My father helped to construct *The Good Ship Motor Town*. My brother was one of the sailors on board who collected money from those who turned out to see the flotilla of sponsored ships steam through the streets of the City. Dressed in sailor suits, my brother would accompany me on the piano and I would sing the song about Sam the sailor man. This was the metal figure of a sailor sold for funds. The more you collected the higher you rose in rank. On reaching a certain figure you were allowed to wear a Sam in the splendidly painted uniform of an admiral of the fleet.

On VE or VJ night, I can no longer remember which, our parents took us into town and we watched the revellers doing the conga in the middle of Church Street.

From 1 February 1947 when the royal family left Britain there were nightly bulletins about what they had been doing during the day and how many miles closer to South Africa HMS *Vanguard* had brought them. Once they had landed in Cape Town their tour was fully reported in the press and over the air. Bunting covered the buildings of Pietermaritzburg. There was a triumphal entrance arch in Church Street near the railway station. School pupils had been rigorously rehearsed in the songs they were to sing. New clothes had been bought and flags to wave. The 18th of March dawned fair and warm. We assembled in front of Merchiston School in Burger Street and walked to the Oval in Alexandra Park. Although it was only a distant view of the royal family that we were able to get, the excitement of the whole experience is with me yet.

In retrospect this seems to be the watershed of a happy youth. In 1948 the National Party came into power. In January 1949, we watched army vehicles drive past the house. They were patrolling the town because of race riots. Thirty-nine years later I no longer live in Loop Street but I still live in a strife-torn land.

Nineteenth-century Loop Street

Shelagh Spencer

Loop Street still has much of its nineteenth-century character, in the buildings that remain from that era, in sites that have strong nineteenth-century associations, and in its side-streets that can trace their names to residents of bygone years. This article focuses on some of the street's earliest nineteenth-century buildings, and on how some of its older streets acquired their names.

The erven in Pietermaritzburg are named according to the street nearest to the Msunduze River, e.g. the first Catholic church in Loop Street, (where the Prince Imperial lay in state in 1879) is on Erf 9 Burger Street, while the erf immediately across Loop Street from it is Erf 9 Loop Street. This holds good for Loop Street through to Greyling Street. Burger Street is the exception. Here the erven furthest from the river run from 1 to 55 (with 111 placed beyond 55), while those nearer the Msunduze run from 56 to 110.

One often reads that the upper end of town, (near Government House and Fort Napier) was the élite part of Pietermaritzburg. However, it would appear that in the early 1850s, Lieutenant-Governor Pine, in the thatched cottage he had recently purchased from Dr William Stanger, the Colony's Surveyor-General, was surrounded by very ordinary neighbours. Looking at the occupants of the erven between the top of town and West Street, one finds from the 1853 *Directory of D'Urban and Pietermaritzburg* that his Longmarket Street neighbours included a wagonmaker, a carpenter and joiner, and two storekeepers. There were three storekeepers between Erven 1 and 5 on the Church Street frontage, together with a watch-maker, a labourer, a tinplate worker, a tailor, a blacksmith and the Quartermaster of the 45th Regiment. Almost on his doorstep there was Visagie's mill which dominated this end of town. The top end of Pietermaritz Street was thinly populated with a market-gardener and seedsman on Erf 1, and William Millward Collins, Pine's private secretary, on Erf 5. The top of Burger Street, also later to become an area in which the upper classes lived, could boast only a tailor, a builder, a labourer, a widow, a farmer and a laundress. The only residents in Pine's immediate neighbourhood to whom, in that era of snobbery, would be given the appellation 'gentleman' were the two clergymen, the Revd James Green of the Church of England in Church Street, and the Presbyterian Revd William Campbell in Longmarket Street.

Loop Street would seem to be the exception. Along the Burger Street side lived Lieutenant-Colonel Edmund French Boys of the 45th Regiment, Theophilus Shepstone, the Diplomatic Agent to the Indigenous Tribes, and Daniel Burton Scott, a gentleman. According to the *Directory* the only occupant on the other side of the street was Margaret R. Day, who defies identification! From the property valuations which appeared in the *Natal Witness* in September 1854 one finds that Colonel Boys' property was now rented by Colonel Cooper (also of the 45th), and that its annual value was £60. Shepstone's property also had an annual value of £60, while Scott's was only £24 (the average value for Erven 1 to 5 in Loop and Burger Streets calculated from the list is £26). To put this in perspective, £5 is the smallest value shown for any property in either Loop or Burger Street, and the largest was £120 for Revd James Archbell's half of Erf 31 Loop Street. The next highest valuation was J.C. Zeederberg's £80 for Erf 25 Loop Street, occupied by Charles Florey. This was the Crown Hotel, now Liberty Tavern.

Walking down Loop Street from Pine Street one can identify many relics of the street's history. The core of the house now numbered 10 Loop Street, on the Pine Street corner, was Colonel Boys' residence. The erf (No. 1 Burger Street) was granted to Boys in 1846. Boys commanded the 45th Regiment in Natal from 1845 to 1853. As Senior Officer Commanding the Forces in the Colony, to him fell the duty of administering the government during the interregnum between the death of Lieutenant-Governor Martin West in 1849 and the arrival of Pine in the following year. With Boys' departure from the Colony ownership passed to another 45th officer, Lieutenant George Stacpole Coxon. Lieutenant Coxon it is that we have to thank for one of the very early illustrations of Pietermaritzburg, a pencil sketch dating to 1848 of the top of Church Street showing Visagie's mill (which was situated on what later became part of Government House gardens). Coxon still owned 1 Burger Street in 1860, and by then it was occupied by Major Williamson of the 85th Regiment. By 1863 Captain Walter Lloyd was the owner and it was being rented by W.M. Collins, by that time Natal's Postmaster-General. By November 1870 the premises were unoccupied, but by 1872 the building was being rented by the newly established Anglican grammar school, Bishop's College. Lloyd sold it to the trustees of the College in the following year. (It is interesting to note that in 1896 the successor to Bishop's College, Michaelhouse, also began its days in Loop Street, further down, in the house now numbered 386.) After the demise of Bishop's College in 1880 the buildings were occupied for a brief period by the Victoria Club. In 1882 Miss Eliza Jane Usherwood purchased Bishop's College premises to house St. Anne's Diocesan School for Girls, of which she was the Lady Principal. She then donated the property to the Anglican Church. During the occupancy of St. Anne's the buildings were extended along both Loop and Pine Streets. St. Anne's moved to Hilton in 1904 and in later years the buildings were altered and segmented forming separate dwellings. These still exist.

Across Loop Street from No. 10 is Macrorie House, on Erf 1 Loop Street, which was granted to Julius Flesch in 1846. Almost immediately it was sold to George Winder, better known on the Durban scene as the proprietor, in later years, of the Masonic Hotel, now the Royal. The succeeding owners, P.J. Jung & Co., subdivided the property in 1854, and Sub A on which the house stands, had four successive owners before October 1861 when it passed into the hands of the trustees of Catherine McLeod, the wife of Edward McLeod, Pietermaritzburg's Acting Postmaster, and later Acting Postmaster-General. Judging from the price paid for the property (£110), and the £700 for which it was sold in 1863, it seems probable that the house was built during the McLeods' tenure. A notorial deed signed by Edward in 1863 makes mention of the house 'recently erected on Sub A, which was purchased with money given Catherine by her mother'. The McLeods had come to Natal in 1851, and with Edward's civil service salary and his wife's private income, had been free of monetary anxieties, unlike many other colonists. There were domestic problems, however, which led to a divorce in May 1863 and the sale of the house and its contents (including 64 yards of Brussels carpeting) in July. The sale notice described the house thus: 'that recently built substantial and commodious dwelling house of two storeys containing seven apartments... together with pantry, kitchen, etc'. The saga of this McLeod family ends with their departure from the Colony, Edward for Australia, and Mrs McLeod and their daughter for Britain.

The house's new owner was Edward Few, that enterprising personality who had established the sawmills at Boston in the early 1850s. It was from the Few brothers' Maritzburg timber depot on Erf 21 Longmarket Street that Timber Street takes its name. It appears that Edward did not live in the house (he was resident in England by 1864), but that it was occupied by his brother Joseph. With Edward's insolvency in 1867, the house, described then as 'the finest and best built family house in the City', was again sold. From Few the property passed to Paul Henwood, and it was from him that Bishop W.K. Macrorie and his wife were renting it in 1870. The Macrories later bought the house and two other subdivisions of Erf 1. They gave their residence the name South Hill, and improved and enlarged it in the 25 years of their ownership.

A short distance below Macrorie House is Fleming Street. In its day Loop Street has known two Fleming Streets, both named after John Fleming (c.1823–1902), carpenter and builder, and Mayor of the City from 1875 to 1877. This Fleming Street runs down the middle of Erf 3 Loop Street. By 1863 Fleming owned and occupied half of Erf 2, while the 1870 valuation roll shows he also had part of Erf 3. His dwelling was on the Longmarket Street frontage. In the early 1850s Fleming had lived on Erf 14 Loop Street, and the street laid out between this erf and Erf 15 was called Fleming Street. It is now known as Ebenezer Street.

Another thoroughfare at the top of Loop Street with nineteenth-century connotations in Shepstone Avenue, on Erf 2 Burger Street. Theophilus Shepstone owned a small piece of Erf 2, his residence was on Erf 3, and he also owned Erf 4. His house stood on Loop Street almost on the corner of Shepstone Avenue. Shepstone was an enthusiastic gardener and his extensive garden was a local show-piece.

When discussing early Loop Street one must include, only briefly, as they are being dealt with elsewhere, the first Catholic Church, dating to 1852, and the adjoining priests' house, completed circa early 1857. The latter, wrote Bishop Allard, Natal's first Catholic bishop in 1857, was considered 'to be the most solidly built one in the town'.

Further down the street on the same side, on Erf 11 Burger Street, is a cottage (No. 118, set right on the street line). This property was granted in 1848 to Robert Lindsay, an ex-corporal in the 45th Regiment, as a discharged soldier. Lindsay later made a living in Pietermaritzburg as a builder before going farming in the late 1850s at Liddesdale in the Boston district. In 1898 he sold part of Erf 11 to his neighbour, John Freeman, while in 1902 after his death, his son James disposed of the rest to Freeman. The cottage has a notorious chapter in its long history, for it was here in 1907 that one of its tenants, Mrs Elizabeth Macdonald, the retired Matron of Grey's Hospital, when trying to protect her Indian maid from his wrath, was murdered by her Indian man-servant.

Adjoining No. 118 is a house that has received much publicity in recent years because of the fine way in which it has been refurbished after years of near-dereliction. This is Overpark (No. 122) on Erf 12 Burger Street. In June 1860 the Presbyterian Church called for tenders for the laying of foundations for a house on Erf 12, and for bricks, brickwork, carpentry and slating. This was to be Revd William Campbell's new manse, the plans for which he had brought back to Natal in 1858 at the conclusion of his two-year tour in North America, Great Britain and Ireland, raising funds for the new church in Church Street, and for the building of a manse. The Campbells moved into the house in April 1862. According to Barbara Buchanan, the manse was for many years the only building on the rise immediately above the loop in Loop Street. A few years after its construction the Prophet Ignoramus in his amusing way recorded: 'Many people thought the house of too much splendour for an humble priest as it was better than the house of the rulers of the land'. Towards the end of Campbell's life there was a split in the Pietermaritzburg congregation and another was formed. Consequently the First Presbyterian Church's finances suffered, and in 1897 the manse, then 'in a chronic state of disrepair', was sold to John Freeman, a prosperous miller originally from Prestbury in Gloucestershire. Freeman renovated and extended the house. It remained in the Freeman family, in the female line, until 1980, but was uninhabited from 1964 when Freeman's daughter, Mrs van Ryck de Groot, died. By 1980 Overpark was once again in 'a chronic state of disrepair' and it was sold. The new owners have restored it to what it must have been like in its heyday under the Freemans.

Another of Loop Street's early residences is Park View on Erf 14 Burger Street, now numbered 146 Loop Street. In 1863 Erf 14 came into the possession of Robert Anderson (c.1818–1878), the land surveyor, who in the early 1850s acted as agent for those British settlers who came to Natal under the auspices of John Lidgett and

The corner of Chapel and Loop Streets. Although taken in the 1890s, this view is still recognizable. Fort Napier can be seen in the distance.

15

16

R.M. Hackett. After the death of Anderson's widow in 1880 the property passed to their second daughter, Mrs Louisa Martha Baylis. Leighton Street, which runs between Erfs 13 and 14, was established in 1899 when Mrs Baylis and the owner of Erf 13, John Mortimer (of the firm Bale & Mortimer, house and land agents), each donated a portion of their land to the Pietermaritzburg Corporation. The street, one presumes, takes its name from Louisa's husband, the dentist, Leighton Baylis. In 1902 and 1903 Erfs 13 and 14 were split. A number of subdivisions were bought by John Harwin (a merchant who traded where John Orr's is today), or by his son-in-law, Clement Horner Stott. Stott was a prominent architect in the City whose surviving buildings include the original Cedara College of Agriculture structure and Harwin's Arcade. It is known that Stott designed No. 30 Leighton Street. As at least five other houses in this street bear a striking resemblance to it, and as far as can be ascertained, are on lots originally owned either by him or by Harwin, one concludes that he is responsible for Leighton Street's pleasing and unique streetscape.

The naming of Ebenezer Street (formerly Fleming Street) also dates to the nineteenth century. Revd James Allison, the founder of both the Indaleni and Edendale Mission Stations, later moved to Pietermaritzburg. To facilitate his ministry to the Africans of the town he built in 1865 a chapel on the site adjoining his house on the corner of Longmarket Street and the then Fleming Street, to which he gave the name Ebenezer Chapel. This still stands.

One house, the oldest part of which dates to 1869, is Dean James Green's Deanery, at present the residence of the Cathedral's Sub-Dean. During the Colenso controversy the Supreme Court in 1868 awarded Bishop Colenso all the church property invested in his name or in that of the Bishop of Cape Town. Consequently the clergy opposing him had to vacate their churches and rectories. The Dean was forced to leave his Deanery in Pietermaritz Street (Deanery Lane indicates its position), and with money he collected in England he built both St. Saviour's Cathedral and a new Deanery. In letters of November 1869 and April 1870 Green wrote of his new house as 'a commodious well-built and very pretty residence' and '... a most excellent house, such as you never saw in Natal. In fact I feel half ashamed of it, not that I have spent money on ornament, but only in solidity. A thorough English parsonage, all on the ground floor... It is on a piece of ground facing the river, and overlooking the park... We have three-fourths of an acre...' In his November letter the Dean described the school chapel for the African congregation which was about to be built in the Deanery garden, while in his second letter he recounted the laying of the foundation stone, and stated that the chapel was expected to be completed within the next two weeks. 'The design though simple is very pretty so that the building is quite an architectural feature.' This, of course, is St. Mark's, which, since enlarged, still stands in the Deanery garden. For a number of years now it has been unused, the congregation having moved to a new church at Imbali.

Diagonally opposite the Deanery is another old house, No. 184, now occupied by the architects Meanwell, Andersson & Jackson. The plot, 32 perches in extent,

A gentleman's residence in Loop Street at the end of the 19th century. (Epworth High School opened in this building in 1898.)

was bought in 1851 by Benjamin Swete Kelly (c.1819–1899), a Byrne settler from Cork, and a cabinet maker. Kelly and his two sons later had an outfitting establishment in Church Street. This land remained in the Kelly family for 69 years, during which time the house was built. From 1920 to 1966 it was owned by the John family of John & Salter's, wine and spirits merchants.

Yet another nineteenth-century house in this region is No. 191 on the corner of Loop Street and Buchanan Street. This cottage, according to a caption to a photograph in the Hattersley collection in the Natal Archives, was in existence before 1860. During the 1860s the property came into the possession of David Lindsay, brother of Robert Lindsay. David and his family came to Natal from Glasgow at Robert's instigation, as did other members of the Lindsay family. David was a carpenter, and in later times, an undertaker. In 1871 Peter Davis senior, printer, and later owner of the Natal Witness, bought the property, and it remained in the hands of the Davis family until 1920. When street numbering was introduced in the 1890s, this house was given the number 187 Loop Street, but in 1903 it was changed to the present 191. In the 1890s Edward Dent, a retired soldier of the 85th Regiment, and his wife lived in this cottage. After the Dents died, Mrs Dent's son by a previous marriage, Benjamin Favell, and his family rented the house for some years in the early 1900s.

Buchanan Street, which runs down the middle of Erf 19 Loop Street, dates back to 1862 and takes its name from David Dale Buchanan, the founder of the Natal Witness, and its editor for many years. He owned a quarter of Erf 19 and all of Erf 20 in the 1850s and until at least 1870.

Another street whose name goes back to the last century is Killarney Terrace which divides Erf 20 Burger Street and runs from Loop Street through to Burger Street. This erf became the property of Johan D. Marquard, Pietermaritzburg's first government teacher, in 1852. In 1856 he divided it and sold half to his assistant, and later successor as government teacher, George Thomson. The other half, after various changes in ownership, was bought in 1861 by James Renault Saunders, the Natal progenitor of the Saunders of

Tongaat. Saunders sub-divided the land into nine small lots, with a right-of-way through the centre. In 1878 Henry James Cooper Hutton, an 1850 Byrne settler ex *Edward*, bought the other half of the erf, (with the Burger Street frontage). He also owned land across Burger Street, and in about 1880 sold some of this to the Girls Collegiate School as the site for their first building. A condition of sale was that he extend the existing right-of-way through his property to Burger Street. The name Killarney Terrace comes from the Huttons. Their farm in the Umlaas Road district was Killarney Isles, and so struck with the name were they that one of their children was baptized Kate Killarney. This happened despite the fact that there does not seem to be any Irish ancestry in the background — Hutton was from Bedfordshire, and his wife, Mary Dicken, from London.

Erf 20 Burger Street is interesting on another score. On the largest of the subdivisions made by Saunders in 1863, Sub E, on the corner of Killarney Terrace and Loop Street, there survives a portion of Marquard's house. For a short time in the 1850s this house was rented by John Bird, the Chief Clerk in the Colonial Office, and later the City's Resident Magistrate. It has achieved local fame because Bird used to wave his handkerchief from the upstairs window (looking on to Killarney Terrace) as a signal for the correct timing of the 9 a.m. gun which was fired daily from the military camp at Fort Napier. In 1863 ownership passed from Saunders to the solicitor, John William Turnbull, in whose family the property remained until 1918. Turnbull, who eventually became a judge in the Supreme Court, added a ballroom on the Loop Street frontage and workshops at the back. The reason for this, as tradition has it, was his desire that his family find their entertainments at home, rather than mix with the *hoi polloi* of Pietermaritzburg.

Just before reaching Commercial Road one encounters Witness Lane on Erf 24 Loop Street, adjoining Erf 25. Erf 24 belonged to J.C. Zeederburg in the 1850s, and sometime in the early 1860s it was subdivided. By 1863 one of the subdivisions was owned and occupied by P. Davis & Sons. They later acquired a second subdivision, and the *Natal Witness* premises are still on this site. The Davis family has strong connections with Loop Street. By 1852 Peter Davis's home was on Erf 35 Burger Street, while his sons, Peter and Alfred, owned various lots on both Loop and Burger Street erfs.

One of Loop Street's old houses which is still in the street, but not on its original site, is Hinton House, part of which has been re-erected in the Natal Museum as one of the exhibits in its Hall of History. Numbered 270 Loop

SERVANTS IN THE 1920s AND 1930s

William Bizley

No doubt a good deal of the idyll that was white life between the wars derived from the well-nigh feudal system of servants and labourers that supported it. It takes probably a century or two of political heat to decide whether the underdogs, in the feudal pyramid, were content or not with their daily existence. The retinues of black servants, delivery 'boys', assistants, launderers, harnessers, wagoners, coal shovellers, grass cutters, who worked for a pittance and were never seen in shops or streets except on errands were probably too close to primitive laws of supply and demand to consider the issue. The rickshaw industry is the controversial area here — in retrospect it seems the most man-impounding and enslaving sort of job, but there was great rivalry for licensed vehicles, especially as, with fares ranging between 6d and 2/- you might, in two or three days, earn as much as the 'head boy' of a household in a month, which was usually £2. (Incidentally the starting pay for a white nurse was then £1.10 a month. For those who had to pay board and lodging, like a brand-new schoolteacher, the starting pay was £11.3s.4d. Of this the board would be about £5 to £6.) The first block of flats in Pietermaritzburg, 'Strathallan', was not yet built and there was a great collection of minor hotels and boarding houses — the Thanet, the Oaks, the Summerville, Warrington House, Palmdene.) One doesn't imply an inveterate contentment, then, if one recalls the colourful picture of the suburban off hours period between 3.00 and 5.00 p.m. when servants and domestics would sit along the pavements, feet dangling in the gutters, chatting, listening, playing Jew's harps, mouth organs, squash boxes or home-made banjos. What did they think of the curfew bell that sounded from the tower above the police station (today's Publicity House) every evening at 10.00 p.m.? That smacks of the old South, and yet . . . the railway station was the exit gate from undesirable employers, just as it was the disembarking point for dozens seeking work.

The servants who withdrew into invisibility at 10.00 p.m. rewarded their employers with a touching honesty. Oxenham's Bakery (owned by Roy Hesketh's father) used to pile each day's takings into huge pots in easy public view and reach, and yet they were never the object of theft. The locking of doors of Maritzburg homes seems hardly to have occurred; only the annual holiday would warrant it. Yet the serene life could take a violent turn, as on Sunday afternoons, when 'kitchen boys' formed gangs to have *skebenga* stick fights.

Many white housewives took an active interest in the uplift of their servants; one made her house *umfaan* recite his homework as he stood on the ladder hanging curtains, before sending him off to night school at the old Colenso Church on Commercial Road. The black serving population was not apolitical in a 'Southern' sort of way. The ICU, the Industrial and Commercial Workers' Union, reached through to all layers of black labour, even to farm workers who, to all appearances, seemed utterly apolitical. In Maritzburg the ICU headquarters were below Scott Street at the upper end of Church Street and invariably there was a milling crowd thereabouts on Saturday nights. Yet residents preferred to walk through this crowd, and in fact often did so, since the alternative, Pietermaritz Street, was dimly lit and dangerous. The ICU obviously provided an important social outlet; but all was not well with its management of funds, which were made up of subs carefully collected every Friday evening from kitchen and garden staff through town and suburbs. The story is that when one of the Maritzburg ICU officials bought a motor car (something beyond the wildest dreams of the ordinary members) many withdrew in disgust.

The composition of the servant population has changed since this photograph of the staff of the Imperial Hotel was taken in the late 19th century. By the 1920s white maids, once top of the hierachy of servants, had effectively disappeared, and today black women have all but supplanted black men in domestic service.

17

Street, its site is now engulfed by the Joshua Doore Centre. According to Professor Hattersley, this house was one of those appearing on a plan of Pietermaritzburg prepared in 1852 by the surveyor, Hughbert Baker, and sent to his friend Isambard Brunel. By the end of 1852 Edward London, a bookbinder from Manchester, was living in this house. By January 1855 he and his wife and daughter were conducting a private school there, to which they gave the name Hinton House Academy. It appears London ran the boys' section, while Mrs London and Emily taught the young ladies. By June 1858, London, whose first teaching experience dated to 1820, had given up his boys' school, as there was too much competition, and he could make a better living with his stationer's and bookbinding business. (He also ran a subscription library.) The academy for young ladies continued under Mrs London until October 1860, when a Miss Ford took over its management. Mrs London, in her early years in Pietermaritzburg, had been the 'female assistant' to J.D. Marquard in the Government School. Hinton House has another claim to fame: it was the site of Maritzburg's first Baptist services, under 'Pastor London'. The earliest reference traced to the Baptist community in Pietermaritzburg appears in October 1861, when an advertisement in the *Natal Courier* informed the public that subscriptions for the erection of a Baptist Church were being received by Mr London and Phillip Ferreira. Nothing eventuated, and after London's death in 1874 the Baptist meetings were discontinued. It was only ten years later that a Baptist congregation was regularly constituted in the Capital. The first minister arrived in 1884, and the church in Chapel Street was completed in the following year.

On the erf adjoining that where Hinton House stood, Erf 28 Burger Street, is another nineteenth century house, No. 284. In February 1852 this property was transferred to John Moss, a Yorkshireman from Burneston near Bedale, who had emigrated to Natal on the *Haidee* in 1850. In April 1851 Moss's tender for the building of the municipal pound was accepted. At that time he offered his services as Poundmaster if required. He was still the City's Poundmaster in 1860. Erf 28 Burger Street was his residence in 1854, but by October 1858 he had a tenant in these premises. Possibly he had by this time moved to Fox Hill, where he certainly was living by 1862. Moss's tenant, according to the *Natal Witness*, was J. Allen (sic).

The evidence points to this being John Allan, another Yorkshireman, from Exelby, near Burneston. Allan and his wife, Martha, emigrated to Natal on the *Jane Morice* in 1851, together with their daughter Martha, and a relation (possibly a son), Thomas Allan and his family. Besides the fact that both the Mosses and the Allans came from the same part of Yorkshire, it seems possible that they were also related. Moss's wife Mary was a Robinson, and so was Thomas Allan's wife, Ann. John Allan died in 1862 and John Moss in 1866. In 1868 Mrs Moss married Richard Baynes (father of Joseph Baynes of Baynesfield). Mrs Baynes died in 1874 and Mrs Allan continued to rent the property until her death in 1878. Only in 1883 was this property transferred from the Moss estate to its new owner Lancelot C. Hodgkins. Subsequent owners for short periods were John Hodgkins and Peter Carbis.

In December 1902 ownership passed to Susan Russom, the widow of John Russom, an auctioneer and storekeeper of Pietermaritzburg, who was Mayor of the City in the 1869-70 municipal year. On Mrs Russom's death in 1905 the house was transferred to her daughter Catherine Augusta, the wife of Robert Isaac Finnemore, who had a distinguished career in the Natal civil service culminating in the post of Chief Justice. It would seem that Mrs Russom never lived at No. 284. From 1903 until her death she was across Loop Street at No. 287, near the corner of Henrietta Street. To this house she gave the name Westbury after the Gloucestershire village Westbury on Trym with which the Russom family had connections. (As an aside — another Loop Street resident, Sir Theophilus Shepstone, was born at Westbury on Trym.) After Mrs Russom's death the Finnemores lived at Westbury. Westbury was still standing during the Second World War, by which time it had been converted into a boarding-house. From Mrs Finnemore, No. 284 passed to her daughter Irene Augusta Violet Cullerne who continued to live there until her death in 1971 when the house, after a period of 69 years, passed out of the hands of the Russom family.

Further down the street, on the other side, one comes across two lanes with names that take one back to the last century. Terry Street, or Terry's Lane as it was once called, runs through part of Erf 30 Loop Street, and is named after Joseph Terry, a builder, who bought part of this erf from Archbell's insolvent estate in 1869. He also purchased portions of Erf 31 from the estate. Most of the Terry land on these erven remained in the family until 1932. Their house, much altered, stands on Loop Street between Terry and Archbell Streets. Archbell Street traverses the middle of Erf 31 Loop Street. It was in existence by at least 1867, when it was known as College Street, presumably because it opened into Loop Street directly opposite the newly-erected building of the Pietermaritzburg Government High School (now Maritzburg College). Archbell owned Erf 30 Loop Street and half of Erf 31. His residence was on the Longmarket Street frontage facing on to the Market Square.

Boshoff Street comes by its name because from the early 1850s Jacobus Nicolaas Boshoff (1808–1881) owned part of the adjoining Erf 35 Loop Street. Boshoff was President of the Orange Free State for a brief period in the 1850s and in the 1870s was the member for Klip River County in the Natal Legislative Council.

Finally we come to the bottom end of town. It would seem that no really early houses survive in this part. Possibly, as it was a sparsely populated, virtually rural area, the structures were not as durable as those in the centre of the town. From the Town Surveyor, Alexander Mair's 1869 map of the City, one finds that of the 42 erfs below Boshoff Street, 32 were not built on on their Loop Street frontage, whereas for the 70 erfs above Boshoff Street, only 25 had no buildings on the street. The rural aspect of this area is endorsed by the fact that in the 1850s and 1860s the last five erfs in Loop Street, together with the last five in adjoining Longmarket Street (52–56), formed a farm or estate. The extensive house forming the nucleus of this property was in the 1870s the temporary lunatic asylum. For many years it was the last dwelling encountered when proceeding down Longmarket Street. It stood on Erfs 52 and 53 Longmarket Street and was called Town End House.

Sobantu Village

Heather Peel

From the earliest days of Pietermaritzburg, the African community provided its own accommodation on the edge of town, or on the properties of its employers, while some Africans were housed in barracks and compounds. White officials and residents generally regarded this as an unsatisfactory arrangement, and for many decades the establishment of a 'native village' was recognized as a possible solution to perceived problems of control and sanitation. However, although discussed periodically from the mid-nineteenth century, no real progress had been made by the time the Natives (Urban Areas) Act was passed in 1923. This Act provided the Council with the necessary incentive and power to move more decisively.

For several years, possible sites for a village had been under investigation, but each suggestion had been greeted by a storm of protest from those burgesses who owned property in the vicinity. By 1925 the Council had isolated two sites: one on the Bishopstowe Road, and the other at Mason's Mill. The latter was favoured by the Africans themselves as it linked up with established locations in the Edendale area, and was on existing transport routes. The main objection to the Bishopstowe Road site was its proximity to the town sanitary depot. Yet the feelings of the Village's future inhabitants apparently mattered less to the burgesses than the greater initial cost of building a village at Mason's Mill. In a plebiscite held in June 1925 they voted for Bishopstowe. The Council accepted this choice despite continued opposition, especially from Africans.

Plans were now prepared, and in 1927 a European contractor began work on the first 100 brick houses. Few voluntary tenants could be found when they became ready for occupation in 1928. Africans living in town were therefore ordered into the Village, and their makeshift dwellings were immediately demolished. In 1931 a further 100 houses were started to allow the 'cleaning-up' of the town to continue.

For that time, the facilities provided by the Pietermaritzburg Council compared very favourably with township development elsewhere. Streets and houses were electrified. Water taps and ablution blocks were communal, but each house had its own bucket-toilet. Properties were individually fenced to encourage gardening. In 1930 a school and market hall were built, and a year later a weekly clinic for infants was started. The 'Pietermaritzburg Native Village', as Sobantu was called until 1947, was gradually becoming more popular. From the mid-1930s there were consistently more applications than places available. This was also a result of the proclamation in 1931 of the whole Pietermaritzburg Borough as an area in which only domestic servants and other Africans with special exemption could live. Those who failed to get a house at the Village, and others who preferred to live under less controlled conditions, all moved to Edendale.

The residents of the Village were subject to a special set of regulations drawn up by the City Council. These were enforced by a white superintendent and his assistant, both of whom lived with their families at the Village until 1959. They were responsible to the manager of the Municipal Native Administration Sub-Committee. The decisions of this body were ratified by the City Council. Other municipal departments and officials, especially the City Engineer and the City Treasurer, were also directly involved in running the Village. The Council remained consistently opposed to direct representation for the villagers on the Council, arguing that the partly elected, partly nominated Advisory Board, headed by the chairman of the Native Administration Sub-Committee, was a sufficient link between the villagers and the Council. The Council itself was subject to the intrusive control of the Native Affairs Department in Pretoria. Apart from changes in name, this structure of administration remained largely the same until the early 1970s. Sobantu was officially part of Pietermaritzburg, but its administration and development were increasingly controlled from further afield.

The Village might have been distinguished from the rest of Pietermaritzburg administratively, but its residents were very much part of the City's working community. In fact, it was specifically intended to cater for married Africans employed in Pietermaritzburg, while single workers were accommodated in the hostels in town. One consequence of moving African families out of town, was that a subsidized bus service had to be provided by the Municipality. Since the prompt payment of rentals depended upon continued employment, a policy of giving preference to villagers, especially in recruiting for municipal departments, gradually developed. However, profits from the municipal monopoly on 'kaffir beer' contributed far more towards financing the Village than rents or other fees.

The first housing schemes were financed with ordinary loans, but later government Sub-Economic and National Housing loans were used. This drew the Council into a bureaucratic maze of protracted negotiations and delays before any scheme could be launched. In the 1940s the Pietermaritzburg Corporation successfully switched to using African artisans for building works at the Village. This innovation was opposed by white trade union interests, but aroused great interest from other local authorities. During the 1940s and early 1950s Sobantu Village grew rapidly from 357 houses in 1940 to 920 in 1956. This necessitated expansion beyond the original boundaries, the largest addition being the incorporation in 1945 of a neighbouring farm called The Finish.

Other developments accompanied the building of houses. Several churches, a recreation hall, an administration block, an old-age home, some sports facilities and three schools were also built over the years. The Marjorie Pope-Ellis Weaving School, started in 1939, provided some women from the Village with training and employment. Municipal Village Police were responsible for keeping control, the most on-going source of conflict being the domestic brewing of beer. As Sobantu Village developed, it acquired a reputation as a 'model community'. Yet, however self-contained it might seem, while most of the residents worked in neighbouring Pietermaritzburg, the inescapable anomaly remained that all the property was owned by the City Council.

Apart from these obvious administrative and

employment links, some Pietermaritzburg citizens did take a more social and charitable interest. Christmas treats were organized annually for the Village children, school bursaries were sponsored, and summer and winter garden competitions were held. Sobantu also participated, albeit separately, in festivities to celebrate royal occasions, Pietermaritzburg's Centenary, VJ Day and Azalea Week. Optimism about Sobantu's place in the wider Pietermaritzburg community would not have seemed misplaced in 1950.

However, difficulty was already being experienced in keeping pace with the demand for housing. This problem was compounded in the early 1950s when the Government decided to reduce losses on African housing by introducing economic rents. No more sub-economic schemes were to be built until all economic class tenants had been catered for. The housing at Sobantu was of a high standard, so many rentals were more than doubled when converted to an economic basis. This measure was obviously fiercely resented, and its implementation was delayed several times.

Yet not only were existing schemes made economic, but great difficulty was now experienced in getting approval for any new projects at all. The Council was informed by the Department of Native Affairs that no further extensions to Sobantu would be approved until the racial zoning of Pietermaritzburg had been completed under the Group Areas Act. A large extension across the Bishopstowe Road was therefore refused, eliminating any possibility of a site-and-service scheme to alleviate the housing shortage. In 1954 the Council was told that Verwoerd, the Minister of Native Affairs, regarded Sobantu as being *finaal afgehandel* — absolutely no more developments would be approved, even on land already included in the location. Pretoria refused even to discuss this policy decision with the Council, and it had to be accepted.

Sobantu consisted entirely of municipal houses. Plots had been allocated upon which Africans could build their own houses, but since the land would remain municipal property, none of the residents had ever been interested. However, with the introduction of economic rentals and the insecurity of a severe housing shortage, some tenants now began to push for a home-ownership scheme. In late 1955 the Council applied to convert a recently finished scheme for 25 superior economic houses to home-ownership. In April 1956, W.W.M. Eiselen, the Secretary for Native Affairs, replied that this would not be advisable for:

> ... whilst the Department appreciated the fact that Sobantu Native Village is a pleasant well-built Native residential area, it is nevertheless felt that it is not ideally situated in relation to the European areas, and that the inhabitants must ultimately be moved to an area specially determined for Native occupation in accordance with the planning under the Group Areas Act.

This threat of removal came as a complete surprise, because even at the hearings of the Land Tenure Advisory Board in May 1954, development at Sobantu had been frozen, but left in its present position. There was a general outcry in Pietermaritzburg about the proposed destruction of the City's 'model village', although some did deem it a necessary sacrifice to the apartheid ideal.

For various reasons, tension had been mounting in the Village for several years. Overcrowding was becoming worse as the Council was unable to expand Sobantu, and a proposed second village could not be started until group areas zoning had been finalized. Rents had increased sharply for economic tenants, and new electricity charges and an education levy were soon to be introduced. These particular local grievances must be seen in the context of the more general frustrations caused by the introduction of apartheid during the 1950s. On the night of Saturday, 15 August 1959, rioting broke out at Sobantu Village. The schools were set alight, and the overall damage was eventually estimated at over £23 500. This was the first serious disturbance to occur at Sobantu, and it marked the beginning of a less happy phase in the Village's history.

In the 1980s there were still only 1 092 houses in Sobantu, exactly the figure for the late 1950s. The 1960s and 1970s were therefore stagnant years, overshadowed by the threat of eventual removal. Population expansion was partly accommodated in unofficial backyard shacks, but from 1965 houses began to become available in the long-awaited second village at Imbali. This did help to reduce the number of lodgers at Sobantu, but houses at Imbali were being occupied as fast as they could be built, so the proposed removal of Sobantu residents to Imbali was never feasible.

In 1973 Sobantu was transferred from the City Council to the control of the Drakensberg Administration Board, later the Natalia Administration Board. This meant that the Village was officially no longer part of Pietermaritzburg, but in practice the residents continued to work and live as before. In fact, many officials simply changed their titles and continued with the same work as previously. In 1979 the Board supervised the election of a Community Council. The low poll at the time indicated

High-mast security lights, installed in 1987, at enormous expense, spotlight Sobantu's run-down streets.

limited initial support, and even this steadily waned. In 1982 there was an outbreak of unrest in the Village. By 1984 the Community Council had been disbanded, and the attempt to set up a town committee also failed. Sobantu had clearly had enough of puppet institutions. The real leadership of the community lay with the unofficial 'Committee of 12'.

In 1986 the Natal Provincial Administration took over official control from the defunct Administration Board. Provided that certain legal requirements were met, money would now be made available for development after years of neglect. However, through its Committee of 12, Sobantu now pushed for reincorporation within the Pietermaritzburg Borough. Negotiations eventually resulted in a compromise in December 1986: the Pietermaritzburg Mayor, Mark Cornell, was appointed as administrator of Sobantu for a trial period of six months. He was to work with an advisory committee consisting of three councillors

and three members of the Committee of 12. The Mayor was quoted in the *Natal Witness* in December 1986 as saying that:

> Our ultimate aim is to look at how we can combine Pietermaritzburg and Sobantu under one city council as it had been in the past, only this time with Sobantu residents represented on the council.

In July 1987 another important breakthrough was made when residents agreed to have the Village properly surveyed. This would pave the way for ownership of land, and hence also for private loans for building.

Two long-standing obstacles to development, true representation and land-ownership, are apparently being confronted as Sobantu approaches its 60th year, and Pietermaritzburg its 150th. Both communities seem to be forging a more promising relationship than before.

1847–1987

140 Years of Family Ties with Pietermaritzburg

Waldy Ahrens

On 25 January 1847, my maternal great-grandfather, the Revd Carl Wilhelm Posselt of the Berlin Missionary Society, and his family looked down from World's View on the small town of Pietermaritzburg. This was to be their home for about three years. During this period he lost three members of his family. His youngest son died on 12 March 1848, his wife Christiane on 17 April 1848, and his youngest daughter, also Christiane, in 1849. The gravestone was still to be seen in 1968 in the old Dutch Reformed Church Cemetery, but has since then weathered away altogether. In 1850 Posselt's English/Zulu phrase book *The Zulu Companion* was published by David Dale Buchanan at 23 Church Street.

In 1859 great-grandfather Casten Heinrich Ahrens and family arrived in South Africa, and went to the Emlalazi Mission Station in Zululand. His wife died in 1860, and he followed in 1864. They were buried near the Nyezane River. Their only son, my grandfather Heinrich Wilhelm, went to stay at the Hermannsburg Mission Station, which great-grandfather Posselt had assisted the Missionary Society in purchasing in 1854.

In 1867 he went to Hermannsburg in Germany, where he worked as a carpenter and wheelwright. In 1870 he joined the Hermannsburg Missionary Society, and in 1874 returned to Hermannsburg in Natal to work as a teacher, becoming headmaster in 1881. Grandfather made frequent contacts with the education authorities in Pietermaritzburg, and during the period 1902–1914, when he was the general manager of the Hermannsburg Mission in South Africa, he was appointed a Justice of the Peace.

My father, Heinrich Wilhelm, was born in 1880, and went to school, first at Hermannsburg, then at Hilton. He joined the civil service in 1903, and from 1912–1920 worked at the Old Supreme Court in Pietermaritzburg. From 1920 he was a magistrate at various places, until in 1936 he and my mother returned to live in Pietermaritzburg. My father died in 1954 and my mother in 1966, and both were buried at the Mountain Rise Cemetery.

Prior to his retirement, my father had been selected to sit as a member of the Native Appeal Court. Its first session took place at the present Umgeni Court. He was a member for quite a number of years.

Revd C.W. Posselt

H.W. (Waldy) Ahrens

During his retirement he kept himself very busy. In his book, *From Bench to Bench* (Pietermaritzburg, Shuter & Shooter, 1948), he stated: 'Pietermaritzburg has changed very little since my first acquaintance with it, which dates back to 1895.' He was a very active member of the Historical Monuments Commission for a number of years, as well as serving on the Rent Board. He also was appointed a Justice of the Peace.

I was born at St. Anne's Hospital in 1913 while the family were living at Scottsville. My younger brother, Louis Hermann, was born at the same place in 1918 while we were living at Sweetwaters. He became a world-famous scientist in the moon-rock saga, and was Professor of Geochemistry and Cosmochemistry at the University of Cape Town. He is the recipient of a number of gold medals, both local and from overseas.

He and I both went to Natal University College in 1937–1939 and 1931–1935 respectively. In 1936 I went to Cambridge, having been awarded an Elsie Ballot Scholarship. From then onwards I worked all over the place, visiting Pietermaritzburg only for holidays, until final retirement in 1983. My sister, Mrs J.G. Hattingh, has lived in Pietermaritzburg for the past 19 years, and my youngest daughter has worked for the Natal Parks Board for the past 8 years, and is resident in Scottsville.

The pomp of Empire in a colonial capital:
the Queen Victoria statue in front of the
Legislative Assembly building, unveiled on
8 July 1890 before a loyal throng.

CHAPTER SIX

Capital City

Colonial capital

John Benyon

'The Capital', today rather a tongue-in-cheek phrase, has real meaning in the historical growth of Pietermaritzburg. 'Port Natal' — Durban — could just as easily have become the principal administrative centre; and Pietermaritzburg might then have languished as a struggling country town, with little to distinguish it from Richmond, Ladysmith, Greytown, and· half a dozen other rural market villages in the colonial uplands of Natal. Instead, its position as the seat of government gave it an immediate primacy in many facets of Natal's development. From the beginning, the political, legal, social, spiritual and even — to a lesser extent — economic life in this remote corner of the Empire came thus to revolve round Pietermaritzburg.

By October 1838 a Voortrekker decision had named the new town and identified it as the control-point of the Republic of Natalia. The consequences were momentous; for when the British formally reimposed imperial authority upon their free-wheeling Boer emigrants in 1842–3, it had naturally to be in, and from, Pietermaritzburg. Yet the process proved difficult and complex, because the Boers did not easily knuckle down to the authority of mere 'captains' and 'commissioners', such as the early agents of British transfrontier authority, Smith and Cloete, respectively were. Nor were the imperial authorities in far-off Cape Town and London in any hurry to pick up their newest hot potato! Though nominally annexed on 8 June 1843, Natal did not learn that its position would be that of an outlying district of the Cape before mid-1845; and its first Lieutenant-Governor, Martin West, arrived in his 'district capital' of Pietermaritzburg only on 4 December. Yet 13 guns properly saluted him, because the military, at least, had literally entrenched its own position at Fort Napier a good two years before the civilian administration had been able to follow.

Early civil government functioned upon a minimal establishment. There were only West and several industrious officials, such as William Stanger as Surveyor-General, and Theophilus Shepstone, who began humbly as 'Diplomatic Agent to the Native Tribes' before becoming the grander 'Secretary for Native Affairs'. But titular modesty here concealed the future centrality of this key post. From Pietermaritzburg Shepstone was to traverse and retraverse the length and breadth of Natal in order to settle returning black refugees in the half dozen 'locations' demarcated by a commission of 1846 — on which, incidentally, he also served. In the locations he reinstituted the elements of a traditional structure of chiefly authority that pyramided up, through himself, to the Lieutenant-Governor as 'Supreme Chief'. He also began devising a loose-knit system of 'native law' to supply a practical solution to the legal incompatibilities between the juxtaposed European and African communities. From its earliest days as colonial capital Pietermaritzburg therefore both taxed and governed much more than the small white community of Natal. Being initially a mere district centre of the greater Cape Colony established certain further precedents that were to determine the relations of the infant Capital with other parts of South Africa and the Empire till at least the end of the nineteenth century. These relations are nowhere more clearly foreshadowed than in the British Secretary of State's declaration in May 1844 that 'the affairs of the whole of South Africa are so intimately connected together' that he had to have 'the assistance of the Governor of the Cape... with the power of control over the neighbouring but inferior colony of Natal'. And soon Sir Harry Smith, who arrived in Pietermaritzburg from the interior in 1848, was invoking just such an authority — as Cape 'High Commissioner' — to exercise control in matters of Natal land policy over an insubordinate Lieutenant-Governor West. But from 1850 onward West's successor, Sir Benjamin Pine, was at least able to assert Natal's right of separate correspondence with Downing Street — though by 1855 another Cape High Commissioner, Sir George Grey, was busy in Pine's new Government House at the top end of Longmarket Street with planning the limited form of 'representative government' constitution that was to apply from the following year.

2

Lieutenant-Governor
John Scott (1856–1864) in
full uniform about to
mount his steed at
Government House
before an imperial
ceremony.

Governor Sir Walter Hely-Hutchinson (1893–1901) wearing the resplendent Civil Uniform.

In the 1850s the system of colonial government in the newly created 'City' of Pietermaritzburg had therefore advanced beyond simple executive domination. While the Natal Colonial Secretary, Treasurer, Attorney-General, and Secretary for Native Affairs remained influential if not entirely ascendant, they had now to share some of their law-making power under the Charter of 1856 with twelve elected members in the public proceedings and debates that henceforth resounded across the Legislative Council Room near the corner of Longmarket and Chapel Streets. Shepstone's attempts to wall off 'native policy' were a particular source of resentment to members claiming to express the popular voice of the white colonists (the multiracial character of the Natal franchise was never more than nominal). And even Lieutenant-Governor Pine found this newly strident popular criticism, in the form of D.D. Buchanan's *Natal Witness*, pursuing his executive policies into the recesses of his own Government House!

The judiciary, too, was more of a bridle upon executive assertiveness. For instance, Lieutenant-Governor Scott's angry suspension of a judicial critic of his prerogative actions in 1859 was to harm the reputation of his administration, and its revenue (in the form of a court suit), rather more than it did the Bench. Between 1873 and 1882 a cumulative series of events was to prick the bubble of adolescent political pretension that marked Pietermaritzburg's early times as colonial capital. The elaborate charade of Chief Langalibalele's show 'trial' for defiance of the Natal Government's arms regulations took place in 1873 amid much panoply in a marquee in Government House grounds. Soon, these irregular proceedings issued in a trial of strength between a disapproving imperial authority, initially represented by Barkly as Cape High Commissioner, and the Natal executive council, with its desire to exert independent power not only over black affairs in the Colony itself but far beyond, over most of south-east Africa. Alas, there was neither the moral right nor the real power to sustain this exalted plan to make Pietermaritzburg's role that of a 'sub-continental' capital.

Just how hollow it all was emerged when Sir Garnet Wolseley arrived in 1875 to assert as Administrator

what was, in effect, the overriding imperial power of a kind of 'sub-High Commission'. But ending Natal's maverick behaviour as prelude to her incorporation as a docile unit of sub-continental confederation involved persuading the colonial legislature to accept as many as eight nominated non-official members into a slightly enlarged Council. Here Wolseley's cynical eye summed up political Pietermaritzburg's desire to see something of a colonial court flourish at Government House, not least after Prince Alfred's royal visit in 1860 had enhanced the City's perception of itself. Pine had set early precedents for official entertainments; Scott had fallen sadly short; and Keate after a good start had spent too much on bricks and mortar rather than public relations. Wolseley knew better: soon, he had deployed his 'sherry and champagne' as well as he ever placed his redcoats, though, as he confessed to his wife, he resented seeing his 'good wine disappearing down the guzzling throats' of the 'pettifogging politicians' whom he so much despised! Pietermaritzburg's surrender to such blandishments would, however, cost her dear; for Wolseley's manipulations were soon to be replaced, in 1878–9, by the more formidable directing power of the Cape High Commissioner himself, Sir Bartle Frere.

During the Anglo-Zulu War which Frere provoked in 1879 in bland contradiction to objections cogently urged by Natal's own Lieutenant-Governor, Bulwer, Pietermaritzburg was to learn that being a capital 'in the front line' held its dangers. Several dozen young white and black men from the City and outlying Edendale were to pay the supreme penalty at Isandlwana; and the laager in the town centre created a siege atmosphere that was to be re-experienced on two subsequent occasions, during the First and Second Anglo-Boer Wars. And when the 'captains and kings' had departed (not least the sad cortège of the Prince Imperial), the Capital would feel strangely deserted. Though now full 'Governor' of Natal, Wolseley in 1879–80 held the Governorship of the Transvaal and the High Commissionership for South-East Africa as well; so he would be largely an absentee while attending to the more demanding affairs of the Zulu, Boer and Pedi peoples. At least his successor as Governor, Sir George Colley, and the latter's presentable wife were more to be seen in Pietermaritzburg — for example, at the grand opening of

C. J. Bird, Principal Under-Secretary in the Colonial Office, at his desk in the first Colonial Buildings in 1897.

GOVERNMENT HOUSE

T. B. (Jack) Frost

The historic Erf 1 Longmarket Street on which Government House stands was originally granted to Willem Neethling in 1839. Eight years later it was sold to Dr William Stanger, Surveyor-General in the first British colonial administration. On it was an unpretentious cottage, single-storeyed under thatch, fronting Pine Street. Stanger, in turn, sold to Benjamin Pine, Natal's second Lieutenant-Governor, from whom the Natal Government subsequently purchased it.

The years brought many changes to Stanger's humble cottage. In the 1850s Lieutenant-Governor John Scott closed Pine Street and had the building transformed into a more substantial shale-built house. Further enlargements followed in the governorships of Keate (1868) and Havelock (1888), while the visit of the Duke and Duchess of York to Natal in 1901 prompted the addition of the red-brick wing (under whose shelter, ironically, the royal party stayed for but two nights).

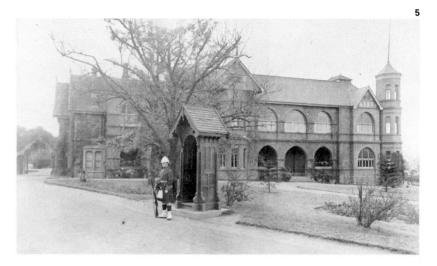

Standing guard at Government House. The 1901 red-brick wing is to the right.

Government House was the setting of many significant moments in Natal history: none more discreditable than the farcical trial of Langalibalele in a marquee pitched in the grounds; none more glittering than when Sir Garnet Wolseley swept away the Colony's constitutional liberties in a flood of sherry and champagne; none more dramatic than the midnight knock which brought Sir Bartle Frere tumbling out of bed to hear the ill-tidings of Isandlwana; none more poignant than the visit of the bereaved Empress Eugénie on her sad pilgrimage to the spot where her only son, the Prince Imperial, had lost his life in the Anglo-Zulu War. The House also entertained many famous visitors: Voortrekker Andries Pretorius and Boer President Paul Kruger; local notables like Bishop Colenso; members of the royal family, Prince Alfred and later the Duke and Duchess of York; Joseph Chamberlain, Lord Milner and the young Winston Churchill.

With the coming of Union the last colonial Governor, Lord Methuen, departed. Government House stood empty. Curiously, it was not occupied by Natal's first Administrator, Charles Smythe, probably because of the refusal of his wife to move from the family farm at Nottingham Road. Accordingly the decision was taken to make it the home of the infant Natal Training College, which it became in 1912 and whose students occupied it continuously until 1987.

Today it provides offices for the staff of NTC's successor, Natal College of Education. No longer a seat of political power, it continues its role in fostering the arts of peace and civilization.

---

the rail connection with Durban. But the trio of poor Colley, the newly established full Governorship, and its linked High Commission were all to come abruptly to an end on the battlefield atop Majuba Hill in February 1881. Instead, Pietermaritzburg learnt to its dismay that it would once more house only a mere Lieutenant-Governor, and that this personage would be a lowly unknighted Mr Sendall! But the experiences of the previous decade had at least taught both Colony and Capital to put a more realistic value on their worth. Pietermaritzburg now knew what it was to be an important decision-point of empire. Prancing 'High Commissioned' proconsuls like Frere and Wolseley spelt trouble; but an appropriate gubernatorial status was non-negotiable! Pietermaritzburg's resulting agitation was therefore orchestrated to play up Sendall's appointment as a permutation of outdated imperial jobbery which a self-respecting colonial public opinion would not tolerate.

Surprised and startled, Gladstone himself had to accept that, as British Prime Minister, he could no longer allow his Colonial Office to ride roughshod over Natal sensibilities. But the colonists were also more sober; the heady days when Wolseley had seemed about to cast Pietermaritzburg as 'Capital of South-East Africa' were over. In a more dangerous sub-continent, where political and, soon, economic restructuring was taking the form of Afrikaner republican nation-building upon a base of gold revenues, the City valued the imperial connection in its existing — reassuring — form of the garrison at Fort Napier. And if the price of retaining the redcoats had to be a moratorium on the creation of a 'responsible' executive of colonists, then so be it! In the meantime — and in anticipation — the Capital could go about raising a new Parliament House next door to the current 'borrowed quarters' in the Supreme Court Building. In 1889 Governor Havelock opened the Council's new home. Four years later, when Sir John Robinson's campaign for 'responsible government' did end successfully, the newly elaborated legislative and executive arrangements required further provision for sittings of the upper chamber and for the work of the colonial civil service. During the Second Anglo-Boer War these extensions of the governing complex in the centre of the Capital were taken into service in the shape of the Upper House Building and the Colonial Office Buildings. Both physically and figuratively the Governor's old locus of power at the top end of town had become remote from the new reality...

Between 1897 and 1902 Pietermaritzburg extended its

sway as colonial capital over Zululand and over the conquered northern districts of Utrecht and Vryheid. Now, not only Dinuzulu as scion of the Shakan royal house, but also former Transvaal republicans might find themselves petitioning assistance or answering charges in what must have seemed to them the alien environment of an English-speaking Victorian colonial city. Yet in spite of this minor 'empire-building', the importance of Pietermaritzburg in relation to the other centres of power in South Africa had paradoxically declined between these years of 1897 and 1902. At first, the Governor of Natal, Hely-Hutchinson, and Hime's colonial ministry had been essential props to the strategy that the High Commissioner, Milner, pursued against Kruger's republic. In October 1899 that strategy passed from a diplomatic to a military character; and Pietermaritzburg came once more into the front line as Buller's force passed northward through it to try to relieve beleaguered Ladysmith. But in 1900 the Roberts/Kitchener 'steamroller' scored a deep new axis of power beyond the Drakensberg; and Milner's subsequent appearance in Johannesburg as virtual ruler of South Africa spelt the end of the importance that he attached to the Natal connection.

Henceforth, Pietermaritzburg would know only apprehension over how favourably — or unfavourably — he or the succeeding Transvaal responsible government would assess the claims of its rail route to the Witwatersrand in relation to the competing Cape and Delagoa Bay lines. To this nagging erosion of confidence the 'Bambatha Rebellion' of 1906 would also add a deluge. When Union was first under debate in 1908, the Natal holiday resort of Durban and not the Capital, Pietermaritzburg, housed the National Convention; and no amount of referendum campaigning by the City's newspaper and politicians could prevent the rest of Natal (and, sad to tell, some of its 'very own') from voting solidly for Union — and an end, in effect, to really significant decision-making and administration in the resplendent government buildings that had so recently come to adorn the City centre. By 1910 power lay in Pretoria; sadly, Pietermaritzburg's days as colonial capital were over — though their atmosphere lingers...

A suitably grandiose setting for the bureaucrats of Empire: the second Colonial Buildings, opened in 1900.

6

Colonial capital to provincial centre, 1904–1912

Jill Raybould

In 1860 a spokesman for the Pietermaritzburg Town Council, fired with patriotic fervour aroused by the visit of Queen Victoria's midshipman son, Prince Alfred, but lacking in geographic knowledge, declared: 'Our City promises at no distant date to be the chief city of Central Africa'. Sadly, or fortunately, depending on one's viewpoint, his prophecy has not come true.

Seat of colonial government and military authority for the whole British Colony of Natal, Pietermaritzburg was afforded the prestige of housing the representative of the Imperial Government, and enjoyed all the attendant social activities, such as the assurance of being on the itinerary of visiting royalty. It also benefited from the financial support and protection of the Home Government in times of need.

Nevertheless, the claim by a correspondent to the *Natal Witness* in 1907 that 'Pietermaritzburg was brought into being through political discord', can certainly be applied to the City's progress, or lack of it, following the conclusion of the Anglo-Boer War when for several years the whole of South Africa was plunged into a severe economic depression. During that time the Colonial Government in Pietermaritzburg suffered repeated verbal abuse, not only from within the boundaries of the Colony itself, but also from neighbouring states and the Imperial Government in Britain. The Government was accused of being incapable of generating the finance necessary to keep the Colony solvent, wasting money on unnecessary public works, introducing impossible taxation schemes, and neglecting the 'native question', which resulted in outbreaks of serious unrest and other related 'crimes'. As for the majority of parliamentarians, they were considered incompetent and not worth the £1 per day they received for expenses. The Town Council of Pietermaritzburg came in for its own fair share of criticism and was blamed for the lack of progress made by the City in comparison with other major centres such as Durban. Out of this discontent with their civic administrators, a group of enthusiastic residents formed the Association for Popularizing Maritzburg, or APM as it was known, with the purpose of attracting much-needed trade and industry to the area and generally making the City more attractive both to the local population and to visitors. The major contributions of the APM included the opening up of the Msunduze River to boating, the staging of gala days and shopping festivals to attract visitors to the commercial centre of the City, sporting events and even an essay-writing competition on Pietermaritzburg as a health and holiday resort. The winning entry was printed and circulated to newspapers, clubs, hotels, steamship companies and railways throughout Natal and the adjacent colonies.

From late 1907, however, the problem that occupied the minds of most South Africans was the growing clamour for a union of the separate states. The burning question was how best to accomplish the amalgamation. The white residents of Pietermaritzburg made their choice very clear in a referendum conducted by the *Natal Witness* in 1908, when 386 out of the total poll of 688 voted in favour of a Federation of the states, 291 voted to stay out of whatever form of Union was agreed upon and thereby risk isolation, whilst only 11 voted in favour of a Union. For maximum effect the results for the whole of Natal, which reflected those of its capital city, were published on 12 October 1908, the same day that the delegates to the National Convention met in Durban for the first time.

When it became evident that there was a strong possibility that a centralized government would take over the administration of the separate states, articles appeared in the local Press suggesting ways and means of compensating Pietermaritzburg for its loss of status as a capital city. These suggestions ranged from the City being made the military headquarters for South Africa, to the transfer from Pretoria of the entire railway construction and repair shops to compensate for the civil servants who would be moved to the administrative centre of the Union. All correspondents to the *Natal Witness* agreed that the South African Government should pay half Pietermaritzburg's municipal debt, approximately £1 169 000 at the end of January 1909, instead of only 2% of the total as proposed in the Draft Constitution. As Pietermaritzburg had been a capital city, large sums of money had been sunk into public works such as the installation of electrified trams, and the erection of imposing buildings to house the machinery of government. Once the City lost the need for these amenities the residents had a right to expect compensation for their outlay. The Mayor suggested that a university be erected and that the City be declared the headquarters of higher education in South Africa.

A commemorative service held in the City Hall and a mayoral 'At Home' in Alexandra Park with sporting events for the children, marked the limited extent of the celebrations held in Pietermaritzburg on the first Union Day. However, although the residents quickly returned to the even tenor of their daily lives after the excitement of the pre-election period, the local Press very soon began carrying articles pointing out the apparently alarming losses that Pietermaritzburg was experiencing as a disrated capital. The City certainly lost status in the transition from being the capital of a British colony to that of a provincial centre of an independent Dominion, and this is amusingly reflected in a report on the opening of the Provincial Council. The *Natal Witness* correspondent deplored the lack of pomp and ceremony as nobody seemed to know, or care, how the Administrator arrived for the occasion, and declared that he might as well have been going to open a Sunday School or a mothers' meeting for all the impact his entry into the House made on the assembly.

The loss of Government House as a social focus in the life of the City was very deeply felt by the residents and the local tradesmen who had benefited from the Governor's patronage. Reductions to the Public Service

Committee of the Pietermaritzburg Closer Union Society, photographed in 1909 before the Senate Building. A remarkably wide cross-section of colonial society is represented.

1   J. M. Egner — Wool & hide merchant, Cnr Timber & Longmarket St.
2   F. Shippey — Merchant of Church St. Furniture, Crockery etc.
3   R. W. Jackson — Tent maker — Commercial Rd.
4   W. H. Griffin — Draper — cnr Church & Chapel St.
5   T. P. O'Meara — Timber merchant. City Councillor.
6   Sir T. K. Murray — Minister under Natal Govt.
7   D. C. Dick — Wood & coal merchant; Mayor & City Councillor.
8   Fred Reid — Grocer (Norrish & Co)
9   Sir Thomas Hyslop — Farmer of Howick. Minister in Natal Govt & Delegate to National Convention.
10 Daniel Sanders — Several times Mayor of P. M. Burg; Propr. of Vause Slatter & Co.
11 R. D. Clark — Head of Maritzburg College.
12 Morton Green — Resident of Loop St.
13 James Whitelaw — Wagon Builder.

14 W. F. Leeson?
15 D. F. Forsyth — City Treasurer (formerly Borough Policeman).
16 D. F. Forsyth — City Treasurer (formerly Borough Policeman).
17 Robt. Dunlop — House and Estate Agent (Secy Chamber of Commerce).
18 Herbert Murray — Solicitor (partner of E. G. Jansen).
19 J. T. Taylor — Manager Henwood, Son, Soutter & Co.
20 Alfred Lister?
21
22 Carter — Builders merchant.
23 John Hardy — Builders merchant.
24 ?
25 J. McGowan — Manager of Steel Murray & Co.
26 R. J. P. Otto — Railway Surveyor — afterwards farmer Otto's Bluff.
27 Geo Tirrel — Cycle Business.

28 J. G. H. Randles — Solicitor.
29 Robt Anderson — Proprietor of Boots Shoe Store.
30 Ernest Goodwin? — Carriage Builder.
31 Marsden — Tailor.
32
33 ?
34 Tennent — (brother of H. D. Tennent)
35 W. A. Matthews — Propr. of Cosy Inn, Church St.
36 H. D. Tennent —
37 E. G. Jansen — Solicitor — partner of H. Murray & later Governor-General of S. Africa.
38
39 Fred B. Shaw — (Foss & Shaw) Ironmongery.
40 Turner — Chemist.
41 A. C. Bell — Builder.
42
43 J. C. Hill — Builder.
44 H. P. McCrystal — Saddler.

This list of names appears to have been added to the photograph at a later date. It is reproduced here unedited. Eds.

91

as departments were closed down and staff transferred to the administrative capital, Pretoria, also had their adverse effect. Besides the financial loss to the City, several public buildings stood practically empty, and private property owners found themselves with unrented houses on their hands.

It would appear that conflicting opinions existed as to the financial position in Pietermaritzburg after Union. F. Reed, Chairman of the Chamber of Commerce, declared that the more settled conditions by the end of the first year under Union had resulted in improved trading and cash flow. The annual inspection reports for the Standard Bank recorded that it was only by mid-1912 that the City's trade showed signs of recovery from the dislocation caused by Union. The Mayor's considered opinion was that any improvements in the City's financial status were 'in spite of' and not 'on account of' Union. So alarming did the situation appear to the City Council that in March 1911 a resolution was passed to form a committee of prominent citizens and councillors to negotiate further with the Government on the requirements of the City. Thus was born the Vigilance Committee which enjoyed limited success during its brief existence. A deputation to the Prime Minister in October 1911 to plead for the fulfilment of promises made by the Government regarding compensation to the City was received with the assurance that the matters discussed would be given very serious consideration. A year later, the editor of the *Natal Witness* reminded his readers that at regular intervals over the last two years the same things had been requested: all deputations to the Government had been received with a flattering display of respect and then promptly forgotten.

A far more positive picture of Pietermaritzburg's progress by the end of 1912 can be gained from a series of articles written for the benefit of delegates to the annual congress of the Association of Chambers of Commerce in South Africa. For example, the reader learnt that the City possessed quite the best 'foot pavements' of any town in the Union; that the City Council was engaged in an impressive scheme to bring waterborne sewerage to as many areas as possible at maximum efficiency, but minimum taxation; that the 'native' beer-houses operating in the central area had largely stopped the illicit sale of intoxicating beverages; that the City Council had introduced the planting of wattles on town land, and that the revenue derived from this scheme was to be used to relieve the rates.

Added to this was information relating to the existing industries operating in the City, which included the impressive clothing factory established by Joseph Baynes in Longmarket Street to compensate for the promised Government Clothing Factory which had never materialized.

Visitors were no doubt impressed with Pietermaritzburg's educational facilities, which by that stage boasted the newly opened University, Teachers' Training College, a Technical Institution, sixteen schools for the white population and several schools run by church groups for the black and Indian children. Adequate sporting facilities and cultural activities, the scenic attractions of the immediate environs of the City, plus a healthy climate, all convinced the visitors that, whilst not exactly a hive of commercial activity, Pietermaritzburg was an attractive city eminently suitable as a residential and educational centre and that in time it would recover from whatever losses it had sustained by the advent of Union.

The centre of the City *c.*1906.

8

The old Natal Parliament

Graham Dominy

The Voortrekker Volksraad, which ruled the Republiek Natalia, met between 1839 and 1845 in a simple building on the site of the present City Hall. For the next eleven years Natal was ruled by British officials as a district of the Cape Colony until, in 1856, it became a separate colony with a measure of representative government. Twelve of the sixteen members of the Legislative Council were elected by male colonists, and the remainder were nominated by the Governor, who was responsible to the British Government and not to the Council. The Legislative Council first met in March 1857 in the Government Schoolroom in Chapel Street opposite the present Metropolitan Methodist Church. Sittings were held after 1873 in the building in Commercial Road which was later to accommodate the Supreme Court, and now houses the Tatham Art Gallery.

Agitation for more control of Natal's own affairs led in 1893 to the granting of responsible government, by which Natal became a self-governing colony within the British Empire. The Natal Parliament consisted of a Legislative Assembly elected by male and almost exclusively white voters, and a nominated Legislative Council or 'Senate'. The Legislative Assembly debated in a magnificent building in Longmarket Street, which the old Legislative Council had completed for its own use in April 1889 at a cost of £28 000, demolishing St. Mary's Church in which Bishop Colenso's Zulu congregation had worshipped. Extensions were made to the Legislative Assembly building in 1898 and 1900. The Legislative Council met in the Supreme Court building and in the City Hall (until it was destroyed by fire in 1898), while its stately new home, known as the Senate Building, was under construction next to the Legislative Assembly. The Senate Building was brought into use in 1901 without ceremony as the Anglo-Boer War was still in progress.

When, at Union in 1910, the Natal Parliament disbanded, the new single-chamber Provincial Council, which was empowered to make laws on specified local matters, continued to sit in the Legislative Assembly building. Provincial civil servants moved into the Senate Building, and remained there until the multi-storeyed Natalia Building opened in 1973. The Provincial Council then used the vacated building as offices and committee rooms.

When South Africa became a Republic in 1961, the position of the Provincial Councils was preserved in the new constitution. The Natal Provincial Council continued meeting for a further 25 years, jealously guarding its traditions and attempting to defend its status in the face of encroaching central governmental authority. However, the Constitution Act of 1983 sounded the death knell for the Provincial Councils. The Natal Provincial Council was disbanded in 1986, and since then the Provincial Executive has been nominated by the State President and is responsible to Parliament. Since 30 June 1986 the premises of the old Natal Parliament have been temporarily tenanted by civil sevants. The buildings are preserved as a national monument, and the interior may be viewed by appointment. The debating chamber is used occasionally by Committees of the Tricameral Parliament.

The Natal Legislative Assembly in session about 1905. This magnificent chamber continued to be used after 1910 by the Natal Provincial Council, until it was disbanded in 1986[9].

The Legislative Assembly building[10], with its classical columns and pediment, was opened in 1889 to accommodate Natal's representative government. The advent of responsible government in 1893 necessitated the construction of an upper house with dome, completed in 1901.

Royal visitors

Ruth Gordon

With the arrival in 1850 of the Byrne settlers, Pietermaritzburg became a thoroughly Victorian City and Natal a loyal Queen's Colony. Britons who had seen England change mood and character after the Queen's accession in 1837 brought with them their enthusiasm for things royal, blue-blooded and conservative. They were a very class-conscious society in the 1860s when it was learned with excitement that Queen Victoria's sixteen-year-old midshipman son was to tour South Africa and visit Natal. It became an occasion for ridiculous social jostling and 'an atmosphere of emotionalism as thick as triple ice-cream'.

The year was 1860. Alfred travelled overland from the Cape escorted by Sir George Grey. He rode up Pietermaritzburg's Church Street under banners displaying the legend 'Thou Royal, we loyal'. The poor, bored boy, later to become the reigning Duke of Saxe-Coburg-Gotha, had to shake hands with dozens of 'important' people, listen to addresses of welcome, plant trees, watch Zulu war dances and lay the foundation stone for the planned City Hall. It became the fashion for some while for boys to wear the midshipman's jacket over white trousers.

A hall was hastily erected on the Market Square: it was decorated with 'extempore chandeliers of painted hoops dangling in all directions', flowers, flags and the lion and the unicorn fighting for the crown over the doorway. It is doubtful whether the boy prince noticed any of this and he was not enthusiastic about the dancing partners selected for him, 'one of whom could not dance and another could not talk'. He asked for and got lovely waltzes and polkas but one observer remarked: 'a general expression pervading his features was one of gentleness and pensiveness, in part, no doubt, due to physical fatigue'.

He slept at the home of an officer of the 85th Regiment on the corner of Loop and Pine Streets. Reminders of his visit are the first foundation stone, now in the Church Street portico of the City Hall, and the street named after him.

The Anglo-Zulu War of 1879 was to see the arrival of another 'royal' — Louis Napoleon, Prince Imperial of France, serving as an additional aide-de-camp to Lord Chelmsford. In Durban he bought a spirited and restive horse which alarmed observers of its antics when he stayed briefly at the Imperial Hotel in the Capital. It was thought that had his horse been steadier he could have got away when he fell into a Zulu ambush on 1 June 1879. His embalmed body lay in state in the little Roman Catholic Chapel in Loop Street, Pietermaritzburg, before being taken away aboard HMS *Boadicea* amid scenes of sorrow and respect.

A year later his mother, Empress Eugénie, was sent by her friend Queen Victoria to visit sites her son had known. It was a sad pilgrimage of mourning conducted very quietly with dignity and without publicity. Her entry into Pietermaritzburg under the escort of Sir Evelyn Wood was decorously attended by a few citizens with doffed hats and curtseys. The Queen had provided

£2 500 for this six month visit to Natal and there was a large train of pack-mules and handlers to organize camps along the route. Government House, where the Empress stayed, was completely cordoned off. A tent was pitched just outside the Longmarket Street gate where sympathizing citizens could sign their names in a book.

When the Pietermaritzburg City Hall was built in 1891, the stripling Prince Alfred of 1860 had become the bearded Admiral and Naval Commander-in-Chief at Plymouth. The first foundation stone was relaid by Sir Charles Mitchell with the Prince, *in absentia*, represented by the Mayor. Then came the disastrous fire of 12 July 1898, after which rebuilding work continued until August 1901 when the City Hall could be officially reopened by the Duke of Cornwall and York, later King George V.

This was a real royal visit, staged with formal pomp and ceremony. The Duke and his wife, 'Princess May', arrived in Natal in August 1901. George was then 36 years old, a serious, straightforward personality, and the tour did much to increase his self-confidence and prepare him for kingship. May was 33, poised and beautiful with great charm of manner and an excellent dress sense, though on this trip she was limited to black in mourning for Queen Victoria. With her towering toques, elaborately dressed

The royal visit of August 1901. One of the four extraordinary triumphal arches erected in honour of the Duke and Duchess of York. This was on the corner of Longmarket and West Streets[11].
The Governor, Sir H.E. McCallum, reading an address from the 'Native Chiefs' to the royal couple in Alexandra Park, named after the Duke's mother[12].

11

12

hair, high collars, fur trimmings, parasols and corseted figure she was every inch royal.

There had been feverish activity at Government House for six months to add the brickwork extensions and a new staircase to provide adequate and up-to-date accommodation for the Duke and his entourage. Students at what was until recently the Natal College of Education proudly referred to the Royal Staircase and Royal Chamber where the royal couple slept.

There was much drilling, bugle blowing and marching hither and yon by the Natal Carbineers, Umvoti Mounted Rifles and Bethune's Mounted Infantry contingents who paraded in Pietermaritzburg. They formed a Guard of Honour at the Railway Station and lined the road to the nearby Government House. It was wet — 'the street was just slush from one end to the other'. But the next day, when there was the function at the City Hall, the weather was clear and beautiful. In the afternoon the royal pair attended a Presentation of Decorations and Inspection at Alexandra Park and a Zulu war dance. In the evening there was a reception at Government House and the party left by train next day with Mary in possession of a table gong made up of three pom-pom shells mounted on rhinoceros horn.

The Victoria Club welcomed an unappreciative Prince of Wales in June 1925[13].

Bayat's store, which stood in upper Church Street, expressed the enthusiasm of some of the Indian community for the visit of George VI and his family in March 1947[14].

13

14

ROYAL VISITS

William Bizley

In 1925 dutiful sons and daughters of the Empire are marched up in droves to the station, there to welcome Prince Edward with his least favourite piece of music, 'God bless the Prince of Wales'. Those in the know discover that the personage in question does not fulfil all the expectations of a future monarch. Edward's renown as a small eater has not, it seems, caught up with him in Pietermaritzburg. The Victoria Club is hurt to the quick when the Prince arrives from polo to a banquet in his honour, takes one apple and loses interest in the meal. But greater scandals follow: at the Reception in the City Hall, he neglects to dance with the Administrator's daughters, since he finds a young reporter from the *Witness* more to his taste (and entertains her, some say, on the royal train...)

During the Anglo-Boer War, Queen Victoria's grandson, Prince Christian Victor, died in 1901 of enteric fever and by his own wish was buried among his comrades in Pretoria. The Prince's mother, Princess Helen, or Christian as she was usually called, came to South Africa in 1904 to visit her son's grave. She was 58 years of age and the least attractive and the least known of Victoria's daughters. But she was an amiable and comfortable person, celebrated for her good works and public spirit and not unlike her mother in appearance and figure.

She travelled through Natal accompanied by her daughter, the 'skinny' Victoria who was rather unkindly nicknamed 'The Snipe'. At Government House where she stayed she was photographed in a group in the portico, in flowered hat and feather boa.

The next royal visit was that of the Prince of Wales in 1925. Between 1919 and 1925 he really saw the world with visits to 55 countries. By the time he arrived in Natal he was utterly weary of so much formality and dull routine — 'always more hands to shake than a dozen Princes could have coped with: such was the substance of my official days'. He never missed a chance of enjoying himself and was pronounced to be less mature, less disciplined, less conscientious and less dignified than his father had been at his age. Nevertheless the 'blonde, blue-eyed and wistful-looking' Prince moved in an aura of adulation. For almost three months the White Train was his home and he was entertained in Durban, Zululand and Pietermaritzburg.

On 17 February 1947 HMS *Vanguard* arrived at Cape Town with the royal family, George VI, his Queen and the two Princesses, Elizabeth and Margaret Rose. In due course General Smuts accompanied them by train to Natal.

They arrived in Pietermaritzburg on 18 March. An attempted boycott by the Indian community came to nothing and the entertainment provided by the Indian people, with fifty girls dancing in colourful saris, eclipsed all other programmes. Their hostess was the Mayor, Mrs E.E.M. Russell, who officiated at a great welcome staged on the balcony over the City Hall portico.

All royal visitors to Natal, with the exception of the Empress Eugénie, have been Queen Victoria's family — children, grandchildren or great grandchildren. No wonder she stands so proudly on her marble plinth gazing onto Longmarket Street with a proprietary look in her eye.

Legal centre of Natal

Peter Spiller

Pietermaritzburg has held the primary place in Natal's legal affairs throughout the one hundred and fifty years of its existence. During the years of the Boer Republic (1838–45), judicial powers lay with the elected Volksraad. From February 1840, this sat in the Voortrekker Raadzaal facing Market Square. The Raadzaal was a small building of unburned brick, whitewashed walls, thatched roof and six small windows, and was described as a 'dog kennel' and 'the most unornamental edifice in the town'. In these unprepossessing quarters, the members of the Volksraad administered justice, according to Roman-Dutch law, until well into 1845.

Following the British annexation of Natal as a separate District of the Cape Colony, a District Court of one judge (styled a Recorder) commenced hearings in January 1846. This Court heard major civil and criminal disputes, while minor matters were assigned to the magistrates' courts which were established in Pietermaritzburg and Durban in 1846. The Recorder and his District Court administered justice in the 'very scrimp and imperfect accommodation' provided by the Raadzaal, although two small rooms were added, for the judge and the registrar. The general conditions of Natal and Pietermaritzburg at this time were aptly described as being 'rude and plain'. For example, in April 1856, such heavy rains fell that the Recorder had to swim the Msunduze River to reach the court-house. He was greeted by a crowd gathered with sandwiches and 'grog' for the eagerly awaited session, but the session was postponed because the witnesses (unlike the judge) were unable to master the floods.

During most of the District Court era (1846–55), the Recorder was the talented and temperamental Cape advocate Hendrik Cloete, and for the remaining period (1855–58) the office was filled by the mediocre public servant Walter Harding. They continued to administer Roman-Dutch law but, especially with the Anglicization of Natal colonial society from the early 1850s, pressures arose to make Natal's legal affairs more English. The resultant tensions contributed significantly to the suspension of Recorder Hendrik Cloete (a staunch Roman-Dutch exponent) in 1853. Though he was restored to office in 1854, his disenchantment with aspects of Natal's legal affairs was such that he returned to the Cape the following year.

The local Bar that serviced the needs of Natal litigants was generally mediocre in legal knowledge but colourful in personality. From the outset, Natal's Rules of Court allowed dual practice, in terms of which advocates and attorneys could act in each other's profession. The result was that, for many years, most Natal advocates were admitted on the basis of being attorneys, either because they were United Kingdom practitioners or by virtue of local practical training. The two most prominent Pietermaritzburg advocates of the early years were Arthur Walker, the former Dublin law clerk and Pietermaritzburg horse-dealer, and David Buchanan, the eloquent and fiery editor of the *Natal Witness*.

The District Court theoretically held jurisdiction over all persons residing in Natal. But, at the commencement of British rule, Theophilus Shepstone, Diplomatic Agent, assumed *de facto* jurisdiction over inter-African affairs, and here African laws and customs were applied. In 1849, Shepstone's administration was regularized and, from his centre in Pietermaritzburg, he presided over a network of administrators of African law (including African chiefs) with appeal to the Lieutenant-Governor. This system remained in operation until 1876.

Natal officially remained a District of the Cape Colony until 1856, when a Charter established Natal as a separate Colony. Calls were then made for the upgrading of the District Court, in keeping with Natal's improved political status. The result was the transformation of the District Court into the Supreme Court, comprising a

The Natal Supreme Court buildings in the 1920s[15] and the Native High Court in Pietermaritz Street during the 1880s[16].

THE TRIAL OF LANGALIBALELE

Bill Guest

One of the earliest 'treason trials' held in Pietermaritzburg took place in 1874, in a tent pitched specially for the occasion in the grounds of Government House. Langalibalele was charged with 'treason' for failing to appear before the Secretary for Native Affairs, Theophilus Shepstone, when summoned to explain the non-registration of firearms which members of his Hlubi chiefdom had acquired while working on the Griqualand West diamond-fields. He was also accused of 'rebellion' for having withdrawn without permission to Basutoland, beyond the territorial jurisdiction of his 'Supreme Chief', the Lieutenant-Governor of Natal, Sir Benjamin Pine.

The indictment was clearly framed in terms of 'native law' yet, when the trial began, immediate recourse was made to English criminal law with the accused being required to plead against the charges indicated. Langalibalele conceded some of the assertions made in the indictment but disputed the conclusions which the prosecution had drawn from them, a plea of 'not guilty' which was interpreted by the Court as an admission of guilt. His 'native judges', comprising six local 'chiefs' and 'indunas', were then permitted to express their contempt for his conduct as well as their unanimous conviction of his guilt, after which the examination of witnesses took place.

Pine subsequently admitted that this 'was not a trial of a prisoner in the ordinary sense, but was an inquiry to ascertain the whole circumstances of the case, and its ramifications so far as other tribes were concerned'. His critics in Britain were not mollified. As Lord Cairns, the Lord Chancellor, observed when the trial was reviewed in the House of Lords: 'The second day was spent in taking evidence, after the man had been pronounced guilty'. During the same debate Lord Carnarvon, the Secretary of State for the Colonies, explained: 'What, my Lords, I so object to is not . . . native law, as the mixture of native and English law. Let us have either the one or the other. To have recourse to both is likely, I think, to be productive of unfairness, for it scarcely seems right when you fail to reach a man by native law to have recourse to English law; and when you fail to reach him by English law to fall back upon native law.'

Pine was adamant that the procedure adopted was in accordance with 'native law', and that this law had been established as the common law of the Colony, as it applied to the 'native' population, by the Royal Instructions of 1848 and Natal Ordinance No. 3 of 1849. On this pretext Langalibalele was initially denied a defence counsel, though this was granted on the third day of the trial 'for the sake of public opinion at home', as Shepstone confided to his son Henrique. The Durban lawyer Harry Escombe was appointed but declined the brief when refused permission to confer with the accused in accordance with normal English court procedure.

The composition of the Court was also hardly conducive to impartiality. Pine himself presided, in his capacity as 'Supreme Chief', although he had already outlawed the accused and led the military expedition launched to secure his arrest. The seven members of the Executive Council who joined him on the Bench included Major Erskine, the Colonial Secretary, whose son was one of those killed at the Bushman's River Pass when the colonial volunteers tried to prevent the escape of Langalibalele's followers into Basutoland. Shepstone, whose authority as Secretary for Native Affairs the accused was alleged to have flaunted, was also among those who sat in judgment.

The sentence of transportation passed on Langalibalele far exceeded the powers conferred by 'native law' upon Pine who, as 'Supreme Chief', had reached the limit of his authority two months before the trial when he deposed the accused from his chiefdom, drove the Hlubi off their location near Ntabamhlope, and seized their cattle and property. In a series of subsequent trials seven of Langalibalele's sons, two 'indunas' and two hundred of his followers were sentenced to varying terms of imprisonment. Their fate was brought to the attention of the British public largely through the efforts of Bishop Colenso, and the Colony of Natal soon found itself in the glare of an imperial spotlight that ruthlessly exposed the inadequacies of its legal system in so far as it affected blacks.

The result was a new Native Administration Act which placed the 'native' population under the jurisdiction of the ordinary criminal law of the Colony and provided for subsequent trials of a political nature to be conducted either in a new Special Native High Court or in the Supreme Court. The Langalibalele episode also prompted the imperial authorities to amend the Colony's constitution, thereby delaying the attainment of the responsible government status that the Cape had acquired in 1872 but for which Natal was clearly not yet ready. The unfortunate Hlubi chief still had to endure a long exile on Robben Island and the Cape Flats before being allowed to return to Natal in April 1887. He was settled in the Swartkop location under the supervision of one of his former 'native' judges, Chief Thetheleku, but died two years later and was buried in the Drakensberg foothills that had earlier formed part of the Hlubi location.

Monument to the colonial troops who died in attempting to suppress the 'Langalibalele rebellion', unveiled in 1874.

17

Sir Michael Gallwey, Chief Justice of
Natal, 1890–1901[21].

Sir Henry Binns, when Attorney-
General of Natal[22].

Chief Justice and two puisne judges. The men selected to pioneer this Court were Chief Justice Walter Harding (the former Recorder), Judge Henry Connor of Ireland and Judge Henry Lushington Phillips of the English Bar. They maintained the basic substratum of Roman-Dutch law, but inevitably English and Natal legal elements infiltrated the legal system.

The Supreme Court was obliged to sit in the Raadzaal building until 1871, when the Court moved into the new government building in Commercial Road. This building was a decided improvement over the old: it was built in the Renaissance pavilion style, with an attractive arcaded front and a well-ventilated, commodious interior. But the Court experienced acoustic problems, and palliatives, such as the erection of a sounding board made out of old packing cases, had little effect. Furthermore, there was the major difficulty that the Supreme Court initially had to share its new premises with the Legislative Council. This produced 'chronic squabbling' between politicians and lawyers, and the interruption and postponement of Court sittings. The problem lasted until the late 1880s, when the Legislative Council moved to the new Parliament Buildings. In ensuing years, there was the occasional disruption of proceedings caused by defects in the court-house: in January 1897, during a wind and rain storm, a leak developed, causing the usher to seek refuge under the registrar's table and finally the abandonment of the court session. But, overall, there was now little public complaint about the chief seat of the Supreme Court.

The Pietermaritzburg Bar continued to be dominated by English or locally-trained advocates-cum-attorneys. Joining Walker and Buchanan at the forefront of the Bar were the Irish-born Attorney-General Michael Gallwey, and 'Offy' Shepstone, the forceful son of the Secretary for Native Affairs. In 1871, the advocates of Natal decided to form the Natal Law Society, to promote the interests and legal knowledge of the legal profession. In ensuing years, meetings were held under the aegis of the Attorney-General, and dinners were enjoyed for the reason that 'no business can be done without eating'.

Three major developments took place in the mid-1870s. First, on the death of Walter Harding in 1874, the Chief Justiceship passed to Henry Connor. During his tenure in office, Chief Justice Connor established himself as one of the finest judges in South African legal history. His three decades on the Natal Bench (including sixteen years as Chief Justice) were marked by profound scholarship, keen and logical acumen, absolute integrity and thorough

dedication to duty. During his Chief Justiceship, he was a dominating presence on the Bench, and, for many decades after his passing, his judgments were quoted in the Natal Court with respect and even reverence. His reputation extended beyond Natal's borders, and such legal luminaries as Chief Justices Henry de Villiers, John Kotze and James Rose Innes praised his ability, intellect and learning. Natal was especially fortunate in having Chief Justice Connor in view of the sharply contrasting performance of certain of his brother judges, whose personal moral standards, judicial ability and notions of impartiality were woefully inadequate. The second major development of the 1870s was that the Shepstonian system of adjudication with the help of African chiefs was replaced by a new, formalized structure. Most civil matters between Africans were now to be heard by administrators of African law, with appeal to a single-judge Native High Court, which also had original civil jurisdiction in certain cases. Specified crimes committed by Africans — such as political offences and faction fights — were also assigned to the Native High Court. The first judge of the Native High Court was the Hon. J. Ayliff, the former Colonial Treasurer and Postmaster-General, and he began proceedings on 27 December 1876. The third important development of this time was the trial of the black chief, Langalibalele, in 1874. The regrettable outcome of this trial had momentous political consequences for Natal.

The 1890s saw further significant changes in legal affairs in Pietermaritzburg. In 1890, Michael Gallwey succeeded Henry Connor as Chief Justice. Chief Justice Gallwey was a talented lawyer, but could not compare with his predecessor in ability and erudition. His tenure as Chief Justice (1890-1901) was undistinguished and, apart from the presence of Judge Arthur Mason (future Judge-President of the Transvaal), the Natal Bench of the time was of a mediocre standard. Then, in 1896, the Supreme Court took over the functions of the Native High Court. This development was partly the result of certain discontent with the workings of the Native High Court, and also the emergence of an ideological commitment to 'one Supreme Court and one law for black and white'. The Supreme Court exercised the functions of the old Native High Court from 1896 to June 1899. During this period, as in no other time during the Supreme Court's existence, its legal business reflected the true nature of Pietermaritzburg and Natal as a multi-racial, multi-

The three Professors Burchell. Frank Bruce ('Binkie') (1923–54), Exton Mabbutt (1954–82), Jonathan Mark (appointed 1987). This dynasty of legal academics is believed to be unique in South Africa.

18   19   20

GANDHI'S ADMISSION AS AN ADVOCATE

Hassim Seedat

M.K. Gandhi wearing the controversial head-dress of the Bombay High Court.

Gandhi entered in his diary for 3 September 1894: 'Was admitted. Had to put off the hat. The application for admission as translator withdrawn. Received about 7 telegrams of congratulations'.

The application by Mohandas Karamchand Gandhi for admission as an Advocate of the Supreme Court of the Colony of Natal was moved by the Attorney-General Harry Escombe. The application was opposed by the Natal Law Society. Mr Greene appeared for the Society. In the affidavit filed in court and signed by W.M. Cameron, the Honorary Secretary of the Natal Law Society, the first ground of opposition was: 'That it was never intended by the Rules of Court dated 2nd January 1893 to admit persons as Advocates or Attorneys of the Supreme Court other than those of European extraction'. The other grounds of objection were that the Certificates produced by the applicant of his admission to the Bombay and English Bar were not sufficient; that there was no proof that he was still on the Rolls of those courts; and finally that the certificates of character produced by Gandhi were not acceptable. The argument was that the certificate of one Max Heilbut (a businessman from Johannesburg) was not sufficient as Heilbut's 'Knowledge of the applicant is derived from casual conversations with him (Gandhi)'. And as for the others 'purported to be signed by Abdoola and others are unknown to the Natal Law Society and they cannot place much value on such certificates'.

The application was heard by Wragg J., Gallway C.J. and Turnbull J. Mr Greene wisely did not advance the objection on the grounds of race for fear, no doubt, of a castigation from the Bench. The question of the suitability of Gandhi's character references was resolved before the hearing when the Law Society insisted on a further affidavit from Abdoola, who attested to the fact that he knew the applicant's family and that Gandhi's father was Dewan (Prime Minister) of the Porbandar, the state in India where Gandhi was born. Mr Greene, however, persisted with the objection on the grounds of the inadequacy of the certificates. During argument when Mr Greene questioned the authenticity of the documents the Chief Justice snapped, 'Is the Applicant being tried for perjury?'

Wragg J. found that the original certificate from the Inns of Court testifying to Gandhi's call to the English Bar should have been produced. However he said, 'I believe the applicant has been called to the Bar and I am anxious not to place any objection in the way'. The other judges concurred.

Gandhi was sworn in, but before he could leave the Chief Justice said: 'Mr Gandhi, you must now remove your turban. Being an Advocate of the Natal Bar, you must, while in it, conform to the rules of the Court with regard to the dress worn by a practising barrister'. Gandhi removed the head-dress, which was that of the Bombay High Court. In later years he rationalized the incident thus: 'I wanted to reserve my strength for fighting bigger battles. I should not exhaust my skill as a fighter in insisting on retaining my turban. It was worthy of a better cause'.

The Natal Law Society came under severe criticism from the Press. Particularly scathing was the *Natal Witness* (5 September 1894):

> We cannot congratulate the Natal Law Society on its attempts to exclude an English Barrister, who happens to be an Indian by birth from practice in this Colony. When the status of a society or an individual is not quite assured, the most foolish thing that either can do is to draw attention to itself and himself. And we make so bold as to say that the legal ability and legal knowledge as well as the educational standing of the majority of the members of this Law Society are not such as to invite comparison.

The paper commented that besides a few members of the Bar of Natal, 'who might almost be counted on the fingers of one hand', the rest did not 'exactly command admiration'. Taking into consideration that the Natal advocates could not even practise as such in the neighbouring territories, it made it 'absurd and contemptible that such opposition should have been raised to the admission of Mr Gandhi'. The paper regretted that 'things were made as nasty as they could be made for the applicant and he had a taste of what he may expect from a section of his "brother practitioners" who had insinuated that Gandhi had tried to be admitted under false pretence'. The *Commercial Advertisers and Shipping Gazette* (6 September 1894) described the Law Society's objection as a 'lawyer's quibble' and asked if objections to the certificates would have been raised if Gandhi had been a European. The *Johannesburg Star* of the same day commented that the Law Society had certainly not 'added lustre to its somewhat doubtful prestige' by objecting to the admission, and added that in all probability Gandhi was better qualified to practise than the vast majority of his local colleagues. A Cape paper about a fortnight later noted that the objection of the Natal Law Society was 'capital advertisement for him', and that it was 'quite within the range of possibility that he may become a judge in Natal...'

Gandhi never became a judge in Natal; nor has any other non-white. Gandhi practised very successfully for a few years in Natal and in the Transvaal, and when public work came to occupy his time he abandoned his career as a lawyer.

---

faceted society. However, the experiment with one Court proved to be a failure. The Supreme Court judges revealed little understanding of or regard for African customs and legal practices, and the result was a developing lack of confidence in the Court amongst African suitors. The result was the resurrection of the Native High Court in 1899. This was to be composed of a Judge President and two puisne judges, who were to hold exclusive jurisdiction over Africans in all except specifically reserved civil suits, and a greater jurisdiction over criminal cases than that enjoyed by the earlier Native High Court. The new Judge President was Henry Campbell, former civil servant, master and acting judge of the Supreme Court, and the Court was to occupy the court-house in College Road that came to be known in later years as the 'Old Bailey'.

The last decade of the Natal Supreme Court saw a Natal-born man at the helm of legal affairs. Chief Justice Henry Bale succeeded Michael Gallwey in 1901, and

remained Chief Justice through to Union in 1910. He was a solid, capable judge, with a reputation for integrity and dedication to duty. The rather pedestrian Bench over which he presided was considerably uplifted in 1904 with the arrival of Judge John Dove Wilson, a talented Scots advocate. Pietermaritzburg was now also the setting for a variety of specially-constituted Courts, notably the treason Courts to try recalcitrant Boers (in 1900–2) and the preliminary examination of the Zulu chief Dinuzulu (in 1907–8) for his alleged part in the 'Bambatha rebellion'.

In the Pietermaritzburg Bar, the closing decades of the Supreme Court revealed a growing sophistication and sense of purpose. The Natal Law Society intensified its efforts to raise the ethical and educational standards of the Bar. For example, it actively developed a library for its members, the collection being housed with certain prominent advocates (notably, at the office of Messrs Hathorn and Mason), and later in the Public Library.

However, the Society did not always exert its efforts constructively: in 1894, it unsuccessfully opposed the admission of Mohandas Gandhi to the Natal Bar, for evidently racialistic motives. Within the ranks of Natal advocates there now emerged men of greater stature and expertise than the leaders of the early Natal Bar. These included the learned politician-cum-advocate William Morcom and the confident and forceful Frederick Tatham.

With Union in 1910, the Natal Supreme Court became the Natal Provincial Division of the Supreme Court of South Africa. By the end of 1910, John Dove Wilson had succeeded Henry Bale as Judge President of Natal. Judge President Wilson, during his twenty years in office, was a highly respected figure in Natal and South African legal affairs: certain of his judgments have remained standing precedents of South African law and he was called upon to assist the Appellate Division in Bloemfontein. His presence helped to compensate for the presence on the Natal Bench of certain judges of lamentable judicial ability. The Native High Court continued to dispense justice for Africans, under the guidance of Judge President Henri Boshoff and his brother judges. But legislation of 1927 and 1929, which established a system of 'native' commissioners, divorce and appeal courts, deprived the Native High Court of all civil jurisdiction and much criminal jurisdiction. Thereafter the Court functioned simply as a superior court to try African crime, and was seen as a 'fossil' survivor of pre-Union days.

Also in 1910, Pietermaritzburg saw the foundation of a legal institution which has had a major impact on Natal legal affairs, namely, the Law Faculty at the University of Natal. Notable members of the academic staff were Robert Inchbold (the founder), and the father-and-son team, Frank and Exton Burchell. The bulk of Natal's legal profession came to be trained at the Pietermaritzburg Law Faculty and (from 1927) its branch in Durban. In 1923, the Natal Law Society established itself in elegant accommodation in Change Lane. By this time, Natal's dual profession had experienced certain stirrings of change: under the leadership of Graham Mackeurtan, one of the greatest lawyers South Africa has known, a separate Bar of advocates had emerged. Another noteworthy development came in June 1929: Caroline Fraser became the first woman to be admitted as an attorney in Natal. In 1930, Richard Feetham succeeded John Dove Wilson as Judge President of Natal. Judge President Feetham was a scholar, at home in Greek and Latin, and his judgments were models of intellect and elegance. He maintained the standards and rules of the Natal Court with icy efficiency. Soon after his appointment he was called upon to draft Rules of Court which were of great importance to the Natal legal profession. The resultant Order of Court of 1932 brought to an end Natal's distinctive system of dual practice, with effect from 1937, although legislation preserved the right to dual practice of those with such right in 1937.

In 1939, Richard Feetham was transferred to the Appellate Division, and Roy Hathorn became Judge President of Natal. His appointment signified a recurring feature of Natal judicial affairs in the twentieth century, namely, the prevalence of judicial dynasties. Judge President Hathorn's father, Kenneth, had served on the Natal Bench from 1910 to 1926, and his son, Anthony, became leader of the Natal Bar in the 1950s. Thus it was said that 'the Hathorn family is part of the tradition of the law in this province — a tradition of keeping the law consistent and certain'.

Judge President Hathorn's retirement in 1950 brought another of Natal's legal dynasties to the fore, namely, the Broome family. Judge President Frank Broome was the son of Judge William Broome, who had served on the Natal Bench from 1904 to 1917, and he was the father of John Broome who was to become a judge of the Natal Bench in 1976. As Judge President he revealed a logical, clear mind, a strong sense of decorum, and a courteous manner. It was during his tenure that the Native High Court passed out of existence. On 15 December 1954, Judge President Brokensha of the Native High Court announced at the end of the Court session that 'the Court will rise and will not sit again'.

In January 1961 Judge President Broome retired, and former Transvaal judge Arthur Faure Williamson served as Judge President for the rest of 1961. However, in January 1962, Williamson was sent to the Appellate Division, and his place at the helm of Natal's legal affairs was taken by Alexander Milne. Judge President Milne passionately believed that the proper administration of justice was one of the main foundations of South African civilization. Contemporaries remarked that he conducted the Natal Court with dignity, courtesy, scrupulous fairness and the conscious disregard of outside pressures and influences. On Milne J.P.'s retirement in 1969, Neville James became Judge President. He was said to possess a pragmatic approach to the processes of the law, an invariable 'nose' for the right answer, and an ability to reorganize the work of the Supreme Court so that delays that had occurred in the times of his predecessors were considerably reduced. His tenure proved to be an interregnum in the reign of the Milne family over Natal's legal affairs. Alexander John Milne, the son of the former Judge President, became Judge President in 1982. Judge President A.J. Milne, the 'kind-eyed judge with a gentle sense of humour', remained Judge President to the end of 1987. During his Judge-Presidency, the Natal Provincial Division has established a reputation for activism and judicial independence in the face of a government intent on exercising a vast array of executive powers.

In July 1983, Judge President Milne and his Court left the Supreme Court building in Commercial Road, which had housed Natal's premier Court for one hundred and twelve years. Judge President Milne spoke of the affectionate regard that the Natal legal profession retained for the old court-house, which was 'rich in memories of powerful battles and human drama'. However, the new Supreme Court premises offered many advantages, with eight acoustically-sound, light, airy and comfortable courts and sumptuous facilities. The result is that Pietermaritzburg approaches its one hundred and fiftieth anniversary well-provided in terms of material legal facilities. Furthermore, it has, in the person of the present Judge President, and in the careers of predecessors such as Chief Justice Connor and Judge President Wilson, much to be proud of. One may be confident that the declaration of Judge President A.J. Milne, that the Natal Supreme Court is one which is dedicated to serving 'all of Natal's peoples without fear, favour or distinction', is indeed carried into effect.

CHAPTER SEVEN

Maritzburg and the Military

Those who died in war are recollected in a peaceful garden in the City's heart: the Second Anglo-Boer War memorial.

Fort Napier

THE IMPERIAL BASE THAT SHAPED THE CITY

Graham Dominy

Hamish Paterson

For seventy-one years, almost half its recorded history, Pietermaritzburg served as an important base for the British Army. Although no battle took place in or near the City, imperial troops marched out to fight in numerous campaigns ranging from minor skirmishes with cattle-raiders and black peasant farmers to the major wars with the Zulu kingdom and the Boer republics.

The Imperial Garrison acted as an important link between the City and the rest of the Empire. The regiments that succeeded each other in the local barracks were liable for transfer to outposts scattered anywhere between Dublin and Delhi, China and the West Indies. This leavened the parochial attitudes of the townspeople and gave them a vicarious interest in exotic places and far-flung battlefields. The seven decades that imperial troops spent in the City also linked Pietermaritzburg with major world conflicts. The first garrison commander in 1843 was a veteran of the Battle of Waterloo and the last, in 1914, led the former garrison of the City, the 1st South Staffordshire Regiment, into the holocaust of the First World War battles in Flanders.

Fort Napier sited in a commanding position over Pietermaritzburg. Note the rectangle of brick barracks, completed in 1845, whose outer walls were loopholed for defence, and flanked by two stone bastions.

British military involvement in Natal began in December 1838, but was sporadic and confined to the coast until 1842. This was a year after Dick King's epic ride to Grahamstown for reinforcements to relieve the beleaguered British force in the 'Old Fort' in Durban. The Voortrekkers submitted to British authority in July 1842, but their Volksraad continued meeting in Pietermaritzburg and some Trekkers still hoped to shake off the imperial yoke. The British envoy sent to Pietermaritzburg in 1843 asked for troops to be despatched from Durban to occupy the Voortrekker capital. The commander of the troops, Major Thomas Charlton Smith, refused to move from Durban until reinforcements arrived. On 22 July 1843 a detachment of the 45th Regiment, newly arrived from Ireland, disembarked through the surf at the port. Nevertheless more than a month passed before Smith could be persuaded to move inland.

On 25 August 1843 Major Smith, veteran of Waterloo and defender of Durban's 'Old Fort', marched for Pietermaritzburg with two companies of the 45th Regiment, some Royal Engineers, a troop of the Cape Mounted Rifles and a half battery of field guns. The troops of the 45th Regiment were under the command of Captain Kyle, a son of the Bishop of Cork, and marched equipped for battle as attacks by the Voortrekkers were feared. The march was, however, uneventful and the force arrived safely in Pietermaritzburg on 31 August. Lieutenant Charles Gibb of the Royal Engineers chose the most defensible position for the camp, the hill at the western end of the town, on which the 45th Regiment planted its standard.

The camp was named Fort Napier, in honour of the Governor of the Cape Colony, Sir George Napier. On the evening of 31 August, Major Smith positioned the artillery to command the town and mounted guards to protect the camp from a surprise night attack. The precaution proved to be unnecessary as the dispirited Trekkers made no aggressive moves. Understandably the Trekkers resented the presence of the garrison, but as the troops settled in and began mixing with the townspeople the atmosphere warmed and eventually many strong bonds of friendship developed between the Trekkers and the men of the 45th.

Toy soldiers? Parade at Fort Napier in 1861 for the firing of the 9 o'clock gun.

The British authorities relied on the garrison not only to overawe the Trekkers with a show of military strength, but to woo them with practical demonstrations of the benefits of British rule. The troops were encouraged to mingle with the Trekkers and were given leave so that they could help on Boer farms. The establishment by the garrison of a theatre in 1846 can be seen as part of this policy. In 1844 officers of the garrison established the Maritzburg Turf Club which advertised its first meetings for 8 and 9 July. The race meet was widely supported by Trekkers and troops alike.

Meanwhile British control over the Voortrekker dorp took physical form. Lieutenant Gibb began construction work at Fort Napier on 1 September 1843, the day after the troops arrived. Barracks were traced out in the shape of a square to provide accommodation for 200 troops from the 45th Regiment, the men of the Royal Artillery, the cavalrymen of the Cape Mounted Rifles and their supporting storemen, cooks, farriers and stable hands. Stone emplacements at opposite ends of the square were constructed first, but work was delayed by heavy rains. The troops had to live in tents for months on end while the officers occupied houses nearby in Loop and Longmarket Streets.

By July 1845 the brick barracks had been completed. The outer walls were loopholed and windowless, while the inner walls that faced the square had windows. On the eastern and western corners were redoubts, mounting three guns on revolving platforms which completely commanded the town. The headquarters of the 45th Regiment moved from Cape Town to Pietermaritzburg during 1845 and the Commanding Officer, Lieutenant-Colonel Boys, was appointed commandant of Natal and a member of the Executive Council, and instructed to act as head of the Government in the absence of Lieutenant-Governor Martin West.

The garrison at Fort Napier played a critical role in changing Pietermaritzburg from a Voortrekker dorp to a firmly Anglophile Victorian colonial capital. Many of the cultural and social amenities were started by the officers while the other ranks laboured to build a new city. The Government School, used in 1856 for the first meeting of the Legislative Council, was built by two soldiers of the garrison, McKeaney and Murphy. The men of the 45th Regiment, the Royal Engineers, the Royal Artillery and the Cape Mounted Rifles improved and built Pietermaritzburg's water furrows, roads, offices and private houses. The Durban detachment of the 45th Regiment built the 45th Cutting which remained the western entrance to the port city for well over a century.

The 45th Regiment left Pietermaritzburg in 1859, but many of the men who completed their period of military service during the Regiment's fifteen-year stay elected to remain in the City as colonists. One such veteran, Thomas Greene, who had arrived in 1843, described the 45th Regiment as the 'real pioneers' of the Colony. Although poorly clothed and fed they were 'ready and willing' to do 'every work that came their way'.

Not only did the garrison provide labour for the building of Pietermaritzburg, but it also provided an important market for the farmers' produce and a very important source of custom to the local shop- and inn-keepers. Pietermaritzburg's economic development would have been far less certain had it not been for the stable market that the garrison assured. This remained true throughout the nineteenth century, despite the overall growth of the City. Shortly before the Anglo-Boer War broke out in 1899, the military authorities threatened to withdraw the garrison from Fort Napier unless the municipality took urgent measures to improve the water supply to the fort. At this stage, because of the political tensions in South Africa

Lancers at Fort Napier in the 1890s. A motley collection of offices and stores surrounds the parade-ground.

COMPENSATION FROM MOSHESH! NATAL 1865

The spoils of war[5]. Troops marching down Chapel Street in 1865 on their return from exacting 'compensation' from the Basutho.

Military duties were coupled with public entertainment: a military concert in Alexandra Park c.1902[6].

The Imperial Garrison holding a review in honour of Queen Victoria's birthday, 24 May 1899.

there were nearly 5 000 officers and men in garrison at Fort Napier with about 500 women and children living with them. The loss of a market of this magnitude would have been a social and economic disaster to the City that had to be avoided at all costs. The City Fathers acted quickly to improve the garrison's water supply.

The men of the garrison who made such a sustained and profound impact on Pietermaritzburg were drawn largely from the two extremes of British society; the wealthy landed classes and the very poor. The middle classes in Victorian England did not join the army.

The officers came from the wealthy upper classes and the landed gentry. Before 1871 officers had to purchase their commissions, which effectively barred all those without substantial resources from military careers. After the abolition of the purchase of commissions the need for a private income kept the exclusive character of the officer corps intact. An officer could not afford on his army pay alone uniforms, servant, mess bills, horses, sporting equipment and other luxuries considered essential to his status as an 'officer and a gentleman'. Under these circumstances it is not surprising that the British officer devoted more time to his own amusements than he did to his regimental duties. Intellectual pursuits were shunned, but young officers enjoyed amateur dramatics, gambling, hunting, shooting and equestrian pursuits. These activities played a great role in shaping the character of Pietermaritzburg.

The strong local tradition of amateur dramatics has its roots in the garrison's theatre begun by young officers. The history of the 45th Regiment claims that the first performance was held on 3 March 1846 before the Lieutenant-Governor, Martin West, but this has been disputed. Nevertheless, the first confirmed performance was also by army officers on 8 August 1846. As has been noted, officers of the garrison organized the Maritzburg Turf Club, polo matches, cricket and other sports. The officers of the 45th Regiment were avid hunters, and in the late 1840s one expedition near the City slaughtered an elephant and twenty-six eland, missing ten lions and two more elephant. Balls and dances were popular entertainments and were often the climax to other social events. In 1844 the Maritzburg Turf Club held an end of year race meeting on 30 and 31 December which was followed by a highly successful New Year's Eve ball

K.R.R.

THE LAST 24'S MAY REVIEW MARITZBURG 1899

organized by the officers. Some officers, such as Captains Garden and Gordon, sketched and painted, and provided Natal with some of its earliest European works of art.

The garrison, however, brought more than a touch of glamour to Pietermaritzburg: it accentuated the class-consciousness and snobbery of Victorian society. Pietermaritzburg acquired the reputation of being the most 'clique-ridden' town in Southern Africa. The officers of the garrison and the very senior colonial officials lorded it over the rest of the City's inhabitants in blatant and cutting ways. Class segregation dictated social events, the Race Ball of the May Season being followed by a Tradesmen's Ball.

At the other end of the social scale the garrison greatly stimulated the liquor trade and the world's reputedly oldest profession — prostitution. Drinking and womanizing were the two most sought-after forms of relaxation for the British soldier. In 1884 the Waterloo Bar in Church Street was a favourite haunt of the garrison and was the scene of numerous brawls and a few deaths. A veteran of the 82nd Regiment, John Mockler, who settled in the City, concluded that the Tommies kept Pietermaritzburg 'alive'; and in 1938 an elderly City innkeeper, Mr Sammy Froomberg, recalled that when cavalrymen visited the Black Horse Bar, they would ride into the bar, down their drinks while still mounted and ride out again.

The 'other ranks' of the Victorian army were drawn from the slums of Britain's industrial cities and included drunkards, criminals and the otherwise unemployable. The army was virtually the only welfare service provided by the Government of Victorian England. It was also one of the most frequently used escape routes for destitute young Irishmen seeking relief from poverty and famine. Irishmen were numerous in the 45th Regiment and provided Pietermaritzburg with its first significant numbers of Roman Catholics.

Another unit that had a very long association with Pietermaritzburg was the Cape Mounted Rifles. From the 1840s until the Regiment was disbanded in 1870 a detachment was stationed at Fort Napier. The CMR was a unit of the Imperial Army. Although many of its men were recruited from the coloureds of the Cape Colony, it had British officers and was a professional, not an amateur volunteer military unit. The CMR had an arduous time in Natal. Often the only cavalry available to the colonial Government, the CMR patrolled the foothills of the Drakensberg, the Zulu and Basotho borders, pursued San cattle raiders and guarded remote farms. It is also likely that the CMR made its contribution to the growth of Pietermaritzburg's coloured population. Many men from the garrison regiments had sexual liaisons across the colour line and so, in addition to enforcing the Pax Britannica, the Imperial Garrison played an important part in developing Pietermaritzburg's multi-cultural population.

The garrison was also concerned with the public health of the City. In 1847 the Regimental Surgeon gave smallpox innoculations to the citizens of the town, and the army doctors generally watched anxiously for signs of communicable diseases and acted vigorously to stamp them out, in the City as well as in the fort. During the Anglo-Boer War it was the townspeople's turn to care for the Tommies. The homes of Pietermaritzburg were flung

Entertaining the citizens. A cavalry display in Alexandra Park, c.1897.

open to the wounded streaming into the City from the battlefront along the Thukela River. The Natal Parliament moved out of its debating chambers so that wounded troops could be treated. St. George's Garrison Chapel and Maritzburg College were also pressed into service as hospitals to supplement the inadequate medical facilities at Fort Napier.

During the first thirty-odd years of its history, Fort Napier was the best protected complex of buildings in the City and the natural rallying point in the event of trouble. During the 1850s the Colonial Treasurer's office was robbed of a large sum of money and the Lieutenant-Governor decided that the Government's funds would be safer in Fort Napier under military guard than in a bank or government office.

In 1861 conflict over the royal succession in Zululand caused the colonists to fear that Natal would be invaded. Lieutenant-Governor Scott marched the 85th Regiment, a troop of the CMR and supporting artillery post-haste from Fort Napier to Kranskop to forestall any Zulu invasion. The citizens of Pietermaritzburg gathered in alarm around the reassuring guns of the fort, and its redoubts were manned by Natal Volunteers. Fort Napier also served to shelter a royal fugitive. Prince Mkungu, a younger son of King Mpande, was a student of Bishop Colenso's out at Bishopstowe where the Government felt he was vulnerable to a possible kidnap attempt by his vengeful elder brother, Prince Cetshwayo. Lieutenant-Governor Scott arranged for Mkungu to be placed in 'protective custody' in Fort Napier until the crisis passed. During the scare the time-gun fired daily from the Fort fell silent. The firing of a gun was to signify the arrival of an invading Zulu force, but Cetshwayo's army never crossed into Natal and Pietermaritzburg soon relaxed.

The garrison found it less easy to do so because facilities at Fort Napier were becoming progressively more over-crowded. During the 1860s the officers still lived in the City, staying in the fort overnight only when they were on duty. In 1864 this practice, and the overall conditions at the Fort, were severely criticized by the General Officer Commanding in South Africa, Lieutenant-General R.P. Douglas. He pointed out the 'mischief' likely to occur when

Paul Thompson

News of the British disaster at Isandlwana reached Pietermaritzburg on the morning of Friday, 24 January 1879. Further information revealed heavy casualties among the Natal Carbineers and heightened the sense of alarm at a possible Zulu invasion. The Maritzburg Rifles (a militia unit), the Natal Rifle Association, and the City Guard (a kind of special constabulary improvised at the beginning of the War) all turned out, but they were too few to protect the City against a Zulu impi. The Colonial Secretary and Commandant of the City, Lieutenant-Colonel C.B.H. Mitchell, RE, decided that the best defence was in laager. At this time 'laager' meant an enclosure behind which settlers with firearms could repel blacks with spears — it might be formed hastily of wagons drawn round, or constructed deliberately of brick or stone or even earth, with bastions and loopholes. Mitchell selected an area in the centre of Pietermaritzburg, the block bounded by Commercial Road, Church Street, Timber Street and Longmarket Street, and part of the adjacent block as far as Pietermaritz Street. Certain larger buildings were designated as refuges for the town- and country-folk who could be expected to come in — the cannon at Fort Napier was to fire a signal if the enemy were in proximity — and careful instructions were circulated for these people telling what and how much to bring of bedding, food and utensils. Special attention was given to sanitary arrangements, and the people were given to understand that the Commandant's orders should be obeyed.

Work on the laager was under way in earnest by Sunday 26 January. Buildings were altered for defence and barricades were erected between them, with passages to be blocked at the last minute. The Colonial Engineer had three wells sunk and checked two 3 000-gallon tanks on top of the court-house for a sufficient water supply. The Town Council provided for quantities of mealies, mealie-meal, rice and salt to sustain the inmates, and had dead trees in the park cut and brought in for firewood. On 28 January Mitchell divided the laager into 'wards', and a fortnight later named regular officers to take charge of them, and designated buildings in each as armouries. Thus was Maritzburg prepared to meet an incursion from over the border. None occurred. There was a scare, based on an incorrect report, on the

Barricading and loopholing the Supreme Court, one of the substantial buildings upon which the improvised laager of barricades was anchored.

night of 3–4 February, and some people did resort to the laager even though there was no signal, and were duly sent home. Soon it became apparent that the Zulu strategy was defensive, and as British reinforcements arrived in the Colony a sense of security returned to the City. In July the laager was dismantled. The *Natal Witness* wondered: 'Could not some portion be left as a monument?' Today the only buildings which were in the enclosure are the old court-house (now housing the Tatham Art Gallery), the old Scottish Presbyterian church nearby, and the old Native High Court (now tenanted by the district surgeon).

The first Colonial Buildings in Church Street with the shutters loopholed against anticipated Zulu attack.

officers were not present overnight. He also described the garrison's hospital accommodation as 'miserable' and the troops' recreation facilities as 'defective'.

A building programme was launched but it took time for the facilities to be improved. In the meantime the troops sought their relaxation in the town and on the sportsfield. On 26 September 1866, Pietermaritzburg had its first football match, between a team of City lads and a team of large soldiers from Fort Napier. The match was a draw despite the shameless bias of the referee, Sergeant Clark, towards his fellow soldiers.

It was not, however, the soldiers who fulfilled General Douglas's predictions of mischief, but the officers. The editor of the *Times of Natal*, William Watson, published some veiled innuendoes concerning a Captain Yardley and a young lady. The captain and four brother officers visited the editor's home and, since he refused to apologize, attempted to tar and feather him. Mr and Mrs Watson and their daughter resisted the military hooligans and the noise brought neighbours and officials to their aid. The officers were charged in the magistrate's court, but the charges were dropped once the officers apologized to Mr Watson and paid damages.

The 99th Regiment (2nd Wiltshire) was in garrison between 1865 and 1867 and, encouraged by the Lieutenant-Governor, Colonel Maclean, coupled its military duties with public entertainment. The highlight of the fashionable 'May Week' Season was the review of the garrison followed by a ball at Government House. The pantomime antics of the garrison and the reaction of the local populace provided a good example of the extent to which the Pax Britannica rested on bombast and bluff.

The parade at Fort Napier on 24 May 1865 was described as the making of 'mimic war' which entertained the audience. The 'shouts and shrieks of astonishment and delight' from the black observers were considered a 'revelation of unaffected barbarism' and the colonial observers concluded that the garrison's military display ought to have a 'wholesome influence' on the minds of the Colony's black population.

Ten years later the garrison was required to exercise a 'wholesome influence' on the minds of the Colony's white population. The 'Langalibalele rebellion' which had shaken

Bringing up supplies. The Pietermaritzburg railway station saw heavy service during the Second Anglo-Boer War.

the Colony in 1873 had seen imperial troops take the field, but the brunt of the action had been borne by the colonial volunteers. The mission of Sir Garnet Wolseley in 1875 was one of the political consequences of the Langalibalele affair. The 13th Regiment (Prince Albert's Light Infantry) was to lend social support to Sir Garnet's political efforts to change Natal's constitution. Wolseley's tactics have been described as 'drowning the liberties of Natal in sherry and champagne'. The band of the 13th Regiment played at the Governor's glittering balls and receptions, and Wolseley's staff of aristocratic officers dazzled the colonial ladies while the Governor browbeat their husbands.

Wolseley decided to attend church services at Fort Napier and endure the tedious sermons of the elderly military chaplain rather than having to choose between the services of the rival bishops, Colenso and Macrorie. Sir Garnet inspected the fort on 5 April 1875 and was not impressed. He described the barracks as a 'disgrace' and the married quarters as resembling 'Irish hovels'.

A new building programme began in August 1876, partly as a result of Wolseley's criticisms, but also because of increasing political tension in the Transvaal and on its

Maritzburg College was used as a military hospital during the Second Anglo-Boer War.

THE GLITTER OF THE GARRISON

Hamish Paterson

The imperial troops at Fort Napier dictated many of the City's pastimes for more than seventy years. In 1938 an elderly pub-keeper nostalgically remembered the days when 'Tommy' reigned supreme in Pietermaritzburg and people did not go to bed early.

Amateur theatricals began in the garrison theatre in 1846, starting a tradition that continues. Regimental bands played in the parks and on the Market Square. This was not always popular as clashes occurred between Nonconformist religious sects, anxious to protect the sabbath, and the troops, backed by music-loving citizens.

Sporting fixtures were arranged by the troops: football, cricket, gymkhanas, croquet, steeplechases and horse-racing. The garrison gave Pietermaritzburg a sparkle that many other South African towns lacked entirely.

The officers escorted the ladies of the town to most of the social events and a young officer was a sought-after catch for the daughters of the City's social leaders. Cavalry officers were married off with some rapidity to eligible ladies in the 1880s and 1890s.

border with Zululand. The fortifications were extended and a ten-foot-deep trench with corresponding earthworks was built around the barracks. Less than three years later the British invaded Zululand in January 1879 and Natal was rocked by the news of the disaster at Isandlwana. The centre of Pietermaritzburg was fortified and Fort Napier was prepared as one of the key points of the City's defences. Women and children were to shelter behind the fort's earthworks while a scratch force of civilian volunteers and military base staff defended the City. As in 1861, Natal was not subjected to a Zulu invasion. In 1881 the Transvaal revolted and the garrison rushed north to attempt to quell the rebellion. The defeat at Majuba led to peace negotiations and the garrison returned to barracks.

During the 1880s and the early 1890s the burning political issue for the Natal colonists was that of responsible government. The position of the Imperial Garrison was one of the important factors in the debate. The Imperial Government insisted that the colonists take over their own defence and that the garrison be withdrawn or reduced. Many colonists felt that the garrison was vital to their security and others felt that it was essential to their prosperity. The debate raged on, but Natal finally received 'responsible government' status in 1893 with an Imperial Regiment still garrisoning Fort Napier.

During the 1880s tensions mounted within the garrison and, in 1887, when the Royal Inniskilling Fusiliers and the Inniskilling Dragoons were both stationed at Fort Napier, serious trouble broke out. A fatigue party from the Fusiliers refused to clean out the Dragoons' barracks and the infantrymen were arrested. A little later some of their drunken comrades stormed the guardroom and released them. The whole party then marched into town and the uproar spread. They attacked a military patrol, killed a corporal and terrified the townspeople. Eventually they were hunted down and arrested by the city police and the Dragoons. The mutineers appeared before civil and military courts and two were sentenced to death. One had his sentence commuted to penal servitude for life, but the other was hanged in the City's prison. His body was removed and given a decent burial by the Roman Catholic nuns of Loop Street.

During the 1890s the political situation in South Africa worsened and the British garrison was reinforced. The buildings at Fort Napier were deteriorating and in urgent need of renovation. In late 1892, the General Officer Commanding in South Africa inspected the fort and described the corrugated iron barrack huts as being like ovens in summer and bitterly cold in winter. He refused to allow troops to live in them as this was 'incompatible with ordinary considerations of humanity'. Another construction programme began at Fort Napier, the most gracious building being the new garrison chapel, St. George's.

The Anglo-Boer War saw Boer commandos within 50 km of Pietermaritzburg, but the City itself was not directly threatened. Fort Napier was used as a supply base for the forces of General Sir Redvers Buller that were trying to relieve Ladysmith. The City was also an important medical centre during Buller's campaign, but after March 1900 the main fighting moved west across the Berg and Natal became a military backwater.

After the signing of the Peace of Vereeniging on 31 May 1902, the garrison at Fort Napier was reduced in numbers and in quality. The better troops were required in the Transvaal and the new Orange River Colony, and Fort Napier was occupied by various detachments of the prosaically named Royal Garrison Regiment.

Fort Napier during the First World War became an internment camp for German prisoners of war and civilians from British colonies in Africa. Censored postcards sent from the camp are now collectors' items.

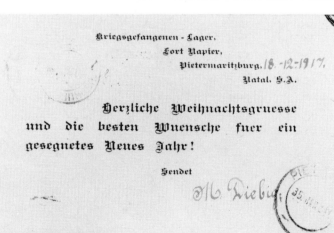

REGIMENTS IN GARRISON AT FORT NAPIER, 1843 — 1914

Graham Dominy

This list is derived from the commemorative plaques in the Pietermaritzburg City Hall. Minor modifications, such as the inclusion of the Cape Mounted Rifles, have been made.

The plaques give the designations of the regiments as they were when the plaques were mounted and not necessarily as they were when the regiments served at Fort Napier. Support units, such as the Royal Engineers, are not included.

During the Anglo-Zulu and Anglo-Boer Wars Fort Napier served as a base camp for the forces in the field and was occupied by a wide variety of units for different lengths of time.

Cavalry

1843—70	Cape Mounted Rifles
1881—90	6th Inniskilling Dragoons
1890—92	11th Hussars
1892—95	3rd Dragoon Guards
1895—98	7th Hussars
1896—97	9th Lancers
1898—99	5th Royal Irish Lancers

Artillery

1884—93	4th Mountain Battery
1893—98	10th Mountain Battery

Infantry

1843—59	45th (1st Sherwood Foresters)
1859—61	85th (2nd King's Shropshire Light Infantry)
1861—62	59th (2nd East Lancashire Regiment)
1863—64	25th (2nd Royal Northumberland Fusiliers)
1864—65	2/11th (2nd Devonshire Regiment)
1865—67	99th (2nd Wiltshire Regiment)
1867—70	2/20 (2nd Lancashire Fusiliers)
1870—71	32nd (1st Duke of Cornwall's Light Infantry)
1871—75	75th (1st Gordon Highlanders)
1875—77	1/13th (1st Somerset Light Infantry)
1877—78	80th (2nd South Staffordshire Regiment)
1878	1st/24th (1st South Wales Borderers)
1878	2nd/24th (2nd South Wales Borderers)
1879—80	3/60th (Kings Royal Rifle Corps)
1880—84	58th (2nd Northamptonshire Regiment)
1881—86	1st Welsh Regiment
1883—85	1st Argyll and Sutherland Highlanders
1884—87	2nd South Lancashire Regiment
1886—88	1st Royal Inniskilling Fusiliers
1888—91	1st Royal Scots
1887—90	1st North Staffordshire Regiment
1891—94	2nd York and Lancaster Regiment
1894—98	2nd Duke of Wellington's Regiment
1897—99	2nd Royal Dublin Fusiliers
1898—99	1st Leicestershire Regiment
1899—02	Anglo-Boer War (no permanent garrison)
1902—03	2nd King's Own Royal Regiment
1902—03	2nd West Yorkshire Regiment
1904—08	1st Royal Garrison Regiment
1906	2nd Cameron Highlanders
1906—07	3rd Royal Warwickshire Regiment
1907—09	2nd Royal Norfolk Regiment
1908—09	3rd Royal Fusiliers
1909—13	1st Wiltshire Regiment
1913—14	1st South Staffordshire Regiment

The outbreak of the 'Bambatha rebellion' in 1906 led to imperial reinforcements being sent to Natal. The 2nd Cameron Highlanders and the 3rd Royal Warwickshire Regiment garrisoned Fort Napier, but imperial troops were not committed to the field. The rebellion was suppressed by Natal colonial forces with the assistance of volunteers from the other South African colonies. One of the results of the rebellion was the realization of the Natal colonists that they needed the safety of a united South Africa to maintain their dominance over the restive black population. Negotiations towards this end began in Durban in 1908 and Natal joined the Union of South Africa on 31 May 1910.

The Imperial Garrison remained at Fort Napier for a few more years consoling the townspeople of Pietermaritzburg, who regretted the loss of their capital status, with performances of regimental bands, balls and sporting events. The outbreak of the First World War resulted in the final withdrawal of the garrison. On 12 August 1914 the band of the 1st South Staffordshire Regiment beat the retreat in front of the Pietermaritzburg City Hall and the troops boarded the train *en route* for the horrors of the Western Front.

The South Staffordshire Regiment saw action all through the campaigns of autumn 1914 and was decimated at the first battle of Ypres in November. By the end of 1914 most of the officers and men that Pietermaritzburg had known so well were dead or wounded. It was the end of an era.

During the First World War, Fort Napier was used as an internment camp for German prisoners of war and citizens from all over the Union and from other British colonies in Africa. In 1918, at the end of the War, the British Government handed Fort Napier over to the Government of the Union, and by 1920 the last military administrative personnel had left Pietermaritzburg.

Relic of an era that had ended, the fort stood empty and in decay. Having unsuccessfully attempted to sell it to the Pietermaritzburg municipality (who thought the price too high), the Government divided it in 1927 into two sections. One was given over to the construction of housing for white railway-workers; and the other — which included most of the now derelict buildings of the old fort — was turned into a mental hospital. There are hopes today that the historic core of buildings might be restored.

The last of the garrison. Officers of the 1st South Staffordshire Regiment at Fort Napier in 1914, just before leaving for the Western Front and the first battle of Ypres.

14

Three camps of World War II

John Deane

From the earliest days of British rule until the departure of the last imperial troops in 1914, the military focus of Pietermaritzburg was Fort Napier, overlooking the City from rising ground to the south-west. But by 1901 the colonial government had bought the agricultural showground near the Commercial Road cemetery for use as a drill ground, and added a large brick drill hall. The site is still used today by the South African Defence Force. The Second World War saw the establishment of three large camps on the southern and south-eastern outskirts of the City, about four kilometres from the centre. They were Oribi Military Hospital and Camp, the Durban Road Prisoner of War Camp and the Hay Paddock Transit Camp.

Though the City has spread outwards, and the open veld of the 1940s and 50s has been covered by residential suburbs and industrial estates, the general location of each of these camps is still easily discovered today. After the War the name Oribi was for a time synonymous with the men's residence of the University of Natal, for part of the hutted camp for some years housed a younger and more carefree population than the sick and wounded soldiers who had occupied it from 1941 to 1944. It also provided housing for returning servicemen and their families; and there were some who were both ex-servicemen and students. Today, known as Oribi Government Village, its buildings and subsequent additions are used for housing, a post office, a shop, a commando unit headquarters and a few light industries. Entrance to the village is still through the shale-built gateway where sentries stood in former days. Not very far away, in the fairly new residential area of Epworth, an interesting landmark is the little Italian prisoners' church. This attractive stone building, with its modest tower and guardian stone lion, is a reminder that this area was once within the barbed-wire enclosure of the prison camp, and is a tribute to the craftsmanship of the prisoners of war who built it. Lastly, on the broad hill slope where Hay Paddock Camp used to be, is the suburb of Hayfields, with only a few road names such as Military Way to remind residents of the thousands of Commonwealth and Allied troops who passed through the transit camp during the five years of its existence.

Oribi Hospital

During the earlier part of 1940 elements of the Royal Natal Carbineers had been in training at a camp at Oribi, but this was a very small establishment compared to what it was to become within a year. The 1st South African Infantry Brigade had its first clash with Italian forces at El Wak, Abyssinia, on 16 December 1940, and British forces faced the imminent prospect of heavy fighting in the

Middle East. The South African Government was requested to assist by establishing two 1 200-bed hospitals and a convalescent depot for 2 000 by the end of December 1940. Events, however, were moving fast, and 500 sick and wounded from the Middle East were expected to arrive in Durban in mid-November, with another 600 a couple of weeks later. Against this background a decision was taken to convert the Oribi infantry camp into a hospital for 2 200 patients. Its situation right on the main Durban-Johannesburg railway line was no doubt a factor in the choice of the site. Carbineers who had left from Oribi for East Africa returned after a year or eighteen months to find the place almost unrecognizable, as an extensive hospital in brick hutments had been established in a very short time.

181 Military Hospital, Oribi, was essentially for imperial troops from various theatres of war, and was staffed by South African, British and Canadian medical personnel. The wards, mess-halls, staff accommodation, YMCA canteen (tea — a penny; dinner — one shilling and sixpence!) and recreation areas can still be seen today, converted to other uses. Even detention barracks were necessary, as illness and injury were not always guarantees of good behaviour.

The popular Officer Commanding, Colonel O.L. Shearer, of the South African Medical Corps (later to be Member of Parliament for Pietermaritzburg City from 1943 to 1961), wanted the physical surroundings at Oribi to be as pleasant as possible, and saw gardening as a useful activity for staff and a therapy for many of the patients. As a result of his encouragement and personal example, the spaces between the hutments were soon transformed into attractive lawns and gardens. The formation of the Oribi Military Hospital Association brought about co-ordination of all entertainments and sports for staff and patients and, together with the fortnightly *Oribi News*, contributed to the strong community feeling which developed.

Fig. 1 The three camps.

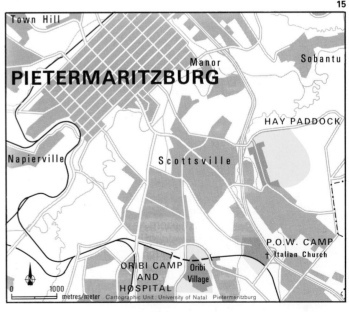

110

Situated outside the perimeter of the hospital itself were the barracks of the Women's Auxiliary Army Service, the headquarters of the Officer Commanding, a Motor Transport Depot, Number 6 Provo Company of the Military Police, and a tented Convalescent Camp for those who had been discharged from the hospital but were not yet fit enough to resume active service. The military police were responsible for policing not only the City, with its various places of entertainment for servicemen, but also the railway as far as Germiston, and the military camp at Ladysmith. They also had to provide additional guards when large contingents of prisoners of war arrived at or left the nearby prison camp. Some Italian prisoners were released on parole, to work at Oribi as orderlies, artisans or in other specialized jobs. The military police, for example, tired of their food being ruined by incompetent cooks, obtained the services of two prisoners. One of them had been personal chef to General Graziani, the Governor of Italian Somaliland, and the other had worked in the kitchen of a large hotel in Rome. The improvement is not hard to imagine!

Khaki battledress was to be seen everywhere in wartime Pietermaritzburg, but the Oribi patients who were able to go into town added a touch of colour with their bright blue tunics and trousers, white shirts and red ties. This uniform was a passport to hospitality, and many a disconsolate Saturday afternoon stroll through the streets ended with an invitation to join a family for a meal and possibly an outing the next day. These often developed into regular visits to the same family, and friendships thus formed continued long after the War. For the less fortunate, who could not leave the hospital, there were regular visitors from town who would bring a few gifts and comforts and a good deal of solace to the badly maimed or seriously ill men who were also very anxious about their families as Britain bore the brunt of German air raids.

For one British casualty, at least, arrival at Oribi Hospital must have seemed unbelievable good fortune. *Oribi News* of 7 June 1941, describes how Private Thomas Jordan of the Royal Army Ordnance Corps, when he boarded a hospital ship in the Middle East, thought it would be sailing to Britain. Their destination, however, was Durban, and then Oribi. Jordan had been stationed in Egypt for seven years, and his wife and infant son had been evacuated from there, together with many other servicemen's families, after war broke out. But of all the many places in South Africa where evacuees were accommodated, Mrs Jordan and her baby were in Pietermaritzburg!

Although most of the patients were British, there were others, too, notably the Poles and Free French, whose continental courtesy impressed the women at Oribi Hospital and in the town generally. At Christmas in 1943 the medical staff were invited to a celebration, with traditional Polish fare, carols and a Nativity play. The words were unintelligible throughout the evening, but the message and the spirit were unmistakable. All was not sweetness and light, however, and it is recorded that fighting in Hay Paddock Camp between Polish troops and men of the Royal Navy kept the Oribi casualty ward busy on several occasions!

In April 1944 the British War Office decided to shut down Oribi Hospital, and by the middle of that year only a handful of patients and nurses remained.

The Durban Road Prisoner of War Camp

During the War, travellers by road between Pietermaritzburg and Durban passed very close to the prisoner of war camp on the outskirts of the Capital, and could see crowds of unhappy men standing at the tall barbed-wire fences, staring at the passing traffic. Some of them were German soldiers captured in North Africa, awaiting transfer to prison camps in Canada, and one incident among them resulted in a murder trial in the Natal Supreme Court. A German officer instructed two of his men to execute a certain Helmuth Haensel who was suspected of disloyalty and passing information to the camp authorities. On 6 June 1942 they gagged and throttled the unfortunate man and then hanged the body on a tent-pole to give the appearance of suicide. At the time no foul play was suspected by the camp authorities, or if it was, no proof was available. Only after the War had ended did the facts come to light, and the two men were brought to trial. The trial judge found them guilty, but with mitigating circumstances, and sentenced them to five years imprisonment; but also reserved appeal on a question of law. The Appeal Court in Bloemfontein was then called upon to consider such matters as offences

A corner of Italy. The shale church, lovingly built by the Italian prisoners of war as a permanent reminder of their long stay in Pietermaritzburg.

PRIGIONIERI DI GUERRA ITALIANI CAMPO DI PIETERMARITZBURG

NUMERO UNICO   1944

The cover of the commemorative booklet published to mark the consecration of the Italian church on 19 March 1944.

committed by prisoners of war, what law governs them, crimes committed by prisoner of war on the orders of a superior officer, and the killing of an innocent person by compulsion. The finding of the trial court was upheld, and the case of *Rex* v. *Werner and Another* passed into South African legal history as a significant case to be quoted in textbooks and subsequent judgments.

With a significant sector of the South African population pro-German in its sympathies, it was no doubt considered unwise to keep large numbers of German prisoners in this country, so their stay in the Durban Road camp was brief. Apart from some Japanese and other oriental prisoners, those in long-term captivity in Pietermaritzburg were mainly Italians, captured in Abyssinia, Eritrea and North Africa. Few were really committed to the War, so it was deemed possible to release quite a number on parole. Some were employed by the military authorities; others worked on farms or in factories. A number of them returned to settle in South Africa after the War. Many Italians were held at the Zonderwater Camp in the Transvaal, and in the opinion of some prisoners who had experienced both places, the Pietermaritzburg Camp was far preferable.

The first contingent of Italian prisoners of war arrived in Durban on 4 April 1941, and after a few weeks at Clairwood were transferred to Pietermaritzburg or Zonderwater. The group of several thousand which settled into the Durban Road camp included officers and men with very many skills and abilities, and this enabled them, even in the restricted circumstances of a prison camp, to create an existence 'behind the wire' which mitigated in some measure the harsh fact of captivity in a strange land. Apart from a chaplain and medical staff, there were men able to run a school and a library, and there were many craftsmen and artisans, able to practise their skills and teach them to others. When one group arrived, they were ordered to deposit all their aluminium water-bottles in a pile. The metal was probably destined for the South African war effort, but the pile disappeared overnight. The prisoners had secretly buried them, and during the next few years the hidden store was drawn upon to provide material for the manufacture of all kinds of useful articles and ornaments, for the prisoners' own use, or for sale to the camp guards.

There was a whole army band, with their instruments, and others whose musical or theatrical talents were also put to good use in a programme of entertainments. The standard of music was understandably very high, and three public concerts, under the baton of Lieutenant Luigi Bezzio, were given in the City Hall in aid of Red Cross funds.

As Pietermaritzburg gardeners know, shale lies very close to the surface in the City's southern suburbs, and this building material was readily available for the construction by the prisoners of a large combined mess and recreation hall, and, later, a camp post office and sick-bay, using dry-walling technique, with roofs of tarpaulins over wooden beams or poles. Areas were levelled for football, tennis, volley-ball and athletics, all of which had their enthusiastic adherents. The project upon which most care was lavished, however, was the church.

The senior Italian officer in the camp wished the prisoners to leave some beautiful permanent record of their longing for *la patria lontana* — the distant home country was decided to build a stone church, and as no cement would be available, '... every stone block would be hewn to fit its surrounding fellows exactly, in the way the Etruscans, Romans and Italians had built for centuries'. The South African military authorities gave permission, and even arranged for the Italian quarrymen and stonemasons to go to a quarry outside the camp to select the stone, which was then taken the two kilometres to the camp by handcart. The master-builders among the prisoners had no need of an architect or quantity surveyor, and soon the work, sustained by religious faith and a longing for *la patria lintana* — the distant home country — was in progress. The chief designer and supervisor of the work was Sergeant Ottaviano Aiello, supported by a team of about forty quarrymen, stonemasons, bricklayers, carpenters, painters and decorators, metalworkers and artists. They had inadequate tools and equipment; there was no scaffolding material, even though towards the end some of the work was being done almost ten metres above the ground; and the work was seriously delayed by three exceptionally rainy months. During the course of the building operations, in September 1943, Italy had surrendered to the Allies, and in the early months of 1944 the heavy fighting at Monte Cassino and Anzio dominated the War news. The foundation stone had been ceremonially laid on 2 February 1943. Thirteen and a half months later, on Sunday 19 March 1944, the Apostolic Delegate to South Africa, Archbishop van Gijlswijk, inaugurated and consecrated the church. The ceremony and the High Mass which followed it were charged with emotion for the hundreds of Italian prisoners who participated — pride in a great creative effort completed, relief that the War seemed to be moving to its end, but also fear that Italy would still have to endure months of bitter fighting as the Allies slowly drove the German forces northwards.

To mark the occasion a commemorative booklet was printed, entitled *In Attesa* (While Waiting), describing the church-building project, giving an account of the many other activities with which the prisoners tried to alleviate the misery of captivity, and ending with a memorial page dedicated to eight soldiers who died in the camp and are buried in the Mountain Rise cemetery. Despite its unhappy associations for the prisoners, and the fact that most of them could have seen little of the City except the admittedly attractive panorama of Swartkop and the Town Hill, there are several complimentary references to Pietermaritzburg, and no doubt there are to this day copies of *In Attesa* in homes all over Italy, nostalgically read by elderly men who were *i prigionieri di guerra Italiani, del campo di Pietermaritzburg.*

Hay Paddock Transit Camp

Hay Paddock Camp was under construction during July 1942, with an authorized expenditure of £157 000 for the various civil engineering works required. By the end of that month 3 212 Polish troops with 34 officers, and 1 484 Royal Navy personnel with 32 officers, were already encamped. As the Union Defence Force camp staff numbered only 4 officers and 12 other ranks, a report to the Deputy Adjutant General considered that 'immediate assistance in the way of increased staff [was] essential'. This was forthcoming, and Hay Paddock was thereafter appropriately staffed except, as we shall see, for security personnel.

The 181-acre (72 hectare) site was divided into twenty blocks, each to accommodate 1 000 men, mostly in tents. It was intended to house Union Defence Force units in readiness for embarkation, to relieve congestion in the Durban transit camps (such as Clairwood), and 'to accommodate troops of the Allied Nations while in transit'. Its average occupancy was 15 000, but at peak periods as many as 25 000 were in camp. Perhaps the largest single influx of South African troops occurred in 1943. On New Year's Day advance parties of the 1st South African Division arrived back from Egypt, and two weeks later the main body of the Division followed. Although they were all dispersed on home leave by 18 January, the camp facilities were temporarily under severe strain, and none more so than the small camp post office as the returning men all wrote to tell their families that they were back on South African soil. Defence Headquarters in Pretoria had been advised that the post office at Hay Paddock should be '... conservatively staffed at first, as the mail of the Allied troops is very small [Polish troops never get any]'.

The short parenthesis of the reporting officer is a poignant reminder of the complete lack of contact between many of the continental troops and their families in occupied Europe. Small wonder, therefore, that their stay at Hay Paddock was hardly a happy time for the great majority of troops. The tented camp was bitterly cold on winter nights, and in spring and summer rain made conditions very trying. The inmates referred to the place as 'Clay Paddock'. Some, after unfortunate experiences in the crowded tents, called it 'Flea Paddock'!

Camp security was a constant problem, with petty theft rife, and the camp authorities unable to bring the culprits to book or take preventive measures. Using members of units in camp for gate duty and general security had proved unsatisfactory, and in March 1943 the commandant, Lieutenant-Colonel Stewart-Dunkerley, made a strong request for police personnel as an integral part of the camp staff.

It was mainly Hay Paddock which accounted for the ubiquity of uniformed troops in Pietermaritzburg streets. Ten different places catering for servicemen and women were listed during those years, run by service organizations such as the YMCA, Toc H, and the South African Women's Auxiliary Services (SAWAS). Perhaps the best known was the Soldiers' Club, in a handsome old commercial building at 168 Longmarket Street, opposite St. Peter's Church grounds. (The building survived for many years after the War, used by various firms, but was demolished to make way for the open-air parking lot now occupying the site.) Every Tuesday night there was a Uniform Dance in the City Hall from 7.30 till 10.30 p.m. Bars and hotels also attracted men with time and money to spare, and the civil and military police often had their hands full when things became too rough. At one time military police were given a list of useful foreign phrases (phonetically spelt) to enable them to communicate with those who were lost, drunk, or both. Even though it was wartime, it was a boom time for 'the bioscope', and on Friday 19 September 1941 the 20th Century Cinema in Longmarket Street opened as the City's fourth and most modern cinema. Not one of these cinemas — the Excelsior, the King's, the Grand and the 20th Century — remains. The 20th Century finally closed its doors during 1986, but there must be many ex-soldiers all over the world who remember it as it was then, with the paint hardly dry and the newsreels providing a carefully controlled description of the War's progress.

Pietermaritzburg, like other South African cities, was far removed from any war zone. There were some food shortages and some rationing; there were blackout regulations and air-raid drills, which citizens observed without for a moment believing that they would ever see the real thing. But the three large camps we have discussed constantly and forcibly reminded even those townspeople who had no relatives in the armed forces that the world was in turmoil. Not only were off-duty servicemen a common sight in the streets, but there were the long columns of men, accompanied, often, by bands playing, armoured cars, guns and gun-carriages, marching to and from the railway station along Commercial Road and Church Street. For the schoolboys who hung over the fences to watch, they simply provided more inspiration for the war games they played with such gusto. Others saw them come and go with the mixture of pride and sorrow which such sights have always brought.

The Natal Carbineers and Pietermaritzburg

Mark Coghlan

Hamish Paterson

The connections between volunteer regiment and community in nineteenth-century Pietermaritzburg was strong in the case of the Natal Carbineers, the oldest existing regiment in Natal. In the absence of modern forms of entertainment, regimental parades, drills and annual camps, as well as balls, gymkhanas and race meetings, were a welcome relief from the daily round.

The outbreak of the Crimean War in 1853 and the attendant possibility of the withdrawal of the Imperial Garrison, gave Natal, concerned as it was with the problem of keeping its own black population down, and the potential threat of the Zulu kingdom, a disturbing insight into its military vulnerability. In response to this situation, the Natal Colonial Government passed an ordinance, on 20 November 1854, enabling volunteer units to be formed for the defence of the Colony.

Preceded in 1848 by a short-lived Yeomanry Corps, the Natal Carbineers was officially established on 13 March 1855. By November, 50 Carbineers were attending parade, resplendent in dark-blue uniform with white facings. (This uniform was replaced by khaki in 1894.) The first Carbineer Ball, on 13 February 1856, was presided over by the first Commanding Officer, Sir Theophilus St. George, a popular Irish baronet, and assistant magistrate. His wife was regarded as Natal's most outstanding horsewoman. His successors were often prominent members of the Executive Council.

The Regiment's peace-time duties included providing escorts to receive Lieutenant-Governors, royal visitors, and other dignitaries, a function they fulfilled until the railway reached Pietermaritzburg in 1880.

During the 1860s the Carbineers took part in the Queen's Birthday reviews, held quarterly drills, and provided a dashing addition to the various balls held in the town. They also upheld Maritzburg's reputation with varying success on the sporting field and shooting range. The Carbineers were also present at the opening of the Victoria Suspension Bridge over the Msunduze in 1860. In December 1875, a contingent attended a ceremony for the cutting of the first sod of the Natal Government Railway. During the 1870s, the Carbineers were given another public duty, that of escorting the Governor to the opening of the Legislative Council, an honour that was to be theirs for almost 40 years.

By the 1890s the Carbineers had become an integral part of Maritzburg life. The Regimental Ball and Gymkhana had joined the Regimental Race Meeting as important social occasions, and the annual encampment had become a major event. The Regiment was adept at mounted sports but had mixed fortunes at cricket. Their

standing in the community was demonstrated when in 1898 they were seen off on the annual camp by Sir Michael Gallwey, the Acting Governor, the Prime Minister, the Attorney-General, and the General Officer Commanding Natal. They had also been inspected by prominent British generals such as Sir Garnet Wolseley and Sir Arthur Cunynghame, and in 1897 a Carbineer contingent travelled to London for the celebrations of Queen Victoria's 60th year on the throne.

In the aftermath of the Anglo-Boer War the Regiment and the City resumed their normal pursuits. The annual Regimental Ball and Gymkhana continued to be social highlights. The Carbineers were present at the opening of the second City Hall in August 1901; and in 1902, a contingent attended the coronation of Edward VII. The Regiment was awarded its Anglo-Boer War medals at a splendid parade in Alexandra Park in August 1903, and in 1904 it received its King's Colour at the same venue. A memorial tablet to Carbineers who had fallen in the War was placed in the City Hall entrance. In 1906 Lord Kitchener, of Khartoum and Anglo-Boer War fame, accepted the Colonelship of the Regiment, which in terms of the Militia Act of 1905 had undergone wide-ranging organizational changes, with staffing, equipment and finance placed on a uniform basis.

The years until the First World War were quiet ones for the Regiment. The Carbineers continued to uphold the City's honour at shooting and to add glamour to the social scene, in spite of losing the privilege of escorting the Governor to the opening of the Legislative Assembly when in 1910 Natal became part of the Union of South Africa. On the other hand, a new duty replaced the old, for they were now called upon to provide guards-of-honour to visiting Governors-General, a duty they would perform for the next fifty years. In September 1910, the Carbineers became allied to the 6th Dragoon Guards (the Carabineers) and as such appeared in the British Army Lists.

After the German South West African campaign, the Carbineers, like all Active Citizen Force (ACF) units, continued to exist only on paper until January 1920 when the *Natal Witness* launched a successful appeal to save the Regiment. The Carbineers were consequently one of the regiments accepted for peace-time training in June 1921. Pietermaritzburg provided the men for 1 and 2 Troops of A Squadron, the machine-gunners, signallers, and the regimental headquarters staff. The 1920s also saw the formation of the Natal Carbineers Veterans Association, which strengthened the links between City and Regiment.

While the Carbineers were being reorganized, the regimental band represented the Regiment in public until, in November 1922, the Regiment paraded for the first time since 1915. The Regiment then resumed its place in the City's life. In August 1923, the Maritzburg detachment's departure for the annual camp once more became a newsworthy item. In the next year a governor-general was again received by a Carbineer guard-of-honour. The Regiment was also affected by the dance craze of the 1920s, and Carbineer dances became part of Maritzburg's social scene. The *Natal Witness* started and supported a fund for regimental standards for both regiments of the Carbineers. The climax of 1925 was the visit of Edward, the Prince of Wales. The Carbineers were accorded two special honours, that of providing an

18

When the Second World War ended in 1945, the Carbineers returned to a City that honoured its Regiment's achievements in practical ways. For example, a bursary plan was started for the sons of Carbineer servicemen. By July 1946 the Regiment was once more a functional ACF unit, and in October the Regiment placed a memorial plaque to their fallen comrades in the entrance to the City Hall. In March 1947 they had the privilege of receiving their Colonel-in-Chief, George VI, in their home town. The Regiment resumed peacetime responsibilities such as providing the guard-of-honour and band for Armistice Day (renamed Remembrance Day).

The National Party's triumph in 1948 directly threatened the Regiment's existence, because it brought into office as Minister of Defence, F.C. Erasmus, a man obsessed with routing out what he called 'foreign influences'. His first victims were the 2nd Regiment Royal Natal Carbineers and the Second Battalion Royal Durban Light Infantry, both of which were sacrificed to save the Umvoti and Natal Mounted Rifles. Despite this threat, the Carbineers celebrated their centenary in fine style, Pietermaritzburg conferring on her Regiment her highest civic honour, that of Freedom of the City. The document was drafted by a man who had brought honour to the Carbineers: the Mayor's Secretary, Henry Guest, MM and Bar. (To win the Military Medal and its Bar was a rare achievement.)

19

Peace-time ceremonial duties. The Natal Carbineer escort at the opening of the Legislative Council in 1880[18].

Life in the field was less elegant. The Carbineers' annual encampment, 1883[19].

The Minister of Defence's obsession continued to threaten the Carbineers. In 1957 they were banned from taking part in Pietermaritzburg's Remembrance Day Service (supposedly because Union Defence Force units could not be present when 'God Save the Queen' was played), and were allowed to return only in 1962. In a further attempt to destroy the ACF Regiment, the sale of alcohol in regimental messes was banned — but the Regiment survived this deprivation. Finally, just before he retired, the Minister tried unsuccessfully to change the name of the Regiment on the unconvincing grounds that the name 'Natal Carbineers' gave no indication of where the Regiment was situated.

Since 1961 the Carbineers have lost their designation of 'Royal', but a tradition became established of performing a Retreat ceremony at the Royal Show, and guards-of-honour were provided for the State President when he visited Pietermaritzburg. The Regiment continued both to preserve tradition and to innovate: in 1976 women joined the Regimental Band; and in 1979 the appearance of the band at the Natal Witness Garden Show revived an old custom (in the 1890s the Carbineer band had played at the Natal Horticultural Society's Spring Show). In 1980 the City Sporting Club reinstated the Carbineers' link with the Sport of Kings by introducing a Carbineer race meeting as part of its summer programme.

The Natal Carbineers were not intended to be merely an ornament to the social scene, and enjoyed numerous periods of active service. During its first 20 years the Regiment's military career was often controversial, and they were probably more suited to a deterrent rather than an active role.

From their inception, the Carbineers were prepared to serve over a wider area than the immediate City environs. The expedition against San cattle raiders in 1856 was the first occasion for a rendezvous on the Market Square,

escort to their Colonel-in-Chief, and of receiving their standards from his hands. Until the Second World War, the Regiment provided the ceremonial arch guard, guard-of-honour, and band for Armistice Day services.

Links with Pietermaritzburg were strengthened when in 1929 and 1935 the Regiment was affiliated with the cadet detachments of Hilton College and Maritzburg College respectively. One aspect of Carbineer tradition was lost when in 1934 the Carbineers exchanged their horses for machine-guns, before becoming an infantry regiment in 1936. During the Second World War they were to serve as a motorized regiment. In 1936, only months after he had indicated that he would be pleased to continue his association with the Carbineers, Edward VIII abdicated as king and with it his responsibility to the Regiment. This intensified the impact of the abdication on Pietermaritzburg. The orphaned Regiment did not remain so for long, for King George VI on his coronation assumed the Colonelcy-in-Chief of the Natal Carbineers along with the other responsibilities his brother had renounced.

always a time of bustle and excitement. In January 1858 the Corps formed part of the expedition against the local chief, Matshana, and was again mobilized in 1861 to meet an apparent invasion threat from Zululand.

Although the 1870s began quietly (with an expedition in July 1873 to accompany Theophilus Shepstone to Cetshwayo's coronation) the decade was to prove a traumatic one for the Carbineers. Ironically, the Carbineers began the 1870s making strenuous efforts to improve their military effectiveness, even appointing a regimental drill instructor. That these efforts were insufficient was demonstrated by the setback at the Bushman's River Pass in November 1873, when Carbineers took part in the expedition against Langalibalele. The debacle plunged Pietermaritzburg into mourning for its lost soldiers (including Robert Erskine, son of Major Erskine, Colonial Secretary at the time and a previous regimental commander of the Carbineers). The Regiment was severely criticized, despite the fortitude displayed during the expedition, and the Corps owed its survival to Offy Shepstone and William Royston, under whose care the Corps recovered and expanded. The City and Corps chose not to glorify the Carbineers but rather to remember them as 'those who fell in discharge of their duty'. A memorial to the fallen was unveiled in November 1874 in the Town Gardens.

The Corps continued to receive praise from the Press on their drill, appearance, and growing numbers, which had dropped temporarily during the Depression of the 1860s and in the aftermath of the Bushman's Pass affair. This affair had its own legacy, for henceforth most drills were conducted in heavy marching order. Increased numbers were equipped when, in October 1878, the Carbineers volunteered to serve outside the Colony against the Zulu kingdom. On 30 November they were given a rousing farewell by their fellow citizens. In later years a Carbineer

recalled how envious he had been of Trooper Fred Jackson, who sounded the call *Boots and Saddle* for the muster at Market Square, thus defying parents and Commanding Officer who felt he was too young at sixteen to go to war. He died with his comrades at Isandlwana on 22 January 1879. Although the Anglo-Zulu War brought little glory to Natal, Pietermaritzburg could take pride in the Carbineers' courage (they had also provided escorts for the Prince Imperial) and showed it in the spontaneous and enthusiastic welcome given the Carbineers who, on their return, had tried to enter the town quietly.

Unlike some other Natal volunteer units, the Natal Carbineers soon replaced their war losses and the Corps continued to grow. 1885 saw the expansion of the Corps into a Regiment, a source of pride to Maritzburg although by then it had to share the Carbineers with other Midland towns.

For the citizens of Pietermaritzburg, the proximity of war in 1899 with the Boer Republics was emphasized by the increased military activities of the Carbineers. They stepped up their drilling, exercised with imperial troops, and held joint field days with the Natal Royal Rifles. Finally, at extremely short notice on 29 September 1899, the Carbineers were mobilized. A force of about 500 proceeded to the front with the Mayor, Major G.J. Macfarlane, in command of a squadron. Their most celebrated actions occurred during the Siege of Ladysmith. The Carbineers' return, in October 1900, was celebrated in fine style. The City was *en fête*, despite the 70 casualties (including 13 dead) which the Regiment had suffered, and the Carbineers were formally welcomed by the Governor and given a welcoming address by the Mayor.

In 1906 the Natal Carbineers were mobilized in a policing role as part of the Natal Government's response to the black unrest in Natal, and in April they were despatched to help put down the 'Bambatha rebellion'. They were in the field until the end of July and on 2 August were publicly thanked by the Governor at a review in Market Square. The Regiment was given little

The Carbineers setting off to form the Royal Escort for the Duke and Duchess of Connaught on 1 December 1910.

WHAT'S IN A NAME

Mark Coghlan

Possible forerunners of the Carbineers include the Pietermaritzburg Yeomanry Corps (1848) and the Umgeni Rangers (1851). The Carbineers were initially formed as the Pietermaritzburg Irregular Horse, but within a few weeks, after the establishment of the Richmond Troop, the name was changed to the Natal Carbineers because the Regiment was no longer an exclusively Pietermaritzburg one. By 1905 the Regiment had grown to seven squadrons throughout the Colony, of which numbers 1 and 2 (the Right Wing) were based at the Regiment's Headquarters in Pietermaritzburg; while the remainder, (the Left Wing) were drawn from the Midlands and based in Ladysmith. The Regiment's most famous squadron during the nineteenth century was possibly that of the Karkloof Troop.

According to the 1912 Defence Act, these wings became separate regiments, the 1 and 2 Mounted Rifles, with continuity of name ensured by the suffix 'Natal Carbineers'. The title 'Natal Carbineers' was restored in 1934. Between 1935 (when the Carbineers became a Royal Regiment as part of King George V's Silver Jubilee celebrations) and 1961, the Regiment proudly bore the title 'Royal Natal Carbineers'. In 1954 the 2 RNC was disbanded, and since 1961 the Regiment has been known as the Natal Carbineers.

opportunity to rest, however, and was mobilized again on 30 November 1907 to assist in arresting Dinuzulu for his part in the 'rebellion'. 'Rebellion Medals' were presented in Alexandra Park on 16 August 1908.

On 20 August 1914, soon after the outbreak of the First World War, the Carbineers were ordered to mobilize and assemble in Pietermaritzburg. This event was overshadowed by popular enthusiasm for raising the war service unit, the Natal Light Horse. The Regiment's return from the South West African campaign, in which it had distinguished itself at Gibeon on 3 May 1915, was the occasion for wild (if sometimes drunken) excitement. The Thanksgiving Service was held in bitter weather, but in spite of this a huge crowd attended.

The Second World War was a long one for Maritzburg and its Royal Regiment. The City responded well to the calls made on it. The Carbineer marches through the City in November 1939 and May 1940 persuaded many to join up. Later, Major R.C. Tomlinson and the *Natal Witness* assisted many to join the Regiment. 'Maritzburg's Own' took part in the first action by South African ground forces, at El Wak in East Africa on 16 December 1940, and were in the field to the end, with a brief respite at home in 1943.

In August 1942 the City was electrified by the news that a Carbineer, Sergeant Quentin Smythe, had been

Royal connections. The Prince of Wales, Colonel-in-Chief of the Natal Carbineers, with the officers of his regiment in June 1925.

Standing, back row, left to right:
Lt. R.S. Miller, 2nd Lt. H. Stewart, Lt. G.W.G. Holmes, 2nd Lt. P.J. McKenzie, Lt. K.G. Winter, Lt. W.G. Holcomb, 2nd Lt. R.M. Slatter, Lt. & Qrm. A. Mason.

Standing, middle row, left to right:
2nd Lt. E.W. Gibson, Lt. H.S. James, T./Cpt. C. Gray, Capt. J.M. Comrie, V.D., Lt. L.N. Hay, M.C., Lt. J. Stewart, Lt. A.W. Gower-Jackson, Lt. & Sig. Off. H. Durham, Lt. D.R. Cresswell, 2nd Lt. V.C. Crooks.

Seated, front row, left to right:
Lt. C.O. Howes, Lt. F.H. Brickhill, M.M., Mjr. H.P. Walker, M.C., Capt. & Adj. W.J. Perkins, Capt. P.A. Comrie, Lt. Col. J.P.S. Woods, D.S.O., V.D., H.R.H. THE PRINCE OF WALES, Col.-in-Chief, Lt. Col. R.M. Tanner, D.S.O., V.D., Mjr. R.A. Lindsay, V.D., Capt. H. Teasdale, Capt. & Q.M.F.R. Cooper, Capt. & Adj. O.B. Jones, M.C., Capt. A. Gordon McKenzie, MC.

Seated on ground, left to right:
Lt. & Sig. Off. B.V.H. Flack, 2nd Lt. W.T. Urquhart.

21

SWEAT AND FUN

Mark Coghlan

The Carbineers combined the fun aspects of encampments with a consistently high standard of manoeuvres, drill and shooting. From 1861 the prize at shooting competitions was a rifle presented by Prince Alfred. The Volunteer Picnic was also a fun-filled occasion, with drill followed by dinner and sports. Skirmishes and mock assaults were popular, and in 1871, the Carbineers were praised for their innovative tactics during a sham fight with the Maritzburg Rifles and members of the 32nd Light Infantry in the vicinity of the racecourse. These mock battles were the centre-piece of the annual encampment, including one in 1904 on the site of the Battle of Colenso. Between the two World Wars the Carbineers continued to impress their home town with performances during mock battles for 'Flag Hill' (near Ladysmith) and between 'Northland' and 'Southland', which were part of ACF training exercises. During the nineteenth century shooting competitions had provided both a test of skill (usually with antiquated weapons) and an opportunity for a day's entertainment. The Carbineers more than held their own. In the 1960s the Regiment won the Gold Cup (a Defence Force shooting competition) eight times in a row. In these competitions, the Carbineers used the same weapons as on active service. In the 1850s these were adapted muzzle-loading Enfields. The Terry and Snider carbines followed in the 1860s and 1870s. The unpopular Swinburne-Henry carbine (1878) was followed by the Martini-Metford, the Regiment's standard weapon during the Anglo-Boer War. During the two World Wars, the Carbineers relied on the British Army stalwart, the Lee-Enfield, and in recent years, standard Defence Force rifles such as the FN/R1 have been used.

awarded the Victoria Cross in the Western Desert. On his return to Natal this unassuming man received, among many other honours, honorary life-membership of his cricket club, the Standard.

After the declaration of a Republic in 1961, and until mobilized for Border service in 1976, the Regiment was called upon only once. This was to deal with post-Sharpville unrest around Durban.

The increased size of the community, changing perceptions of newsworthy material, and the restrictions of military security, have in recent years distanced Maritzburg's Regiment from the public eye. Yet over the last 133 years the links between the City and the Carbineers have become cemented. To this day, local men fill the ranks, the Regiment provides NCOs to drill cadet detachments, and military contingents continue to add lustre to civic occasions.

Carbineers up North. Sergeant Quentin Smythe who was awarded the Victoria Cross in the Western Desert in August 1942[22], and Carbineers on leave at Gizah in 1942. *Left to right:* Capt. Peter Francis, Lt. Derrick Norton and Lt. R.K. (Sandy) Moir[23].

With colours flying and drums beating, the Natal Carbineers paraded through the centre of the City on 28 April 1988[24]. Among those taking the salute was Lt.-Col. Peter Francis MC, ED, honorary colonel of the regiment (second from left, standing behind the Mayor, Mr Mark Cornell). During World War II when he commanded the Carbineers in Italy he was, at 27, the youngest colonel in the South African land forces. He was the officer in command in 1955 when civic honours were conferred on the regiment.

CHAPTER EIGHT

Economic Hub of the Midlands

The Market Square in the 1890s, the commercial focus of Pietermaritzburg, teeming with draught-oxen. The Market Hall, demolished in 1972 despite vigorous protest, is in the background.

1

Economic development

OF THE CAPITAL CITY 1838–1910

Bill Guest

The establishment of Pietermaritzburg as the spiritual and political capital of the Republic of Natalia ensured that it would also become a focal point for social and commercial exchange. Yet the City's emergence as a significant economic centre proved to be a gradual process. The Nagmaal observances at the Church of the Vow and the quarterly meetings of the Volksraad attracted a periodic influx of burghers from the surrounding countryside which generated some commercial activity, though not sufficient to encourage the development of large trading stores. Moreover, the resident civil service was almost non-existent. It involved an expenditure of less than £500 a year, including the salaries of the port captain, the collector of customs, the white police officers, and the landdrosts of Pietermaritzburg, Port Natal and Weenen. This modest civil list appealed to the Boers, who had complained of being over-governed in the Cape Colony, but it meant that the Capital of the new Republic did not immediately acquire a large civil service around which a hard-core permanent population could coalesce. There was also very little money to spend on public works and buildings in a state that was based on a traditional pastoral economy which yielded only limited and irregular revenues. Tax evasion, exemptions and postponed payments were commonplace; so too was the delayed payment of civil service salaries and of debts to government suppliers.

Consequently, in its early years Pietermaritzburg offered little incentive for the launching of business enterprises. Gradually, however, the palisaded camp of wagons and mud huts was transformed as the Volksraad initiated the construction of water furrows, organized its Capital into wards, and began to press for the erection of permanent brick or stone dwellings. Timber was felled and transported from the yellowwood forest forty kilometres to the north-west, and C.W. Pistorius began to supply bricks and tiles from his brickyard at the foot of the Town Hill. A powder magazine and prison were constructed and a site was chosen at the western end of the Market Square for the erection of a Raadzaal. The latter took some years to complete, but by mid-1840 a church built of local stone and fifteen houses made of local sun-dried brick had been constructed. Eventually all the burghers abandoned their wagons in favour of more comfortable accommodation, though the majority of them remained farmers at heart instead of becoming townsfolk, surviving by the cultivation of their allotments and by pasturing their livestock on townlands. Local agricultural production was almost entirely at a subsistence level, in view of the Republic's isolation and the absence of any significant market incentive to produce a surplus.

Initially no attempt was made to reproduce the taverns, clubs and coffee-houses of Cape Town and Grahamstown, for Pietermaritzburg's rustic founding-fathers felt no sense of deprivation in this regard. There was only a trickle of trade, most of it conducted by itinerant hawkers or *smouse* who had followed in the wake of the Trekkers and maintained their commercial links with the Cape economy. They were able to provide a few groceries, some clothing and a little wine and brandy, but their prices were high, for the overland route to the Cape was tenuous and, in the absence of any bridges or even a recognizable road, the eighty-odd kilometres to Port Natal involved a five-day journey by wagon.

Some farsighted Cape merchant-houses bought land in Pietermaritzburg in the hope of generating business in the new Trekker Republic. The first shop was opened by C. Ortmann, followed by the Zeederberg brothers who established a store on the site later occupied by the Crown Hotel (now Liberty Tavern). The first local industrial enterprise was Kritzinger's mill, erected in 1841 for the purpose of grinding corn and powered by water which was led in furrows from the Swartkop valley. This property, which adjoined what was later to become the grounds of

Transport-riding, the usual means of moving produce before the coming of railways, provided a livelihood for many colonists. Here wagons are moving down the Town Hill towards the City.

Government House, was subsequently sold to C. Visagie. He, as well as Tobias Smuts, was awarded a grant by the Volksraad to mill maize at a fixed rate for all its burghers, but also found time to crush tobacco and make snuff. In 1842 Smuts built his mill on the northern bank of the Msunduze, below its confluence with the Dorpspruit. A few years later the property was acquired by John Vanderplank, the Natal wattle pioneer, who named it Milton. Other early enterprises included Ortmann's shale quarry, which was situated to the east of the town; wagon-, furniture- and cask-making; treefelling in the Karkloof forest to provide the necessary timber; and the specialized hunting of selected species of game such as elephant, hippopotamus and buffalo to provide the ivory and skins which at that time were the only local products for which there was a strong foreign demand.

The commercial hub of Pietermaritzburg and, indeed, of the Republic of Natalia was the Market Square, between the Church of the Vow and the Raadzaal, where visiting burghers halted their wagons alongside those of the *smouse* and the hunter-traders who were *en route* to or from the Port. The formal establishment, in 1843, of a market with a salaried market master provides some indication of the extent of trading activity there by the time of the British annexation. Thereafter the tempo continued to quicken as Pietermaritzburg's status as a political capital was confirmed by the new colonial regime. Many, though not all of the Boers who remained in Natal, settled in the town, whose population was further increased by a small but growing colonial civil service. In addition, from 1843 Pietermaritzburg was also a garrison centre. This not only engendered a greater sense of physical security, which inspired business confidence, but also gave it an additional resident population that made its presence felt in the economic life of the Capital. In the course of seven decades prior to the departure of the garrison in 1914 many local businesses, not all of a respectable nature, benefited from the expenditure of the garrison's pay, while the City as a whole became indebted to various imperial regiments for the part that they played in the construction of watercourses, roads and public buildings. There were many individual members of the garrison who were so enchanted by Pietermaritzburg that, after leaving the army, they became private residents and, in some cases, set up local businesses.

The stimulus provided by the British annexation manifested itself in various ways. In March 1844 Cornelius Moll brought a small printing press from the Cape and, with Charles Etienne Boniface, launched a weekly newspaper *De Natalier*, though unlike the *Natal Witness* established in 1846 by David Dale Buchanan, it did not survive its infancy. The first turf club and theatrical functions were held in 1844, and in 1847 McDonald opened the first coffee-house, followed in 1855 by J.D. Holliday's in Longmarket Street. Other businesses appeared, including hostelries, watchmakers and a few more shops, though the resident population increased very slowly after the departure of those Boers who were not willing to live under the British flag. By January 1849 only 167 of Pietermaritzburg's 486 erven were occupied, of which a mere 44 could be described as being wholly cultivated. Many of the remainder had been handed over by the emigrant Boers to their

In the days before the combustion engine, saddle- and harness-making was an essential industry. The premises of J. Christian in Church Street.

creditors, while others were left fallow under the ownership of absentee speculators who were investing in land all over the Colony in expectation of a massive influx of British immigrants that would enable them to make a handsome profit.

There was indeed a mid-nineteenth-century wave of emigration from Britain to her colonies, as a result of the unemployment and social distress experienced during and immediately after the 'hungry 1840s'. However, Natal was unable to match North America and Australasia in attracting the flood of settlers that was anticipated, and the glowing emigration propaganda published by land speculators and immigration agents was soon counteracted by the reports of early settlers concerning the primitive conditions which still prevailed in the Colony. By 1852 various immigration schemes, including that organized by Joseph Byrne, had increased Natal's white population to only 7 600. Many of the new arrivals lacked the capital necessary to develop the land allotted to them and were unsuited to the rural environment in which they were

The Pietermaritzburg Fire Brigade in 1902.

expected to take root. Even those with previous agricultural experience were soon struggling with unfamiliar farming conditions and undeveloped access to local markets. Large numbers abandoned their land and either left the Colony or opted for a more familiar urban lifestyle in Pietermaritzburg or Durban.

Consequently, although the 1850s did not witness a successful large-scale settlement of British immigrants on the land, there was a noticeable increase in the population and commercial activity of Natal's two main urban centres. In 1854 one-third of the white population lived there, the majority of them in Pietermaritzburg which then had a total population (including blacks) of approximately 2 000 inhabitants. In that year it acquired the status of a city when, with the arrival of J.W. Colenso as Bishop of Natal, it became an episcopal see. This reinforced Pietermaritzburg's claim to be a spiritual centre, a tradition initiated by the erection of the Church of the Vow and perpetuated by the various other religious denominations which subsequently established places of worship there. It ensured for the City a permanence denied other embryonic settlements and thereby consolidated its growing economic importance.

By 1854 there were 300 houses and 265 shops in Pietermaritzburg, most of them 'general stores' which dealt in a variety of goods such as hardware, clothing, boots, draperies and groceries. Some catered specifically for the 'Boer trade', serving the needs of the Transvaal and Free State farmers who visited the City each year during the winter months to sell their 'Dutch produce' to the local stores in exchange for payment half in cash and half in goods. Their wagons were a familiar sight on the Market Square between April and July, until the late 1860s when the discovery of diamonds in the interior induced them to take their business elsewhere. Other newly-established enterprises in Pietermaritzburg included E.R. Dixon's drapery, John Palmer's retail store, and the chemist shops set up by J.W. Akerman and Robert Dawney, all in Church Street. The first hotel, the Crown, had been conducting a brisk trade since opening in 1849 in Church Street, although Commercial Road, where it moved in 1850, was opened to vehicular traffic only in 1851. It was followed by the establishment of several other hostelries, in response to the influx of new arrivals and the steady if unspectacular flow of travellers into the interior. The rural character of the City was nevertheless revealed by the first burgess roll, compiled in 1854, according to which there were more

P. Davis and Sons[5], booksellers, stationers, music sellers, pianoforte dealers and proprietors of the *Natal Witness* in 1895.

The post cart in 1896[6], ready for its journey to Durban.

farmers living in Pietermaritzburg than persons of any other occupation, though storekeepers, merchants and clerks were also fairly prominent. A few bankers were listed on the roll, reflecting the establishment in 1854 of the Colony's first bank, the Natal Bank, which thereafter played an important role in the colonial economy to the benefit both of the Government and of the local business community.

In contrast to the developing commercial sector, during the 1850s there was still very little industrial enterprise in Pietermaritzburg apart from the production of building materials and the manufacture of wagons, furniture and a few household necessities. In the absence of sufficient skilled labour and investment capital, other forms of industry were not attempted until later in the century, while ivory continued to be exported unworked and hides untanned. Few of the Colony's ten water-driven mills were equipped to produce flour and in Pietermaritzburg most of the commercial milling was undertaken for a time by Paul Anstie at his Belvidere Mill, situated below the Victoria Bridge weir on the northern bank of the Msunduze. It was an enterprise which unfortunately went bankrupt within a couple of years, though such occurrences were rarer in the 1850s as the City continued to prosper and expand than during the depression of the 1860s. In 1851 the Pietermaritzburg Agricultural Society and the Natal

A gentleman's oufitter in 1895. John Polglase,
231 Church Street.

Society were established, in 1855 Grey's Hospital was opened, followed in 1858 by the Supreme Court and in 1859 by the Victoria Club. All bore testimony to the increasing sophistication of life in the Capital and enhanced its importance to the Colony as a whole.

Pietermaritzburg's emergence during the second half of the nineteenth century as a major legal and educational centre further enlarged its resident population and generated additional demands for goods and services which gave even more impetus to the growth of its commercial section. More important, economically speaking, was the City's emergence, from the 1850s, as the economic hub of the Natal Midlands farming community. Its proximity to both sweet and sourveld pasturage was undoubtedly an important factor influencing the Boers in their choice of a site for the new republican capital. However, by the end of the century Pietermaritzburg had become the centre of an agricultural region that was characterized not only by cattle-farming but also by the production of wool, most of the Colony's wattle, and the cultivation of maize, barley, millet, oats, beans, potatoes, turnips and other root crops. In addition to serving as an entrepôt for the Midlands, the City's own increasing population provided a ready market for local products, such as beans, potatoes and maize from Richmond, butter from Nottingham Road, and timber cut into planks at the sawmills in the Dargle and Karkloof valleys.

When the increase in commercial activity continued into the 1860s Pietermaritzburg's future as the capital of an expanding colonial economy seemed assured. Exports overberg and overseas continued to gather momentum as Coastlands sugar and Midlands wool production began to indicate a capacity to do more than merely compensate for the declining supply of ivory and skins. The era of the hunter-trader in Natal was drawing to a close but in 1860,

when Prince Alfred visited the Colony, he was fêted by a settler community that was fiercely proud of the imperial connection and confident of its own economic future, though he personally considered the region to be decidedly backward. In Pietermaritzburg he was called upon to lay the foundation stone of a new Town Hall. Sadly, the slab was subsequently fenced off, a tangible reminder of misplaced expectations that were to be long delayed by a shortage of public revenues and a severe depression during the 1860s. Similarly, in 1860 it was confidently assumed that southern Africa's first railway line from the Point to Durban would soon be extended to the Capital but, due to financial and topographical difficulties, the initial survey was not completed until 1867 and the line itself reached Pietermaritzburg only in 1880.

The road link between Natal's two main urban centres was steadily improved, with the help of the military authorities. The frequency with which their commissariat wagons overturned on the rough wagon-track via Sterk Spruit and Uys Doorns prompted them to assist the Surveyor-General, Dr Stanger, in planning a route which avoided the steepest and stoniest gradients. By 1860 the traffic on it was sufficient to justify passenger service in the form of John Dare's horse-drawn omnibus *Perseverance* which carried twelve passengers, ten inside and two on top with the driver. Privately-owned open gigs could hazard the journey in a breathtaking six hours and Dare managed to reduce his transit time from fourteen to an admirable twelve hours, including a lunch-stop at the 'Halfway House' on Johannes Potgieter's farm. However, passengers were obliged to walk on the hilliest sections and, on occasion, even the women had to assist in heaving the vehicle out of muddy patches. High running expenses, aggravated by horse-sickness, obliged Dare to raise his fare from twenty to thirty shillings and forced him out of business within a year. His equipment was taken over by J.W. Welch, who had previously driven mail coaches between London and Worcester. From 1862 he provided a service operating three times a week in each direction but, ably assisted by his two sons, he was soon offering a daily service which began at the Plough Hotel on the Market Square and completed the journey to Durban in eleven hours at a fixed rate of twenty-five shillings. The vehicles in which he subsequently invested, including the *Prince Alfred* and *Cock of the Walk*, carried more passengers than Dare's *Perseverance* and being heavier were less prone to overturn, as Dare's bus once did at the foot of Botha's Hill. In 1868 Welch had to stave off the challenge of a Mr Jessup, who tried to gain a monopoly for his *Good Hope* bus by offering lower fares, but was defeated when his rival threatened to charge even less and to provide passengers with free meals at the popular 'Halfway House' run by his wife and two daughters.

Apart from the improving link with the Port, the roads radiating from Pietermaritzburg were still little more than wagon-tracks. The 'iron tension' bridge constructed across the Msunduze at the entrance to the Capital in 1858 was one of only two in the Colony and was destroyed by a herd of oxen driven across it in 1866. The new Commercial Road nevertheless continued to be used as the main exit to the south-east, but the north-westerly exit up the old Voortrekker road into the interior was unsatisfactory because of the vlei at its foot which often impeded the passage of wagons and necessitated the development of a

THE ECONOMIC DEPRESSION OF THE 1860S

Julie Parle

The early 1860s were years of expansion and development for Pietermaritzburg. It was in this decade that the City underwent the transition from Afrikaner dorp to a bustling English commercial centre. In fact, most of Pietermaritzburg's citizens in the 1860s were involved in trade and commerce rather than production, and it was for this reason that the Pietermaritzburg area was the hardest hit by the depression of the 1860s.

The depression was caused by a number of factors: Natal's inability to produce a staple export product, and the consequent imbalance of imports over exports; the effects of a crisis in British banking circles which led to a contraction of trade and credit throughout the Empire; Natal's reliance on the overberg trade; a general depression throughout southern Africa; and, above all, the unsound financial system in Natal as a whole which relied heavily on an overextended credit system whereby bills and promissory notes had become more common than hard cash.

Although the Colony was apparently prosperous during the early 1860s, with exports and revenue rising, many institutions were actually already heavily in debt. This was true of the Pietermaritzburg Town Council as early as 1863, which in that year nevertheless took over Grey's Hospital from the Government and opened Alexandra Park. When the financial crash came in 1865, its effects were immediate and far-reaching. The large auction firm of Raw and Wilkinson was declared insolvent with debts of over £61 000; the oldest financial institution in Natal, the Natal Fire and Life Assurance Company, also went into liquidation, as did two banks and many other businesses. Trade came to a standstill, all public works were halted and unemployment, amongst both blacks and whites, was widespread. Real poverty was common and Grey's Hospital was used as a Poor House, accommodating several hundred people a year. Crime and drunkenness were rife, and many people left the City to work on the land. The few attempts to deal with the crisis made by the Government and Town Council proved ineffectual, and dissatisfaction with the authorities ran high.

Recovery was slow, but trade was subsequently carried out on sounder principles, credit being carefully restricted. The cessation of the Orange Free State-Basotho War and the discovery of diamonds in the Cape in the late 1860s did not effect an immediate recovery in Natal, but by 1870 trade had revived and Natal was well on the way to recovery from its first major economic crisis.

The 1860s were unfortunate years for the City. In 1866 the original Victoria Bridge (an iron tension bridge across the Msunduze) collapsed when a large herd of oxen was driven over it[8]. The sturdier second Victoria Bridge is shown in 1875[9].

8

9

During the depressed 1860s, the second Dutch Reformed Church stood watch over an often empty Market Square[10] and wagonmakers, such as Merryweather & Sons[11], suffered from the loss of trade.

10

11

more suitable alternative route over Ketelfontein. Natal's first postal service was provided by the military authorities, followed in 1846 by the *Natal Witness Express* which established weekly communication with Durban through the medium of native runners who initially took two days to complete the journey. The advent of the horse-drawn omnibus in 1860 offered a speedier alternative, though the lighter 'postcart' provided an even faster and more efficient service between the Port and the Capital and thence to Newcastle. In 1864 a privately-operated electric telegraph line from Durban to Pietermaritzburg gave the local business community a further means of prompt communication.

These infrastructural improvements were vital to the economic development of Pietermaritzburg but could not prevent the depression of the middle and late 1860s. It was hoped that the increased transit trade generated by the discovery of the Kimberley diamond-field in 1870 would provide the local economy with a much-needed boost. Instead, the immediate effect was to draw population away from the Colony and create, for a time, a serious shortage of manpower. Most families were infected by diamond fever and even the Colonial Secretary, David Erskine, privately confessed to a desire to join the stampede of fortune-seekers. Mrs Colenso recorded 'great excitement over the diamonds', observing to a private correspondent that 'the diamonds are draining off so many of our heads and hands — we hope it will be but a temporary evil ... Our congregation is depleted because of the diamond fields attraction'. However, the discovery of diamonds, and of gold in the eastern Transvaal, did eventually have the desired effect. The increased through-traffic did help to revive the City's commercial sector and, within a few years, at least some former residents were sufficiently affluent to return and either repurchase properties which they had been obliged to sell during the depression or else invest their newly-acquired wealth in new residences and commercial ventures, as well as in agricultural land. In consequence, the 1870s developed into a fairly prosperous decade for Pietermaritzburg, which in 1877 was described by the widely-travelled novelist Anthony Trollope as 'perhaps the best of all South African towns', where one could live as inexpensively as in London.

The discovery of diamonds also had a significant impact upon the City's small but growing black community. There was a heavy demand for labour at the diggings and many blacks returned from them with cash in hand and with a variety of purchased articles, including firearms which were more readily supplied in Kimberley than was the case in Natal. The enterprising *kholwa* (convert) members of the black community, who since the 1850s had been supplying urban markets like Pietermaritzburg with surplus produce for cash, were quick to extend their transport-riding activities inland to the diamond-fields and eventually over other parts of the subcontinent in favourable competition with whites. However, from 1872 J.W. Welch continued to conduct a thriving business with his Royal Mail buses that operated on a weekly basis from Durban through Pietermaritzburg to Kimberley. Commercial links were further strengthened in 1873 when the colonial Government bought the privately-owned telegraph line operating between the Port and the Capital and extended it from there in different directions. The overland link with Cape Town

H.V. Marsh, builders' merchants, one of the City's longest surviving businesses.

via Kokstad and King William's Town was completed in April 1878. By the end of 1879 Pietermaritzburg was also connected by telegraph through Newcastle to Pretoria, and by submarine cable from Durban through Delagoa Bay and Suez to Britain. The railhead from the coast had penetrated only as far inland as Botha's Hill when the Anglo-Zulu War broke out in January of that year.

From September 1878, when the British High Commissioner, Sir Bartle Frere, established his temporary headquarters at Pietermaritzburg in order to plan the provocation and prosecution of war against the Zulu kingdom, the City and its environs enjoyed a minor boom as it began to swell with imperial forces and with local volunteer corps being readied for the impending conflict. While the War lasted it continued to be a hive of commercial activity, only briefly interrupted by the temporary panic which followed the news of the British defeat at Isandlwana. The amount of coin in circulation increased due to expenditure by military personnel *en*

J. Alexander, farriers, a thriving undertaking in the days of horse transport.

route to and from the War zone and by military authorities engaged in provisioning the large Imperial Army with wagons, draught animals, meat, fresh produce and various other necessities. Local suppliers took advantage of the demand, while it lasted, inflating prices so much that the cost of living increased by more than 50 per cent during the first eight months of 1879. Although the collective wealth of the Colony increased and some individuals, primarily in business or transport-riding, benefited enormously from these artificial wartime conditions, both blacks and whites in salaried employment were adversely affected and were soon demanding wage increases.

In 1880 the arrival of the long-awaited railhead from Durban raised expectations of a new and more prolonged era of economic prosperity in Pietermaritzburg. Unfortunately, in the same year the post-war recession began to make itself felt, primarily as a result of the departure of the imperial forces from the region and a consequent decline in the amount of money being spent in the Colony. There was also a decline in the volume of shipping calling in at Durban as more and more vessels switched to the alternative Suez route between Europe and the Far East. To add to Natal's economic woes, there was a slump in the overberg trade following a crisis in the diamond industry and a drop in the exportation of Free State wool caused by severe drought conditions. The outcome of the First Anglo-Boer War (1880/81) aroused

fears in Natal that the Transvaalers might assert their newly regained independence by developing external trade links through Delagoa Bay. Unlike the Anglo-Zulu conflict, the War was too brief to make an impact upon the local economy, other than to disrupt the overberg trade and expose the extent of its value to the Colony. It took some time to restore commercial relations but the effort was worthwhile, for it was the overberg trade with the Transvaal which subsequently pulled Natal out of the economic doldrums when the discovery of the main Witwatersrand goldreef in 1884 initiated another boom and revived the interest of foreign investors in southern Africa.

In Pietermaritzburg there was again a rapid increase in the amount of currency in circulation as the commercial sector benefited from the heavier flow of through-traffic to and from the Transvaal, much of it conveyed by large British and American-type stage coaches that were capable of carrying twelve passengers inside and six on top. The emergence of a rapidly expanding market on the Witwatersrand encouraged Natal's farming community to increase production by rationalizing agricultural methods and bringing more land under the cultivation of those crops for which there was now a ready and growing demand. Investment syndicates were formed in Pietermaritzburg (as elsewhere) to buy up promising claims on the Reef and several gold mining companies were floated to work the properties acquired. Share-dealing became so extensive that a stock exchange was established in the City, as well as a diamond market, and some individuals lost considerable sums of money through inexperience and overspeculation. As had been the case

Central Longmarket Street in the early 20th century[14] with Reid's famous cabinet works to the left.

God and Mammon? The Natal Brewery[15] in upper Longmarket Street across the road from the first St. Mary's Roman Catholic Church.

with the earlier discovery of diamonds, the gold boom prompted an exodus of fortune-seekers from Natal, with many Maritzburgers prominent among the first wave who established the Natal Spruit Camp near the present-day Jeppestown. Some of the wealth subsequently acquired by individuals and by companies based in Pietermaritzburg was invested in the City through the acquisition of property and the erection of new buildings.

The development of a major gold industry in the Transvaal also provided the necessary incentive for the completion of Natal's main railway line into the interior, in order to ensure that the Colony would be able to compete on at least an equal footing with the Cape for the lucrative transit trade in goods and passengers between the Witwatersrand and the coastline. An incidental consequence was that Pietermaritzburg and the harbour at Durban could now both be supplied in bulk from the Klip River coalfield in northern Natal. The ensuing emergence of a large-scale commercial coal industry there had already been anticipated by the establishment in 1887 of a Natal Mines Department, under a Commissioner of Mines based in the colonial Capital. A further consequence of railway extension inland was that Pietermaritzburg lost the importance it had enjoyed since 1880 as the terminus and therefore no longer served as a base for the transport-riders and forwarding agents who acted for those commercial houses engaged in the overberg trade. As the era of the transport-rider and the forwarding agent like that of the hunter-trader became a thing of the past, Pietermaritzburg was no longer the commercial focal-point of Natal and, within the broader context of the colonial economy, declined in importance as the nineteenth century drew to a close. There was a shift in the region's economic centre of gravity away from the Capital towards Durban as the latter expanded more rapidly and as the Colony became increasingly more dependent upon revenues generated by

the transit trade between the Port and Johannesburg. During the 1880s Durban's population began to forge ahead of Pietermaritzburg's and by 1911, when the first Union census was taken, it totalled 89 998 compared to the Capital's 30 555, including all ethnic groups.

Yet Pietermaritzburg did not become a commercial backwater as some of its residents initially feared. It retained an economic significance by virtue of its continued status as the political capital of the Colony. It remained an important spiritual and educational centre adding, in 1910, the Natal University College to its many other institutions of learning. As the seat of the Supreme Court it was still a major legal centre and it continued to be a garrison city. Not least, it remained the economic heart of the Midlands, whose farming community continued to make a valuable contribution to Natal's foreign exchange earnings, particularly through the production of wool and, to a lesser extent, of wattle bark. Despite having to contend with a variety of natural disasters, notably drought, locusts and rinderpest, the farmers of the Natal Midlands enjoyed a rising, if unspectacular level of prosperity during the last three decades of the colonial era and this was shared by the firms in Pietermaritzburg with which they did business.

During that time the City's commercial sector was further enriched by the presence of a growing Indian community which increased from less than a thousand in 1880 to approximately 6 500 in 1903. Despite the hostility of some white traders who opposed the granting of trading licences to Indian competitors, by 1891 there were 141 Indians registered as hawkers in Pietermaritzburg, 60 as storekeepers, 51 as other traders, 16 as goldsmiths, 8 as eatinghouse-keepers and two as cigar-makers, as well as an indeterminate number of basket-, shoe- and dress-makers, blacksmiths, tinsmiths, carpenters, tailors, bookbinders and potters. Following Natal's attainment of

15

responsible government in 1893, the Indian community was subjected to legislation that was intended not only to inhibit its trading activities but also to limit Asiatic immigration into the Colony. It nevertheless continued to grow, establishing a virtual monopoly in catering to the needs of local Indians and indigenous blacks, and attracting an increasing white clientele as well.

Kholwa entrepreneurs experienced similar hostility and found it increasingly difficult to compete with white farmers when they began to apply their superior capital resources to the production of food crops in response to improving market demand. However, the 1890s did witness a new black business initiative in Pieter-maritzburg when rickshaws began to appear in the City's streets. Unlike the familiar horse-drawn cabs and post-carts, they survived the advent of the motor car in Natal — in 1904 the editor of the *Natal Witness*, F. Horace Rose, drove to Durban by car in just five hours. By the late 1890s all of Pietermaritzburg's main thoroughfares had been macadamized and the dim oil lamps introduced as street illumination from 1866 were rapidly being replaced by electric lamps. By the end of 1904 the central streets were also being served by an electric tram system which was extended to Scottsville and to Prestbury in order to promote the sale of townlands in those suburbs. Communications within the City and with the outside world were further strengthened by the introduction of a telephone system, and by 1910 an aerodrome was being planned on the Oribi flats.

During the 1890s and early 1900s there was a marked increase in banking activity in Natal, and in Pietermaritzburg branches of the Standard Bank of South Africa and of the Bank of Africa began to compete for business with the long-established Natal Bank. Their presence helped to promote local industrial enterprise, for although most of the Colony's manufacturing industries were established in Durban it was during the 1890s that the Capital experienced its first taste of industrialization. In 1890 the highly successful Natal

Brewery was established by the appropriately named Frederick Mead, and in 1891 the Natal Tanning Company began producing leather from locally supplied hides treated with tannic acid derived from locally grown wattle bark. Samuel Green erected Natal's first iron ore smelting furnace at Sweetwaters and smelted a ton of ore a day using locally discovered ore deposits and coking coal from northern Natal. After prolonged argument concerning Pietermaritzburg's claim to the Natal Government Railways main workshops, premises were erected there with the assurance that they would henceforth be regarded as the headquarters of the Colony's entire railway system. In 1907 the office of the NGR's general manager was duly moved to the Capital, though most construction and repair work continued to be done in Durban.

In the early 1900s a group of concerned citizens formed the Association for Popularizing Pietermaritzburg in an effort to attract more commerce and industry to the City, but they met with only limited success. Nevertheless, in addition to the enterprises already mentioned, by 1903 Pietermaritzburg boasted several brick, pottery and printing works, as well as mills, bakeries, carriage and wagon manufacturers, and a variety of smaller businesses. Many of these were established during the boom (reminiscent of 1879) that followed the outbreak of the Second Anglo-Boer War in October 1899. While the colonial government suffered a severe loss of customs and railway revenues due to the disruption of the overberg trade, the Capital benefited from a large influx of imperial troops and of refugees from the Transvaal, which substantially increased the local demand for accommodation and for a wide range of consumer goods. Immediately after the War property sales soared as the inflow of immigrants and capital continued. However, between 1903 and 1909 the whole of Southern Africa experienced a prolonged recession from which Pieter-maritzburg did not escape. It was due in large measure to the wartime closure of the Transvaal gold industry and the difficulties encountered in putting it back into full production. In Natal it was due also to the decline in wartime expenditure and to the cessation of imperial funds which had previously flowed into the Colony to pay for the repatriation and settlement of refugees. In Pietermaritzburg several businesses failed as credit was curtailed and merchants were caught with large quantities of cash invested in goods for which there was now only a limited demand. The situation was aggravated by the dumping of surplus military stores onto the local market.

It was not until 1909 that there were some indications of an economic revival, when local consumption again began to exceed available supplies and the Colony recovered from the additional destabilizing blows of East Coast fever in 1904 and the 'Bambatha rebellion' in 1906. When, in 1910, Natal entered Union the misgivings expressed by many of Pietermaritzburg's residents were understandable considering the loss of political status involved. Yet in spite of this and of the declining economic importance which the City had experienced since the mid-1880s, the palisaded camp formed by the Voortrekkers had been transformed out of all recognition and Pietermaritzburg was firmly established as the economic pivot of the Midlands.

The west side of Commercial Road between Church and Pietermaritz Streets in the 1920s. The delivery van of the East Griqualand Meat Supply can be seen in the left foreground; the firm is still trading at the same premises, just to the left of this picture.

16

THE GREAT DEPRESSION AND WHITE UNEMPLOYMENT

David Owen

John Sellers

Not until September 1930 did Pietermaritzburg begin to feel the effects of the Great Depression, which had followed on the collapse of the New York Stock Exchange in October 1929. Yet in responding to the escalating rate of unemployment among all sectors of the City's population, there was a lack of official concern for the plight of any besides the whites, at whom all attempts to alleviate the condition of the jobless were aimed.

Not that the white unemployed considered these efforts sufficient. Disgruntled with the fumbling measures undertaken by the municipality, province and central government, an action group called The Grousers was formed in December 1930. Its intention was to work independently of official organizations and charitable institutions for the alleviation of distress among white families. Soup kitchens and similar services gained it much favourable public support, and by December some 1 000 Grousers were feeding 600 hungry. Within two months The Grousers had done more than anyone else to relieve the effects of unemployment. Despite this undoubted success, February 1931 saw the demise of The Grousers in a series of scandals involving financial irregularities and cases of assault.

The corporation now took up the burden on a more orderly basis, and on 17 February 1931 formed the Central Council for the Relief of Unemployment and Distress to coordinate all relief efforts. Only the 'deserving' unemployed and residents of twelve months' standing were eligible, for there were fears that layabouts might benefit, and that there might be an influx of 'poor whites' from elsewhere. Private citizens were encouraged to offer odd-jobs to the unemployed, but the municipality's chief effort was in the provision of relief work. This scheme was initiated in January 1931 with relief work on the roads, and in 1932 the municipality spent £10 000 on relief capital works, primarily in the Botanic Gardens, Fort Napier and Alexandra Park, where the great rock gardens were built. In September 1931, as a consequence of the Government's insistence at the Pretoria Conference that more 'civilized labour' be employed, the municipality retrenched 20 per cent of its African labourers and gave their jobs to unemployed whites. Those blacks that remained had their salaries reduced to a sum half that paid the whites. Not that the latter were particularly grateful. Relief work, because it entailed manual labour — 'kaffir work' — remained extremely unpopular.

Nevertheless, relief work, and charities like the Mayor's Unemployment Distress Fund, remained necessary for some time. In May 1932 there were 185 registered unemployed white men, a drop from the 200 in February 1931. But by July 1932 the figure had risen to 280, while by November it stood at 506, with 300 on the waiting-list for the despised relief work.

When in December 1932 the Government at last abandoned the Gold Standard, there was a dramatic economic improvement throughout South Africa. This, and the Government's policy of eliminating relief works and providing more permanent employment (in Pietermaritzburg's case particularly in the Roads Department and on the Railways), ensured that by 1934 the problem of white unemployment in Pietermaritzburg had been alleviated.

17

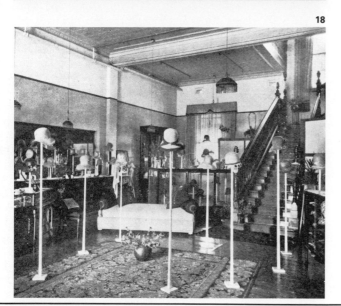

18

19

H. Witney's Clothing Factory at 255 Pietermaritz Street[17]. It is not known whether these employees retained their jobs once the Depression began to bite[19].

Despite difficult economic times, certain businesses, such as Mesdames McFarlanes' 'millinery establishment'[18], and Christie's 'Cafe-de-Luxe'[20], continued to flourish in the 1930s.

20

The Pietermaritzburg market

AND THE TRANSFORMATION OF THE NATAL MIDLANDS IN THE COLONIAL PERIOD

John Lambert

Although the development of Pietermaritzburg was linked to its status as the political capital of the Colony, its growth was also encouraged by its position as the economic hub of the Midlands district of Natal.

This district, comprising the Pietermaritzburg and Umvoti Counties, consists of a wide diversity of climate and terrain, ranging from riverine lowlands to the highlands of the interior. The former are exceedingly steep, broken and rocky with low annual rainfalls and high temperatures. The soils are subject to excessive erosion and are unsuitable for commercial agriculture unless irrigated. In the 1850s most of these lands were set aside as African locations.

The most important of these were the vast Inanda, Umvoti and Tugela locations in the eastern Midlands. Even in the 1850s they were too densely populated to support their occupants. Virtually isolated from the rest of the Colony, there was no inducement for Africans to plant except for

Chief Thetheleku of the Mphumuza in Swartkop Location, who benefited from the proximity of the Pietermaritzburg market.

subsistence purposes and many became migrant labourers in Pietermaritzburg and elsewhere.

There was also a large concentration of Africans in the Upper Umkomaas locations of the south-west Midlands. Although climatic conditions here were not as extreme as in the eastern locations, they too were subject to drought and erosion. In the early decades of British rule they remained isolated from the rest of the Colony and surrounded by Crown Lands.

The rest of the Midlands consists of a mist belt which merges in the north-west into the moist uplands and the highlands of the Drakensberg foothills. With numerous streams and a good annual rainfall, it is rich in water and has deep soils suitable for intensive farming and afforestation. The mist belt stretches from the village of Ixopo (colonial Stuartstown) in the south-west, through Richmond and widens to include most of the Umgeni, Lions River, and New Hanover divisions and includes Greytown in the far east.

The mist belt is particularly suitable for dairy farming but in the nineteenth century lack of transport made it economically unfeasible. Roads throughout the Midlands were little more than tracks, while the railway reached Pietermaritzburg only in 1880. Thus, despite its potential, until the 1880s much of the south-western mist belt in the Ixopo and Upper Umkomaas divisions remained in the hands of the Crown and inhabited by African squatters.

To the east, Umvoti County was inhabited mainly by Afrikaner farmers. Most of their farms had been granted by the Volksraad of the Republic of Natalia, and confirmed by the colonial administration. They were large, each approximately 6 000 acres in extent, and on them pastoralism was the norm. A lungsickness epizootic of 1855 encouraged a switch from cattle to merino sheep and the county became one of the foremost wool-exporting districts in Natal. Generally high temperatures and poor communications discouraged commercially viable cultivation and it has been estimated that as little as five per cent of the average farm was used for crops.

By contrast, the central mist belt had ideal conditions for intensive farming. Its fertility, combined with its proximity to Pietermaritzburg and to the main road from

The Market Square before the building of the City Hall, appropriately dominated by the Market Hall.

130

Durban to the interior, ensured that it would attract white settlers. In the 1850s, the British Government encouraged immigration schemes such as the Byrne in order to introduce close settlements with small allotments similar to those held by tenant farmers in England.

There was considerable mismanagement of the schemes. For example, many of the Byrne settlers were provided with allotments which were too small and often not worth the survey fee. In addition, lack of capital and knowledge on the part of the settlers militated against success. By the 1860s many farms were in the hands of speculators, while the depression of 1865-70 saw many hitherto successful farmers forced to mortgage and then surrender their lands. By the late 1870s, most of Lions River and large pockets of land in the Umgeni division were owned by speculators, foremost among whom was the Natal Land and Colonization Company. Although a few absentee-owned lands were farmed by white tenants, the great majority were occupied by African squatters.

The low price of land in the 1860s, combined with a failure on the part of the agricultural interest to find a lucrative export crop in the Midlands, meant that there was little incentive for merchants in Pietermaritzburg to encourage the development of farming. Important city firms such as Barnes and McFie and even the Natal Bank found it profitable to engage in land speculation, holding on to their lands until it became profitable to sell them while relying in the mean time on rents from squatters to bring in an income.

After the opening of the diamond-fields in the late 1860s, many white farmers or their sons became transport-riders. Although this helped many to recover from the depression, in the short term it continued to depress agriculture. As a result, Pietermaritzburg in the 1870s was dependent on imports for most of its milk, butter and meat supplies.

The stock of a prosperous white farm near Greytown in the Natal Midlands, arrayed before the eye of its proud owner.

The difficulties of supplying the market meant that those farmers who stayed on their land were reluctant to invest in improvements. Until the 1880s, travel to Pietermaritzburg from outlying parts of the Midlands was usually confined to one or two trips a year to dispose of wool or produce. Even farmers closer to the City were faced with similar transport problems. Although Nel's Rust (later Baynesfield) was only 24 kilometres from Pietermaritzburg, it took Joseph Baynes one and a half days to send produce by wagon to the market. The discomfort and inconvenience of making the journey discouraged many farmers' families from attempting it. For example, in 1884 John and Janet King paid their first visit in 34 years to Pietermaritzburg from their Nottingham Road farm, Lynedoch.

The inability of most farmers to provide the Pietermaritzburg market, caused a remarkable flowering of the African homestead economy in the 1850s to 1870s. In pre-colonial times, this economy had made provision for the production of a surplus to meet contingencies such as tribute or drought; now, particularly with the introduction of the plough which made possible the cultivation of a larger acreage, Africans on private lands close to Pietermaritzburg, or in the Swartkop location a few miles west of the City, began cultivating for markets. As early as 1850 they were providing potatoes, maize, sorghum, beans, fruit, forage, timber, and a variety of vegetables for the market, while hawkers were selling fowls, eggs, milk and firewood to homeowners.

In general, Africans were not as hard hit as were Europeans by the depression of the late 1860s, while the growing prosperity of the 1870s increased their ability to compete. Like their white counterparts, many invested in wagons and became transport-riders. A chorus of complaints arose from farmers that they were unable to compete with Africans as '... they are large growers, all have wagons and oxen, and having so few wants can afford to sell and trek at a much cheaper rate than the English'.

23

Africans close to Pietermaritzburg were able to make use of their contributions to the market to enable them to resist the demands of farmers and of the City for labourers. Access to the market also encouraged a growing differentiation within African society. For example, part of the money used by Chief Thetheleku of the Mphumuza in Swartkop to accumulate cattle to enable him to marry his 23 wives, came from access to Pietermaritzburg. He and other Swartkop chiefs such as Hemuhemu and Mzimba were also prepared to innovate to take advantage of the market.

Although chiefly lineages were well placed to obtain the land and labour resources necessary for participation in the market economy, the mission-educated *kholwa*, with their access to white technology, responded particularly well to the needs of the market. *Kholwa* in a village like Edendale were ideally situated to provide Pietermaritzburg with produce. The example of Edendale encouraged land purchases elsewhere and by 1878 Africans in the Midlands owned 17 366 acres.

The prosperity of many Africans, and particularly of the *kholwa*, had a positive effect on the development of Pietermaritzburg and its environs. The missionary James Dalzell estimated that the average homestead bought £2 worth of imported goods annually while an individual *kholwa* purchased £20. The latter were extensive purchasers of European clothing and manufactures and did much to stimulate trade. Shops to supply African needs proliferated — by 1879 there were 40 in Umgeni alone.

By the end of the 1870s, however, the growth of Pietermaritzburg saw demands for a more regular supply of produce than most African suppliers could provide. The influx into the City of colonists and troops during and in the years after the Anglo-Zulu War, and the arrival of the railway in 1880, provided a market which encouraged the subdivision of farms and the proliferation of market gardens. By the 1880s the City was surrounded by a belt of small farms occupied by Europeans or Indians, while the German immigrants of the New Hanover-Wartburg area were also becoming a major source of supply. Butter and eggs, flowers, fruit and vegetables were now all regularly available in the Market Hall, while the railway ensured

Black women offering sugar-cane for sale in the Market Square in 1879.

24

25

Supplying the African market has always been a lucrative element in Pietermaritzburg's economy. Hoes and iron cooking pots can clearly be seen outside this store.

that produce that could not be supplied locally could be sent from Durban.

By 1886 the railway had reached Ladysmith and had opened up the district on either side and stimulated economic growth in towns such as Estcourt and Ladysmith. The Colony's Crown Lands were also opened for sale in 1880 under a ten-year instalment scheme (extended to twenty years in 1889).

Although few branch railways were built in the nineteenth century (by 1898 the only one in the Midlands was to Richmond), the opening up of formerly inaccessible parts of the Midlands by the sale of Crown Lands did much to create a viable white farming community. This encouraged merchants to support the commercialization of agriculture in order to provide the food requirements of the Colony's towns and villages, and of the newly-opened gold-fields of the Witwatersrand. The following years also saw rapid development in Pietermaritzburg, and by 1891 the City had 11 544 inhabitants. Prices were rising and the Market Square became a flourishing business place.

A demand for better produce encouraged more careful cultivation. As a result, farming in Pietermaritzburg County became more scientific and more intensive. On many farms horses replaced oxen in farming while mechanical appliances and the use of chemical fertilizers became commonplace.

Although the growing prosperity of white farmers was most marked in Umgeni and New Hanover, the late nineteenth century saw Upper Umkomaas emerge as an important agricultural district. Many of its farmers responded eagerly to the opportunities offered by the expanding colonial and Johannesburg markets. Prominent amongst these were men like the Nicholson brothers with numerous, prosperous farms; or Joseph Baynes who derived much of his wealth from lucrative contracts to supply the Imperial Garrison at Fort Napier. The latter's Baynesfield estate, comprising 23 418 acres by the end of the century, was the most progressive agricultural enterprise in the Colony.

Families such as these and the Smythes, Methleys and Suttons, were able to accumulate sufficient capital to invest in land and become part of a prosperous land-owning class. Unlike small farmers who continued to face strong competition from African cultivators for markets, these landowners exercised a firm control over their tenantry. This control could be used by a man like Charles

26

P. Henwood, Son, Soutter & Co., 241 Church Street, ironmongers, specializing in agricultural implements.

Smythe to exploit the labour of his tenants; or by Joseph Baynes to encourage his tenants to produce cash crops and to arrange for their sale in Pietermaritzburg.

These families had close links with the City and with the colonial authorities. From their ranks were drawn justices of the peace, members of parliament, and, after 1893, cabinet ministers. It was partly through their influence that the white agricultural interest was able to triumph over its African counterpart by the end of the century.

The rising fortunes of these families were reflected in the growing importance of the Midlands. This was largely tied to two developments. The first resulted from the world-wide dairy revolution of the 1880s. In the following decade pasteurizing, refrigeration. and the centrifugal cream separator were introduced into the Midlands. These encouraged farmers near the railway to import better breeds of cattle for dairy rather than slaughter purposes.

The introduction of wattle was more important than dairy farming for the transformation of the Midlands. By 1887 George Sutton had ascertained the value of black wattle (*Acacia mollissima*) as a tanning agent. The soil and climate of the mist belt were ideal for its cultivation and the 1890s saw the grasslands of the mist belt steadily yield to plantations. The country between Pietermaritzburg and Greytown in particular became one continuous line of plantations.

The commercialization of white agriculture stimulated industrial activity throughout the Midlands, and particularly in Pietermaritzburg which had to cope with the influx of goods from the farms. By the end of the century the City and its environs were able to boast grist and saw mills, wood-turning machines, brick works, jam factories, bone crushers, wattle bark cutting machines, boot and shoe factories, a brewery and an iron foundry.

Few Africans had either the political or the economic advantages to benefit from the changes in agriculture and maize remained their standard crop. As the extension of the railway, however, made the importation of cheap American grain feasible, there was a steady decline in the price African suppliers were able to get. This had serious implications for an economy based on maize, and the resultant undermining of African prosperity did much to weaken their ability to compete with white farmers.

In addition, the late 1880s saw the start of a drought

cycle which resulted in a decrease in the average annual acreage of maize cultivated, and in the crop yield. Yet despite this, rents were steadily rising (in 1888 the average rent paid by Africans in Umgeni was £3.15 per hut compared to a colonial average of £2.10), and in order to raise the cash for rents and taxes Africans were having to increase their sales on the Pietermaritzburg market. This need also forced many to sell sub-standard grain resulting in frequent complaints from the Market Master about inferior, mushy and dirty mealies.

With better quality produce supplied by whites and, increasingly, by Indians, purchasers were reluctant to buy from Africans. The latter accordingly were receiving far lower prices on the City market than they had in the past.

By the late 1880s, Africans not only had to contend with low prices; they were also debarred from selling in the Market Hall (this restriction applied to Indians as well), and were faced with a situation in which the Market Master was deliberately manipulating his charges. The average charge to suppliers was 4,5 per cent of the selling price, but as Africans tended to supply small quantities they were charged a much higher rate, often as high as 31 per cent. The corporation claimed that it was necessary to charge high rates on small supplies in order to keep the average rate at 4,5 per cent, but the African small supplier, who could least afford the charges, was in fact subsidizing the white supplier.

As a result, neither the 'traditionalist' nor the *kholwa* African was finding it easy to raise sufficient money to cover his needs. Most *kholwa* in the vicinity of Pietermaritzburg supplemented their income by wage labour in the City, while an increasing number were leaving agriculture and finding full-time employment as artisans, clerks, teachers and clergymen.

From the homesteads one or two men were being sent out to work for a short period each year. Although the wages offered in Johannesburg acted as a magnet, relatively high wages attracted many to Pietermaritzburg as *togt* or domestic labourers.

Although farmers complained bitterly that their

A homestead in the later 19th century at Elandskop. Many of the men would have been migrant labourers.

labour was being lost to the towns and mines, they seldom offered reasonable wages. In addition, the adoption of intensive market gardening, and of wattle and dairy farming also increased the need for seasonal, well-trained labour and made it uneconomic to continue to allow squatting. Africans were either evicted from farms or, if allowed to remain, had their gardens and grazing lands reduced, and were obliged to agree to labour contracts which severely limited the freedom they had previously enjoyed. The result was a further weakening of the economic independence of the African peasantry, and a growing polarization between farmers and tenants. By the 1890s the frequency of complaints by African tenants of unreasonable demands and ill-treatment reflect a steady deterioration of labour conditions on the Midlands' farms, and also goes far to explain the preference for working in Pietermaritzburg. At the same time the position of Africans was being undermined by a growing influx of Indians into the Midlands. They were providing the Africans with additional competition for the City market and by 1891 the Market Master estimated that Indians were supplying one-third of the produce sold in Pietermaritzburg.

The economic and social balance in the Midlands between whites and blacks finally tilted decisively in favour of the former at the turn of the century. The granting of responsible government in 1893 effectively placed the control of the Colony's Government in the hands of the representatives of the farming community. At their instigation a series of laws was introduced which restricted the Africans' ability to compete with white farmers by limiting their access to land and to the resources available to farmers, and by increasing the burdens of taxation and of labour service.

At the same time, the great rinderpest epizootic of 1897/8, followed by East Coast fever in the early twentieth century, virtually destroyed the ability of the homestead economy to compete for access to the Pietermaritzburg market. By the 1900s there was such a decrease in the amount of maize cultivated by Africans that their sales on the Pietermaritzburg market had plummeted and they were forced to buy much of what they consumed.

By 1910 migrant labour was becoming the norm among Africans in the Midlands and the destruction of black agricultural independence had been assured. Europeans had been protected from agricultural and industrial competition from Africans and the pattern of a dominant and prosperous white landowning class and a dependent black labouring class had been secured in the Midlands.

UNEMPLOYMENT IN PIETERMARITZBURG, 1986

Norman Bromberger

It is apparent to all that unemployment in Pietermaritzburg and in the area which provides its labour force has risen in recent years. While it is difficult to obtain exact estimates of the number of people affected, a survey undertaken in July-August 1986 does so with reasonable precision. This survey covered the borough of Pietermaritzburg (including the coloured and Indian residential areas), Sobantu, Imbali, Ashdown, Edendale and Vulindlela (excluding Mphophomeni township near Midmar Dam). Parts of KwaZulu east of the City, such as Table Mountain, were not covered. Of the estimated population of 376 110 in the area surveyed, 50,2 per cent were in the working-age group: males, 15 to 64 years; females, 15 to 59 years. Of these, some 131 000 to 135 000 were in the labour force, meaning that 34,8 per cent of the population of all ages, or 69,4 per cent of the working-age group, were working or seeking work.

If the unemployed are defined as those within the working-age group who are not working, but who describe themselves as seeking employment, then the number of unemployed stood at 36 353, or 26,9 per cent of the labour force. The percentage rose to 30,9 when whites were excluded. Unemployment varied greatly across the population groups. That among coloured and African groups was in the region of 30 per cent, among whites below 5 per cent, and among Indians at between 15 and 20 per cent.

Unemployment among blacks as a whole grew by 3 to 4 per cent over the twelve months prior to the survey. Indians appear to have suffered the most, unemployment among them having risen by 20 per cent over earlier levels. Sobantu had the lowest unemployment rate (28,7 per cent), and Ashdown the highest (39,3 per cent). Unemployment in Vulindlela (31,9 per cent) was lower than that of the townships, apart from Sobantu.

Unemployment was more severe among women than men. In the black labour force 35,5 per cent of women were unemployed, as opposed to 27,3 per cent of men. The unemployed were mainly the young. About 80 per cent were under 35 years. The age-class with the highest rate of unemployment (31 per cent of the total) was that between 20 and 24 years. It seems 31,6 per cent of unemployed males had never been employed, and 56,5 per cent of the female unemployed were in the same situation. Of those who had been employed before, about one-half had been without a job for periods of up to a year. Among those who had been without work for over a year, 22,3 per cent had been unemployed for over eighteen months. About one quarter of the unemployed in coloured and Indian cases were the household head, and only 11 per cent in the case of Africans.

Of unemployed persons 42,6 per cent had at least some secondary school education. A further 34,2 per cent had reached some level in the higher primary stage of schooling. Only 5,5 per cent had no formal education.

Young unemployed men walk aimlessly down a road in Vulindlela.

28

The coming of the railway to Pietermaritzburg

Bruno Martin

During the 1860s trial surveys were carried out on several routes for a railway to run from Durban to Pietermaritzburg, and for an extension in the direction of Ladysmith and the northern Natal coalfields. It was not before 1873, however, that a detailed survey was undertaken, which delineated much of the route the main railway line ultimately followed. Locating a route through the rugged terrain that would be least costly to build and maintain was indeed no mean achievement for the early railway engineers, who had set about this daunting task without the aid of aerial surveys and accurate topographic maps. Since the engineers could not afford to indulge in elaborate works of civil engineering, a track alignment was devised which twisted and turned in every direction by closely following the curves and contours of the land. The length of the line between Durban and Pietermaritzburg as originally surveyed was to have been 124 km, but when

The inaugural train arrived in Pietermaritzburg on 1 December 1880 to the welcome of an excited crowd.

the route was pegged out for construction several improvements to the alignment reduced the distance to 113 km. Although the first stretch of railway to be built in Natal, that from Durban to the Point, adopted the 4 ft. 8½ in. (1 435 mm) gauge, the advantages of the narrower and more flexible 3 ft. 6 in. (1 067 mm) gauge in the hilly terrain were realized, and this accordingly became the standard of construction.

In 1875 loan funds of £1 200 000 were allocated for the construction of 168 km of railways in Natal, £606 749 of which were earmarked for the Durban-Pietermaritzburg rail link. The customary sod-turning ceremony was held in Durban on New Year's Day, 1876, to initiate work on the railways. Some 4 000 men were employed in the building operation, using picks and shovels to excavate the cuttings and wheelbarrows to remove the soil. The line was opened for traffic in sections as work was completed. On 4 September 1878, a regular train service from Durban to Pinetown was introduced and extended to Botha's Hill on 24 March 1879. A particularly difficult stretch lay in the vicinity of Inchanga, where in addition to the sinuous location work and a short tunnel, nine iron girder bridges were required. The longest bridge was 173 m long and spanned the valley of the Sterkspruit, towering about 27 m above the bed of the stream. Following the completion of the bridges, the railhead was advanced to Camperdown by the beginning of October 1880. Finally, on 21 October, after nearly five years of intense labour, the rails reached Pietermaritzburg station. The construction contractors arranged an impromptu ceremony to mark the arrival of the first train to the City that day. The official opening of the rail link with Durban, which followed on 1 December, was an occasion of great festivity and excitement. From

30

Natal Government Railways

Opening throughout, for Passenger Traffic,

OF THE

MAIN LINE TO PIETERMARITZBURG,

ON

THURSDAY, 2nd DEC., 1880.

The Public is respectfully informed that the Main Line will be op ned throughout for Passenger and Parcel Traffic between

DURBAN AND PIETERMARITZBURG

On Thursday, the 2nd December, 1880.

For the present, the Train Service will be limited to one Daily Train each way,

AS UNDER :—

TO PIETERMARITZBURG :		Fares from Durban to Pietermaritzburg, and vice-versa :—
	P.M.	**SINGLE JOURNEY.**
Durban - - - - dep.	12.20	
Pietermaritzburg - - arr.	6.34	1st Class. 2nd Class. 3rd Class.
TO DURBAN :		17s. 9d. 11s. 9d. 6s.
	NOON.	**RETURN JOURNEY.**
Pietermaritzburg - - dep.	12.0	1st Class. 2nd Class.
Durban - - - - arr.	5.46	26s. 9d. 17s. 9d.

For alterations consequent upon the above and minor changes, see Time Tables exhibited at the Stations.

GOODS & GENERAL TRAFFIC.

The Date of Opening for Goods and General Traffic to Pietermaritzburg will be subsequently announced ; in the meantime, Goods Traffic will continue to be conveyed to and from Camperdown.

REVISED GOODS CLASSIFICATION & SCALE OF RATES.

On 1st December, 1880, a Revised Goods Classification and Scale of Rates applicable generally to all Stations will be brought into operation, and changes will be made in Season Ticket and other Rates. Full particulars of the Rates will be given in printed Notices exhibited at the various Stations.-

DAVID HUNTER, General Manager.

Durban, November, 1880. 817an

In its climb up from the coast, the line to Pietermaritzburg had the characteristics of a mountain railway with its ruling gradient of 1-in-30 and curves of 91 m radius. Although there were no great mountain passes to overcome, the topographical difficulties were nonetheless formidable. After an initial level start, the line gained 73 m in elevation in 45 km and reached its highest point between the Bay of Natal and Pietermaritzburg, 931 m above sea level, near Thornville Junction. It then descended 275 m in 17 km to the bridge over the Msunduze River. It is not surprising that in the 1880s the journey from Pietermaritzburg to Durban took 6¼ hours! The 453 m climb from Pietermaritzburg station to the top of the Town Hill was the most tortuous stretch of railway alignment on the entire Natal Main Line. For the most part this 18 km stretch was benched out of the hillsides on a 1-in-30 grade and abounded with so much curvature that it averaged 250 degrees per kilometre. It follows that trains negotiated this curving alignment at a snail's pace. The maximum safe speed on the best portions of the line was limited to 24 kilometres an hour with severe restrictions for crossing the Inchanga bridges.

Major reconstruction work over the years, necessitated by the demands of the increasingly heavy traffic flow, has resulted in considerable changes to the alignment around Pietermaritzburg and to the route taken to Durban. On 8 July 1906, a 6,4 km-long deviation was opened between Umsindusi and Pietermaritzburg Stations to circumvent the steep climb from the Msunduze bridge to the entrance of the yard. Work on an easier-graded ascent of the Town

The Foxhill viaduct[31]; and the viaduct over the Mkhondeni[32].

31

32

---

the early hours of the morning the city centre was bustling with activity. Business concerns closed their doors for the day and many buildings in Church Street were decorated with banners depicting railway scenes. Shortly after 1.30 p.m., the inaugural train from Durban, conveying a bevy of dignitaries, was given a rousing welcome by a large crowd as it pulled into the station. After the opening ceremony, the dignitaries sat down to a sumptuous luncheon in the engine shed, while the townspeople proceeded to Alexandra Park to celebrate the event. In the evening a giant fireworks display on the Market Square brought the day's festivities to a close.

The arrival of the railway in Pietermaritzburg in 1880 was an important milestone in the construction of the Natal Main Line. This remarkable engineering feat was the first instalment of what subsequently became the chief rail artery to link the port of Durban with the Witwatersrand gold-fields. Work on the 191 km extension to Ladysmith was started in July 1882 and taken into service in June 1886. Construction of the line was continued in 1888 and by April 1891, the railhead had advanced to Charlestown near the Transvaal border. The rail link to Johannesburg was completed in December 1895, and became fully operational on 2 January 1896.

136

Hill was begun in 1912 and entailed building 19 km of new line. Notable engineering features were the double horseshoe curves near Boughton, where the alignment turned to 180 degrees each time to gain altitude, and two tunnels, one of 90 m and another of 831 m. The 6,5 km stretch from Pietermaritzburg Station to Boughton was built as double track and opened on 28 May 1916, together with a short link to the old main line. The main portion of the Town Hill deviation was taken into use for goods traffic only on 6 December 1916. To the south of Pietermaritzburg, a 31 km line linking Pentrich directly to Umlaas Road was opened on 9 January 1919.

A major innovation in motive power in the 1920s was the application of electric traction. The Natal Main Line served as the testbed for the electrification of South Africa's railway system. It was first introduced to the Ladysmith–Mooi River section in 1925 and extended to Pietermaritzburg in April 1926. The first electrically-hauled passenger train arrived in the City on 14 June 1926, and was greeted with hearty cheers and the crash of breaking glass, as the Administrator, George Plowman, broke a bottle of champagne on the leading unit. By 1932, electric traction was extended to Cato Ridge and all the way to Durban in 1936.

The next major development in track relocation in the vicinity of Pietermaritzburg came in 1955 with the construction of the Cedara twin tunnels, each bore measuring 6 023 m. On 17 July 1958 the bore for the 'up' tunnel was holed through. Four months later, the headings of the 'down' tunnel met perfectly. A ceremony was held at the south portals on 28 March 1960, officially to open the tunnels to traffic. The tunnels not only made redundant most of the Town Hill deviation of 1916, but also reduced the length of track required for the ascent from Boughton to Cedara by 6,8 km. The Cedara twin tunnels have the distinction of currently being the longest railway tunnels in Africa.

More recently, the Pentrich–Umlaas Road section was rebuilt on a more direct route in conjunction with the doubling of this part of the Natal Main Line. In addition to the extensive earthworks, five pairs of tunnels, varying in individual length from 161 m to 1 310 m, were driven through the hillsides. The principal engineering work, however, was the construction of the colossal viaducts needed to take the line over the valleys of the Mpushini and Mkhondeni Rivers respectively. Both structures are of the open spandrel type with 30,5 m span semi-circular arches. For bridging the valley of the Foxhill Spruit, a viaduct consisting of fifteen 20 m deck spans was built, which towers 18 m above the houses in the Bisley residential suburb. The new alignment was opened on 5 December 1965, and is 10,4 km shorter than the circuitous line completed in 1919.

Many of the abandoned railbeds around Pietermaritzburg are still clearly visible, although heavily overgrown and eroded in places. In the World's View area, the Upper Linwood Trail makes use of the old railway alignment which includes a short, curved tunnel.

Fig. 1 Natal Main Line: Durban-Pietermaritzburg section.

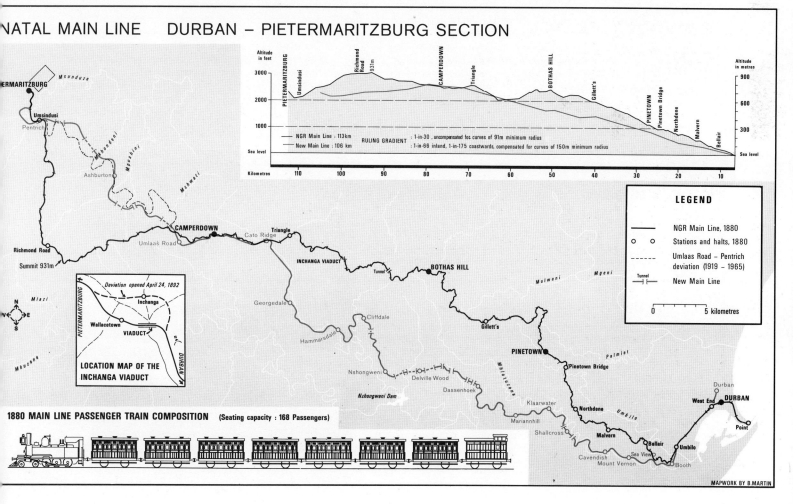

137

FROM RICKSHAWS TO MINIBUS TAXIS

Trevor Wills

In a city of 'magnificent distances', as J. Forsyth Ingram described it, transport has always been important; no more so than in the contemporary metropolis, where the poor especially have long distances to travel daily to and from work.

In 1892 rickshaws were introduced and soon became a ubiquitous feature of the Capital's streets. The rickshaw provided a means of transport for all but the very poor, and a livelihood for many. Ingram records that in 1898 there were 21 official rickshaw ranks, with space for 144 rickshaws (one such rank marker remains today outside St. Mary's hall in Burger Street). Rickshaw sheds were built, as well as barracks for rickshaw pullers. The numbers of rickshaws licensed reached a peak in 1902, when 912 plied their trade (with 8 800 men registered as rickshaw pullers), but declined after the introduction of the tram system in 1904. Still, 305 rickshaws were licensed in 1930, and they did not disappear from city streets until well after the Second World War, being used particularly by less affluent citizens to transport purchases home from the Market Square, or up to the railway station. The pony rickshaw was an early competitor, particularly on the longer routes to and from the suburbs prior to the opening of the tram system.

The electric tram system was opened with great ceremony on 2 November 1904. Initially the trams operated from sheds in Havelock Road down the centre of Church Street as far as Retief Street, and the full length of Commercial Road from Victoria Road, crossing the Msunduze on a specially constructed bridge alongside the Victoria Bridge, and continuing out past the racecourse in the new suburb of Scottsville (where a small loop allowed special race-day trams to await their loads without interrupting the normal service) to its terminus below the NUC grounds. Here the backrests of the seats were flicked over for the return journey. Within a year the system had been extended to the Botanic Gardens and Prestbury, with small branches into Alexandra Park and to the Showgrounds beyond Victoria Road.

The popularity of the tram system was not matched by patronage and after many years of losses the system was finally closed on 17 December 1936. Since 1924 the municipal bus service had been making inroads on the routes and patronage of the trams. The first municipal bus, a 40 hp diesel-electric charabanc seating 20 persons, was acquired in 1913, but was used for sight-seeing trips only around town — the Tramways Manager also being responsible for the Information Bureau. Curiously the Transportation Department was also responsible for the racecourse, leasing the premises to the City Sporting Club.

Bus transport became the pre-eminent mode of travel in the City for those without private transport. Bus services had linked Edendale with the city centre before the first municipal service linked the Town Hall and Roberts Road, and in 1938 an Indian entrepreneur started a service to and from Sobantu Village. The development of Willowton Industrial Estate to the north of the Dorpspruit, although adjacent to Sobantu, shifted the centre of gravity of employment in Pietermaritzburg even further away from the bulk of the labour force who were African and lived south of the City, and increased their reliance on the bus services.

The heavily subsidized bus transport system needed to prop up the 'apartheid city' with the poorest people relegated by legislation to the outer reaches, also led to monopolies developing, and thus to the disappearance of private transport companies serving the metropolis. Today the municipal bus system, and that of the KwaZulu Transport Company (collectively serving the metropolitan area), face a threat from the drop-off in patronage by white commuters, and more seriously from the proliferation of minibus taxis, locally known as 'Kombi' taxis. Spawned by discontent with the inefficiency of existing bus services, and by the spate of bus boycotts which have afflicted many South African cities, these taxis carry, speedily and in relative comfort, some 22 000 passengers a day in the Pietermaritzburg area (municipal statistics). Between 1984 and 1985, the number of minibus taxi operators awarded permits rose from 148 to 186, while estimates of the number of illegal operators on city streets rose from 200 in 1984 to 300 in 1985. The taxis serve not only the African residential areas such as Imbali and Edendale, where the roads and relatively low density of population are generally more suited to the smaller vehicles than buses, but also the Indian and coloured suburbs. Whereas taxi operators used to favour large American cars, they are a rarity today amongst the 12- to 16-seater minibuses. Taxi associations have emerged to bring some sort of order to the flourishing trade, which is highly competitive. At peak periods the 'ranks' used by minibus taxi operators ring with the cries of the usually very youthful drivers' assistants who hang out of doors and windows announcing the route to be followed and exhorting people to climb aboard. Although the upsurge in the taxi trade provides many enterprising individuals with a potentially lucrative occupation, albeit at a high risk, there are signs that the very success of the new industry has attracted those with substantial capital, and, unfortunately, members of the underworld.

Before any other options opened to them, the poor in Pietermaritzburg walked to and from work — and many still do so today. The City has an essentially radial pattern of transport, requiring often that workers travel into the city centre and then out to, for example, the Mkhondeni industrial area. As a consequence a network of footpaths laces the City, providing the shortest routes on foot from residential areas to workplaces.

Minibus taxis dominate the traffic in Longmarket Street.

33

Pietermaritzburg and the railway

William Bizley

There is no better way to approach Pietermaritzburg than on a train from the 'interior' — the term used by our forebears to indicate those dim and distant parts west of the Drakensberg. Like a celestial vision in a Bunyanesque dream, Maritzburg floats and dazzles in one's compartment window, and then is gone as the train buries itself in unhallowed regions, passes through sloughs of despond (one of the tunnels is in fact the longest in the southern hemisphere) until, suddenly, the radiant vision fills the window again, giving stupendous glimpses not only of the City itself but of half of Natal, a mantle of tropical green stretching far beyond Table Mountain. Thereafter the visionary 'Capital' starts to assemble itself as an actual place of brick and mortar, with leafy backyards and genial groves of pawpaws and banana trees. After a good twenty minutes, the descent is complete. With much squealing of brakes and groaning of flanges the 'yards' come into view that bespeak the City's importance as an intersection of branch-line railways.

Those branch lines spell one fact about Pietermaritzburg that — if I may go back to my notion of Ariel's lsland, filled with unseen music — was for many decades obvious more to the ear than the eye. It is a truism that, for the best part of a century, the magical sound of labouring steam-engines was never long out of earshot of the City of Pietermaritzburg. I can give my personal assurance that there was no better way for a schoolboy to fall asleep on a Sunday night in the 'fifties and 'sixties than with the faraway ever-changing voices of double-headed Garratts, tackling the tortuous curves below Claridge with (at a distance, at any rate) a dreamy lullaby effect, able to empty one's mind of the doleful prospect of the coming week. Indeed, for the railway historian, the City's distinction lies in what (to the unconverted) might seem a rather marginal fact. For several decades, Pietermaritzburg was the 'Garratt capital' of the world with a wonderful grimy stud of Garratt locomotives, engines whose single boiler and two sets of driving wheels make together a three-part chassis, and whose performance on the climbs out of Maritzburg was so prolonged and thrilling as to bring photographers from far and wide to witness their efforts.

This somewhat esoteric claim to fame will not, perhaps, convince the general historian, nor would it have been anticipated by those solid worthies of the town who, early in the 1880s, after much flagwaving and festivity, found the iron horse to be firmly established on their landscape. As a matter of fact, the brand new ribbon of steel that coiled up from the coast proved to be not quite the boon and herald of a new era that they had hoped. Personal tax came in as a direct result of the railway, and the NGR (Natal Government Railway — though irreverently nicknamed 'Never Goes Right') was subject to a great deal of satire, if not out-and-out criticism, right from the start.

There was for instance the fairly astounding fact that the first trains knocked off only half an hour from the schedule for Mr Welch's horse-drawn mail service, and since these were the days when railway carriages were of a peculiarly unsprung and boxy variety, there was no guarantee that the ride behind the iron horse would turn out to be the more comfortable experience.

Since the speeds attained on what was called the 'Cape' gauge were never glamorous, we might ask why the first shrieking little tank engines, that weren't allowed to hit it beyond 24 kilometres an hour, couldn't give a better account of themselves. In answering that we have to make one or two points about the topography of Natal, not so obvious to the human eye, but all too obvious to a railway engineer, who has to restrict gradients and curvature to practical limits. African terrain is of such a great scale that it swallows height, with huge horizons that erase the great altitudes that are contained within them. The first night-train from Pietermaritzburg to Ladysmith, which the governor and his wife up there at Government House heard whistling its departure at 11 p.m., back in 1889, would, by the time it reached Hilton, be only 24 m lower than the Gotthard tunnel, and, by Lidgetton, higher than any point on the Gotthard route, or on the mainline from Zurich to Vienna. Of course this really demonstrates that European engineers had far more capital to sink into their broad-gauge routes, so could afford the elaborate tunnelling necessary to avoid bridging the mountains themselves. The Gotthard route, opened in 1882, required a capital outlay of £9 million, whereas the line from Pietermaritzburg to Ladysmith, opened in 1886, and 32 km longer than the Gotthard, had to be built and equipped with £1½ million. So the driver of that first 11 p.m. train to Ladysmith, toiling round the curves above Pietermaritzburg (would he have seen a candlelight glow in the valley as he got towards Hilton?) must have been considerably taxed to get into Ladysmith by 6.30 next morning.

The climb out of the colonial Capital had an epic quality. A journalist who accompanied the inaugural train wrote:

> Halfway up the hill, the serpentine track bewilders one, and then the line strikes towards Kettlefontein. A splendid view of the City is had as the labouring engine skirts ahead of the Zwaartkop Valley. The top of Town Hill is reached at the 12th mile, and looking down in the far away valley, the passenger begins to wonder what manner of invention is this that can overcome such obstacles and yet have strength enough to go further...

The topography of Natal helps to explain, then, why Mr Welch's horse cart that disappeared down Polly Shortt's every day to Durban had only 54 miles ahead of it, while the new line up from Durban was in excess of 70 miles.

But this *apologia* for the railway explains only half the case. The other half lies in the principle of what I call railway amnesia, the principle defined by one Mr Pinson in the Legislative Council of 1888 (by which time parliamentary debates had become a major entertainment for the citizenry of Pietermaritzburg). Mr Pinson complained that:

> [the] time and expenditure in wages and coal lost in waiting at stations must be very considerable indeed. There is no necessity for it ... There is not a single thing done, and nothing to stop for, and you look out, and wonder what is the meaning of it.

It is a mystery that lies intact to this day, but in the first decades of the NGR it was the source of much satire, as we can soon discover in the colonial newspapers. Thus for instance the 'Man in the Moon', writing for the *Natal Mercury* in July 1884:

> *Scene: 1st Class Carriage between Durban and Maritzburg.*
> *Characters: A visitor to the colony and a railway manager.*
> *Visitor*: Does the management of this concern allow passengers to give them advice, if it is rendered in a respectful manner?
> *Manager*: The Management is very glad to receive suggestions for the improvement of the railway.
> *Visitor*: Well, it occurs to me it would be as well to detach the cow-catcher from the front of the engine, and hitch it to the rear of the train, for you see, we are not liable to overtake a cow: but what is to prevent a cow trotting up to the rear and butting us off the track.
> *(Collapse of Manager.)*

When it was discovered that the several viaducts on the new line showed a tendency not to maintain their rigidity, the railway debates drew even greater audiences. Maritzburgers revelled in such picturesque news as that provided by Mr Binns, Member for Victoria County, who said that the bridges on the main line were 'standing in every position but the right one, and altogether presenting a most miserable spectacle'. One found 'some in plasters, the next in splints, and the next in bandages'. No wonder a *Natal Witness* for June 1884 asks darkly: 'Who are "the women" in the railway scandal? Answer: Misconstruction and Mismanagement'.

One *Witness* editorial illustrates the general enjoyment of Natal's own railway crisis when it reports 'the crowded condition of the galleries. It is seldom nowadays that our Senators reach the small hours...' Amongst those who relished the atmosphere were, it appears, 'boys too young to understand anything... some alone, and some brought by thoughtless parents'. It seems that the Huck Finns and Tom Sawyers of Pietermaritzburg found the railway debate a choice venue for illicit breakaways.

One rapidly discovers, in these debates, how much rhetorical mileage there was to be had from the nice fact that Pietermaritzburg was, in colonial parlance, the 'City' and Durban merely the 'Town' (or, at best, the 'Port'). It was, therefore, an undoubted blow to the 'City's' pride that the chief colonial civil servant, the General Manager of Railways, held sway and ruled his kingdom of iron from the town of Durban. Could Maritzburg get the mighty Sir David Hunter to entertain the notion of residence in 'the City'? It tried to do so by the erection, in the Capital, of a new NGR Engineers' Office, a building that would stand, in due course, next to the Natal Museum, and which indeed presently serves as the SAP central charge office. But this building was originally intended for grander personages than engineers; it was conceived as a sort of Maritzburg blandishment to bring the General Manager up to the 'City', and break him in to the notion of actually being directed by the Government.

Hence some undisguised faction fighting in the House. The eloquent member for Pietermaritzburg City (Mr O'Meara) asked the Minister of Railways:

> Now I would like my honourable friend to tell us what is lost in Durban by the general manager not residing there. These Durban gentlemen pay none of the railway carriage. Not a single merchant in Durban pays one single sixpence in railway rates... I tell these gentlemen they pay nothing at all, they simply pay upon what they use in their own houses for their own consumption. What did we find Sir David Hunter doing (and this is why I want the general manager removed from that unholy influence with which Sir David Hunter is surrounded in the town of Durban). We find him carrying sugar for the planters for 15 years and giving them threepence a ton for sending it to the railway to carry. Is that a management this country is prepared to put up with? No sir, I hold that the proper place for the General Manager is in this city, where he can be controlled by the city...

To further protests from 'the Port', the City's MP asked:

> I want to know who is running this country. Are these few gentlemen from Durban going to govern the general manager of railways? Now we have had some experience of this great gentleman, Sir David Hunter, that we hear so much about... I have the greatest respect for Sir David Hunter as a private gentleman, but as a public servant that gentleman ought to have been pensioned off ten years ago or he ought to have been brought to Maritzburg and controlled by the Government of the day.

The unsteady Inchanga viaduct, *c*.1886.

34

Alas, the 'unholy influence' proved more durable than Mr O'Meara's eloquence, and the General Manager did not add to the various glories of his office that of residence in Pietermaritzburg.

Another 'hardy annual' amongst 1890s railway debates concerned the 'Extension to Howick Railway Bill'. Should a spur be built off the main line at Merrivale to take in Howick, especially now that the Falls had earned themselves a reputation as inland Natal's chief natural spectacle? (The Drakensberg became generally accessible only with the building of the Winterton branch in the 1900s.) We must remember that, in the last years of the nineteenth century, the Thomas Cook euphoria took Kodak-wielding imperialists to the Rockies and the Pyramids, and now it had even reached the sleepier quarters of the Southern Hemisphere. The Colonial Secretary argued that a line to the Falls was necessitated since 'tourists from Great Britain and other countries are coming to South Africa more and more every year, and we want to encourage traffic of that kind'. But, in a colonial parliament, to move solid Victorians to any sort of action you had to enlist a moral principle rather than a pleasure principle, and this Mr T. Kirkman, member for Alexander County, was well able to do. In his vocabulary, the proposed four miles of branch-line took on a neo-Kantian hue. 'I have looked upon this railway,' said Mr Kirkman, 'and still look upon it, as an educational railway'. This certainly sounds better than a 'tourist' railway, and in fact our nineteenth-century idealist gives us one of the earliest hints that, by now, 'industria' had enveloped the colonial Capital. The new branch to the Falls would take city-dwellers — so Mr Kirkman claimed:

> ... away from this humdrum place in which there is nothing whatever on which to spend their time or to interest them. ('Oh, oh' from several Hon. members, and 'Shame' from Mr Tatham.)

Apparently Mr Kirkman's colleagues were reluctant to discover in Pietermaritzburg a sort of tropical Leeds, but their dissension only spurred him on further:

> The railway will enable people to see something more than public houses ... It will lead to the non-necessity for such places as inebriate retreats ...

(At which point, of course, he veritably echoes Thomas Cook, whose tourists were sent off to the ends of the Empire with much 'prohibitionary' enthusiasm.) But was Pietermaritzburg of the 1890s so squalid that a railway line should be built for its moral health? Mr Kirkman thought so:

> Young men and others ... should have an opportunity of seeing something other than the walls of churches, something which will appeal to them far more eloquently from nature, from the running water and from anything that appeals to one's inner senses, something above the life of a city like this.

One could hardly deny that Howick would provide the spiritually starved with the sight of running water. But Mr Kirkman's radical secularism was too much for a colonial assembly, and to everyone's relief Mr Hulett quickly moved closure.

In some smoky and steely heaven, which blends incipient Wordsworthianism with the 'Cape' 3 ft. 6 in.

gauge, I hope that I survive to assure a spectral Mr Kirkman that no one derived more joy from his 'educational' picnic line (it was completed, eventually, in 1911) than I did. But of course the motive power — by the time the ride to Howick became my chief means to witness 'running water' as a spiritual refreshment — was electricity, and I must now observe another historical fact that will seem of relevance only to the most 'smitten' sort of historian. Maritzburg was, for nearly two decades, the chief town on the longest electrified line in the world. Even the development of the Garratt locomotive could not defer the decision, in the early 1920s, to surmount the extraordinary difficulties of the Natal route by using the new-fangled traction that was now proving itself in the Alps and the Rockies.

The result was the 'units'! This was the Natal nomenclature for the excellent 1 200 hp Metro-Cammell electric engines that, single or in multiple, worked the chief arterial line of the Union, and then the Republic, of South Africa. The 'units', (which word rather imitates their characteristic grinding whine) did not generate their power on board, and so were not, by Stephenson's principles, 'locomotives'. I have to confess — as a well-worn steam-lover — that, in the conditions of sub-tropical railway travel, one did fairly gasp with relief when, after a long grimy day behind steam on any of the branches, one at last boarded a mainline train behind the units.

In fact, if I may finish on an outrageously personal note, let me take you to Maritzburg station in the early fifties, with the mail train for Johannesburg about to arrive just after 7.00 p.m. First came the sound alone, the exhilarating high whine of the units, and then, peering round the curve, a single yellowish headlamp. Then, in a nice exhibition of railway dramatics, the train spent an aeon creaking slowly into the station, since Maritzburg was a city so portentously important that the carriage wheels must be checked here all along the train. When it was at last 'landed' one took up one's position beneath the driver's cab, to savour the panting and spluttering and coughing of the hydraulics, together with various clatter-clatter interludes as the vacuum was restored.

And then, some acrobatics of shunting in the eight-minute wait. The Maritzburg situation was a veritable feast, especially in winter. The units unlatched and hurried off, making their whining and throttle-belching noises, to pick up a steam heater truck. Quickly one scampered down the platform to where a steam shunt was adding a coach or two from East Griqualand at the back of the 'mail'.

Then a scamper back to the units for take-off — as thrilling with those first-generation units as with steam engines. Two bells and a green light, and then — none of the complacent gliding of their modern successors. It could take up to five explosive punches on the driver's control before the two units would at last move the long brown train behind them. If the driver got to the fifth slot on his control, he would have used up all the coupling slack that he had carefully prepared when the train first got in. So the 'mail' would leave with a great heave felt right down the train, persuading the anti-steam faction, perhaps, that the electrics weren't such heaven-sent creatures after all.

Last sight of the mail train would be a string of lights 300 m above Pietermaritzburg, whining gloriously into the night ...

African reaction to the beer halls

Paula du Plooy

In 1960, fifty-one years after beer halls were established in Pietermaritzburg in 1909, black women armed with sticks marched into them and forced the male customers to leave. The women then picketed the beer halls so effectively that for days the men were too scared to return.

Beer halls have been both resented and frequented by the urban Africans. They perceive them as instruments of their poverty and symbols of government oppression, yet recognize that they meet certain social and recreational needs.

Long before the arrival of the whites, the brewing and drinking of beer had been an integral part of African social life in Natal. A wide variety of beers had been produced, *utshwala* being the generic name given to them. This thick reddish-grey brew was usually made from sorghum, which is laid between damp mats until it begins to sprout. The grain is then dried, ground to a fine powder, fermented and boiled. The result is, in the words of the South African Native Races Committee, 'a beverage hardly as alcoholic as the lightest European-beer and extremely wholesome'.

Besides being an essential element of diet, beer also played a significant role in the community life of blacks. Beer was a common means of exchange or payment for services rendered. It was used to sweeten social intercourse and was, moreover, vital to religious rituals of the community.

After colonization, Africans began increasingly to move from the rural areas to cities like Pietermaritzburg, where traditional ties were broken under European influence. Africans began to consume European spirituous liquor and to sell their traditional beer, a thing they had never done before. They also began to add spirits to their beer, making it much more potent. The Natal Government, in response to pressure from whites, prohibited the sale of European liquor to all Africans while at the same time gradually increasing restrictions on African production and sale of *utshwala* in the cities. After 1908 Africans in urban areas were no longer allowed to brew their beer domestically. Instead, city councils were permitted either to monopolize the manufacture or sale of beer or to provide licences to individuals to brew and sell it. Pietermaritzburg, along with Durban, decided on the former system.

The Pietermaritzburg City Council adopted the monopoly system ostensibly to control African consumption of alcohol and to curb the drunkenness and crime apparently so prevalent in the borough at that time. While Council was determined to protect its white citizens from the ravages of African drunkenness, it was also influenced by the knowledge that a great deal of profit could be made out of the monopoly system, and that this profit could be used to finance the increasing costs of African administration in the borough. There was also an element of paternalism in the Council's decision, for by establishing municipal controlled beer halls, African beer-drinkers were to be protected from unscrupulous illicit liquor dealers and to be provided with 'good and wholesome' beer in 'clean and hygienic' conditions.

On 14 February 1909 a brewery and four beer halls were opened in the City. The beer halls were established in areas where large numbers of Africans lived or worked, such as outside the Togt (day labourers) Barracks and near the Power Station. Soon afterwards a fifth beer hall was opened in Commercial Road for domestic servants and other Africans who lived in town.

The establishment of beer halls was resented by the African community, which initially indicated this by boycotting them. Amongst their reasons were the exclusion of women, the inferior quality of beer on sale and the prohibition on the brewing of beer at home for domestic consumption. Yet according to the Mayor's Report of 1909, the boycott did not last long and beer halls soon became 'fairly popular'.

Beer halls were forbidding, cold, concrete establishments, but the people who attended them made them warm. Initially Pietermaritzburg beer halls were just what their name implies — halls where beer was sold. Within a year, however, the beer halls on Commercial Road and outside the Togt Barracks had eating rooms attached to them. African entrepreneurs could hire a table and sell food to all who cared to eat there. This was the first step in the evolution of beer halls into social, recreational and entrepreneurial centres for Africans in the borough.

This process took place over several decades, and culminated in 1934 in the building of a model beer hall in Berg Street. Ever since the establishment of beer halls, African traders have used the area outside to sell their wares. Inside the halls, the City Council provided stalls, at a price, to would-be entrepreneurs. This opportunity to do business legally attracted many Africans to the halls and still does today. Among goods traditionally sold are medicines, snuff, groceries and trinkets.

Besides selling their wares, Africans also used the beer halls for wedding receptions, dances and meetings. These were all monitored by the white supervisor of the beer halls who would not allow any African political activists to use the halls as meeting places.

In their leisure time, which was limited, African labourers nevertheless found the opportunity to drink copious amounts of beer, as is borne out by the large profits made from its sale. It was in the 1950s though, when a new brewery was established and the quality of beer improved, that beer sales really soared. In 1955 beer worth £61 758 was sold. After the prohibition of African consumption of European liquor was lifted in 1961, the Council decided that whites could also drink African beer, but not in the beer halls. The beer was sold in containers in liquor stores. Africans quickly began buying this beer in huge quantities.

While a great many Africans spent as much time as they could in the beer halls, the beer halls were never totally accepted by the community. Different sectors of the African community had different reasons for disapproving of them. The educated African élite felt uncomfortable in the beer halls which were crowded, noisy and often dangerous as other customers became drunk and unruly. There was no place for the élite to conduct dignified conferences or enjoy quiet conversations. It appears that the Pietermaritzburg City Council was aware that the beer hall system failed to meet the needs of the African élite, and tried to rectify the situation by providing facilities such as rest rooms and special accommodation for the sole use of educated Africans. But the innovation failed to achieve its purpose.

The reluctance of 'respectable' Africans to enter the beer halls was not only based on class prejudices. Many regarded the whole practice of drinking *utshwala* with abhorrence, and recommended that the consumption of all forms of intoxicating liquor should be prohibited. It was claimed that beer halls were responsible for 'ruining our people' and lowering moral and social standards.

Council's use of the beer hall profits served to increase criticism by educated Africans. They were aware that the sale of *utshwala* enabled the Council to administer Africans without using much money from the general revenue account. Conscious that they were thus paying for their own administration, Africans deplored the lack of consultation between the authorities and themselves. As Mr Selby Msimang told the 1941–2 Native Affairs Commission, it was unfair that 'Europeans know how much they get and how it is used but natives don't'. The Council's protestations that beer hall profits were used to provide essential services for the African community did not diminish criticism.

The wives and daughters of African labourers also disapproved of the beer halls, although their reasons for doing so differed from those of the educated African élite. Economic conditions in the first decades of the twentieth century forced a great many women into the urban areas where they suffered under the triple discrimination of race, class and sex. Work was hard to come by and wages usually only a third of what men received. Women, who had to manage the home as well, struggled to make ends meet. What made the struggle particularly heartbreaking was that their husbands and sons often squandered what little money they had in the beer halls. The Council's prohibition of the presence of women in the beer halls increased female animosity. Unlike their menfolk, they had no time or opportunity for relaxation.

African women made public their discontent with this unjust situation in 1929 and again in 1960, when they forced men to boycott the beer halls, demanding that these be closed. They believed that if municipal beer halls were shut down, the men would spend more time at home and that there would be more money for food.

While the boycotts and violence of 1929 and 1960 received a great deal of publicity, they were not the only form in which women protested against the beer hall system. Shebeens were the female symbol of defiance in a male-dominated society. The origins of shebeens lie in the traditional gathering of men at the homestead to drink *utshwala* brewed by women. This tradition changed in the urban environment. Prior to 1908 great confusion existed regarding the liquor laws and African labourers were unsure of how to obtain beer legally. To lessen their men's thirst, women brewed *utshwala* in the homestead and transported it into town by railway. *Utshwala* was then sold by the male members of the family.

When women were forced into the cities they took over the selling of *utshwala*. Shackled by unemployment,

women brewed *utshwala* in their backyards for sale to male customers in an effort to earn enough money to live. The name given to women who ran such establishments was, and still is, 'shebeen queens'. It was often stated that inadequate wages was the reason for the proliferation of shebeen queens, but this cannot be totally accepted. The better quality beer brewed by these women and the fact that it was far more potent than Council beer also contributed to the enormous popularity of shebeens. Also contributing to their popularity was the fact that they offered African labourers the opportunity to relax away from the constant vigilance of European supervisors and away from the stabbings, beatings and pick-pockets of the beer halls.

Nevertheless, the fact that beer halls up to 1939 were solely the retreat of men, and that the culture that developed there was dominated by masculine activity, possibly accounts for their abiding popularity amongst African labourers. A more feasible explanation concerns the siting of the beer halls. The Council established them not only where large numbers of African labourers were gathered, but also where they had to pass as they travelled to and from work. After an arduous day's work the temptation to step into a beer hall and have a drink proved hard to resist. The shortage of alternative recreational facilities in the City was another contributing factor.

While the Council maintained that the beer hall system was essentially voluntary it can be regarded as coercive. It intruded directly into the lives of urban Africans, if only because it monopolized the sale of their traditional beverage and provided a few other forms of amusement. Even so Africans were quickly able to modify and adapt the beer halls to fit into their lifestyles.

Women selling food in a Pietermaritzburg beer hall.

Industrialization 1838–1987

Carlo Torino

The Boers, who had left the Cape Colony and founded Pietermaritzburg as their capital in 1838, developed the locality largely as an agricultural village. The earliest recorded industrial activity in the area was the milling of grain, grown both on the townlands and the surrounding farms. In 1845, when Natal became a British Colony, many of the original Voortrekkers retraced their steps over the Drakensberg. In the late 1840s a new element was introduced in the form of British immigration schemes. Many of those settlers who were unable to make a success of farming gravitated to Pietermaritzburg. Amongst their numbers were many craftsmen and traders, who had been encouraged to emigrate, partly because of a depression in the textile industry in Britain. Consequently in addition to the farming community, there were now also blacksmiths, tailors, 'straw hat and bonnet manufactures' and saddlers in the City. These pioneers prepared the ground for future industrialization.

One of the first industries of importance was the wagon and coach building firm of Merryweather's, established in 1854. Wagon-building was a fundamental industry throughout the major part of the nineteenth century, when the ox-wagon represented the dominant means of freight transport. Between 1862 and 1880, Pietermaritzburg had up to 12 wagon manufacturing companies. During this time there was also a rapid escalation in the number of related enterprises, such as blacksmiths, farriers and cycle works.

The development of railway transportation in Natal served as a key factor in the advancement of its commercial and industrial activities. By 1895 the railway system had been extended to the Transvaal, and the substitution of cheaper Natal coal for the previously imported coal provided an incentive for businesses to use the railways. One local concern which took advantage of this expansion of the market was Reid's Cabinet Works. Established in 1880, this company supplied all types of furniture to clients in the inland states and beyond. Hay's Biscuit Factory, set up in 1888, was another well-known concern which took advantage of these communication improvements, and its products were dispatched as far afield as Rhodesia.

A major development was the establishment in 1890 of the Natal Brewery in Pietermaritzburg. This firm distributed special barley seed to farmers in the surrounding grain-growing districts for production into malting barley. The addition by the late 1890s of a boot and shoe factory, a cannery, and several brickworks and printing works gave Pietermaritzburg a more diverse industrial structure.

The period before the Anglo-Boer War turned out to be a prematurely important phase in the City's evolving economy. After the War, a general business depression set in. In response to this economic downturn, the City Council set up a Commission in December 1909 to investigate the promotion of industry. The Commission was composed of equal numbers of councillors and businessmen, and met chiefly to discuss proposals put forward by the local Chamber of Commerce. One of these proposals requested Council to appoint a Commissioner to interview overseas industrialists, with a view to attracting their investment to Pietermaritzburg. Nothing much happened in the wake of Council's first industrial investigation committee, but it did establish a precedent for future political intervention in the local economy.

Although the Council of the time was not averse to further industrial growth, it was apparently more orientated to maintaining Pietermaritzburg as an educational and administrative centre. The City's businessmen, however, were keen to consolidate their power as an interest group. In 1910, W. J. Laite, the General Secretary of the South African Manufacturing Association, arrived from Cape Town to address local industrialists. His efforts culminated in the formation of a Pietermaritzburg branch — the antecedent of the local Chamber of Industries.

From water power to electricity. Visagie's mill in upper Church Street, *c.*1844[(36)]; and Pietermaritzburg's power station, 1904[(37)].

Wagon-building was a major industry in the City throughout the 19th century.

The outbreak of the First World War resulted in the immediate departure of soldiers and a concomitant decline in business for the City's commercial outlets. However, because it placed a considerable premium on shipping space, the War also provided the necessary stimulus to implement a wattle extraction process which had been discovered in Pietermaritzburg in 1913. Previously, the green bark had been exported to extract manufacturing firms in England and Germany, but difficulties in marketing the wattle bark overseas were already being experienced by local wattle growers. In 1915, the Natal Tanning Extract Company erected a factory in Pietermaritzburg and South Africa's first solid wattle extract business was launched when operations commenced the following year.

After the War, the Council appointed a sub-committee to review Pietermaritzburg's industrial development. As a consequence, it offered special electricity and water discounts to new industries for the first five years. Although the conflict over the nature of the City's identity persisted, the Council was keen to foster industry. Pietermaritzburg's industrial potential was obvious: the City possessed adequate land for industrial expansion; it had electricity and water supplies as well as labour resources; and it had a less corrosive atmosphere than the coastal areas; as well as a transport infrastructure for access to markets or raw materials.

In 1928 the City Council gave renewed attention to the question of offering further inducements to industrialists. Another Industries Sub-committee was appointed. Members of the Natal Chamber of Industries (a body which had close links with the Pietermaritzburg branch) were invited to participate directly in the proceedings. In addition to the existing special water and electricity rates, Council was now also prepared to offer land at a nominal fee to prospective industrialists.

Although industrial investment in the City was hailed as beneficial to all sections of the population, blacks still experienced disproportionate hardships. In 1920 for example, the Municipality's Medical Officer of Health noted the existence of slums in the City. In 1922, he reported on the appalling housing crisis faced by Africans and Indians. By 1926, when the Municipality's first housing project for whites was completed, conditions for 'non-whites' remained substantially unaltered. Response to unemployment also depended on race. Relief Works were initiated for unemployed whites in April 1922, but little or nothing was done for blacks out of work. Only in 1933, two years after the commencement of the Great Depression, were members of other race groups included in the scheme. This state of affairs was symptomatic of a racially exclusive City Council.

In December 1933 a turning point was reached in the City Council's efforts to promote industry. A separate Industries Committee of the Council was created, specifically to encourage the launching of new ventures in the City. It consisted of three members of the City Council, together with a representative from the Chamber of Industries, Commerce, and one from the Publicity Association. In contrast to the City Council's vacillation in 1910, this Committee decided almost immediately to have a brochure produced publicizing Pietermaritzburg as *A City of Industrial Opportunity*. Despite these efforts, there was no marked upsurge in industrialization.

Pietermaritzburg was not stimulated by a war economy during the Second World War, and the wave of post-war industrialization that surged through the rest of the country completely bypassed the City. Lack of material and a general increase in prices meant that new water and electricity services could not be supplied, and also that the tarring of roads had to be suspended. Though faced with these restrictive conditions, and the accompanying deterioration of infrastructure, the civic authorities contemplated the future with undaunted spirits. In 1941, a new textile factory commenced operations, and negotiations for further ventures were under way.

Some still believed that Pietermaritzburg would most likely achieve success as an agricultural, educational and residential centre. This viewpoint probably contributed to the City's 'Sleepy Hollow' image, but it must also be seen as a rational response by the City's ratepaying public. Long before industrialists could be urged to set up new factories in the City, considerable funds were required to plan and lay out new industrial sites, and to cover the advertising costs.

In 1943 the new Mayor, Mrs E.E.M. Russell, was brought to office, backed by her Scottsville ratepayers, who had the majority on the City Council. This group was opposed to industrialization, and tended to perceive Pietermaritzburg as a place for civil servants, students and farmers. In September 1946, however, when Mrs Russell was seeking re-election as mayor, the Mkhondeni and

THE ROYAL SHOW

Ruth Gordon

In 1851 the Natal Society organized the first agricultural show in the City, held on vacant land on what is now the Town Gardens. From 1854 the Market Square became the venue, until in 1886 the site of what was later to be the Drill Hall was secured. When the government bought the site in 1901, the show moved to its permanent home at the bottom of the Town Hill. In 1904 King Edward VII granted it the title of The Royal Agricultural Society of Natal.

The Royal Show has, from its beginning, given a sense of direction to the farming community in Natal and offered incentives in the form of prizes and trophies. Increasingly, it is also becoming a showcase for local industry. Since its inception in 1923 the Arts and Crafts section has grown enormously, while arena events, especially equestrian, have always featured prominently.

The Royal Show today is firmly established in popularity, and in 1988 no less than 221 974 people visited it.

The Royal Show highlights the importance of agriculture and related industries in the economy of the Natal Midlands. This picture shows a cattle parade in 1986.

Fig. 2 The City's industrial areas in 1987.

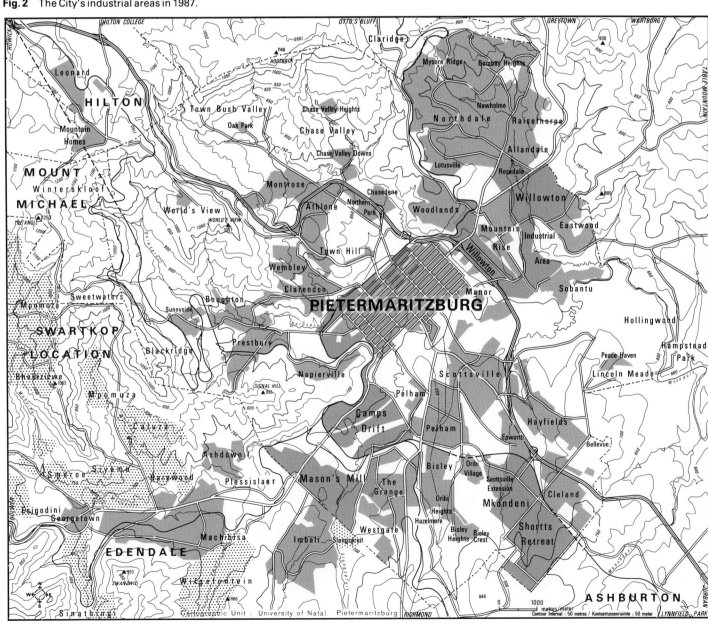

Mason's Mill areas were made available to industry (possibly as part of an election deal) and later developed by Rhodesian Cables (now Scottish Cables), Alcan Aluminium (now Huletts Aluminium) and Rexo Manufacturing Company.

With Mrs Russell firmly as Mayor in 1947, further industrial expansion in the Mkhondeni and surrounding areas was halted, with one important exception. This was the case of Hay Paddock, the site of the present-day Hayfields residential area, an army camp during the War. The City Council purchased the army's buildings, and let them out to ex-soldiers and immigrants, who turned the area into the fountainhead of various small industries and businesses. Some barracks were also converted into residential flats to alleviate the acute housing shortage.

With the election of Allan Hirst as Mayor in 1948, the Council made a more concerted effort to promote further industry. There were several reasons for this shift in attitude. Pietermaritzburg's industrial progress did not match the extraordinary development that had occurred in other areas of the country after the War, and it was becoming clear to the City Council that without a greater range of commercial and industrial development, the local economy would stagnate. Accompanying this economic decline in the late 1950s, was a wave of black peri-urban population growth in the Edendale-Vulindlela area to the west of the City. The Council was forced to acknowledge that genuine grievances such as unemployment and overcrowding did exist. At the same time, Pietermaritzburg's white urban population structure was adversely affected by an increasing tendency for younger people to advance their careers by moving to the larger cities.

The Council's initiative proved successful for two main reasons. Firstly, in 1960 it allocated sufficient funds for the development of the first stage of the extensive Willowton industrial estate. Secondly, prolonged negotiations with the central Government eventually resulted in 1963 in Pietermaritzburg being declared a 'Border Area', which provided financial concessions to new industries locating in the City. These incentives played a vital role in attracting some notable industrial development to the area, beginning for example in 1964 with a new R1 million rice mill.

The City Council's sustained campaign to attract industries was increasingly successful. A peak was reached in 1969–1970, when approximately 33 industrial sites were sold. This was partly attributable to the shortage and much higher price of similar industrial land in the Durban area at the time. As early as 1966, however, the City Engineer complained that expenditure on the provision of new industrial sites was becoming potentially detrimental to the maintenance of other essential services in the City. When industrial development slowed down temporarily in 1967, the Estates Department welcomed this as an opportunity to concentrate on the City's housing backlog.

In 1970 the central Government, believing that the City's industrial progress was assured, decided to withdraw the Border Area concessions. No immediate effect was felt in Pietermaritzburg, as several transactions were still in the process of being concluded. But within two years it became evident that new investment had declined steadily. In addition, some of the long-established industries began retrenching their workers. In 1978,

SOMETHING FOR THE ELEPHANT TO REMEMBER

The declaration in 1963 of Pietermaritzburg as a 'Border Area' attracted considerable industrial development.

unemployment had reached such high levels that a relief fund, the 'Need Fund' was inaugurated. In the interim, the size of the black population in the Pietermaritzburg metropolitan region, which extends into the adjacent KwaZulu territories, was nearing an estimated 250 000.

In 1979, economists were anticipating a revival in the South African economy, and this gave grounds for cautious optimism in the year ahead. To take advantage of this mood, and any potential upswing, a Co-ordinating Committee for the Development of the Pietermaritzburg Region was formed. This body consisted of the City Council, representatives of Afrikaans industrial interests, the Chambers of Commerce and Industries and the Drakensberg Administration Board. Its membership has altered over the years, but its greatest feat has been the effective reinstatement of the Government's concessions.

The concessions were the means by which the City Council planned to attract numerous additional industrial enterprises to Pietermaritzburg. The incentives were only introduced in April 1982, but in the interlude, the City Council continued in its own endeavours to stimulate industrial progress. Several promotional seminars, both in Johannesburg and overseas, were undertaken, and a follow-up programme was made feasible by the appointment of an Industrial Promotions Officer. As a result, 1982-1983 turned out to be unusually successful, with nearly 20 industrial transfers being concluded.

Pietermaritzburg today presents a picture of sophistication and bustling activity as one of the main centres of commerce and industry in Natal. This transition from a predominantly agricultural, educational and administrative centre, to one with a distinctive industrial bearing, reflects the increasingly vigorous industrialization policy embarked upon by the City Council, and the crucial role played by the central Government's decentralization incentives. The recent completion of Phase 1 of the Camps Drift project at a cost of some R12 million, is the Council's guarantee that sufficient land and infra-structural services will be available for future industrial growth.

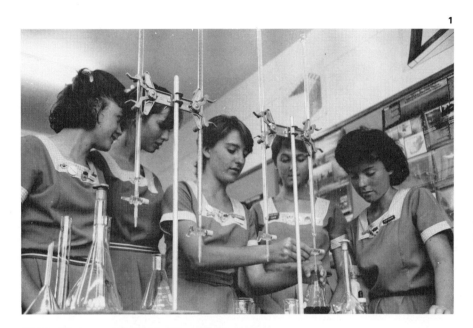

Girls' schools now offer most of the subjects once considered suitable only for boys. Matric science pupils at Pietermaritzburg Girls' High School, 1988.

Thanet House School flourished between 1882 and 1908. Founded as the Old Deanery Ladies' School, it was renamed when it moved to Thanet House at the corner of Longmarket and Chapel Streets.

CHAPTER NINE

Educational Capital

Educational capital of white Natal

Sylvia Vietzen

With the demise of the Provincial Councils on 30 June 1986, Pietermaritzburg as an educational capital experienced a jolt which passed almost unnoticed by the public at large. The administrative machinery for white education in Natal proceeded to vacate its headquarters in Natalia and, though relocated in another part of the City, it embarked on a new era as a satellite of Pretoria. Despite assurances to the contrary, it is reasonable to assume that a chapter has closed and, technically at least, Pietermaritzburg will no longer call the educational tune in Natal.

Yet this development has come at a time when the Pietermaritzburg City Council has identified publicly with the Natal/KwaZulu Indaba negotiations and, in so doing, has declared its intention for power sharing and for social and political change. Other forces for change are vigorously at work. Whatever form this change might eventually take, it would signify a removal of racial divisions in education. Thus, to speak of white education in the Pietermaritzburg of 1988 is an anachronism of no mean proportions. It is nevertheless true that in the first 150 years of its formal existence, Pietermaritzburg's paramountcy in white education in Natal is an historic reality.

It began when the Voortrekkers chose the site in January 1838 and established Pietermaritzburg as the seat of the Volksraad in February 1839. Although preoccupied with matters of defence, by 1842 they claimed to be placing government as well as religion and education on a secure footing. In practice this amounted to little more than the usual brief period of family-based Trekker education — occasionally supplemented by a spell at the feet of the rather dubious itinerant 'meester' — producing an elementary literacy necessary for church membership. Given the rudiments of civic life in Pietermaritzburg, small schools gradually appeared. In April 1844, H.A. Repsold launched classes, and evening classes for adults, in the home of A.W. Pretorius opposite the church. The Revd Daniel Lindley and his wife did likewise, as did Miss Olivier, later Mrs Louis Nel. The increasing English population in Pietermaritzburg by 1845 is reflected in the project of an enterprising lady, Mejuvrouw Catharina Muller, who offered a basically Trekker education of 'Spellen, Lezen, Schryven and Cyferen', in both Dutch and English.

The change from Trekker to British administration and the related exit of Dutch and influx of British settlers during the 1840s and 50s were soon evident in the Colony's social attitudes. As a predominantly white centre and seat of the Establishment — Government, Garrison and Church — Pietermaritzburg was poised to reproduce a colonial version of what Kitson Clark calls that 'common civilization' or 'English-speaking culture' of Britain's 'expanding society' in the years 1830 to 1900. This was particularly observable in the variety of educational projects which emerged. There were dame schools and ladies' academies which could have come straight out of *Vanity Fair*. There were governesses who mirrored Jane Eyre. All were epitomized, for example, in the Hinton House Day and Boarding Schools at 27 Burger Street opened for girls by Mrs Emily London and her daughters in 1854. A separate section for boys was conducted by Edward London, a thwarted Byrne settler, who, though publicizing a library which would inspire 'noble sentiments and purity of style', was soon back in his occupation of bookbinding and stationery. The London ladies continued to the 1860s, offering advantages of a 'superior order' involving a 'liberal and solid education'. Extravagant claims to the building of character and moral and religious training, together with tuition in violin and flute, seem to have reduced themselves in practice to a fairly simple business of teaching manners, including curtseying, and a little reading and writing in the confines of one rather closely packed room. It was to one of many such seminaries in Pietermaritzburg that Ellen McLeod was sent for six months in 1852 from Byrne to receive the rudiments, only to be sent home again when the schoolmistress succumbed to fever. Unstable though they might have been, the governess, the dame school and the young ladies' or gentlemen's seminary or academy remained a feature of Natal education throughout the century, catering to the needs of scholars in remote areas, and girls in particular, but also to the pretensions of assumed social class. Many preferred the solicitude of a small private seminary or academy to the rough and tumble of government schools, even when these became available.

It was in the development of government education that Pietermaritzburg assumed a central position. The first government school was opened in a thatch-roofed building at the corner of Longmarket and Chapel Streets in 1849 with Johan David Marquard as Government Teacher. The school — another was opened in Durban the following year — was to be managed by a government-appointed School Committee consisting of the Secretary to

Dr Robert Mann, first Superintendent of Education in Natal.

Government, the minister and churchwarden of the Church of England and the minister and senior elder of the Dutch Reformed Church. In this it differed from England where issues of church and state prevented a state system of elementary education until the 1870s. Colonists debated the advisability of government education, but the absence in those pioneering years of other agencies to provide elementary education, the need for facilities for Dutch and English alike and the differing needs of rich and poor gave the impetus to government involvement.

The way was set for the tradition which has developed in Natal of using 'Pietermaritzburg' and 'education' synonymously. In 1858 a Select Committee of the Legislative Council recommended a Chief Central Board of Education consisting of eight leading government and church dignitaries with a system of local committees to administer grants-in-aid. The system did not prove effective. Full responsibility devolved on the Superintendent whose mammoth task it was to recommend, allocate, supervise and account for grants, examine and report on tuition, appoint and dismiss teachers, regulate courses of study, approve and organize school books, and do all the clerical work. This was centralization indeed, and it follows that the character of Natal education during its formative period was greatly influenced by the individuals who held the position of Superintendent: first, Robert James Mann MD, FRAS and then Thomas Warwick Brooks. From Pietermaritzburg they rode out on their horses to remote country schools, returning to the Capital to negotiate, single-handed, the minutiae of administrative detail. Mann, a medical doctor and an astronomer, and Brooks, '... a man of the world polished by letters and by travel', were indeed men of education. Sir John Robinson recalls accompanying Mann on one of his tours of inspection:

> Ambling along the bridle paths that connected outlying centres in secluded districts, the good doctor's companionship was not less entertaining than profitable, for to him nature was an open book and his work a delight. Like all true colonists, he lived in the future not less than the present ... The tiny barnlike structure, in which the few humbly clad children gathered under their homely teacher to learn such rudiments of knowledge as he or she could teach them, became in the doctor's presence the birthplace of a future seminary, and the wondering but eager-faced pupils, struggling with their alphabets and primers, their slates and copybooks, amidst the sylvan surroundings of a South African wilderness, were the coming citizens of a new state, the heralds of a new order. Sometimes arrangements would be made for the instruction of the elder folk in the form of a popular lecture on some scientific or literary subject, which would be handled by the doctor with wonderful ease and graphic charm.

It was the beginnings of a bureaucratic centralization rather than a personal one which emerged when the Education Laws 15 and 16 of 1877 were promulgated and the Superintendency was succeeded by the Council of Education in 1878. This Council consisted of ten members nominated by the Lieutenant-Governor of whom five should be members of the Executive Council and the Legislative Council. A precaution, probably reflecting the denominational difficulties of the Colenso controversy, precluded membership of the Council by any 'Clergyman or Minister of Religion'. The secretary of the Council was to be the 'Superintendent Inspector' who was responsible

to the Council. He was to be assisted by inspectors who would visit the schools. In fact, in the person of Robert Russell, the Superintendent Inspector proved to be hardly less influential than the Superintendent. He held the position throughout the period of the Council of Education and continued to do so after Responsible Government when the Education Act No. 5 of 1894 placed supreme control in the hands of the Minister of Education and a Department of Education.

The Russell regime was one of marked expansion and consolidation. By the turn of the century there were government primary schools in no fewer than fifteen of Natal's rural centres. Perhaps the most notable development of the period was the provision of 'model' primary schools in Pietermaritzburg and Durban. In Pietermaritzburg, for example, the Girls' Model Primary School which opened at the corner of Chapel and Berg Streets in 1879 under the principalship of Miss Eleanor Broome, exists to the present day as Russell High School. With its extension class for pupil teachers, it gave just a little more than the usual elementary education provided in government primary schools. This was exceeded for girls — in the Capital — only when Girls' High School was opened in August 1920.

The truth is that, for girls and boys alike, the focus of government education in nineteenth-century Natal was essentially primary. There was a strong belief in the Colony that a secondary education, especially of the classical type, unfitted its charges for the practicalities of a pioneering society. Russell was its chief protagonist. He commended the headmasters of Maritzburg College and Durban High School in 1866 for devoting more attention to the 'ordinary' subjects which, he contended would furnish youth with 'the tools and weapons necessary for the work and battle of life'. Not that the headmasters agreed with him. R.D. Clark, Headmaster of Maritzburg College, for one, came into direct conflict with the Council of Education and threatened resignation unless the high schools were allowed to pursue secondary education undisturbed by an

Boarders at Maritzburg College, Nathan House, c. 1940.

T. B. (Jack) Frost

Until the establishment of the Indumiso College for Education for blacks in the 1980s, the story of teacher education in Pietermaritzburg was one of white endeavour only. In 1909 teacher training classes were started by the Natal Education Department in the old YMCA building in Longmarket Street, from where they moved to the recently vacated premises of the Legislative Council. Charles Smythe, Natal's first Administrator after Union, chose not to live in Government House which, after suitable alterations, became in 1912 the home of what was then called the Natal Training College. Until 1954 NTC was to be the sole institution for the training of white primary school teachers in Natal.

Initially a two-year course of training was offered. In the early 1930s, when economic hard times attracted a higher calibre of student into education, all took three first-year university courses in their second year. In return, university students training for teaching received some of their method lectures at NTC. In 1936 the first specialized third-year course was offered, a quaintly-styled 'Rural Diploma'. Later, more appropriately, it was transferred to Cedara. It was only in the 1960s that a full three-year course became standard. In the 1970s a fourth-year course became first optional, then standard. This immediately placed newly qualified students at an advantage over serving teachers,

and obliged the Education Department in 1977 to establish a College of Education for Further Training, whereby serving teachers could improve their qualifications by means of part-time study.

During the same period, however, it was becoming apparent to education planners that their earlier blithe confidence in the untrammelled growth of the white school population was misplaced. Repeated attempts were made from 1975 onwards to close NTC in favour of the palatial facilities, embarrassingly under-utilized, at Edgewood College of Education in Pinetown. To these proposals the provincial Executive Council (EXCO) was implacably opposed. In 1986, however, the old elected system of provincial administration was ended. One of EXCO's last decisions, the amalgamation of NTC and CEFT as the Natal College of Education, failed to save the former. A petition of 10 000 signatures left Pretoria, where control of education now resided, unmoved. Opening the College to meet the needs of all races was equally unthinkable in terms of the Government's 'own affairs' mentality. Nevertheless, at the time of writing pressure from various quarters does seem to have persuaded the minister to allow the College to enrol a limited number of black correspondence students. The end of 1987 consequently marked not only the end of an era with the loss of the historic NTC, but offered hope of some small adjustment to the educational realities in Natal.

---

annual primary examination. Yet Russell approached the close of his voluminous career well satisfied with his product. Speaking at the Education Congress of the Victoria Era Exhibition in London in 1897 — with the licence of old age and the sentiment of the occasion — he made the most of his facts:

> Our little colony of Natal may be said to have existed since the beginning of our noble Queen's reign. When Her Majesty ascended the throne the streets of what is now the Capital of Natal were occupied by the huts of native races, and the streets of our seaport, where we now have dozens of schools whose attendance ranges from 700 downwards, were then the haunts of the elephant and other wild animals, roaming about in the primeval forests.

Sometimes supplementing and sometimes reacting against this rather basic provision of government education was a variety of private educational activity. This ranged from the small privately-owned seminaries already mentioned to the private secondary schools, many of which continue to play a special role in Natal education today. It included the public pressure to provide a better quality education of a secondary type and it included the public pressure for élitist and sectarian projects related to the strong class and denominational consciousness of 'Victorians', in Natal as in Britain. Pietermaritzburg, and its environs, was the focus of most of this activity. Thus, in the movement for a Collegiate Institution, a correspondent to the *Natal Witness* in 1860 wrote:

> Certainly it seems but natural, that if anywhere the initiative is taken to found a seat of learning in Natal, it should begin in Maritzburg, itself the seat of Government and a Cathedral City.

Summing up his rationale, he continued:

> An endowed College, perfectly unsectarian, free, and open to all sections of the community, whether English or Dutch,

Jew or Christian — aspiring to literacy or professional distinction, and qualifying its alumni to occupy a respectable standing in society, and in positions of civic honor [sic], and in our Legislative Council; producing educated men, of good manners and good breeding, of whom we need not be ashamed or doubtful — this is the desideratum, we have long felt, must sooner or later be met and supplied.

Supported by Lieutenant-Governor Scott and the City Council, the Pietermaritzburg Collegiate Institute was provided for by the Law of 1861. No effect was given to it, however, and Dr Mann, recognizing the need, took steps to start the Maritzburg High School. It opened in 1863 in temporary premises in Longmarket Street with William Calder as headmaster. In 1866 the school moved to new premises in Loop Street built by the Collegiate Trust but rented by the Government. By means of the Bill of 1886 the Colonial Government appropriated the funds of the Collegiate Institute to build a new school. Not without heated debate did the public and private sectors thus join forces in the establishment of Maritzburg College on the site where it flourishes today with close on 1 000 pupils.

At the other extreme were the private schools established to meet special needs. Such, for example was Bishop's College, an essentially 'high church' enterprise opened by Bishop Macrorie in a house opposite his own in Loop Street, probably in 1871. The first headmaster was the Revd Pritchard. The last was Canon Bowditch who, shortly after the school's demise in 1880, entered into a fiery three-cornered press debate with a parent and R. D. Clark of Maritzburg College in defence of sectarian as against secular education. The implication of the row was that the 'advanced church' affiliation of Bishop's College caused its failure in a way that the more Protestant basis of the other Anglican schools — St. Mary's Diocesan College at Richmond and St. Anne's in the City — had not. It is significant that diocesan education for girls survived, while that for boys did not. St. Anne's actually moved into the vacated Bishop's College in 1882, and in 1889 Bishop Macrorie felt bound to report to Synod, 'I have to lament year by year the want of a high-class Diocesan School for boys'. Only in 1901 when Michaelhouse, founded as a private venture in 1896, became a diocesan school, was this balance redressed.

It was in the area of private schools for girls that Pietermaritzburg made its best, if not a unique showing. While the precedent of Miss Beale and Miss Buss in the secondary girls' school movement in England was a key influence, the rash of girls secondary schools which appeared between 1875 and 1877 in Pietermaritzburg and, to a lesser extent, in Durban must relate to other factors. Chief among these was the mid-Victorian obsession with denominationalism. The arrival of the Sisters of the Holy Family in 1875 and the founding of the Convent Schools in Pietermaritzburg and Durban set in motion a prompt Protestant reaction against the snares of '... the Scarlet Lady, and of her acknowledged hand-maid — Ritualism'. So intense was the apprehension of Catholic influences on the unsuspecting Victorian female, that the opening of the Convent in Pietermaritzburg precipitated the circulation of a pamphlet entitled, 'Give the Cat the Cream to Guard'. Hence the founding in 1876, by the businessmen of Pietermaritzburg, of the Natal Evangelical Protestant Ladies' School Association (Ltd) which gave birth to Girls' Collegiate School, and a similar body in Durban which launched Durban Girls' College in 1877. Continuing alongside was the Anglican specialization, pioneered at Richmond with the opening of St. Mary's Diocesan College in 1869 and given fresh impetus with the opening of St. Anne's Diocesan College in Pietermaritzburg in 1877. In 1892 yet another variation of Anglicanism emerged when the Sisters of the Society of St. John the Divine founded St. John's Diocesan High School for Girls to cater for those of slightly lesser means than attended St. Anne's. Spreading the net was Epworth High School, begun in August 1898 by Miss Mason and Miss Lowe in collaboration with the Wesleyan-Methodist Church. Not always related to denominationalism but rather to the fact that nineteenth-century girls' education was seen to be a specialized, protected, even luxury commodity reflecting and promoting the nineteenth-century female image, more private secondary girls' schools continued to be established in Pietermaritzburg. There was the Old Deanery School opened by Mrs Edmonds and Miss Maas in 1882 which later became Thanet House School. There was Miss Rowe's Maritzburg High School for Girls, opened in Chapel Street in 1894 and reopened at Swartkop in 1899 as Uplands High School. There Miss Rowe, who had resigned as Lady Principal of Girls' Collegiate owing to a disagreement, openly promoted her new venture as the Newnham of Natal. There was Wykeham School opened in 1905 by Miss Mary Moore — also in high dudgeon — with a nucleus of girls from St. Anne's where she had been since 1891.

That Pietermaritzburg could sustain this hive of private female educational activity was as much an interesting phenomenon then as it is today when all but the Holy Family Convent, Thanet House and Uplands continue to vie for support both in the City and the Natal hinterland. Still select, and of English tradition, but government-aided and examination orientated, the private girls' schools of 1988 are by no means the social features that they were in Victorian Pietermaritzburg. At Thanet House in the 1890s, new teachers were expected to leave their visiting cards at Government House. And what could be more indicative of tone than Miss Mary Moore's slightly cynical snippet in a letter to her sister on the Government House reception which she and her colleagues at St. Anne's Diocesan College attended late in 1892?

> Last Thursday Lady Mitchell held a reception ... The receptions are most odd. You go to Government House and on the road outside you see a miscellaneous collection of vehicles and horses, awaiting their owners. You enter the grounds, walk up to the house and in the hall a soldier salutes you and requests you to write your name and address in two books, you lay cards on a table covered with similar bits of paste-board and stroll through the house into the garden, where on a bit of grass, of limited dimensions but proudly spoken of as 'English grass', you are presented to Lady Mitchell. She gives you a hand, squaring her elbow to an acute angle, murmurs that she is very glad to see you etc. and you pass on to look for friends. Under a tree is a tea-table with tea, coffee and cakes. When we left Lady Mitchell we came upon Sir Theophilus Shepstone and Miss Heaton who introduced me. He is a dear old man, he asked me to go and see his garden. Lady Warden and Miss Heaton were calling on Lady Shepstone the other day and they say the ferns are lovely.

Private schools were preferred for girls and relieved the government of full responsibility in that area. This remains partially true today.

During the 1890s Pietermaritzburg was overtaken by Durban in population. This was increasingly reflected in educational statistics. But Pietermaritzburg was the Capital and, as such, remained the educational nerve-centre of Natal. Tradition has it, though evidence is not easily available, that at Union in 1910 Pietermaritzburg was to be made the educational capital of South Africa to correspond with the capitals granted to the other provinces. While this did not materialize, it is true that in the National Convention negotiations, the Natal delegation secured the control of education 'other than higher education' for the provinces. When the Jagger Commission of 1915 recommended that the Provincial Councils be dissolved after their allotted ten years and education be transferred to the Union Government, G.T. Plowman, Administrator of Natal, submitted a minority report pleading for their retention. His argument hinged on the importance of catering to local needs in education

Girls' Collegiate, founded in 1878. In 1963 the school moved from these premises in Burger Street to a new site in Clarendon.

5

Epworth High School, like other private schools, now admits pupils of all races.

and the possibility that under the more remote control of a less interested parliament, educational considerations would be sacrificed to party politics. He pointed to the strides made in the Provinces in primary, secondary and technical education since Union. Plowman's was a Natal point of view for it would seem, according to E.G. Malherbe, that many educational leaders favoured a national approach to education. With the National Education Policy Act of 1967 which aimed at co-ordinating education in South Africa, anxiety concerning Natal's identity in education again surfaced. It was to no avail. A decade later Roger Whiteley, a former MEC for Education in Natal, wrote in the *Daily News* of 6 April 1978:

> The process of conditioning the South African voting public to the point of view that Provincial Councils are not necessary has begun ... This is one issue that the people of Natal, especially the English speaking people must resist with everything at their disposal. The people of Natal generally want the retention of the Council and they want more powers — not fewer powers.

When the Provincial Councils were finally due to go in 1986, the President of the Natal Teachers' Society voiced his dismay in an article entitled 'Pretoria takes over from Pietermaritzburg'.

Meanwhile it is possible to make certain broad observations about white education in twentieth-century Pietermaritzburg while the Province held the reins.

Clearly, there has been marked expansion. Pupil numbers have grown, indicating not only a steadily increasing population but greater use of more varied facilities and differentiated courses. Secondary education and matriculation have become the norm. No longer do pupils leave school at Standard 6 or Standard 8, a development which went hand in hand with the elimination of the Primary School Certificate and Junior Certificate examinations respectively. Schools have increased in size. Maritzburg College and Girls' High School have exceeded the 1 000 mark and certain primary schools have approached it. Geographical and demographic factors have caused pioneer schools in the city centre — Boys' Model in the original Maritzburg High School building, Longmarket Street Girls' and Harward Boys' — to abandon their gracious Victorian or Edwardian red-brick buildings to other purposes and close or relocate.

New schools have sprung up in the proliferating suburbs. Alexandra Boys' High and the co-educational Carter High form part of this trend, as do many primary schools. Junior Primary sections have in some cases become separate, new schools and pre-primary schools have made their appearance. The Afrikaans speakers have been catered for at the Voortrekker and Gert Maritz Schools in particular. A white government school population — excluding government-aided schools — which stood at 1 650 in 1900, at 1 892 in 1910, at 4 408 in 1948, stands at 12 017 in 1987. These figures take account of 4 schools in 1900 and 28 in 1987.

The educational establishment has grown even more markedly, giving rise to a suspicion that there are 'more chiefs than Indians'. Warwick Brooks, reputed to have taken his life in 1866 because of overwork and lack of clerical help, would have viewed with incredulity the hierarchy of directors, inspectors, planners, advisers, support services and administrative personnel now resident in Pietermaritzburg, forming a notable enclave of its society. Though jealous of its own identity as a province, the Natal regime never extended the principle of decentralization to local school committees and guarded jealously its centralized control in the Capital.

Perhaps the most notable trend of the twentieth century has been the gradual advance of Nationalist Government ideology on the educational stronghold of Pietermaritzburg since 1948. No longer would it be easy to picture the school population of the City turning out in full force to the Alexandra Park Oval to perform morris dances and sing, in massed choir, *Land of Hope and Glory* and *Will Ye No' Come Back Again* as it did for the visit of the British royal family in 1947, even though what appears to be a Union Jack still flies above the Victoria Club. Natal has worked assiduously to retain its educational prerogatives: the element of choice against compulsory mother-tongue education; the favourable pupil-teacher ratio; its priorities in syllabus content and teaching method; and its positive attitude to critical thinking and its critical approach to examining. Gradually, and often with subtlety, it has been brought into line. It remains to be seen whether, as an 'Own Affair' under the Department of Education and Culture: House of Assembly, and with School Committees and Regional School Committees now a reality, the Pietermaritzburg regime in Natal education will live on — with its wings clipped — or be snuffed out. Perhaps it will be transfigured in a form as yet unseen. That is the gate at which it stands in the 150th year of the City's history.

Pietermaritzburg is generally acknowledged as an educational centre, in the same league, for example, as Grahamstown. It was regarded as the natural place in Natal for the first high school in 1863, the first college for training teachers in 1904 and the first university in 1910. It has lost a great deal. It has lost the headquarters of school education. It has lost the administrative headquarters of the dual-centred University of Natal to Durban, and at the end of 1987 the resident section of the Natal College of Education — the original Natal Training College — was closed. Yet Pietermaritzburg retains an educational ethos, even if, at times, this seems to be of an age gone by. One only has to see grown girls in green uniforms still cycling to school in 1988 to realize that tradition, in Pietermaritzburg, dies hard.

An appraisal of black education

IN THE PIETERMARITZBURG AREA, 1987

Deanne Lawrance

In recent years comprehensive reports prepared for the Buthelezi Commission and by the KwaZulu/Natal Planning Council have outlined the picture of black education in the region, which includes schools in the Pietermaritzburg area. The assessment that follows, while aware of the main points in these documents, is a more personal appraisal of the situation.

For several years I have travelled daily from our First World city to Sinathing, an area in Edendale some fifteen kilometres away, to a high school that caters for 1 000 pupils in a Third World community. Matric pupils and others can daily be seen carrying buckets of water and firewood on their heads. As I make this journey, I am often aware that certain tensions are receding as I enter an area where a joyous sense of being human is still evident in faces along the way. This is not an attempt to glamorize a situation filled with hardships encountered in facing the requirements of a First World education system, but an appreciation of the human warmth and generosity of spirit I have come to know.

Black schools in the area fall under either the KwaZulu Department of Education and Culture, based in Ulundi, with a local Circuit Office in Edendale; or the Department of Education and Training, which is Pretoria based, and locally controlled by the Pietermaritzburg West Circuit. The KwaZulu Edendale office controls schools in the greater Edendale area; while the DET office controls those in the local townships of Imbali, Ashdown and Sobantu. The latter also runs those further out in the Camperdown and Greytown areas as well as over a hundred farm schools — but these have not been included in the following statistics. Students move freely between areas, those from Imbali, Ashdown and Sobantu often seeking places in KwaZulu schools, which tend on the whole to have a better teacher-pupil ratio. The DET controls 6 secondary local schools, with a total pupil enrolment of 4 697, and 12 primary schools (including lower and higher primary) with a total enrolment of 8 397. In addition it controls the Plessislaer Technical College which currently enrols 463 students doing technical, commercial or teacher training courses as well as the Indumiso College of Education which has a current enrolment of 1 080 students.

The KwaZulu Edendale office is in charge of the following local schools: 11 high and 20 junior secondary schools; 30 lower primary, 15 higher primary and 23 combined primary schools. In addition they run 3 special schools for handicapped children. The total enrolment at the high schools is 9 038, at the secondary schools it is 9 200. The total for all the primary schools in the area is 48 358. This staggering figure is given by one circuit office and obviously gains meaning only when related to the number of teachers. Suffice it that one school has an enrolment of 1 821 under one principal, and that a few schools still operate on a platoon and double-session basis.

The Department of National Education, after meeting with heads of Education Departments across the country, has devised a funding policy which is designed to allocate funds to all education departments on a more equitable basis. This should have significant implications for local black schools, but needs to be viewed against the enormous lacks that still characterize most of them. The following tend to be norms: crowded class-rooms, with inadequate seating; a poor pupil-teacher ratio; school buildings in need of basic repairs; inadequate or non-existent sports facilities; and an overburdened teaching staff, most of whom are improving their qualifications through correspondence or other courses and so have neither the time nor energy to give their wholehearted commitment to their schools. A further common feature is that most pupils catch one or two buses to and from school, a costly addition to their day in terms of time and money.

A significant factor was highlighted by the KwaZulu Minister of Education and Culture, Dr O. Dhlomo, in his 1987 Policy Speech to the KwaZulu Legislative Assembly. He reported on the phenomenal increase in enrolment in KwaZulu schools for the preceding year, which stood at 80 per cent. He said, 'This tremendous growth has adversely affected our financial resources at all levels'. He went on to express his Department's appreciation to the communities for their sacrificial struggle to provide class-room accommodation for their children. Money raised for this purpose is refunded to them on a rand for rand basis, once the building is completed. In the Pietermaritzburg area alone, this financing system accounted for 18 class-rooms in KwaZulu schools last year. Whites can hardly imagine having to provide the finances needed for establishing a school.

A representative black school in Vulindlela. Facilities in black schools in the Pietermaritzburg area generally compare unfavourably with those at white schools.

Money is more readily available for schools under the Department of Education and Training, and in 1983 it completed one of its most impressive complexes. Between Imbali and the main Edendale highway, it comprises a High School, Sukuma, planned originally to accept boarders from primary farm schools in their local areas; the Plessislaer Technical College; and the Indumiso College of Education. This complex with its impressively equipped buildings, modern technology and sports facilities, displays an efficiency and stature not equalled by other black schools in the area, and which it will take them some years to achieve.

The majority of the DET schools have electricity. This obviously affords tremendous advantages in terms of educational aids, which tend to be almost non-existent in the majority of KwaZulu schools. So for the latter, quite apart from not being able to turn on lights or heaters, there are no overhead projectors and much laboratory equipment is rendered ineffective. However, a costly generator is sometimes available, providing for the occasional film, an item of comparative luxury, and greatly appreciated when available.

While Resource Centres are an established feature at most other schools, at black ones they are relatively new in concept and provision. READ (Read Educate And Develop) is an organization reaching into schools in this and other areas to help provide facilities and train teacher-librarians. The transition for many pupils from a non-literary to a literary background is being positively promoted by this organization.

Inadequate facilities reflect in measurable results such as those of the matriculation examination, which year by year shows up the disparities in the different education departments. In his recent policy speech, Dr Dhlomo said:

> It is still a matter to be regretted that the matriculation examination results in Black schools are lamentably lower than the results in Coloured, Indian and White schools in our country. Despite this unsatisfactory position, our department has continued with its motivation programme for principals, heads of departments, teachers, pupils, parents and the members of the inspectorate, in order to improve the standard of teaching and learning.

Dr Dhlomo was able to report that, unlike in the previous years, the 1986 examination results improved considerably from a 35 to a 55 per cent pass rate. The sad reality for a great number of the students who gain such a pass is that they still battle to gain employment of any kind.

CITY OF LIBRARIES

Jennifer Verbeek

Pietermaritzburg is sometimes referred to as a city of schools. Perhaps it would be more apt to call it a city of libraries.

The Natal Society Library (established in 1851) provides the main thrust of public library facilities for the City, and is also one of the five South African legal deposit (copyright) libraries. The libraries of the Natal Museum, Natal Law Society, Nederduitse Gereformeerde Kerk (Natal), Supreme Court, Cedara Agricultural College and Allerton Regional Veterinary Services also predate Union and provide comprehensive specialist services. These libraries, as well as more recent ones such as those of the Voortrekker Museum and the Natal Archives depot, hold rich special collections, particularly of Africana and Nataliana. The library of the University of Natal (1912) serves the academic community.

Pietermaritzburg hosts the Natal Provincial Library Services, which provide professional support and the stock for 122 public libraries, 102 library depots, 151 school library depots and 40 departmental libraries in Natal. There are also libraries for teachers of the Natal Education Department and the Teachers' Centre (House of Delegates) in Pietermaritzburg. Schools under their control in the City, as well as seven private schools, all have functioning Media Resource Centres.

In response to changing needs in education, the Natal Society Library has established the Lambert Wilson Project Library which makes specially-chosen reference material available to children engaged upon self-study assignments; while the embryo library of the Sached Trust plans to concentrate on material for new literates and students studying by correspondence. In another departure, there has been an increasing tendency towards private industrial libraries, with Hulett's (S.A.) leading the field.

Perhaps the most novel recent development is the Natal Parks Board's attempt to recreate the colonial library of the now deserted village of York at the Midmar Historical Museum.

In 1913 R.D. Clark, headmaster of Maritzburg College, presented his library to the school at a ceremony attended by many of the City's notables.

Top Row: Dr Ward, A.G. Douglas, L. Line, A. Eicke, C. Hime, A.O. Kufal.

Middle Row: Prof. Denison, C.G. Lund, Supt. Barrow, Prof. Petrie, G.W. Sweeney, Y. Worthington, F.H. Rose, W.J. Shawe, C. Bird, Sir J. Dove-Wilson, Dr. Hyslop, Revd Dr. Smith, D. Saunders, W. Shepstone, Maj. O.W. Elsner, R. Robb, D. Walker, Sir T. St. George, A. Head, W. Falcon, C.A. Bangley.

Front Row: P.F. Payn, J. McGibbon, R.D. Clark, E.W. Barns, Col. G.J. Macfarlane, J. McAuslin, W. Abbit.

8

The University of Natal and Pietermaritzburg

John Sellers

The Act which gave birth to the University was promulgated on 11 December 1909. Subsequently the Pietermaritzburg City Council granted 40 acres of land in Scottsville on which the first university building was erected. Designed by the local architect J. Collingwood Tully and built at a cost of £30 000, its foundation stone was laid on 1 December 1910 by the Duke of Connaught. Ever since it was completed in August 1912 the Main Building with its clock tower has dominated Scottsville ridge. So perfect is its location that one can gaze down on the whole central area of the City spread out below. Yet what helped determine its position in those days when the motor car had barely arrived in Pietermaritzburg was the existing tramway system, which extended along King Edward Avenue and had its terminus at the pedestrian entrance to the University.

The University began with only 8 professors and 57 students, 'the Aboriginals'. One can only marvel at the range of expertise expected of the original professors. J. W. Bews, for example, was at the age of 26 Professor of both Botany and Geology; while R. B. Denison felt he held not the 'chair' but rather the 'sofa' of Chemistry and Physics.

During the First World War the advancement of the University was minimal, but an important landmark was reached when on 2 April 1918 the Natal University College became a constituent college of the University of South Africa, established as a federal university. The next phase in the growth of the NUC (as it was known in those days) was the establishment of new departments in Durban, primarily Engineering. They were housed in Howard College, opened in August 1931, and destined within a few decades to outstrip those in Pietermaritzburg.

The appointment of Dr E. G. Malherbe as Principal in 1945 signalled the dawn of the post-Second World War renaissance. With the cessation of hostilities came a rapid growth in the student population which rose from 340 on the Pietermaritzburg campus in 1945 to 654 in 1946. Even more startling were the plans of Malherbe himself, formerly Director of Military Intelligence. His two main aims were to advance the status of the NUC to that of a

Staff and senior students of Natal University College, 1921.

Bottom Row: C.P.W. Douglas de Fenzi, G.W. Sweeney, A.D. Mudie, A.F. Hattersley, R.U. Sayee, G. Besselaar, J.W. Bews, O. Waterhouse, W.N. Roseveare, R. Beckett Denison, P.A. Guiton, R.D. Aitken, D. Dyer, V.C. Harrison, F. Smith.

Second Row: L.V. Thorrold, P.A. Menzies, O.M. Thorrold, N. Marshall, E. Grundy, E.A. Thorrold, W.L. Saville, I.D. Cochar-Hall, K.M. Holmes, M.G. Rhodes, N.W. Benson, D.E. Serruijs, M.H. Holderness, A.I. McKenzie, M.E. Calder, C.D. Scott.

Third Row: R.O. Pearse, A.S. Paton, C.J. Armitage, L.M. Dugmore, S.R. Dent, S.F. Bush, G.W. Gale, K.A. Fishlock, E.H. Goodall, R.W. Whitelaw, R. Jay Browne, J.B. Colam, W.S. Shaw, C.E. Peckham, W.H.C. Hellberg, A. Gardner, W.M. Adams.

Top Row: L.E. Morin, A.W. Bayer, L.P. McGuire, M.E. Pennington, F.N. Howes, L. Egeland.

fully-fledged independent university, and to realize to the fullest extent Durban's potential as a university centre. To further these aims he successfully badgered the corporation and private enterprise for financial assistance, and through the Press made the public aware of the great potential asset they had in the University.

His first significant achievement was the establishment of the Faculty of Agriculture in 1947. Housed originally in converted hutments in what had been the Oribi Military

10

E.G. Malherbe, acclaimed educationist, Principal of NUC and the University of Natal, 1947–1965.

University Hall (built in 1922), the first residence for women, with the clock tower of the original College building in the background.

11

Hospital, by 1954 the faculty was in its impressive building adjacent to the main campus. Subsequently the Ukulunga experimental farm near the Oribi aerodrome was acquired for its use.

As a result of the passing of the University of Natal (Private) Act no. 4 of 1948, piloted through Parliament by the local MP Colonel Oswald Shearer, the University was at last established. It was formally inaugurated on 15 March 1949 in the Grand Theatre (since demolished) by Dr A. J. Stals, Minister of Education in the new Nationalist Government. The Hon. Denis Gem Shepstone, the then Administrator of Natal, was elected the University's first Chancellor.

Perhaps the most controversial decision Malherbe took was to remove the centre of the University's administration from Pietermaritzburg to Durban, a project carried out during the long vacation of 1953–54. Understandably the City Council and citizens of Pietermaritzburg were up in arms when the decision was first announced, and more particularly when it seemed that all the teaching departments then in the City — with the exception of Agriculture — were to be moved down to Durban. In the end, this transfer was not implemented, but from 1954 it was obvious that the main focus for growth and development would be at the Durban centre. Although further development has continued to take place on the Pietermaritzburg campus, there is no disguising its dependent status.

During the 1960s and 1970s the University grew considerably: in 1967 the Government approved the University's plan to acquire the Scottsville golf course and in 1973 the City Council sold it the site of the Isolation Hospital. During the 1960s some academic buildings were extended and a new library, student residences and Students' Union were completed. The buildings for the Faculty of Education and the Department of Psychology on the new campus were completed in 1970, and were followed by those for the Faculties of Commerce, Law and Arts. Denison, a new residence for men and women, is still growing, and in 1983 the J. W. Bews Biological Sciences Building was opened adjacent to the Faculty of Agriculture. This steady march of new buildings along the former golf course has been matched by a similar, but less obvious, form of territorial expansion. Since the Second World War the University has been progressively buying houses in its vicinity, and either demolishing them to make way for developments such as the Malherbe Residence, or converting them to its own use, especially to the benefit of the burgeoning administrative staff, which in 1985 numbered 52 to the 231 academics and 85 technicians employed by the University.

On the whole, relations have always been reasonable between the City and the University so inextricably in its midst. Certainly, the University has tried to maintain contact, and through Inaugural Lectures, the Wednesday University Lectures, the Extension Lecture Programme, the Schools Lecture Programme, plays, concerts, and exhibitions of various kinds, has shared its expertise with the public.

Inevitably, though, it has been the presence of university students which has had the most obvious impact on the City. Many citizens would associate the University most readily with the annual Rag Procession which took its modern form in 1932, and with its magazine *Nucleus*.

Neither necessarily are greeted with much approval, though the purpose of both is to collect money for charity. The students involved are too easily perceived as being disorderly and irreverent. Students impinge on the public in other ways too. Their favourite pubs are places to be avoided by the older and more conventional citizens, and it is many a householder's fear that a students' digs be established next door. In earlier times the majority of students lived in university residences or boarded in homes which had been officially approved. But escalating fees, a degree of selection by residences that cannot cope with growing student numbers, and a greater spirit of independence among the young, has led to the establishment of digs or communes all over town, though particularly in the Scottsville area. Some communes, in large rented houses, are systematically organized and effectively run. Others are not. A deteriorating house full of students is perhaps too common a sight, and neighbours have suffered all too often from the sounds of revelry from large and uncontrolled 'digs parties'.

At certain stages students' clothes and hair styles have been a real source of irritation to respectable citizens. In the 1930s and 1940s the dress of women students was still conventional and men wore slacks and sports jackets. Dinner jackets and long dresses were worn at university balls, and suits on other formal occasions. The striped NUC blazer (which one hardly sees today) was worn by both men and women to informal functions and sporting events. Gowns were worn to morning lectures and to meals. This dress code was strictly adhered to. In the 1950s the trend was towards greater informality: dresses and sandals; or shorts with long stockings for the men. With the advent of the Beatles in the 1960s the student fashion scene changed dramatically. Long hair for men became commonplace and remained so for over a decade, much to the fury of many of the local conservative burgesses. Abbreviated shorts or jeans became the norm for men, as did 'slops' instead of shoes. Women took to the abbreviated mini-skirt. Student fashions in the 1970s and 1980s have been less *outré*, and have reflected what is normally worn by young people elsewhere, though the 'ethnic' look with beads, sandals and shawls has survived among some of the women. Essentially, dress today is informal, and the academic gown has disappeared from the campus. Even the lecturing staff has abandoned them, the last member to do so being Professor Mark Prestwich, who retired in 1976.

Now, as the City commemorates its 150th anniversary, many citizens will critically examine the role played by the University that has been in its midst for nearly eight decades. Surely their considered verdict will be that a worthwhile and positive co-existence has generally been maintained between 'town and gown'.

The float procession and student antics during the annual Charity Rag have changed little over the years. What is different is the composition of the student population. Now dedicated to serving all the people of Natal, the University has begun to move away from white exclusivism. In 1988 it enrolled at its Pietermaritzburg campus 465 black, 64 coloured, 419 Indian and 3 502 white students (total 4 450).

The Natal Museum

Brian Stuckenberg

The notion of a Natal Museum arose from a desire to maintain cultural standards in a small and highly isolated community of English settlers just established in the nascent town of Pietermaritzburg. Victorian ideals regarding the value of education, and the great public popularity of museums in Britain, would have contributed to the high priority given to such an institution. A museum was deemed a necessity also because it would promote the economic development of the Colony through making its natural resources better known and utilized.

The founding of the Museum in Pietermaritzburg lay in the formation of a local literary society. In May 1851, when the white population numbered about 1 500, the Natal Society was inaugurated, its main objectives being the dissemination of improved knowledge about the physical, climatic, agricultural, historical and commercial characteristics of the Colony. Clause 14 of the Society's Rules provided for a museum, but no real progress was made until 1854 when the President, Henry Cloete, began to press for such an institution. A 'Natal Museum', in his view, would be '... a source of rational amusement and interest to the stranger and visitor', and '... a school of practical information and instruction'. A collection of natural history specimens was started and grew rapidly through donations encouraged from the public, as well as through the zeal of local naturalists. Soon the collection crowded the reading-room of the Society's Library, and by 1891 a nearby room had to be rented to gain more space for it. In 1894 the Society then erected a Museum Hall behind the library premises, where the collection continued to

grow. By the turn of the century this Hall was full, and there was considerable support for the establishment of a government museum. Attempts to interest the legislature had been made previously but had failed, as they commonly do when the question of spending public money on cultural projects arises. Largely through the efforts of Morton Green, however, the Natal Government agreed eventually to accept the Society's collection as the nucleus for an official museum. This decision was soon implemented through the purchase of land and the approval of plans for a building in Loop Street, which was started in February 1902 and completed in July 1903, at a cost of £17 500.

Although this new museum building was well suited to its purpose, its external architectural features, in a Flemish Renaissance style, were hardly appropriate; one modern commentator, noting the sculptured friezes and entrance archway, and the gables over the end sections festooned with flowers and fruit tied with bows, considered the design to be 'particularly hideous'. The ornamental friezes designed by Alfred Palmer offended the columnist 'Topics of the Town' who commented in the *Natal Witness* of 2 July 1901:

> I am still lost in amazement at the ineptitude of these frieze arrangements, on which are represented a mob of underclothed boys in impossible attitudes, going through a kind of curious circus performed with scientific instruments unknown to Gods or men.

The first Director of the Natal Museum, Dr Ernest Warren, was appointed in 1903. He had a distinguished academic background and soon revealed a determination to make the new Museum a thoroughly scientific experience for visitors. Wasting no time, he purged the old collection of the Natal Society of all the bad specimens, monstrosities and irrelevancies which had accumulated over the years. Towards the end of 1904 the new cases had been stocked with acceptable specimens, and the Natal Museum could be officially opened; this great event took place on 30 November 1904 with the Governor, Sir Henry McCallum, officiating, and with the Natal Carbineers' Band in noisy attendance.

An immediate inflow of visitors indicated a favourable public response, but there was some adverse comment in the Press. The informality of the old museum, with its many 'curiosities' donated by the public, had gone. Here now was a scientifically structured collection, replete with daunting names, completely academic and formal. 'Anthropologist' wrote in the *Natal Witness* of 6 December 1904: 'It seems to me that the Museum is arranged to give the seal of approval to a few petty narrow-minded scientific men, and that the public interest is sacrificed to pander to this.' Warren was unmoved and embarked on a vigorous programme of collecting, public education, and research.

Specimens flowed in from many sources. Examples of sable and roan antelope were donated by the famous hunter, F. C. Selous. The Museum's own taxidermists were sent on a trip to the wilds of northern Zululand to gather examples of game animals; they incurred the displeasure of the Director by travelling first-class in the train ('Only second class rail is allowed and you must not let this occur again'). A 'native employee' sent in 1909 to Zululand to obtain the skin and skeleton of a hippo, died of 'malarial fever'. Warren was particularly proud of a

The Natal Museum, Loop Street, completed in 1903.
The building on the left was finished in 1905 for the Natal Government Railways.

fine lion acquired from Rhodesia (now Zimbabwe), which a reporter described in the *Natal Witness* thus:

> It has a noble cast of countenance, and the expression upon its features suggests that this king of beasts must have been at peace with all the world when it received its death wound.

So successful was the acquisition programme that Warren was soon pressing for a substantial enlargement to the building. A large new hall, designed especially to house the comprehensive collection of African mammals, was completed in 1912. Although this hall was visually impressive, it was museologically inapt and posed intractable problems in later years. The mammal collection, nevertheless, filled much of it quite effectively, and on 20 July 1914 the *Natal Witness* could report with moderate hyperbole that 'Almost every accessible variety of animate and inanimate nature is to be found within the four walls of the building'.

When Warren was appointed, the staff comprised seven people (other than the cleaners), but financial constraints reduced it to four by 1910, at which level it stayed until 1949! The Museum's grant-in-aid remained virtually unchanged from 1909 until 1935 when Warren retired. Despite such discouraging circumstances, his accomplishments were extraordinary. In the 31 years of his directorship he built up a remarkably comprehensive and internationally known museum, and he fostered research on the fauna and did his own research so proficiently that regular publication of the *Annals of the Natal Museum* (which he launched in 1906) was assured. In various other ways Warren also made the Museum a significant force in the community: he opposed the wanton slaughter of wildlife by the 'sporting' public and pressed for the first local ordinances protecting birds and other animals, and he formed the first Game Protection Association (in 1909); he played a major part in the proclamation of the Mont-aux-Sources Park and of the St. Lucia Bird Sanctuary; he fought determinedly against the misguided policy of game eradication as a means of controlling tsetse fly; and he sought to stop the destruction of natural forest and the despoliation of Bushman paintings. Warren evidently played a role in the establishment of the Natal University College in Pietermaritzburg; he was concurrently the first Professor of Zoology (giving his lectures in the Museum), and he was the first professor to hold office as Chairman of the Senate.

Dr Warren was succeeded by Dr Reginald F. Lawrence in 1935. This was an unpropitious time for a new Director; the depression of the 1930s and then the Second World War kept funding at a miserably low level, and when Dr Lawrence resigned in 1948 to devote his time to research, the staff still numbered only four and the grant-in-aid had hardly improved on the amount for 1903! It was not surprising that the institution had to mark time over this period. For Dr Lawrence, however, opportunities for research were still there, and his studies on the spiders, scorpions, millipedes and mites thrived. The Natal Museum came through this difficult time with its scientific reputation undiminished. An unsettled interlude then followed when problems arose over finding a new Director. Phillip A. Clancey came from Scotland to take up the post in April 1950; in a short time he renovated the bird exhibits and embarked on a general overhaul of the other galleries, but he left in December 1951 for the Durban Museum and a distinguished future in African ornithology.

With the arrival of the next Director, Dr John A. Pringle, in 1953, a new era started during which the institution underwent a significant transformation. With the aid of some constructive reports by commissions of enquiry into national museum affairs, and also of upsurges in the national economy, the staff could be expanded to 22 by 1972, and to 37 by 1978 when Dr Pringle retired. State funding soared, reflecting a better level of support and the larger staff, but also the growing effects of inflation; by 1978, the grant-in-aid had risen forty-fold in comparison with 1948. The institution could expand and flourish in every possible way. There was a transforming addition to the building which provided new display halls, a fine lecture theatre, and accommodation for research, library and technical staff. This addition, the design of W. L. Chiazzari, had to be planned for optimal use of the only vacant ground available, so in style it was quite different from the original building against which it was juxtaposed. Its modern rectangular form was made interesting by a distinctive ornamental frieze based on ancient fossil organisms, definitely a better choice than the 'mob of underclothed boys' of 1904!

The older research departments of Arachnology and Entomology could now be joined by new departments of Malacology, Archaeology and Ethno-Archaeology, the last-named being an innovative field of study in South Africa, with its focus on the understanding of indigenous communities through a combination of modern, historical and prehistorical research. An Education Department was also started, and the original Technical Department was greatly increased in size and expertise. Collecting of European cultural material was initiated by Dr Pringle and proceeded so successfully that a large display devoted to white settlers in Natal could be created. A highly original and much acclaimed Marine Gallery was then undertaken and was completed in time for the Museum's 75th anniversary in 1979.

The past decade has seen further growth. Design flaws in the main mammal hall, which had inhibited the exhibit programme, were eventually eliminated when the Trustees took the bold step of restructuring the hall. Exhibits on dinosaurs and African ethnology were set out, and major new galleries for archaeology and geology were embarked on. Departments of Cultural History, Conservation and Lower Invertebrates, have been opened. An interesting new sideline has been research on sixteenth-century Portuguese shipwrecks, which resulted in the identification of some of the oldest wrecks on the South African coast, and the acquisition of magnificent bronze cannons from the *Santiago* which was lost on the Bassas da India reef in 1585.

It would be appropriate in this anniversary year to attempt a review of the Museum's accomplishments and its role in the community it serves. When Dr Warren took up his appointment, he formulated three objectives:

> ... the Museum should be an educational force in the Colony ... the collections should be of practical utility ... and the Museum should in time become a centre for scientific research.

To what extent can it be claimed that these objectives have been met? Public education received priority from the outset. The exhibition galleries offered opportunities

161

for formal and informal education for everyone, and they were immediately popular. In the opening year 16 318 visitors were recorded, of whom 45 per cent were children; such a level of attendance was creditable, as the total population of the town at the time was about 30 790. The throng of visitors has continued; a modern survey revealed the following visitor profile: whites 46 per cent, blacks 27 per cent, Indians 24 per cent, coloureds 3 per cent; 63 per cent lived in Natal, 38 per cent lived locally, 34 per cent were scholars, 42 per cent were children, 13 per cent were housewives, 88 per cent came in company with somebody else, and 90 per cent were enthusiastic about their visit. Of particular note is the fact that the Museum has always been open to all races; indeed, it can claim to have been Pietermaritzburg's first non-racial amenity. From time to time complaints were received about the presence of blacks, but such disapprobations were firmly rejected by the Trustees.

Public talks had been a feature of nineteenth-century Natal Society days, and were continued by Dr Warren; he lectured also to agricultural students, ambulance classes, and student nurses. Today, many thousands of scholars (18 084 in 1986) benefit from the curriculum-enrichment programme provided by the Education Officers; many talks, slide-shows, guided tours and field excursions are arranged for the public; special-interest groups, students and school clubs, with audiences drawn from across the province, and many members of staff participating.

That the Museum has an international reputation for research is beyond doubt. Vast extensions of knowledge in various fields of natural history have been achieved, and the work of our archaeologists has transformed knowledge of the Iron-Age and Stone-Age inhabitants of Natal. By the end of 1986, 16 559 pages of original research had been published in the *Annals of the Natal Museum*. Basic research of this kind is fundamental to progress in the applied sciences.

The Council of Trustees recently made a fresh examination of the Museum's role, and formulated the following restatement of objectives: the Natal Museum aims:

> To increase and to diffuse knowledge and understanding of Man and nature in Southern Africa, through the collection, conservation, study and display of original objects in the fields of natural and cultural history.

This statement encapsulates the traditional functions of a general museum and reaffirms the intrinsic importance of such functions, but it does not imply that the Natal Museum will remain rigidly in its present form or never embark on significantly new developments. Examinations of purpose, roles, and social obligations, are the contemporary concern of museums worldwide; in South Africa such matters are especially urgent because of the rapidly changing and deeply divided nature of our society. Demographic trends presaging changes in the racial composition and distribution of our society, the continuing loss of traditional values, and the possible emergence of new economic orders, as well as a mounting debate about education, among many current issues, are forcing a phase of critical self-evaluation in South African museums. It is already apparent that their traditional form, cast from British and European moulds, may by now have resulted in their having little appeal and uncertain relevance for disadvantaged communities. Developing patterns of urbanization will probably leave the museums in the old city centres, remote from new areas of population growth and settlement; providing a service to such areas will not be possible on traditional lines. The provision of satellite museums in the manner of the American 'neighbourhood museum', in which local communities have a major voice in determining form and content, appears to be a promising solution.

Tribute should be paid to those many citizens of Pietermaritzburg who served on the Council of Trustees. Their contribution to the progress of the Natal Museum has been invaluable. Many City Councillors, university professors and other eminent local persons have been Trustees. A revealing demonstration of their dedication is the fact that there have been only eight Chairmen of the Council in 86 years: Arnold Cooper (1902–14), Sir George Plowman (1914–36), Colonel J. Fraser (1936–38), Professor S. F. Bush (1938–69, a South African record !), Professor G. S. Nienaber (1970–76), Professor R. G. MacMillan (1976–85), Professor J. A. Meester (1985–87), and John M. Deane (1987 to date). The impressive size of the institution today, its high standards, and its good level of public support, would have gratified those earlier citizens of Victorian Pietermaritzburg who laboured in the cause of a museum for the people of Natal.

The Museum has three functions: preservation, research and education. These pictures show archaeologists at work [16] and an Education Officer with a group of school children [17].

16

17

The Voortrekker Museum

Ivor Pols

The continuous hardships and fear which marked the journey of the Great Trek were provisionally brought to a close at Blood River where King Dingane's might was finally broken. For the Voortrekkers, this victory heralded the start of a 'new life'; or at least the opportunity of being able to settle down to a relatively peaceful existence at Pietermartizburg, where the Trekker Council decided, on 23 October 1838, to develop their first town.

Arriving from Blood River, the Voortrekkers soon constructed temporary buildings out of wood and thatch to serve them as a place of worship and a school. Although no permanent church existed at the time, this nevertheless is seen as the first parish formed to the north of the Great River; a development which is akin to the growth of the City of Pietermaritzburg.

Mindful of the Vow which they made before Blood River — should they be successful in breaking the Zulu power — that the day of victory would be regarded by them and their descendants as a day of thanksgiving and as a sabbath, the Voortrekkers during 1839 expressed the wish for a church to be built. For this purpose subscription lists were issued by the Volksraad and building commenced on the modest Church of the Vow, with construction of yellowwood and shale walls two feet thick, enclosing an area 50ft. by 30ft. On 15 March 1840, the consecration took place and the Revd Erasmus Smit who accompanied the Great Trek was installed as its first minister.

In 1861 the building ceased to be used as a place of worship after a new church had been built adjoining the old one. It then became a school and was sold in 1874. On the instigation of Dr G. M. Pellissier, a commission was appointed in 1908 by the council of the Dutch Reformed Church, to investigate means whereby the church could be rescued from desecration, bought back for the people of South Africa and made into a permanent memorial. This was brought about and on the 16 December 1912 it was taken into use as a Voortrekker Museum.

The most impressive and interesting celebration of the Day of the Covenant which has ever been held at Pietermaritzburg was that which took place that day. From country and town Natalians of both language groups assembled to show their appreciation of the Voortrekkers who had held it a sacred duty to fulfil their pledge. On the platform a seat had been given to Aia Jana, an old 'coloured' woman who had accompanied her mistress on the Great Trek, and who was evidently much affected by the proceedings.

The church, completed in 1841, has been remarkably preserved. The building was restored subsequent to its repurchase in 1910, when a front gable and porch were added. The exhibits displayed in the Museum represent various aspects of Voortrekker life. Taking pride of place in the old Church of the Vow stands the pulpit which was prized by the first Dutch Reformed community. It had been removed to the new church in 1861, and thereafter was in regular use until 1955. It is itself a historical monument and is an exquisite piece of workmanship.

The Voortrekkers had advanced with rifle in hand and this aspect of Trekker life has a leading place in the Museum. There is a muzzle-loading elephant gun which had been found in Dingaanstad in December 1838 by Jacobus Phillipus Moolman and which had obviously belonged to one of the Retief party killed by Dingane on 6 February 1838; a flintlock pistol and a powder flask, silver mounted and with gold inscriptions, which had been the property of Trekker Paulus Maree, ancestor of the Maree family of Greytown; a muzzle-loading gun used at the Battle of Blood River, a powder horn, bullet moulds, trimmers and actual bullets.

Voortrekker transport is represented by a wagon chest, among others, which had belonged to Jacobus Odendaal, who had brought it from the Cape in 1836; a tar bucket, originally the property of Voortrekker J. B. Rudolph, which was hung below the wagon and contained tar for greasing the wooden axles; a wagonslipper, used as a break, originally the property of Coenraad Lukas Pieterse who is mentioned in the diary of Erasmus Smit.

Also represented is the Voortrekker at work. In this group is a collection of miscellaneous articles: a square made of stinkwood by Trekker L. Robbertse in 1816; handmade nails used in the construction of the Church of the Vow; a ploughshare made by P. W. Jordaan, blacksmith among the Trekkers in 1852; an old hammer and pointless screws.

Not forgotten is the Trekker woman at work. Here there is a Trekker coffeepot, there an old copper kettle (the property of Jan Thomas Martens); a porcelain meatdish which had been brought from Klaasvoogds River, Robertson district, in 1836 by Mrs Martha Maria Bruwer; a calabash for storing tea-leaves; a meat mincer; an old work-box complete with secret drawer, which was made by Trekker Rautenbach while on his way to Natal; and a workbasket made by Elsie Hendrina Nel, the wife of Jeremias Nel.

The Voortrekkers were a highly religious community. Although it is somewhat difficult to arrive at the true state of their literary attainments, some light can be shed on this by a study of the literature in their possession at the time of the Great Trek, a considerable amount of which has fortunately been preserved and is now housed in the Voortrekker Museum. The impression generally held that their literature was limited to the Bible, the Book of Psalms and Hymnal, is not valid. The books in their possession would appear to have included: biblical commentaries, homilies, religious meditations, anthems and an occasional literary work. A book which the Voortrekker housewife would have consulted regularly was the seventeenth-century recipe book *De Volmaakte Hollandsche Keukenmeid* written by 'Eene Voorname Mevrouwe' (an Important Woman). Many examples of the literature read by the Voortrekker children are preserved in the museum, for instance *De Kleine Printbybel*, which uses lively illustrations to explain a Bible text.

Varying views are held with regard to the fashions of the Voortrekkers. There is a tendency to lay down hard and fast rules. Like modern women the Voortrekker mothers and their daughters also exhibited a taste for dainty clothing and pretty colours and usually selected material with attractive floral designs. The dress material of the early days shows marked superiority in quality if compared with that of the present day. This is evident if we look at the present state of dresses and material of the period in the Voortrekker Museum. Pieces of bright coloured taffeta and satin frocks and shawls of the same material dating more than a hundred years back are still in a state of good preservation. The dress worn by the first Voortrekker woman who arrived in Natal is on exhibit.

Dresses for daily use were made of floral, checked or striped cotton material, with silk, satin, velvet and brocade being kept for best. Closely connected with the dresses were the aprons which were worn on all occasions. The Voortrekker women were passionately fond of neckerchiefs and scarves which served as the only decoration of these frocks of simple cut. They were pinned together with a gold, silver or ivory brooch. The Voortrekker bonnet, although simple in itself, ranks amongst the most picturesque and artistic items of Voortrekker dress. The bonnets still remain as evidence of the skill and artistic taste of the past generation. No photograph or description is capable of doing justice to the art displayed in them.

The Voortrekker men were also fond of fine clothes and of soft, becoming material. The type of trousers worn was known as flaptrouser. Felt hats with broad brims and flat crowns were usually worn. Waistcoats worn on special occasions were made of rich satin, silk, velvet and satin brocade and so on. The Voortrekker Museum has the wedding waistcoats of Sarel Cilliers, Pieter Lafras Uys and Commandant-General Andries Pretorius. Their ordinary working clothes were of coarser material, such as tweed and moleskin. The men, as well as the women, wore handmade leather shoes.

The Voortrekker Museum was proclaimed an historical monument in 1937. During the past six years the Voortrekker Museum has undergone vast changes and greatly expanded.

Under the auspices of the Voortrekker Museum, many projects have been undertaken to preserve the Voortrekker heritage in Pietermaritzburg and its environs. The house of Andries Pretorius, first double-storey built outside the Cape Colony, was situated on the farm Welverdiend some 20 kilometres from the City. This house has been reconstructed adjacent to the Museum, using as much of the original building material as possible. With Museum funds and help from many private firms, this project was completed in 1981.

Voortrekker House was another addition to the Voortrekker Museum complex. Situated at 333 Boom Street, this is the oldest double-storey Voortrekker house in Pietermaritzburg, and was probably the first dwelling in the City to be painted in colour inside (light blue on the ground floor and pink upstairs). The old house, a declared national monument, was purchased by the Museum and completely restored.

The complex was extended in 1984 by the erection in the courtyard of Andries Pretorius House of a double-storey building to house a workshop, library and offices. In addition, negotiations have just been concluded to incorporate the huge property of Longmarket Street Girls' School. A project being planned at the moment is the restoration of the historical portion of the Voortrekker farm Zaaylager on the outskirts of Escourt, which was saved at the eleventh hour by private citizens.

The Voortrekker Museum was the first in southern Africa to receive the full accreditation of the South African Museum Association.

Two Voortrekker-period houses are now annexes of the Museum. Next to the Museum is a replica of Andries Pretorius's Edendale farmhouse [18] and at 333 Boom Street an early double-storey house [19].

18

19

The Presbyterian Church in Church Street was one of the City's earliest churches. Though much altered, it is still readily recognizable. In this picture Theophilus Shepstone can be seen conducting an indaba with chiefs outside the church, which, in 1865, was still in its original form.

CHAPTER TEN

City of Diverse Faiths

1

World religions in Pietermaritzburg

Ian Darby

Patrick Maxwell

Pietermaritzburg is a place where people from Europe and Asia have met those of Africa. These people have all brought with them languages, customs and beliefs, so it is not surprising that most of the world religions are represented in Pietermaritzburg. Although Christianity with its various strands predominates, African indigenous religion, Hinduism and Islam also have strong support. Judaism has had a small following since the beginning of European settlement. Buddhism has made its appearance during the present century.

Indigenous African religion has existed since earliest times. The high God *uMvelinqange* was worshipped by the Nguni people who venerated their ancestors, believing them to possess a mediatorial role between people and God. The ancestors' good pleasure was invoked and any anger appeased at the regular ceremonies of slaughtering and praise song. By means of the ancestors, community was maintained. The ceremony of *imbeleko* which followed the birth of a child gave it personhood and identity. Likewise after death *ukubuyisa* ensured that the deceased was accepted by the ancestors.

African religion easily assimilated the Christian gospel, with Jesus as mediator, Saviour and Lord being given most of the ancestors' role. Nevertheless the ancestors continue to be venerated and the traditional ceremonies are practised side by side with the Christian rites and sacraments. Worship in the medium of Zulu is expressed with a spirit and vigour unmatched by anything in the European languages. The African Independent churches abound in all cities in southern Africa, displaying the rhythm, life and colour of this continent.

Christianity came to Pietermaritzburg with the different streams of European settlers. The Dutch introduced the faith and the British settlement contributed the many different denominations. The Trekkers who gave the place its name in 1838 were devout adherents of the Dutch Reformed Church, but they had set out on the Great Trek without the support of the Cape synod. Those who came to Natal were accompanied by a former missionary, Erasmus Smit, who served as their *predikant*. A church was built to commemorate the vow taken before the military success at Blood River. Called the Geloftekerk, it was completed in 1840, the first service being conducted on 15 March. On account of failing health and doubtful ordination, Smit was replaced by Daniel Lindley of the American Board of Missions.

The Church of the Vow continued to be served by missionaries for some years. Then in April 1861 a new church was completed. The original church was later reacquired and restored, and in 1912 it was opened as the Voortrekker Museum.

Following the British annexation of Natal in 1842, Christian denominations of the English-speaking variety were introduced. The Reverend John Richards arrived in 1846. He had been sent by the Wesleyan Missionary Society to evangelize primarily the indigenous Zulu, but was immediately appointed chaplain for the military and civilian British. The Wesleyan Church had acquired erf 15 Longmarket Street and, in 1848, they opened a chapel — hence the name Chapel Street — which is still standing. Fronting onto Church Street the Wesleyans built a mission in which Richards conducted worship in both Zulu and English.

In the meantime in Edendale the Reverend James Allison established his mission farm. After starting work

Chapel Street takes its name from the Wesleyan Chapel and mission premises which were well established by the 1850s.

2

at Ndaleni near Richmond he had fallen out with the Wesleyans and so had moved to Edendale to start an independent venture. It was based on the idea of a self-contained agricultural and craft community. In 1854 Bishop Colenso inspected the enterprise and was determined to follow the same pattern at his own mission station.

Revival in true Methodist fashion necessitated a new chapel for Pietermaritzburg. It was opened in 1859 and is substantially part of the present Metropolitan Church. The gallery was erected in 1878 to cater for the increasing congregation. Four years later a further church was opened in Boshoff Street.

The first major influx of British settlers brought about the establishment of a further four Christian denominations in Pietermaritzburg. In 1849 and 1850 the Anglicans, Congregationalists, Presbyterians and Roman Catholics gathered congregations. Although most of the British already in Pietermaritzburg were adherents of the Church of England, the first Anglican clergyman arrived only in 1849. The Reverend James Green was sent by Bishop Gray of Cape Town as the colonial chaplain. His services were conducted in the government schoolroom at the corner of Chapel and Longmarket Streets. Land was acquired — the present cathedral site — and plans were prepared for the first Church of England.

Bishop Gray visited Pietermaritzburg in 1850 and saw the need for division of his diocese to enable the missionary work to progress. In 1853 John William Colenso was appointed and consecrated Bishop of the Natal Colony. Colenso was a mathematician with a critical enquiring mind but was not endowed with tact or statesmanship. Believing that the Zulu were already inspired with religious beliefs and principles, he commenced his mission on that basis and so clashed with fellow missionaries and church authorities.

Colenso had, however, brought with him to Natal a team of gifted people. One such person, Henry Callaway, was both medical doctor and priest and he started the first

Anglican Zulu mission in the City. St. Mary's Church was erected near the corner of Longmarket Street and Commercial Road and served the Zulu both there and in its subsequent site in Burger Street. Callaway left Pietermaritzburg in 1858 to found a mission near Ixopo. Colenso continued to work his own mission station, Ekukhanyeni, at Bishopstowe. In 1855 he opened St. Andrew's Church in Pietermaritz Street and in 1857 St. Peter's Cathedral.

As a result of the Colenso controversy and the church schism, St. Saviour's in Commercial Road was opened in 1868. William Kenneth Macrorie, as Bishop of Maritzburg, arrived in the following year and created St. Saviour's as his cathedral in 1877. Also during his episcopate St. Mark's in Carbineer Street, St. Luke's, Boshoff Street and the convent of St. John the Divine, Loop Street were all established. It was only after Colenso's death in 1883 and Macrorie's resignation ten years later that the churches of St. Peter and St. Saviour were reconciled. Although continuing as separate parishes, both now came under the Bishop of Natal, who chose St. Saviour's as his cathedral. St. Peter's became known as the Old Cathedral.

In October 1849 a meeting was held in a private home to organize Pietermaritzburg's first Congregational Church. Services were conducted from that date in hired buildings in English for the settlers and Dutch for the 'coloured population'. Land was acquired and a church was completed in 1863. The building in Longmarket Street opposite Buchanan Street still stands and serves as an annex to a health studio. It was used by the Congregationalists for two long periods. Further churches were opened in Boshoff Street in 1884 and in Greyling Street for the Zulu in 1890.

Congregationalists were of an independent nature and were usually known by that name. Freedom of religious interpretation and practice was allowed. Their minister, the Reverend S. Waterhouse, refused to condemn Bishop Colenso's teachings. Both infant as well as believer's baptism were permitted, thus providing a home for those of

3

WESLEYAN MISSION PREMISES, PIETERMAURITZBERG, VICTORIA.

the Baptist persuasion. Intercommunion was practised from early times. Independent attitudes can have their drawbacks as well, and Congregationalists had some difficulty in forming a denominational structure in Natal. Some members could become too independent, as did the Reverend W. Berry, who resigned and broke away in 1883 to form a short-lived rival congregation at St. Andrew's Church.

The first meeting of Presbyterians in Pietermaritzburg was held in Congregationalist premises in October 1850. The Reverend William Campbell arrived in the following year to be the first minister and services were conducted in various places, including the Dutch Reformed Church. In 1852 the Presbyterian Church in Church Street opposite the Colonial Buildings was opened. It still stands today, although it has not been used as a place of worship since 1942.

In 1865 William Campbell was joined by the Reverend John Smith as an assistant. Regrettably, disagreements led to his resignation in 1870. Together with supporters, Smith started a new congregation at St. Mary's. Three years later they opened St. John's Presbyterian Church in Longmarket Street next to St. Peter's. Several attempts were made to unite the two congregations but it was only in 1942 that this was achieved. In the meantime a mission of the Free Church of Scotland was opened in Loop Street in the 1860s with the Reverend John Bruce as its first minister.

Almost simultaneous with the introduction of Presbyterian worship was the celebration of the first mass of the Roman Catholic church. Father Thomas Murphy officiated in the home of Captain John McDonnell in Loop Street in November 1850. In July of the following year Jean Francois Allard was consecrated Bishop for Natal. Being an Oblate of Mary Immaculate he commenced a tradition whereby the Oblates have since served many of the Natal churches. On Christmas Day 1852 a chapel in Loop Street opposite the present St. Mary's was opened for use. A larger church in Longmarket Street was later erected and the building now serves as St. Mary's hall.

Bishop Allard initiated much missionary and educational work in his far-flung jurisdiction which included Lesotho, Zululand and the Transvaal, in addition

A newly married couple in the 1880s leaving the Metropolitan Methodist Church, corner of Longmarket and Chapel Streets.

4

to the Colony of Natal. In 1874 he was succeeded by Charles Constant Jolivet. The work was consolidated during Jolivet's episcopate with the opening of St. Joan of Arc's Church in Ohrtmann Road, the original St. Anthony's in Berg Street, the establishment of a convent next to the original Catholic Church by the Holy Family sisters, and a school for girls attached to it. Later in the century the Augustinian sisters opened the Sanatorium, which later became St. Anne's hospital.

Having accommodated themselves with the Congregationalists, the Baptists were rather late in forming their own church. Following a meeting in February 1884, land was bought in Chapel Street and in July 1885 the City Tabernacle was opened. Financial problems and a revival congregation, the Bethel Tabernacle, forced the City Tabernacle to close temporarily, but in 1893 it reopened as a united Baptist Church. The congregation grew from strength to strength and the revivalist preaching of the Reverend F. G. West drew such large crowds that on occasions the Town Hall had to be hired to accommodate the numbers.

A small number of Jews was present among Pietermaritzburg European settlers. Jonas Bergtheil, after establishing a settlement at New Germany, opened a store in Pietermaritzburg in 1845. The Jewish cemetery in Clarendon provides a record of Jews who lived and died in the town, but the small numbers meant that the first Hebrew congregation was established only in 1884, with James Henry Isaacs as its president. It was still without its own premises, the annual Jewish festivals having to be observed in the Masonic hall. A rival congregation was formed in the early 1900s but the two were united when the synagogue in Pine Street was consecrated in 1914.

With the expansion of Pietermaritzburg towards the end of the last century it was necessary for the different denominations to plant new churches. It seems as if the Methodists and Anglicans were often equal to this task, although in Boshoff Street they were joined by the Congregationalists. In lower Longmarket Street both Anglicans and Methodists built churches to serve as missions for Asians. In Victoria Road and Prestbury their buildings appeared almost simultaneously and not quite opposite each other. A later divergence emerged with the Methodists building in Mountain Rise and the Anglicans dedicating their church at Allerton in 1908. The Roman Catholics expanded with the opening of St. Anthony's and its school in Loop Street in 1901. A regrettable move on the part of the Catholics was the decision that from that year onwards the Bishop would be based in Durban instead of in Pietermaritzburg.

Many smaller religious groupings made their appearances early in the present century. The Salvation Army built its present headquarters in Chapel Street. The Seventh-day Adventists met in Stranack Street and the Old Apostolics in Pietermaritz Street. The Spiritualists gathered in Loop Street, and the Christian Scientists took over the original Congregational Church. In 1905 the Congregationalists, having outgrown their premises, moved into their splendid new edifice at the corner of Chapel and Loop Streets. By 1945 the building was too large for their needs and so they exchanged with the Christian Scientists, returning to their original church.

The German Lutherans built their church in Pine Street in 1913. In more recent years the Jehovah's Witnesses and Mormons have established themselves as flourishing congregations, the Jehovah's Witnesses in their local kingdom halls and the Mormons in Alexandra Road. The Christadelphians now worship in the original Nederduitsch Hervormde building in Boom Street.

Mainly as a result of the missionary campaigns of Pastor J. F. Rowlands, Bethesda congregations of the pentecostal movement have been established in the City and elsewhere. In July 1925 the first was formed in Pietermaritzburg and subsequently several more were founded. Since the Second World War many other pentecostal groups have also been thriving throughout the city: Calvary Full Gospel Church was opened in 1952 in Victoria Road; and more recently a second congregation was started in Chase Valley. In Chapel Street the Apostoliese Geloof Sending Kerk was opened in 1960. In 1964 the Assembly of God was established in Scottsville.

The growing suburb of Scottsville had possessed St. Alphege's Anglican Church since 1927. The Presbyterian Church was opened in Ridge Road in 1950. The Baptists opened their church later. The establishment of Sobantu Village between the two world wars attracted churches for the Baptists, Congregationalists and Anglicans.

Expansion of the Dutch Reformed Church has been noticeable since the war years. In 1939 the foundation stone for the Eeufees Kerk was laid in Boom Street for the Pietermaritzburg West Congregation. In more recent years *gemeentes* have been established in Prestbury, Napierville, Scottsville, Northdale, Woodlands and Hayfields. The smaller sister church, the Gereformeerde Kerk van Suid-Afrika, opened its present building in Greyling Street in 1952. After worshipping in their church in Boom Street for many years, the Nederduitsch Hervormde Kerk moved round the corner into Pine Street to take over its elegant new building in 1965.

Most of the long established denominations of the City have recently replaced their churches. The Roman Catholics built their splendid St. Mary's in 1928. The Presbyterians built on the site of St. John's to house the now united city congregations. The Baptists and Dutch Reformed have been in modern style churches for some years. St. Alphege's and St. David's have both been replaced. The Congregationalists once again moved out of their original building to take over the Anglican Convent Chapel and premises in 1968. The German Lutherans have moved to a new building in Hayfields. The Hebrew congregation consecrated their new synagogue in Clarendon in 1982 after their property in Pine Street was expropriated by the municipality.

The implementation of the Group Areas Act has meant dwindling numbers of Zulu-speaking worshippers in the city centre. The mission churches have all been closed but Anglicans, Methodists, Presbyterians and Roman Catholics conduct services in the Zulu medium in addition to English. Large churches of all denominations have been built at Imbali and Edendale. In addition to expanding in those areas, the Church of England in South Africa, after selling Bishop Colenso's St. Mary's to the Provincial Administration, has developed a flourishing congregation in the Alexandra Road area.

The suburbs of Woodlands and Northdale have both mushroomed in recent years, as has the number of churches. St. Luke's was moved from Boshoff Street to Woodlands. Roman Catholics, Anglicans and Methodists have had their places of worship in Raisethorpe and Mountain Rise for some years.

A moving towards greater understanding and working together has been a characteristic of the recent Christian scene. Two bodies, the Presbyterians and the Anglicans, have been able to reconcile their hitherto divided city congregations, with the latter building a new cathedral to symbolize by its cylindrical shape the unity of the church. Two missions, in 1963 and 1975, have been conducted by Pietermaritzburg's home-grown Africa Enterprise incorporating most of the Christian churches. The charismatic movement, emerging in Pietermaritzburg in the 1970s, brought about greater understanding and cooperation between older denominations such as Anglicans and Roman Catholics and the pentecostal bodies. In November 1974 thousands of members of the Presbyterian, Methodist, Congregationalist and Anglican bodies covenanted to work together for unity. United churches have been established at Eastwood, the Grange and Athlone. Shared buildings exist in Scottsville and Hayfields. Arriving in 1976, the Federal Theological Seminary in Imbali trains students for the ministry on an ecumenical basis. The Evangelical Bible Seminary in Pine Street commenced similar work in 1980 on non-denominational lines.

The ever changing pattern, however, is by no means only in the direction of unity. At all times there is the formation of new groups, often the result of division and splintering. Reactions to the racial and political upheavals of the country produce further divisions with many of the traditional lines of demarcation becoming blurred and being overshadowed by new formations. The Christian Centre is a movement which has only recently emerged. Thousands have been attracted to its lively services, many

The Ebenezer Chapel in Ebenezer Street in *c.*1867. It was built by the missionary James Allison for his black congregation, and was administered by the Free Church of Scotland.

5

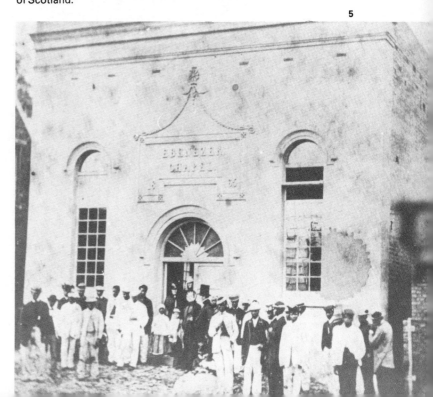

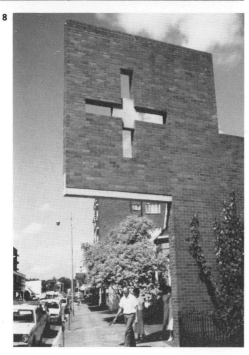

abandoning traditional denominations. Other new groups follow in its wake.

Hindu Indians started to arrive in Pietermaritzburg in about 1870. Freed from their indentures on the coastal canefields, many Indians took up market gardening and the hawking of fruit and vegetables in the various centres of the colony.

Hinduism is renowned for its almost bewildering diversity. The Natal Hindu religious scene illustrates this in microcosm, with its wide variety of religious and cultural organizations, temples, shrines and halls. As it is impossible to deal with every facet of Pietermaritzburg Hindu life, attention will be concentrated mostly on three broad religious groupings — the so-called Sanathanists or traditional Hindus, the neo-Vedanta groups, and those who follow the uncompromisingly monotheistic way of Arya Samaj.

The overwhelming majority of Pietermaritzburg's earliest Hindus, as well as many of their modern descendants, are often referred to as Sanathanists, i.e. those who feel at home with the traditional Hinduism of the popular Scriptures, the colourful rituals and religious cermonies, and the myths and stories about the deities of classical and medieval Hinduism, notably the great gods Vishnu and Shiva. An important local organization representing this sort of Hinduism is the Pietermaritzburg Sanathan Ved Dharam Sabha. The term 'Sanathan' comes from the age-old Sanskrit name for what westerners refer to as Hinduism, namely Sanatana Dharma, the Eternal Way. The Sabha has its hall and shrine on the corner of Bombay Road and Lotus Road, Northdale. Its aims and objectives are similar to those of the national body Shree Sanathan Dharma Sabha of South Africa. These two *sabhas* (*sabha* means 'association') try to encourage the development and understanding of traditional Hindu religion and culture.

Local Hindu temples which exemplify Sanathanist Hinduism include the Sri Siva Soobramoniar and Marriamen Temples on the corner of lower Longmarket Street and Williams Street, and the Sri Vishnu Temple in Longmarket Street on the opposite side of the road. The Siva temple complex celebrated its centenary in 1985, while the diamond jubilee celebrations of the Vishnu Temple took place three years earlier.

The Siva temple complex includes two main temple buildings, both of which were officially opened in 1925. The Siva Soobramoniar Temple, the one closest to Longmarket Street, contains images or *murtis* of Soobramoniar or Muruga, the elephant-headed Ganesha (remover of obstacles), Vishnu, and the great god Shiva himself, both in his aspect as Cosmic Dancer and in his *lingam* (sacred pillar) form, which represents luminosity, infinity or fertility. Soobramoniar and Ganesha are both important sons of Shiva. The Marriamen Temple contains images and representations of many female manifestations of deity, among them Marriamen herself, who is divine patron of rain and the healing of diseases, Draupadi (goddess of firewalking), many-armed Durga, the fierce goddess Kali, and Ganga. The annual firewalking ceremony, in honour of Draupadi, takes place every Good Friday. Devotees demonstrate their faith by walking across the fire-pit in front of the Marriamen Temple.

The two most famous master-builders of South African Hindu temples, Kistappa Reddy and K. R. Pillay, were to some extent involved in the construction of these two temples.

The Vishnu Temple, with its traditional north Indian veranda to enable devotees to walk around the shrine, was completed by 1922, and consecrated in 1924. The temple contains images of the great god Vishnu and his consort Lakshmi, goddess of good fortune, as well as representations of Vishnu's two most important incarnations in human form, Rama and Krishna. Rama's heroic exploits are narrated in the religious epic known as the *Ramayana*, while Krishna is famed as the central figure of the celebrated *Bhagavad Gita* (Song of the Lord), the most popular of all the Hindu Scriptures. Other representations in the Vishnu Temple include Hanuman, the monkey-god who championed Rama's cause, Shiva, his son Ganesha, Shiva's *lingam* (sacred pillar), and the Divine Mother.

South African Hindus are often classified into four basic linguistic-cultural groups: Hindis and Gujeratis, originally with north and central Indian links; and Tamils and Telugus, originally with south Indian links. The Siva temple complex has traditionally catered mostly for Tamils, in contrast to the Hindi orientation of the Vishnu Temple.

Hinduism is predominantly a religion of the home: the traditional temples are not often used for congregational worship. Nonetheless, popular Hindu festivals are celebrated at the various temples as well as at most of the other local Hindu religious institutions. These festivals include Krishna Asthmee (Krishna's birthday), Deepavali (Festival of light), Shivarathri (Night of Shiva) and Ramnaumee (Rama's birthday).

Popular Pietermaritzburg Hinduism is also well represented by the Siva Nyana Sabha, established in the late 1960s. The Sabha encourages the promotion of south Indian religious culture, and one of the highlights of its year is the ten-day Navarathree festival in honour of the Divine Mother. The Sabha's hall and shrine are on the corner of Chetty and Nulliah Roads, Northdale. The shrine contains representations of Shiva, Ganesha and the Divine Mother herself in some of her important

The magnificent nave of St. Mary's Roman Catholic Church in Loop Street.[6]

The mihrab in the City's oldest mosque, the Soorti Suni,[7] or Top Mosque.

The Anglican Cathedral of the Holy Nativity reaching out to passers-by in Longmarket Street.[8]

The *cella*, or tower, of the Sri Siva Soobramaniar Temple.[9]

A little piece of India in Pietermaritzburg: the temples, minarets, gables and trees of lower Longmarket Street.[10]

The City's older mosques are unobtrusive. The Soorti Suni is located down a lane off upper Church Street.[11]

manifestations. The consecration of the shrine was performed in March 1976 by a revered sage and mystic from India.

The Gujerati Vedic Society is responsible for a recently-built temple, the Radha-Krishna Mandir, in Royston Road, Mountain Rise. The main images are Krishna and Radha. The temple is open to all worshippers, regardless of religious affiliation. A proposed Mahatma Gandhi hall is to be built alongside the temple.

Many Sanathanist householders, especially Hindis, occasionally engage in a ceremony known as *katha* and *jhanda*. This ceremony, conducted by a Hindu priest, involves the erection of a three-cornered flag on a bamboo pole, as well as the telling of a sacred story whose central theme is the triumph of good over evil. *Katha* and *jhanda* may be performed as a result of the fulfilment of a specific religious vow, or it may simply be an expression of thanksgiving.

Until the turn of the century, local Hinduism was exclusively Sanathanist in orientation. The twentieth century has seen the establishment of various renewal (or neo-Hindu) movements in South Africa, particularly in Natal. Local examples of such movements include Hare Krishna, the neo-Vedanta groups and the Ayra Samaj.

The Hare Krishna movement, known officially as the International Society for Krishna Consciousness or ISKCON, has taken solid root in South Africa during the last decade. Their magnificent temple in Chatsworth, near Durban, is now a significant national religious landmark. Although no Hare Krishna temple exists in Pietermaritzburg there are a number of local devotees,

The Shri Vishnu Temple
where Hindi-speaking Hindus worship.

12

SHRI VISHNU TEMPLE

some of whom are no longer related to ISKCON. Hare Krishna represents a reformed Hinduism which takes the *Bhagavad Gita* as its central Scripture. It emphasizes the all-encompassing reality of Krishna, the eternal yet essentially personal God who can grant release from the cycle of reincarnation to all who approach him in love and devotion.

Two important neo-Vedanta organizations based in Durban are the Ramakrishna Centre of South Africa (founded in 1942) and the Divine Life Society of South Africa (founded in 1949). The Ramakrishna Centre has a Pietermaritzburg branch in Northdale at the corner of Sarojini and Hardev Roads. The basic message of the Centre has been summed up by Swami Vivekananda (1863-1902) in terms of the divinity within every human being as the basis of spirituality, human dignity and service to others. Vivekananda was the chief disciple of Sri Ramakrishna, the God-intoxicated nineteenth century Indian mystic. In the words of Ramakrishna:

> Many are the names of God and infinite the forms through which He may be accepted. In whatever name and form you worship Him, through that He will be realized by you.

The two local centres of the Divine Life Society are in Loop Street and in Northdale on the corner of Mysore and Lahore Roads. Each centre is called Sivanandashram after the late Swami Sivananda, the revered spiritual Master of the Divine Life Society's *ashram* and headquarters in Rishikesh, India. A recently-produced revised version of the publication *Sivananda's Gospel of Divine Life* gives an excellent impression of the spiritual concerns of the Society, which include a life of compassion and service, and a dedicated willingness to tread the path toward God-realization.

The Ramakrishna Centre and the Divine Life Society aim to promote spiritual knowledge by means of relevant literature, regular religious services, educational and cultural programmes and yoga/meditation facilities.

The Saiva Sithantha Sungum of South Africa, which was founded in 1937, has its headquarters in Durban. Its Pietermaritzburg centre, on the corner of Veerappa Road and Gangalu Place in Northdale, was officially opened in 1980. Although there are strong historical links and continuities between the medieval Indian 'Saiva Siddhanta' (a religious and philosophical tradition emphasizing the supreme, incomparable yet gracious God Shiva) and the contemporary Saiva Sithantha Sungum, the Sungum today is probably best known for its emphasis on the essential unity, universality and fellowship of all religions — an emphasis which it shares with the Ramakrishna Centre and the Divine Life Society. The various living faiths are all believed to lead towards the same ultimate divine goal.

The Ramakrishna Centre, the Divine Life Society and the Saiva Sithantha Sungum are all constituent members of the recently-established Hindu Alliance of South Africa. The first issue of the Alliance's newspaper, *Hindu Dharma*, contains an editorial which endorses basic neo-Vedanta themes such as the divinity of every human being, a sense of responsibility to others, and the validity of the various world religions as complementary pathways to God.

No survey of the local Hindu scene can afford to neglect one of the most impressive religious structures in Pietermaritzburg, namely the Gita Mandir in Privet Road, Raisethorpe. It was conceived, planned and built by members of the Hindu Prayer Circle, a religious organization formed in 1953. The Gita Mandir was officially opened in August 1975. For many years its spiritual head and revered guru was the late Guru Rambaran, who was also the founder and leading light of the Prayer Circle.

The structure of the Gita Mandir has a symbolic and spiritual significance. An impressive library, housing scriptures and religious books from a variety of living faiths, dominates the lowest of the Mandir's four levels. On the ground floor is a large congregational hall for religious services, with an impressive image of Lord Krishna which stands 1,8 metres high. A meditation room is to be found on the next highest level; it contains representations of Krishna, Rama and other manifestations of Absolute Deity. On the topmost level of the Gita Mandir stands the small empty Temple of Silence, where practitioners of yoga seek to realize inner union with the Divine. The Gita Mandir's religious life tends to be oriented towards the Vedanta dimension of Hinduism, and the *Bhagavad Gita* is valued as the primary Scripture.

What distinguishes the Hindu Prayer Circle and the Gita Mandir from the world of Sanathanist Hinduism is their conviction that certain Sanathanist beliefs and practices are unnecessary or spiritually misleading, e.g. the mediatorial role of traditional priests, the allegedly unedifying mythology of the Scriptures known as Puranas, and the many so-called 'superstitions' and popular rituals which preoccupy most Sanathanist worshippers.

After Guru Rambaran's death in 1984, a group of his disciples from the Gita Mandir established a society known as Guru Rambaranji's Vedanta Satsang Society of South Africa. The Society's centre, which operates under the guidance of Sri Roopchand Dhanilal, is in Royston Road, Mountain Rise. Mr Dhanilal emphasizes that the life of the Society is spiritually inspired by the teachings of Guru Rambaran and Sri Sathya Sai Baba of India. Sai Baba is regarded as the present incarnation of God on earth.

Before leaving the world of neo-Vedanta, mention should be made of Pietermaritzburg's Sathya Sai Baba groups, two examples of which are the Sri Sathya Sai Baba Centre in Newholme and the Bhagwan Sri Sathya Sai Baba Centre of Pietermaritzburg Central. Their religious and cultural life focuses on Sai Baba, who is revered as a spiritually realized God-man. His teaching promotes the fatherhood of God and the brotherhood of man, and encourages people to identify with the Divine. This is seen as the basic purpose of the various world religions.

In April 1984 the Veda Dharma Sabha of Pietermaritzburg celebrated its 75th anniversary. The Sabha, founded in 1909 by Swami Shankaranand, is one of the most significant Ayra Samaj organizations in South Africa. It controls two local *mandirs* or temples: the Vedic Mandir in lower Longmarket Street, and the Vedic Mandir in Nohar Road, Northdale. The consecrations of these temples, in 1958 and 1978 respectively, were performed by the well-known Arya Samaj scholar and educator Pandit Nardev Vedalankar of Durban.

Arya Samajists are often referred to as 'Vedic' Hindus because of their conviction that the Scriptures known as the four Vedas contain universally and eternally applicable teachings, that the infallible divine knowledge which they enshrine was revealed by God to four sages in times immemorial. It is over a hundred years since Swami Dayanand Saraswati founded a reforming movement in India named Arya Samaj (Society of the Righteous) to bring Hindus 'back to the Vedas' and to the truths they contain. The Arya Samaj emphasis is on one formless, almighty, unchanging God who has intelligence and will, who has created the universe out of pre-existing matter, and who now sustains it. Each human being possesses an eternal soul, and can find fulfilment and peace through knowledge of the truth, through prayer, worship and meditation, and through an ethically disciplined life. Although individual souls can never become God, they can advance spiritually to the point where they attain full God-realization and eventually break free from the limitations of ordinary existence.

Other Arya Samaj organizations in Pietermaritzburg include the Raisethorpe Arya Samaj, with its Ved Mandir on the grounds of the old Baijoo and Maharaj school, Old Greytown Road; the Plessislaer Arya Samaj, with its Ved Mandir on the corner of Gandhi and Madurai Roads in Northdale; the Vedic Vidya Pracharak Sabha in Mountain Rise; and the Mt. Partridge Arya Samaj in Northdale. These four organizations, along with the Veda Dharma Sabha, are members of the Arya Pratinidhi Sabha, a national Arya Samaj association with its offices in Durban. The Sabha was established in 1925.

The Plessislaer Arya Samaj, the Vedic Vidya Pracharak Sabha, and the Mt. Partridge Arya Samaj were significant victims of the Group Areas Act, which forced them to move from Plessislaer, Pentrich and Mt. Partridge respectively to their present homes.

While the main goal of Arya Samaj Hinduism is the upholding of Vedic Truth, the various organizations also emphasize the importance of promoting Indian culture in general and the study of Indian languages in particular, especially Hindi.

What clearly distinguishes Arya Samaj adherents from virtually all their fellow Hindus is their conviction that the eternal, formless God can never take on any form, whether human or non-human. This means that God has no incarnations, nor can he ever legitimately be represented by any image or idol. Arya Samaj temples therefore contain no images.

If the central Scriptures of the Sanathanists are the Puranas and the Epics, and the most philosophically relevant Scriptures for many neo-Vedantists are the Upanishads, then the Arya Samaj lays great emphasis on the very earliest sacred writings of India, namely the four Vedas. Nonetheless, what unites all Hindus is: first, a belief in the interminable process of repeated reincarnation, which is governed by karma, i.e. the impersonal law of spiritual cause and effect; second, the conviction that, in the last analysis, there is one

THE CONTROVERSY SURROUNDING
BISHOP COLENSO

Ian Darby

John William Colenso,
Bishop of Natal (1853—83).

Pietermaritzburg in the nineteenth century was the unlikely venue of an ecclesiastical controversy which caused ripples over much of the British Empire. It would have been unexpected in any quarter; yet with hindsight we can see that such a chapter of conflicts was inevitable.

The controversy surrounding the first Anglican Bishop of Natal was caused primarily by disputed interpretations of the Bible. Nevertheless Bishop Colenso's personality would in any case have attracted controversy, as would the nature of his chief opponent, Dean James Green. They were both hard-headed, zealous pioneers determined to establish the church in the infant Colony according to principles which were diametrically opposed to each other. John William Colenso was a liberal thinker and desired his missionary work to be based on the idea that all people were members of a human family under God.

Christ had redeemed them from the curse of Adam's fall and it was the missionary's task to take this good news to the Zulu. Dean Green on the other hand was determined to build the church on the foundation of orthodox doctrine and tradition and to be free from any state control. Both leaders were on an obvious collision course.

Although tension was present within church circles since the Bishop's arrival in 1854, matters came to a head in the 1860s when he published his commentaries on Paul's Letter to the Romans and the first five books of the Bible. Colenso's novel doctrine of salvation and his doubts about the accuracy of the Bible led to an ecclesiastical trial presided over by Bishop Robert Gray of Cape Town. Colenso was found guilty of heresy and upon refusing to retract, he was excommunicated. The civil courts ruled that because of defects in their appointments, Gray had no authority over Colenso, who was entitled to retain his bishopric and properties. Dean Green and others loyal to Gray were forced to leave and establish their own church, St. Saviour's. A schism resulted and it persisted until almost the end of the century.

Once the two church factions settled down to exist side by side, Bishop Colenso became embroiled in a campaign for a just treatment of Chief Langalibalele who he considered had suffered a mockery of a trial. Colenso succeeded in being heard, with Lieutenant-Governor Pine being recalled, but he lost much popular support among the colonists as well as the valued friendship of Theophilus Shepstone. Colenso's protests at the war with the Zulu, which he thought the British had deliberately provoked, were even stronger and the last years of his life were spent in campaigning for King Cetshwayo. Colenso died in 1883 and was buried in St. Peter's Cathedral.

St. Saviour's Cathedral in Commercial Road, *c.*1885. In its short history Pietermaritzburg has had three Anglican cathedrals. The first, St. Peter's in Church Street, was completed in 1857 by J. W. Colenso, Bishop of Natal. At the height of the Colenso controversy W. K. Macrorie was appointed Bishop of Maritzburg and he chose St. Saviour's Church (first opened in 1868) as his cathedral in 1877. With the healing of the schism after 1891 and the recent building of the new Cathedral of the Holy Nativity, St. Saviour's was deemed redundant and demolished in 1976. Part of this very fine brick-built edifice was re-erected at Halfway House near Pretoria; while the remaining bricks went to the building of a new house in Pietermaritzburg. Some of the stained glass was incorporated in the new cathedral.

Ultimate Divine Reality who is the spiritual goal of all creaturely existence, and that it is only by coming to terms with this Reality that anyone will be enabled to break free from the chain of reincarnation; and third, the recognition that the *Bhagavad Gita* is one of the best loved and most used Hindu Scriptures. Although different branches of Hinduism interpret the *Gita* in different ways, there is common agreement that one of its fundamental themes is 'action without attachment'. The important thing is not to try to cease all action by literally renouncing the world, but to carry out all the acts of life in a spirit of equanimity and selflessness. What attracts negative karma is the selfishness and desire that lie behind action, and not the mere fact of action itself.

While prior to the 1920s the number of Buddhists in Pietermaritzburg was very small, thereafter adherents increased as a result of a revival of Buddhism in many parts of the world. The Natal Buddhist Society was founded in 1920, and a short time later an equivalent group was established in Pietermaritzburg. Buddhists have tended to be almost entirely of Asian origin but more recently, in Natal and elsewhere, members of other races have shown an interest in Buddhist meditation and philosophy. Visitors to the Buddhist Retreat Centre at Ixopo include people from the Pietermaritzburg area.

In the seventeenth century the earliest South African Muslims were brought to the Cape as slaves from parts of the Far East. It was during the 1860s that Natal saw the arrival of the first substantial group of Muslims from India. Some of these Indian Muslims began to settle in Pietermaritzburg from about 1890.

Central to Islam is the reality of the one true God who is the creator, sustainer and sovereign determiner of all existence. Throughout history God has never left mankind in ignorance of His will, but the last and greatest of his messengers, among whom were Abraham, Moses and Jesus, was Muhammad (AD 570-632). For Muslims the Qur'ān is the infallible and comprehensive written record of God's revelations, which were communicated to the world through the prophetic agency of Muhammad. The word 'Islam' means submission, and a Muslim is one who sincerely and obediently submits to the will of God in all aspects of life. Islam accepts no sharp distinction between the spiritual and the everyday dimensions of human existence.

The fundamental religious duties of the Muslim are the so-called Five Pillars of Islam:

1. Confession of the *kalima*, i.e. 'There is no God but God, and Muhammad is the messenger of God'. Such a confession implies not only the reality of the one sovereign God and the finality of Muhammad's prophethood but also other basic Muslim beliefs such as the Day of Resurrection, the final Judgment, heaven and hell, God's angels and prophets, and the revealed Books of God, of which the Qur'ān is the last and greatest.

2. Worship or prayer before God five times a day. Although Islam has a lunar calendar, the times of the daily prayers are fixed according to the position of the sun. Each of the five daily prayers includes a set of prescribed prayer movements (bowing, prostrating, etc.) as well as a number of utterances of praise to God.

Once a familiar sight in any Voortrekker dorp: Boer families camped on the Market Square during *Nagmaal*. The Dutch Reformed Church, completed in 1861, is in the background. It was demolished in 1955.

PIETERMARITZBURG CEMETERIES

Robert Haswell

Crumbling tombstones and straggling cypress-
trees: the Commercial Road cemeteries are in need
of repair and conservation.

*We rode over the bridge . . . and passing the burial
grounds (where differences which separated
Christians during life are still permitted to part their
bodies after death) we entered the broad streets of
the city.*

BISHOP COLENSO, 1854.

Pietermaritzburg's historic central cemetery was sited, as
was the norm in Voortrekker dorps, on the edge of the
original street layout. The subsequent British takeover of
the dorp resulted in the construction of numerous
churches, but rather than each having its own adjacent
churchyard, as was the custom in British settler towns
such as Richmond, the Voortrekkers' cemetery was
enlarged, and, in 1859, divided into seven denominational
compartments straddling Commercial Road.

Unlike Durban's historic West Street Cemetery wherein
the Christian, Hindu and Moslem faiths each have their
own section, Maritzburg's non-Christians were banished
to a burial ground which was set aside on the Town Hill in
1863. In 1896 this latter cemetery was reduced in area to
make way for suburban growth on the hill, and builders
unearthed unmarked graves and skeletons in the process.
By the 1920s the City's cemeteries were almost full and
the Cremorne Cemetery was established. The
Commercial Road Cemetery was in regular use then
during the period 1840–1920 and therefore clearly reflects
nineteenth-century formal garden design features. It is
thus a special landscape with the gravestones and
monuments in particular constituting a distinctive kind of
art and craft.

Tombstones provide a fascinating record of who is
buried, how long they lived, where they were born and
occasionally the cause of death. Many of early
Maritzburg's leading citizens are buried in the
Commercial Road Cemetery, and thus the origin of many
of the City's unusual street and place names are revealed.
Hunting, wagon accidents and drownings are recorded in
epitaphs, and the high rate of infant mortality is readily
apparent. Furthermore, tombstones have always been
related to contemporary styles in art and architecture, and
the symbolism in the decorations of historic tombstones
often expresses the changing notions of death, very
different from one era to another. In the Commercial Road
Cemetery tombstones range from the upright largely
unadorned sandstone slabs of the period 1840–1880 —
reflecting the mortality and stark fate of man — to grander
and more imposing monuments of the latter half of the
nineteenth century, when granite and marble were the
most commonly used stones, and when funerary
symbolism was favoured as a decorative element. The
cross, clasped hands, dove, anchor and draped urn are
symbolic of man's eternal reward after having shuffled off
this mortal coil. Examples of local and imported cast-iron
work can be seen in the many grave-enclosing fences,
which may reflect Western society's preoccupation with

private property. Victorian opulence in the form of
sculptured marble monuments, complete with encaustic
tiles, characterize turn-of-the-century memorials. The
German penchant for iron grave markers, with floral
decorations, stands in sharp contrast to the many Celtic
crosses. The few Germans buried in the Commercial Road
Cemetery are possibly descendants of the settlers
brought in by the firm Bergtheil and Jung in 1848.
According to his memorial, Jonas Bergtheil 'was a
Legislative Councillor during the years 1856-1866 and sat
in the Natal Parliament before Jews were admitted into
the English Parliament'.

But, above all, a walk through the cemetery can be a
transcendental experience. As one strolls among the
gravestones one is almost shielded from the outside
world by the high hedges. One peers down intently,
reading faded inscriptions on weathered and aged
gravestones, and yet one's glance is often drawn
towards the lychgate. Imperceptibly one transcends both
time and space, and is walking in a different age — when
there was still a Natal Police Force (NP) — and in a far-off,
exclusively Christian, land where the trees and hedges are
immortally evergreen. But the use of local red brick for
drainage channels — and for one or two graves which are
unmistakably Maritzburg — along with the chatter and
antics of myna, bulbul and drongo, and the
appropriately melancholic song of the turtle dove and
symbolic waiting and watching of the 'Jackie Hangman'
are there, as are the black staff, to remind you of just
where you are.

All of this suggests that the Commercial Road Cemetery
is a special place warranting careful management. A
management programme could include the relettering of
inscriptions in order to extend their 'readable life', and the
straightening of leaning or falling gravestones. Rising
damp has resulted in layers of sandstone spalling off the
surface of many of the older gravestones, and unless the
stone is to fall away entirely, hydro-epoxy consolidants
will have to be used. In the case of cast iron the best
protection against weathering is the routine application of
fish oil. Our main aim however should be to preserve the
layout and features in their entirety with as little
disturbance as possible.

3. Fasting during the month of Ramadan.

4. The obligation to give to the poor and needy, if one can afford this.

5. The performance of the pilgrimage at Mecca at least once in a lifetime, if one can afford this.

These pillars should all be performed with sincerity of intention.

The overwhelmingly majority of South Africa's Muslims are Sunni Muslims. Most of the world's Muslims are Sunnis, in contrast to the minority Shiite group, which is predominant in Iran. Sunnis believe that the God-ordained pattern of belief and practice, which covers all areas of life, is laid down in the Qur'ān itself and also in the Sunna, the traditional record of Muhammad's teaching and example.

The mosque is an important centre of Muslim religious and social life. It is the venue of the important weekly service, which takes place every Friday. The five daily prayers should be performed in a mosque, unless special circumstances make this impossible. The word 'mosque' translates the Arabic term *musjid*, which means 'place of prostration'.

There are seven mosques in Pietermaritzburg (and one in Edendale). The old Top Mosque, with its distinctive plaster mouldings, was opened in 1903. This mosque, which stands just off upper Church Street, has recently been restored. The most recently built mosque is the Olympia Way Mosque in Primrose Road, Northdale, which was completed in 1982. The other five mosques are:

- the Habibia Soofie Mosque, in East Street between Longmarket and Loop Streets. This mosque has historical links with a well-known Natal Muslim saint called Soofi Saheb.
- the Central Mosque, in Lower Church Street.
- the Northdale Mosque, on the corner of Chetty and Nulliah Roads, Northdale.
- the Raisethorpe Mosque, in Old Greytown Road.
- the Mountain Rise Mosque, in Royston Road, Mountain Rise.

Although these seven mosques differ in size and architectural detail, they share certain features which are virtually universal in Islam. Each has adequate facilities for the required ablutions, a mihrab or niche indicating the direction of Mecca, a staircase-like pulpit from which the Friday sermon is delivered, and an elevated place (in most cases the traditional minaret) from which the faithful are summoned to prayer.

Each mosque is controlled by a Muslim society, e.g. the Central Mosque has behind it the Islamia Muslim Society. An active *madrasah* is attached to each of the mosques except Top Mosque, where the *madrasah* is now used for storage purposes. A *madrasah* is a special Muslim school, run by Muslims for Muslim children, which operates in the afternoons after the normal state or state-aided school day is over. *Madrasah* pupils are given instruction in subjects such as Islamic history, Islamic belief, the reading and reciting of the Arabic Qur'ān, etc.

One of the influential groups within South African Islam is known as the Tabligh Jamaat. This Tablighi movement, which was consolidated in India by Maulana Muhammed Ilyas (1885–1944), is well represented in Pietermaritzburg. Endeavours which would be supported by Tablighis, as well as by other Muslims concerned with the spiritual renewal of Islamic life, include spreading the word of Islam, increasing the vitality and sincerity of worship and belief, and maintaining the purity and living orthodoxy of Islam by discouraging allegedly questionable innovations of belief and practice.

Two South African Muslim organizations in Pietermaritzburg which are of special relevance to younger people are the Muslim Youth Movement and the Muslim Students' Association. Many of the recent publications of these organizations have emphasized Islam as a way of life which has religious, economic and socio-political relevance. The message of Islam is held to be incompatible with apartheid and the denial of human-worth.

The Muslim Youth Movement publishes a Muslim newspaper called *Al-Qalam*, which is read by many Natal Muslims. However, some of the local Muslims with a Tablighi concern prefer *The Majlis — the voice of Islam*, a Muslim newspaper based in Port Elizabeth.

The Sunni Muslim religious year includes a number of festivals, of which the most universally celebrated and the most locally relevant are the following:

- the Birthday of the Prophet.
- the Night of the Ascent, commemorating the journey of Muhammad to the heavens.
- the Night of Power, during the month of Ramadan, commemorating the issuing of the first of the Qur'ānic revelations.
- Eid-ul-Fitr, just after the end of Ramadan, to mark the breaking of the Ramadan fast and to give thanks to God for enabling the Muslim to observe the fast.
- Eid-ul-Adha, the festival of sacrifice. On this day, which marks the end of the pilgrimage at Mecca, Muslims all over the world make a sacrifice, normally in the form of an animal, in commemoration of Abraham's willingness to sacrifice his son.

In South Africa there are a number of provincial or regional Islamic councils whose task it is to supervise, control and deliver authoritative judgements on various aspects of Muslim life and practice. One example of this is the issuing of rulings that specify precisely which foodstuffs are *halaal* (permitted) and *haraam* (forbidden). Many aspects of Pietermaritzburg Islamic life fall under the jurisdiction of the council known as the Jamiatul Ulama, Natal.

The remarkable diversity of faiths that Pietermaritzburg enjoys is almost a microcosm of the full spectrum of the main world religions with their different denominations and subdivisions. Most of these worldwide groups are represented in the City, thus enabling the faithful to remain in touch with wider developments. Most new religious movements and revivals eventually find their way to Pietermaritzburg, affecting and shifting the religious scene. Like a kaleidoscope, the diverse faiths of the City are forever vibrant, dynamic and subject to adaptation.

The Roman Catholic centres

Joy Brain

The first Roman Catholic priest to visit Natal in modern times was Father Thomas Murphy who arrived in November 1850 on an official visitation on behalf of the Catholic Bishop of Grahamstown. It was he who applied for a grant of land in Pietermaritzburg for a chapel. This was granted in July 1851, being Lot 9, Burger Street, and was to become the centre of the Loop Street Roman Catholic complex.

In March 1852 the vicar-apostolic, Bishop Jean Francois Marie Allard, arrived from France with a party of priests and brothers belonging to the Missionary Oblates of Mary Immaculate. Allard and his companions were initially guests of John Bird and Captain John McDonnell at their cottage, Lot 7 Burger Street, later moving to rented accommodation. Within a few years, and despite a chronic shortage of funds, Allard showed himself to be an astute purchaser of properties.

The simple chapel opened in December 1852 and erected on Lot 9 Burger Street, was the first of the buildings which eventually made up the Roman Catholic complex. This chapel was altered and improved several times and had a moment of glory when the body of the Prince Imperial lay in state there in June 1879. By 1890 it had become too small for the growing Catholic community and was replaced by a brick church in Longmarket Street.

In 1854 Allard purchased a site adjoining the chapel, Lot 8 Burger Street, where in the next three years the missionaries themselves erected a large double-storey dwelling capable of accommodating 24 persons. This building was of solid construction and is still in existence, forming part of the convent until recent years. In 1857 Michael Hayes, one of Allard's flock who several times acted as his agent, bought the site opposite the chapel, Lot 9 Loop Street, on Allard's behalf. Later the buildings of St. Charles Grammar School were erected on this site as well as the presbytery erected by Bishop Jolivet. In 1859 half of Lot 10 Burger Street was acquired. It had belonged to Charles Logue who was obliged to mortgage it, and again Michael Hayes acted as the Bishop's agent. It was on this property next to the Augustinian sanatorium that Holy Name Chapel was erected. The final purchase on the Burger Street side was Lot 7 on which Captain McDonnell's cottage stood. It came onto the market in 1860 and was bought by the Bishop for £600. Later it became part of the land used for the Holy Family Convent. Four years later the site of the present St. Mary's, Loop Street, was acquired from Thomas Horn, who continued to occupy a cottage on part of the property. The first church built on this site, facing Longmarket Street, served the Catholic congregation until 1927 and is now used as the church hall. Within twelve years Bishop Allard had bought three

On 8 and 9 June 1879 the body of the Prince Imperial of France lay in state in the Roman Catholic Chapel in Loop Street. Fr. Joseph Gerard (beatified in 1988) was among the Missionary Oblates of Mary Immaculate who built the house next door. Fort Napier can be seen in the distance.

plots on Burger Street and two on Loop Street.

Allard's intention in acquiring these properties was to provide for the future religious needs of Catholics in and around Pietermaritzburg, and a Catholic school for their children. St. Mary's Church and the co-educational parish school supplied these needs during Allard's episcopacy. This school, run by Father Justin Barret with the assistance of a series of lay teachers, was originally situated in Pietermaritz Street on Patrick Hayes' property until the Bishop acquired land for it in Loop Street. It also enabled his successor, Bishop Charles Jolivet, to provide more sophisticated educational institutions for the children of the middle class, while maintaining the parish school for those unable to pay the fees of the convent or St. Charles Grammar School. It was Jolivet who brought the Holy Family Sisters to Pietermaritzburg in 1875 to take over the teaching in the parish school, and later to open a convent school for girls in the land adjoining St. Mary's Church. The convent continued to offer a solid education to generations of girls for nearly 100 years. St. Charles Grammar School was opened at about the same time as the convent school, catering for boys who sought a general education with a Christian outlook. Despite the support the school received, the Bishop had great difficulty in finding efficient teachers and his hopes of finding a community of teaching brothers to take it over did not materialize until long after his death in 1903. St. Charles Grammar School was finally closed in 1912, and in 1914 the Marist Brothers opened St. Charles College, originally in Loop Street and later in Scottsville.

The 1970s proved to be years of crisis in Catholic education when shortage of staff forced the closure of the Holy Family Convent, while St. Charles College was taken over by the Natal Education Department.

Roman Catholic institutions have always included hospitals and orphanages and the Loop Street complex under Bishop Jolivet provided both. A small orphanage was run by the Holy Family Sisters for about 20 years until in the late 1890s the Sisters of Nazareth opened an orphanage and old age home in Durban and the orphans from the Capital were transferred there. The hospital or Holy Name Sanatorium, run by the Augustinian Sisters, was opened in 1898 and survived until the 1970s when a shortage of nursing nuns and the financial demands of modern medicine made it impossible for them to continue.

Although the Loop Street complex was the most extensive, it was not the only Catholic centre in Pietermaritzburg. The needs of the black community were not forgotten. Nor were the successive vicars-apostolic likely to forget that they had originally been sent to undertake mission work among the Zulu as a priority. Much of the pioneer work among the Zulu in the Capital was initiated by Father Franz Mayr, a Zulu linguist of some ability, who in 1893 raised the money to build Holy Name Chapel in Loop Street for the use of blacks living in Pietermaritzburg itself.

Apart from religious services, Mayr ran an elementary school for black children in a building attached to the chapel and on Sundays provided catechetical instruction for adults and children after Mass. However, Mayr is best remembered for his work in establishing Maryvale (or Marievale), a Catholic communal village, in the vicinity of the present Ohrtmann Road. He travelled to Europe and raised the money needed to purchase land and erect simple

buildings and to launch his scheme. The chapel-school was the first project to be completed. Like its model, St. Francis Xavier Mission on the Bluff, Maryvale was a success from the start and additional property had to be rented to provide a piece of arable land and a dwelling for forty families who settled there. Maryvale provided for the spiritual and educational needs of the Zulu Catholics in the same way as the Loop Street complex, and if the facilities were simpler, the effort put into Maryvale was no less great.

Simple health care was provided by sisters from the Augustinian Convent in Loop Street who visited Maryvale once a week to run a clinic. St. Joan of Arc Church still exists in Ohrtmann Road but the 'village' disappeared as the City grew and its residents were required to move into locations. Maryvale African Primary School, originally part of the village, continued to exist until 1977. The Ohrtmann Road complex has recently taken on a new lease of life with the renovation of the church and the extension of the presbytery to form a small monastery for the Capuchin Fathers who now serve the Catholics of that area.

The growth of the small Christian Indian community in Pietermaritzburg led to the establishment of a third complex. In 1885, when there were approximately 1 600 free Indians, most living in the lower part of the town, Father Barret opened a small school for Indian children in hired premises. In 1892 a more substantial building was erected on the corner of Pietermaritz and Retief Streets. About 40 children attended in the first year but there was a shortage of teachers able to speak Tamil and only after the Holy Family Sisters took over the running of the school in 1888 did the school prosper. This school, St. Anthony's Primary Day School for Indian and coloured Children, continued to exist until 1973. Older Catholic residents of the Capital retain affectionate memories of Sister Beatrice who served as principal for many years and who became known as the 'Empress of India'. St. Anthony's school buildings were in frequent use for congresses and gatherings at a time when facilities, especially for the Indian community, were in short supply. It was closed because pupil numbers dropped after the removal of a large part of the Indian community from Pietermaritzburg itself to Raisethorpe, and the building was eventually demolished.

The first church specifically for Tamil-speaking Indian Catholics was a simple chapel, St. Anthony's, opened by Father Barret in 1886. Under Father August Chauvin a more substantial building, St. Anthony's Church, was erected on the corner of Retief and Loop Streets, and completed in 1901. This church, extensively renovated in 1976, is still the centre of Catholic worship for the Indian community in Pietermaritzburg. This complex was enlarged with the erection of the Marian Centre in Loop Street to provide a venue for the Marian Indian Government-Aided School (until 1970), a church hall and accommodation for catechism classes. Many of the parishioners moved from Pietermaritzburg centre in 1946 when the Indian township of Raisethorpe was established. In that year Our Lady of Health of Vailanganni Church was built, thus dividing the Indian Catholics geographically. St. Anthony's Church, the priest's residence, the schools and later the Marian centre formed the third Roman Catholic complex in Pietermaritzburg.

CHAPTER ELEVEN

Health in the City

1

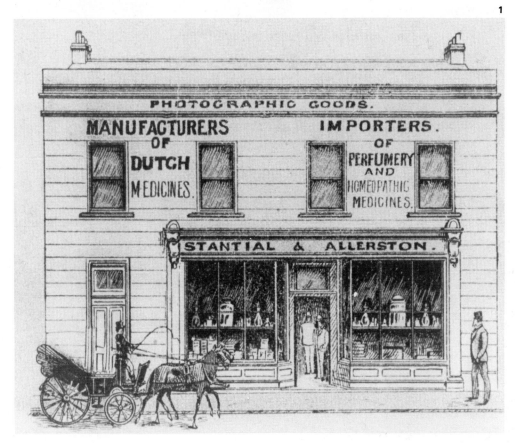

Grey's Hospital

Angus Rose

Until 1855, Pietermaritzburg's sick had to rely solely on the care available in their own homes. Those suffering from both mental and financial disorders languished in the local gaol. That this was built long before Grey's Hospital, an institution now indissolubly linked with the name of our City, throws an interesting light upon the social perspectives of the period.

Sir George Grey, Governor of the Cape, and High Commissioner for the Adjacent Territories, had already been instrumental in establishing a hospital in Port Elizabeth, and after his visit to Pietermaritzburg in 1855, he made a grant of £1 000 towards a hospital in the City. Peter Sutherland, both a qualified doctor and the Surveyor-General of Natal, chose a site bordered by the Msunduze River, the Dutch cemetery and what is now Alexandra Park. Building began in February 1856, hurried along by Doctor Sutherland's material contributions. The original hospital was a simple six-roomed construction, of stone and brick, topped by a thatch roof. Dr Samuel Gower was appointed the first hospital surgeon and, at the queenly salary of £3 a month, Mrs Isabella O'Hara became the first matron.

In May 1857 Matron O'Hara, several medical patients and some insane patients moved in. Not surprisingly, patients entering the hospital did so with considerable qualms, believing that survival was infinitely more likely at home. No water was laid on, needs being supplied by the Commercial Road spruit. Lavatories were far removed from the wards, and patients needing water at night fetched it themselves as there were no night staff.

The hospital's administration, which the City Council took over in 1863, soon realized the dire need for proper nursing staff, English-trained. Changes for the better were immediate. A vegetable garden was started, and separate accommodation for the 'lunatics' provided. Clean water was supplied from a well. Iron beds were ordered from England, and five major operations were all successful. The commonest diseases were fever, diarrhoea, dysentery, rheumatism and consumption. By 1867 Grey's accommodated 25 white patients (5 of them insane) and 13 black (3 insane). Amenities soon included a library of some 600 books, a tiled roof, a veranda and an imposing entrance porch in Prince Alfred Street. In 1870 the black patients were provided with a separate building, enabling the hospital to give succour to 19 whites and 32 blacks. Various toilet facilities — enamel baths, hot and cold water, some hand and foot basins — enhanced the patients' comfort considerably. An operating theatre, a shower and a 'vapour bath' were installed in 1872.

Matron Elizabeth Macdonald is now an ineffaceable aspect of Grey's history. She was the last of the 'lay' matrons, and her tenure of 27 years saw not only vast improvements and changes, but the realization that here was a woman worthy of the profoundest respect and love. Under her guidance the training of nurses began — the first nurse to qualify being Kate Driver who was registered in November 1891. Several structural alterations were put in hand: gables on the front of each wing, and waiting and consulting rooms. In 1899 electric lights were installed, a considerable boon, as can well be imagined.

Wars always accelerate development. The Second Anglo-Boer War increased the number of patients and added to the medical and nursing staff. Hours were improved, duty lasting from 7 a.m. to 9 p.m. with two hours off. Starched aprons and caps featured prominently. Grey's nurses formed part of the Army Nursing Service Reserve, later to

2

Grey's Hospital *c.*1895.
Matron Elizabeth Macdonald is standing on the extreme right.

be known as Queen Alexandra's Imperial Military Nursing Service. Queen Alexandra granted Grey's nurses the privilege of wearing their scarlet capes with a rosette at the back, a tradition which — honoured in its day — has now fallen away.

As time went by, both the size and scope of Grey's increased to a point where, in 1905, 12 wards housed 51 patients, and a 'Kaffir Hospital' 32. At this point, after 27 years' service to Grey's, Matron Macdonald retired. She went to live at 118 Loop Street (which still stands) but was, sadly, murdered by her Indian servant on 10 May 1907. She lies buried in the cemetery close to the hospital she served so devotedly. The children's ward, opened in 1907, bears her name in proud and lasting tribute.

In July 1905 the elegant Nurses Home, fronting Prince Alfred Street, was completed. Now, alas, demolished, this lovely example of double-storeyed Victorian building boasted graceful cast-iron railings along its balconies and a covered way linking the home with the hospital. Here 24 nurses and their matron were accommodated. In 1910 the waterborne sewerage connection was at last made. A year later doctors' quarters were erected between the Nurses Home and the hospital, and in the same year, some private wards were built on the banks of the Msunduze. The operating theatre was housed in a small isolated building behind the hospital. The river banks were cleared and grassed and a boat purchased for the relaxation of convalescents and staff. In 1913 the new X-ray machine arrived from England, while 1914 saw the completion of the new 'Native Ward' — later E Ward — housing 32 beds. A year later, radiators replaced the open fires in the wards. Then, because of the War, building operations abruptly ceased.

The outbreak of the War in 1914 saw the opening of a military ward. In 1917 nurses approached the Board with an objection to 'nursing the enemy', but the Board compassionately ruled that serious cases had to be treated. Despite the impetus given by the War, nurses' very poor conditions of service changed little. Nevertheless, between 1913 and 1915, 25 Grey's nurses qualified, and in the next year some 17 Grey's nurses were serving with the armed forces in South Africa and Europe.

With the end of the War, the world was about to enter an unhappy period of recession, so few major improvements were feasible. However, in 1919 Grey's largest building up to that time, the new European Wards, A and B, were opened. This was a double-storey building facing Commercial Road, and contained the first lift to be installed at Grey's. In 1920, the Outpatients Department was extended, and in 1927, thanks to a generous bequest from Albert Nathan, Nathan Ward was begun. In the same year a second floor was added to the 'Native Wards' and a second Nurses Home built. In 1929 a house was built for the medical superintendent, opposite the Nurses Home.

Administrative changes also occurred. It was decided in 1922, largely for financial reasons, that Grey's should be placed under the wing of the provincial authority. Accordingly, the old Hospital Board was reconstituted, though with substantially reduced powers. The economic stringencies of the era delayed many of the hoped for improvements. Among these were greatly needed alterations to the kitchens, where conditions were little short of appalling. Because of the evidence that all was not administratively well, the Hospital Commission recommended the immediate appointment of a medical superintendent. The appointment of Dr R. E. Stevenson in June 1928 saw an appreciable improvement in affairs — thanks to the energy, devotion and dedication of this remarkable man, who held his post until 1936. Dr Stevenson, in retrospect, stands out as one instrumental in raising both the standards and status of Grey's among South Africa's hospitals.

Outpatient and casualty facilities were added, together with a reception hall, a telephone exchange, a dispensary and two new operating theatres. With three subsidiary

Grey's nurses with a military doctor on the veranda of the hospital in 1915.

theatres, Grey's could now boast that — with the exception of the Johannesburg General — it possessed the most modern and best surgical equipment in the Union. In 1933 new kitchens were at last opened. In the same year the X-ray unit was updated and a maternity ward added — later known as J Ward. Three years later saw the addition of a second storey, and Lakhi Ward opened partly funded by a bequest from M. E. Lakhi. In 1938 the new Nurses Home, 'C' Home, was built on a property once owned by Professor Alexander Petrie. This had two lecture rooms on the ground floor and a further 127 rooms on four floors. One year later, the non-European outpatients building was erected.

The pre-war period was distinguished by the outstanding successes of several Grey's nurses, largely as a result of the tuition given by Sister-Tutor Sybil Marwick, appointed in 1930. The Kenneth Gloag Medal, awarded to the nurse with the highest marks in the South African final examination, was won seven times between 1931 and 1937 by Grey's nurses. In January 1933, out of nine nurses awarded first class passes, five came from Grey's. Nurses' salaries were still unchanged, though uniforms had become all white, with canvas shoes that required regular doses of Blanco. Caps still covered all the hair, and sleeves, rolled up for working, had to be rolled down countless times every day, whenever the matron, a staff nurse or a doctor appeared. Hours were from 7 a.m. to 8.30 p.m., with one day off—never a Saturday—each week.

The war years brought several developments, many as a result of a generous bequest by Miss Martha Welch, whose name adorned one of the new wards. The military asked for beds for 200 military patients who were housed in four huts. These huts, no longer needed after 1943, were then used for white civilian patients. Staff shortages, overcrowding, blackouts, air raid warnings and other deprivations and inconveniences characterized these days. Grey's troubles increased with an outbreak of diphtheria in 1943, and the much more serious polio epidemic the year after. Yet despite these handicaps, two Grey's nurses won the Kenneth Gloag Medal in 1945 — a splendid tribute to the quality of nursing education they received.

On 6 June 1944 the Government passed the Nursing Act of South Africa, by which the control of all nursing affairs passed to two statutory bodies, the South African Nursing Council and the South African Nursing Association. Under the provisions of the Act, all nurses and midwives were obliged to register. By 1955 Grey's was staffed by 4 matrons, 19 sisters, 42 staff nurses, with 38 student midwives and 207 student nurses — an astonishing growth. A strong, dedicated panel of visiting surgeons, physicians, pediatricians, ophthalmologists, anaesthetists, obstetricians, orthopaedic surgeons, a radiologist and a pathologist ensured that standards of medical care and tuition were not allowed to lapse.

The military huts were finally removed at this time and the new three-storeyed Maternity Block, completed in 1957, begun. In 1954 Edendale Hospital opened and Grey's saw the last of the many black patients who had been treated over the years.

The year 1955 was an important one for Grey's since it

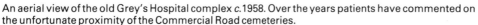

An aerial view of the old Grey's Hospital complex c.1958. Over the years patients have commented on the unfortunate proximity of the Commercial Road cemeteries.

4

marked its Centenary, an event celebrated in many ways, not the least of which was the publication of Professor A. F. Hattersley's *A Hospital Century*. The numbers of student nurses continued to grow and for several years, places for their accommodation were at a premium. This necessitated the construction of a new block. With its opening in 1968, 378 beds were available for staff.

But still it was not enough. Nurses were put into 'prefabs' (known as Fort Knox because of the high wire fence surrounding them), rooms were doubled up, some nurses went to 'Old Merchiston', others to 'The Villa' in Burger Street. The old Merchiston School became the College of Nursing in 1965.

The end of the sixties saw the arrival of nurses in short sleeves, with disposable paper caps adorned with the Grey's badge. Staff nurses' caps were trimmed with a maroon stripe, while sisters wore the new cap-veil. Hours were down to 44 a week, and off-duty time could be spent in the library, at the hairdresser on site or on the squash court. Waiters — in white suits and bow ties — served meals, though later a 'cafeteria' system put paid once and for all to meals at set times. The iron lung — forever associated with John Odams — gave place to the ICU. But these changes were nothing compared with what was to come.

Since 1930 it had been considered desirable that a large, modern hospital complex replace the agglomeration that was the old Grey's. The obvious site for a new Grey's was the Town Hill, where a large open area belonging to Town Hill Hospital stood invitingly vacant. In 1971 the Government finally released 56 acres, and the great decision was taken to build an entirely new Grey's Hospital there, despite the recent purchase of the site of the old Girl's Collegiate opposite the existing hospital.

The immense new project began in 1976 with the levelling of the site and the installation of stormwater drainage. From this point the thoughts of those working in Grey's were cruelly split between past and future. The 'old' Grey's began to assume an air of somewhat shabby gentility, like a ship on her last voyage home. The long-awaited move — after several delays and postponements — was not without its pangs of sadness and nostalgia, even though such emotions were tempered by healthy anticipation.

Close on 10 million bricks went into the new building's fabric with 75 trucks full of stone quarried near Empangeni; millions of rand worth of equipment was installed, for surgical, medical, X-ray, culinary, cleaning, cooling, heating and countless other purposes. Gardens were dug and planted; floors polished, windows cleaned, curtains hung and . . . at long last, the first patients were admitted on 11 July 1984. Eleven days later, on 22 July, a huge crowd assembled for The Great Grey's Walk — a moving (in more than one sense) pilgrimage in gratitude for the love and service given to so many by so many since the first days of Grey's back in the 1850s. It was also a symbolic advance into a future that will no doubt hold as much interest and human drama as the past. A spirit of dedication and devotion to Grey's — old and new — infused all who participated in that walk.

The new Grey's Hospital contrasts with the 19th century Town Hill Hospital in the background.

Mental health in colonial Pietermaritzburg

Gustav Fouché

On 27 July 1855, the Mayor, Counsellors and burgesses of the City of Pietermaritzburg resolved to grant a piece of land, in extent 50 acres, of that part of the City known as Townlands, to the Colonial Government of Natal, for the sole purpose of establishing a Public Lunatic Asylum, later known as the Natal Government Asylum or Town Hill Hospital, and more recently forming part of the Midlands Hospital Complex.

It was not till 19 November 1873, however, that the deed of transfer was signed in which the Mayor formally ceded the land to the Colonial Secretary. On 1 July 1876, the Colonial Engineer was requested to submit a suitable design for approval by the Legislative Assembly so that the necessary money could be voted for building a Public Lunatic Asylum. A week later he replied that he had written to the Colonial Office in England requesting plans and estimates of the latest and most approved design for hospitals and lunatic asylums in Great Britain. Although he had not had a reply, the Colonial Secretary urged him to submit plans anyway since no money could be voted by the Legislative Assembly in the absence of plans or designs. On 18 July three designs were submitted by the Colonial Engineer's office. The first design was estimated to cost about £20 000 and designs two and three about £15 000. On 5 August 1876, 16 days later, the Colonial Secretary authorized the acceptance of design no. 1 and instructed that the necessary provisions be made in the 1877 Estimates for the erection of the building on the 50 acres granted by the City Council of Pietermaritzburg. The commendable speed with which the local bureaucracy expedited the matter must have gratified the City Fathers. The necessary surveying of the site was equally expeditiously completed and further instructions were issued from the Colonial Secretary's office to plant a large number of trees on the site to create a parklike setting for the building.

In February 1880 the inmates were transferred to the New Asylum on Town Hill from the Temporary Asylum, which had initially been attached to the gaol and had subsequently been relocated to a house at what is now 525 Longmarket Street. The Temporary Asylum had been opened on 1 February 1875 with 37 inmates who were moved from the actual gaol. The Lunacy Law of 1868 had made provision for the detention of the insane in gaols. Only a few 'idiotic, epileptic and paralytic' cases were treated in hospitals in Durban and Pietermaritzburg.

By the time the Colonial Government of Natal was legislating for the care of the insane, through the Lunacy Law of 1868, there was already a well-established system of state and private institutions in Great Britain for the care of the insane. In 1815 the House of Commons appointed a committee to inquire into abuses in these institutions. This resulted in certain reform measures which were again reviewed in 1828. These measures were partly initiated by medical/psychiatric experts, based on their changing views of the origin of mental illness and the proper treatment of the insane. A major change in the treatment was, for example, the abolition of physical restraints like handcuffs. These restraints were replaced by 'external reorganisation, proper nourishment, good ventilation, baths, more and better-paid attendants'.

Social activities like 'outdoor entertainment, concerts, even dances were introduced and the public was invited'. In addition, physical work was encouraged and the 'moral welfare' of the inmates was attended to by regular Christian worship. Instead of the unacceptable methods of 'personal restraints', a system of surveillance by attendants, in a building constructed to enhance this watchfulness, was introduced.

In how far these practices were applied in the colonial setting of Natal, can be gleaned from the annual returns and the Reports of the Lunatic Asylum Board submitted to the Office of the Colonial Secretary. In the first report of 1877 it is noted that handcuffs were still being used, but only in 'extreme cases'. A year later the District Surgeon directed that the use of handcuffs be discontinued in future and only seclusion under lock and key be resorted to.

It is further noted that provision had been made for various sources of amusement. The Colonial Government donated musical instruments (two concertinas), a chess set, a draughts board, 4 lbs. of marbles and 6 packs of playing cards! Ministers of various denominations were conducting church services on Sundays but the attendance was no more than 6 inmates at a time. White inmates refused to do any physical work.

The diet of the inmates was recorded in these early reports. Separate diet sheets are noted for 'Europeans, Kaffirs, Coolies and Hottentots' for the three daily meals. Judging by contemporary nutritional standards, these rations were deficient in certain essential vitamins, proteins and minerals. The nutritional status of long-term patients must have been appalling and could have induced pellagra, a condition with known psychiatric complications!

The staffing and management of the Lunatic Asylum was a matter which required the attention of the colonial authorities right from the beginning. A Board of Management for the proper running of the Temporary Asylum was appointed in 1875, consisting of the Colonial Secretary, the Resident Surgeon, the Mayor of Pietermaritzburg (ex officio) and a private citizen. The Male Attendant of the Temporary Asylum, and later first Keeper of the New Asylum, was John Smithwick, formerly a sergeant in the 75th Regiment, and recommended for appointment on 19 February 1875. Within a month of his appointment on 20 March 1875 he wrote a letter to the Colonial Secretary's Office requesting certain staff changes. In the same letter he recommended that the 4 'Coolies' employed as servants at the opening of the Temporary Asylum be dismissed and that two 'natives' be employed instead as general servants.

In reply the Resident Magistrate agreed with some of the proposals, adding that it was not desirable that the Keeper should be the only European in charge since he would have to leave the patients under the protection of

'Coolie and Native' men should he leave the premises. When the matter was put to the District Surgeon for comment, he supported the Keeper's recommendation adding 'it is not in accordance with the arrangements which received the approval of the Colonial Government... to employ Coolies for the purpose'. He suggested that 'two intelligent Zulus, if procureable... should be employed instead of the Coolies'.

With an ex-army sergeant in charge, assisted by servants and guards, the care of the inmates could not have been much different from that of ordinary prisoners. It was not till the appointment of Dr J. Hyslop, as the first Resident Surgeon on 21 June 1882, that a more professional approach to the hospital care of the insane was instituted. Dr Hyslop came from the Royal Asylum in Edinburgh and would have been familiar with current care practices in Great Britain. He accepted the position at a salary of £400 per annum. In 1886 Miss E.M. Schaffer from England was appointed as Matron but only 'after some considerable difficulty owing to the smallness of the salary offered'. She arrived in Pietermaritzburg on 3 November 1886.

An Official Visitor, Brigade Surgeon Robinson, from the Fort Napier Garrison, was appointed in the capacity of Commissioner for Lunacy in accordance with the practice in Great Britain at the time. Some strained relationships developed between the Visitor and Dr Hyslop over the interpretation of the rules of visitation. The Colonial Secretary had to employ all his diplomatic skills to restore amiable relationships. The incident which started a minor feud between these two government officials arose from the fact that the Visitor wanted the identification of the inmates, according to race, to be done more frequently. He wrote on 16 August 1889:

> Identification of the Coloured people and Kaffirs is desireable more frequently than once a month as required by the instructions issued to the Official Visitor. The identification of European inmates and Africanders should not be of a formal character but each patient should be seen by the Official Visitor... The visits should be fortnightly.

One such visit led to considerable distress amongst the patients and Dr Hyslop wrote a critical note to the Colonial Secretary's Office complaining of the practice. He suggested less frequent visits by the Visitor and that the visits should be by appointment rather than of the nature of a surprise. The Colonial Secretary cautioned that

> Common sense would appear to show that an identification carried out on the principle that obtains in a regiment on 'general muster' day must have a deleterious effect on lunatics.

The Lunacy Law of 1868 for the Colony of Natal made provision for procedures for the admission of patients via the office of a Resident Magistrate. Two medical officers had to examine the patient before admission could be finalized.

A very crude classification system was applied by the medical officers to identify the particular illness from which the patient was supposed to be suffering. The system provided for only four categories viz. (a) maniacal and dangerous (b) quiet, chronic (c) melancholy and suicidal and (d) idiotic, paralytic, epileptic. There was obviously great concern over 'dangerousness' since the Returns of the years 1877 and 1878 reflect the highest numbers of

The original Town Hill Hospital, opened in 1880 to house the City's mentally ill.

6

inmates classified in either category (a) or (b). This is not entirely surprising since the Custody of Lunatics Act No. 1 of 1868 provided mainly for the detention of the 'dangerously insane'. If seclusion and restraint did not prove to be effective, drugs were resorted to. From Case Books kept at the Public Asylum it is evident that potassium bromide, chloral hydrate and *Cannabis indica* (dagga) were frequently prescribed to patients who were 'wild and maniacal; restless and suicidal'. These drugs have potent sedative effects and are addictive if prescribed indiscriminately.

A particularly inhuman method of seclusion was devised by Dr Hyslop in 1887 to control female black patients. A large pit 30 feet long, 15 feet wide and 6 feet deep was dug, into which difficult patients were dropped daily. Hyslop found it necessary to justify this medieval method by saying that 'although at first sight it might appear a rather barbarous proceeding, the result fully justified the treatment adopted'.

An early example of a challenge to the system of classification/certification involved the rights of patients. It is to be found in a petition which a patient directed in 1901 to the Colonial Secretary requesting to see the papers by which he was committed. In refusing this request the Medical Superintendent wrote:

> I was following the universal practice at home. In this as well as in most cases where a similar request is likely to be made, the exhibition of the papers would have a most prejudicial effect on the patient.

The Attorney-General, when asked to comment, concurred with the opinion of Dr Hyslop but at the same time wished to have the right of patients for access to their lawyers to be upheld. To settle the matter, the Colonial Secretary wrote to the Agent General for Natal in London asking for information about the practice in Great Britain and other countries on this issue. On 3 May 1901 the reply came from London:

> The Commissioners for Lunacy state that in this country there is no fixed rule about regulations on the point. The power is left to the Medical Superintendent to use his discretion. The request is rarely conceded.

With the increase in the number of patients (by 1901 there was a total of 366 of all races) extensions and new buildings became necessary. A new main building was completed in May 1891. By 1916 the number of patients was 746.

MIDLANDS HOSPITAL

Gustav Fouché

The founding of the Union of South Africa in 1910 brought to an end the close administrative relationship which the City and the Colonial Government had with the Natal Government Asylum on Town Hill.

All psychiatric services were transferred to the central Government Department of the Interior. The foundations of custodial care of the insane with differential standards for the different races were established by the Colonial Government. The Mental Disorders Act of 1916 put the responsibility for the implementation of the care of the insane in the hands of a Commissioner for Mental Health. In 1943 psychiatric services were transferred to the Department of Health. The pressing need for increased accommodation for the mentally ill could no longer be met by Town Hill Hospital. In 1927 the vacant and somewhat derelict buildings of Fort Napier were designated as a mental hospital and the first patients arrived the next year. In spite of the poor environment, the dedication of the medical and nursing staff helped to develop the Fort into a hospital.

The Second World War interfered with the planning to rebuild the institution. The temporary wood and iron structures built to accommodate German internees during the War were retained as wards. There was an acute shortage of medical and nursing staff and overcrowding became a serious problem. A modern 4-storeyed nurses' home, later to be converted into wards, treatment units and offices was opened in 1953.

Advances in the psychiatric treatment of patients were introduced by successive medical superintendents so that a more 'therapeutic environment' now prevails in both the Town Hill and Fort Napier Hospitals. The care of patients is now in the hands of a multi-disciplinary team consisting of medical specialists, psychiatrically-trained nurses, clinical psychologists and occupational therapists. Both Hospitals serve as training institutions for psychiatry and clinical psychology and the nursing college attends to the specialized training in psychiatric nursing.

An extensive building programme at Town Hill Hospital, which now admits white patients only, has been undertaken over the past five years. Accommodation for patients of other races at Fort Napier Hospital has not yet been fully modernized.

The care for a special group of patients, namely the mentally defective, was opened in 1949 at the Umgeni Waterfall Institution in Howick in a disused hospital built by the British Government as a convalescent unit during the Second World War. It now serves the needs of the white population.

In 1978 Fort Napier Hospital, Town Hill Hospital and Umgeni Waterfall Institution were amalgamated into one hospital complex known as Midlands Hospital.

CARING FOR CHILDREN

7   8   9

There are always children needing care. Peter Davis Infants' Home, 1924[7]. Mthuthuzeli Crèche, Edendale, 1987[8 and 9].

Edendale Hospital

David Robbins

Hardly ten kilometres from the City Hall, Edendale Hospital is an apt and often disturbing reminder that Pietermaritzburg is indeed an African city. The feel at the hospital is unmistakably Third World. In many ways it is a monument to the uneasy interface between the Third and First Worlds.

I went to Edendale Hospital one Friday evening to see what it was like. The hospital buildings stood dark and square against a fading sky, yet the buildings, like the buildings of all big institutions which operate at night, hummed with life. The lights in the wards were already on; escaping steam hissed high up on a side wall somewhere; people and vehicles passed continuously along the driveways which led to and from the main entrance. The flashes from an ambulance, picking its way carefully through pedestrians, illuminated the uniforms of nurses, the small perched caps they wore. Headlights confronted the growing darkness and weird shadows fluttered on walls. I went inside to find out what the ambulance had brought.

It was a young woman who had been stabbed in the stomach. She lay, while some paper work was done at Admissions, on her trolley, her lifted face a blank mask, although sometimes you could see the pain in her eyes. Her small child, sound asleep, was wheeled in on another trolley. A passing doctor said 'What's the trouble with this one?' The ambulance woman said, 'Nothing, doctor. He belongs to the woman. We had nowhere to leave him.'

The woman and her child were then wheeled to the Surgical Outpatients Department. A doctor turned her over to look at the wound, while a nurse fondled the child briefly, tucking the blanket more firmly about the tiny body. You notice the wounded woman's eyes searching for her child as she is wheeled away. The nurse pins a card onto the sleeping child's clothes so that people will know to whom he belongs.

Surgical Outpatients Department on a Friday night. A polished passage with people sitting on benches. Doctors and nurses hurry about. Then, in a sudden tightening of focus, you see blood on the foot-rest of an empty wheelchair. In another place, a young man whose head is swathed in bright red bandages. Blood trails over his face in a multiplicity of little rivers; it drips from his chin to splash in the pool on the floor. He slumps to one side. Nurses tend him. He tries to fight them off. They laugh and scold. They insert a drip and hang the bottle on a wire. In due course he is wheeled away, and when he returns he is unconscious and his head has been shaved and stitched. The drip bottle now lies tangled in his legs.

A nursing sister smiled and said, 'Have you come to see what it looks like here on a Friday night?' She indicated the unconscious young man and smiled again. 'That's just the beginning. Most of them are still drinking. They'll come though.'

They did. They came in their dozens. Old and young. Stabbed and beaten. Stabbed in the head, in the face, in the groin, in the back, in the arms. Sometimes they would admit themselves, waiting while the paper work was done, then walk or stagger, clutching their cards in bloodied hands, to the benches in the polished passage where the doctors and nurses never rested.

Sometimes I would go outside to watch the ambulances arriving, or simply for some fresh air. You look at the scattered lights of the Edendale valley and you wonder what is happening out there. And you wonder about the hospital, too. As a referral hospital, it copes with a vast area which stretches from Umtata in the Transkei to Newcastle in the north. Closer at hand, a population of more than half a million relies on Edendale for its basic medical needs. Like sewing up heads, you think. But there is more to it than that. On the seventh floor, 'lodger mothers' sleep on the floor in the passage while their children are being treated in the wards. Lodger mothers, and their sick children, are from outlying districts; they sleep on the hospital floor because they have nowhere else to stay. On the seventh floor, sick babies from the bush; battered city dwellers below.

A young man approached me and said a little wildly: 'I am going to get into trouble because I am not at work. I was on my way when the *tsotsis* grabbed me. Can you telephone my work?' His breath smelt faintly of liquor. I agreed to telephone. As he walked away, I saw he had been stabbed high up in the centre of his back. 'We live with danger all around us,' a nurse said. Two doctors talked to me:

> The frequently-made suggestion that violent behaviour is a particular characteristic of the black population here has no real validity. Almost identical situations exist in any other country among the poor and unemployed sector of the population. The magnitude of the problem here merely indicates that the poor sector of the population forms such a large part of the whole society.

A police van approaches Edendale Hospital.

A sign in the always-crowded entrance hall of Edendale Hospital appeals, not always with much success, for: Silence, *Thula Umsindo*, and the request is repeated in Hindi, a reminder that the hospital served Pietermaritzburg's Indian population before one was built in their own group area in the late 1970s. 'We used to get a first class service there at Edendale,' an Indian once told me, and he was right. For decades, Edendale enjoyed a reputation as one of the best hospitals in the country.

But this reputation has declined in recent years. Perhaps the situation can best be summed up like this: Edendale used to be a First World hospital ministering very largely to Third World needs; now, although still ministering to Third World needs, Edendale has become a Third World hospital. But it is a summing up which requires considerable explanation.

We must start at the beginning. Edendale admitted its first patients in March 1954. As early as the second staff-meeting that year, mention was made of a shortage of space at the 620-bed hospital. The subsequent history of Edendale has been one of 'persistent accommodation shortage and expansion', according to an article in the *South African Medical Journal* by Dr J. E. Cosnett in 1975. In consequence, the hospital grew in 20 years to 1 645 beds. Now in the mid-1980s it has posts for 140 doctors and an all black nursing staff of 1 277.

It also enjoyed for many years an international reputation as a teaching hospital. As well as attracting thousands of South African doctors of all races, Edendale patients have been tended by young interns from Germany, New Zealand, Canada, Australia, India, Pakistan, Greece, Cyprus, the United Kingdom and the United States.

'There were two reasons for our international reputation,' a senior doctor told me. 'Firstly, Edendale offered a concentrated form of experience for young doctors which could hardly be equalled anywhere in the world. The second was the quality of the teachers, the consultants and specialists, which the hospital attracted.'

To these reasons can be added a third: Edendale always functioned reasonably efficiently and was well-equipped. It had, for example, 'probably the first intensive care unit in any hospital in South Africa', again according to Dr Cosnett.

But as the hospital moved towards the middle 1980s, deterioration began to set in. A 1983 report described surgery equipment at Edendale as 'adequate' but requiring repair and updating. At one stage during the same year, all four monitors in the obstetrics ward, used to measure the heartbeat of babies about to be born, were broken.

In 1984, Edendale had a serious ambulance crisis; its stores, holding over R7 million worth of essential medical supplies, had no administrative officer and inadequate stock control; and many salary mistakes (delays in increases, for example, and sometimes no salary at all) were being made each month.

What was going wrong?

To understand, we need to look at the administrative history of the hospital. It was originally built and administered by the Natal Provincial Administration, and subsequently by State Health and Welfare. After KwaZulu was created in 1970, the hospital was jointly administered by the KwaZulu and State Health Departments, but with KwaZulu's stake in the business gradually increasing until 1977 when the KwaZulu Health Department assumed full control — full control, that is, of everything save the non-black staff who were, and still are, considered as being seconded from Pretoria.

The inevitable conclusion is that Edendale's autonomy, in other words its ability to administer itself, was being smothered. Important decision-making — whether in the spheres of expenditure within a set annual budget, recruitment, or long-term planning — had passed firmly into the hands of what someone described as 'extra-hospital officials' who worked 300 kilometres away in Ulundi.

It is not necessary here to go into detail about a particularly unhappy period in the history of Edendale; suffice it to say that the white administrators of the hospital began to resent increasing KwaZulu control, and

Children's ward, Edendale Hospital[11]. This mother [12] had nowhere to sleep while her child was being treated.

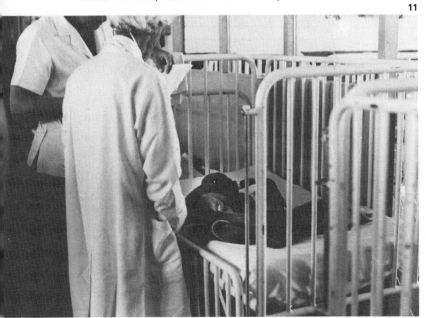

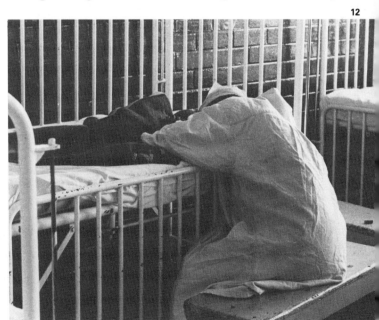

especially the aggression with which it was assumed. Records and other documentation were burned and an attempt was made by Ulundi officials to introduce new, and generally inadequate, administrative procedures. To aggravate matters, Edendale's resentment turned to stubbornness and an attitude of non-cooperation, while on the other hand it appeared that the KwaZulu Department of Health and Welfare was intent on pursuing a vigorous policy of Africanization.

'This was fair enough, but in the running of such a large hospital all races need each other,' a white doctor said. 'There was even talk of placing non-specialist doctors in charge of departments. This would inevitably have led to an appalling drop in standards.'

It was definitely the power struggle between a hospital used to arranging its own affairs and a KwaZulu department anxious to wield its new-gained authority, which resulted in the erosion of the hospital's autonomy, and the placing of more and more power in the hands — sometimes incompetent hands — of Ulundi officials.

Perhaps the hospital was beginning to pay for the

African nurses, and later Indian, have led the women of their communities into the wider world.

NORTHDALE HOSPITAL

Lal Dwarkapersad

Northdale Hospital was commissioned in 1974 to provide medical services for the coloured and Indian communities in Pietermaritzburg. Overlooking the sprawling townships of Northdale and Allandale, the Hospital, which is continually expanding, covers an extensive site. The wards are all in the style of army barracks, and are almost unbearable in the summer months because no adequate cooling system has yet been installed. On the other hand, the Hospital boasts some of the most modern equipment and sophisticated services. Only speech and occupational therapy services are lacking. The numerous medical departments cater for every other need.

The number of out-patient attendances has risen from approximately 85 000 in 1975 to 175 000 in 1986. In-patient numbers have increased from 1 300 in 1979 to 18 000 in 1986. In recent years Northdale Hospital has been inundated with many motor accident victims and violent trauma patients, not to mention the drug-abuse and para-suicide pathologies. Because behavioural problems, personality disorders, child abuse and geriatric difficulties seem to be on the increase in the coloured and Indian communities, much emphasis is given to the holistic approach to patient care, and the Clinical Psychology Department, Psychiatric Clinics, Depression Clinic and Social Worker render very necessary services.

Conscious of the competitive environment of the hospital world, Northdale is approaching the future with an awareness of the need for constant change and growth. A Nursing College with a very fine library is attached to the Hospital, and the Nursing Department initiated and is taking a lead in redefining the future of nursing at the national level. A ward was opened at the Hospital for the treatment of private patients by their own doctors. The Hospital took over the East Street Clinic and commissioned a detached wing of the old Infectious Diseases Hospital to accommodate geriatric patients at Eastwood. It has recently opened Community Health Centres at Richmond and Underberg.

In all, Northdale Hospital is a vibrant institution, doing its best to meet the growing demands of the communities it serves.

decades of neglect of black education, or perhaps, as a doctor put it: 'The Zulu people won't ride the independence bicycle, therefore we must punish them with unnecessary red-tape and inadequate budgets compared to those people who have opted for the South African style of independence for blacks. If you ask me, the underlying cause of Edendale's problems is political.'

A high-ranking KwaZulu Department of Health and Welfare official said: 'The problems of Edendale must be seen against the background of an emerging government and administration, and more specifically of an emerging health and welfare department. I'm not trying to say that we haven't got our problems. We have. But we have some extremely keen people who would like to see the department — and Edendale Hospital — work well.'

Meanwhile, life at the hospital had to go on.

Edendale was running on an annual budget (1983) of R6 million, excluding salaries, plus R300 000 for equipment. Some of the equipment purchased was R80 000 worth of surgical instruments, a deep-therapy machine (R72 000), electro-surgical units and a portable X-ray machine. The hospital's medicine bill came to R3 million, food R1,12 million, clothing R300 000, and so on.

Hospital activity was increasing all the time. Admissions rose by more than 60 per cent between 1978 and 1982, while the number of operations performed rose from just under 3 000 in 1979 to nearly 12 000 in 1983 (an average of 32 a day). Hospital administrators, however, were not allowed to recruit above the laid-down manning levels — manning levels, incidentally, which had not been substantially changed for a decade simply because there was insufficient money to finance any increases. According to nurse/patient ratios laid down in the 1982 new dispensation for nurses, an increase of at least 800 was required to staff Edendale adequately. The hospital got nowhere near that.

Listen to the Health and Welfare official again: 'KwaZulu gets only one-fifth of the money used by Natal for health services, but must spread this money over three times as many people.'

'The other difficulties at Edendale,' he went on, 'are clearly administrative. It all boils down, I think, to middle management. To fully appreciate the problem, however, you must remember that people here are learning the game. They're naturally cautious, reluctant to be innovative. But when forms are returned because someone has written N/A instead of "not applicable", there is definitely room for improvement. The exciting thing though is that you frequently come across people who are exceptional in every way. Given time, training and opportunity, they will make it fantastically.'

What does the future hold for this great hospital and its many thousands of dedicated staff?

In May 1986, a suspected African National Congress terrorist was admitted to Edendale for major surgery after being shot in the stomach. At about 8.30 one evening shortly after the operation, several people dressed in white coats entered the hospital and made their way to the second floor where the ANC man was being treated in the intensive care unit. They opened fire, wounding the two police guards and killing a young visitor to the hospital before making off with the critically ill ANC man.

Is this incident the harbinger of the sort of future which Edendale Hospital can expect? The sound of gunfire in the corridors? The rough-shod invasion of that medical sanctum — where life is indivisible and always worth striving to save — by the ideologies and gangsterism of acute social turbulence?

Will it be a future in which promising young doctors can still be kicked out for refusing to take, not the Hippocratic oath, but that other oath of allegiance to Inkatha? In which the need for more space and more staff will remain as acute as it has always been? In which administrative problems will continue to bedevil the day-to-day business of care and healing?

Yet, whatever the future seems to hold, one thing is certain: Edendale Hospital will remain. It is, after just over thirty years of existence, an indispensable part of the fabric of greater Pietermaritzburg. The traditions of dedication and care which pervade the crowded corridors and wards will not be easily undermined.

In his 1975 article on Edendale, Dr Cosnett observes that in spite of many problems and perplexities, the workers of Edendale, 'paradoxically and inexplicably, under the circumstances, seem to have enjoyed themselves, and continue to do so, most of the time'.

This sense of purpose is still evident today. It is perhaps the one thing which comforts as the hospital peers forward into an uncertain future.

As in all South African cities, there are many people in and around Pietermaritzburg who live below the breadline. Some needs are being met by numerous charitable organizations. This cheerful resident of Emuseni Home is cared for by the Edendale Society for Family and Child Welfare.

Infectious diseases in Pietermaritzburg

Joy Brain

Influenza

Everyone knows of the great influenza epidemic that followed the First World War; it has been described as 'the greatest disaster in South African history', and probably killed a quarter of a million people in the Union. Maritzburg, however, got off rather lightly. In the report of the Medical Officer of Health for the year ending 31 July 1918 there is no mention of influenza in the City, although the newspapers were already reporting an epidemic which had begun in Spain (hence the popular name 'Spanish influenza') and spread throughout Europe. By the end of September, however, he reported a 'serious epidemic' of influenza in Pietermaritzburg, which lasted two months; there were 343 deaths. Although the situation was grave, the death rate in Natal, as far as it could be estimated, was much lower than in the 'Black October' epidemic in the Cape, in which about 7 per cent of those attacked were believed to have died; the figure for Natal was about 2,5 per cent.

Deaths apart, the other effects of the disease were bad enough. Probably nearly half of the total population of South Africa went down with it, leading to widespread disruption of essential services. A second brief epidemic broke out in June and July 1919, which at first appeared less severe, though the death rate among those attacked

was higher; 883 cases were notified in the City, with 31 deaths among whites. Not many blacks were attacked on this occasion.

By October 1918 the epidemic, particularly in the Cape, was causing widespread alarm, and measures were taken in the City on the advice of the MOH, Dr W. J. Woods. The public were advised not to attend gatherings, and were later actually prevented from doing so by the closure of theatres, cinemas and schools. Children were instructed to keep in the open air and many remember the long and exciting hikes enjoyed during this unexpected holiday. A district nurse was appointed and free medicines provided for the poor. A free vaccination station was opened (it is unlikely that any vaccine then available would have had any effect, however) and some of the hutments on the University campus were converted into an emergency hospital. The Epidemic Hospital was prepared for black cases, and a relief committee was formed with headquarters at the Ladies' Club, YMCA Buildings.

The Mayor's report for 1919 expressed the gratitude of the City to those who had devoted themselves to the treatment of the sick and the relief of distress. Correspondents in the Press suggested that the epidemic had been a form of divine retribution for fighting a destructive war, or alternatively for fighting on the British side. After representations from local authorities, the central Government agreed to bear four-fifths of the expense of dealing with the outbreak, and in the report for 1920 things were almost back to normal.

Typhoid fever

Smallpox, plague and cholera were diseases that caused consternation or even panic, yet typhoid or enteric fever was the most serious and persistent disease endemic in Pietermaritzburg in the nineteenth and early twentieth centuries. It affected all ages and its causes were the subject of discussion and speculation among doctors and laymen alike. The symptoms were severe vomiting and diarrhoea, stomach cramps, and high fever lasting five or

16

The public lavatories that once stood conveniently in the middle of Chapel Street.

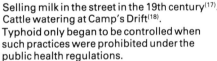

Selling milk in the street in the 19th century[17].
Cattle watering at Camp's Drift[18].
Typhoid only began to be controlled when
such practices were prohibited under the
public health regulations.

six weeks. In the nineteenth century between 10 per cent and 30 per cent of those attacked by the disease died.

The first person in Natal to formulate the theory that there was a connection between enteric fever and cows seems to have been Dr James Allen. He found that the disease was more common among householders who kept their own milch cows or who lived close to dairies. Since there were at the time 23 dairies within the municipal boundaries and many families kept two or three cows for domestic use, it seemed obvious that enteric fever was not going to be easy to eradicate. The apparent connection between cows and typhoid fever was based on observation and no scientific study was carried out.

Outbreaks of the disease were more common in summer and epidemics occurred every few years. A graph of the admissions and deaths in Grey's Hospital covering the years 1870 to 1910 shows that epidemics of typhoid occurred in 1874, 1879–80, 1892, 1897 and in 1900. One of the most serious outbreaks took place during the Anglo-Zulu War and was blamed on impure water supplies. British troops were then transferred from the Capital to the military camp at Pinetown to avoid the dangers of enteric fever and they remained there until 1887. Another serious epidemic occurred in the German internment camp in 1918 when 3 persons died and 30 were seriously ill. The City itself had 17 cases and 1 death.

As in the United Kingdom, the eventual decline of the disease in Pietermaritzburg was brought about not by new drugs and treatments, but by greatly improved sanitation. Dairies moved out of the City itself, fewer people kept cows as the health regulations were tightened, water supplies were protected and purified, the open canals were closed, houses began to have running water laid on instead of

depending on tanks and streams and improved sewage removal was introduced. Nevertheless as late as 1934 there were 23 cases among borough residents and 6 died; in addition 32 people living outside the municipal area died in the City. The Medical Officer of Health declared in 1933 that enteric fever had become a disease mainly of rural districts in process of development; the Balgowan road camp and Edendale had particularly high incidences.

Typhoid fever is unusual in that some convalescent patients continue to carry bacilli in their intestines and gall bladders for months and years and can infect others by contaminating food, milk or water supplies with their excreta. This accounts for the association with dairies; the milk was contaminated by human carriers, or by contaminated water used to wash the cans. The problem of the carrier seemed to be insoluble up to quite recent times and it was suggested that known carriers be prevented from handling, preparing and selling food. It was accepted that until the carrier problem had been addressed there was no chance that Pietermaritzburg would ever be free of sporadic cases in the three or four hot summer months.

Improved sanitation of all kinds has made enteric fever almost a rare disease in Pietermaritzburg and cases that do occur can be effectively treated today. Fifty years ago, however, it was certainly something to be dreaded.

Malaria

Malaria is endemic in many parts of the world, including Africa, and although nowadays everyone accepts that it is spread by the bite of anopheline mosquitoes, this was not known in the first half of the nineteenth century. Only in the 1880s did it become possible to examine blood smears for malaria parasites and thus identify the disease positively. It was a decade after this that doctors outside the established medical centres routinely examined the blood of patients suffering from 'fever'.

In Pietermaritzburg the hospital records regularly report cases of fever throughout the nineteenth century, the first positive mention of malaria appearing only in 1893. The cases of fever peak about every five years and occasionally there is a reference to Delagoa Bay fever or the remittent variety, but there is no certainty that these were cases of malaria or, if they were, whether they had been contracted in the City. In fact, Dr Mann, (who tried to persuade sufferers from tuberculosis that the Capital was the ideal place for recuperation), and Ingram (*Portrait of an African City*) deny that Pietermaritzburg had any malaria at all. Ingram, quoting the famous Dr James Allen, declared the most important thing is that we have no endemic disease, and malaria, the endemic disease of other parts of Africa, is unknown.

Despite this confident pronouncement, 11 cases were seen at Grey's Hospital in 1893, but there was apparently no investigation of their origin. Three years later 40 cases of malaria and beriberi were admitted to Grey's and two died. Twenty-seven cases were treated in 1898 and 34 the following year; thereafter the number of cases reverted to single figures until 1904. Pietermaritzburg was unaffected by the serious malarial epidemic which hit Durban and the coastal districts in 1905–1907 and there was only a slight increase in cases. Until the 1920s, when their complacency was rudely shattered, Pietermaritzburg residents and health authorities continued to believe that the patients had been infected in outlying areas, or in Zululand or even on trains.

In 1928/29 the Medical Officer of Health reported that:

> although during the summer months a few natives and Indians are usually admitted to Grey's suffering from malaria ... our previous experience of outbreaks in the coastal belt would indicate that any serious outbreak of this disease in Maritzburg is very unlikely.

The first warning came in that year when there was a considerable increase in cases and especially when six were reported from the City itself, including four white children living within a few yards of each other. This was explained as being 'probably caused by the introduction of infected mosquitoes from malarial areas'. The following year, with serious outbreaks reported from Durban, Zululand and the North Coast, malaria was made a notifiable disease again, though an examination of the low-lying areas of the Capital showed no mosquito larvae.

In 1930/31 malaria in epidemic form appeared in the Pietermaritzburg district for the first time: 105 cases were admitted of whom 14 died. The parts of the town most affected were those bordering the river and Dorpspruit, particularly Camp's Drift, Fox Hill and Blackburrow Road. In 1931 the report of the visiting expert Swellengrebel was issued and Pietermaritzburg health authorities introduced the preventive measures recommended — spraying breeding places with oil or Paris green. In the first five months of 1932, 1 500 cases were identified, all of which were noted as first infections, and there were 92 deaths. By the end of May the peak had been

reached and the epidemic suddenly subsided. In the first five months of 1933, 239 first infections within the Borough were reported, again mostly in parts bordering the rivers and spruits, with 37 deaths, 16 of which were attributed to relapses of old infections. One block of the hospital for epidemic diseases was lent to the Provincial authorities to accommodate convalescent malaria patients from Grey's Hospital during April and May.

The real breakthough in the prevention of malaria came when Dr Park Ross and his team decided to introduce indoor spraying with a mixture of kerosene and pyrethrum. The practice was ridiculed by many, including the American epidemiologist Dr Fred Soper, who asked whether the mosquitoes were expected to fly indoors to be exterminated at the approach of the spray teams. Later he was to change his opinion and Park Ross's method of spraying every dwelling at least once a week during an epidemic became accepted practice in the 1930s and 40s. In 1934 heavy breeding of larvae was observed along the Msunduze; 472 cases were reported within the Borough and 1 201 in patients who contracted the infection outside it. In spite of these high figures, the death rate was notably lower than in 1932. This was attributed to the more efficient discovery of cases, mostly because of the free service for routine examination of blood slides in the municipal laboratory introduced for the first time in that year.

In 1935 no fresh infections were reported from the City. Since then there have been very few infections originating in the Borough, and its inhabitants can again feel secure in their belief that Pietermaritzburg is the healthiest place in the inhabited world.

Anopheles funestus, the mosquito which carries malaria. **19**

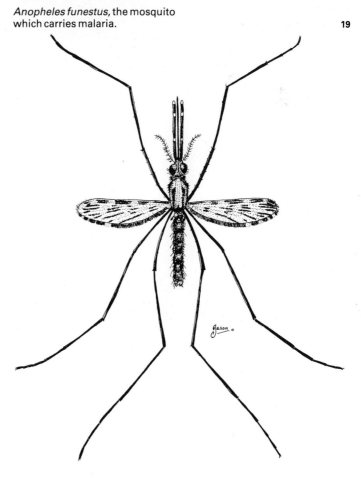

1

The only known photograph of M. K. Gandhi in Pietermaritzburg.
Left to right: M. K. Gandhi, H. Kellenbach, Mr Glask and
Mrs M. Polak, all leading figures in the Satyagraha (Passive
Resistance) Campaign. They are standing on the platform of
the station in 1913, not far from where Gandhi was thrown
from a train in 1893 — an event which transformed his life.

Natal's first Legislative Council elections,
10 February 1857: polling on the Market Square, for
the two Pietermaritzburg seats. J Bergtheil and
J. Henderson were elected. The Presbyterian church
can be seen on the left.

196

CHAPTER TWELVE

Politics and Protest

2

The Pietermaritzburg voter

AND PARLIAMENTARY ELECTIONS

Paul Thompson

Pietermaritzburg has been regarded as the seat of the quintessentially English Natalian. Certainly the architectural heritage suggests that, although as a caricature of Natal *anglais*, Durban may be closer to the mark historically. There is no doubt that the Pietermaritzburg electorate of the House of Assembly has exhibited a British imperial bias throughout the Union and Republican eras, in that the majority has consistently rejected Afrikaner nationalism and republicanism up until the general election of 1987. Apart from that, the pattern of voting is rather more complex.

The polity of Natal in the colonial period has been likened to a large English village. Not numerous, and scattered, the white electorate was dominated by a controlling social élite. Pietermaritzburg was the focus of colonial society, and remained important as the capital in the provincial period although outpaced in growth by the port of Durban. The parliamentary franchise extended to white male adults, and after 1930 to white female adults as well. The Act of Union allowed for numerical variations in parliamentary constituencies, favouring rural voters; Pietermaritzburg, along with Durban, suffered discrimination in this respect, but it was less than had been the case during the colonial period. Nor is there evidence of gross gerrymandering in the delimitation of constituencies. From the time of Union until the general election of 1924, the borough was neatly separated between two parliamentary divisions, Pietermaritzburg North and Pietermaritzburg South. From 1929 until 1970 the separation was between Pietermaritzburg North (1929–1933) and then City (1938–1970) and Pietermaritzburg District. From 1974 there has been a return to the North and South divisions.

The accompanying chart records election results for the Pietermaritzburg electoral divisions. A scholarly analysis of the returns in order to ascertain the bases of shifts in sentiment and opinion, as well as demographic influences, has yet to be made, but even a cursory look at the returns reveals certain interesting features.

First, there have been periodic shifts in the voting pattern. The data for the elections of 1910 and 1915 suggest that the selectors, still partial to Natal's colonial separateness, moved towards the party that would assure its position in the Empire, not just the Union, and the sentiment is reflected in the issues and votes of the 1920s. The data for the elections of 1929 and 1933 suggest that the Great Depression and the Statute of Westminster had divided sentiment with regard to both Union and Empire. This first generation of Natalians of the Union was not integrated in the white South African polity, and the Pietermaritzburg constituency attests it. In 1948 the elections indicated a closing of ranks in the United Party against Afrikaner republicanism and apartheid, and for most of the next twenty years Pietermaritzburg was practically a pocket borough of that party. The fourth shift in the vote pattern is the most recent, beginning in 1974 and marking the full integration of the present generation in white South African politics.

Second, there have been remarkable divisions in the electorate, notwithstanding the prevailing patterns. These suggest that the Pietermaritzburg electorate is not monolithic and that 'Englishness' does not preclude differences of opinion. From 1915 to 1929 the Labour Party was a force, and from 1920 represented the Pietermaritzburg North division; it might have continued to do so after 1929 had there not been a split in the Party at the national level. From 1933 to 1948 the Dominion Party, drawing on devolutionist and home rule support, challenged the imperial bona fides of the United Party; but in the Second World War the United Party proved its fidelity and at its close absorbed the Dominionites. The United Party's monopoly of parliamentary representation was subsequently challenged by the Nationalists in the elections from 1943 to 1958 and again from 1966 to 1974, but without success; however, the Nationalist effort *per se* is notable, suggesting the more favourable conditions for the Party with an increasing Afrikaner population within the borough and a decreasing allegiance amongst the predominantly English speaking community to the old party of Smuts. From 1961 the Progressive Party also challenged the United Party, although not in the same dogged manner as the Nationalist, and with the dissolution of the United Party it carried both divisions in 1981. In 1987 it allied with the New Republic Party (the successor to the United Party) against the National Party and lost both seats. The death knell of the traditional bias against Afrikaner nationalism may have been sounded in the last election, but it would be imprudent to generalize so soon afterwards. In any event, the New Republic Party having become identified as a 'Natal Party', the Progressive Federal and National Parties' victories may be regarded as a further proof of the integration of Natal *qua* Pietermaritzburg with the rest of white South Africa.

Third, the role of political personalities should not be underrated. To what extent voters preferred a man to a party remains to be examined. The British-style political system does not place a premium on individualism in politics, but the durable careers of such United Party fixtures as W. A. Deane and W. J. O'Brien, O. L. Shearer and B. H. Henwood, and latterly W. T. Webber, suggest personal popularity, or at least influence, as well as party regularity. T.G. Strachan's career as the Labour MP for Pietermaritzburg North from 1920 to 1929 also suggests a certain hardihood of political character, for after 1921 the Party was on the defensive in the province.

Election	Electoral Division	Registered Voters	Votes Registered	Parties and Candidates					Remarks
15.9.1910 (General)	PMB. (NORTH)	2 229	1 447 (64,9%)	INDEPENDENT T. Hyslop 489	INDEPENDENT H. Wiltshire 493				UNION AND EMPIRE
	PMB. (SOUTH)	2 185	1 357 (62,1%)	INDEPENDENT W.H. Griffin 519	INDEPENDENT H. Ryle Shaw 119	INDEPENDENT C.A.S. Yonge 357	NATIONAL (Natal Party) T.P.O' Meara 290	SOCIALIST L.H.H. Greene 72	
20.10.1915 (General)	PMB. (NORTH)	1 979	1 267 (64,0%)	SOUTH AFRICAN T. Orr 880				LABOUR F.G.E. Tilbury 379	SAP. v. LABOUR 1915–1929
	PMB. (SOUTH)	1 912	1 309 (68,5%)	SOUTH AFRICAN W.H. Griffin 424	SOUTH AFRICAN R. Buntine 868				
21.11.1918 (By)	PMB. (SOUTH)	2 402	1 426 (59,4%)	SOUTH AFRICAN W.J. O' Brien 654	UNIONIST P.H. Taylor 375			LABOUR T.G. Strachan 384	
10.3.1920 (General)	PMB. (NORTH)	2 222	1 519 (68,4%)	SOUTH AFRICAN T. Orr 572				LABOUR T.G. Strachan 917	
	PMB. (SOUTH)	2 172	1 328 (61,1%)	SOUTH AFRICAN W.J. O'Brien 891				LABOUR W. Cox 424	
8.2.1921 (General)	PMB. (NORTH)	2 229	1 503 (67,4%)	SOUTH AFRICAN W.A. Deane 740				LABOUR T.G. Strachan 752	
	PMB. (SOUTH)	2 181	UNOPPOSED	SOUTH AFRICAN W.J. O'Brien					
17.6.1924 (General)	PMB. (NORTH)	1 997	1 694 (84,8%)	SOUTH AFRICAN F. Banks 724				LABOUR T.G. Strachan 963	
	PMB. (SOUTH)	1 808	1 464 (81,0%)	SOUTH AFRICAN W.J. O'Brien 1 000				LABOUR G. Stobie 446	
12.6.1929 (General)	PMB. (DISTRICT)	2797	UNOPPOSED	SOUTH AFRICAN W.J. O'Brien					
	PMB. (NORTH)	2 897	2 408 (83,1%)	SOUTH AFRICAN W.A. Deane 1 456			COUNCIL LABOUR N.P. Palmer 65	PACT LABOUR T.G. Strachan 875	DEPRESSION AND STATUS UP (Coalition → Fusion) 1933–1948 Home Rule/Dominionite challenge
17.5.1933 (General)	PMB. (DISTRICT)	6 265	4 500 (71,8%)	SOUTH AFRICAN (COALITION) W.J. O'Brien 2 389	HOME RULE C.G. Leftwich 2 087				
	PMB. (NORTH)	6 031	3 971 (65,8%)	SOUTH AFRICAN (COALITION) W.A. Deane 2 170	HOME RULE T.J. Cook 1 782				
18.5.1938 (General)	PMB. (DISTRICT)	5 824	4 611 (79,2%)	UNITED F.N. Broome 2 755	DOMINION C.G. Leftwich 1 839				
	PMB. (CITY)	6 539	4 628 (70,8%)	UNITED W.A. Deane 2 848		INDEPENDENT R. Dunlop 1 721			
12.9.1939 (By)	PMB. (DISTRICT)	5 802	3 077 (53,0%)	UNITED C.F. Clarkson 148 (Withdrew)	DOMINION C.F. Stallard 2 893				
7.7.1943 (General)	PMB. (CITY)	8 128	6 229 (76,6%)	UNITED O.L. Shearer 5 130	PURIFIED NATIONAL J.G.M. Richter 1 027				1st Nationalist Challenge 1943–1958
	PMB. (DISTRICT)	6 693	''4 980 (74,4%)		DOMINION C.F. Stallard 3 493		LABOUR A.S. Knox 169	INDEPENDENT R.G.L. Mathias 1 234	
26.5.1948 (General)	PMB. (CITY)	9 269	7 530 (81,2%)	UNITED O.L. Shearer 5 681	NATIONAL J.G.M. Richter 1 793				
	PMB. (DISTRICT)	7 923	5 815 (73,4%)	UNITED B.H. Henwood 4 928	SOUTH AFRICAN W.J. Walker 843				APARTHEID AND REPUBLIC (Dominionite demise = UP monopoly)
15.4.1953 (General)	PMB. (CITY)	11 751	10 182 (86,6%)	UNITED O.L. Shearer 7 802	NATIONAL J.G.M. Richter 2 340				
	PMB. (DISTRICT)		UNOPPOSED	UNITED B.H. Henwood					
16.4.1958 (General)	PMB. (CITY)	11 596	10 044 (86,6%)	UNITED O.L. Shearer 7 317	NATIONAL C.C.L. Klopper 2 707				
	PMB. (DISTRICT)	9 778	7 403 (75,7%)	UNITED B.H. Henwood 6 717				LIBERAL P.M. Brown 604	Progressive challenge 1961–1974
18.10.1961 (General)	PMB. (CITY)	13 621	7 326 (53,8%)	UNITED H.G.O. Odell 3 915	PROGRESSIVE W.G. McConkey 3 282				
	PMB. (DISTRICT)	11 488	7 936 (69,1%)	UNITED B.H. Henwood 4 014	PROGRESSIVE G.D.B. Forder 3 839				
30.3.1966 (General)	PMB. (CITY)	13 279	10 163 (76,5%)	UNITED W.J.B. Smith 4 987		NATIONAL H.G.O. Odell 4 935	NATIONAL FRONT J.R.N. Swain 201		2nd Nationalist challenge 1966–1974
	PMB. (DISTRICT)	10 834	8 826 (81,5%)	UNITED W.T. Webber 4 807	PROGRESSIVE L.L. Boyd 1 108	NATIONAL J.G. Leppan 2 710	NATIONAL FRONT E.S. Dawson 169		
22.4.1970 (General)	PMB. (CITY)	14 154	10 807 (76,4%)	UNITED W.J.B. Smith 6 257		NATIONAL C.C.L. Klopper 4 517			
	PMB. (DISTRICT)	13 027	10 214 (78,4%)	UNITED W.T. Webber 7 524		NATIONAL K.R.H. Eggers 2 633			
24.4.1974 (General)	PMB. (NORTH)	13 169	10 029 (76,2%)	UNITED G.W. Mills 3 825	PROGRESSIVE I.H.M. Balfour 96	NATIONAL H.G.O. Odell 2 570		DEMOCRATIC T.J.A. Gerdener 3 431	
	PMB. (SOUTH)	13 764	10 574 (76,8%)	UNITED W.T. Webber 6 429	(Withdrew)	NATIONAL H.B. Klopper 4 178			CRISIS DISPENSATION Dissolution of UP = Div. betw. NP & PFP 1977–present
30.11.1977 (General)	PMB. (NORTH)	13 422	10 062	NEW REPUBLIC G.W. Mills 2 808	PROGRESSIVE FEDERAL S.A. Pitman 3 304	NATIONAL D.P.A. Schutte 3 854			
	PMB. (SOUTH)	13 792	10 231	NEW REPUBLIC G. de Jong 5 523		NATIONAL V.A. Jordaan 4 409			
15.5.1981 (General)	PMB. (NORTH)	13 679	10 280 (75,15%)		PROGRESSIVE FEDERAL G.B.D. McIntosh 5 423	NATIONAL D.P.A. Schutte 4 622			
	PMB. (SOUTH)	13 602	10 175 (74,8%)	NEW REPUBLIC L.H. Smith 2 050	PROGRESSIVE FEDERAL M.A. Tarr 4 159	NATIONAL R.C. Anderson 3 921			
6.5.1987 (General)	PMB. (NORTH)		12 649		PROGRESSIVE FEDERAL G.B.D. McIntosh 5 531	NATIONAL Schutte D.P.A. 6 652	HERSTIGTE NASIONALE A.R. Stephenson 414		
	PMB. (SOUTH)		13 778		PROGRESSIVE FEDERAL M.A. Tarr 5 927	NATIONAL B.V. Edwards 7 436	HERSTIGTE NASIONALE P.J. van Rooyen 352		

Finally, splinter parties have fared badly. Pietermaritzburg voters have not been responsive to dubious runners. The Liberal (1958) and National Front (1966) candidates lost badly; however the Democratic (1974) candidate, personally popular and influential, came close to a victory.

In conclusion, it can be said that despite rivalry among English-speaking parties, the predominantly English-speaking constituency of Pietermaritzburg rejected Afrikaner nationalism — indeed, the inter-party rivalries may reflect the confidence of the polity that Afrikaner nationalism was an alien menace, not one to be fought on the home ground. The 1987 election and the National Party victories in Pietermaritzburg would seem to mark the end of an era. This is a remarkable, perhaps momentous, development, but it should be noted that in the most recent election the National Party was no longer perceived to be the Party of extreme Afrikaner nationalism, which distinction was shared by the Conservative and Herstigte Nasionale Parties; also, that the 'alliance' of the Progressive Federal and New Republic Parties produced a major defection from the latter and consequently the Nationalist Party might be likened plausibly to the United Party of 1934; and finally, that neither party in the last election was disposed to cater to the particular Natal interest or outlook, and so the electors of Pietermaritzburg went to the polls presumably thinking and, perforce, voting in 'national' and not Natalian terms.

Bearing this in mind, it may be useful to recall how Pietermaritzburg electors voted in the national referenda. In 1909, 1 844 out of the 3 896 who were eligible voted on entry in the Union — only 59,6 per cent of the electorate. Of these 1 122 voted for the Union, when political and especially economic arguments for doing so were particularly strong. In 1960, however unionist the electors might be, they were definitely anti-republican. In Pietermaritzburg City, 12 751 electors in a 92 per cent poll rejected the Republic 8 987 to 3 689; and in Pietermaritzburg District 10 679 voters (94,9 per cent poll) by 8 705 to 1 890. The statistics on the vote for the new constitution in 1983 do not tell the bias of the City, for the Pietermaritzburg division includes the interior of Natal. Of the 70 945 who voted, 50 519 were in favour of the new dispensation. How much of the 28,3 per cent negative vote was cast in the City is a matter of speculation, at least until a more precise breakdown of returns is made available.

LIBERALS IN PIETERMARITZBURG

Peter Brown

Some of South Africa's greatest liberal figures have had their roots in the City. Bishop Colenso worked in Pietermaritzburg; Edgar Brookes, Alan Paton and Selby Msimang were born here. Everyone knows about the contribution they made to the defence of liberal values in Natal and South Africa. What is probably not so well known is the contribution other people from this area made to giving South African liberals a coherent and organized political voice in this country.

Not a few people came out of the Second World War thinking that white South Africa would now start to take the first steps towards creating a non-racial society. The Nationalists' surprise victory in 1948 put an end to all that, and it soon became apparent that the United Party, the only possible source of such a change at that time, was very unlikely to win the next election or to embark on such a course if it did. Liberals began to ask themselves what they should be doing in these circumstances.

In Pietermaritzburg the response was the calling of a non-racial meeting of a small group of people on 21 June 1952. The group continued to meet regularly, drawing in new members, amongst them Alan Paton, who was finishing off *Too Late the Phalarope* at Bulwer, and who used to come in from there to attend. On 8 December the group took the daring step (for such it certainly was felt to be at the time) of holding a public meeting in the Conference Room of the City Hall. Geoffrey Durrant, Professor of English at the University, and Hugh Carey, a master at Michaelhouse, were the speakers. A non-racial committee was elected, a rather modest 'manifesto' and appeal for support was sent to the Press, and organized liberal politics had come to Maritzburg. A week later, at much the same kind of meeting, Durban set up a similar group. In January 1953 both groups sent representatives to a meeting in Cape Town at which the South African Liberal Association was formed, bringing together in one body liberals throughout the country. Later that year, after the Nationalists had been returned to power for the second time, the Association voted to convert itself into the Liberal Party of South Africa. The two Natal delegates to the meeting which took the decision were Selby Msimang and Peter Brown, both from Pietermaritzburg. They returned to set up the provincial office of the Party in the old Ireland's Building in Church Street (now Edgars), and from there slowly to extend the membership and influence of the Party throughout the Midlands and Northern Natal.

In time four branches were established in and around the City: in Pietermaritzburg itself, Edendale, Raisethorpe and Pentrich. It is a reflection of what apartheid and the Group Areas Act has done to us that the Pentrich community, which was the base of that branch, no longer exists, and that Edendale had a branch with black, white, Indian and coloured members who lived happily together in that area. Today a branch based on people living in Edendale would be black only.

The Party fought two elections in the City, one provincial and one parliamentary, both with disastrous results in terms of votes received, but notable for the fact that they introduced to Pietermaritzburg something it had not seen before: a non-racial election campaign. Most Party activity was, however, extra-parliamentary, fighting blackspot removals, the Group Areas Act and the host of intrusions into their lives with which apartheid was confronting its growing black membership. In these fields a close working relationship developed with the Congress Movement, the Black Sash and, later, the Progressive Party.

In response partly to its membership's reflecting more accurately the racial composition of South Africa at that time than was the case in the other provinces, the National Headquarters of the Liberal Party were moved to Pietermaritzburg in 1956. They were set up in the building at 268 Longmarket Street, which now houses the Lambert Wilson Library — and the HNP office! Alan Paton, then living at Kloof, became National Chairman that year and, in 1958, was succeeded by Peter Brown. He held the position until his banning in 1964, when he was succeeded by another local citizen, Edgar Brookes. Dr Brookes held the position until the Improper Interference Act, preventing non-racial politics, forced the Party to close in 1968.

Nearly twenty years later organized liberalism has again surfaced in the City with the formation of the Liberal Democratic Association. It is committed to keeping liberal ideas alive in the period of transition to a non-racial society, and hopes to see that their importance is recognized and enshrined in the civil liberties and legal, constitutional, and economic arrangements of that society.

Selby Msimang.

GANDHI: THE PIETERMARITZBURG EXPERIENCE

Hassim Seedat

It was in Pietermaritzburg in 1893 that a young Indian lawyer, Mohandas Gandhi, took a decision that irrevocably committed him to his political and religious destiny as a leader. After he left South Africa in 1914 he led the struggle for the national independence of India, and the non-violent methods he used earned him world-wide recognition as one of the greatest men of this century.

Just before his seventieth birthday in 1939, Gandhi was asked by the missionary, Dr John R. Mott, to single out the most creative experience of his life. This was Gandhi's reply:

> Such experiences are a multitude. But as you put the question to me, I recalled particularly one experience that changed the course of life. That fell to my lot seven days after I had arrived in South Africa. I had gone there on a purely mundane and selfish mission. I was just a boy returned from England, wanting to make some money. Suddenly the client who had taken me there asked me to go to Pretoria from Durban. It was not an easy journey. There was the railway journey as far as Charlestown and the coach to Johannesburg. On the train I had a first-class ticket, but not a bed ticket. At Maritzburg when the beds were issued, the guard came and turned me out, and asked me to go into the van compartment. I would not go, and the train steamed away leaving me shivering in the cold. Now the creative experience comes there. I was afraid for my very life. I entered the dark waiting-room. There was a white man in the room, I was afraid of him. What was my duty? I asked myself. Should I go back to India, or should I go forward, with God as my helper and face whatever was in store for me? I decided to stay and suffer. My active non-violence began from that date.

The event Gandhi described had taken place nearly forty-six years before, on the night of 7 June 1893. It is not surprising that after all that time there should have been some errors in Gandhi's recollection. He had arrived in Durban from India earlier than he remembered, on 23 May 1893, and it was not the railway guard that had turned him off the train at Pietermaritzburg station. In fact, the guard had summoned the aid of a police constable when Gandhi had refused to budge from his seat, and the constable had unceremoniously pushed him out of the compartment and pitched his luggage after him.

That wintry night in the waiting-room of the Pietermaritzburg station, Gandhi made the fateful decision not to accept his ignominious treatment but to stay on and fight racial injustice. In the morning he sent a telegram of protest from the Pietermaritzburg Post Office to the General Manager of the Railways. Gandhi had initiated his public career.

A late 19th century architect's drawing of the Pietermaritzburg railway station.

4

The *Natal Witness* and 'Open Testimony'

Basil Leverton

There is only one source which covers, and in detail, 142 consecutive years of the history of Pietermaritzburg. That is the *Natal Witness*.

Established in February 1846 in the geographical heart of a fledgling British colony, and at a place where the Queen's representative ruled with wide powers over a populace then largely non-British (Dutch and Zulu), the *Natal Witness* from its very first issue stood for what it called 'open testimony', a philosophy which was appropriately backed by a masthead motto of 'The Truth, The Whole Truth, and Nothing But the Truth'. To be sure, this motto was not chosen at random nor, indeed, in mere flamboyant fashion. It related directly to the significant advances made in the Cape Colony.

In the 1820s men like Thomas Pringle and others had felt very strongly that to collaborate with a government-controlled Press was merely to compromise those liberties which British subjects held most dear. They had fought unflinchingly against any control whatever of people's written thoughts. Their victory in 1829, which brought the first South African freedom of the Press, resulted in the mushrooming of journals in Cape Town itself, then spreading in an ever-widening arc to Graham's Town in 1831 and to Natal fifteen years later. The birth of the *Natal Witness* was thus the direct outcome of the work of several idealists at the Cape who opposed with heart and soul the machinations of a closed society in which the basic civil liberties did not apply.

Two years after the founding of the *Natal Witness*, the townsfolk of Pietermaritzburg stared as a cheering party carried a smiling man shoulder-high through the streets in a wreathed armchair, a copy of his newspaper tied to it by a bright ribbon. The man in the chair was David Dale Buchanan who was on his way from prison, his fine having just been paid by his supporters.

Buchanan was a rollicking, pugnacious editor who steadfastly refused to bridle his tongue — or his pen —in serving what he regarded as the public interest; he was also the exemplification of the colourful and irrepressible editorial character which emerged from the pioneering years of the South African Press at the time of growing freedom of written thought. When the Cape Press was freed in 1829, D. D. Buchanan was an impressionable lad ten years of age attending John Fairbairn and Thomas Pringle's evening classes, as well as being an avid Latin pupil of Dr John Philip. His close collaboration with the *Cape Town Mail* (edited by George Greig) was later to be of exceptional value when he came to set up the *Natal Witness*. It was while working at Cape Town that Buchanan first attracted attention, especially after he reacted very strongly against the Cape Government's intended imposition of a newspaper tax.

202

It was fortunate for Natal and Pietermaritzburg that 'D. D.' did not become a missionary in the Christian field, but left the Cape to become a missionary for the freedom of the Press and Cape liberal thought in his new home.

Throughout his long stewardship of the *Natal Witness*, which lasted for several decades, Buchanan wrote under a two-pronged and continuous threat: one was the supposed threat of a Zulu invasion from the north; the other the lieutenant-governor and his appointed aides. Buchanan regarded the latter threat as the more potent. He was fully aware of the official establishment's attitude to Pietermaritzburg's first newspaper, *De Natalier*, whose editor had been accused of the spreading of a 'seditious spirit' among 'this ignorant people'. Buchanan did not intend them to remain in ignorance.

Buchanan possessed wit, charm and eloquence, and these characteristics came to the fore in his *Natal Witness* editorials. But he was also capable of penning some of the most vitriolic leading articles which have ever appeared in print in South Africa. His relationship with Natal's first lieutenant-governor, Martin West, was not too abrasive, and he waged his most controversial campaign against Lieutenant-Governor Benjamin Pine, a man whom he suspected of despotic intentions. Under the startling headline of PINE AND RAPINE he wrote of Benjamin Pine as follows:

> Our mountebank governor has returned from his drinking and dancing friends at Durban, where he has been again bedewed with showers of pothouse popularity.

Buchanan succeeded in making Pietermaritzburg the hub of the anti-Pine party and the nucleus of the movement towards constitutional reform. The white inhabitants of Natal loved to read in the *Witness* that they were the victims of 'Downing Street despotism', and Buchanan's success from his editorial chair in persuading the British Government to grant representative government to Natal in 1856 was perhaps in many ways due to his ability to 'read' public opinion and to express popular ideas in his own words.

Critics of D. D. Buchanan have averred that he misused the *Witness* to pursue a private vendetta against Lieutenant-Governor Benjamin Pine and it has been suggested that he tried to manipulate the people of Pietermaritzburg for his own personal satisfaction. It is true, indeed, that on several occasions his editorial conduct degenerated into licence for abuse and slander. But to his credit it should be remembered that throughout his career he displayed a strong determination to retain for the Press its hard-fought-for freedom of expression. He set a standard in the Natal capital and elsewhere for courage in the face of the official penchant for oppression, and he was noted for his strength in not succumbing to government pressures. During his editorship there was never any threat of the

5

David Dale Buchanan, founder of the *Natal Witness* and editor 1846–71.

Mark Prestwich,
editor 1953–6.

closure of the *Natal Witness*. Even his critics praised the high standard and quality of editing which he set for his newspaper, and Lieutenant-Governor Robert Keate commended him on 'his fair and clear' exposition of Natal politics and upon his 'honest convictions'.

When he died in 1874 Buchanan was hailed throughout the South African Press. This was the real measure of the success of his policy of 'open testimony'. The *Natal Witness* itself called him an 'honest hater' and remarked: 'Public offenders had to be punished and the press was the only means at his disposal. It was the only corrective for wrong-doers either in high or low places.' That was praise indeed for a man who not only laid the foundations of a long-lasting newspaper but also etched out a new 'press conscience' in Natal.

As representative government in Natal proceeded along its tortuous trail from 1856 onwards, and as the Colony's financial situation improved and Pietermaritzburg grew in size and population, the opposition of the *Natal Witness* to the workings of officialdom toned down considerably. In 1873, however, an event occurred which tested the newspaper's stand on 'open testimony'. This was the 'Langalibalele rebellion', which brought the 'native question' of the Colony to the political forefront.

The British Government considered, in view of the judicial debacle which followed the rebellion, that the time had come to deprive Natal of some of its mismanaged constitutional advantages. Sir Garnet Wolseley was despatched to Natal to arrange for the so-called 'Jamaica reforms'. This visit brought the *Witness* into the fray once more, and on one occasion the editor complained bitterly of the 'bellowings' of the Exeter Hall faction in England — a complaint aimed at the constitutional threat to Natal, rather than being any objection to the improvement in the position of the black population of Natal.

The controversy brought to the fore Ralph Errington Ridley, a tanner by trade, who had come to the Colony in 1861. Ridley, a disciple of John Stuart Mill and Herbert Spencer, was dubbed in Natal 'that would-be Cobden'. After stints at the editorial desks of the *Natal Mercury* and the *Times of Natal*, he became the editor of the *Natal Witness*, a position which he held from 1873 until his death in 1875.

In his editorial columns Ridley stoutly opposed the Shepstonian system of black administration as he felt

that this was a system which, if not properly backed by proper education and upliftment, would entrench backwardness and poverty. He was also a great supporter of British constitutionalism, and it was his consistent aim that Natal should proceed without problems or delay to responsible government. He was convinced that this kind of government would enable the Colony to solve some of its racial problems. It was not to be wondered at, then, that before long editor Ridley became to be regarded as a 'nuisance' by Natal officialdom. This opinion of him did not change when, with the coming of bad financial times, his attacks upon authority increased.

The coming to Natal of Sir Garnet Wolseley transformed Ridley from a somewhat pedestrian critic of authority into an almost rabid anti-government activist. He argued that the Langalibalele affair had been purposely used by the British Government for its own political objectives, and began a merciless editorial attack upon Sir Garnet Wolseley. That 'very model of a modern major-general' came to regard Ridley as the most able man in Natal, though a very dangerous leader and the sort of 'demagogue with great brains' who could very easily upset the British applecart in Natal. By urging in the *Witness* that the Natal Parliament adopt delaying tactics in approving constitutional changes, Ridley succeeded for a while in thwarting the aims of Sir Garnet Wolseley. But in the middle of this great constitutional debate Ridley took ill and died. Such was Wolseley's real hatred of the *Natal Witness* editor, that he refused to attend the funeral. He could not have paid Ridley a better tribute.

Somewhat like D. D. Buchanan, Ridley was often impervious to any counter-arguments, and like his illustrious predecessor, refused in his editorials to compromise on what he thought right for Natal. Yet Ridley had strengths which Buchanan did not possess: he was an excellent orator and a man who went down well as a public representative in the Natal Parliament. Though often an impulsive editor, he was earnest in his beliefs and, what was more, he succeeded in greatly boosting the circulation of the *Witness* in the Natal capital. What more could one demand from a newspaperman?

In the years between the death of Ridley and the outbreak of the Anglo-Zulu War of 1879, the *Witness* gave its support to the conciliatory policies of Lieutenant-Governor Sir Henry Bulwer. It strenuously opposed the British policy of seeking a confrontation with the Zulu kingdom in the interests of its plans for confederation. The *Natal Witness* was dubious all along about the wisdom of the annexation of the Transvaal in 1877, and it complained about the utter folly (from the point of view of the Natal colonists) of antagonizing the mighty Zulu king, with whom, it averred, the people of Natal had never had any quarrel. On many occasions it crossed swords with the British military authorities concerning the conduct of the Anglo-Zulu War. The *Witness* was outraged when, after the end of the War, the British Government (to placate home opinion) demanded from Natal a Zulu War payment, as if the Colony had in some way been responsible for the outbreak of the War. Anger was turned to fury when the British Government threatened Natal with no help with its railway if the payment was not made.

At this juncture there stepped into the editorial chair of the *Natal Witness* a man whom Sir Garnet Wolseley described as a 'most amusing ruffian, full of Irish stories which he tells inimitably'. Alfred Aylward, an Irish Fenian who had had a varied career in South Africa, campaigned in and out of season against British treatment of the Transvaal Boers. This was, indeed, in keeping with public thinking in Natal, for strong trade ties bound the two communities together, and there was a common anti-British feeling in both territories. In 1881, when the First Anglo-Boer War broke out, the *Witness* strongly advocated that Natal should wash its hands of any further British adventures in the interior of South Africa.

Francis Reginald Statham had briefly been editor of the *Natal Witness* in 1877 and, after an interval, he returned in July 1881 to further his declared policy that 'one man, with justice on his side, is a majority'. This conviction made him a fearless editorial writer and accounted for his frequent feuds (both in and out of the editorial columns) with the authorities, and explained his general inability to get on with people. With characteristic vehemence he opposed Sir Garnet Wolseley's post-war settlement of Zululand, supported Bishop Colenso (who was also highly critical) and angered Sir Henry Bulwer and the Natal official establishment, especially the Shepstone family. So violent were some of his views and words that someone in the Colonial Office described him as 'that pestilent journalist' — an indication that his editorial barbs were reaching their mark. Yet he was also a man of vision: his forecast of the political situation in Natal in 1889 (as published in the *Natal Witness* in 1879) was so remarkably true that his prognostications were reprinted in full in the *Witness* columns in 1889.

In 1881 the British Government sought a replacement for Sir Henry Bulwer as Governor of Natal and appointed one W. J. Sendall. The *Witness* complained in very loud voice that this gentleman had never been an administrator, never mind a governor. The newspaper saw Sendall as a nominee of the Governor at the Cape and the appointment as a ploy to make Natal subservient to Cape Town. After some very heated editorials the proposed appointment was cancelled. The *Natal Witness* rightly regarded this as proof positive of the effectiveness of its prompt protest.

The decade between 1883 and 1893 was taken up in Natal by the continued struggle for responsible government, which would confer upon the Colony complete control of its own affairs. In this campaign the *Witness* took a decided stand. Responsible government was attained in 1893 but Britain retained *de facto* control of 'native policy'. The *Witness* argued that this was a mistake and that the Natal blacks would have been better off if the colonists had been given control of them — which in the light of normal colonial practice was a dubious assertion.

After 1893, Natal affairs assumed the decided characteristic of what was called 'parish pump politics', and the *Witness* considered that this was the inevitable result of a 'sham' form of popular representation. The newspaper was not surprised when the colonial Parliament put up a poor performance, particularly as regards black affairs. When the question of the unification of South Africa came up after the turn of the century, the *Witness* studiously opposed the idea of Union on the terms offered by the National Convention. It favoured rather the federal form of unification as it considered that the interests of English-speaking South Africans and the blacks under Union would ultimately become subjugated to those of the Dutch. The *Natal Witness* considered itself not surprised that eminent English politicians were omitted from the first South African cabinet.

During the early years of Union, editorial attention in the *Witness* was devoted mainly to the country's inter-white relationships. Several custodians of the editorial chair touched upon this subject, but the man who was perhaps representative of them all was G. H. Calpin, a confirmed progressive in all spheres of development. On 'native policy' he was far ahead of public opinion and the generality of his readers. At this juncture the *Witness* was possibly the only South African English newspaper which admitted the legitimacy of the claims of the Afrikaans republican Press, and Calpin believed that the *Witness* could possibly form a bridge between the two sides. Calpin was not a man for journalistic 'stunts', but he made much of the belief that the 'streams' policy in South Africa made sure that English and Afrikaans in the country would never converge and, by implication, that the same applied to white-black political and social relationships. Via the columns of the *Witness* he argued that in South Africa there was far too much of the 'gesture attitude', which left nobody completely satisfied.

The coming to power of the Nationalist Party in 1948 shifted the editorial emphasis of the *Witness* from white politics to black politics, and there was much stress laid upon the deterioration of the rule of law and the concomitant loss of Press freedom. During the period February 1953 to January 1956 Mark Prestwich occupied the editorial chair of the *Natal Witness*, and of all the editors of the period he is perhaps the most singular. Mark Prestwich was a truly civilized and liberal man. Full of wit, with a peerless command of language and an encyclopaedic knowledge of history — all supported by an analytical frame of mind of the highest order — he gave to his prose a bite and acuteness which would be difficult to emulate. At a time when the Torch Commando was active in its opposition to proposed Government curbs, he wrote on 21 February 1953: 'It is impossible to criticise these laws adequately without using plain language. It may even be impossible to criticise them effectively without arousing strong moral indignation — for moral indignation has been the driving force behind a multitude of reforms.' In an editorial entitled 'The Attack on the Constitution' on 10 March 1953 he wrote: 'It is hardly worth while to comment on Dr Donges's idea that parliament and not the courts should protect the rights of the individual.' In February 1953, with typical wit, in relation to a news item that the then prime minister had had twelve teeth removed, he penned an editorial which he entitled 'The Tiger Still Has Teeth'.

It may seem an injustice to have singled out individual *Natal Witness* editors who have followed D. D. Buchanan's 'open testimony' dictum, for it needs to be said that all the *Witness* editors have continued the war against injustice, social, legal, political and otherwise. As D. D. Buchanan once wrote: 'Whether an editor is ill or well, happy or miserable, cheerful or melancholy, he must come up to the mark. There is no discharge from his warfare.'

Richard Steyn

On founding the *Natal Witness* 142 years ago, David Dale Buchanan promised to bear 'fair and open testimony' in matters of public interest and committed his newspaper to 'the cause of sound progress, just government and constitutional liberty, without regard to persons or parties'.

Those brave and noble sentiments have guided successive proprietors and editors of the *Natal Witness*, now South Africa's oldest continuously published newspaper. But how capable of attainment are they today? In his efforts to keep readers informed, Buchanan clashed frequently with the authorities; but he did not have an Internal Security Act, a Police Act, a Prisons Act or Emergency Regulations to contend with. In promising that his newspaper would bear witness to the truth, Buchanan did not foresee a time when government would seek to monopolize the truth and force public opinion into a strait-jacket of its own making.

CENSORED

News about politics, unrest and labour activity is seriously affected by the emergency regulations.

A sign of the times.

It is one of South African history's unhappier coincidences that Pietermaritzburg's 150th birthday should be celebrated amid the most serious civilian strife in the life of the City. The very denial of sound progress, just government and constitutional liberty over many decades has led to near anarchy on the City's outskirts, where respect for the constitution and the rule of law no longer exists. The violence in the black suburbs, and officialdom's attempts to suppress it, have posed special difficulties for the *Natal Witness* — the newspaper of record of the area. While the authorities believe that suppressing news of violence helps to contain it, the reality has proved otherwise. Despite the absence of detailed news coverage, the death toll has mounted steadily.

In trying to stay true to its traditions, the *Natal Witness* faces challenges as daunting as any in its long history. Reporters — especially those who are black — have to weave their way through a thicket of legal restrictions, ignoring threats to life and limb, harassment from police officers and advances from people intent on using the Press to advance their political cause. The emergency curbs prevent journalists from going to the scene of the fighting and interviewing people directly affected. Reporting and commenting on the conflict means expanding on the terse 'unrest reports' put out for public consumption, and trying to decide — in the absence of legal precedent — what the regulations do and do not permit. If the authorities had their way, the media would report no more than the barest details of the conflict, confining it to the inside pages at that.

Other significant influences are the demands of the combatants themselves, locked in a struggle not only for political supremacy but for public sympathy as well. From Ulundi, Chief Buthelezi keeps a critical eye on newspaper coverage, as do various government bodies monitoring the media. Commerce and industry in the capital are concerned at the City's image as a focus of unrest. The security police are ever watchful and suspicious of what appears in print. All these pressures weigh upon a small though determined editorial staff. As one remarked ruefully, it is rather like having to cover the Falklands War from a distance in a manner which satisfies both the British and the Argentinians.

The *Natal Witness's* response down the years to the manifold political and legal constraints placed upon the media has been to do its utmost to preserve an independent stance and keep its readers informed to the maximum extent permitted by law. In its comment and feature articles, the newspaper has attempted to uncover the underlying causes of the current conflict, in the hope that diagnosis might lead to cure. It has thrown open its opinion and letters columns and tried to be a channel of communication between races and factions. Regrettably, successive security clampdowns have made fairness and balance virtually impossible to achieve.

Despite these vicissitudes, the *Natal Witness* will remain faithful to the ideals of its founder. It will continue to proclaim the virtues of just government and personal liberty under the law, however distant those goals may seem at present. It will continue to be a witness to events in the City, an affliction sometimes to the comfortable and a comfort to the afflicted. In so doing, it will endeavour always to retain the goodwill of our readership without whose loyal support the *Natal Witness* would not have survived and prospered for almost as long as Pietermaritzburg itself.

Afrikaners in Pietermaritzburg

CULTURAL PATTERNS AND POLITICAL AWARENESS

Pieter Prinsloo

At the turn of the century, Natal was predominantly English-speaking. Of the 97 109 whites living in Natal in 1904, only 16 000 were Afrikaners. English social and cultural patterns dominated community life. Only a small number of Afrikaans-speaking people lived in the Capital at that stage, and had no influence on the community. Their activities were centred mainly on the Dutch Reformed Congregation and church organizations like the Christian Endeavour Society.

It was J. S. M. Rabie, the editor of *De Afrikaner,* published in Pietermaritzburg, who carried the post-Anglo-Boer War countrywide Afrikaner cultural awakening into Natal by means of his newspaper. His clarion call was not without success. From 1906 the Afrikaners in Pietermaritzburg became progressively organized, laying the foundation for the establishment of their cultural patterns. This in its turn led to a singular cultural awakening among the broader ranks of the Afrikaner in Natal.

Opening of the Church of the Vow as the Voortrekker Museum by General Schalk Burger, 16 December 1912.

7

During June 1906 a few Afrikaners, under the chairmanship of D. P. Boshoff, and with the encouragement of the Afrikaners in Vryheid and Babanango, founded the Pietermaritzburg Boer Society, a quasi-political organization. This movement was the first sign that the Afrikaners in Pietermaritzburg were busy leaving their church laager and becoming involved in matters concerning the community. The editor of *De Afrikaner* regarded this as an indication that the old Boer capital, long since regarded as lost to any Dutch-Afrikaans influences, had started to lift its head to let its particular voice be heard. The Pietermaritzburg Boer Society linked up with the overarching governing body, Het Kongres. For the few years it lasted, this society existed as an essential interest group of the Pietermaritzburg Afrikaner, and as such laid the foundation for organized action in Pietermaritzburg. The founding of the South African Party in 1911 presented the Afrikaners of the Natal Capital with a new forum from which to further their interests. On 17 June 1915 the National Party of Natal was constituted, presenting the Afrikaners with an additional political platform. General Hertzog explained the dogma of Afrikaner nationalism to the Natal Nationalists in October 1918, thus applying the Natal Afrikaner's struggle for maintenance of culture to practical politics, and igniting the latent power of their selfconsciousness.

This was the reason that the proposal to send a Deputation of Liberty to the 1919 Peace Conference at Versailles roused such enthusiasm in the ranks of the Natal Afrikaner. Although the *Natal Witness* regarded the idea as extreme arrogance, it was carried into the Natal capital by Advocate E. G. Jansen and other Nationalists. On Saturday evening, 4 January 1919, Jansen addressed a public meeting on the development of the political consciousness of the Afrikaner and the Deputation of Liberty. Afterwards the Nationalists enthusiastically founded a National Party branch for the capital. E. G. Jansen and A. T. Spies were chosen as Natal representatives for the Deputation of Liberty. Despite the disdain of some English-speaking citizens *Die Afrikaner* regarded this deputation as symbol of the Afrikaner's deep-rooted sense of freedom. After eight months had elapsed, the Pietermaritzburg branch of the National Party organized a reception at the Creamery Hotel for the returning Deputation members. While the guests were being treated on Wednesday 3 September 1919 to a seven-course meal, tributes, patriotic speeches and musical items, a hostile crowd of about 800 people gathered outside the hotel. Shortly after the speeches and dinner, the Deputation members were led through an unguarded exit, while the mob entered the hotel, searched it and bombarded it with eggs and other 'weapons'. It was not without reason that some of the English-speaking citizens unfavourably regarded Jansen and the Pietermaritzburg Nationalists as the source of the unfolding national self-consciousness and political activity of the Natal Afrikaners.

Meanwhile, another cultural pattern was developing in the ranks of the Pietermaritzburg Afrikaner. It revolved around the upholding and development of the Afrikaner's spiritual values. It was centred mostly in social gatherings of societies, for example the Pietermaritzburg Debate and Literary Society and the Christian Young People's

Association. Furthermore, Afrikaans-speaking leaders in Pietermaritzburg united Afrikaners and encouraged participation through the South African Academy, the Organization of Dutch and Afrikaans Language Friends, the Pietermaritzburg Vigilance Committee and the Saamwerk-Unie. These societies and organizations not only kept the Afrikaans language culture in Pietermaritzburg alive, but also established new cultural patterns among Afrikaners. The monthly meetings served as convivial social and post-school training-centres for young and old. The approximately 100 Afrikaners who supported these activities entertained and spiritually strengthened one another by means of recitations, singing, musical items, dialogue, speeches, literary readings, historical anecdotes, debates, plays, receptions and religious readings. An entire generation of Afrikaans-speaking people was enabled to develop their language proficiency, eloquence, patriotism, piety and Afrikaner nationalism, naturally and spontaneously. The value of these societies can hardly be overestimated. They not only improved the quality of the Afrikaans-speaking population's cultural life, but together with societies in the English-speaking community such as the Young Men's

Christian Association, Friendly Society, Victoria Club, and the Mechanic's Institute formed the dynamo of white cultural life in the Capital.

These culture-orientated activities enabled a group of Pietermaritzburg Afrikaners to emerge as local leaders, and to go on to achieve fame on the provincial and national level. E. G. Jansen, his wife Mabel, Professor G. Besselaar, G. Nienaber, J. J. le Roux and the Revd G. M. Pellissier were the most prominent and, with their new vision, caused a renaissance in Afrikaner culture in Natal.

The Pietermaritzburg Vigilance Committee introduced the first phase of the Afrikaans mother-tongue struggle in Natal schools. The Organization of Dutch and Afrikaans Language Friends in Natal, which was founded in 1917 as a result of these activities, successfully carried through the protest movement for equal language rights in Natal. This agitation was aimed at the Natal Provincial Council which did not acknowledge Afrikaans as a language medium in schools, as did the other Councils in the country. The recognition of Afrikaans as an instruction medium and the establishment of Afrikaans-medium schools was a direct result of this agitation.

The endeavour of a few men who, under leadership of

Dr E. G. JANSEN,
the Doyen of Afrikaner Culture in Natal

8

Pieter Prinsloo

Dr E. G. Jansen.

E. G. Jansen was born in the Dundee district of Natal on 7 August 1881. He matriculated at Durban Boys' High in 1898, and obtained an LL B degree in 1905. In 1906 he started to practise as an attorney in Pietermaritzburg and in 1908 he was called to the bar.

Adv. Jansen soon discovered that Pietermaritzburg was not the ideal place for him to live, because of racial prejudices against Afrikaners:

> I am powerless in fighting the prejudices against my fellow citizens, and living in this unsympathetic environment day after day has disheartened me. To leave this place would be regarded by our enemies [the English] as defeat, and I do not want to run away. Is it my fate to pass my days in an environment where I do not feel at home? At times I experience an intense longing to be in an Afrikaner-environment! Yet, I am positive that my duty lies here.

Precisely these uncomfortable circumstances caused E. G. Jansen to devote his life to serving his fellow Afrikaans citizens, and to carry his singular philosophy of life into Natal. He encouraged his fellow citizens to be

intellectual builders. He believed that if one's mind is developed, one's spiritual eyes will also be opened. He believed that if one is given a true understanding of life, of the universe and of oneself, then one's complacency will also wilt. Jansen also believed that if one's self-esteem is to be elevated, one must be loyal to oneself, to one's people and to God.

As cultural leader, Jansen taught his fellow Afrikaners that they had within themselves the power which would enable them to maintain a footing and which would protect them against influences alien to their people. Being a moderate person, he also believed that the future of this country lay in co-operation between people. He did not regard conciliation as a political trump card, but as an attitude towards life which he himself practised.

Although E. G. Jansen served his people on a national level, he mainly served his fellow Afrikaners in Natal. In a gripping public career, he was one of the first persons to further Afrikaans as a spoken and a written language; he established Afrikaner nationalism in Natal; he furthered the symbols of the Afrikaner culture in words, achievements and writing, committees and diverse organizations; he united the memory of the Voortrekkers in a museum, in monuments and in books, and in doing so he gave form to the mythologization of the role played by the Voortrekkers.

Above all, E. G. Jansen was a sensitive person, a gentleman *par excellence* in thought and conduct, polished and sincere, one who carried the hallmark of good breeding with distinction. This made him an exceptional advocate, a fighter for his language, a cultural leader and a leader of the people, conservationist, editor, Speaker of Parliament, Minister and Governor-General from 1951–8.

E. G. Jansen, were struggling for the maintenance of Afrikaans culture, led to the founding of the first culture federation in the country. The Saamwerk-Unie of Natal Societies had been a cultural power-house among Afrikaners in Natal since 1917. Under the leadership of Jansen and a so-called 'Pietermaritzburg culture junta', the Cape Language Association was opposed with a modern language initiative. The establishment of Afrikaans language examinations was a countrywide success, which accelerated the official recognition of Afrikaans.

Pietermaritzburg was also the centre from which the cultural flame of the Natal Afrikaner was kept burning by means of the written word. The fortnightly newspaper, *Die Afrikaner*, was a social political and moral champion in the Afrikaner ranks. This paper mirrored the Afrikaans community in Natal. After its swansong on 29 April 1932, this role was performed by *Die Natalse Afrikaner* from October 1937 till March 1942, and from March 1945 till January 1951. The first post Anglo-Boer War Dutch magazine, *De Kondschapper*, also appeared in Pietermaritzburg for four years, from October 1908. The editorial staff under leadership of the Revd Pellissier and E. G. Jansen then published *De Bode. Die Voortrekker*, published in Pietermaritzburg, succeeded these magazines and was regarded as the cultural binding agent in Afrikaner ranks.

Another group of Pietermaritzburg citizens, among whom were B. Vorster, E. G. Jansen, Mrs F. D. de Beer (wife of the Revd F. Z. de Beer), the Revd G. Pellissier, J. M. N. A. Hershensohn and others, had honoured the memories of the Voortrekkers since 1908. Due to them, a committee was formed which repurchased and restored the Voortrekker church with the aid of Afrikaans and English-speaking citizens and also established it as a museum. The completed project was described proudly by *De Kondschapper* as follows:

> When all the memories of the Voortrekkers of Pietermaritzburg have disappeared, this small white building will still lift its pointed gables high and call to every visitor, every traveller: 'The Voortrekkers! Don't forget them!'

This committee also pursued the ideal of building a monument in commemoration of the Voortrekker leaders. This attempt, under the leadership of E. G. Jansen, eventually led to the Voortrekker Monument ideal being taken up nationally. Monuments commemorating the Voortrekkers in Pretoria, Winburg, Blood River and Pietermaritzburg were the rich harvest of the mustard seed, planted in the Natal capital in 1908.

The abovementioned cultural patterns formed the basis of the so-called 'struggle for the maintenance of culture' of the Natal and Pietermaritzburg Afrikaners. A process aimed at the preservation of a language and national identity, it prevented the collapse of the Afrikaner's culture in Natal.

Re-enacting the Great Trek:
Voortrekker wagons, 1938.

9

208

Opposing apartheid

IN THE PIETERMARITZBURG REGION

Peter Brown

John Aitchison

In the struggle for black rights in South Africa, Pietermaritzburg is probably best known to the world as the place where Gandhi was thrown off a train for sitting in a seat reserved for whites — an experience which changed the course of his life and sowed in his mind the seeds from which grew his policy of *satyagraha*, perhaps the noblest strategy for political emancipation the world has seen.

The Gandhi incident was an exceptional and dramatic event, but the fight to preserve what rights black people had, and to win those others which were theirs by right, has been carried on in and around Pietermaritzburg since that day in less spectacular fashion by many other individuals and organizations.

Blatant petty apartheid signs have disappeared from the City, though the fundamentals of apartheid are still entrenched.

On 13 December 1886, seven years before the train incident, Selby Msimang was born at Edendale. He died on 29 March 1982. Most of Msimang's middle years were spent out of Natal. For instance, he was living in Johannesburg in 1912 when he was one of those who helped found the predecessor to the African National Congress, the South African Native Congress. It was in Bloemfontein that he was arrested in 1917 for leading a strike of municipal workers. In the Cape he helped Clements Kadalie launch the Industrial and Commercial Workers' Union in 1920, and was elected its first President. But Edendale and Pietermaritzburg remained his home and to there he returned to become election agent for Edgar Brookes, another great local fighter for black rights, when he decided to stand as Natives' Representative for Natal in 1937. Selby himself was elected one of the Natal members of the Natives' Representative Council and was present when Dr Verwoerd abolished it. He was actively engaged in the ANC in Natal and was one of the group which sponsored

Chief Luthuli for the Presidency of the Natal Branch of the ANC. Later he went as a Pietermaritzburg delegate to the meeting in 1953 at which the Liberal Party was launched, became chairman of its Edendale Branch and served on its provincial and national committees up to the time that the Improper Interference Act forced it to close in 1968. Still later he joined Inkatha, hoping that it would establish a working arrangement with the ANC, in spite of his fundamental objection to the latter's armed struggle.

Other important African political figures were the Gumedes, whose home for many years was in New Scotland Road, off College Road. James Gumede, who was part of the 1919 ANC delegation to Great Britain seeking the repeal of the Natives Land Act of 1913, was elected President of the Congress in 1927. During his term of office he visited Moscow and formed a close working arrangement with the Communist Party. This led to considerable strain between him and some of his ANC colleagues, particularly as at that time the Communist Party was advocating the creation of an 'Independent Native Republic'. The result was that Gumede was challenged at the 1930 presidential elections by the ANC's founder, Dr Seme, and defeated. But that was not the last to be heard of the family. Archie, son of James, was born in the City in 1914 at 5 George Street. The family soon moved to 400 Berg Street, to a house owned by Joe Soobiah, Maritzburg's famous 'potato king', and in 1921 to New Scotland Road, where they remained until the Group Areas Act evicted them.

The young Gumede was soon active in ANC affairs, becoming secretary of the local branch under the chairmanship of A. B. Majola. Mr Majola, former manager of the Umgungundhlovu Co-op, now lives at Imbali, another victim of the Group Areas Act, which drove him there from his home in the now-forgotten freehold area of Maryvale, on the outskirts of town off the Wartburg road. Archie Gumede went on to become assistant secretary of the Natal ANC under M. B. Yengwa, and was very active in the Pietermaritzburg area in the build-up to the Congress of the People. He later faced charges for this action in the Treason Trial, the case against him eventually collapsing, as it did in every other case. Now he has emerged, after numerous bannings and detentions, as a President of the United Democratic Front. Remarkably, his experiences at the hands of the Government have left him quite unembittered and, despite pressures from friend and foe alike, totally opposed to violence.

Other important figures in the Pietermaritzburg ANC, and later in the 1950s and 1960s in the South African Congress of Trade Unions in the Pietermaritzburg area, were Moses Mabhida and Harry Gwala. The former has recently died in exile; the latter is serving a life sentence.

Both the Natal Indian Organization and the Natal Indian Congress were active in Pietermaritzburg up until the 1960s. Then the NIO began slowly to wither away when its moderate stance was challenged on account of its failure to halt the advance of apartheid and particularly the application of the Group Areas Act in the Pietermaritzburg area. The NIO represented primarily the commercial interests in the City. Its leading figure was S. R. Naidoo, who had his offices in Chancery Lane, and

Personalities at the Natal Convention, 1961.

who was highly regarded even by his critics in the Indian community, and certainly by many other Pietermaritzburg citizens, white and black.

The NIC drew to it the more radical members of the Indian community, particularly young professionals and trade unionists. Its first post-Second World War campaign was the Passive Resistance Campaign against the Smuts Pegging Act, forerunner of today's Group Areas Act. Initially only five volunteers could be found in the whole of Pietermaritzburg. They were Suthie Mungal, a tailor by trade but at that time involved in the Municipal Workers' Union; L. T. Ramdeen; Naicker of Eddels; S. B. Maharaj and G. R. Naidoo, son-in-law of 'S. R.' of the Natal Indian Organization. They formed themselves into a Passive Resistance Council and at a meeting at Sutherlands Tannery, Plessislaer, where S. B. Maharaj was employed, launched (with the permission of the owners) their appeal for volunteers. At this and subsequent meetings, 120 volunteers were recruited. They were sent in batches to Durban where they set up camp in Gale Street. There the police, who had been warned in advance, arrested them. They were sentenced to 30 days in gaol, 7 days of which would be remitted for good behaviour — a far cry from the treatment they could expect today.

Pietermaritzburg provided no volunteers for the Defiance Campaign of 1952, but later in the 1950s the NIC in the City was heavily involved in the preliminaries to the Congress of the People and in anti-Group Areas Act agitation. A Congress of the People Committee, jointly chaired by Dr Chota Motala and Archie Gumede, with Messrs Mungal and Mabhida as secretaries, was set up. Their campaign led to a delegation of 30 being sent to the Congress, and to Archie Gumede and Chota Motala being charged with treason. The Group Areas campaign persisted throughout the decade and on into the early 1960s. It led to a remarkable degree of co-operation between the Congress Alliance, the Liberal Party and the Black Sash in the Pietermaritzburg region. From Pietermaritzburg this campaign was extended into the outlying areas of the Midlands and Northern Natal. Weekend protest meetings were almost a weekly event. Dr Motala was not often missing as a speaker, and would be joined by ANC speakers and by some Liberal Party representative such as Alan Paton, Leo Kuper or Ken Hill. This co-operation spilled over into other fields. In 1959 a massive protest meeting against the banning of Chief Luthuli filled the City Hall to overflowing. It was the most spectacular of many such joint meetings and demonstrations during the 1950s and early 1960s, in which the Progressive Party later joined.

In 1961 the Natal Convention was held at the University. Initiated at another mass meeting in the City Hall, presided over by Archbishop Denis Hurley and chaired by Dr Edgar Brookes, it brought together as wide a variety of political views at one gathering — from United Party supporters to Congressites — as Natal had ever seen. They managed a surprising degree of agreement, even the unanimous acceptance of the aim of universal suffrage on a common role. One of the consequences of the Convention was the drawing for the first time of members of the Pietermaritzburg coloured community into the mainstream of South African anti-apartheid politics. Most of them were ex-servicemen active in the local branch of the British Ex-Servicemen's League, which eschewed political involvement. But led by Dempsey Noel, a local plasterer, they began to involve themselves in other organizations, notably the Liberal Party and the Coloured Convention Movement.

Later in 1961, Edendale provided the venue for the meeting of the All-In African Conference, where Nelson Mandela emerged from a recently-expired ban to make one of his last important speeches as a free man. The Non-European Unity Movement, notably through the Christopher and Hassim families, and its successor the African People's Democratic Union of South Africa (APDUSA), have been active and vocal in Pietermaritzburg politics for many years. The Azanian People's Organization (AZAPO), the heir to Steve Biko's Black Peoples Convention, also made its presence felt in the Pietermaritzburg area, though it has been greatly eclipsed since the rise of the United Democratic Front (UDF). Inkatha has become a real force to be reckoned with in local black politics, since the resurrection of this Zulu cultural organization as a political movement with wider and national ambitions. Many members of the Congress Movement, their organization shattered by the bannings of the 1950s and 1960s, have found a new home in the UDF. Archie Gumede was on the platform at its Natal launch at Edendale, and Dr D. V. and Mr A. S. Chetty, who were leading figures in the Natal Indian Congress (NIC), are now in the UDF.

The declaration of the 1986 State of Emergency had a grievous impact on organizations and individuals associated with the UDF, with over 950 people detained in the Pietermaritzburg region over an eighteen-month period. The trauma of the 1986 and 1987 emergencies was heightened by the seemingly continuous fratricidal conflict between 'vigilantes', alleged to be the agents of Inkatha, and the UDF and radical youth. The bloodletting reached horrifying proportions in 1987 and the first two months of 1988 with over 550 people killed for political reasons in the Natal Midlands, the majority of those whose political affiliation could be identified being supporters of the UDF. Peace negotiations between Inkatha and the UDF/ COSATU alliance started in late 1987 brought little respite and there was growing anxiety at the State's evident unwillingness to take legal action against vigilante 'warlords'. Detentions were equally one-sided with 754 detentions of UDF and COSATU supporters in 1987 but no Inkatha members. In February 1988 the UDF and a number of other organizations were effectively banned.

It is over a hundred years since Selby Msimang was born, and very nearly a hundred since Mohandas Gandhi was unceremoniously bundled off that train onto our station platform. In that time the individuals and organizations of this City, which have fought for full rights for all its citizens in a non-racial South Africa, have acquitted themselves with considerable credit in different circumstances. It is a sad fact that this record has in the past few years been marred by a dangerous factionalism and violence, where opponents of the Government spend more time fighting each other than it. The politics of non-racialism could do no greater service to South Africa and Pietermaritzburg in its 150th year than by recreating the broad spirit of co-operation against apartheid which was such a feature of the City in the late 1950s and early 1960s. *There* is the real challenge for 1988.

THE UNIVERSITY AND POLITICAL PROTEST

Deneys Schreiner

There have been a number of occasions on which constituent parts of the University of Natal have taken part in political protest and the University supports their right to do so. The University itself is only involved on those occasions when education is concerned, or its own autonomy is threatened, or the academic freedom of its members is in danger. Many occasions on which the University has acted as a whole have concerned fundamental freedoms that are widely accepted as essential for a university to function properly. Briefly stated, these are freedom of access to information, freedom to choose what shall be taught, who shall teach and who shall be admitted as students. In South African universities the major concerns that have arisen have been censorship; the banning of people and therefore their writings; restrictions on academics from teaching; and the denial of admission of students either as individuals or because they belong to certain population groups. It is around these matters that concerted university action has centred.

In its earlier days the University did not act consistently in support of these freedoms. From its inception the Council of the University had sole discretion about admission of students. Nevertheless, during its first two decades the only two applications from 'other-than-white' students were refused, the first by Council and the second on Senate's recommendation. It was not until 1936 that the first black students were admitted. In Durban, Dr Mabel Palmer persuaded the then Principal that the University must undertake the training of black teachers. This the University accepted. In Pietermaritzburg a threat from the Law Society to withdraw its recognition of the University as a training centre led to the admission of two Indian students. After the Second World War the student composition in the University changed markedly under Dr E. G. Malherbe. Separate but identical lectures for black students were started and this together with the establishment of the wholly black Medical School meant that by 1959 the University of Natal provided tertiary education for more black students than any similar institution south of the equator. The Pietermaritzburg campus contributed very little to this change.

In 1957 the government moved toward the establishment of socially or ethnically restricted universities. For the University of Natal this would have meant the excision of the Medical School, and that new black students would only be admitted by ministerial permit. Strong and public protest by the University as a whole, and the staff of the Medical School in particular, avoided the excision, but the second threat became law in 1959. Malherbe's policy of parallelism prevented any close co-operation with the Universities of Cape Town and Witwatersrand at this time of need for a common stand. But this period of protest, coupled with the detention of some members of staff in 1960, which involved combined student and staff marches of protest in Pietermaritzburg, created a new awareness in the University. This grew, although not without some setbacks, until the present time.

In 1983 the government introduced a law which empowered the Minister to apply a quota limitation to the number of black students in the University. This led to a major march of the University from the Anglican Cathedral down Church Street to the Pietermaritzburg City Hall where the packed hall was addressed by Dr Alan Paton. Off-campus marches have been restricted by emergency regulations, but in 1987 the University held assemblies of both the Durban and Pietermaritzburg centres, to protest against the introduction of a Bill which had the effect of making the University Council an extension of government law enforcement against its staff and students for political actions they might take whether within the University or not. The Bill became law and the University Council successfully challenged the matter in the Supreme Court.

Throughout the period of increasing tensions in the country and the growth of restrictive legislation, the University has successfully carried out its annual and long-term educational function. It has attempted to protect its own position as a member of the international university community and, also, the rights of each of its constituent parts, and those of the individuals who make up those parts. It has had varied success but it will not weaken in its continuous endeavours.

The University protests against the 'Quota Bill', June 1983. Staff and students processed from the grounds of the Cathedral of the Holy Nativity to a public meeting in the City Hall.

12

Students protesting against government action in June 1988. An all too familiar sight during the last twenty years.

13

Mrs E. E. Russell

AND THE ROLE OF WOMEN IN THE CITY'S PUBLIC LIFE

Pat Merrett

In the year that Pietermaritzburg gained the status of a provincial rather than a colonial capital, Mrs E. E. M. Russell, then Miss Columbine, arrived from England to take up a teaching post. She was in her early twenties, and during the next fifty years was to play a leading role in a number of organizations relating to education, women and charities. But her reputation rests most securely on eighteen years' service on the City Council. These years are remembered not just for the fact that she became the City's first woman Mayor, but also for the solid contribution she made to civic affairs. Nevertheless, an assessment of her contribution to the City must encompass all her many activities, for they overlapped to a considerable extent, and all were founded, it would appear, on a fundamental commitment to the ideals of public service and common justice.

She was born Eleanor Ethel Mariella Columbine in 1882 into a society undergoing fundamental social and political changes. These affected the role of women in certain limited respects, for conventional familial and social restrictions persisted. Legal rights were granted to married women, local government reforms gave female ratepayers the vote (single women in 1869 and married women in 1884); while in 1907 a special Act of Parliament enabled women to become city councillors. Suffrage societies were engaged in a sustained campaign for equal political rights for women, although these were not to be gained until 1918. From the 1870s educational opportunities for upper middle class girls outside the home expanded, though formal education remained permissive and not prescriptive. Interest in social and 'sanitary' issues widened their acceptable philanthropic activities, though broadening occupational opportunities were essentially limited to charitable work and to poorly paid positions, particularly in teaching. Yet there was one category of women able to escape the rigid subordination of sex and class. This was the single woman of means, and Miss Columbine seems to have been one of them, whether in terms of her education, public activities or employment.

She was apparently educated at Bedford High School (for girls), which had been founded in the late nineteenth century. She therefore gained a reputable school education and is said to have acquired a teaching qualification. At some stage she attended lectures at London University where she obtained the Inter-BSc. which was not a full university degree. She gained teaching experience of mathematics and science in at least two schools in England and was Vice-Principal of one of them. She was also active in charitable organizations for children and the needy in the East End of London. Miss Columbine also took an interest in the suffrage movement, although she is said to have disapproved of the violence of the Suffragettes, and

Freemen of the City of Pietermaritzburg, 1965
Left to right: A. T. Allison, D. G. Shepstone, Montgomery of Alamein, H. Collins, H. C. Franklin, G. R. de Carle (OC, Natal Carbineers), E. E. Russell, H. G. Tatham (representing NU Regiment).

the full extent of her involvement is not clear. It has however been claimed that she continued her membership of the Fawcett Society throughout her life.

Thus when she arrived in Natal in 1910, Miss Columbine was imbued not only with the common English middle class devotion to humanitarian causes, but also with an appreciation of the role that women (particularly educated women) could play in society. She had also acquired a number of years' experience in those areas of concern to which she remained devoted for the rest of her life. To what extent, however, did Maritzburg society in 1910 offer her opportunities for active involvement in those concerns, and in a wider sphere such as local politics?

On the one hand, South African women in the early twentieth century (and black women in particular) were in an inferior position relative to men, in the political, economic and legal spheres. White women had neither the municipal nor parliamentary votes. The Act of Union, which in de Kiewiet's words, was 'dedicated to the European community', could also be said to have been dedicated to white masculine authority, for it excluded female suffrage. Legally, women were also subordinate to men, and in the economic sphere, employment opportunities had been restricted to the traditional areas of feminine concern: teaching, domestic and charity work. Furthermore, despite the large pool of easily exploitable black labour, which relieved many women of domestic drudgery, the tradition of community service does not seem to have been deeply entrenched in white South African middle class women.

On the other hand, there were significant developments in the economic sphere which, as in Britain (although at a later date), were to alter social attitudes and the position of women, and these arose out of the industrialization, economic growth and urbanization of South African society in the wake of the late nineteenth century mineral discoveries. Wider employment opportunities opened for women, and educational facilities improved. Natal University College (Pietermaritzburg) for instance, opened in 1910 with 8 women and 49 men students. The First World War and the growth of secondary industry were greatly to stimulate these processes.

It was the increasing involvement of women in activities outside the home, particularly economic activities, which influenced the growth of a South African women's suffrage movement. The first society to be organized specifically on female suffrage was the Women's Enfranchisement League (WEL) in Durban in 1902. Other leagues were established in the major cities, Maritzburg following in 1910. When the Act of Union excluded votes for white women, the leagues affiliated in 1911 to form the Women's Enfranchisement Association of the Union (WEAU). Given the fact that this was essentially a conservative white, urban, middle class movement, and that Miss Columbine had been interested in the British suffrage movement, it would be surprising if she had remained aloof. Clearly the opportunity for active involvement in wider issues was available in Maritzburg, and there is evidence that Miss Columbine participated in at least one campaign organized by the WEL in the Capital City, and was a member of a deputation in 1912 to table 'a bill' in the Natal Provincial Council giving the municipal vote to women. Two years later, such an ordinance (No. 11 of 1914) was passed, and the other provinces followed Natal's example. There were

thus close links between the British and South African suffrage movements, for another member of the deputation was Lady Barbara Joanna Steel, ex-member of the Women's Social and Political Union of Britain, who came to South Africa in 1911, and became President of the WEAU from 1916 to 1930.

Two years after the ordinance granting white women the municipal vote was passed, the first female councillor in South Africa was elected. She was Mrs Sarah Ann Woods of Maritzburg who defeated retiring Councillor Mr J. M. Forrester. In 1917 she was joined by Johanna Catherine Watt. Mrs Watt became the first woman Deputy Mayor in Maritzburg when she was elected to that office in 1926. In that year, Miss Columbine married Mr W. A. D. Russell MPC and five years later — one year after white women in South Africa were granted the parliamentary and provincial votes — she was elected to the City Council, the fifth woman to achieve this distinction. The tradition of female involvement in local politics had been established, and was to be strongly entrenched by Mrs Russell.

By 1931, when she became a City Councillor, Mrs Russell was a well-known public figure in Maritzburg, having been associated with Girls' Collegiate for sixteen years and with a number of local women's organizations. She had arrived as Second Mistress in 1910 and in 1914 had been offered the post of Lady Principal, a position she had retained until her marriage in 1926. The impact she had on the school may be judged by her obituary which recorded 'her foresight and understanding of the place of women in modern society and the need for a broad and comprehensive education to fit them for this place'. The school named the Eleanor Russell Memorial Library after her, and it seems that in 1961 (in her 79th year), Mrs Russell played a significant role in the decision to build a new Girls' Collegiate, the foundation stone of which she laid in 1963.

The eighteen years she spent on the City Council, from 1931 until 1948, as representative for Ward 5, were probably the most active and significant years of Mrs Russell's long life. She served on the Native Administration Standing Committee for many years, and became the first woman chairperson in City Council history when she was elected to head that committee for nine consecutive years. She played a major role in the development of the educational, social and health facilities in the 'Native Village' which had been founded two years before she was elected to the City Council, and which was later named Sobantu Village. Her membership of two other committees, Finances and General Purposes (which she chaired for two years), and Public Health, also spanned a number of years. In the midst of the Second World War she was elected Deputy Mayor for 1940 and 1941, and in late 1943 became the first woman Mayor of a municipality in Natal when she was elected Mayor of Maritzburg, a position she held for four years.

The range of Mrs Russell's involvement in Council affairs went beyond the traditional sphere of female concerns in health and education, and is revealed in the conferences she was delegated to attend on behalf of the City Council. These included, amongst many others, Conferences of the Natal Municipal Association, on TB in Natives, 1936, and of Municipalities on the Urban Areas Act, 1937. In 1936 she was the only woman member of the Broome Commission which enquired into the provincial system of education. The list of government commissions to which she gave evidence is impressive and includes the following: the Native Affairs Commission on Land Matters, 1937; the Inter-Departmental Enquiry into the Invalidity Scheme and Relief of TB, 1939; the Inter-Departmental Committee *re* Economic Conditions of Urban Natives, 1941; and the Sale of Kaffir Beer, 1941. In 1946, according to one report, she was nominated by the Minister as a member of the Native Affairs Commission (Fagan Commission) but was unable to accept due to the pressure of her duties as Mayor. In 1947 Mrs Russell hosted the royal family during the royal visit (she was an ardent monarchist), and the following year, at the age of 65 years, she voluntarily retired. In 1952 and 1954 she tried to make a comeback to local politics, but on both occasions was defeated at the polls.

In his address on the occasion of the conferring of the Freedom of the City on Mrs Russell in 1960 (she was the second woman to be so honoured, Miss M. J. 'Nettie' Parker being the first in 1942), the Mayor, Councillor C. B. Downes, mentioned her 'outstanding services to the City'. As Mayor, he said, she had revealed 'administrative competence, moral courage and those intangible qualities so necessary in a leader of men — and women', and he paid tribute to her pragmatic but far-sighted ambitions for the City.

Mrs Russell's interests in women, education and charitable organizations had been maintained during her years in the City Hall. In the realm of black education she had taken a keen interest in schooling in Sobantu Village — the Russell Lower Primary School being named after her — and in June 1946 she had addressed the Natal Bantu Teachers' Association Conference in the Village. She is acknowledged to have been an outspoken critic of the Bantu Education Act of 1953 which she recognized as offering an inferior education to blacks. In the context of her times this probably indicated a limited commitment to a good quality, but separate, educational system for blacks. Mrs Russell had also taken an interest in adult education in Maritzburg, representing the City Council in 1947 on an interim Committee on Adult Education, chaired by Dr W. G. McConkey. From 1936 until 1948 she represented the City Council on the Natal University Development Fund and, as Mayor, had been a member of the Natal University College Council. In recognition of these services, the University conferred on her the degree of Master of Arts (*honoris causa*) in 1950, and in 1963 the Eleanor Russell Women's Residence was opened by her.

When the South African Women's Auxiliary Services were formed on the outbreak of the Second World War, Mrs Russell had joined, and on one occasion declared her belief that 'in the present terrible days of war women could rightly take their place on an equal footing with men'. On the occasion of her funeral, the Dean of Pietermaritzburg was reported to have said that Mrs Russell was a staunch supporter of St Peter's Church, but nevertheless he recalled that 'she was ever conscious of the fact that women *per se* did not have that equality she dearly prized and were discriminated against as far as ordination was concerned and in other aspects of church life'. This progressive concern with the role of women in society continued to be given active expression in her years of 'retirement'. From 1958 to 1960 she was

Gwladys Terry,
City Councillor 1949–74.

15

Pamela Reid, who gave distinguished service as a City Councillor 1954–88, and who was Mayor 1981–4.

16

elected Natal President of the SA Association of University Women, and in 1959 represented that body at the International Federation of University Women Triennial Conference in Helsinki. In her presidential address of 1958, Mrs Russell stressed that a university education conferred on one an obligation to serve the community. The duty of the SAAUW she declared was to uphold 'cultural and intellectual standards' in South Africa, and to be informed on international affairs so as to foster 'international friendship'. Significantly, she also had practical suggestions to make in this regard.

A few of the other organizations to which Mrs Russell belonged, or in which she held office, included the National Council of Women of South Africa (of which she was a foundation member in 1912, President from 1948 to 1952, and Life Vice-President, and which she represented at the ICW Conference in Athens in 1951), the Girl Guide Association (of which she was a founder member), the Federation of Women's Institutes, and the South African Institute of Race Relations (of which she was an Executive member).

It has been claimed that Mrs Russell belonged to no political party. Although she was a member of the Black Sash for a while, her commitment was most likely founded on nineteenth-century notions of justice and fair play; and while she seems to have believed in the equality of the sexes (though this was doubtless limited in some respects), there is no evidence that she was prepared to support the dismantling of the fundamental structures of a society based on racial privilege and power. Given the context of her times, this is not to be wondered at.

A number of contemporaries have paid tribute to Mrs Russell's courage and humanitarianism. One particular incident in 1943 reveals considerable resolution on her part, and in popular memory it has become embellished into the myth that she once 'quelled a riot'. On the night of 20 November 1943, a group of 200 to 300 European transit troops rioted outside the City Hall. They were in the habit of attending a public dance every Saturday evening, but on that occasion the Coloured Welfare League was to hold their annual dance. Mrs Russell, as Mayor, was the guest of honour. She confronted the troops from the front steps of the City Hall to try and explain why they could not attend the dance, but could not be heard above the tumult. Finally the dance had to be cancelled, reinforcements called in and teargas used to disperse the rioters. Mrs Russell ensured that all the League members had been evacuated safely before herself departing. She publicly criticized the behaviour of the troops and received formal apologies from Col. MacKenzie, OC of the troops. When she suggested to the Colonel that racial animosity had contributed to the disturbance, he was forced to agree.

Her pragmatism and humanitarian qualities on the other hand are revealed in an article she wrote for *Outspan* in 1950, on the subject of female alcoholism, which was on the increase in the wake of the war. She made a conventional bow to the traditional idealization of women by writing that a drunken woman 'was infinitely more dreadful' to see than a man, for 'she is the source of life, defiled and debased into a mockery'. Then she firmly put aside that symbol of woman and tackled her as a flesh-and-blood individual, displaying an unusually enlightened attitude towards alcoholism as a disease and the need for a well funded rehabilitative social service. As to whether or not it was worth the considerable effort, she concluded that 'if you believe that any waste of life is a diminution of all life . . . there is no question'.

Not least of Mrs Russell's memorable qualities were her wit and fluency in public speaking (which were never supported by written notes), and her informed grasp of committee work. No assessment could fail either to mention that to most contemporaries she appeared an imperious and formidable personality, who was outspoken in her opinions and would not suffer fools gladly. To what extent such qualities were unusual, or were exaggerated by observers due to an unconscious bias against women who exercised authority and leadership at a time when such women were rare, is uncertain. By education, personality and experience, she enshrined the attributes of leadership, and it is perhaps significant that the decade after her career on the City Council came to an end, that is the 1950s, was the heyday of female participation in local politics. In that decade there were never fewer than three, and for three years, up to five, women councillors, out of a total of fifteen representatives. Furthermore two of them were elected Deputy Mayor: Isabel S. Beardmore (1956 and 1957), and Pamela Ann Reid (1958 and 1959).

Nevertheless, the numbers of women contesting Council seats in Maritzburg has always been small, and it is noticeable that the few stalwarts who have gained seats have held on to them for many years, often being unopposed when elections fell due. Gwladys Elizabeth Terry, for instance, served on the Council for twenty-six years, from 1949 to 1974. Since 1973 the number of women on the City Council has dropped to two, and only five other women have since then unsuccessfully contested seats (one of whom lost to a successful woman candidate). Furthermore, in the last twenty-five years, only one woman has emulated Mrs Russell's career. Miss Reid entered local politics in 1954 and is at present still active on the City Council. She was again elected Deputy Mayor in 1978 and 1980, and was Mayor from 1981 to 1984, the second woman to hold that post in the City's history. For five years she chaired the Finances, Policy and General Purposes Committee, and is at present Director of the Pietermaritzburg Chamber of Industries.

In recent years other boroughs in Natal have elected women mayors, but it is still unusual for women to achieve prominent positions in local politics. For a woman to have attained the highest position in the 1940s is therefore remarkable. Clearly Mrs Russell's education in a society at a relatively advanced level of industrialization, with vociferous feminist movements and wider opportunities for privileged single women, stimulated her interest in public affairs. The comfortable middle class lifestyle she led in Natal, particularly after her late marriage in 1926, also gave her the freedom from onerous domestic duties (including childbearing) to participate in public life. But in the final analysis, it was personal dedication to public service, fair play and the role women could play in society, however limited these may seem from the perspective of late twentieth-century political and social standards, which enabled her to grasp the opportunities afforded to women of her calibre in post-World War South Africa. At the very least it can be said that, having supported the struggle to extend equal opportunities to women, she demonstrated the justice of that cause.

'I REMEMBER MISTER GANDHI'

Robert Haswell

There are still elderly Indians living in Pietermaritzburg who well remember some of the activities of 'Mr Gandhi' in the City. One such person is Mr T. Ramkolowan Singh, known to many as 'Tommy'. Born in Pietermaritzburg in 1901, he was a pupil at the Hindi Vernacular School which used to occupy the barracks at the corner of Greytown and Fitzsimmons Roads (now the site of the M.L. Sultan School). Tommy remembers that he and his classmates pulled a carriage containing Gandhi in 1909: 'Mr Gandhi was released from the Burger Street Prison, after being transferred there from the Transvaal, and we pulled a four-wheel carriage, a Cab Victoria, all the way down Longmarket Street to Boshoff where we turned and then made our way down Church Street to the school, where Mr Gandhi shook hands with each of us.'

Tommy also remembers being seated in the gallery of the City Hall in November, 1912, when Mr Gandhi, Mr Gokhale and the Mayor addressed a meeting. 'I can still hear the power of Mr Gandhi's high-pitched voice. He did not need a microphone at all. Mr Gokhale, a member of the Indian Civil Service, had come to Natal, to examine conditions, and we formed a guard-of-honour when he was met at the station by Mr Gandhi.'

Incredibly, Tommy's memory is razor-sharp, for all I had to do for confirmation was to open the Mayor's Visitors Book, and there sure enough, dated 7 November 1912, are the signatures of Gokhale and Gandhi. The latter gave his address as Lawley, Transvaal, which was the nearest station to Tolstoy Farm.

The *Natal Witness* of 8 November 1912 supplied more information.

> The Indian community of Maritzburg turned out in force yesterday afternoon to meet the down mail conveying the Hon. Gopal Gokhale.
>
> It was a clear case of 'best bib and tucker' for the occasion and the result was almost paralysing to the occidental eye. There was a bodyguard of young Indians in pink puggarees, a detachment with saffron headgear, and a variety of other able-bodied colours to help matters out.

Barracks at the corner of Greytown and Fitzsimmons Roads where the Hindi Vernacular School was situated.

> The Town Hall was thronged last evening when the Hon. Gopal Gokhale addressed a meeting, which included all the leading citizens of Maritzburg, and a great number of Indians.
>
> Mr M.K. Gandhi said he had been a resident of South Africa for the past 18 years. The Ganges was a holy river, and, if its waters had flowed into the Umsindusi in the person of Mr Gokhale, then it was a proud day for the City. If Mr Gokhale had been an Englishman he would have been where Mr Asquith was to-day; if a Frenchman, then he would be President of a great Republic, if a South African — and born somewhere near the Transvaal (laughter) — he would have been where Gen. Botha was today. That was the spirit of veneration in which his fellow countrymen held Mr Gokhale (applause). He had not the slightest doubt but that his message — which was one of goodwill and peace — had already succeeded. Whether his mission towards helping the Indian would be successful still remained to be seen. It would rest a good deal with those in South Africa as to whether that devoutly-hoped for success of Mr Gandhi's visit would materialise. Entered into with a generous noble spirit his mission should be signally successful (applause).

In November 1912 the *Natal Witness* reported further.

> At an early hour yesterday, (Friday) the Hon. Gopal Gokhale was interviewing a multitude of deputations and visitors. At 10 o'clock there was a large gathering of Indians at the Indian High School, Willow Bridge. They were gathered to give the Indian view of the grievances to which it was desired to draw the visitors' attention. The spokesmen were Ismail Bayat, the Rev. Joseph, Mr Royappen, Mr Naik, Nr P. Naidoo and M. K. Gandhi.
>
> A lunch was arranged at the Camden Hotel... Among the company were his Honour the Administrator, the Mayor, Cr. D. Sanders, The Attorney-General, Mr C. W. F. Bird.
>
> Mr M. K. Gandhi, in proposing 'Our European Friends' said he spoke as an Indian and on behalf of the Indians. He voiced their feelings when he said that they were doubly indebted to the Europeans who had so heartily assisted the Indians in welcoming and assisting their visitor, an illustrious son of India. Wherever Mr Gokhale had gone there had been a spirit of peace. He could only hope that that spirit would not vanish with his departure, but would continue and intensify, because there was not, after all, any reason why they should not all live together under the same flag in peace, amity and friendship (cheers).

Perhaps there are others who recall Gandhi in Pietermaritzburg, and it seems that scholars have largely ignored the *Natal Witness* as a source of information on Gandhi. And surely there should be some memorial to Gandhi in this City?

17

'Tommy' Ramkolowan Singh holding the Mayor's Visitors Book.

18

Governing Pietermaritzburg

Ralph Lawrence

In Pietermaritzburg's city centre and its surrounding garden suburbs, the business of everyday government is carried out smoothly and unobtrusively. Electricity flows, water is piped, drains carry away waste, garbage is collected, and mayors and mayoral cars enter and leave service at regular intervals. But this easygoing rhythm does not extend throughout the Pietermaritzburg area, especially not of recent years. As the present decade has unfolded, Sobantu to the east and Edendale, Ashdown, Imbali, and their neighbours to the west, have all been wracked by increasingly bloody conflict. South Africa seems to be at civil war and the events of 1987 demonstrated that its epicentre has shifted to Pietermaritzburg. The situation remains unchanged in early 1988, with three people, on average, dying daily. Countless more suffer injury and loss of possessions. Civil administration, itself a major focus of political discontent in the strife-torn territory, has been seriously disrupted, even undermined, by the raging battle. Every essential public facility and service, be it education, health, housing or transport, has fallen prey to violence. These townships are now under siege. Military forces were despatched by central government in a determined endeavour to quell the unrest and institute order by whatever means deemed necessary. Thus, for the time being, real administrative power no longer lies with the government officials of Imbali and elsewhere, but with the South African Defence Force.

Nothing could illustrate more starkly Pietermaritzburg's divided political character. Whereas at City Hall, 'parish pump' politics dominates, in the outlying regions the stakes are much higher, for politics there really is a matter of life and death. Why this extraordinary contrast? Apartheid is the answer. South African society, shaped for three hundred years by settlement and conquest, has consistently practised segregation, whereby the European colonists and their descendants have sought to maintain social, political and economic ascendancy over the indigenous inhabitants. The National Party, which came to power in 1948 and has remained in office ever since, has tried to pursue segregationist policies to a logical conclusion. The upshot is apartheid, the ideology of separate development. Distinguishing between people according to arbitrarily defined racial criteria is fundamental to the Nationalist plan. Each resulting racial group should develop according to its own dictates, preferences and interests. With this vision in mind, the Nationalist Government in the early 1950s embarked on

19

The City Council of 1858.
Left to Right: J. Anderson, J. Russom, R. Dawney, J. Archbell (Mayor), Mr George, E. Buchanan, J. Raw, E. Tomlinson.

countrywide social engineering schemes designed to make apartheid a reality.

The effect on cities like Pietermaritzburg was profound. The population was reorganized into racially exclusive enclaves, where people were supposed to lead most of their lives within the confines of their assigned ghetto. And so the government of Pietermaritzburg took on a split nature. Today the City's political universe comprises insiders and outsiders. The insiders are the whites, whose fifteen elected white representatives on the City Council, with the assistance of senior bureaucrats, all of whom are whites as well, govern the municipal area that is officially Pietermaritzburg.

The outsiders are not ranked identically. According to orthodox Afrikaner Nationalist thinking of yesteryear, Indians would be 'repatriated' and coloureds, those of mixed racial descent, would be herded into their own state. Both objectives were abandoned. But how could the political aspirations of Indians and coloureds be accommodated, particularly at the level of local government? Rather than creating a distinct, exclusive city government for both the Indian and coloured racial groups, which the ideology of apartheid requires, the Nationalist leaders in 1966 opted for Local Affairs Committees. The thinking was that Indians and coloureds had to learn the business of local government and administration at the knee of white officialdom before being granted autonomous powers. Originally members of these committees were all Nationalist Government appointees, but election soon replaced nomination as the method of selection.

The Local Affairs Committees have enjoyed little success, largely because they have failed to gain the support of the communities for which they are intended. Not surprisingly, Indian and coloured people reject the inferior status conferred on them in the system of apartheid rule and, therefore, shun the racially separate political institutions devised by the Nationalist Government. Moreover, Local Affairs Committees have been granted only advisory powers; final decisions are taken by the City Council. This also discourages participation. What incentive is there either to become a member of a toothless body, or, indeed, to vote for it? The City Council in recent times has made efforts to upgrade the status of the Local Affairs Committees, to draw them into Council deliberations. In September 1987 the Council resolved to introduce a 'consensus' system whereby members of the Local Affairs Committees were invited to attend all committee and council meetings. At such meetings a 'consensus' vote, in which everyone could cast a vote, would be taken, followed, if legally necessary, by a white councillors only vote. However, such manoeuvring within the confines of the apartheid framework has had limited success. Clearly, the Indian and coloured Local Affairs Committee members will not participate willingly or fully, until they have full voting rights.

The worst placed outsiders in Pietermaritzburg are the Africans. The Nationalist Government's intention was to include all Africans in Natal in a Zulu independent state. Thus, KwaZulu came about in 1970. It was given territorial expression and delegated legislative powers in 1972 and granted further executive authority two years later, but sovereignty has yet to be ceded. African residential areas in the western sector of Pietermaritzburg

echo sounds in maritzburg

sounds of '76 soweto hinted
and haunted my dreams as i was
once more
in the midst of gunsmoke
overwhelmed by the avalanche
of tearsmoke
inhaling and exhaling
bullet smoke
in this city
a former oasis
of passiveness
once more i heard the gun
coughing death at
ntombela's son
the gun that walloped
graham hadebe
the gun has harnessed
my people together
the gun has fuelled the struggle

the soweto spectre has haunted maritzburg
the spectre has permeated
when teargas spread
and disrupted sermons
when funerals started to be banned
all hell has broken loose
oppressors are now standing to lose
for i have
once more
seen union taking root
at the stroke of death
once more there is
awareness, togetherness
solidarity, fraternity

take heed for
once more
foes have turned to comrades
movement has gained ground
take heed
you have mobilised your foes
a task applauded by insurgents
beware!

MLUNGISI MKHIZE

were scheduled to be absorbed into KwaZulu. Both Edendale and the Vulindlela region now come under the aegis of the KwaZulu Government which administers their affairs.

By contrast, Imbali is in limbo, beyond the official boundaries of both Pietermaritzburg and KwaZulu. It falls under the control of central government and is managed by regional bureaucrats stationed in Pietermaritzburg. Over the past decade, the Nationalist Government has come to accept that certain Africans are permanent settlers rather than temporary sojourners in South African cities. Accordingly, organs of political representation, initially community councils, then city councils, were envisaged for the African urban townships. In Imbali, as elsewhere nationwide, such structures never took root. Few stood for office, few voted for them and councillors and council alike were swept aside in the conflict that in the course of the last five years has built up to civil war. Sobantu's experience has been similar. Originally the creature of Pietermaritzburg's City Council, Sobantu Village was erected in 1927 and 1928. Zealous apartheid planning meant that the City Council had to transfer its responsibility for Sobantu to central government in 1973. An elective community council was set up in Sobantu in 1979, but proved shortlived. Councillors resigned in the wake of the civil unrest of 1982. No replacements emerged and thus the council could not be resurrected. However, because the land occupied by the Village was never surveyed out of the borough, the City Council had to agree to a transfer of the land to the provincial authorities in the first instance, thereby enabling individuals to purchase property in Sobantu. After much debate, the Council, upon the request of the Sobantu Committee of Twelve, agreed to the transfer and the Mayor was appointed as the Administrator of Sobantu. It would appear then that in order to facilitate individual property ownership, Sobantu has had to pay the price of being legally excised from the City.

While the apartheid system has never been fully implemented, and probably never will be, it has proved remarkably effective in casting people into different social worlds. Whites, coloureds, Indians and Africans occupy, for the most part, separate political universes, each encouraged to impinge on the others as minimally as possible. Civil war has broken out in the African areas over how best to end the apartheid they reject, and a deadly struggle is being waged for support and territory in the afflicted townships. In the minds of many of Pietermaritzburg's white citizens, the civil war is remote, for it is erupting beyond the City's municipal boundaries, hence outside the political universe reserved for whites.

The violence, seemingly so remote, is further testament to the relative powerlessness of the City Council. A local government's authority is determined by the South African Parliament or, in effect, by the Nationalist Government. Jurisdiction over the African areas was taken away from the City Council at the stroke of a pen. Local Affairs Committees were conjured up just as easily. The City Council is hemmed in: the manner of Indian and coloured representation has led to these communities becoming alienated from city government. The remedy lies ultimately in the hands of the central authorities, while the City Council is a hapless bystander. Modest efforts to play a conciliatory role in the conflict have been made but, here again, the might of central government will carry the day. Perhaps most disturbing of all is that in the interests of so-called security the shadow of the military deepens over the battle-scarred suburbs. Recent findings revealed the existence of a National Security Management System, with a network throughout the country, extending to mini Joint Management Centres in cities like Pietermaritzburg. These bodies have a strong military flavour. Their role is to stamp out, even to pre-empt, civil unrest, by assuming extraordinary powers and commandeering whatever resources are necessary. What is the effect of this shadowy organization on the governance of the Pietermaritzburg region? The public at large does not know. Surely here, alone, are grounds for disquiet?

Sadly, Pietermaritzburg's commemorative year finds it an embattled, divided city, a city of insiders and outsiders. The challenge ahead is to eradicate the boundaries between the different political universes, to forge a unified, united, inclusive community embracing the whole Pietermaritzburg area, so that all who live and work there can enjoy as equals what is on offer. But where politics is truly a question of life and death for some, it can never merely be 'parish pump' politics for others. The sooner the citizenry of Pietermaritzburg fully realizes this and acts appropriately, the more contentedly all will sleep in the hollow.

City Council 1988. This Council is unique in South Africa in that it operates by consensus: members of the Indian and Coloured Local Affairs Committees attend committee and Council meetings and may speak and vote.

Front row (left to right):   Cllr. L. Simon, Cllr. L. Gillooly, Cllr. P. C. Cornell, Mr L. S. Moodley, Mr H. D. White (Town Clerk), His Worship the Mayor Cllr. M. H. Cornell, Cllr. R. F. Haswell (Deputy Mayor), Mr J. Petersen (Chairman CLAC), Cllr. R. D. Dales, Cllr. P. C. Harwood and Cllr. G. D. de Beer.

Second row: Mr H. E. Baxter, Cllr. V. D. Mason, Mrs M. Brennan, Cllr. B. V. Edwards MP, Mr B. R. Jawahar, Cllr. N. M. Fuller, Mr H. Dannhauser, (Mace Bearer), Cllr. H. Dyason, Cllr. E. L. Bennett and Cllr. I. H. M. Balfour.

Third row: Mr F. W. Quayle (Director of Parks), Mr C. M. Hobbs (Estate Manager), Mr M. T. Hoskins, Mr A. G. Narayadu, Mr S. N. Naidoo, Mr C. C. C. Robinson (Director of Market), Dr I. Walters (Medical Officer of Health).

Back row: Mr C. J. M. Chandler (Licensing Officer), Mr R. Green (Quarry Manager), Mr P. F. F. Cox (City Treasurer), Mr G. W. Pascoe (Chief Traffic Officer), Mr K. G. Nicol (Associate Town Clerk), Mr R. B. Cairns (Forestry Manager), Mr J. B. Robbins (City Engineer).

Background to political violence

PIETERMARITZBURG REGION 1987–8

John Wright

Pietermaritzburg approached the 150th anniversary of its founding in the aftermath of one of the greatest crises in its history. From the beginning of 1987 to the early months of 1988 some 600 people were killed in an outbreak of political violence in the townships to the west of the city and in the adjoining peri-urban areas of KwaZulu. Hundreds more were maimed and injured, and thousands driven from their homes. Damage to property ran into millions of rand. In many areas round the City organized community life broke down and education systems collapsed. Overall, the violence was the worst experienced in any one region of South Africa since the revolt of 1976-7. In the Natal Midlands it was probably the worst since the 'Bambatha rebellion' of 1906.

Numerous attempts were made by commentators in the Press during and after the fighting to explain its causes. The most incisive analyses were those which were concerned to place the Pietermaritzburg violence in a broader political context. The argument put forward here is that the conflict that took place in the local townships in 1987-8 cannot adequately be explained without reference to, firstly, the history of African politics in Natal since at least the mid-1970s; secondly, the role of the South African state; and thirdly, the role of 'big business' interests in the region.

The first political organization since the banning of the ANC and PAC in 1960 to attract a mass following among African people in Natal was Inkatha, formed by the leaders of the new KwaZulu bantustan in 1975. By the later 1970s it was emerging as essentially a political vehicle for the material aspirations of the rising KwaZulu-based middle class of civil servants, small entrepreneurs, tribal chiefs and other local authority figures. The leadership successfully used appeals to a common Zulu heritage to win emotional support from large numbers of working-class Zulu people in Natal.

In the first few years of its existence, Inkatha was also able to win wider popular support outside Natal by keeping on good terms with the African National Congess, which was reviving its presence inside South Africa after the Soweto revolt of 1976-7. But as support for the more militant and nationally-rooted anti-apartheid stance of the ANC increased, so the wider appeal of local, bantustan-based organizations like Inkatha began to fade. In 1979-80 the two organizations broke off relations and began to take an increasingly hostile line towards each other.

The rapid growth of independent trade unions in Natal in the late 1970s and early 1980s, and the formation of the United Democratic Front in 1983, posed a threat to Inkatha's hold on popular support in its home area. As an organization dominated by an emerging privileged class, with a vested interest in the comfortable jobs, protected business opportunities and patronage networks provided by the bantustan system, Inkatha was unable to act effectively in the long-term material and political interests of the mass of African working-class people in Natal. In spite of its increasingly 'Zulu-ist' rhetoric, numbers of Zulu-speaking people began to give their support to the trade unions and to anti-apartheid community organizations outside Inkatha's and KwaZulu's range of bureaucratic controls.

After the break with the ANC, the Inkatha leadership made the conscious decision to establish a wing of its youth organization on para-military lines to 'safeguard those things we erect in the national interest'. Increasingly, Inkatha supporters began to use strong-arm methods to suppress the growth of rival quasi-political organizations in Natal. In 1980 armed gangs of Inkatha supporters were active in stamping out a schools boycott in the townships round Durban. In 1983 an attack by Inkatha supporters on anti-Inkatha students at the University of Zululand left five people dead.

Towards the end of 1984 co-operation between important sections of the trade union movement and community organizations aligned with or affiliated to the UDF began on a national basis. In response, Inkatha began to operate more vigorously to establish itself as the sole effective political organization in the African townships round Durban. In August 1985 a series of attacks by Inkatha supporters on trade unionists and members of youth organizations culminated in violent confrontations between youth groups and well-organized bands of vigilantes. Several days of fighting ended with 75 people dead and Inkatha in control of the major Durban townships.

In the townships round Pietermaritzburg, civic associations and youth organizations with UDF sympathies began to emerge in 1985. From the end of the year they received increasing support from local branches of the newly formed COSATU group of unions. Tensions between these organizations and Inkatha began to mount, particularly after large numbers of workers staged a successful stay-away in July 1985 in support of strikers at the BTR-Sarmcol factory in Howick. This was followed in August-September by a consumer boycott, which was opposed by Inkatha, of white-owned shops in Howick and Pietermaritzburg. Another stay-away in Pietermaritzburg on May Day 1986 signalled that working-class political consciousness was rapidly increasing in a region where Inkatha had never been particularly strong.

Meanwhile the South African government was beginning to take increasingly forceful measures to try to stamp out the popular revolt against township administrations that had flared in many parts of the country from 1984 onwards. Under emergency regulations, thousands of UDF and COSATU activists and supporters were rounded up by the police. Individual opposition leaders were murdered, communities that were strongholds of resistance to the state were broken up, and numbers of townships were occupied by the South African army. From late 1985 there was a wave of vigilante attacks, many of them apparently connived at by the state, on community organizations all over the country.

At the same time the state was beginning to shift away publicly from its bantustan policies, which had patently failed to produce either economic development or political quiescence in the 'homelands', towards a policy of 'regionalization'. In terms of this the bantustans were to be linked with neighbouring urban and industrial centres to form 'development' regions, and bantustan governments could expect to have more powers devolved on them to negotiate the necessary arrangements with white local and regional authorities. In Natal this policy converged in important respects with an initiative taken by big business and industrial interests to draw the rising and politically ambitious middle-class stratum which dominated KwaZulu politics into an alliance against the anti-apartheid and partly socialist popular movement which was beginning to take organizational form in the region. To begin negotiating the terms of this alliance, the so-called KwaZulu-Natal Indaba was set up at the beginning of 1986. More than ever it became important for Inkatha to establish undisputed control over African people in Natal in order to be able to present itself as their sole representative organization.

At the end of 1986 Inkatha began to go onto the offensive against the growing challenge to its political position in the townships round Pietermaritzburg. In December of that year a group of vigilantes invaded Mpophomeni township outside Howick and killed four members and supporters of a COSATU union. Early in 1987 vigilante gangs in Mpumalanga, near Hammarsdale, began to turn on local youth organizations, and a long series of killings followed.

In the Edendale region, conflict between Inkatha supporters on one side and youth organizations and COSATU members on the other began to spill over into violence in the early months of 1987. It was intensified by the success in Pietermaritzburg of a national stay-away called by the UDF and COSATU for 5 and 6 May in protest against the white general election held on the 6th. By the end of August some 80 people had been killed in the Pietermaritzburg area. The available evidence indicates that in most incidents of violence the aggressors were supporters of Inkatha.

In about July or August 1987 local Inkatha leaders seem to have begun a drive to suppress resistance to Inkatha in the townships round Pietermaritzburg and the neighbouring Vulindlela area of KwaZulu, and to increase

An incident in a township
during the stayaway of July 1985.

22

the organization's local membership. A number of vigilante leaders, often men of little education, seized the opportunity to expand their personal power bases. They recruited gangs of armed followers from the large number of unemployed men and youths in the townships, and proceeded to establish their domination over territories in which they terrorized the inhabitants into joining Inkatha and paying them 'fees' of various kinds.

Little effective police action seems to have been taken to check the vigilante violence, and the youth organizations which were bearing the brunt of the attacks began to step up the organization of communal self-defence committees. Retaliation against the vigilantes became more frequent. Both sides attacked 'soft' targets and forced numbers of apolitical people to support them in the mounting conflict, but again it is clear that most of the violence was provoked from the side of the vigilantes. In spite of the virtual absence of any on-the-ground UDF structures capable of co-ordinating a response to the attacks, large numbers of people who had previously known little or nothing about the UDF came to see it as a symbol of resistance to Inkatha and to apartheid. Lack of evidence, due largely to state restrictions on the reporting of the violence, makes it impossible at this stage to analyze the social patterns of the conflict in any depth.

In the period from September 1987 to February 1988 some 500 people were killed in the fighting. Two-thirds of the victims whose political affiliations are known were supporters of UDF-linked organizations, and one-third of Inkatha. When, from late October, the vigilantes began to suffer reverses, the security forces intervened by systematically detaining hundreds of anti-Inkatha activists. By contrast, very few, if any, Inkatha supporters were detained, and in spite of a series of court injunctions against them, the vigilante leaders were allowed to remain at large and active.

At first most white people in Pietermaritzburg took little notice of the fighting which was raging in the townships. White political and business leaders in Natal, though increasingly embarrassed by the association of numbers of Inkatha supporters with the violence, were generally committed to Inkatha's side through their support for the KwaZulu-Natal Indaba. When the escalation of violence threatened to disrupt industry and commerce in Pietermaritzburg, local business leaders attempted to arrange peace negotiations between leaders of Inkatha, the UDF and COSATU. These initiatives had little effect, and in the event they were torpedoed by the South African state when, in February 1988, it in effect proscribed the UDF.

By March 1988, for reasons that are not yet clear, the level of violence in the townships was diminishing. In the Edendale area and in parts of Vulindlela, unlike the main Durban townships in 1985 and Crossroads-KTC near Cape Town in 1986, state-backed vigilantes had been unable to destroy organized popular resistance. In effect the vigilantes had been fought off by the young men and boys who called themselves the 'comrades', though at horrific cost to the latter. The state of 'violent equilibrium' that followed was maintained only by the deployment of a large security force contingent. It was unlikely that real peace would return to the townships without a major realignment of political forces both in Natal and in the wider South African context.

The glamour of *fin de siècle* theatre in Pietermaritzburg. Scott's Theatre in Theatre Lane, which was built in 1897, could seat 1 500 people and boasted nine boxes for the socially prominent.

CHAPTER THIRTEEN

Arts and Entertainment

1

The performing arts

Michael Lambert

If it were possible for inhabitants of Victorian Pietermaritzburg to have scanned the entertainment sections of the *Natal Witness* in November and December 1986, they would have felt completely at home: Handel's *Messiah* performed by the Pietermaritzburg Philharmonic Choir, the Charles Dickens Singers in a Christmas Promenade Concert, Dickens's *A Christmas Carol* at the Cygnet Theatre, the University Madrigal Singers in a Christmas recital, the Herald Players' pantomime *A Sleeping Beauty* and the Pietermaritzburg Choral Society in a carol programme at the Imperial Hotel.

Had our Victorians attended any of these performances, they would readily have identified with each cultural offering and would probably have revelled in the continuity of the Empire's cultural institutions. After all, *Messiah* had first been performed in Pietermaritzburg in 1864 and has been performed regularly ever since; a Philharmonic Society (arguably the legitimate ancestor of the present one) had been established in 1868; a year before, a reading of *A Christmas Carol* was presented in the old Town Offices; the Madrigal Singers would probably have recalled the 75th Regiment's Madrigal Club of 1872; the first Christmas pantomime was performed in 1877; a Pietermaritzburg Choral Society had been formed in 1863 and the Imperial Hotel was established in 1878!

Continuity of cultural taste, reinforced by the tragic absurdity of apartheid with its notion of the rigid separateness of cultures, characterizes the history of the performing arts in Pietermaritzburg. In relatively prosperous times, prosperous in the light of the depressed 1840s, the early British colonists, exploiting the availability of black servants, created the opportunities for leisure in which they did not sow the seeds of a new Anglo-African cultural tradition, but effected the awkward transplantation of the culture of a provincial British town.

As the Roman armies prepared the way for the Romanization of Britain, so the various regiments stationed at Fort Napier between 1843 and 1914 paved the way for the systematic Anglicization of this corner of Africa. This was not difficult. The Trekkers had had neither the time nor the energy to establish a strong Dutch cultural tradition in Pietermaritzburg. Zulu culture was simply ignored or burlesqued. Furthermore, as our own times have shown, military power can prescribe cultural taste in a devastatingly effective manner.

Thus, perhaps as an outlet for what James Morris calls 'the irrepressible randiness of the British soldier abroad', the 45th Regiment produced the first play in Pietermaritzburg, in a large room of the barracks on New Year's Day, 1846. The play was *Zorinski*, which was followed by an interlude of music and dancing (a Highland fling, naturally), and a farce, *The Honest Thieves*. This combination (play, musical interlude and 'screaming' farce) was to prove enduringly popular in both amateur and professional theatricals. So the soldiers of the garrison helped to shape a taste for the melodramatic and farcical which is still evident in Pietermaritzburg theatre-going audiences today.

When various regiments with good theatrical traditions left, the townsfolk formed amateur dramatic clubs whose fortunes were and still are closely linked to socio-economic circumstances and to the challenges provided by professional touring companies. In 1854 the first amateur group in the City appeared in a programme of melodrama and farce, the musical interlude being provided by the band of the 45th Regiment. Co-operation between the soldiers and civilian groups became more frequent after the closure of the two garrison theatres (the Victoria and St. George's). Significantly, of the 29 pieces presented by the Amateur Dramatic Club in 1865 – 1866, 28 were either farces or burlesques. The soldiers had made their influence felt.

That this tradition still survives is evident if one examines the work of the Natal Society Drama Group, currently the most active amateur group in the City. Formed in 1930, the group found its permanent home in the Cygnet Theatre in 1953. Apart from farces, light comedies and thrillers form the backbone of the group's repertoire. Plays such as *Good Night Mrs Puffin* (1965), *I'll get My Man* (1971) and *Big Bad Mouse* (1981) have their dramatic antecedents in such pieces as *Love à la Mode* (45th Regiment 1848), *Done On Both Sides* (5th Fusiliers 1864) and *Slasher and Crasher* (Amateur Dramatic Club 1865).

Whilst a taste for vapid, escapist fare with little or no intellectual content predominates in Pietermaritzburg's theatrical history, serious theatre, in particular the performance of the 'classics', is also part of the inherited British tradition. To the soldiers of the 45th Regiment must go credit for the first performance of a Shakespearian tragedy (*Macbeth* 1847) and for the introduction of comedies of worth, such as Sheridan's *The Rivals* (1848). However, a taste for serious theatre was never rigorously developed, chiefly because of the cultural impoverishment of the settlers. During a professional production of *Hamlet* in 1879, the audience was lifeless except when a pumpkin was brought on to represent Yorick's skull. The curtain-raiser, *Little Toddlekins*, was better received than performances of *Hamlet* and *Macbeth* in 1882. One could not have expected anything else of an audience trained only to appreciate farce and burlesque.

In its early days, the Natal Society Drama Group did not confine itself to farce or thrillers. Ibsen's *The Master Builder* (1949), *The Merchant of Venice* (1948), Shaw's *Man and Superman* (which opened the Cygnet in 1953) and Pirandello's *Six Characters in Search of an Author* (1975) reflect the group's attempt to develop a taste for serious theatre. Regrettably, productions of this kind have been too infrequent to succeed.

Student productions at the Natal Training College (as it was formerly known) and at the University of Natal, because of their rather esoteric and élitist appeal, seem to have made little impression on the taste of the average theatregoer either. The University Dramatic Society, which tackled everything from mediaeval mystery plays to Jean Anouilh, ended its history with a sorry production

Programme of Music.

By the Band of the King's Own (R.L.) Regiment,
The Borough Organist (Mr. Alfred H. Day),
and Mr. Alfred Heather.

Band Items during Dinner.

OVERTURE	-	"Mirella"	-	*Gounod*
SELECTION	-	"The Gondoliers"	-	*Sullivan*
GAVOTTE	-	"Old Windsor"	-	*Godfrey*
MORCEAU	-	"Turkish Patrol"	-	*Michaelis*
AMERICAN SKETCH	"Swanee River"	-		*Middleton*
SELECTION	-	"A Country Girl"	-	*Monckton*

After Dinner.

SOLO	-	National Anthem	-	
	Mr. ALFRED HEATHER.			
SONG	-	"When other Lips" (*Maritana*)		*Wallace*
	Mr. ALFRED HEATHER			
CORNET SOLO	"The Lost Chord"			*Sullivan*
	BAND.			
ORGAN SOLO	-	"Andantino"	-	*Lemare*
	Mr. A. H. DAY.			
SONG	-	"Evening Song"	-	*Blumenthal*
	Mr. ALFRED HEATHER.			
ORGAN SOLO	-	"Fantasia"	-	*Hewlett*
	Mr. A. H. DAY.			
ENTR'ACTE	"La Colombe"	-		*Gounod*
	BAND.			

The City's musical preferences exposed
in a concert programme of 1902.

of *Macbeth* in 1981 — regrettable, as the society had acquired a fine reputation for its 'Shakespeares' in the fifties and sixties. Like university drama departments in Britain and America, the Department of Speech and Drama has been responsible for producing plays of a wide range of authors whose work reflects major trends in the history of European theatre. Plays by Aeschylus and Aristophanes, Stoppard and Pinter, Lorca and Brecht, Berkoff and Benmussa have provided rare challenges for Pietermaritzburg audiences. However, although the Department is committed to a form of theatre which is not trivial and escapist, the theatrical tradition at the University, like the tradition at the Cygnet, is still fundamentally Eurocentric. Despite its experimental work, the University also perpetuates the inherited tradition. Wycherley's Restoration comedy *The Country Wife* opened the Hexagon Theatre in 1977 and nothing could have been more unashamedly British than the musical *Salad Days* which was the University's 75th anniversary production in 1985.

Of black South African amateur theatre, the average white Pietermaritzburg theatre-goer sees very little. The University has hosted a number of original plays and musicals (*Born Free* 1977; *Hhay' Hhashi!* 1979) which testify to a vibrant and original mode of theatrical expression in the community halls of the black townships flanking the City. Poetry readings and extracts from township drama are not uncommon at the cultural evenings of various non-racial groups in the City. Interestingly, anyone who has seen township theatre will recall the roars of delight which greet slapstick farce. Although there is evidence that some performances in the Victorian era were non-racial, separate performances for 'natives' given by the many professional tricksters, circuses and visiting companies were more common. It is tempting to believe that these companies helped develop a similar taste for farce in black audiences which endures to the present day.

Pietermaritzburg has always relied on visiting professional companies to enliven the theatrical scene, ever since the Sefton Parry Company arrived in the Capital in 1862. It did not take long for these companies to assess local taste, to pander to it and so reinforce it firmly. Many companies had to use local amateur performers in their productions and these amateurs took back to their clubs a taste for the sensational special effect, an abiding feature of Victorian professional theatre.

This taste for the sensational was nourished even more assiduously by the visits of circuses, by the appearance of woeful 'professors' of electro-biology and mesmerism and by infant prodigies like Annie May Abbott, the little Georgia magnet, who lifted five seated men in the audience. Grotesque human and animal shows such as the appearance of Och-a-Mah, an Ashanti dwarf, who could play the violin with his toes, and the troupe of musical baboons which danced the hornpipe on a tight-rope, helped inculcate a taste for spectacle.

Although this taste is today catered for by television, films, wrestling-bouts and the excesses of the religious fringe, vestiges of it endure in theatre-going audiences. It is, for example, exploited by impresarios like Pieter Toerien whose tiresome British comedies, which visit the City periodically, are encased in elaborate sets, usually enthusiastically applauded by Pietermaritzburg audiences. Napac too has often journeyed to the City with rococo productions of the 'classics' or of dated thrillers in which special effects often make up for the lack of substance.

With the formation of Napac's experimental Loft Company in 1985, it was hoped that challenging and provocative South African theatre would be presented in the Capital. Indigenous plays which attempt to explore the realities of the South African situation have been attempted by this company but poor scripts and mediocre acting have detracted from their impact. Other visiting companies have presented indigenous theatre of a much higher standard. Excellent productions of *Siswe Banzi is Dead* and *Master Harold and The Boys*, as well as of the dynamic *Woza Albert!* and Ackerman's *Somewhere on the Border*, have shown Pietermaritzburg audiences what issues can be creatively confronted by an indigenous theatrical tradition which Pietermaritzburg sadly lacks.

The histories of musical and theatrical performance in the City are inextricably linked. Consequently, the evolution of a taste for farce, melodrama and the sensational is matched by the development of a taste for the light music of the comic operetta and for the sentimental schmaltz of 'songs from the shows'.

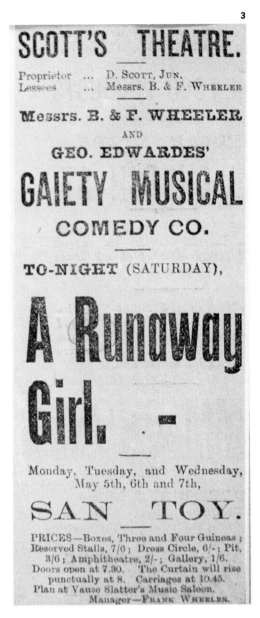

SCOTT'S THEATRE.

Proprietor ... D. Scott, Jun.
Lessees ... Messrs. B. & F. Wheeler

Messrs. B. & F. WHEELER

AND

GEO. EDWARDES'

GAIETY MUSICAL

COMEDY CO.

TO-NIGHT (SATURDAY),

A Runaway Girl. -

Monday, Tuesday, and Wednesday,
May 5th, 6th and 7th,

SAN TOY.

PRICES—Boxes, Three and Four Guineas ;
Reserved Stalls, 7/6 ; Dress Circle, 6/- ; Pit,
3/6 ; Amphitheatre, 2/- ; Gallery, 1/6.
Doors open at 7.30. The Curtain will rise
punctually at 8. Carriages at 10.45.
Plan at Vause Slatter's Music Saloon.
Manager—Frank Wheeler.

Theatre boxes for 'carriage-folk' were an expensive luxury.

Regimental bands and civilian players, some of whom had emigrated along with their instruments, were responsible for the first concerts in Pietermaritzburg, held at the garrison. When soldiers and civilians began to work together in the theatre, the repertoires of the various regimental bands which played in the interludes determined the direction of the City's musical taste. Some of the bands had excellent bandmasters (like Signor Faccioli of the 45th) and these bandmasters ensured that the bands did not merely play martial music extolling the Imperial Idea. Operatic overtures by composers like Mozart, Weber, Meyerbeer, Verdi and Rossini helped develop a taste for the brief, tuneful overture which still endures, as a glance at recent programmes of the Pietermaritzburg Symphony Orchestra and of the Natal Philharmonic Orchestra will testify. At the inaugural concert of the NPO in the City Hall in October 1983, two overtures (Dvorak's *Carnaval* and Tchaikovsky's *1812*), both noisily exhilarating, were rapturously received.

Regimental glee clubs, madrigal groups, minstrels and church choirs perpetuated the Victorian tradition of choral singing, a tradition which is still strong today. A choir of between 30 and 40 voices performed extracts from *Messiah* in January 1864. Incidentally, the performance was not well attended in contrast to modern performances of *Messiah* which are invariably sold out. The Pietermaritzburg Philharmonic Society in 1881 had 60 'singing members' whereas, in true imperial style, a choir of 250 voices inaugurated the new City Hall in 1901. In pre-Republican days, royal birthdays and visits were celebrated by choral concerts on a grand scale. A sure indication of the enduring Britishness of musical taste in Pietermaritzburg was the fact that Elgar's *Land of Hope and Glory* could be sung at a concert in 1986 with no apparent sign of incongruity.

The present Philharmonic Choir has approximately 120 members and large choral works which are Victorian in spirit (such as Stainer's *Crucifixion* and Mendelssohn's *Elijah*) are in the choir's repertoire. However, although the choir has attempted musically more demanding works such as Verdi's *Requiem* and Bach's *B Minor Mass*, extracts from Gilbert and Sullivan and Rodgers and Hammerstein are the especial favourites of Pietermaritzburg audiences.

The other large amateur choir of note in the City at present is the Pietermaritzburg Choral Society. Winners of a national choral competition in 1986, this choir was the first black choir to perform with the Pietermaritzburg Symphony Orchestra. Under the baton of the choir's conductor, Joshua Radebe, the choir performed extracts from Mozart's *Coronation Mass*, to critical acclaim. Although there is record of a Zulu choir performing in Durban in 1892, it seems to have taken Pietermaritzburg a further 94 years to recognize officially the importance of the Zulu choral tradition which exists in schools, training colleges and churches in and around the City. A great deal of European music (and much of it noticeably Victorian in taste) is sung by these choirs, but works by indigenous composers are also performed, particularly at the keenly contested choral competitions regularly held in community halls in the various townships.

Pietermaritzburg music lovers have always revelled in operetta and light musicals and, for this tradition as well, the soldiers of the 45th Regiment, who produced the comic opera *Love Laughs at Locksmiths* in 1847, must bear responsibility. As in the realm of theatre, visiting professional companies exploited the audience's taste and the Poussard Bailey Company were the first professionals to stage an operetta in 1868 (*The Painter and his Model*). Gilbert and Sullivan seem especially to have delighted Pietermaritzburg audiences, ever since *Trial by Jury* was produced by the 80th Regiment in 1879. A juvenile production of *HMS Pinafore* at the Theatre Royal in 1885 anticipated the fashion for all-child casts set by Pollard's Lilliputian Opera Company in 1898, and so set a pattern for school productions of 'G & S' which endures to the present. Significantly, apart from university productions, the only major Pietermaritzburg amateur contribution to the Grahamstown National Festival of the Arts was *Trial by Surjury*, a zany medical send-up of the original, performed in 1985.

A taste for the superficial music of the operetta was strongly developed by Charles Lascelles Grey,

THE CHRISTY MINSTRELS

Michael Lambert

Visiting professional companies also helped to encourage the various regimental and amateur minstrel or 'nigger burlesque' groups which flourished in Pietermaritzburg, following the visit of the Christy Minstrels who played to packed houses in 1865. An American export, the Christy Minstrels consisted of a small group of performers with blackened faces (and hands and necks, if professional) who sang in close harmony and parodied what they considered to be 'negro oddities'. Whilst these groups were musically proficient (one of the Christy's in 1874 delighted the congregation in St. Saviour's with a rendition of *I Know That My Redeemer Liveth*), they unfortunately reinforced British colonial racist attitudes. Instead of understanding the 'native', the settlers preferred to burlesque him. Significantly, one of Baby Benson's hits in Pietermaritzburg was *Old Black Joe*, sung in Christy Minstrel attire.

Rather condescendingly, the 75th Regiment chose to introduce some local colour by forming the Isivimbo Minstrels in 1872, a title which suggests parody of a Zulu *impi*. This was, of course, before Isandlwana. It would be untruthful to state that this tradition no longer survives. A group called the Chase Valley Darkies, smeared in black and festooned with skins and feathers, has performed unharmonious Zulu impersonations during Azalea week float processions. Furthermore, when Pieter-Dirk Uys, in 'golliwog' wig, attempted a brief impersonation of Archbishop Tutu during a revue in the Hexagon Theatre in 1986, one could not help wondering whether the uproarious laughter which greeted this parody reflected a trace of Victorian Pietermaritzburg's taste for 'nigger burlesque'.

4

Pietermaritzburg's most colourful musical character who was introduced to the City in 1876. A concert version of Offenbach's classical operetta *The Grand Duchess of Gerolstein* began Lascelles' brief but creative acquaintance with the City, during which he was involved in the production of operettas and operas such as *The Bohemian Girl, The Rose of Auvergne, Maritana, Les Cloches de Corneville* and *The Daughter of the Regiment*. Even in the post-Lascelles era, Luscombe Searelle's production of *Maritana* managed to run for 24 nights at the Theatre Royal in 1888 — a sure sign that a taste for operetta had been well nurtured. In true Lascelles tradition, Lehàr's *The Merry Widow* opened the Winston Churchill Theatre in 1971. The Herald Players, with productions of musicals such as *Brigadoon* and *The Sound of Music*, continue to foster Pietermaritzburg's preference for light popular music.

Serious opera was first introduced to Pietermaritzburg audiences by the Miranda-Harper professional company in 1870 with a production of Verdi's *Il Trovatore*. As travelling theatrical companies used local amateur actors, so this company trained and used a local amateur chorus, thus reinforcing a taste for Italian opera initiated by the regimental bands. For production of serious opera, Pietermaritzburg still has to rely on visits from professional companies like Napac. The healthy practice of using local amateurs in the chorus is no longer possible or practical. In the last decade or so, operas like *Nabucco, Madama Butterfly, The Barber of Seville* and *Don Pasquale* have continued the tradition of Italian opera. However, as with serious theatre, productions of opera have been too sporadic to have developed a critical appreciation of this genre.

Military bands aside, the origins of orchestral music in Pietermaritzburg can be traced back to the small ensembles which accompanied hymns and psalms at Trekker services, a practice later continued (for example) in Colenso's church where the congregational singing was reinforced by a small orchestra consisting of violin, cornopean and seraphine! Clearly, no fully-fledged symphony orchestra accompanied Lascelles' operatic productions. He himself appears to have directed at the piano with the assistance of a violin and a few other instrumentalists. One cannot speak of an orchestra in Pietermaritzburg until the inauguration of the Philharmonic Society (which incorporated the Pietermaritzburg Orchestral Society) in 1881. Under the baton of bandmaster Rowlandson, 30 players visited Durban in 1885 but, apparently, the strings of the orchestra were not strong enough to balance the other instruments. Rowlandson's visit to Durban exemplifies a musical tradition common in the late nineteenth century. Many early orchestral groups in Durban were augmented with players from Pietermaritzburg.

Today the reverse is true. The Pietermaritzburg Philharmonic Orchestra, which has approximately the same number of players as Rowlandson's orchestra, is often augmented with players from the professional NPO, based in Durban. This very expensive practice has resulted in cutbacks in the number of concerts given by the local orchestra — so much so that only one performance of *Messiah* could be held in November 1986. Like Rowlandson's orchestra, the present symphony orchestra (as well as the NPO) does not have a strong enough string section. The violins in both orchestras are especially thin, although the quality of playing in the PPO has improved noticeably under the orchestra's most recent conductors, Errol Girdlestone and John Mitchell. Girdlestone and Mitchell are both good organists and this continues a tradition established by Pietermaritz-

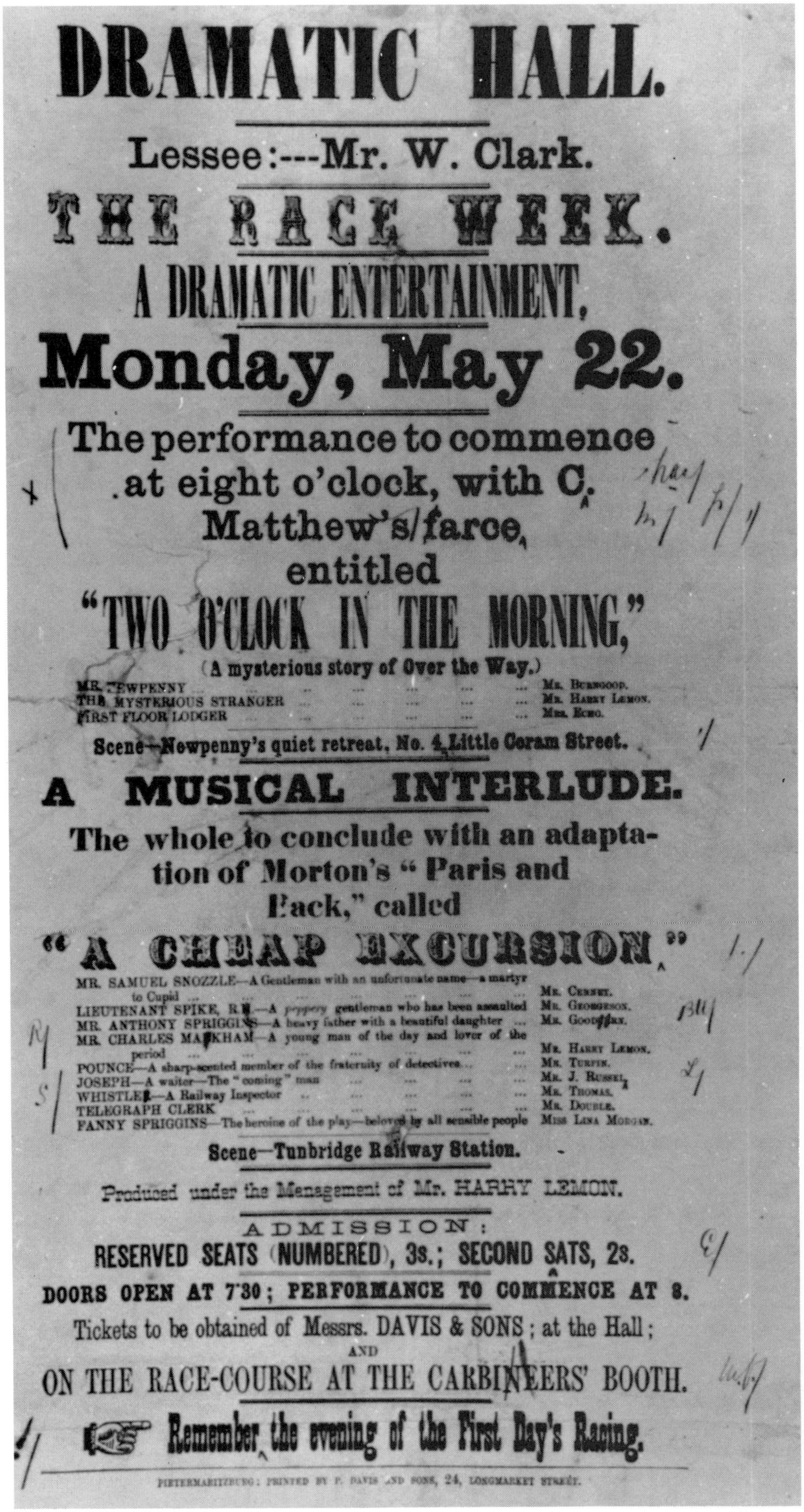

DRAMATIC HALL.

Lessee:---Mr. W. Clark.

THE RACE WEEK.

A DRAMATIC ENTERTAINMENT,

Monday, May 22.

The performance to commence at eight o'clock, with C. Matthew's farce, entitled

"TWO O'CLOCK IN THE MORNING,"

(A mysterious story of Over the Way.)

MR. NEWPENNY ... ... MR. BEARGOOD.
THE MYSTERIOUS STRANGER ... ... MR. HARRY LEMON.
FIRST FLOOR LODGER ... ... MRS. ECHO.

Scene—Newpenny's quiet retreat, No. 4, Little Coram Street.

A MUSICAL INTERLUDE.

The whole to conclude with an adaptation of Morton's " Paris and Back," called

" A CHEAP EXCURSION."

MR. SAMUEL SNOZZLE—A Gentleman with an unfortunate name—a martyr to Cupid ... MR. CERNEY.
LIEUTENANT SPIKE, R.N.—A peppery gentleman who has been assaulted MR. GEORGESON.
MR. ANTHONY SPRIGGINS—A heavy father with a beautiful daughter ... MR. GOODJOHN.
MR. CHARLES MARKHAM—A young man of the day and lover of the period ... MR. HARRY LEMON.
POUNCE—A sharp-scented member of the fraternity of detectives... MR. TURPIN.
JOSEPH—A waiter—The "coming" man ... ... MR. J. RUSSEL.
WHISTLER—A Railway Inspector ... ... MR. THOMAS.
TELEGRAPH CLERK ... ... MR. DOUBLE.
FANNY SPRIGGINS—The heroine of the play—beloved by all sensible people MISS LINA MORGAN.

Scene—Tunbridge Railway Station.

Produced under the Management of Mr. HARRY LEMON.

ADMISSION :

RESERVED SEATS (NUMBERED), 3s.; SECOND SATS, 2s.

DOORS OPEN AT 7·30; PERFORMANCE TO COMMENCE AT 8.

Tickets to be obtained of Messrs. DAVIS & SONS ; at the Hall ;

AND

ON THE RACE-COURSE AT THE CARBINEERS' BOOTH.

☞ Remember the evening of the First Day's Racing.

PIETERMARITZBURG : PRINTED BY P. DAVIS AND SONS, 24, LONGMARKET STREET.

burg organists in the nineteenth century. In 1881, C. T. Varley from Pietermaritzburg gave the first organ recital in Durban and in 1894, A. H. Day, the first Borough Organist, performed at the inaugural recital on the new Durban Town Hall organ.

A glance at the composers on the programme of the piano recital given by J. C. Dunster (conductor of the Pietermaritzburg Philharmonic) in 1883 confirms that taste in serious music has not altered. Beethoven, Weber, Mendelssohn or Chopin (or any other romantic composer) have remained firm favourites with lovers of classical music in Pietermaritzburg. The NPO, which plays in the Capital during its seasons, tends to reinforce this taste by performing works by romantic composers like Brahms, Dvorak, Tchaikovsky, Liszt and Rachmaninov. The orchestra has included 'moderns' in its Pietermaritzburg performances, such as piano concerti by Prokofiev and Shostakovich. These works are usually politely received, if the performance is restrained, and enthusiastically applauded (with the requisite foot-stomping) if the performer is a Russian defector and flamboyantly Hoffnungesque. The Victorian taste for spectacle lives on.

Visiting professional musicians, unaware of the prevailing penchant for romanticism, often encounter very sparse houses if their programmes have works by composers of the Second Viennese School in them. Over the years, the University Music Society has attempted to develop an appreciation for contemporary serious music by inviting composers from the Department of Music at the University of Natal in Durban to perform their works, but Pietermaritzburg music-lovers are not ready for works scored for crying baby, doctored piano, ping-pong ball and ululating soprano!

String quartets and *Lieder* recitals have also not been favoured with packed houses by Pietermaritzburg audiences who, like their Victorian predecessors, want a big sound laced with hummable tunes. A performance of *Lieder* by Richard Strauss, Schubert and Wagner at the Winston Churchill Theatre in 1986 was attended by approximately 25 people. Interestingly, the *Natal Witness* critic in 1864 complained that, when a certain Mr and Mrs

Paris gave a very respectable performance of Beethoven's *Kreutzer Sonata*, there was an audience of 20 people — in the back seats!

This taste for the grandiose and romantic is nowhere more apparent than in the kind of ballet which attracts the most favourable reception in Pietermaritzburg. Visiting professional companies like Pact Ballet are invariably successful with productions of romantic classics such as *The Sleeping Beauty*. It is hoped that the newly-formed Napac Dance Company, which gave its inaugural performance in Pietermaritzburg in the Winston Churchill Theatre in July 1986, will develop a taste for modern experimental dance. Other companies have presented programmes of contemporary dance at the University and students in the Department of Speech and Drama there usually present a dance programme annually, which is exclusively devoted to original, modern dance, some of which is choreographed by the students themselves. However, it cannot be said that experimental dance is wildly popular in Pietermaritzburg. Performances of traditional Zulu tribal dance and of Indian classical dance are not uncommon in Pietermaritzburg but are rarely seen by white audiences.

This discussion of trends in the major performing arts in Pietermaritzburg over the past 150 years seems to confirm that audiences in the City have been, and are still, chiefly interested in theatre which is escapist and unchallenging, in music which is sentimental and romantic, and in dance which is traditional and spectacular.

In a City of diverse cultures, Eastern, Western and African, an imported British cultural tradition has been perpetuated, protected by apartheid legislation. So far, the First World has been culturally insulated from the Third. However, no culture, although it may seem comfortably and even complacently established, can survive without creative and critical interaction with the realities of the environment in which it finds itself. The British cultural tradition in Pietermaritzburg has yet to achieve this. If it does not, it will die of sterility. If it does, Pietermaritzburg will cease to be, as Hattersley once called it, 'a corner of Victorian Britain under an alien sky', and will become a truly African city with its own specific cultural identity.

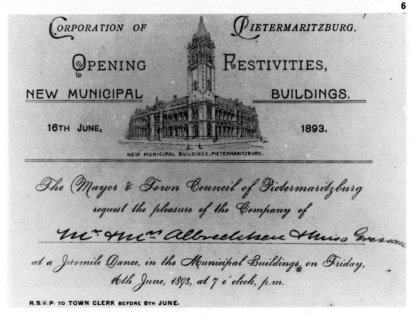

Pietermaritzburg's taste in entertainment, in the 1880s as today, can hardly be described as 'highbrow'[5].

The diversions of the City's youth were once innocent and strictly supervised[6].

CHARLES LASCELLES GREY

John Mitchell

'Pietermaritzburg — the city of scandal, religion and theatricals.' So it was dubbed a hundred years ago and, excluding religion, owed much of this reputation to Charles Lascelles Grey.

Grey, the foppish Bohemian son of a distinguished English family, was an accomplished musician. A brilliant pianist and vocalist, he also composed and was a respected orchestral conductor.

It was his unusual voice which drew the attention of Madame Anna Bishop. This redoubtable lady, singing star of her day and estranged wife of composer Sir Henry Bishop, made an international career singing the famous song composed by her ex-husband — *Home Sweet Home*. Lascelles was the perfect partner, accompanying her at the piano, directing the orchestra if available, singing duets and also composing. In January 1876, their peregrinations brought them to Pietermaritzburg for five performances at the Bijou Theatre, a converted shop. The programmes changed nightly and Lascelles's popularity grew with every show.

Within two weeks Anna and Charles recruited and trained a local orchestra, chorus and soloists and on 17 January they presented a concert version of the operetta *The Grand Duchess of Gerolstein*. A tradition was born that night and two purpose-built theatres were soon under construction.

Anna retired shortly afterwards but Lascelles returned permanently to Maritzburg in 1879 and quickly established himself. Tracking down the participants of *Grand Duchess* he formed a permanent amateur company, 'Opera de Camera', and after only a month he produced the first operetta at the Dramatic Hall — *HMS Pinafore*.

The New Bijou Theatre, now the Theatre Royal, could not compete, so a deal was struck. Opera de Camera became the Theatre Royal Company with Charles directing. His energy was amazing and new operettas were staged monthly. Lascelles was a charismatic genius and artists and public alike were entranced.

In 1880 the Royal presented Balfe's *The Bohemian Girl* — the first fully-staged grand opera in South Africa; and in 1881 the Pietermaritzburg Philharmonic Society gave its first performance under Lascelles's direction.

Unfortunately Maritzburg was also reputed to have the worst behaved audiences in the world and Lascelles himself stopped a show to inform the patrons that even in Australia and America he hadn't met 'such an ill-conducted, shameless, disorderly and disreputable set of people as those who compose the gallery audience'.

However, Lascelles himself was somewhat responsible for the situation. 'Poor Charlie' was 'thirsty' and it proved his undoing. Trading insults with an inebriated maestro may have been fun for the gallery, but performances suffered and things finally came to a head in Durban when Charlie failed to make the show and disappeared with the leading lady.

He eventually lurched back to Maritzburg but it was really all over. Arrested by a black policeman for drunkenness, he was subdued with a blow on the head and spent the night in a cell. He died a few days later, perhaps from the after-effects.

The Philharmonic Society, his most enduring legacy, honoured their founder with a monument, so if you're passing the Commercial Road Cemetery, why not pay Charlie a visit? Take a bottle!

Dedicated musical amateurs: the Pietermaritzburg Philharmonic Society orchestra rehearsing under the baton of John Knuyt, who was Music Director in the 1960s and early 1970s.

The Tatham Art Gallery

Lorna Ferguson

The Tatham Art Gallery is one of only seven art museums in South Africa. It was established in the early twentieth century with all the enthusiasm and gusto that many colonial late Victorians brought to idealistic and high-minded projects.

In November 1900 Mrs George Thresh presented the City Council with its first recorded painting. The work was a water-colour entitled *Rabbits*. Several portraits followed, including those of Lords Milner and Kitchener and various city councillors. A work by John Lomax with a typically Victorian anecdotal title, *A fortune on a throw*, was also acquired.

Then in 1903 the City Council Minutes reflect discussion on the proposed formation of an Art Gallery, followed speedily by a conditional offer (again by Mrs George Thresh) of two paintings worth 300 gns each — *La Mascotte* and *Preparing the Maypole* — if two other citizens were to make like contributions. By this stage Mrs Ada Tatham, wife of the Judge President of Natal, had set about energetically collecting funds from the citizens of Pietermaritzburg for an art gallery. In 1949 she wrote of this:

> It was as long ago as 1903 that I collected, through the generosity of friends interested in the formation of an Art Gallery a sum of £500 and the Corporation very generously added another £500, and as my husband and I were going to England at that time, I was asked to purchase the pictures.
>
> Several donors wished their gift should be specially chosen as from them. Before sailing, I wrote to my husband's cousin, Sir W.B. Richmond, R.A., to tell him of the venture and he invited several of the members of the Royal Academy, as well as its President, Sir E. Poynter, P.R.A., to meet me. So the way was made easy for me to deal directly with gentlemen, who were interested in the foundation of an Art Gallery in an English colony, so far away as Natal.
>
> I had decided whose pictures I hoped to acquire through reading of their work, in my Art Journals, and this was made possible, by meeting many of the Royal Academicians in a friendly manner.

Mrs Tatham travelled as far north as Aberdeen in Scotland to secure paintings from Royal Academicians and, with the £1 300 she had collected for the Art Gallery funds, she negotiated for and bought paintings to the value of £3 236. It is apparent that she moved around Britain with indomitable confidence, for she acquired on loan for a huge exhibition those paintings which she saw and admired but could not purchase. Over 100 paintings were shipped to Natal. On arriving in Pietermaritzburg the paintings were displayed in the Natal Society Library's building in Theatre Lane. For the following year lectures on art and music were arranged once a week as a draw card, and citizens were encouraged to choose and donate a painting from the exhibition. It appears from Council records that despite public enthusiasm, a permanent home for the Corporation pictures was not found for many years. After the loan collection returned to England, Mrs Tatham had to watch as a new collection, donated in 1923 by Lieutenant-Colonel Robert Whitwell, made its way onto the second floor of the City Hall, while the paintings that she and her supporters had amassed were hung in a tight arrangement in the stair-wells.

Whitwell's taste, particularly in post-Victorian British painting, was refined and selective. He donated a collection of superb vitality and quality which ranged from the Barbizon School to Oriental carpets. He also had donated a sizeable collection to the Durban Art Gallery, and gave several reasons for his gift to Pietermaritzburg. The most commonly repeated was gratitude for the warmth of hospitality he had received here. However, in correspondence with his friend, Sir Thomas Watt, the High Commissioner for South Africa, who also played an active role in securing the donation for the Capital, Whitwell wrote of his

> ... great admiration for General Botha and his efforts to bring the two white races in South Africa into the common fold [and] conceived the idea of expressing appreciation of the General's work by presenting a collection of pictures etc. to South African municipalities.

The Whitwell gift is particularly distinguished for including a painting entitled *L'Etude d'arbres en fleur* (*Study of trees in bloom*) by the Impressionist painter Alfred Sisley. Pietermaritzburg's good fortune in owning it is illustrated by the following quotation from Whitwell's correspondence with the Mayor in 1923:

> A certain very beautiful picture of mine by Sisley is at present in the Tate Gallery on loan for 12 months from 1st August of this year. It may be that the National Gallery would like to have it. If not, do not forget to claim it for Maritzburg on the 1st August 1924. I am not at all desirous of letting the Tate Gallery own it though they have often asked me for it.

Petite Venus debout, 1913.
Bronze by Pierre-Auguste Renoir.

8

Some six months after Whitwell began sending consignments of works to Pietermaritzburg, he gave the City another collection of 42 works, originally destined for Victoria in British Columbia. This fine collection included Wilson Steer's *The Sofa*, Sickert's *Asparagus* and Boudin's *Mussel Gatherers*. They had been offered to British Columbia on condition that a special fire-proof building was built to house them. On 6 December 1923 the time given by Whitwell to Victoria, British Columbia expired, and at midnight he sent to Sir Thomas Watt offering the works to Pietermaritzburg. The following afternoon a rather distraught Agent-General for British Columbia, telegram in hand, tried in vain to rescue the collection for his government. The scrupulous Whitwell wrote to Sir Thomas: 'I had to reply they were too late. There will be a hell of a row now between the two ends of the cable'. Through the persuasive appeals of Sir Thomas, Pietermaritzburg was not immediately required to build a new fire-proof gallery, but instead arrangements were made to cover windows on the second floor of the City Hall and an electric lift was installed. More than fifty years later this situation still persists.

Plans to accommodate the art collections of the City have been under way in various forms for 85 years. An almost successful attempt to build a gallery in honour of the 'fallen' in the Great War was narrowly defeated and the memorial arch in the Old Supreme Court gardens was built instead. A public swimming pool was the successful outcome of 'fierce town council debate' concerning a proposed art gallery to be built for the centenary celebrations in 1938. The most concrete evidence of Council's intention to build is a foundation stone which was relaid in 1977 for decorative purposes in the city councillors' car park. The inscription reads:

CENTENARY MEMORIAL ART GALLERY
This foundation stone was laid
on the 21st June 1939 by
General the Right Hon J C Smuts P.C., C.H., K.C., D.T.D.,
Deputy Prime Minister and Minister of Justice
of the Union of South Africa.

A new art gallery complex was again proposed for the sesquicentennial celebration of the City. In 1985, after twelve years of negotiation with the Government, the City Council finally acquired the Old Supreme Court and surrounding gardens together with the Old Presbyterian Church for this purpose. These buildings are planned as the new art gallery, sculpture garden and a visual arts training centre.

Consultant architects have been appointed and plans drawn up for the conversion of the buildings, but at the time of writing lack of Council funds appears to be the decisive factor in preventing the project from being satisfactorily completed. The Old Supreme Court building was nevertheless put to immediate use by Art Gallery staff who, with the help of 40 singing and brush-wielding women (employed on a government unemployment scheme), cleaned and renovated the derelict shell. Temporary exhibitions have been held which increased the Art Gallery's annual attendance by over 40 per cent, proving that ground floor and week-end access to the Art Gallery are vital.

Although unsuitable and cramped premises on the second floor of the City Hall have made the Art Gallery more inaccessible to the public than street-level premises, the collections owned by the Pietermaritzburg City Council are held in the highest esteem both nationally and internationally because of the calibre and aesthetic value of the works. The present cohesive character of the collections is the fruit of a proposal in 1961 by Councillor Pamela Reid to upgrade the Art Gallery. As a result the Council appointed its first curator, as well as a select committee, to study the City's painting and sculpture. Their working brief was the establishment of an art museum to function as a show-piece for art treasures of educational value. Mrs E. Lorimer, the curator of the newly established Art Gallery in Port Elizabeth, was also brought in to assist. The existing collections were radically culled (except for the Whitwell collection which was legally protected) and sold off at auction. The main casualties were South African and many Victorian paintings of minor relevance. At the time, the Victorian school commanded little academic interest, and market value had reached its lowest ebb. The moralistic, anecdotal and highly representational nature of the works was not fashionable. Many of Mrs Tatham's original selection of paintings paid the price of being too specifically Victorian in character for the progressive-spirited art panel, who worked feverishly to accession, catalogue and rationalize the collections into a coherent homogenous unit. The value of this exercise, despite the unfortunate sale of many Victorian paintings, is borne out by the clear vision which the City's art holdings now display. A disciplined collecting policy was formulated, based on what are now apparently some of the best examples nationally of 'modern' British, turn-of-the-century paintings.

The Gallery was re-opened in 1962 and officially named the Tatham Art Gallery in honour of the woman whose prodigious energy had been the main motivation behind the establishment of a gallery in Pietermaritzburg. A Purchase of Art Fund was instituted, and the City Council fully accepted the responsibility of running and maintaining an art museum. New paintings reflecting the more adventurous spirit of the selection committee were purchased, including works by Manessier and Ivon Hitchens. In 1968 the South African school of painting was re-established with a strong selection of the Everard family of woman painters. Not since the mid-1930s, when public reaction to expenditure on the proposed new art gallery was vociferous, had such an outcry been witnessed in the local Press. Many Pietermaritzburg citizens have subsequently spent years complaining to the Press of their sense of helpless indignation at the City Council's increasingly generous, progressive attitude, and determination to offer the capital a facility which is of primary educational importance.

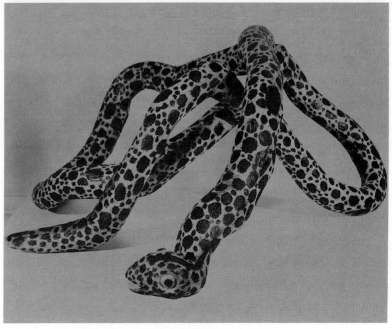

L'Etudes d'arbres en fleur, c. 1880. Oil on canvas by Alfred Sisley. [9]

The Sofa (detail), 1877. Oil on canvas by Phillip Wilson Steer. [10]

Edith picking flowers, 1904. Oil on canvas by Bertha King Everard. [11]

Four cairn terriers and a long basket, c. 1912. Oil on board by Duncan Grant. [12]

The Ring, c. 1890. Oil on canvas by John Bacon. [13]

The Snake, 1986. Wood carving by Vuminkosi Zulu. [14]

16

17

Untitled, 1987. Khoki pen on board by Derrick Nxumalo. [15]

Elephant with baby, 1979. Lino by John Muafangejo. [16]

Zulu doll, 1960. Msinga district (artist unknown). [17]

The re-establishment of the South African school, although initially extremely selective (in that the works of art purchased related predominantly to the existing British and French collections), nevertheless launched collecting policy in a new direction. The 'colonial' stamp, which hitherto had been an exclusive mark of the Gallery, had begun to change. There can be no doubt that the extraordinarily valuable donations amassed in the early part of this century will remain the core of a collection which has drawn academic attention to Pietermaritzburg's Art Gallery. Nevertheless, the general acceptance that the Art Gallery serves the community as a whole has led to the recognition that South African art in all its forms, including traditional and contemporary black art, has to be presented to generate interest and research into our visual cultural heritage. The change, it is hoped, reflects a broader overview of the rich diversity which has led, and will lead in the future, to a unique cross-cultural adaptation of our artistic output. If the Tatham Art Gallery succeeds in reflecting this ideal it will be an educational institution of which we can all be justly proud.

SLEEPY HOLLOW?

George Candy

O little town of Maritzburg,
how snugly dost thou lie –
a hazy mile of tar and tile
beneath the bright blue sky;
though sometimes when the wind forgets
to stir itself and jog
the air on high, the bright blue sky
is blotted out by smog.

We love thy busy streets where ears
grow deaf from hooters barking,
since every truck and car is stuck
because of double parking.
We love thy charming narrow lanes,
a hideaway from hawkers,
where air fans tall, built in the wall,
expectorate on walkers.

We love thy parks where on the green
young lovers kiss and cuddle,
and gentle 'Duzi winds its oozy
way through pool and puddle.
We love thy forest trails which give
a thrill to rural ramblers,
when forced to flee down scarp and scree
to 'scape the wheels of scramblers.

We love thy humid summer warmth –
no need for stove or sauna –
when roaches pry and flea and fly
augment the local fauna,
when termites to the nearest lamp
on fluttering wings are drawn,
and skeeters' hum keeps sleepers glum
and wide awake till morn,

when tempers in the torrid heat
approach an all-time high,
as 'neath the hills the city grills
like boer'wors at a braai.
Aware of these insomnious traits,
we find it hard to follow
why carping clowns from other towns
should call thee 'Sleepy Hollow'.

Afrikaans authors of Pietermaritzburg

Wilfred Jonckheere

Ina Rousseau.

D. J. Opperman while a
student at NUC.

Natal has sometimes been regarded as the Cinderella province of Afrikaans literature, a view which was certainly valid fifty years ago. However, since then some of the Afrikaans community's greatest poets have hailed from or have spent important parts of their creative lives in this province, more specifically in Pietermaritzburg.

As it happened, C. E. Boniface, author of the first comedy written in a mixture of Dutch and Afrikaans (*De Temperantisten*, 1832) settled in Pietermaritzburg in 1843. This brilliant Frenchman had learned Dutch and Portuguese at the Cape, where he was the soul of the local theatrical scene. He was equally well known in Cape Town as editor of several newspapers. In 1844 he and his friend C. Moll started Natal's first paper, *De Natalier*, which was superseded in 1846 by the bilingual the *Natal Witness — De Natalsche Getuige*. (Only in 1931, six years after Afrikaans became an official language, did the *Witness* drop its Dutch section.) Boniface's writings were mainly in Dutch, English and his native French, or a mixture of all three, and only in situations where he wanted to record scenes from daily life did he make use of Afrikaans, which was still in an early stage of development. In this vein, he published a conversation between two Afrikaans-speaking farmers, which has now become a unique piece of realistic writing and, ironically, the humble beginnings of Afrikaans literature in Natal.

The Anglicization of Pietermaritzburg, originally a Voortrekker town, and the growing popularity of Afrikaans, meant that Dutch as a spoken language — more so than its written form — was on the decline by the second half of the nineteenth century.

A handful of minor authors in Natal using Dutch or early Afrikaans are on record, and it is not until the mid-1940s, and the appearance of D. J. 'Dirk' Opperman (1914-1985), born on a farm in the district of Dundee, that the Natal Afrikaans community could make any claims to literary fame. Opperman's high school career in Vryheid was succeeded by studies toward a BA and later an MA at the then Natal University College in Pietermaritzburg (1935–1939), after which he taught Afrikaans at the local Hoerskool Voortrekker until 1945. Most of his later life was spent far from his native Natal, in the Western Cape (Cape Town, Stellenbosch), where he taught and trained generations of university students, some of whom followed in his footsteps as poets and literary critics.

Opperman, who is reckoned amongst the greatest Afrikaans poets, started his literary career in Pietermaritzburg. Some of his earliest poems appeared in the *Natal University College Magazine* (1935), of which he was to become the editor in 1938. Contributions of his also appeared in the *Natal Witness* and *Die Natalse Afrikaner*. Stimulated and inspired by G. S. 'Oom Gawie' Nienaber, who headed the Department of Afrikaans and Nederlands, Opperman tried throughout the war years to publish his first volume of poetry. He succeeded only in 1945, when *Heilige beeste* appeared in Cape Town. This collection immediately established his literary mastery. It also brought fame and success, and Opperman was awarded the highly coveted Hertzog prize two years later.

Heilige beeste proved to be a break with the preceding Dertiger (thirties) generation, which had raised Afrikaans poetry for the first time to an international standard. Opperman broke new ground with a compact, unembellished verse (yet rich in imagery), earthy and concrete, structured to contain multiple layers of meaning. His themes revolve around what he regarded as the three elementary forces: namely the earth, women, and the Great Spirit, all being the main driving forces of man. Whereas the sterile city with all its attractions is the great destroyer of man, woman is his regenerative force. A typical Natal feature of this volume is the epic poem 'Shaka', in five parts, on the life and death of this famous Zulu leader.

Opperman has proved to be one of South Africa's greatest and most prolific poets. Remarkably, many of his later poetical themes had their roots in literary work that was produced in Pietermaritzburg. He also wrote a number of verse dramas and critical essays.

Ina Rousseau's poetry is different in character, content and texture from Opperman's, being quieter and more introspective, like herself. Born in the Transvaal in 1926, Rousseau lived in Pietermaritzburg from 1966 until her departure in 1984 for Cape Town. Her self-effacing and withdrawn nature may have contributed to the fact that her poetry, published in four volumes, has remained relatively unknown and is certainly underestimated by many. In some ways, for example, thematically, it forms a link between that of Elisabeth Eybers, a Dertiger, and that of Antjie Krog or Lina Spies, both of a younger generation. The volumes published during her stay in Pietermaritzburg were *Taxa* (1970), *Kwiksilwersirkel* (1978), *Heuningsteen* (1980) and finally her *Versamelde gedigte 1945-1984*.

Rousseau excels in her fine command of language, which is apparent in her skilful play with images, multiple meanings and sound effects. At the same time a great sensitivity and an ability subtly to create atmosphere are apparent in her verse. She is a fine chiseller of language, chipping away all the unnecessary parts, leaving only the essence in a beautiful form. Small wonder that she often shows a predilection for sonnets and quatrains. Her themes vary from a longing in her earliest poetry for a lost paradise or purity, to a greater earthiness in her later verse on married life, the family and primordial nature (fossils and animals typical of the African continent). All this is at the same time counter-balanced by a reaching out to God.

The search for God is more prominent in the poetry of Sheila Cussons, born in 1922, who also has Pietermaritzburg links. Cussons hails from Piketburg but studied at NUC where she obtained a BA in Fine Arts in 1942, only a few years after Opperman qualified at the same institution. Like him, she also made her literary debut in this City, teaching until 1947 in the Fine Arts Department of the University. From then on most of her life was spent in Europe, primarily in Spain. Her poetry, collected so far in seven volumes, was published from 1970 onwards. In the first volume, *Plektrum* (1970), which is a harvest of 25 years of poetical activity, some of the poems originated in her Pietermaritzburg days and reflect her great love for the pictorial arts. Cussons, who became a fervent Roman Catholic in the mid-1950s, is largely known for her religious poetry and its unique expression in Afrikaans literature of her mystical longing for God. Her poetry is generally very highly acclaimed and its author is regarded as one of the foremost amongst the ever-growing group of female poets in this country.

Another Afrikaans writer, who lived in Pietermaritzburg from 1949 to 1959, is Henriette Grové (born 1922), wife of the well-known literary critic A. P. Grové, who taught in the University's Department of Afrikaans and Nederlands. Henriette Grové distinguished herself in the writing of children's tales, short stories, novels and dramas. Two of the latter originated in Pietermaritzburg. Written for radio, *Die goeie jaar* (1958) and *Die glasdeur* (1959) have farm settings and are fairly traditional in concept and content. Her best work is found in her collections of short stories and later radio dramas, for which she has won several literary prizes and awards. Some of the earliest stories appeared in *Kwartet* (1957). Grové is yet another case of a well known Afrikaans writer whose literary career started in Pietermaritzburg, but whose literary fame was only gained later in other places.

The same can be said of John Miles (born 1938), now of Johannesburg, who spent part of his early academic life

SINJALE

Deur die late stilte
van my kamer jaag
motors en teen die mure
wankel en tol
Plato se skadu-figure;

iemand op die ondervloer katrol
die drade van sy gloeilamp
uit my rug en maag;

om my skryn die kil morse-kode
van nagdiertjies
en soos oor Sappho twee duisend jaar gelede
kantel die Sewegesternte
oor na die dode.

D.J. OPPERMAN

Opperman wrote his poem while living in this gracious house at 20 Longmarket Street. Despite its literary associations and architectural merit, it was demolished in 1988.

20

ALAN PATON AND PIETERMARITZBURG

Colin Gardner

One of the striking features of Alan Paton's literary style (and a writer's style illuminates his deepest personality) is a certain vivid directness. When he portrays a person, an object or an event — whether in fiction or in biography — he manages somehow both to grasp firmly what he is describing and at the same time to allow it to be itself, to have a life of its own. He is especially skilful in bringing out the dignity of simple and natural things.

These characteristics, which helped to make him famous with the publication of *Cry, the Beloved Country* in 1948, are admirably displayed in *Towards the Mountain*, the first volume of his autobiography, published in 1980. In the opening chapters he evokes his childhood and young manhood in Pietermaritzburg in the first quarter of this century. He sketches the City itself — its central rectangular grid of streets, the countryside just outside which moved him so profoundly, some of the events that he remembers (for example, the soldiers from Fort Napier marching past his home in Pine Street and, when at ease, nodding and winking at young African women, to the disapproval of the white citizens). He also pictures the City as the stage upon which many significant formative incidents in his early life were acted out: he dramatizes, for example, an acutely embarrassing experience at a primary school in Berg Street, the effects upon his conscience of a very minor theft at a bakery in Retief Street, various quietly telling episodes at Maritzburg College, and midnight poetry discussions with Neville Nuttall in 'the little arched building among the graves' in the cemetery in Commercial Road. In these chapters Pietermaritzburg, brought to new life by Paton's pen, acquires an almost mythical quality. It enters the world of the literary imagination.

From school he went on to what was then the Natal University College and took a science degree and a teaching diploma. The University too — especially the Old Main Building, which was then the whole of the teaching institution — gains enrichment from Paton's memories and from his clear, glowing phrases. He taught at Ixopo for several years, then returned to the City to be a science master at Maritzburg College from 1928 to 1934.

After that he went north to be principal of Diepkloof Reformatory. When after 1948, however, he had become a professional writer and a public figure, he returned to Natal. He did not live in Pietermaritzburg again, but he was always within striking distance of it, and he visited it frequently — to deliver memorable political speeches, to see his sisters and other friends, to be honoured by his old school and by the University. He died in April 1988; the first of several memorial services for him was held at the Cathedral of the Holy Nativity in the City.

In *Cry, the Beloved Country* and in *Towards the Mountain* Alan Paton calls Pietermaritzburg 'the lovely city'. Clearly that loveliness was important to him; but at the same time he himself contributed to it, intensified it.

Alan Paton was born on 11 January 1903 at 19 Pine Street, and lived there until 1914. The house has suffered alterations since then.

21

in Pietermaritzburg where some of his first short stories originated. One of them, 'Lucy', is set in the City. Miles was to become one of the angry young men of Afrikaans literature. Some of his controversial modernistic short stories and novels were, and still are, banned.

In the course of the past fifty years a number of heads of the University's Department of Afrikaans and Nederlands and their colleagues have played a key role in Pietermaritzburg, either as stimulators of other authors, or as writers and critics in their own right. Gawie Nienaber, famous linguist and author of numerous books on Afrikaans language and culture, was vital in his encouragement of D. J. Opperman's talent. C. J. M. 'Stoffel' Nienaber, brother of Gawie, and his wife Miep also became well-known literary critics during their academic careers, which led to the publication of numerous books. Stoffel Nienaber's psychological novel *Keerweer* (1946), dealing with the inner life and fears of a mentally deficient person, heralded a breakthrough in Afrikaans literature, especially because the Afrikaans

prose of those days was still preoccupied with traditional characters and subjects. Illustrated by Sheila Cussons, this short novel is now regarded as a forerunner of the work of the Sestigers, which grew out of the younger writers' interest during the 1960s in existentialist philosophy and literature.

The present head of the Department of Afrikaans and Nederlands, W. F. Jonckheere, has also published extensively on Afrikaans and especially Dutch literature. A major portion of his writings discusses the works of the well-known Afrikaans author J. van Melle. Another member of the Department, H. J. Vermeulen (born 1942), has contributed to Afrikaans drama with his surrealistic play *Bus-stop* (1973).

One must agree with Stoffel Nienaber when he wrote that Natal — and for that matter Pietermaritzburg — was a type of training college for Afrikaans writers who subsequently settled elsewhere. Yet in this, the City has played an important role as the birthplace of many a significant work in Afrikaans literature.

Cinema and theatre in the 1920s and 30s

William Bizley

Scott's Theatre could count on visiting stars of international repute. It was the venue, for instance, for a touring Macbeth with Sybil Thorndyke and her husband Lewis Casson in the lead roles. Scott's Theatre managed to cater for every social rank in its small domain, having not only boxes and stalls and a dress circle, but also a 'gods' high in the rear of the building. You climbed up to it by dark wooden stairs and sat on hard wooden forms, but you could avenge yourself on the affluent below by chucking down toffee-papers during the course of the show.

What the intelligentsia of Maritzburg might not have conceded was that the chief passage of talent through the City came to the picture-houses, and that not because of the films they showed, but because of the international quality of the vaudeville troupes who did the circuit of bioscopes right through the Empire. Admittedly these were often the soapbox virtuosi who conjured and yodelled and played any tune on request, but along with them there came such durable stars as Harry Lauder, the De Groot string trio, and Heifitz himself who fiddled to the Grand Cinema in 1933, some five years after talkies had arrived.

There were two picture houses in Maritzburg through the silent era, the Rinko (so called because it was converted from a Victorian roller-skating rink) and the Excelsior. The latter, the 'bughouse' — built, it was said, out of wattle and daub — held the agency for MGM ('Makes Good Movies') but couldn't match the Rinko for the quality of its vaudeville. (Nor could the King's Theatre which came later, and whose gimmick was to place two huge blocks of ice in front of fans on either side of the stage and advertise itself as air-conditioned.) The Rinko catered for a noisy junior clientele in the afternoon (order sometimes restored by one of Maritzburg's best-known characters, the Mental Hospital inmate 'Tom Mix'); but in the evening it took on a metropolitan respectability so great that Mr Line the stockbroker (who imported lace curtains from England and carnation plants from France) could hire his own permanent row of seats for the entertainment of his friends. Mr Line himself slept peacefully through the film; when the talkies came he gave up his row, because he couldn't sleep through the show.

At the beginning of a Rinko evening you would be handed a programme announcing an overture to be performed by the Rinko's own orchestra. This was not a large ensemble, but its names engraved themselves on Maritzburg's memory — Stanley Ricketts on piano, Tommy Cragg on cornet, A. G. Lugsdin (later a City Councillor) on clarinet, and so on. In the silent era a good cinema orchestra varied the music with the action on the screen. The great master of fitting the tune to the film was William Bohm, playing on the Wurlitzer at The Prince's in Durban. Otherwise many a Natal cinema hired the local

piano teacher, who simply played unending syncopation for the length of the film. The vaudeville circuit included names of such prestige as the British baritone George Baker (who, after failing with opera, 'wowed' his audience at the Grand with the nightmare song from *Iolanthe*), Amelita Galli-Curci, Mark Hambourg, John McCormack, Richard Tauber, the D'Oyly Carte Opera Company, and Maritzburg's own 'girl made good', Garda Hall, daughter of the proprietor of Hall's Cycle Works in upper Church Street, who was now so illustrious that she recorded for HMV and lived in England.

Loud hammering accompanied the last silent film shown at the Rinko as the speakers were fixed in place for the first talkie, Al Jolson in *The Singing Fool*. This was cinematic progress, no doubt, but it was doom for the Rinko. Its great iron roof meant that the merest patter of rain drowned any talkie. Certainly it didn't survive the coming of the Grand, which opened in 1928, and was quite the most opulent building that Maritzburg had seen, with plush seating, ornate panels and even twin projectors — now you could show a film without stopping to change reels. To the Grand in the thirties came the dance bands of Jack Payne and Debroy Somers, and the military band of the Grenadier Guards.

The most memorable *non*-cinematic entertainers that passed through Maritzburg belonged to fairs and

The Grand Cinema in Commercial Road, which opened in 1928. It was designed in the opulent style of the period, though it was in a sad state of decay by the time of its demolition in the 1970s.

THE IMPERIAL HOTEL

J. André Labuschagne

The Imperial Hotel was originally a private residence built in 1877 by a Mr T. W. Woodhouse, who was later Mayor of Pietermaritzburg. In 1878 Mr George Thresh converted it into a hotel. It was named after the Prince Imperial of France who stayed there during the Anglo-Zulu War. One early traveller (1894) considered it '... a charming old hotel, an inn quite after Ruskin's heart'. A description of this old red-brick hotel followed:

> ...a rambling old house, which has been added to at various periods to suit the increasing number of visitors, and each wing has its own stoep and veranda. All the rooms are bright and airy, and nicely furnished, the walls of the large dining-room being adorned with branding horns and other trophies of the chase... The Imperial is to my mind the perfection of a colonial hotel, with its comfortable, airy, well-furnished bedrooms, excellent cuisine and scrupulous cleanliness.

Another visitor, also in 1894, spoke of it as a long, low, straggling building. Having passed the kitchen he came upon an uncovered space forming three sides of a quadrangle. Across the courtyard was a new building which resembled nothing so much as a Swiss chalet, built of 'clean, homely delicious pine wood'. The staircase of the upper rooms was outside and the roof above was slanting and eaved.

Three years later, in 1897, there were additions because of a general want of accommodation in the Colony. Remodelling was begun with the erection of a substantial double-storeyed block containing forty bedrooms. When the scheme was finished there were one hundred rooms, eighty-five of them bedrooms. Provision was made for a 50 ft. x 30 ft. dining-room. The plans were drawn by architect Powell and the building erected by the well-known Pietermaritzburg masonry firm, Jesse Smith and Son. The frontage was to be considerably extended and the general appearance improved and rendered 'a more handsome, solid, and substantial character'.

In 1902 the Imperial Hotel Co., Ltd, was formed and it soon proposed rebuilding the front portion, providing four large reception rooms on the ground floor and several complete suites of rooms on the first floor consisting of sitting room, bedroom and bathroom. There were to be several other rooms and lounges in the proposed building. In 1924 the hotel was taken over by Monsieur T. A. Ettelin who had been managing director of the Carlton Hotel in Johannesburg in 1909. The old building was eventually removed as the new building grew into the structure it is today.

The Imperial Hotel in 1938 during transition. The new wing, begun in 1928, is to the left, and contrasts with the earlier, stone-faced building. After World War II the latter was reconstructed to conform with the more recent structure.

24

circuses, which usually camped on the Market Square or in Victoria Road. Pagel's Circus hardly needed a show inside the tent, since Mr Pagel's ride through town with a lion was spectacle in itself, and the antics of Mrs Pagel — who had diamond rings on every finger, who sold the tickets but never gave change, who swore like a trooper and was more terrifying than the lions — drew an audience at the gate just to watch her alone. The fiery Pagels were apparently not daunted, in Maritzburg, by the proximity of that splendidly eccentric society, the Order of the Golden Age, which used to wring public conscience with a poster on which a tiger uttered pathetically, under the ringmaster's lash, 'How long, Oh Lord, how long?'

With the picture houses went a whole ritzy sub-culture of before-and-after-show snacks and teas. One got one's sweets at Lewis's Sweet Corner on the way to the theatre, but on the way back one had the choice of Christie's, the Creamery, Kean's or Perk's, all of which stayed open till 10 o'clock (the white waitresses being only too pleased to get the late-hour jobs in the years of the Depression). Excellent live music could be had from 'The Red Hungarian Band' which played on Fridays and Saturdays in the classy decor of the upstairs lounge of the Creamery. (A change of personnel later required that they rename themselves 'The Lisbon Gypsy Orchestra'.) Their *coup* was to legalize after-church concerts on Sunday nights by charging a shilling for entrance. No wonder Mr J. Withers Carter, who gave the organ recitals in the City Hall, had a variable audience. The Athenaeum and Christie's, the tea-lounges in Church Street, both employed, at various times, their resident bands. (Mrs Christie had another modest gimmick; she dressed her waitresses in the same colour as each day's table-linen.) The sub-culture in theatre music spilt over into a demand for sheet music and gramophone records, Simkins's for HMV, Kemp's for Columbia.

Strauss under the trees. Of a Sunday morning in the 1930s customers at the Botanic Gardens Tea-room were treated to an informal light classical music concert. The Curator played his records on his HMV wind-up gramaphone with its shell-shaped horn.

23

The pubs of Pietermaritzburg

Nancy Ogilvie

At the beginning of the century, Pietermaritzburg appears to have been a very thirsty place, because at almost every corner of our main streets one came across a public house where liquid refreshment could be enjoyed.

Pietermaritzburg at this time was a garrison town and Fort Napier saw many regiments come and go, so that there was no lack of healthy, thirsty young soldiers to fill the many pubs. Let us go back in time and imagine the Tommies taking a stroll through the two main streets to call in on some of the bars. Setting off from Fort Napier at a brisk pace along the road that crossed the railway line at the top of Longmarket Street, they would not have gone far before they came across the sign of a beautiful prancing black horse painted on the side of the building at the corner of Longmarket Street and West Street: this was the Black Horse Bar. This public house remained in the hands of the Froomberg family until a few years ago when the building was sold. The bar was filled with many historical relics, regimental badges and emblems and old photographs.

Having quenched their thirst here, the Tommies would then cross over Longmarket Street, and at the corner of Deane Street, they could see the sign of a rampant red lion hanging from an attractive red-brick building with a pan-tiled roof: the Red Lion Tavern. The proprietor at one time was a Mr Lee who lived with his wife and daughter on the premises. Crossing the street once more, they came to a family hotel known as the Commercial Hotel. It was a long, low building with a veranda on the street front. It later became a private boarding house called Whitby Lodge.

Further down Longmarket Street stood the Victoria Bar at the corner of Timber Street, which had a few rooms for lodgers. Allied House now stands on this site. Across the road from there one could see the Victoria Club, founded in 1859, with its initial effective maximum membership being put at sixty gentlemen. Here the officers from Fort Napier were made welcome.

Leaving the Victoria Bar the Tommies walked down to Commercial Road. In the direction of Loop Street stood the Crown Hotel, a busy spot, as it was from here that John Dare and later John Welch started off with the omnibus on the journey to Durban. (This hotel was run by Mr and Mrs Florey at one time.)

On returning to Longmarket Street the soldiers would find another hotel, the City and Port on Erf 27 Loop Street. J. C. Boshoff had owned this erf since 1846. By 1872 L. Torgins owned the Hotel on the Longmarket Street frontage, though by the end of 1875 E. Warwick had taken over the lease. He changed the name to the Woolpack. In 1879 H. P. Jones became the lessee. The property was sold to George Hesom in 1897. Padaychee's greengrocer shop was in this building for many years, as was D. M. Forbes' pharmacy. The rounded carriage-way door leading to the stables can still be seen on Longmarket Street.

The garrison's pub. The Black Horse Bar, on the corner of Longmarket and West Streets, was a favourite with the soldiers of Fort Napier, and retained its unforgettable ambiance into the late 1960s.

25

In the early 1850s, Pitchers' British Hotel in Longmarket Street was a popular rendezvous. This hotel later became the Plough Hotel. It was a wood and iron building and very popular with the farming community.

Further along Longmarket Street, at the corner of Archbell Street, was an interesting building originally owned in the early 1840s by J. N. Boshoff, and probably one of the first half-dozen substantially built houses in Pietermaritzburg. When Lieutenant-Governor Martin West arrived in December 1845 it was rented to him as a suitable Government House for £100 a year, and he died there in 1849. After his death the building became a superior type of boarding house and later became the Prince of Wales Hotel, proprietor G. Salmon.

Crossing through Market Square to Church Street, the Tommies would have seen the welcome sign of the Market Inn. After a visit there they could start their return trip to Fort Napier. Fortunately for them, there were several more pubs to visit *en route* before returning to Barracks. On the corner of Commercial Road was the Corner Bar.

Drinks could be served on a Sunday at the Star and Garter Hotel on the Durban Road, just outside the City's bounds. (26)

The Horse Shoe Hotel (with gable) in Church Street. (27)

The Horse Shoe Hotel prepared for a banquet to be held by the Natal Caledonian Society in the late 19th century. (28)

26

27

A little further on, next to Edgars, formerly Irelands, was another pub known as the Masonic Bar.

Across the street, on the site of the present Sanlam building, was a really enchanting hotel known as the Horse Shoe. Its large open entrance with its brightly tiled floor gave it a look of luxury and coolness. Inside the bar there was plenty of entertainment too, as the Horse Shoe was known to have the prettiest barmaids in town.

On leaving this fascinating place, the soldiers would work their way up Church Street where the Central Hotel would welcome them. At the corner of Raven Street was the Phoenix Bar, and on the opposite side higher up was the Carlton Bar. In 1887 it was a tavern known as the Waterloo Music Hall, owned by Mr Samuel Froomberg. A very dramatic incident occurred here in that year, when after a brawl at the Fort, a drunken party carrying rifles with bayonets fixed made their way down Church Street, passing Government House. Outside the Waterloo Music Hall they bayonetted a military policeman. Mr Froomberg, hearing the confusion, closed his door and held it shut with the aid of his wife and daughter. One of the soldiers thrust his bayonet through the door, scratching Mrs Froomberg's face. Then the drink-crazed men made off, to be finally captured at the Star and Garter on the Durban Road.

On the same side of the street at West Street corner stood the Royal Oak Bar. The original owner was Mr Zederburg and later on it was owned by Mr Benjamin. Today it is called the New Watson Hotel. Higher up Church Street towards the railway station was the Norfolk Hotel, which still exists, a useful stopover for railway travellers. The Tommies' final call could have been the Railway Bar at the station.

Numerous other bars lay dotted around the town, and two must be mentioned: one was the Polo Tavern at the corner of West and Greyling Streets near the old Polo Ground; the other was the First and Last in Victoria Road. From its name we know that farmers and travellers called there on their way into and out of town.

The opening and closing hours of pubs in the City were closely controlled; however, five km out of the City one could get drinks at any hour of the day or night, at Sutherland's Hotel on the Edendale Road, the Ketelfontein Hotel on the way to Hilton, the Cremorne Hotel on the Greytown Road and the Star and Garter on the Durban Road.

Did the existence of so many pubs first give rise to the City's sobriquet, Sleepy Hollow?

28

The second day of the
'Umsinduzi Swimming Sports'
in the early 1900s.

A panoramic view of The Oval during the New Zealand vs. Natal Rugby match played on 23 June 1928. Nowadays our City is not even a regular venue for provincial, let alone international, sport.

CHAPTER FOURTEEN

Sport and Recreation

The Sporty Hollow!

Robert Haswell

Pietermaritzburg is indeed located in a hollow, but far from that setting inducing lethargy, the City can in fact lay claim to the title of a sporting capital. After all, it has given birth to two of the world's most popular and formidable feats of endurance — the Comrades and Duzi Marathons; it has produced two world motorcycle racing champions in Kork Ballington and Jon Ekerold; it has in Maritzburg College a school outstanding in sporting prowess; and it has aspirations to being the basketball capital of the country.

Maritzburg College Old Boys have captained South Africa at cricket (Jackie McGlew and H. G. Deane) and rugby (Philip Nel), and in all College has produced some ninety Springboks. Keith Oxlee captained the Natal rugby team and was vice-captain of the Springbok team, while both Darryl Bestall and Brian Edwards captained Springbok hockey teams. Brian Irvine, head prefect in 1950, went on to captain both the Natal rugby team and the Junior Springboks, and to become President of the Natal Rugby Union. Craig Jamieson, head prefect in 1979, is the current Natal rugby captain and the tradition seems sure to continue. In 1987 Maritzburg College boasted eleven South African Schools players — four each in rugby and basketball, two in cricket, and one each in squash, polocrosse and hockey. In addition, Jonty Rhodes was selected as captain of the South African Schools hockey XI and vice-captain of the corresponding cricket XI, 'Vimmy' Visser captained the South African Schools basketball team, and Brent Catterall captained the South African Schools rugby XV, to make it a bumper and surely unequalled year for College.

The Pietermaritzburg campus of the University of Natal has also produced a significant number of Natal rugby players, coaches and administrators. Since its inception in 1912 the University rugby club has regularly produced the most exciting young players in the province, but perhaps even more importantly two of its players, Basil Medway and Peter de Villiers Booysen, made outstanding contributions to the administration of rugby in the province, and rose to become presidents of the Natal Rugby Union. Two Varsity players of the 1930s, 'Skonk' Nicholson and Izak van Heerden, became legendary coaches in this country and also helped spread the game in South America.

Although there is currently a paucity of Maritzburg cricket players in the Natal and Springbok XIs, it should be remembered that the names Jackie McGlew, Roy McLean and Vincent van der Bijl are known wherever the game is played. Perhaps the recent decline in the local production of provincial cricketers is partly due to the decline in the number of provincial matches played in the Capital. Year in and year out our schools produce the cricketing talent, and in the Oval and Jan Smuts Stadium we have two outstanding venues. Thus it would seem that the current decline is due to forces beyond the City.

244

Basketball evolved in the USA in the 1890s and was named because peach baskets were all that was available for use as goals in a YMCA gym. Interestingly, the pioneers of the game in Maritzburg played rudimentary basketball during the gym classes run by John Stirling in the Buchanan Street YMCA in 1943-44.

In 1953 the first basketball team, the YMCA Comets, was formed by John Armitage and Albert Feinstein. The other original Comets were Ted Clarke, Mike van Rensburg, Ron Stone and Val Ashworth. Apart from one game in the City Hall in 1954, the Comets had to travel to Durban for games. Nonetheless they won the Natal League and knock-out trophies for seven consecutive years. Increasing frustration with the amount of travel, and Durban's dominance of the Natal team's management and coaching, resulted in the formation in 1963 of a new association, Northern Natal, based in Maritzburg.

In order to promote the game the Comets disbanded and four new clubs were formed: Dynamoes (led by Errol Mantle and Gisbert Dittmar); Harlequins (led by Val Ashworth and Bert Bowen); Wanderers (led by Barry Harrison and Errol Todd); and Collegians (led by Ted and Billy Clarke and Mike de Klerk). Courts were marked out in the Arts and Crafts Hall of the Showgrounds; on a concrete court laid by the players themselves at the Wanderers Club; and even on a concrete slab in Hay Paddock. Since then the University Sports Union and the YMCA have provided players and spectators with ever-improving facilities. At present 36 teams, divided into three men's and three women's leagues, compete under the auspices of Natal Midlands (the name change took place in 1983).

Natal Midlands club and representative teams have enjoyed considerable success. In 1971 Harlequins (men) won the National Club Championships, and in 1987 Natal Midlands (men) won the National Championship. The local University team won the South African Universities title (men) in 1980 and 1986. Even more impressive is the number of Midlands players who have been awarded Springbok colours: 13 men and 7 women.

Maritzburg's position as the capital of basketball is further enhanced by its dominance of the game at school level. In 1974 Alexandra High, St. Charles College and Technical High School (now Linpark) launched school

A uniquely Maritzburg College tradition? On Friday nights coloured rugs and blankets are spread on the stands to reserve seating for Saturday's rugby matches.

3

basketball in the City. With Eric Frangenheim, Carl Pachonick and Darryl Smith at the helm the game grew steadily, and by the late 1970s six boys' schools had adopted the game, and Val Fowler had done much to stimulate schoolgirl basketball in the City and indeed throughout the country.

Carl Pachonick's enthusiasm and coaching skill resulted in his school, Alexandra High, emerging as the basketball powerhouse, especially during 1978-1985. In 1985 Maritzburg College managed for the first time to defeat Alexandra High at basketball, and the bi-annual clash between these two schools is now a major event on our sporting calendar, attracting some 2 000 spectators into the indoor Sports Centre.

The enthusiasm of the basketball fraternity, and their determination to prove that Maritzburg can stand alone, surely carries a message for all sportsmen and women in the City. The success achieved by the Natal Midlands

Most of the City's sports facilities are located along the banks of the Msunduze and are thus within the floodplain! This aerial view shows Collegians Club, Woodburn Rugby complex and the YMCA in the foreground, and Kershaw, Alexandra and Camps Drift Parks in the background[4].

Pietermaritzburg's three Springbok cricketing Macs at a Merchiston School reunion in 1951. *Left to Right*: Roy McLean, Frank Lambert (national selector), Jackie McGlew, Reg Evans (Headmaster) and Cuan McCarthy[5].

Edendale's Joe 'Axe Killer' Ngidi, the former (black) South African welterweight champion[6].

4   Women's Hockey Association adds further strength to the break-away argument.

Motor racing in the Capital also has a long and interesting history. Many readers will remember races at the Roy Hesketh circuit, and some will even remember those at the Alexandra Road Circuit. Kork Ballington and Jon Ekerold are local riders who won world motor cycle championships, and the national successes of the Gray family have kept the tradition alive, despite the present lack of a local circuit.

There are many other sports in which Maritzburg has excelled, but space dictates the mentioning of only a few here. Cycle racing has been a favourite local pastime, and the City has produced some outstanding performers. In the field of amateur boxing the City has a long and succesful history. Some will recall the skills of Laurie Backhouse (junior), the Knoessen brothers (Paul and Ricky) and Norman du Plessis (senior and junior).

Although the story of sport in Maritzburg contains many triumphs, it is also marred by several lamentable chapters. Thus two locals, Joe 'Axe Killer' Ngidi and Leslie McKenzie, both world class boxers, were obliged to seek recognition overseas because their non-white status precluded them from competing against 'white' champions in 'white' venues. Towards the end of his career, Ngidi boxed in Britain and Australia. Similarly, to overcome the restrictions of segregated boxing, Mackenzie had to campaign overseas where he became the leading contender for the British Empire Welterweight Title. Tragically we will never know just how far either he or Ngidi could have gone had they not been denied opportunities while in their prime. In the field of weightlifting, Leslie's younger brother Precious, who also grew up in Maritzburg, was clearly the best in his division in South Africa in 1960, but, despite earlier promises, an all-white team was selected to 'represent the country' at the Rome Olympics. In frustration Precious emigrated to England and won Commonwealth Gold Medals in 1966, 1970 and 1974. The 'Precious McKenzie story ranks right alongside that of Basil D'Oliviera as an indictment of discrimination in sport.

It can thus be concluded that: Maritzburg's sporting fraternity has excelled in those sports which make use of 'natural' facilities, such as rivers and roads, rather than expensive stadiums; Maritzburg sport can survive and prosper on its own; we should never again allow discrimination, whether it be based on race or sporting affiliation, to deny sportsmen and women the opportunity to reach their full potential; and, it is perhaps high time that Maritzburg took stock of its sports strengths and weaknesses, not so much to copy other places, but rather to further strengthen and market its assets.

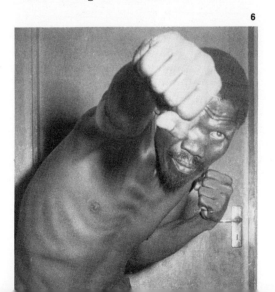

245

Problems of black sport in an apartheid city

Chris Merrett

Given the range of problems facing South Africa, study of the development of sports facilities might appear somewhat irrelevant: a survey conducted in the Eastern Cape townships in 1981 showed that recreational facilities ranked fourteenth in importance among twenty-one categories of which housing, jobs, electricity, transport, lighting and roads were rated more highly. However, consideration of sport is of value when it is assessed as an indicator of the way resources are allocated, and while this is a national phenomenon many revealing aspects are apparent at the local level.

It is generally accepted that sport is a major component of the white South African way of life: rugby has often been described as a national religion and a form of social and political expression. All sports, and rugby in particular, have been used to emphasize white virility and dominance in the South African political order. More recently it has been used as a form of escapism; and where possible as a gesture of defiance towards those trying to isolate South Africa. Just as white South Africans have expropriated labour, space and resources to build a dominant position, so they have appropriated and dominated sport. The economic structure of the apartheid state has rewarded whites with health and leisure while the proletariat, largely black, has lacked political power to achieve satisfactory material needs. Poor diet, disease, lack of facilities and racial prejudice have all hampered the development of black sport. This stimulated the development in the 1960s and 1970s of anti-apartheid (or non-racial) controlling bodies espousing the sporting boycott and arguing that recreation could not be divorced from the general liberation struggle. Such bodies have attained considerable influence in Pietermaritzburg sport.

Enormous capital resources have been poured into white sport. The most important resultant feature of the local sporting landscape is the 'Club', usually based on rugby, cricket, bowls, golf, tennis or hockey. These institutions are an important symbol of white power, economic dominance and racism. Their immaculate buildings and facilities in the choicest locations are founded upon cheap black labour, but by legal, social and economic sanctions they are mostly closed to all but whites. Their officials and members have frequently been well placed in municipal politics and local business and there is considerable evidence to show that attractive financial assistance to them is a time-honoured Maritzburg tradition. The white fraction of the municipal population has declined steadily from one-half at the turn of the century to about one-third at present.

White sportspeople have enjoyed permanent, quality facilities with support from the Corporation since Alexandra Park was established in 1863. Cricket, golf, athletics and cycling were accommodated and the Pietermaritzburg Sports Association, an autonomous management body, was established in 1901. In the same year the Scottsville Racecourse was acquired from the Grand Stand Company. A bowling green was established in 1904 in Alexandra Park and the Msunduze was cleared to provide five kilometres of boating. In 1908 the Scottsville Golf Course was awarded rent free to the Maritzburg Golf Club, and before the First World War Alexandra Park was extended north of the river for hockey. The aftermath of the War was the era of the private club and saw the foundation of Kershaw Park, 1917 (Maritzburg Lawn Tennis Association); Maritzburg East Bowling Club, 1917; Maritzburg West Bowling Club, 1921; Maritzburg Croquet Club, 1921; and Victoria Bowling Club, 1922. From 1925 to 1926 rugby grounds were established at Woodburn and an open-air pool at Alexandra Park.

In each case land and considerable financial aid were provided and all these facilities remain well established today. In some instances the loans were large: by 1929 the Maritzburg Golf Club and the Maritzburg Lawn Tennis Association were in debt to the Council to the tune of £3 250 and £2 900 respectively. In the cases of golf and rugby no security was provided and in 1934 the City Treasurer was threatened with surcharge for exceeding provincial ordinances to an amount of £3 500, although a rectifying ordinance was passed in 1935. Such loans were defended as a means of improving derelict land but they also implied undisturbed tenure and a pre-emptive right to land. The history of the loans was one of slow redemption with deferments, failure to pay off the principal and extensions. Kershaw Park and the now defunct Mountain Rise Golf Club (whose debt of £23 000 was written off in 1961) loom large in the City Auditor's reports before and after the Second World War. In the post-war period, particularly large sums were extended to the City Sporting Club (whose rental of the racecourse was remarkably small), the Country, Wanderers, Lynwood and Collegians Clubs, Maritzburg Croquet Club, Maritzburg Rugby Sub-Union, Maritzburg Golf Club and most bowling clubs.

White sports bodies also received regular if modest grants. In 1930 the Country Club was granted land at Ketelfontein and the Mountain Rise Golf Club was established in 1932, initially for white municipal employees. In the meantime facilities at Alexandra Park were regularly extended or improved: for example, the Burger Street hockey fields (in 1935) and cricket and cycling facilities. During the War repayments were suspended or reduced on the grounds of declining membership. The overall impression is thus one of the transfer of considerable amounts of capital and land from the common municipal wealth into the hands of a racially defined, politically dominant élite. Most of this wealth remains entrenched today mainly in a zone of recreational activity alongside the river, although some white facilities have been overtaken by urban expansion: two polo grounds (by housing and industry) and two golf courses (by industry and the University).

There is an absence in Pietermaritzburg of municipal facilities such as those found in social democracies which have played a part in redistributing resources and creating opportunity. The history of sports facility provision for Indian and coloured Maritzburgers shows startling contrasts compared to that for whites: tardy provision, under-capitalization and impermanence. General sports fields were provided at Chatterton Road and Fitzsimmons Road but specialized facilities were absent. In 1913, when the Buchanan Street indoor baths were being repaired, the head of the Waterworks Section reported: 'I would like to see some provision made for the practice of this healthful exercise [swimming] by the coloured section of the community, even if it were only by adapting a portion of the Msunduze River for this purpose. The cost would not be much'. The following year there was a proposal that a bankside shelter be erected but no evidence of its building. Ten years later a second white, open-air facility was built at Alexandra Park. In 1928 consideration was given to the use of Buchanan Street Baths by the coloured community, but in 1929 it was handed over for the use of white schoolchildren.

By 1930 the Indian Sports Association was in receipt of an annual grant of £10 and it and the Coloured Sports Ground Association were granted loans of about £600. In 1937 J. V. Marsh donated £1 000 as a contribution towards a coloured swimming bath but the offer was rejected, 'it being felt that the cost of erecting and running a Bath would be too great a burden on the City'. The previous year the white Country Club had been granted a £500 loan for a bowling green. The impermanence of coloured and Indian facilities was demonstrated in 1939 when the Coloured Sports Ground was moved to Berg Street from Pine Street; and Indians were allowed use of the old Native Sports Ground east of Fitzsimmons Road. Cricket and soccer fields were provided at Camps Drift in 1945. By July 1947 £14 570 was owed to the Municipality by sports bodies, all of them white except the Coloured Welfare (Sports) Association (£219). In 1948 the former municipal dump at Chatterton Road was levelled as a coloured sports ground. It was handed over, as a bare field, in 1952, the same year in which yet another addition to the Alexandra Park complex, Jan Smuts Stadium, was completed and a year after a floodlit soccer match had been held at the Oval. Large loans to white sports bodies continued, and in 1961 a third swimming pool for whites was opened, in Pine Street.

The first substantial sports complex outside the white sphere was opened at Northdale in 1963. In 1965 further space was made available at Chatterton Road and in September the Berg Street swimming pool was built. With the official opening of Northdale Stadium in 1966 the Berg Street recreation ground was closed, symbolizing the move of facilities to the suburbs and the hardening of racial divides. The Woodlands Sports Centre and the R. G. Pilditch swimming pool were commissioned in 1968, although vandalism soon forced their closure for a year; and the consequent handover of the Brookside ground to the Maritzburg Indian Sports Association in 1971 had to be postponed because of subsidence. The Olympic size pool at Northdale was handed over in July 1978 and during 1986 a second sports complex, at Khan Road, was opened.

The price of acceptable facilities in terms of the ideology of the anti-apartheid sports movement has been high: such facilities have been placed in racially defined suburbs while white sportspeople have continued to benefit from long established facilities in central, accessible areas. Clear attempts have been made by the Municipality to place new facilities under the control of groups with an interest in racial separation, such as the Coloured Local Affairs Committee (CLAC) and the Indian Local Affairs Committee (ILAC). The imprint of apartheid upon sport in Pietermaritzburg has thus ironically hardened. Facilities used by anti-apartheid groups which remain in the City are temporary: Tatham Memorial Ground is threatened by road development; Brookside is earmarked for a bus station; and Chatterton Road's future is uncertain. In each case impermanence has provided an excuse to avoid capital investment. By contrast, in 1982 R27 000 was spent on upgrading floodlights for the Jan Smuts cricket ground, and this was one of the reasons why a match involving the sanctions-busting Arosa Sri Lankan team was vigorously boycotted in 1983, causing an outburst from the white establishment.

In 1896 it was noted in the Mayor's Minute that blacks were not permitted to use Pietermaritzburg's footpaths. It is consequently hardly surprising that the City's attitude to black recreation has been characterized by racism, paternalism and political and social expediency. Initially the only contact between blacks and Pietermaritzburg's recreational facilities was as a result of the cheap black

African labourers planting grass on The Oval in preparation for the 1902 cricket season.

AURORA CRICKET CLUB

Chris Merrett

Aurora, the multiracial Pietermaritzburg cricket club, was formed in early 1973 to challenge the idea that mixed sport was illegal and to test the attitude of white dominated sporting bodies. A careful approach was made for affiliation to the Maritzburg Cricket Union (MCU) in order to ensure that if Aurora's case were rejected it could only be on racist grounds. In an unusual move the MCU passed it on to the Natal Cricket Association (NCA) for advice. Considerable press coverage ensued and the white provincial and national cricketing bodies refused to make unequivocal policy statements, being wary of confrontation with Government. In spite of warnings from Government, the MCU admitted Aurora to its second division on 11 September 1973, having been advised by lawyers that the club could play on public grounds. It thus became the first mixed club to be admitted into a white league, and there was considerable Press speculation on the intriguing possibility of fixtures with the Police Cricket Club, which had abstained from voting.

The reaction from Government was aggressive, interpreting the move as a challenge to its 'multinational' policy, referring to Aurora members as politically motivated agitators working toward confrontation, and arguing that it had to consider interests higher than sport. Friendly matches passed without incident: against a University of Natal Invitation Side at Dalry Park, at which uninvited spectators had to be turned away; versus Michaelhouse at Balgowan; and against a Kloof Invitation Side. A projected match against a touring Rhodesian Stragglers team was cancelled as some of the visiting players were wary of upsetting the South African Government. Dr Koornhof, Minister of Sport, invited three club committee members to Pretoria, entertained them at his home and tried to persuade them to withdraw Aurora from the white league. After a general meeting of the club it was decided to defy the Government. The latter issued Proclamation R228 (1973) altering the provisions of the Group Areas Act in an attempt to prevent Aurora playing, although lawyers felt that multiracial sport had not been made illegal as the Proclamation was vaguely worded and probably *ultra vires*. Dr Koornhof saw the situation differently, though in a statement devoid of any measure of prophecy: 'I have had Aurora googlies and bumpers . . .

but I am still here and not out. Figuratively speaking I am going to score a century for my country and get us back into world sport'.

Bad weather thwarted Aurora's first appearance in white league cricket until 13 October 1973, when University of Natal was met at Alexandra Park, and Aurora became the first club to play a multiracial match on a public ground in South Africa. During the day policemen had been spotted lurking in bushes around the ground and watching the match from a distance through binoculars. At 5.15 p.m. they took the names of the players and some spectators. They temporarily confiscated the film of a press photographer, took the name of the twelve-year-old scorer and had to be persuaded not to remove the scorebook. No prosecution followed, probably through Government concern about publicity.

Aurora continued its multiracial activities under the MCU, but the basic structure of Pietermaritzburg cricket remained unaltered. One team, Voortrekker, twice failed to fulfil fixtures against Aurora in the light of the Koornhof proclamation. In a bizarre twist to the normal traditions of the game, a team list was handed in to the police after each league to keep them away from play. In the season 1976-77 'normal' cricket was played by amalgamating the white, African and non-racial bodies, but few clubs were mixed and various tensions caused its collapse before the end of the season. The main cause was the general nature of apartheid society and more specifically its intrusion onto cricket grounds. Most black clubs withdrew to form the South African Cricket Board affiliated to the South African Council on Sport (SACOS). Although Aurora continued to play under the banner of the MCU, opinion within the club doubted if it was achieving its original aim: no other club had followed its lead; normal social relations had proved difficult in terms of the Liquor Act; and racism had appeared in the form of selection policy and personal insults. Encouraged by the clear non-racial principles and practice of the SACOS aligned bodies, Aurora affiliated to the Maritzburg District Cricket Union in June 1978. It so became and remains to date a significant contributor to anti-apartheid sport in Pietermaritzburg in terms of both players and administrators.

8

Aurora Cricket Team 1973.

Left to right. Back row: Vish Chetty, Mike Hickson, Deva Pillay, Andy Manson, Deva Moodley, Tony Croudace.

Second row: Farouk Ally, Neil Painter, Roy Bunwarie (President), Gopaul Manicum (Captain), Chris Davis (Secretary), Justin Gordon.

Front: Morgan Pillay (Scorer)

labour policy. The Parks Curator commented on the racecourse in 1902 that 'owing to the great scarcity of native labour, there is much I should like to have done that I have been unable to do'. The importance of black labour is emphasized by a report by the Borough Engineer six years later indicating that it was twice as productive as a white labour gang. It is doubtful if the children's playground constructed in the Market Square for 'Citizens and Visitors' was intended for anyone but whites. During the 1920s a sports field for blacks was provided east of Fitzsimmons Road, and in the financial year 1929/30 the Native Football Association was awarded a grant of £10. In the same year a Council grant was made to the Maritzburg and District Bowling Association to assist in the entertainment of visiting British bowlers. In January 1933 the Edendale Road Native Soccer Ground was provided for the Maritzburg and District Native Football Association (later the African Football Association) at a time when £35.17.11 of the Native Affairs Department revenue account of £12.776.1.9 (0,3 per cent) was spent on recreation. In 1930 cricket equipment was supplied and used at the Fitzsimmons Road ground. Although the Native Village (named Sobantu in 1946) was founded in 1928, a start was not made on the football ground until 1935.

It is not unreasonable to suppose that the gradual provision of facilities in the 1930s was connected to white complaints about black use of the Market Square on Sunday afternoons for 'political meetings, rough and ready cycle races and football matches'. 'Native dances' were encouraged on Sunday afternoons on open ground next to the Berg Street Men's Hostel while the Berg Street Native Recreation Ground, which had facilities for the African Tennis Association, was opened in 1938. The pavilion at the Tatham Memorial Ground was built in 1937 to serve two soccer pitches (Bantu Football Association) and an athletics/cycle track. Black facilities emerged at least partially from white fears that central areas would be used by blacks for recreation and from a paternalistic urge to provide for 'less developed' groups. Paternalism is evident in the sports days organized to celebrate imperial events such as Royal Weddings and Coronations: annual jamborees, and the soccer competition for the Governor General's Silver Jubilee Shield persisted until the late 1950s. The annual sports day in 1950 gave the Native Affairs Department the opportunity to comment: 'The meeting was well attended and the Natives were very well behaved'. Self-satisfaction was added to paternalism with a report from the same department the previous year: 'When conducted round the various Municipal Native Institutions in the City visitors are loud in their praise of the amenities offered, and say that it is not hard to see why this City should have earned such a good reputation for inter-racial harmony'. A more revealing official view is, however, provided by the admission that 'The Council has continued to give its full support to sport to entertain the Natives in their leisure hours, and so keep them from drifting to political meetings'.

9

Siyabonga Nkosi bowls under the critical eye of Aurora coach Roger Friedman.

In the meantime the Edendale Road football ground had been expropriated by South African Railways in 1951 and the players moved to a ground near the Indian School in Greytown Road. Temporary facilities were found at Woodburn in 1956, but the short era of Africa facilities in the City was coming to an end. The Maqaleni ground was expropriated for the National Road in 1961, for example. The new black suburb of Imbali was proclaimed in 1965 and soccer field and boxing ring were finally provided in 1971, by which time African use of the Tatham Memorial Ground had ceased. On 1 August 1973 the City's responsibility for urban African affairs was handed over to the Drakensberg Bantu Administration Board.

The advent of the Administration Boards signalled a hardening of long-established economic differentials and spatial segregation. During the 1980s control was reformed in such a way as to make black South Africans acceptable as participants and spectators at many sports venues. At the same time for residential purposes they are still pushed as far as possible from the white City centre to peripheral locations dependent upon public transport. Thus 'the lives of poor people in cities are as they are because they form part of a wider whole'. The very existence and control of space creates inequality, and in Pietermaritzburg this is reinforced by an ideology whose political economy demands a geography of control.

This obliges black citizens to spend considerable portions of their lives commuting from work to their dormitory suburbs, which are required to be self-financing from an extremely narrow resource base with revenue from rents, beerhall profits and, in the past, labour regulation. Some of the profits from inebriation thus manifest themselves as sports facilities. However, from 1981–1983 nothing was spent on sport and recreation by the Drakensberg Bantu Administration Board, although a levy had raised over R1 million. From 1983 to 1985 levy income reached R3 million and expenditure on sport amounted to R4 million, of which 58 per cent was spent on capital development. Recreation was allocated a mere 1,5 per cent of the budget to which beer hall profits made the largest local contribution. Imbali Stadium is reported to be in a decaying state, able to accommodate only a fraction of its supposed 5 000 capacity. Although soccer is the dominant township sport, the stands at Imbali Stadium are rotten and there is no weather protection, nor floodlights as for example are found at Woodburn Stadium, the white rugby ground, Jan Smuts cricket stadium and Collegians Club tennis courts. Sobantu with 8 180 residents (1980 census) has a soccer field, tennis court and a children's playground.

Those areas of Greater Pietermaritzburg which fall under the KwaZulu Government are also poorly served. Wadley Stadium and two other grounds have to cope with 53 teams from the Edendale Football Association. Wadley has no showers, security fence, nor shelter for spectators. There has been conflict over the use of Woodburn Stadium by black soccer largely because of the objections of neighbouring whites. The 260 000 Africans of the Greater Pietermaritzburg area are provided with eight soccer fields and six tennis courts. The Indian/coloured section of the community (63 000) has eleven soccer fields and four tennis courts, two squash courts, one facility each for bowling, hockey and rugby and two swimming baths. Fifty-three thousand whites have at least seventeen bowling greens, forty-four tennis courts, eleven hockey fields, eight rugby fields (four floodlit), nine soccer fields, eighteen squash courts and three swimming pools (one heated). Swimming has always been a particularly sensitive sport and suggestions that white facilities be desegregated have met considerable opposition: in a straw poll in the City Council in 1982 desegregation of Alexandra Pool was rejected; the use of a referendum as a delaying tactic was however avoided, and at the end of summer 1986 the pool was opened to all of Pietermaritzburg's people.

As one would anticipate, disparities at school level are just as great. While white parents assume that their children will receive high quality sports instruction, black schools have struggled to provide the most fundamental recreational resources for their pupils. Black schools in the Pietermaritzburg area often lack all facilities except the bare veld and homemade goalposts which constitute the soccer pitch. Leading white schools each have a wider range of sports facilities and equipment than entire black suburbs.

The carefully tended turf of a white school's soccer or rugby fields, compared with the rough grass and stones of the black, is a graphic indication of the social and political process. Apart from a few desegregated private schools, education in the Pietermaritzburg area is rigidly segregated: in 1982/3 the national per capita allocation by race group was R1 385 for whites, R871 for Indians, R593 for coloured children and R193 for 'non-Bantustan' Africans. In 1983 the Government spent R9,84 on sports facilities for each white child, but only R0,42 on each African child. The 1980 HSRC report on sport found that 72 per cent of all school sports facilities were possessed by whites. This position can be illustrated by Pietermaritzburg examples. In 1971 white schools controlled 89 per cent of Pietermaritzburg facilities; although by 1985 this had declined to 63 per cent. Maritzburg College has facilities for eighteen sports including shooting. Raisethorpe has nine and Georgetown High only one of its own. This crude assessment of quantity ignores quality, where the disparities are as great. For example, one of the problems faced by black schools is the fact that their sports facilities are often the only ones in the area. Consequently, and particularly at weekends, they are invaded by local residents who use them in an uncontrolled fashion.

As a result of the history of expropriation of economic and social resources, sport has become the object of civic struggle in the name of social justice. This initially manifested itself in support for the anti-apartheid South African Council on Sport (SACOS) and latterly for community organizations directly or indirectly linked to the United Democratic Front. This development explains why belated attempts by white-controlled sports bodies to entice blacks into their ranks have failed signally: discrimination in sport has become indissolubly linked to political, social and economic inequity. Only whites have ever enjoyed municipal political rights; while Indian or coloured electors have since the early 1970s voted for, or more probably boycotted, representatives on discredited Local Affairs Committees which have only a token, observer status on the City Council. Whites have controlled both the revenue raising process and allocation of funds, and the distribution of sports facilities and other symbols of social welfare is clearly linked to the concentration and exercise of political power.

The Comrades Marathon

Mark Coghlan

At the start of the 1986 Comrades Marathon in Pietermaritzburg, a sea of over 10 000 runners stretched back hundreds of metres from the City Hall. The scene was lit by banks of floodlights, and television crews on tall platforms recorded the drama for those who chose to remain in bed. Runners milled around in tense excitement, warmly-clad spectators crowded every vantage point, and officials applied the final touches to another smooth start. Traffic police manned intersections to clear the way for the huge field. In the pre-dawn darkness, many athletes had donned T-shirts and arrived as early as 4 a.m. to ensure a favourable position. Families and friends bade their charges a final farewell, and as the City Hall clock chimed 6 a.m., a tape-recording of the late Max Trimborn's traditional 'cock crow' released the tidal wave of athletes down Commercial Road.

Led by a phalanx of escort vehicles, the 'hares' sped out of the city centre, across the Victoria Bridge, and over the Scottsville ridge, past the University of Natal. At the City Hall stragglers were still passing the start banner 15 minutes after the gun. Beyond Scottsville, the field joined the Old Main Road near the Market, and left the City at the crest of Polly Shortts Hill, *en route* for Kingsmead Stadium some 90 kilometres away in Durban.

The year before, the 1985 Jubilee Comrades Marathon had started in Durban, and when the leader, Bruce Fordyce, and the weary thousands behind him crested Polly Shortts, the most gruelling test on the up-run, to see the City spread out below, it was a welcome sight at the end of a long run. The runners wound their way through the Mkhondeni industrial area, down Oribi and Jesmond Roads, finishing at the Jan Smuts Stadium in Alexandra Park. Cheering crowds lined the route and refreshment tables 'refuelled' depleted runners. A large and enthusiastic crowd greeted Fordyce's 5th successive win, and as finishers streamed onto the final grass circuit, the stadium was a bustling crush of humanity.

On a smaller scale, these scenes have been repeated on 61 occasions since Empire Day, 24 May 1921, when 38 intrepid pioneers, in boxer shorts and 'takkies', were sent on their way by the Mayor of Pietermaritzburg, Councillor D. Sanders. Their kit was carried to Durban on a motor trolley, which also served as transport for the only reporter to follow the race. A sizeable crowd watched the start, which was also recorded by a cinema cameraman, Jack Stodel.

It was train-driver Vic Clapham's third attempt to launch the 'go-as-you-please' event, under the auspices of The League of Comrades of the Great War. Clapham was granted £1 (refundable) for expenses!

The Comrades Marathon has become Pietermaritzburg's biggest and most prestigious annual sporting event. Thousands of visitors crowd the City which takes on a festive air, and the race enjoys lavish media coverage. The race alternates annually from a 'down' run to Durban to an 'up' run to the Capital.

The start of the Comrades Marathon and the Pietermaritzburg City Hall have become synonymous.

However, special occasions, such as anniversaries, have seen consecutive 'up' or 'down' runs. Thus in 1988, the race finished for the second consecutive year in Pietemaritzburg, in order to commemorate the City's 150th anniversary.

Many interesting and amusing anecdotes have emerged from the City's close association with the Comrades Marathon. The present finishing venue was preceded by the Collegians Club, the Alexandra Park Oval, its adjoining Track Ground (the 'duckpond'), and the Royal Showgrounds.

For many years the race was organized by Vic Clapham, then by the local Collegians Harriers Club and, since 1982, the Comrades Marathon Association, a non-competitive body that concentrates on this event alone.

A Comrades Museum and administrative centre has been established at 8 Connaught Road in Scottsville. The architect involved with this project is former Springbok rugby captain, Wynand Claasen, whose father, George, won the race in 1961. Comrades bric-à-brac and *memorabilia* were formerly housed in the Natal Museum.

Towards the end of his first win in 1922, Arthur Newton stopped at the Star and Garter Inn, near the present drive-in, for his second half-tot of brandy to see him home. He was almost crushed by crowds at the City Hall intersection — police had to keep a lane open. Newton was escorted down Commercial Road by an army of cyclists, and welcomed into the Showgrounds by a 3 000-strong crowd. Despite fluctuating fields, the large and enthusiastic Pietermaritzburg crowds have become a feature of the race.

The year 1923 saw 16 entrants from the Maritzburg Comrades' Athletic and Cycling Club, special trains for spectators, and the first unofficial woman competitor, Frances Hayward.

Interest in the 1924 up-race was such that arrangements were made to display race progress reports at the Park pavilion, near the new finishing venue at the 'duck-pond'. The first prize, a 4-piece silver tea-set, was donated by the *Natal Witness*.

On the eve of the 1925 race, Pietermaritzburg was reported to be as full as on a Friday night (Friday evening shopping was popular at the time). Special early trams, cars, bicycles, motorcycles, horses, and even rickshaws, crowded roads to the start. Competitors lined up close to the lamp at the Church Street/Commercial Road intersection. George Robinson of Rietvlei near Greytown completed the course on his horse, 'Why Not?', in 5 hours and 14 minutes.

Often, as in 1926, a sports day was organized at the finishing venue, presumably to attract and entertain spectators before the competitors arrived. The 1926 race was won by Maritzburg's H. J. Phillips, who handed Arthur Newton his only defeat in 6 races. He had been runner-up three times.

In 1927 Arthur Newton ran his last Comrades, but returned as guest-of-honour in 1956, when the race finished at the site of his first win in 1922, the Showgrounds.

In 1928 a first prize of £25 was donated by the *Natal Witness*. Prizes fluctuated widely according to economic circumstances.

Darrel Dale, the City's second winner, won as a novice in 1929, when the route was tarred for only 4 miles.

252

HERMAN'S DELIGHT

Mark Coghlan

At dusk on any Tuesday evening throughout the year, runners of all shapes and sizes (and ability) can be seen streaming through Alexandra Park, pitting themselves against the stop-watch in a weekly time-trial known as Herman's Delight. The time trial was started on 26 July, 1960, the brainchild of Herman Delvin, a prominent Pietermaritzburg athlete who had lost a leg in an accident in 1958.

The 6,4 km distance was considered ideal for improving a runner's general ability. On 21 October 1969, well-known athletes Johnny Halberstadt and Dave Piper set a record of 18 minutes and 33 seconds. This time was only bettered in 1986 when Ashley Johnson completed the course in 18 minutes and 10 seconds.

Herman's Delight was one of the first regular time trials in the country, and has since grown into a Pietermaritzburg institution. It is a 'must' for local runners, canoeists, triathletes and rugby players, and attracts visitors to the City, lured by the challenge of the course. This test of fitness is, however, also a social occasion that unites City sportsmen of all races and abilities. The only reward offered is the publication of times in the local newspaper. Its popularity is such that the combined fields for the 2,7 and 6,4 km events sometimes exceed 200. If Herman's delight was to see others suffer, then there are certainly many volunteers!

Jackie Mekler, Dennis Morrison and Gordon Baker contesting the lead.

11

During the 1930s, pre-race gatherings meant tea-and-biscuit socials at Vic Clapham's home. With the large fields of recent years, these have been replaced by seminars and 'carbo-loading' suppers.

1931 saw Pietermaritzburg's next victor, Phil Masterton-Smith, who won in a thrilling final sprint from Colenso's Noel Buree. Masterton-Smith seldom trained on the roads, and was nicknamed 'Umogwaja' (the hare) by local blacks who saw him bounding across the hills. In 1933, the depression year, he cycled from Cape Town to Pietermaritzburg to save the train fare, but this effort sapped his energy and he finished only 10th. Masterton-Smith ran for the Carbineers. He was later killed in action during the Second World War. At 19, Masterton-Smith remains the youngest winner of the race. Pietermaritzburg Comrades fans were disappointed when their idol failed to record a 'double' in 1932, but with his exciting second win in 1931, and his powerful finish in 1930 when he failed by only 37 seconds to catch the winner, Wally Hayward, Masterton-Smith had secured his place in the Comrades Hall of Fame.

The keenly-contested team competition for the Gunga Din trophy was started in 1931 when it was won by the organizers, the Maritzburg United Athletic Club. Its successor, Collegians Harriers, won the trophy in 1950. The familiar baton containing mayoral messages was apparently first handed to the Mayor of Pietermaritzburg by Hardy Ballington, winner of the 1936 up-run. Unbeaten five-times winner, Wally Hayward, received a special centenary cup for his 1954 victory on the occasion of the City's civic centenary.

Since 1968 an inter-varsity competition has been held for the NUAC Shield. The local campus of the University of Natal has won this competition on a number of occasions. Many students in the green and blue colours of the University take up the challenge of Comrades, led in the 1980s by 4-time gold medallist, Danny Biggs. In 1981 Biggs also won the Hardy Ballington trophy for the first novice, when he finished 5th. Lindsay Weight won the 1983 Comrades Bowl trophy for the first woman home, while running for the local campus.

Maritzburg's most recent winner since Reg Allison (1949) was Piet Vorster in 1979, when in a courageous effort he ran despite an injured ankle. He was welcomed by the home-town crowd as a popular winner. The most talented city athlete never to win the race must be Gordon Baker, a consistent gold medallist between 1967 and 1974.

As is the case with the Duzi Canoe Marathon, Pietermaritzburg now shares much of the Comrades glory with Durban. However, many City landmarks and personalities have become part of the folklore and history of the Comrades.

13

The agony and ecstasy of finishing the Comrades[12].

Jonny Halberstadt on the way to setting the half-way up-run record in 1979[13].

A familiar sight in recent years: Bruce Fordyce and Hosea Tjale locked in battle[14].

12

14

253

The Duzi Canoe Marathon

Mark Coghlan

The gruelling Duzi Canoe Marathon, held annually in late January on the Msunduze and Mngeni Rivers, starts in Pietermaritzburg's Alexandra Park, and has become canoeing's answer to the Comrades Marathon. Completing the 'Duzi' has become synonymous with fitness, stamina and skill. It is South Africa's biggest and best known canoe race, and attracts the country's top paddlers.

The first recorded trip down the Msunduze and Mngeni Rivers was attempted in January 1893 by two Pietermaritzburg adventurers, William Foley and Paul Marianny, whose seven-day journey featured prominently in the *Natal Witness*. They used 16-foot canoes weighing 36 pounds each. Their pioneering effort is commemorated by the Marianny-Foley bridge over the Mngeni. In 1910 two other Pietermaritzburg men, 'Timber' Wood and Sonny Mitchell, also completed the journey, using a steel canoe with watertight compartments fore and aft.

Danny Biggs, the fastest runner with a canoe[15].

Yeka lamandla agangayo! (Goodness! what a waste of strength!)[16].

Graeme Pope-Ellis, 'The Duzi King', and John Edmonds, 'The Duzi Prince', at the end of their titanic duel in 1987.

Since the days of Foley and Marianny, the river itself has been altered considerably, and this in turn has influenced the character of the Duzi Marathon. The Msunduze has only one dam, Henley Dam, situated in the Edendale valley above the City. City paddlers train on this dam which is closer than Midmar and more sheltered. Water is usually released to boost the water level for the start if the river is low. Sprint events are at present held at Henley. From Edendale to the low-level bridge near the SPCA, canalization has considerably altered the meandering 'Duzi', especially above the West Street bridge and below the Commercial Road weir. Photographs of Victorian boating parties suggest that the river, in Alexandra Park and below, was deeper than it is today. During the 1950s, canoe races were held between Mason's Mill and the low-level bridge. This

To shoot or not to shoot?

stretch of river is seldom fully navigable today. Shale has been dumped in the river in places (for example, on the bend at the O'Brien footbridge), and elsewhere the river is only knee-deep due to silting.

The release of industrial effluent has been minimized, but pollution and dirty-brown water have become a characteristic of the Duzi. In Victorian times swimming was popular in the Alexandra Park section of the river, but today even canoeists avoid falling into the murky water, which harbours bilharzia. Water-sports were banned on one occasion due to the cholera threat. Litter is a problem, and canoeists have to contend with broken bottles and other hidden hazards.

A few kilometres from the start, and just below the Dorpspruit confluence, Duzi paddlers encounter their first major obstacle, Musson's Weir. Intended to provide water for irrigation and depth for boating, the weir was demolished in 1967, but jagged rocks remain to trap unwary or daring canoeists. A pool below the weir was known by early paddlers as Barbel Pool. The long Bishopstowe portage, starting at the low-level bridge and ending beyond the City boundaries, at Campbell's Farm, was unknown to early Duzi paddlers, who had to negotiate a maze of entangled logs amid the stench of the sewage farm. The present portage skirts Sobantu Village.

In 1986 the City Council decided to complete the Camps Drift canalization scheme above Alexandra Park and this has considerably altered the start. The Ernie Pearce weir — 2 metres high — has been constructed at the West Street bridge. The 2 000 metre-long canal is intended to provide the City with a watersports facility of international standard and the race with a spectacular and spacious new start near Dalry Park. This replaces the cramped starts opposite the Old Grey's Hospital, and Kershaw Park. However, despite a second weir at the upper end of the canal to minimize silting, the tons of debris left by the devastating floods of September 1987 have so far prevented the satisfactory completion of the project. Apart from the start, the river itself is barely recognizable, with many features familiar to 40 years of Duzi paddlers swept away completely. The new Inanda Dam has also contributed to the changed face of the river.

Many Duzi pioneers were Pietermaritzburg personalities, with Ian Player, Ernie Pearce, Bob Templeton and Fred Schmidt founding and dominating the race during the 1950s. During the 1970s and 1980s local canoe-builder Graeme Pope-Ellis has reigned supreme. Up to and including the 1988 event, he has won the race 11 times in a doubles canoe and three times in a single. His impressive story has been told by Clive Lawrance in *Graeme Pope-Ellis: The Duzi King* (Pietermaritzburg: Shuter & Shooter, 1987). His doubles partners have been Richard Hackland, Ernie Clarke, Peter Peacock, and Tim Cornish, a former British international. Pope-Ellis's most recent singles triumph was his narrow 1987 win over local student, John Edmonds, who won in a single canoe in 1985. Other Pietermaritzburg paddlers to feature prominently include Comrades' gold medallist Danny Biggs, Springbok Rory Pennefather, Mike Tocknell, and Mark Jamieson. Biggs won the race in 1982 with his brother Tim, and the Biggs-Pope-Ellis duels were exciting contests. Pennefather won the singles title in 1978.

Dr Ian Player, presently head of the Wilderness Leadership School, was the pioneer of the modern Duzi Marathon. The river flowed past his workplace in Pietermaritzburg. 'Every day I crossed the river on my way to work and wondered about its course through the gorges and ravines until it joined the Mngeni.' Player's enthusiasm survived an exciting and traumatic trip from the Bulwer Street Boating Club to the sewerage farm, in December 1950.

Despite enthusiastic support from the Press, the idea of a race was greeted with ricidule. 'No one in his right senses would think of people chasing one another down two boulder-strewn rivers.' On 23 December 1950, Player launched his fragile wood and canvas canoe, *Umthakathi*, into the muddy Msunduze. Packed into watertight containers were the supplies for what was to prove a devastating week-long ordeal. Included was a pistol that was to come in handy to dispatch a snake.

> Representatives from all three of Natal's newspapers were there to see me off. Photographers took pictures, reporters shouted good luck and pulled my leg about getting washed over a waterfall, thus making a really good story.

Player remarked on the tranquil stretches above Musson's Weir and the careful task of nursing the fragile craft down the rapids.

On 22 December 1951, eight paddlers set off on the inaugural race, under the aegis of the newly-established Natal Canoe Club. Player described the start:

> Some three hundred people were gathered on the banks of the Mzunduze in Alexandra Park. Although there were only eight of us we made quite a colourful scene: bright shirts and shorts and multi-coloured canoes. All contestants wore the leopard-skin hatband, the insignia of the Natal Canoe

Club... The Mayor inspected us, made a short speech prophesying that the race would become as popular as the Oxford-Cambridge Boat Race, whereupon there were howls of derision from the crowd.

The Mayor, Mr Warmback, wrote messages of greeting for the canoeists to pass on to his Durban counterpart. Rules were harsh: no assistance was allowed, and all provisions were packed into the canoes at the start. The craft weighed up to 70 pounds laden. There were no overnight stops and single canoes had to travel in pairs (until 1969). Canoeists seldom trained seriously for early races and often underestimated the ordeal. One competitor bought tickets for the cinema in Durban that same afternoon, but scarcely made it out of Pietermaritzburg. (On other occasions carrier pigeons were brought along, and a steel-framed canoe proved a disaster.) Player was the only finisher of the first race, in six exhausting days.

The Duzi has become part of two Pietermaritzburg-associated competitions. The first, the Gary Player trophy for the best combined Comrades and Duzi performances, introduced in 1962, has often been won by local athletes such as Danny and Tim Biggs, Graeme Pope-Ellis, Piet Vorster, and Tim Cornish. Danny Biggs holds the record for this competition which he won in 1981, 1982, 1984 and 1985. The second competition, for the Iron Man award, comprises the Comrades, the Duzi, and the Midmar Mile swim.

Optimistic predictions for the future of the Duzi have been vindicated. Fields have grown steadily, and the race itself has undergone many changes, especially in the increasingly sophisticated equipment used. Pietermaritzburg has shared in the growing popularity of the race and of canoeing in general.

19

Messrs Wyllie and Ledeboer checking their wooden canoe before the start in 1965[19].

Ian Player[20], the founder of the Duzi Marathon.

20

Clubs and societies

Angus Rose

To judge from the list of clubs and societies in Braby's 1986 *Directory of Pietermaritzburg*, the City's inhabitants would have delighted Samuel Johnson with their 'clubbability', though not all institutions provide the kind of conversational intermingling he had in mind, where the verbal 'tossing and goring' of local personalities constituted a major part of his friends' activities. No doubt plenty of 'skindering' does take place, though much else clearly motivates those who belong to many of the City's such organizations.

High on the list of priorities stands service to the community. The nature of the times we are passing though has increased dependence on those bodies which succour and relieve those lacking even the most basic necessities of life. Round Table (3), Rotary (3) and Lions International (4) are chief among these, with activities ranging from organizing the supply of corneas for grafts and the distribution of spectacles, to fund-raising for all manner of worthy causes.

Hardly a Saturday passes without the stationing of good people at various vantage points throughout the City, with their collecting boxes held at the ready in aid of the needy, the sick, the orphaned, the homeless. Regular letters of thanks to the *Witness* acknowledging Pietermaritzburg's contributions indicate that, if the community is not quite as concerned as it might be, many yet realize the unhappy lot of those not as fortunate as themselves. Such organizations as SANTA, Cancer Research, the Red Cross and St. John Ambulance, Cripple Care, Hospice and many others (not forgetting the SPCA) all command the loyalty of supporters, devoted helpers and those sufficiently caring to appreciate the kind of work done.

Two World Wars, the Korean War and our current Border war all left their legacy, both of distress and of companionship. These doubtless account for the numerous MOTH and other ex-service organizations, numbering more than 30, which flourish in this area. Some are charitably orientated; others function purely socially, allowing friendships tempered in the heat of conflict or under more peaceful circumstances to be renewed and preserved. Remembrance Sunday and the Anniversary of Delville Wood bring forth the legions of these otherwise subterranean beings (are not their separate entities known as 'shellholes'?) when, bemedalled and ramrod-backed, they parade with a dignity at once uplifting and saddening, at the City's two chief memorials in Church Street and in the MOTH Garden of Remembrance alongside the United Services Club in Leinster Road. At the latter, the Memorial Cross, hewn from a tree once part of Delville Wood, annually on or near the Anniversary sheds its 'medicinable gum' like tears of grief.

The great bulk of the clubs devote themselves to the provision of sporting facilities, to the extent that virtually no one living in the City (among the whites, that is) could claim to be uncatered for. You can learn to fly; you can vent your spleen on the shaven lawns of the second-oldest croquet club in South Africa; you can squash, sail, boardsail, shoot, car rally, moto-cross, shake your bones on a BMX circuit if you happen to be spry enough. You can swim, lose your money on the horses, race pigeons, leap from an aeroplane five kilometres above Oribi and land quite gently (if you've done your packing carefully). You can kick, whack, roll, bounce or throw inflated (and solid) balls of various shapes and sizes; you can ramble for miles (or kilometres) under the aegis of a club which has flourished for close on seven decades. You can throw darts, catch (or claim to have caught) fish of varying mass, shape and colour, with fly, worm or mealiemeal; paddle your own, or someone else's, canoe once a year from here to the sea; run non-stop (if you like that sort of thing) from Pietermaritzburg to Durban and back again the year after. You can even, at certain times of the year, walk on red-hot embers or indulge in do-it-yourself acupuncture among the Indian community. You can hit or wrench into knots your fellow citizens, provided you do so in a roped ring. You may not, under any circumstances, pit your pet dog or prize cockerel against other similar creatures.

Should all this violent physical activity daunt you, then you can turn your attention to activities consuming fewer kilojoules: you can play bridge (or whist, or canasta, dominoes or mah-jong); meditate transcendentally (or even horizontally and vertically); you can scout, guide, cub or brown, depending on your age, sex and inclination. You can learn how to draft speeches, and deliver them to captive audiences; play chess, or war games thereby demolishing civilization — and perhaps other areas as well. You can collect stamps; make model aeroplanes, ships, cars or trains and ride on some of them; and in the evenings, if the weather clears, you can learn about, gaze and marvel at the wonders of the heavens. You can play — that is, you may play if you can — all manner of musical instruments with the Philharmonic or the Carbineers, or oompah yourself into the Blaskapelle or other brass ensembles. You can sing with the Philharmonic, or with Joshua Radebe's marvellous prize-winning Pieter-maritzburg Choral Society or with the University Madrigal Singers. You can make pickles, jams, cakes, flowers from sugar, tapestries and other woollen articles with the Women's Institute, and display your prowess at the Royal Show in May; do all sorts of good works with Kupugani and the National Council of Women; stand up (or sit down) for Women's Rights; work for the improvement of your own residential area through the numerous Ratepayers' Associations.

If your predilections tend towards exposing yourself to public scrutiny on the stage, then you will do so through the auspices of either the Natal Society Drama Group, whose intimate little theatre, the Cygnet, is a deservedly popular Am-Dram venue, or the Herald Players, whose annual Christmas Pantomime and other ventures are usually staged in that all-purpose-but-not-entirely-suitable-for-anything-except-bear-baiting building, the Winston Churchill Theatre.

If your bent is towards the conservation and preservation of the environment, you will hie yourself along to join the ranks of the Pietermaritzburg Society, which fights pollution and other detrimental and destructive practices but accentuates the positive. The Natal Society (founded more than a century ago) provides,

257

Snug in the Victoria Club.

at the behest of and with financial assistance from the municipality, lending library facilities, which also include all the major local newspapers and some from overseas, records and tapes, videos and valuable children's and reference sections. The Natal Society Library also arranges regular monthly lectures on topics of general interest. Other organizations offer you tuition in drawing, painting and modelling — like the Tatham Art Gallery and the Midlands Arts Club; or classes in Zulu, Gujerati, Hindi, Tamil and, of course, Afrikaans. If you doubt your linguistic competence in English, then Grammarphone's aid is but a telephone call away.

Should none of these appeal to you, then you can join the Victoria Club. Not if you're female, of course; or if you find it hopelessly difficult eating peas with a fork; and not if you happen to be averse to tortoises. The Victoria Club, founded well over a century ago in 1859, now stands next to the Post Office in Longmarket Street, where it flies its own special flag from morning till evening. This flag, not to be confused in any way despite its similarity to another flag flown elsewhere in the world, was adopted by the Club as its emblem on 25 March 1960, a date also noted for matters wholly unconnected with the Club's functions. Members enjoy the opportunity to eat, drink, read, play squash, billiards and snooker and otherwise retreat, albeit temporarily, from the bustle and jostle of the City's streets. Of all Pietermaritzburg's social institutions, the V.C. probably comes closest to providing for those with clubbable inclinations.

We began with Johnson; let us end with him. 'A man who is tired of London,' said the Doctor, 'is tired of life'. He might well, given our changed circumstances and times, have been willing to change London for Pietermaritzburg.

The grandstand at Scottsville racecourse in 1886[22], and a sketch of the new grandstand being built on the same site in 1988[23].

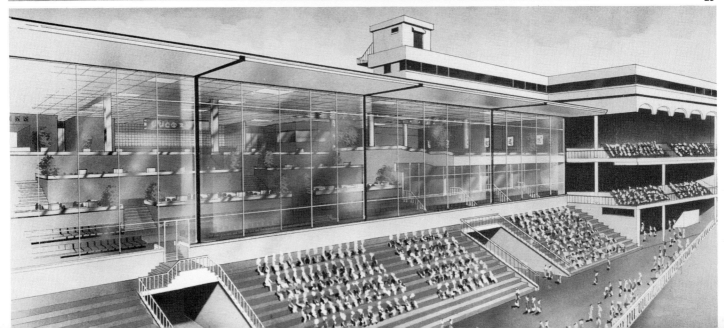

THE MARITZBURG CROQUET CLUB

Paul Murgatroyd

Pietermaritzburg is one of only five localities in the whole of South Africa which possess Association Croquet Clubs, so that the Maritzburg Croquet Club and its members, adept in the arcana of bisques, roquets and peels, make a distinct and distinctive contribution to the ambience of the City. The popular view would be that the club, together with the Pavilion opposite, adds to Pietermaritzburg's Victorian character in particular, but such an impression is substantially erroneous. Although most people associate croquet with vicarage tea-parties of the Victorian era, the game originated long before and continued to flourish long after; and in fact there was no croquet club in Pietermaritzburg until after the First World War.

Some authorities maintain that croquet derives from *Paille-Maille*, a rather similar sport which was known in Languedoc in the thirteenth century. It was a favourite in the seventeenth century of King Charles II of England who reportedly played it with 'high arches of iron' for hoops and on lawns that were 'dressed with high-powered cockleshells'. Alternatively, and on a more plebeian level, croquet may descend from a pastime of seventeenth-century French peasants (the reapers during their midday break tied ears of corn together to form hoops, made a ball from rolled up corn and struck it with shepherds' crooks). The game died out in France after the Revolution, surfaced in Ireland in the early nineteenth century, and then travelled to England and thence to Australia, New Zealand, America and South Africa.

The Maritzburg Croquet Club was founded in 1921, largely by ladies, and largely because ladies then were not welcomed as members of bowling clubs in Pietermaritzburg and, even if accepted, were not allowed to play on Saturdays, unless there was a rink available after all the men had been accommodated. The club was initially called The Maritzburg Ladies Croquet and Bowling Club; but the ladies, who were above the type of discrimination practised by the bowling fraternity of the period, permitted thirteen gentlemen to join and subsequently changed the club's name to its present one. The annual subscription was one guinea, and original patrons included a mayor of Pietermaritzburg and Sir George Plowman, Administrator of Natal.

The Maritzburg Croquet Club is the second-oldest surviving club in the country, and, although in the early 1960s membership dropped so drastically that it had more trophies than players, it has now recovered and boasts 32 members, with a solid core of younger people (the club president and champion is aged 37, and the youngest player is 18). The grounds add to the beauty of Alexander Park and the club adds to the credit of Pietermaritzburg as a whole. Its three well-kept lawns are regularly used as the venue for the Natal Championships and the National Championships; nine of its members have won the Lady Steel Silver Salver (for the South African doubles title); and three have carried off the Belcher Cup (which is awarded to the South African singles champion).

MOTOR RACING IN THE 1920s AND 1930s

William Bizley

With private motor transport came the advent of motor racing, a sport that was very much suited to that mixture of adventure and under-bonnet know-how that the car brought with it in the twenties and thirties. Not a few Maritzburg boys brought up in this milieu would be mending, some years hence, tanks and troop-carriers in the Western Desert. Pietermaritzburg had a stake in two of the country's best-known races. At Merchiston (then, of course, overlooking Commercial Road) crowds of boys lined the school fence every year to see the Durban—Johannesburg motorcycle race go through. The leaders would have all passed by 8.30 a.m., and then of course lessons would be disrupted through the morning as boys rushed to the windows to see the stragglers go by. A great fan was the young Roy Hesketh, who even as a boy made his fanaticism clear by coming to Merchiston Sports Day in a model racing-car decked out in house colours.

He would soon take part in another racing event that was Maritzburg's very own, the annual motor-races, run on a circuit of streets around Parkside, Maritzburg College and the Girls' High School. This drew nation-wide interest: the hotels were full, and various corners and bends became national bywords, such as Angels' Angle (at the corner of Topham and College Roads) and Devils' Bend near the Msunduze — which had to be well padded with sandbags. There were drivers from overseas, like Lord Howe with his Bentley, and the line-up included Auto-Unions, Maseratis, Alpha-Romeos, and of course MGs, the staple fare for drivers like Roy Hesketh.

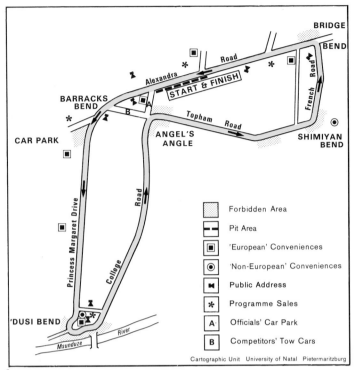

Fig 1 Map of the course.

Rounding Devil's Bend. The stone pier in the background still stands on Park Drive.

A cityscape which has been created over a century or more can be oblitered in a matter of days. This happened in Longmarket Street in 1985 when almost half a block of historic houses was demolished for a shopping centre.

CHAPTER FIFTEEN

Building the Future

1

Architectural conservation

THE CHALLENGE

Henry Davies

Town planners tell us that town planning is a dynamic discipline. Many who in the last decade have lived in Pietermaritzburg or re-visited it, agree: the architectural evidence of change is everywhere. Similarly, few will dispute that over the next decade, the dynamic force of town planning will increase in potency as political, social and economic changes are brought to bear on foundations that have seemed solid and steadfast since the days they were laid. The evidence of these changes is yet to come. The City lies, as it were, on a fault.

If by their renovation one implies protection and preservation for the future, Pietermaritzburg's public buildings are threatened on two fronts. Firstly, many of its finest examples are symbols of a colonial past. Also, in many cases continued state occupancy has resulted in antipathy towards them by the majority of the population for whom the buildings' symbolism and architectural merits are vastly different to the minority's. Secondly, the finance required for the renovation of old and out-dated buildings is vast, so no government of an essentially under-developed country can justify the amounts of money required when the basic needs of the bulk of the population are still to be met. Renovation under such circumstances must be viewed as an act of faith or folly.

Despite their uncertain future, Pietermaritzburg's buildings, public or other, are probably no more at risk from attack by political extremists, vandals, developers, planners and pollutants, feathered or atmospheric, than those in the City's more illustrious counterparts in developed countries. London's High Court suffered a bomb attack as did Pietermaritzburg's Old Supreme Court. The former required extensive renovation to safeguard it; the latter's salvation has proved to be a change of use less likely to provoke hostile acts. Renovators of prominent public buildings world-wide have long since abandoned the principle of refurbishing with identical materials, in favour of facsimiles, the composition of which ensures public safety in the event of violence and attack. Examples are armour-plate glass, reinforced concrete with the appearance of hewn stone, and cast aluminium railings incapable of being used as offensive weapons.

In tomorrow's South Africa, when the general upliftment of its huge population will have to be met from a limited budget, there will be little state expenditure on ordinary, let alone extraordinary, renovations to many public buildings. State owned, occupied but largely uncared for, they will decay to the point where the exponents of cost-effectiveness bay for demolition. The only safeguard for the buildings will be through public subscriptions, if permitted. It is an act of faith to expect people to renovate some of the very buildings that serve to order their lives; it may be folly to expect this in the African context.

The previously tried and trusted safeguard of the authorities, state or civic, that of declaring a building or an area a monument or protected, will no longer suffice. Such action will serve to give only temporary security. It must be accepted that anything that has been proclaimed or zoned in the past, can surely be de-proclaimed and re-zoned in the future. Likewise, in no way will a bronze plaque pinned to a wall guarantee that a building remain economically self-supporting.

2

Pietermaritzburg before the pressure of modern transport and development: the almost rural tranquility of West Street in the early 1900s.

262

With civic buildings, there will be two ways in which to ensure that a building of merit survives. The first is to accept that today's ideal of renovation is a luxury. The cost of ensuring a building's perpetuation will in future have to be borne by those who can afford the luxury. The second is to ensure that the finest buildings of the past will be used by a larger community in the future, so that all will share in the cost.

Let us return to the Old Supreme Court as an example of a building which could be safeguarded either way, and consider its destiny as it passes from state to civic control. Can we expect the civic authorities to spend large sums of money on schemes that will benefit only the few? To the cultural élite, it is a building of outstanding architectural merit, although regrettably lying vacant. Feasibility studies have shown that it could be renovated to form an ideal new home for the Tatham Art Gallery, whose valuable and expanding collections contribute greatly to part of the City's cultural life. The larger community,

however, for whom art and architecture have little or no value, would no doubt argue otherwise: 'who needs art, let's have a community centre'. Both approaches would ensure that the building still stood, but what would the nearby effigy of Queen Victoria say if she could?

It would be naïve to assume that a majority of Pietermaritzburg's community sees any relevance in the conservation and restoration of the City's architectural heritage. If this is the case today, what will be the case tomorrow when the Group Areas Act is revised or dispensed with? If the protagonists of architectural renovation have won so little under the false, but in a sense more protected conditions of the past, what can be their hope for the future?

It is difficult to instil what is popularly termed 'a sense of cultural awareness' into groups of people who are struggling to survive. Such is the level of cultural impoverishment generally, that even were there no disparity between groups, it would be a mistake to hope to

The City is internationally renowned for its architecture, yet countless buildings of merit have been torn down. They are often replaced by modern buildings, out of scale and sympathy with the landmark buildings which have survived. Even more regrettable is the demolition of historic buildings to make way for parking areas. A case in point was the destruction of the Market Inn and the Otto Street warehouse, both in close proximity to the City Hall. The City Council's identification of meritorious buildings — and especially groups of buildings — should now ensure that unnecessary demolitions cease.

ensure a future for our architectural past through education. Neither will sufficient pressure to stir the civic conscience come from amongst the ranks of a concerned minority writing to the local newspapers.

Future decisions regarding renovation are likely to be governed entirely by economic considerations. Can income from local and international tourists to the remains of 'the world's finest Victorian city' feed, clothe, house and create employment for more people as successfully as can a booming light industrial city with anachronistic vestiges of a colonial architectural past? Only economic facts will show if a combination of both kinds of city is preferable, or if one is worth more than the other. To prove this, incentives will have to be offered to renovators as they

The ornate yet harmonious façade and veranda of the stylish Nathan Bros. building on Church Street is today masked by a bland cladding.

4

5

have been to industrialists. In exchange for adopting approved renovation programmes, businesses which own architecturally valuable buildings should be awarded rates' rebates and tax deductions on a sliding scale relative to the importance of the building. In addition, owners of these buildings should be encouraged, financially if need be, to transfer building bulk factors to less valuable buildings or sites.

A further hope for the City's architectural past will depend on the continued existence of foundations and societies dedicated to the cause of renovation in its broadest sense. These organizations should be nurtured, for they have valuable experience, expertise and advice to offer those prepared to listen. The current popular notion that these organizations' memberships consist of meddlesome fools, totally committed to the maintenance of the architectural status quo at the expense of progress, will have to change.

If economic factors dictate that the City's future architectural form should incorporate its past, many home owners will have to be encouraged and given incentives to make more sensitive renovations. Does the majority of owners whose Victorian residences are leased and left to rot, really share Joad's opinion of their residences' English counterparts?

> Sheltered and screened, retired and reserved, discreet, pretentious and respectable, keeping themselves impeccably to themselves, as dull as they are ugly and as ugly as they are dull, these residences are an abiding expression of the civilization that produced them.

Unfortunately, the crime rate is likely to rise rather than fall in the future, so more and more beautiful properties will become surrounded by concrete walls and festooned with ironmongery. However, with incentives and planning controls when and where necessary, the prevailing insensitive attitude towards renovation of the majority of homeowners could be changed. Every attempt should be made to make renovation fashionable and here the architects should take the lead. Homeowners should be persuaded that there is adequate scope for them to make what has now become an obligatory 'personal statement' out of their homes without doing permanent damage to it. One home renovator, rather than one home wrecker per street, would provide adequate proof that concrete mixers, chain saws and the like are not essential tools for home ownership. The home renovator would also demonstrate that renovation can prove to be a healthy, informative, often inexpensive pastime and a challenge to any individual's imaginative and creative powers. Renovation need not be in conflict with the desire for space, comfort and security.

Should the City's future ratepayers see no need for or benefit in acting as custodians and renovators of their architectural past, there will be none. An analogy can be drawn between renovation and wild life conservation. Certain types of buildings and animals which once enjoyed widespread distribution are now confined to specific localities, some state and some privately owned. A number of these areas and the specimens they contain are under threat from changes in land use, business interests and a rapidly expanding population. It is an act of faith to assume that ways will be found to prevent their vanishing forever.

PIETERMARITZBURG RED BRICK: THEN AND NOW

Alex Duigan

The use of red bricks in the Municipal Office Building at 333 Church Street in 1969 heralded the start of a movement towards using similarly coloured bricks in a number of large buildings in the central area. While the brick used in the Municipal Office Building was a light red in colour and matched the earlier Victorian pink brick, the bricks used in later buildings were darker in colour and tended to be dull in comparison with those used on the Municipal Office Building. There were exceptions, such as the Cathedral of the Holy Nativity in Church Street and the Supreme Court Buildings, also in Church Street.

Red brick is said to be used in these large buildings in order to enhance and maintain the red-brick tradition in Pietermaritzburg. However, the net result has been the erection of a number of large buildings in dull red brick, devoid, in the main, of the details found in most Victorian red-brick buildings.

Prevalent in Victorian buildings, ranging from dwelling houses to commercial buildings and public buildings, was the use of moulded and shaped bricks, terracotta roofing tiles and terracotta roof cresting. An important fact concerning these early buildings was that brickwork was load-bearing, so that wall thicknesses were greatest at ground floor level and decreased in width with increased height, while in modern buildings bricks are used as an external cladding and as in-fill panels on perimeter walls.

During the Victorian period there were many skilled craftsmen and artisans in and around Pietermaritzburg and their skills are evident in the many fine buildings existing in the City today. The work of these craftsmen can be seen in such buildings as the Old Supreme Court and City Hall, both in Commercial Road, McNamees in Church Street, and in McAuslin's Building, Reid's Building, Poole's Fruiterers and the former Longmarket Street Girls School, all in Longmarket Street. In all these buildings the Pietermaritzburg 'pink brick' was used in a combination with plaster plinths, string courses, window and door reveals and cornices, resulting in a continuity of detail and the creation of an architectural style that is Pietermaritzburg.

By contrast the recently erected commercial buildings, in which large areas of much darker and indeed dull red brick are used, have overshadowed the smaller Victorian buildings in the central area by their large scale and massing. Little attempt has been made to reduce the impact of large areas of brick walling and in-fill panels, and only in certain instances has shaped and patterned brickwork been used to relieve the monotony of these large areas of brickwork.

Compare these new buildings with the Victorian buildings and note the lack of detail and depth of shadows on sunlit walls. Perhaps the most striking change has been the use of red brick with exposed concrete columns, beams and lintels, as at the Cathedral of the Holy Nativity in Church Street and the two-storey building at 295 Pietermaritz Street.

In the case of the latter building, the exposed concrete elements, combined with deep recessed openings, result in an interesting play of light and shade on red-brick walls, blending to form a modern interpretation of a red-brick Victorian building.

Clearly the use of a variety of red bricks for facing large-scale buildings has not been a success. It is to be hoped that in future better judgement will prevail.

'Nooitgedacht!' Piet Retief's statue gazes in consternation at the monolithic red-brick Symons Centre.

6

Towards a new Pietermaritzburg

Robert Haswell

Pietermaritzburg's past might possess unique aspects, but its history has much in common with many other cities, particularly those in South Africa. So too its future. Thus we will have to improvise solutions to our own peculiar problems, while at the same time addressing challenges no different from those facing any other apartheid city.

The conservation of the City's environmental and architectural heritage is an important local issue. Few cities straddle ecological boundaries as does Maritzburg. The drainage pattern of the streams and spruits puts the connection of elevated forest areas with low-lying thornveld areas within reach, by means of trails along the watercourses. Nature can consequently be allowed to survive and indeed flourish within our City if we so desire. It is worth recalling that our City, as the Capital of Natal, has long been in the forefront — and indeed a pioneer in the field — of nature conservation. The challenge facing urban conservationists is therefore to emulate the success of their rural-focused counterparts. Furthermore, the Natal Parks Board, which was born and nurtured in this City, could now direct more of its attention and expertise to nature conservation within the City of Pietermaritzburg. The Bisley Valley Conservation Area comes immediately to mind.

In terms of the conservation of our architectural heritage, Pietermaritzburg can claim to lead the country, though much remains to be done. We have identified all of the remaining significant buildings and areas within our central City, have amended our town planning scheme to prevent their hasty demolition, are about to introduce a package of incentives to encourage and reward conservation activity, and have embarked on a plan to upgrade and commercially revitalize the heart of the City by capitalizing on its architectural and historic attributes. Few cities contain Voortrekker, British colonial and Indian vernacular period pieces, but we have neglected many of them, as well as the equally important spaces which surround and connect them. We have allowed a townscape of immense richness to become tatty, and therefore increasingly less attractive to residents, shoppers, workers and visitors. With increased pride and care we can reinstate our townscape for the benefit of all.

However the townscape will have to be altered if the centre of Pietermaritzburg, which (particularly in the vicinity of the City Hall) contains so many colonial relics,

Today's tatty townscape: the corner of Commercial Road and Loop Street — scarcely a block away from the City's historic core.

7

is to become a place where all feel comfortable, and indeed proud. Statues and memorials to heroes other than white ones need to be erected, and in this regard the design proposals for a new civic square are commendable. By linking the three main buildings (the City Hall, the Old Supreme Court and Publicity House) with paths and paving, and by enclosing the area with gates at the Longmarket and Church Street intersections of Commercial Road, a square of character will be created. Even more important the focus of the central square, and therefore the City, could be the mosaic which is planned for Commercial Road. This mosaic will feature symbols such as the lotus blossom, the wagon wheel and the Zulu shield in order to acknowledge the contributions of several cultures to the growth of the City and, by virtue of its focal location, could well become the new symbolic heart of the City — a multi-ethnic rather than a legally separated one.

More important than these environmental concerns is the distorted basic structure of our City. Sociologists, economists and geographers have analysed residential patterns in cities and have detected three layers: an economic layer, measured by occupation and income variables, which is divided into distinct sectors; an urbanization layer, measured by age, marital and family status variables, arranged in concentric rings around the central business district; and an ethnic layer, with ethnic groups each tending to concentrate in different locations. These layers are found in most cities, but they are grossly distorted in the apartheid city by the enforced separation of ethnic groups which has almost obliterated other patterns, dividing our City into slices and banishing most blacks to beyond its legal boundaries.

The tragic paradox of the apartheid city is that those who can least afford it live furthest from their places of work. In particular our urban African population has been forced to become commuters — long distance commuters! Because of the low rung they occupy on the socio-economic ladder they are unable to pay realistic fares, and thus their transportation costs have to be subsidized. Despite the state subsidization, which amounted to more than R13 million from 1983-1987, the City Council's black bus service still ran at a loss of more than R9 million in that same period. In the face of this financial burden, and the increasing competition offered by minibus or 'Kombi' taxis, the City Council disposed of its transport department in 1988, but that merely transfers the cost of the service to another operator, who still has to be subsidized. The truth of the matter is that no city can afford to pay the inflated transport costs which arise when ethnic groups are separated by law, and the poor are obliged to travel furthest.

It is also abundantly clear that no city, let alone Pietermaritzburg, can be planned or governed in isolation from its metropolitan hinterland, and that some form of non-racial regional/metropolitan administration is called for.

Pietermaritzburg certainly has the necessary balance of numbers to foster non-racial government. Within the present City boundaries are virtually equal numbers of white and Indian potential voters, with black and coloured minorities, therefore, of considerable importance in terms of the balance of power. Wards could be so delimited that no one racial group could be assured of electing a 'racial' candidate. Candidates with appeal across racial lines could

well emerge, and a local government elected by and responsible to all is certainly within our grasp. The relaxation of residential segregation would also contribute to the growth of a non-racial local government, and would allow blacks in particular to live in the City, and to have an increasingly larger voice in local affairs. By the year 2000 the City of Pietermaritzburg could be home to an almost equal number of blacks, whites and Indians, and thus have a built-in political balance even if racial voting prevailed. The Buthelezi Commission of the early eighties sat in Pietermaritzburg, and in late 1986 a local indaba was announced, and enthusiastically received. A number of events resulted in the postponement in 1987 of the proposed Pietermaritzburg Conference, and perhaps much of the recent violence would have been avoided if the protagonists had indeed been brought then to the negotiating table. It is surely time to revive that initiative.

The fundamental challenge facing this City, therefore, is how to facilitate, most efficiently and equitably, the transformation of a city which has been forceably separated into a voluntarily integrated post-apartheid city. If a commitment to equality does not induce such a transformation then economic good sense surely will. We must begin to question whether, in the face of enormous housing, employment and educational backlogs, we can afford an apartheid city structure, in which certain sectors have vacant land and dwellings, whereas others are dramatically overcrowded. Furthermore, while most of the vacant land within the City's boundaries has ready access to water, sewerage and electricity, outlying housing developments have to take place on sites which are far more expensive to service. In other words, if we continue to plan housing extensions within the concept of black, coloured and Indian areas our City's ratepayers and taxpayers will have to subsidize not only the enormous initial costs of construction but also the subsequent transportation costs.

Council is currently attempting to alleviate the housing shortage among the Indian and coloured communities by means of building projects which are extensions of existing suburbs within the City's established Group Areas. However, private companies seem intent on developing housing areas for each group beyond the City's boundaries, and in combination these two initiatives will not only perpetuate but extend, at enormous cost, the apartheid city structure, with the poor still being treated as outcasts. Without any change to the existing town planning scheme, more than 14 000 additional housing units could be built within the present white residential areas, not to mention the vacant buffer strips of land which were set aside to separate group areas, and which could now be developed as high density residential areas within the City's boundaries. If, on the other hand, whites remain wedded to the idea that blacks, and soon coloureds and Indians, must live beyond the City, then they will have to pay for it. For instance, there are 40 000 housing sites in Edendale and the cost of electrification is currently estimated at R1 000 per site, or a total of R40 million to electrify just Edendale proper. If whites persist in restricting black residence to the greater Edendale area, which includes Imbali, Willowfountain and Vulindlela, then the introduction of electricity alone will cost some R130 million. Clearly there is a financial as well as a moral imperative to transform the apartheid city.

One can only speculate about the character of post-apartheid Pietermaritzburg, but it is likely to be even more flavourful than the present one, and we could all be enriched by interaction with other cultures. People will still tend to live where they feel comfortable, and a mosaic of ethnic congregations seems likely. It will take decades to redress the wrongs — the incalculable costs of the apartheid era — and in so doing establish a healthier rates base for our City, but what sane alternative is there?

Pietermaritzburg could lead other South African cities into the new era — the Capital of the Last Outpost could become the Capital of the New Society. Gandhi, whose philosophy was shaped by events and circumstances in South Africa, and in particular Pietermaritzburg, once wrote:

I do not want my house to be walled in on all sides and my windows to be stuffed; I want the cultures of all lands to blow about my house as freely as possible; but I refuse to be blown off my feet by any.

I humbly submit that a new creed for our City should be adopted:

We do not want our City divided and our windows burglar-proofed against those who could be our neighbours; we want all the people of this land to move about our City as freely as possible, knowing that none of us will be blown away.

The 1906 plan of Pietermaritzburg by D. Seccadanari, engineer and cartographer, shows every property and building in the central area, and is an indispensable source of information in dating the City's historic buildings.

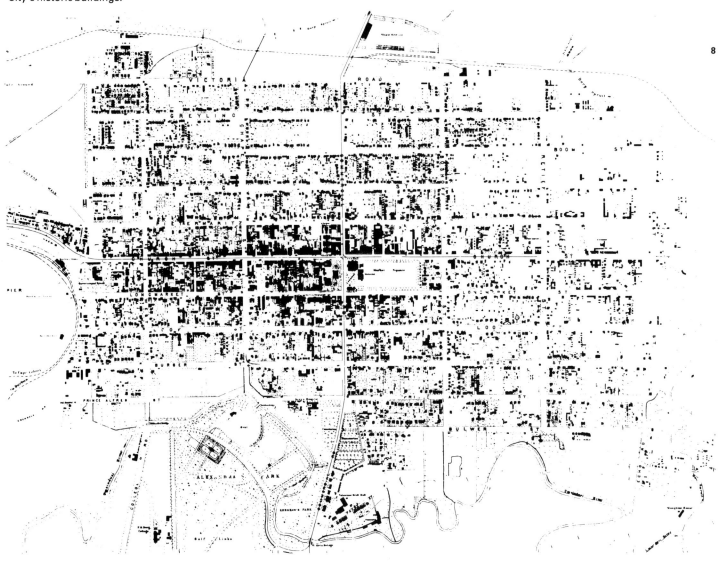

8

A myna bird's-eye-view of the proposed civic square. In this architect's drawing the gates of the intersections of Commercial Road and Longmarket Street (in the foreground) and Church Street (in the background) are closed, thus creating a pedestrian environment for a special event, such as a market. The new square focuses on the circular pavement motif, which has a multi-ethnic theme celebrating the contribution of all citizens to the City.

Sponsors, Donors and Subscribers

Sponsors

1. M.R. Woollam
2. Robert Allen Dyer
3. Dr H.B. Dyer
4. The Brenthurst Library
5. Hulett Aluminium Ltd
6. University of Natal, Pietermaritzburg
7. University of Natal, Durban
8. The Board of Executors
9. Graham H. Volans
10. Pietermaritzburg Chamber of Commerce
11. R.K. Collins
12. J. Leslie Smith & Co.

Donors

P.M. Brown
Mr & Mrs Douglas Cook
Coopers & Lybrand
Dicks Radio
Dr H.B. Dyer
Mr & Mrs Peter Francis
General Accident Insurance Co. S.A. Ltd
Dr R.E. Gordon
Nursing Staff, Grey's Hospital
Greyhound Coach Lines (Pty) Ltd
Maritzburg College
Mutual & Federal Insurance Co. Ltd
Nampak Corrugated Containers (Pietermaritzburg)
Natal Associated Collieries (Pty) Ltd
Pfizer Laboratories (Pty) Ltd
Royal Agricultural Society of Natal
Prof. G.D.L. Schreiner
Simba-Quix Ltd
Syfrets Trust Limited
Tarboton, Holder, Ross and Partners
Tennant & Tennant (Architects)
Truworths
Venn, Németh & Hart

Subscribers

AECI Explosives & Chemicals Ltd
H.W. Ahrens
The Air Survey Co. of Africa Ltd
Helen & Joe Alfers
C.F. Alfers
Mr & Mrs J.J. Allan
B.W.A. Alleson
Waldo Altern
Miss Diana Anderson
Mr & Mrs L.M. Arnold
G.D.J. Atkinson
M.D. Barker
A.M. Barrett
Clive Basson
C.A. Becker
B.L. Bernstein

Lionel Blomeyer
I.A.N. Bloy
Mr R. Bodger
Edna & Frank Bradlow
Prof. J.B. Brain
A.P. Brice Bruce
N. Bromberger
J.E. Broster
Denis J. Brothers
M.D.M. Browne
B. & E. Buckles (Pty) Ltd
Helen Calder
Mary Calder
David A. Campbell
Peter & Mary Campbell
Campbell, Bernstein & Irving
Dora Campion
G.A. Chadwick
Christine M. Chapman
Mr Alan Chettle
Mrs C.V. Cockburn
M.M. Coke
Mr & Mrs C.V. Comrie
John H. Conyngham
M.H. Cornell
Michael Geoffrey Cowling
Graham & Jillian Cox
Pierre C. Cronjé MP
R.G. Crossley
Mrs B.J. Cunningham
Prof. D.H. Davies
Mr & Mrs R.H.D. Davies
G.R. de Carle
G.T. de Lange
Gerrie & Barbara de Jong
Mrs J.M. Dent
Mr A.V.R. Dicks
A.J. Dickson
David E. Dix
D.E. Dobson
Dr Campbell Downie
Dr T.B. Doyle
Mrs P. du Plooy
Michael F. Dutton
Dr H.B. Dyer
Mr & Mrs Roy Eckstein
Edgars Stores Ltd
Mr B.V. Edwards MP
Mr G.E.B. Elliott
Beverley Ellis
The Exporters Club of Pietermaritzburg
Stuart G. Fair
Tony & Janice Farquharson
Mrs L.M. Fatti
K.R. Fawcett
J.E. Feely
Feralloys Ltd
Floccatan (Pty) Ltd
P.A. Forrest
D.N. Forsyth
G.W. Fouché

Mr S.J. Francis
T.B. Frost
Gallagher, Aspoas, Poplak, Senior
Garden City Commercials
C.O. Gardner
R. Gathorne
R.J.B. George
I.F.G. Gillatt
Girls' Collegiate School
Girls' High School, Pmb
S.D. Girvin
I.R. Glashan
H.L. Goedeke
Jo Goodwill
E.M. Gordon
E.B. Gould
Mrs J.W. Griffin
Haesloop Agencies
Prof. R.J. Haines
Mrs E. Hamman
Graham Harrison
R.C.D. Hawkins
Mrs J.E.D. Hay
C.C.R. Heard
B.W. Hellberg
K.A. Herbert
A.R. Hesp
R.B. Hindle
M.J.C. Hodgen
Dr U. Honrath
René & Peter Howe
J.H. Hughes
J.S. Gericke Library, University of Stellenbosch
Neville James
Angus Johnston
E.D. Jones
S. Keyser
Dianne King
Basil & Pauline King
E.N. Kisch
Ken Knowles
A. & J. Koopman
Johan & Paula Krynauw
Michael Lambert
G.D. Larkan
Mrs G.J. Larsen
Mrs J.A. Lavers
Deanne Lawrance
H.R. Lee
Dr G.S. Lennox
I.A. Le Roux
P. Lindeque
R.I. Lister
V.B. Lund
Dennis Lyle
Ian Mackenzie
G.L. Maclean
Ailsa Marcham
S.C. Maree
Mrs B.J. Marlow

E.B. Marriott
M.E. Masojada
Sally Mason
Councillor Vernon Mason
Mrs K.M. McAlister
Duncan & Heather McKenzie
K.R. McCall
Dr Donal P. McCracken
Barry McGarr
L. McGregor
Graham McIntosh
Mr A.R. Mills
D.B. Mitchell
M.P. Moberly
Mr & Mrs C.R. Morewood
Roy & Amber Mottram
Mr M. Najbicz
Natal Museum *for* Dana Beth Oswald
Cecil Nathan, Beattie & Co.
Laurence Nathan
Mrs M.G. Nathanson
Dr E.E. Naude
W.R. & B.A. Nelson
L.A. Németh
Mrs H.C. Nevill
B.M. Nevin
J.M. Nicholson
Keith Nicol
Dr & Mrs R.C. Nixon
R.H. Nourse
Michael Nuttall
Dr M.J. O'Connor
A.C.H. Oellermann
Dr J.M. O'Grady
Mr E.F. Oltmann
P.J.F. Oscroft
Miss E.H. Paterson
Mr & Mrs H.A. Peel
The Pietermaritzburg Society
The Pietermaritzburg Turf Club
Ian Player
Miss B.A. Pooley
Wendy Francis Powell

J.F.W. Price
Dr & Mrs J.A. Pringle
Prof. M.H. Prozesky
Dr J.G. Raftery
A.J. Rall
H.S. Raybould
James Posselt Reekie
Mr & Mrs D.A. Rees
Pamela Reid
Dr A.L. Rencken
Renfreight Aircargo
Renfreight Forwarding
E.J. Richardson
J.S.N. Roberts
Roodepoort City Library
E.P.P. Rose
Bridget Rose
Joan Rosenberg
Mr & Mrs D. Round
Graham & Denise Rusk
Benedick E. Samways
Camilla Z. Samways
C. & U. Scogings
T.P.R. & M.T. Scogings
I.C. Scott
Scott & De Waal
D.S. Shepherd
E.G. Simkins
W.J. Simpson
B.J. Skelton
Christopher D. Smallie
J.R., J.R.Jn, J.E., W.M.G. Smith
P.M. Smythe
J.B.A. Smith
J.S. Snaith
South African Wattle Growers' Union (2)
St. Anne's Diocesan College
W.D. Stanley
R.A. Stanway
Petite Stewart
P.G. Stewart
R.S. Steyn
Dr H.H. Stott

J.A. Stubbings
Stucke, Harrison & Partners
    Architects
Mr D.A. Symington
C.G. Tarboton
Mrs J.B. Tarboton
F.St.G.A. Tatham
H.R. Thompson
Thornton-Dibb & Partners
G.C. Tomlinson
Leda Troedson
Umgeni Water Board (2)
University of Natal, Arts Students'
    Council, Pietermaritzburg,
    for Prof. D.A. Maughan Brown
University of Natal, School of
    Architecture
University of Witwatersrand Library
Viv's Mobile Auto Electrical
E.A. von der Meden
Dr & Mrs C.F.T. von Ziegenweidt
Miss Philippa von Ziegenweidt
Mr Jan von Ziegenweidt
Mr Maarten von Ziegenweidt
Mr Robert von Ziegenweidt
Justin C. Waldman
A.S. Warren
D.R. Wassenaar
Ivan E. Watton
C. de B. Webb
A.S. Webster
S.A. White
Les & Yvonne Wilkins
Trevor Wills
J.C. Wimbush
T.M. Winn
Mrs M.E. Woolley
Wykeham School
Robert & Audrey Wyllie
N.C. Yeats
Maurice & Athene Zunckel

Contributors

Waldy Ahrens
Born in Pietermaritzburg and attended
NUC. First Natal student to be awarded the
Elsie Ballot Scholarship to Cambridge.
After forty-six years as an industrial
chemist he returned to the City when he
retired in 1983.

John Aitchison
Member of the Liberal Party at its
dissolution. Deputy Director, Centre for
Adult Education, UNP. One of the Centre's
current projects is the monitoring of the
unrest situation in the Natal Midlands.

Prof. John Benyon
Professor of Historical Studies, UNP. His
research field is imperial and South African
colonial history and he has had books on
settlers, proconsuls and South African
constitutional and local history published.

Dr William Bizley
Born and bred within sound of the
Maritzburg shunting yards, so it is not
surprising that his chief loves are trains and
music. Senior Lecturer specializing in
Shakespeare and Eliot in the Department of
English, UNP.

Prof. Joy Brain
Head of the Department of History at the
University of Durban-Westville. She is
active in three fields of research: the history
of the Roman Catholic Church in southern
Africa; immigration into southern Africa
(particularly the indentured Indian people)
and, in collaboration with her husband, Dr
Peter Brain, medical history, especially in
Natal and Zululand.

Michael Brett
Works for the Town and Regional Planning
Commission. Specialist in nature
conservation and the provision of open
spaces in cities.

Norman Bromberger
Senior Lecturer in the Department of
Economics and Head of the Development
Studies Research Group, UNP. He has
undertaken field research on socio-economic
life in Vulindlela and Ximba (near Cato
Ridge) since 1980.

Peter Brown
Chairman of the Liberal Party in the 1960s.
Then and now very actively involved in the
fight against resettlement.

George Candy
Senior Lecturer at Natal Training College,
he retired in 1976. He has written serious as
well as humorous verse and has been
published in *Contrast, New Coin, Upstream*
and the *Natal Witness*.

Mark Coghlan
Works for the Natal Provincial Museum
Services, Pietermaritzburg. He is
particularly interested in running and has
researched the social and organizational
aspects of the Natal Volunteers.

Ven. Dr Ian Darby
Anglican rector of Port Shepstone and
Archdeacon of the South Coast. His research
interest is southern African church history.

Henry Davies
Senior Lecturer in Sculpture, UNP. He and

his wife, Sue, live in a fine Scottsville house
built about 1903 during the first phase of the
suburb's development. They have made it a
masterpiece of sensitive and informed
restoration.

John Deane
Deputy Director of Education in the Natal
Education Department. Has lived in
Pietermaritzburg for more than forty-five
years and has vivid memories of World
War II.

Graham Dominy
Works for the Natal Provincial Museum
Services and is doing research on the
Imperial Garrison at Fort Napier for his
doctorate.

Paula du Plooy
During her History Honours year at UNP
she wrote a research essay on beer halls in
the City.

Alex Duigan
Held the post of Chief Town Planner
(Conservation and Urban Design) in the
City Engineer's Department,
Pietermaritzburg. A red brick enthusiast,
he has published a number of articles on the
conservation of Victorian Pietermaritzburg.

Dr Lal Dwarkapersad
Senior Medical Superintendent at
Northdale Hospital, which he intends to
make the best Provincial Hospital in the
Natal Midlands.

Beverley Ellis
Combines teaching Biology at
Pietermaritzburg Girls' High School with
research for an MA in History on the subject
of white settlers and the natural
environment of Natal.

Lorna Ferguson
Director of the Tatham Art Gallery,
Pietermaritzburg.

Prof. Gustav Fouché
Head of the Department of Educational
Psychology, UNP.

Dr Hans Fransen
Senior Lecturer in Art History, UNP.
Though better known for his publications on
the Cape (e.g. *The Old Buildings of the Cape*
written with Mary Cook and published in
1980) and general South African art (*Three
Centuries of South African Art*, 1981), he has
established himself as one of the authorities
on Pietermaritzburg architecture.

T.B. (Jack) Frost
Senior Lecturer in History at the Natal
College of Education which, like its
predecessor, the Natal Training College, is
housed in the once Government House.
Editor of *Natalia: the journal of the Natal
Society*, and author of *A Brief History of
Government House and Natal Training
College* (1982).

Prof. Colin Gardner
Head of the Department of English at UNP.
He worked with Alan Paton in the Liberal
Party and on the editorial board of *Reality*,
and in 1975 he edited *Knocking on the Door*,
Paton's collected shorter writings.

Dr Ruth Gordon
Trained and inspired many History teachers

during her years as Head of the History
Department, Natal Training College. Her
numerous publications on settler Natal and
Pietermaritzburg include *The Place of the
Elephant* (1981) and *Natal's Royal Show*
(1984).

Prof. Bill Guest
Associate Professor in the Department of
Historical Studies, UNP. In addition to
various articles on Natal's history, he is the
author of *Langalibalele: the Crisis in Natal*,
(1976), and co-edited with John Sellers,
*Enterprise and Exploitation in a Victorian
Colony: Aspects of the Economic and Social
History of Colonial Natal* (1985).

Robert Haswell
Senior Lecturer in Geography, UNP, with a
special interest in historic towns. Elected to
the City Council in 1984, he has been
Chairman of the Planning and Development
Committee since 1985 and is currently
Deputy Mayor.

Dr Melanie Hillebrand
Director of the King George VI Art Gallery,
Port Elizabeth, and formerly on the staff of
the Tatham Art Gallery, Pietermaritzburg.
She is an expert on the architecture of Natal
and of colonial Pietermaritzburg in
particular.

Prof. Wilfred Jonckheere
Head of the Department of Afrikaans-
Nederlands, UNP. Has edited and published
widely in the field of Afrikaans literature.

Kerri Jones
Formerly Information Officer for the
Department of Environmental Affairs,
Forestry Branch, Pietermaritzburg. Free-
lance journalist and photographer.

Adrian Koopman
Senior Lecturer in the Department of Zulu,
UNP. He is fascinated by Zulu names and
has lectured and published on Zulu
surnames and bird-, tree- and place-names.

John Laband
Senior Lecturer in the Department of
Historical Studies, UNP. Has published
extensively on nineteenth century Natal
and Zulu history.

J. André Labuschagne
Teaches Geography and the use of
computers at Alexandra High School, and is
an authority on the conservation of Voortrekker and Victorian architecture in
Pietermaritzburg.

Dr John Lambert
Senior Lecturer in the Department of
History, UNISA. He is revising his doctoral
thesis, 'Africans in Natal, 1880–1899:
continuity, change and crisis in a rural
society' for publication.

Michael Lambert
Lecturer in Classics, UNP. Occasional
drama and music critic for the *Natal
Witness*, and director of the University
Madrigal Singers.

Deanne Lawrance
Has taught in Natal and KwaZulu schools
and has written for the *Natal Witness* on
educational topics.

Ralph Lawrence
Lecturer in the Department of Political

273

Studies, UNP. Currently engaged in a comparative study of urban politics and patterns of governance in major Third World countries.

Dr Basil Leverton
Head of the Natal Archives Depot for sixteen years. An indefatigable researcher and writer on Natal history. Probably no one has such an intimate acquaintance with the *Natal Witness* — he has known every editor since G.H. Calpin and has read every issue of the paper from 1840 to 1928!

Dr Tim Maggs
Head of the Department of Archaeology, Natal Museum, Pietermaritzburg. His interest is southern Africa pre-colonial history with special emphasis on the Iron Age, and he is active in historical and cultural conservation in Natal and KwaZulu.

Bruno Martin
Swiss-trained cartographer whose fine skills have enhanced numerous publications on Pietermaritzburg and Natal. Also a railway history enthusiast. Formerly cartographer in the Department of Geography, UNP, he now works in Queensland, Australia.

Patrick Maxwell
Senior Lecturer in the Department of Religious Studies, UNP, with a special interest in Indian religions in South Africa.

Dr Donal McCracken
Senior Lecturer in History at the University of Durban-Westville. He has undertaken research on Irish and South African botanical history and has recently published a book on the history of South African botanic gardens.

Prof. Owen McGee
Associate Professor in the Department of Geography, UNP. In addition to publishing numerous scientific papers in physical geography, he enjoys writing popular articles on meteorology.

Christopher Merrett
Deputy University Librarian, UNP. His main research interest is state censorship in the general context of human rights and the politics of information. From 1981 to 1985 and 1986 to 1987 he was Honorary Secretary, Maritzburg District Cricket Union.

Pat Merrett
Lectures in History at UNP. She is actively researching the role of women in colonial South Africa.

Sheila Meintjes
Has lectured in History at the University of Natal. Presently completing a doctorate for London University on the social and economic history of Edendale from the 1850s to the turn of the century.

John Mitchell
Director of the Pietermaritzburg Philharmonic Society.

Mlungisi Mkhize
Having qualified at the Indumiso Training College at Imbali, he became a very successful teacher, prepared a volume of his poems for publication, and gained a reputation for his community work. He died in 1988 from an asthma attack, at the age of twenty-four.

dikobe wa mogale
Poet, artist, essay-writer and political activist. *Baptism of Fire*, his first book of poems, was published in 1984.

Dr Paul Murgatroyd
Formerly Professor in the Department of Classics, UNP. Now teaching at McMaster University, Canada.

Nancy Ogilvie
Born in Pietermaritzburg a few days after the City Hall fire in 1898 and has lived here all her life. A fount of lively information on the City's past.

David Owen
During his History Honours year at UNP he wrote a research essay on the 1930s Great Depression in Pietermaritzburg. Presently teaching in Kimberley.

Julie Parle
Completing a Master's thesis at UNP, where she is a student in the Historical Studies Department, on the impact of the 1860s depression.

Hamish Paterson
Curator of Uniforms and Accoutrements, South African National Museum of Military History, Saxonwold, Johannesburg. He has researched the military organizations of Natal and their uniforms.

Heather Peel
Examined the administrative history of Sobantu Village during her History Honours year at UNP. She has chosen a teaching career.

Dr Ivor Pols
Director of the Voortrekker Museum, Pietermaritzburg, which has expanded significantly under his direction.

Dr Pieter Prinsloo
His article is based on his 1978 doctoral thesis for Potchefstroom University 'Die Rol van E.G. Jansen in Belang van die Afrikaners in Natal'. He is presently Senior Researcher in the Department of History at the Vaal Triangle campus of Potchefstroom University, where he is investigating the industrialization of the Vaal Triangle.

Jill Raybould
Teaches Mathematics at Pietermaritzburg Girls' High School and is completing her MA in the Department of Historical Studies, UNP, on Pietermaritzburg's conversion from colonial capital to provincial centre.

David Robbins
Assistant editor of the *Natal Witness*. His article on Edendale Hospital is drawn from *Inside the Last Outpost*, which he produced with Wyndham Hartley in 1985.

Angus Rose
While English Editor at Shuter & Shooter he contributed regularly to the *Natal Witness* as Columnist at Large, music critic etc. Now Rector of the new Giyani College of Education, Gazankulu. Also President of the English Academy of Southern Africa.

Prof. Deneys Schreiner
Formerly Vice-Principal, UNP.

Hassim Seedat
Like M.K.Gandhi, he trained as a barrister in London; now a practising attorney in Durban. Researching for a doctorate on the development and practice of *Satyagraha* in South Africa.

John Sellers
As a student and as a member of staff he has spent a large portion of his life on the Pietermaritzburg campus. While Senior Lecturer in the Department of Historical Studies, he edited *Enterprise and Exploitation in a Victorian Colony: Aspects of the Economic and Social History of Colonial Natal* (1985) with Bill Guest. Edited *Natalia* for three years.

Brian Spencer
Grew up in Pietermaritzburg and was educated in the City. Now Don Africana Librarian, Municipal Library, Durban.

Shelagh Spencer
Authority on British settlers in Natal. The first four volumes of *British Settlers in Natal, 1824, 57* have been published and a further sixteen are in preparation.

Dr Peter Spiller
Formerly Associate Professor in the Department of Public Law, University of Natal, Durban; now at the University of Canterbury, Christchurch, New Zealand. Much of his research on the legal history of Natal appears in his book *A History of the District and Supreme Courts of Natal, 1846–1910* (1986).

Richard Steyn
Law graduate of Stellenbosch University and Nieman Fellow, Harvard University. Editor of the *Natal Witness* since 1974.

Dr Brian Stuckenberg
As Director of the Natal Museum he is largely occupied with administration, public education and exhibition development, which leave him less time for his first profession —entomology.

Dr Paul Thompson
Senior Lecturer in the Department of Historical Studies, UNP. His primary research is in Natal history, and he is the co-author with J.P.C. Laband of several books on the Anglo-Zulu war of 1879.

Carlo Torino
Completing a Masters thesis on the politics of industrialization in Pietermaritzburg up to the 1960s in the Department of Political Studies, UNP.

Jennifer Verbeek
Senior Lecturer and Acting Head of the Department of Library Science, UNP. With her husband she has compiled a book of photographs entitled *Victorian and Edwardian Natal* (1982).

Dr Sylvia Vietzen
Formerly Vice-Rector of Edgewood Training College, Pinetown. Now Principal of Pietermaritzburg Girls' High School. Author of *A History of Education for European Girls in Natal, 1837–1902* (1973).

Trevor Wills
Lectures in Urban Geography in the Department of Geography, UNP. His current research in urban historical geography and the contemporary South African city focuses on the impact of the Group Areas Act and the social geography of the late colonial/early post-Union city.

John Wright
Senior Lecturer in the Department of Historical Studies, UNP. His main research interests are in the pre-colonial history and historiography of southern Africa.

Select list of sources

This list of references makes no claim to being a comprehensive and up-to-date bibliography of Pietermaritzburg. Such a guide is clearly needed and it is to be hoped that one will be compiled in the near future to replace Margaret Vowles' valuable but now rather out of date *The City of Pietermaritzburg: A Bibliography* (Pietermaritzburg, 1946).

In the meantime this list of references — based on published works used in the writing of this book — will be extremely useful to anyone wanting to read more about Pietermaritzburg and its life and times. In the main the list has been restricted to published books, articles, theses, conference papers and any other items that are reasonably readily accessible in libraries and other depositories.

Most of the articles in this book, however, are based on extensive original research, and much of this made use of collections of unpublished private and official papers held in archives depots, libraries etc. Pietermaritzburg is fortunate in its libraries and is rich in special collections (see p.156).

The Natal Archives Depot contains a great many collections of significant papers: there are official papers such as those of the Colonial Secretary and the Secretary of Native Affairs for Natal, City records such as the Mayor's Minutes and the Pietermaritzburg Corporation Minute Books, and there are private papers including those of John Moreland and Kit Bird. In addition to the friendly assistance offered by the staff, researchers will find an indispensable guide to some of the collections in *Webb's Guide to the Official Records of the Colony of Natal*, second edition (Pietermaritzburg, 1984).

The Natal Society Library, with its special collections of relevance to Pietermaritzburg and its back files of old newspapers, is an obvious starting point for local history research. Other repositories outside the City also hold documents relating to Pietermaritzburg: for example, the Killie Campbell Africana Library in Durban holds the papers relating to the Pietermaritzburg Botanic Society; and in the Archive of the Royal Botanic Gardens at Kew are the records of Outward exchanges and the Natal correspondence. In all these collections there are many documents and records that have barely been touched, and researchers into Pietermaritzburg are assured that there is no shortage of fascinating and important topics still requiring investigation and writing up. Indeed, some of the Editors' ideas for this book had to be abandoned as the necessary research has still to be undertaken.

This list is arranged in 23 categories. Fifteen of them are directly related to the themes of the chapters of this book, while the other eight are either more general in content or reflect particular forms of material such as maps or newspapers.

General

Barker, Mary Anne, *A Year's Housekeeping in South Africa*, Leipzig, 1877.
Bird, J., ed., *The Annals of Natal*, vols. 1 & 2, Pietermaritzburg, 1888.
Bird, J., 'Natal, 1846–51', Pietermaritzburg, 1891 (reprinted in *Natalia*, 1, 1971).
Brookes, E.H. & Webb, C. de B., *A History of Natal*, Pietermaritzburg, 1965 (reprinted 1987).
Buchanan, B., *Natal Memories*, Pietermaritzburg, 1941.
Bulpin, T.V., *To The Shores of Natal*, Cape Town, 1954.
Chase, J.C., *The Natal Papers*, reprint, Cape Town, 1968.
De Kiewiet, C.W., *A History of South Africa: Social and Economic*, London, 1941.
Harrison, C.W.F., *Natal: An Illustrated Official Railway Guide and Handbook of General Information*, London, 1903.

Hattersley, A.F., *The British Settlement of Natal: A Study in Imperial Migration*, Cambridge, 1950.
Hattersley, A.F., *A Camera on Old Natal*, Pietermaritzburg, 1960.
Hattersley, A.F., *Later Annals of Natal*, London, 1938.
Hattersley, A.F., *More Annals of Natal*, London, 1936.
Hattersley, A.F., *The Natalians: Further Annals of Natal*, Pietermaritzburg, 1940.
Hattersley, A.F., *Portrait of a Colony: The Story of Natal*, Cambridge, 1940.
Holden, W.C., *History of the Colony of Natal*, London, 1855.
Ingram, J.F., *The Colony of Natal: An Official Illustrated Handbook and Railway Guide*, London, 1895.
Kitson-Clark, G., *An Expanding Society: Britain 1830–1900*, Cambridge, 1967.
'Life in Natal, by a lady', *Cape Monthly Magazine*, 1872.
MacKeurtan, G., *The Cradle Days of Natal, 1497–1845*, Pietermaritzburg, 1948.
Mann, R.J., *The Colony of Natal*, London, *c.* 1859.
Morris, J., *Pax Britannica: The Climax of An Empire*, Cambridge, 1950.
Nathan, M., *The Voortrekkers of South Africa*, London, 1937.
Preston, A., ed., *Sir Garnet Wolseley's South African Diaries: Natal, 1875*, Cape Town, 1971.
Robbins, D., & Hartley, W., *Inside the Last Outpost*, Pietermaritzburg, 1985.
Robinson, J., *A Life Time in South Africa*, London, 1900.
Robinson, J., *Notes on Natal: An Old Colonist's Book*, Durban, 1872.
Russell, R., *Natal: The Land and Its Story*, Pietermaritzburg, 1911.
Spencer, S.O'B., *British Settlers in Natal, 1824–1857: A Biographical Register*, vols. 1–4 (Abbott to Coventry). Pietermaritzburg, 1981–7. Further volumes in preparation.
Tatlow, A.H., ed., *Natal Province: Descriptive Guide and Official Handbook*, Durban, 1911.
Theal, G.M., *History of South Africa since 1795*, vol. 6, Cape Town, 1964.
Trollope, A., *South Africa*, London, 1878 (reprinted Cape Town, 1973).
Twentieth Century Impressions of Natal: Its People, Commerce, Industries and Resources, Natal, 1906.
Webb, C. de B. & Wright, J.B., *The James Stuart Archive of Recorded Oral Evidence Relating to the History of the Zulu and Neighbouring Peoples*, vols. 1–4, Pietermaritzburg, 1976–86.

Pietermaritzburg

Bizley, W., 'Pietermaritzburg — the Missing Decades', *Natalia*, 17, 1987.
Black Sash, *This Is Your City . . ., Pietermaritzburg, 1974*, n.p., 1974.
City of Flowers and Progressive Capital of Natal South Africa, n.p., 1949.
The City of Pietermaritzburg, Johannesburg 1968.
Evans, S.A., comp., *Maritzburg for Business and Pleasure*, n.p., 1915.
Gordon, R., *The Place of the Elephant: A History of Pietermaritzburg*, Pietermaritzburg, 1981.
Gordon, R., *Victorian Pietermaritzburg*, see Louwrens, M.
Harris, V.S. & Harris, K., eds., *Pietermaritzburg in Profile, 1987*, n.p., n.d.
Hattersley, A.F., *Pietermaritzburg Panorama: A Survey of One Hundred Years of an African City*, Pietermaritzburg, 1938.
Hattersley, A.F., *Portrait of a City*, Pietermaritzburg, 1951.
Ingram, J.F., *The Story of an African City*, Pietermaritzburg, 1898.
Laband, J.P.C., editorial introduction to 'History of Pietermaritzburg', by G.H. Calpin, reprinted in *Natalia*, 17, 1987.
Louwrens, M. *Victorian Pietermaritzburg*, with text by R.E. Gordon, Springfield, 1984.
Meineke, E.N. & Summers, G.M., *Municipal Engineering in Pietermaritzburg: The First Hundred Years*, Pietermaritzburg, 1983.
Pietermaritzburg 1838–1938: Centenary Souvenir Hand-Book, Pietermaritzburg, 1938.
Pietermaritzburg, Capital of Natal: The City of Flowers, n.p., 1963.
Pietermaritzburg: City of Beauty and History, n.p., 1984.
Pietermaritzburg for the Visitor: City of Beauty and History, n.p., 1970.
Pietermaritzburg Publicity Association, *Your Future Lies in Pietermaritzburg*, n.p., 1972.
Pietermaritzburg Publicity Society, *Pietermaritzburg: The Progressive Capital of Natal*, n.p., 1934, reprinted 1941.
Pietermaritzburg: The Capital of Natal, Durban, 1929.
Pietermaritzburg: Tourist, Residential, Education and Health Resort. Official Illustrated Guide Book, Johannesburg, 1912.
Ridge Women's Institute, *Annals of the Scottsville Area*, unpublished, 1984.

Biographical References

Dictionary of South African Biography, vols. 1–5, Cape Town, Durban, Pretoria, 1968–1987.
Natal Who's Who, Durban, 1906.
The South African Woman's Who's Who, Johannesburg, 1937.
Spencer, S. O'B., *British Settlers in Natal, 1824–1857. A Biographical Register*, vols. 1–4 (Abbott to Coventry), Pietermaritzburg, 1981–7. Further volumes in preparation.

Official Publications

Human Sciences Research Council, *Report on Legislation Hampering the Normalization of Sports Relations in the Republic of South Africa*, Pretoria, 1980.
Natal Government Gazette, 1849–1910.
Pietermaritzburg: A Town Planning Report for the Borough, Durban, 1973.
Report of Commission of Enquiry into the Extent and Conditions of the Forest Lands in the Colony, Pietermaritzburg, 1880.
Report of the General Manager of Railways, Pietermaritzburg, 1912, 1919.
Reports of the Immigration and Crown Lands Commission, Government Report, Pietermaritzburg, 1892.
Report of the Native Affairs Commission appointed to enquire into the workings and provision of the Native (Urban Areas) Act relating to the use and supply of Kaffir Beer, 1941–2.
Report of the Native Economic Commission, 1932.
Reports of Superintendent, Superintendent Inspector and Director of Education, 1858–1987.

Annual Publications

Blue Book for the Colony of Natal, 1850–1883.
Blue Book for the Colony of Natal and its Supplement, 1884–1892/3. (Vol. 1, Statistical Returns; Vol. 2, Departmental Reports).
Statistical Year-Book, 1893/4–1909.
Departmental Reports, 1893/4–1900.
Directory of Durban and Pietermaritzburg, 1853.
Natal Almanac and Yearly Register, 1867–1870.
Natal Almanac, Directory and Yearly Register, 1871–1905.
Natal Directory, Almanac and Yearly Register, 1906–1912.

Newspapers and Periodicals

De [Die] Afrikaner, 1886–1932.
De Natal Bode, 1852–1862.
Dagbreek, 1947–1948.
De Kondschapper, 1908–1912.
Natal Courier and Pietermaritzburg Advertiser, 1859–1865.
Natal Independent and General Advertiser, 1850–1855.
The Natal Mercury, 1852–present.
The Natal Witness, 1846–present.
De Natalier and Pietermaritzburg True Recorder, 1844–1846.
Die Natalse Afrikaner, 1937–1951.
Sondagnuus, 1947.
South African Labour Bulletin, 1974–present.
Times of Natal, 1865–1927.

Historical Maps

Government Surveyor, General Plan of Pietermaritzburg, 1845.
Mair, A., Map of Pietermaritzburg, 1869.
Fitz Henry, Capt. C.B., Map of the Country around Pietermaritzburg, 1897.
Seccadanari, D., New Map of the City of Pietermaritzburg, 1906.

Personal Communications

Mr R. Bizley
Mrs S. Bizley
Mr D. Clapham
Mr R. Curtis
Miss L. Davies
Mrs L. Duffin
Ms M. Dyer
Mrs H. Grenfell-Mitchell
Mrs J. Lloyd
Mrs M. Morton
Mrs N. Ogilvie
Miss N. Ormond
Miss P. Reid
Mrs V. Ridge
Mr J. Sellers
Mrs K. Sellers
Mrs L. Ward

Chapter One

Bayer, A.W. & Coutts, J.R.H., 'Morning and midday relative humidities at Pietermaritzburg, South Africa', *South African Journal of Science*, 35, 1938.
Coutts, J.R.H., 'Meteorological observations at Pietermaritzburg, Natal: rainfall intensity and atmometry', *Royal Society of South Africa*, Transactions, 32, 1950.
King, L.C., *The Geology of Pietermaritzburg and Environs*, Geological Survey, Department of Mines, Pretoria.
Liebenberg, H.M., *The ventilation potential of the atmosphere over Pietermaritzburg and environs*, CSIR, APRG/76/5, Pretoria.
Tyson, P.D., 'Southeasterly winds over Natal', *Journal for Geography* 3 (3), 1968.

Chapter Two

Bryant, A.T., *Olden Times in Zululand and Natal*, London, 1929.
Gardiner, Allen F., *Narrative of a Journey to the Zoolu Country*, Cape Town, 1966 (first published London, 1836).
Isaacs, N., *Travels and Adventures in Eastern Africa*, Cape Town, 1970 (first published London, 1836).

Chapter Three

Barter, C., *The Dorp and the Veld: Or Six Months in Natal*, London, 1852.
Chadwick, G.A., 'Die Voortrekkers vestig Pietermaritzburg', *Lantern*, 23, 1974.
Cloete, H., *Five Lectures on the Emigration of the Dutch Farmers*, Cape Town, 1856.
Daniel, I. & Brusse, R., *Pietermaritzburg*, Pietermaritzburg, 1977.
Delegorgue, A., *Voyage dans L'Afrique Australe*, Paris, 1847.
Drayson, A.W., *Sporting Scenes Amongst the Kaffirs of South Africa*, London, 1858.
Haswell, R.F., 'Indian townscape features in Pietermaritzburg', *Natalia*, 15, 1985.
Haswell, R.F., 'South African towns on European plans', *The Geographical Magazine*, LI, 1979.
Haswell, R.F. & Brann, R.W., 'Voortrekker Pieter Mauritz Burg', *Contré*, 16, July 1984.
Jansen, E.G., *Die Voortrekkers in Natal*, Cape Town, 1938.
King, A.D., *Colonial Urban Development*, London, 1976.
Labuschagne, J.A., 'The oldest houses in Pietermaritzburg reconsidered', *Natalia*, 16, 1986.
Lewcock, E.B.F., 'Pieter Mauritz or Piet Retief?', *Simon Van Der Stel Foundation Bulletin*, 10, 1964.
Liebenberg, B.J., *Andries Pretorius in Natal*, Pretoria, 1977.
Mikula, P. et al., *Traditional Hindu Temples in South Africa*, Durban, 1982.
Notule Natalse Volksraad, (met bylae), 1838–45, South African Archival Records, Natal No. 1, Cape Town, 1953.
Schoon, H.F., ed., *The Diary of Erasmus Smit*, Cape Town, 1972.
Schoon, H.F., *Uit Het Dagboek van Erasmus Smit*, Pretoria, 1967.
Smith, D.M., *Geographical Perspectives on Inequality*, New York, 1979.
Thom, H.B., *Die Geloftekerk en Onder Studies oor die Groot Trek*, Cape Town, 1949.
Van Zyl, M.C., 'Pietermaritzburg: sy onstaan en ontwikkeling', *The Public Servant*, 35,(6), June 1955.

Chapter Four

Bassett, B., ed., *The Buildings of Pietermaritzburg*, Pietermaritzburg, 1986.
Bryant, J., 'Wylie Park', *Park Administration*, July, 1978.
Forsyth, H.G., 'Botanic gardens, Pietermaritzburg', *Park Administration*, January 1952.
Fownes, G., 'Chips from a Karkloof forest', *Natal Almanac and Yearly Register*, 1892.
Greig, D., *A Guide to Architecture in South Africa*, Cape Town, 1971.
Grout, B.R., 'History and horticulture', *Park Administration*, July 1976.
Hillebrand, M., 'Art and architecture in Natal, 1910–1940', unpublished Ph.D. thesis, Pietermaritzburg, 1986.
Hillebrand, M., 'Aspects of architecture in Natal, 1880–1914', unpublished MA thesis, Pietermaritzburg, 1975.

Kearney, B., *Architecture in Natal, 1824–1893*, Cape Town, 1973.
Law, P.A.S., 'Natal Botanic Garden: a brief history', *Journal of the Botanical Society of South Africa*, part 57, 1971.
Methven, C.W., 'Domestic architecture, with special relation to the requirements of Natal', *The S.A. Master Builders Journal*, January 1906.
Paton, W., 'The progress of architecture', in *A Century of Progress in Natal*, 1924.
Quayle, F., 'Alexandra Park', *Park Administration*, April 1978.
Quayle, F., 'Pietermaritzburg's water problem', *Park Administration*, October 1983.
Tarr, B., 'Natal Botanic Garden: an old garden with a bright future', *Veld and Flora*, March 1985.
Wright, A.F., *The City Hall Clock*, n.d.

Chapter Five

Bromberger, N. & Bhamjee, Y., 'Unemployment in Pietermaritzburg, with special reference to Sobantu', paper presented to the 18th Annual Congress of the Association for Sociology in Southern Africa, Cape Town, 1987.
Dick, W.M., *The Four Books of the Prophet Ignoramus . . .*, Pietermaritzburg, 1872.
Feilden, E.F., *My African Home*, London, 1887; 1973 reprint.
Gordon, R., ed., *Dear Louisa: A History of a Pioneer Family in Natal, 1850–1888*, Durban, 1976.
Mason, G.H., *Life with the Zulus of Natal, South Africa*, London, 1862.
Mason, G.H., *Zululand: A Mission Tour in South Africa*, London, 1862.
Smith, E.W., *The Life and Times of Daniel Lindley (1801–80)*, London, 1949.

Chapter Six

Broome, F.N., *Not the Whole Truth*, Pietermaritzburg, 1962.
Pyare-Lal, *Mahatma Gandhi: The Early Phase*, Ahmedabad, 1965.
Radhakrishna, S., ed., *Mahatma Gandhi: Essays and Reflections on His Life and Work*, London, 1939.
Spiller, P., *A History of the District and Supreme Courts of Natal, 1846–1910*, Durban, 1986.

Chapter Seven

Barnett, C., *Britain and Her Army, 1509–1970: A Military, Political and Social Survey*, London 1970.
Carew, T., *Wipers: The First Battle of Ypres*, London 1974.
Crossley, R.G., 'The imperial garrison of Natal', *S.A. Military History Journal*, 2,(5), June 1973.
Dalbiac, P.H., *History of the 45th: 1st Nottinghamshire Regiment*, London, 1902.
De Watteville, H., *The British Soldier: His Daily Life from Tudor to Modern Times*, London, 1954.
Fiasconaro, G., *I Would Do It Again*, Cape Town, 1986.
Haswell, J., *The British Army: A Concise History*, London, 1975.
Laband, J.P.C. & Thompson, P.S., *A Field Guide to the War in Zululand and the Defence of Natal*, 2nd revised ed., Pietermaritzburg, 1983 (reprinted with minor revisions, 1987).
Lucas, T.J., *Camp Life and Sport in South Africa*, London, 1878; reprinted 1975.
Martin, H.J. & Orpen, N.D., *South Africa At War*, Cape Town, 1979.
Nourse, G.B., 'The Zulu invasion scare of 1861', unpublished MA thesis, Pretoria, 1948.
Prigionieri di Guerra Italiani, Campo di Pietermaritzburg, 1944, various authors.
Stalker, J., *The Natal Carbineers*, Pietermaritzburg, 1912.
Tylden, G., 'The Cape coloured regular regiments, 1793–1870', *Africana Notes and News*, 7(2), March 1950.

Chapter Eight

Bizley, W., 'All aboard for Howick', *Natalia*, 7, 1977.
Bizley, W., 'The life and times of the Inchanga Viaduct', *Theoria*, May 1978.
Bradford, H., 'We are now the men: women's beer protests in the Natal countryside, 1929', in *Class, Community and Conflict, South African Perspectives*, ed. Bozzolli, B., Johannesburg, 1987.
Campbell, E.D., *The Birth and Development of the Natal Railways*, Pietermaritzburg, 1951.
Child, D., ed., *A Merchant Family in Early Natal: Diaries and Letters of Joseph and Marianne Churchill, 1850–1880*, Cape Town, 1979.

Cook, A.J., *The Durban Beer System: Building Locations on Kaffir Beer*, Cape Town, 1921.
Gordon, R., *Natal's Royal Show*, Pietermaritzburg, 1984.
Guest, B. & Sellers, J.M. eds., *Enterprise and Exploitation in a Victorian Colony: Aspects of the Economic and Social History of Colonial Natal*, Pietermaritzburg, 1985.
Heydenrych, D.H., 'Natalse spoorwegbeleid en-konstruksie tot 1895', unpublished Ph.D. thesis, Stellenbosch, 1981.
Kennedy, R.S., 'Doubling and deviation of the Natal Main Line between Umlaas Road and Pentrich Stations', *The Civil Engineer in S.A.*, June 1968.
Kondczacki, Z.A., *Public Finance and Economic Development of Natal, 1893–1910*, Durban, 1967.
La Hausse, P., 'The struggle for the city: alcohol, the Ematsheni and popular culture in Durban, 1902–1936', unpublished MA thesis, Cape Town, 1984.
Martin, B., 'The opening of the railway between Durban and Pietermaritzburg — 100 years ago', *Natalia*, 10, 1980.
Morgan, I., 'A city that courts industry', *Management*, February, 1980.
Owen, D.R., 'White unemployment and poor relief in Pietermaritzburg from 1919 to 1934 with special reference to the depression period', unpublished BA (Hons.) thesis, Pietermaritzburg, 1982.
Schmidt, N.F.B., 'The construction methods used on the twin railway tunnels near Pietermaritzburg', *The Civil Engineer in S.A.*, June 1961.
Wilson, D., 'Pietermaritzburg–Riet Spruit deviation, Natal Main Line', *S.A. Society of Civil Engineers*, 1915–1917.

Chapter Nine

Archer, R.L., *Secondary Education in the Nineteenth Century*, Cambridge, 1921.
Armytage, W.H.G., *Four Hundred Years of English Education*, Cambridge, 1970.
Barrett, A.M., *Michaelhouse, 1896–1968*, Pietermaritzburg, 1969.
Brookes, E.H., *A History of the University of Natal*, Pietermaritzburg, 1966.
Kent, R.W., *College, 1863–1963*, Pietermaritzburg, 1963.
Le Roux, A.L., 'Pretoria takes over from Pietermaritzburg', *Mentor*, June 1985.
Malherbe, E.G., *Education in South Africa*, vol. 1, 1652–1922, Cape Town, 1925.
Malherbe, E.G., *Education in South Africa*, vol. 2, 1923–1975, Cape Town, 1977.
Randall, P., *Little England on the Veld: The English Private School System in South Africa*, Johannesburg, 1982.
Tait, M., *Collegiate: The Story of Girls' Collegiate School, 1878–1978*, Pietermaritzburg, 1978.
Vietzen, S., *A History of Education for European Girls in Natal*, Pietermaritzburg, 1973.

Chapter Ten

Bhana, S. & Pachai, B., eds., *A Documentary History of Indian South Africans*, Cape Town, 1984.
Brain, J.B., *Catholic Beginnings in Natal and Beyond*, Durban, 1975.
Brain, J.B., *Christian Indians in Natal, 1860–1911: An Historical and Statistical Study*, Cape Town, 1983.
Buijs, G., 'The role of the mother-goddess Mariamma in Natal', *Religion in Southern Africa*, 1(1), January, 1980.
Burnett, B.B., *Anglicans in Natal*, Durban, 1953.
Colenso, J.W., *Ten Weeks in Natal*, Cambridge, 1855.
Cox, G.W., *The Life of John William Colenso, D.D., Bishop of Natal*, London, 1888.
Gordon, R.E., Gericke, Estelle & Gericke, Elaine, *Macrorie, Gentle Bishop of Maritzburg . . .*, Pietermaritzburg, c. 1973.
Guy, J., *The Heretic: A Study of the Life of John William Colenso, 1814–1883*, Johannesburg and Pietermaritzburg, 1983.
Hinchliff, P., *John William Colenso*, London, 1964.
Hofmeyr, J., 'Directions in the evolution of Hinduism in South Africa', *Journal of the University of Durban–Westville*, 3(2), 1979.
Hofmeyr, J.H., & Oosthuizen, G.C., *Religion in a South African Indian Community*, Durban, 1981.
Kuper, H., *Indian People in Natal*, Pietermaritzburg, 1960.
Kuppusami, C., *Religions, Customs and Practices of South African Indians*, Durban, 1983.
Lewis, T.A., *Since 1849: A Short History of the Congregational Church, Pietermaritzburg*, Pietermaritzburg, 1949.

Meer, F., *Portrait of Indian South Africans*, Durban, 1969.

Miller, A., ed., *The Jewish Community in Natal*, Durban, 1981.

Naidoo, T., 'Arya Samaj in South Africa', *Religion in Southern Africa*, 6(2), July 1985.

Naidoo, T., 'Kavadi: worship through ceremonial festival', *Religion in Southern Africa*, 2(2), July 1981.

Naud, J.A., *Islam in Africa*, Johannesburg, 1978.

Nowbath, R.S. et al. eds., *The Hindu Heritage in South Africa*, Durban, 1960.

Oosthuizen, G.C. & Hofmeyr, J.H., *A Socio-religious Survey of Chatsworth*, Durban, 1979.

Petrie, A., *Presbyterian Church of Pietermaritzburg, 1850–1950: Centenary Review*, Pietermaritzburg, 1950.

Sooklal, A., *A Socio-religious Study of the Hare Krishna Movement in South Africa*, Durban, 1986.

Stones, C.R., 'A South African community of Hare Krishna devotees', *Theologia Viatorum*, 8(1), June 1980.

Van Loon,, L.H., 'The Indian Buddhist community in South Africa', *Religion in Southern Africa*, 1(2), July 1980.

Wilkinson, C.E., *One Hundred Years: The Story of the Chapel Street (Wesleyan) Methodist Church. Pietermaritzburg, 1846–1946*, Pietermaritzburg, 1946.

Chapter Eleven

Doerner, K., *Madman and the Bourgeoisie*, Oxford, 1981.

Duckworth, J.G., *Grey's Hospital, Pietermaritzburg, 1855–1985*, Pietermaritzburg, 1985.

Hattersley, A.F., *A Hospital Century: Grey's Hospital Pietermaritzburg, 1855–1955*, Cape Town, 1955.

Minde, M., 'History of the mental health services in South Africa', Part V, *S.A. Medical Journal*, 1 March 1975.

Town Hill Hospital, 1880–1986, Pietermaritzburg, no date.

Chapter Twelve

Aitchison, J., 'Numbering the dead: patterns in the Midlands violence', unpublished seminar paper, Centre for Adult Education, University of Natal, Pietermaritzburg, April 1988.

Caine, B., *Destined To Be Wives: The Sisters of Beatrice Webb*, Oxford, 1986.

Countess of Warwick, ed., *Progress in Women's Education in the British Empire*, London, 1898.

Erikson, E., *Gandhi's Truth*, London, 1970.

Gandhi, M., *An Autobiography:The Story of My Experiments with Truth*, London, 1949.

Gwala, N., 'Inkatha, political violence and the struggle for control in Pietermaritzburg', unpublished workshop paper, Department of African Studies, University of Natal, Durban, January 1988.

Haysom, N., *Mabangalala: the Rise of Right-wing Vigilantes in South Africa*, Johannesburg, 1986.

Herschensohn, 'Hollands in Natalen in Zuid-Afrika', *De Afrikaner*, 22 April 1909.

Jansen, E.G., *Die Natalse Boerekongres, 1906–1911*, Pietermaritzburg, 1940.

Labour Monitoring Group (Natal), 'Monitoring the Sarmcol struggle', *South African Labour Bulletin*, 11,(2), Oct.–Dec. 1985.

Leverton, B.J.T., 'Government finance and political development in Natal, 1843–1893', *Archives Year Book*, 1, 1970.

Mar, G., & Hamilton, G., *An Appetite for Power: Buthelezi's Inkatha and the Politics of 'Loyal Resistance'*, Johannesburg, 1987.

McCarthy, J.J., 'Progressive Politics and Crises of Urban Reproduction in South Africa: the Cases of Rents and Transport', unpublished Southern African Studies Seminar paper, Pietermaritzburg, 1985.

Niddrie, D., 'Into the valley of death', *Work in Progress*, 52, March 1988.

Nienaber, G.S., 'Die Afrikaanse beweging 1', *Geskiedkundige oorsig*, 1931.

Nienaber, G.S., 'Ernst George Jansen', *Oordruk: Jaarboek van de Maatshcappij der Nederlandse Letterkunde te Leiden*, 1961–2.

Nienaber, G.S., *Honderd Jaar Hollands in Natal*, Pretoria, 1933.

Nienaber, G.S. & Nienaber, P.J., *Die Opkoms van Afrikaans as Kultuurtaal*, Pretoria, 1943

Omond, R., *Apartheid Handbook*, Harmondsworth, 1985.

Prinsloo, P.J.J., 'E.G. Jansen se rol in belang van die Afrikaners in Natal', unpublished D. Litt. thesis, Potchefstroom, 1987.

Pugh, M., *Women's Suffrage in Britain, 1867–1928*, London, 1980.

Walker, C., *The Woman's Suffrage Movement in South Africa*, Cape Town, 1979.

Chapter Thirteen

Jackson, G., *Music in Durban*, Johannesburg, 1970.

Malan, J.P., ed., *The South African Music Encyclopaedia*, vol. IV, Cape Town, 1986.

Schauffer, D.L., 'The establishment of a theatrical tradition in Pietermaritzburg prior to the opening of the first civilian playhouse', unpublished Ph.D. thesis, Pietermaritzburg, 1980.

Stopforth, L.D.M., 'Drama in South Africa, 1925–1955: A critical survey', unpublished, D.Litt. thesis, Potchefstroom, 1950.

Van der Spuy, H.H., 'Die Musieklewe van Pietermaritzburg', unpublished, Ph.D. thesis, Stellenbosch, 1975.

Chapter Fourteen

Alexander, M., *The Comrades Marathon Story*, Craighall, 1985.

Archer, R. & Bouillon, A., *The South African Game: Sport and Racism*, London, 1982.

Bale, J., *Sport and Place*, London, 1982.

Bate, F., 'Pmb. clubs get low interest bonus', *Maritzburg Mail*, Nov.–Dec. 1984.

Hattersley, A.F., *The Victoria Club, Pietermaritzburg, 1859–1959*, Cape Town, 1959.

Hickson, M., 'The Aurora Cricket Club and South African cricket since isolation', *Reality*, 11,(4), 1979.

Lawrance, C. & Pope-Ellis, G., *The Duzi King,* Pietermaritzburg, 1986.

Pietermaritzburg: Apartheid and Sport in a South African City, Pietermaritzburg, 1985.

Swart, B., 'The first Comrades', *S.A. Runner*, June 1986.

Chapter Fifteen

Joad, C.E.M., *The Book of Joad*, London, 1943.

Labuschagne, J.A., 'Pietermaritzburg and preservation: a cultural geographic appreciation', unpublished MA thesis, Pietermaritzburg, 1984.

Sources of Illustrations

The publishers acknowledge with thanks the assistance of the following organizations and individuals who have provided illustrations for this book.

Frontispiece

E. Shariff, City Engineer's Department.

Introduction

1,2 Natal Museum; 3 D. Wills; 4 Africana Museum, Johannesburg; 5 Natal Museum; 6 Killie Campbell Africana Library, Durban; 7 Natal Museum; 8 H. Fransen.

Recasting the Portrait of Pietermaritzburg

1 University of Natal Library, Pietermaritzburg; 2 A. Nixon; 3 Natal Museum; 4 Natal Witness; 5 R. Gordon; 6 Natal Witness.

Chapter 1

1 J.W. Colenso, *Ten Weeks in Natal* . . . (1855); 2 Africana Museum; 3 M.Brett; 4 Natal Parks Board; 5 G. Maclean; 6 M. Brett; 8,9 O. McGee; 10 N. Gardiner; 11–14 O. McGee; 15,16 Natal Witness; Fig. 1–3 O. McGee and Cartographic Unit, Department of Geography, University of Natal; Fig. 4 P. Tyson, 'Southeasterly winds over Natal' *Journal for Geography,* 3, 1968; Fig. 5 O. McGee and Cartographic Unit.

Chapter 2

1–9 T. Maggs; 10 N. Gardiner, *Narrative of a Journey to the Zoolu Country* . . . (1835); 11 T. Maggs; Fig. 1–5 T. Maggs and Cartographic Unit; Fig. 6,7 J. Wright and Cartographic Unit.

Chapter 3

1 Local History Museum, Durban; 2 D. Wills; 3 Natal Museum; 4 Local History Museum; 5 Transvaal Archives Depot; 6 Natal Archives Depot; 7 Local History Museum; 8 J.A. Labuschagne; 9 H. Fransen; 10 Natal Museum; 11 L. and P. English; 12 R. Haswell; 13 T. Wills; 14 Town Clerk; 15 R. Haswell; 16 Local History Museum; 17 D. Wills; 18 Local History Museum; 19 D. Wills; 20 R. Haswell; 21 T. Wills; 22,23 D. Wills; 24 E. Shariff; Fig. 1 Natal Archives Depot; Fig. 2 Cartographic Unit; Fig. 3,4 Natal Archives Depot; Fig. 5–10 Cartographic Unit.

Chapter 4

1,2 Africana Museum; 3 R. Haswell; 4 Cape Archives Depot; 5 Natal Archives Depot; 6,7 R. Porter, postcard collection; 8 M. Hillebrand; 9 H.Fransen; 11 D. Wassenaar; 11 Natal Museum; 12 E. Shariff; 13 Natal Society Library; 16 City Engineer's Department; 17 R. Porter; 18 H. Fransen; 19 R.Porter; 20 J. van Zyl; 21–23 H. Fransen; 24,25 J. van Zyl; 26 H. Fransen; 27,28 J. van Zyl; 29 Natal Archives Depot; 30 Local History Museum; 31,32 N. Gardiner; 33 R. Gush; 34 N. Gardiner; 35 J. van Zyl; 36,37 R. Porter; 38 Natal Witness; 39 Natal Museum.

Chapter 5

1 J. van Zyl; 2 Natal Archives Depot; 3 J.W. Colenso, *First Steps of the Zulu Mission* (1859); 4,5 Natal Museum; 6 M. Moberly; 7 Priscilla Francis; 8 R. Poonsamy; 9–12 Subsistence Agriculture Study Group/Development Studies Research Group, University of Natal; 13 B. Spencer; 14 E. Shariff; 15,16 Natal Museum; 17 Local History Museum; 18 T. Wills; 19,20 H.W. Ahrens.

Chapter 6

1–3 Natal Archives Depot; 4 Natal Museum; 5 Maritzburg College; 6–8 Natal Museum; 9 Natal Archives Depot; 10,11 Natal Museum; 12 Natal Archives Depot; 13 P. Owen; 14 R. Haswell; 15 *Pietermaritzburg: A Century of Progress* (1929); 16 Natal Museum; 17 Natal Archives Depot; 18–20 Prof. J. Burchell; 21,22 Natal Archives Depot; 23 Local History Museum.

Chapter 7

1 R.Holliday; 2 Local History Museum; 3 Natal Archives Depot; 4 Natal Witness; 5 Natal Archives Depot; 6 Natal Witness; 7 S. Watt; 8 Natal Archives Depot; 9 Natal Society Library; 10 Natal Museum; 11 Natal Society Library; 12 Natal Museum; 13 R. Porter; 14 Natal Archives Depot; 15 D. Wassenaar; 16 South African National Museum of Military History, Johannesburg; 17 Natal Archives Depot; 18,19 Natal Museum; 20,21 Natal Carbineers; 22 Peter Francis; 23 Natal Witness, Fig. 1 Cartographic Unit.

Chapter 8

1 Natal Witness; 2 Natal Museum; 3 Natal Archives Depot; 4 Natal Museum; 5 Natal Society Library; 6 Natal Museum; 7 Natal Society Library; 8 Natal Archives Depot; 9 Natal Archives Depot; 10 Natal Society Library; 11 Natal Archives Depot; 12 Natal Museum; 13 Natal Museum; 14, 15 Natal Society Library; 16 R. Haswell; 17–20 Natal Society Library; 21 Natal Museum; 22 Natal Archives Depot; 23 Natal Museum; 24 *Illustrated London News* 1879; 25,26 Natal Society Library; 27 Natal Archives Depot; 28 SASG/DSRG; 29 South African Transport Services; 30 Natal Witness; 31,32 B.Martin; 33 R.Haswell; 34 B.Martin; 35 Natal Witness; 36 Natal Museum; 37 Natal Archives Depot; 38 Natal Museum; 39 Natal Witness; 40 Mr Jock Leyden; Fig. 1 B. Martin, Fig. 2 Cartographic Unit.

Chapter 9

1 J. van Zyl; 2 Natal Witness; 3 Natal Archives Depot; 4 Maritzburg College; 5 Natal Museum; 6 J. van Zyl; 7 SASG/DSRG; 8 Maritzburg College; 9–14 University of Natal Archives; 15 Local History Museum; 16, 17 Natal Museum.

Chapter 10

1 Natal Museum; 2 J.W. Colenso, *Ten Weeks* . . .; 3 Old House Museum; 4 Natal Archives Depot; 5 Natal Museum; 6, 7 J. van Zyl; 8 H. Fransen; 9,10 R. Haswell; 11 J. van Zyl; 12 R. Haswell; 13 Killie Campbell Africana Library; 14, 15 Natal Museum; 16 J. van Zyl; 17–27 R. Haswell; 28 Natal Archives Depot.

Chapter 11

1 Natal Society Library; 2, 3 Grey's Hospital Archives; 4 Natal Witness; 5 Grey's Hospital Archives; 6 Natal Museum; 7 Mrs E. Nieuwenhuis; 8,9 Edendale Society for Family and Child Welfare; 10–13 W. Hartley; 14 J. van Zyl; 15 Edendale Society for Family and Child Welfare; 16,17 Natal Witness; 18 Maritzburg College; 19 J. Londt.

Chapter 12

1 S. Narayan, *Satyagraha in South Africa* (1981); 2 Natal Society Library; 3 J. Aitchison; 4 Natal Archives Depot; 5 Natal Museum; 6 University of Natal Archives; 7 Natal Society Library; 8 Natal Archives Depot; 9 Natal Archives Depot; 10 Natal Witness; 11 Mr Jock Leyden; 12 UN Archives; 13 Natal Witness; 14,15 Town Clerk; 16 P. Reid; 17 R. Haswell; 18 Natal Witness; 19 Natal Museum; 20 Town Clerk; 21 Natal Witness.

Chapter 13

1 Natal Witness; 2–5 Natal Society Library; 6 Natal Archives Depot; 7 Pietermaritzburg Philharmonic Society; 8–17 Tatham Art Gallery; 18 D. Noel; 19 Department of Afrikaans/ Nederlands, University of Natal, Pietermaritzburg; 20,21 J. van Zyl; 22 Local History Museum; 23 P. Owen; 24 Natal Witness; 25,26 Natal Museum; 27 Natal Archives Depot; 28 Natal Society Library.

Chapter 14

1 Local History Museum; 2 Natal Museum; 3,4 R. Haswell; 5 W. Lambert; 6 Natal Witness; 7 South African Institute of Race Realtions; 8 R. Haswell; 9–20 Natal Witness; 21 J. van Zyl; 22 R. Haswell; 23 Pietermaritzburg Turf Club; 24 J. van Zyl; 25 D. Norton; Fig. 1 Ridge Women's Institute, *Annals of the Scottsville Area* (1984).

Chapter 15

1 Natal Witness; 2 Maritzburg College; 3 Natal Witness; 4, 5 City Engineer's Department; 6 R. Haswell; 7 J. van Zyl; 8, 9 City Engineer's Department.

Natal Archives Depot Reference Numbers

52/1, 108/83, 109/1, 118, 141, 176.2, 205, 317, 320, 382, 395, 399, 432, 437, 439, 710, 914, 1097, 1233.28, 1267.01, 1285.2, 1289, 1358, 1983, 2071, 2072, 2075, 2208, 2445, 2447, 3265, 3537.03.

Index

Page numbers in italics refer to illustrations

1st South African Division 113
1st South Staffordshire Regiment 102, 109
2nd Cameron Highlanders 109
3rd Royal Warwickshire Regiment 109
13th Regiment (Prince Albert's Light
    Infantry) 107
45th Regiment 102–5, 224
6th Dragoon Guards 114
85th Regiment 105
99th Regiment (2nd Wiltshire) 107

A

Abbott, Annie May 225
Acheulian industry 15
Adlam, R.W. 62
Africa Enterprise 169
African Football Association 249
African independent churches 166
African law 69, 96, 98
African National Congress (ANC) 209, 221
African People's Democratic Union of South
    Africa (APDUSA) 211
African religion 166
De Afrikaner 206
Agricultural show *see* Royal Agricultural
    Show
agriculture 123, 130–4,
Ahrens, Casten Heinrich 84
Ahrens, Herbert Waldemar 84
Ahrens, Heinrich Wilhelm 84
Ahrens, Louis Hermann 84
Aiello, *Sgt.* Ottaviano, 112
Akerman, J.W. 122
Alexandra Boys' High School 154, 244–5
Alexandra Park 60, *61*, 61–2, 246, 247, *247*
Alfred, *Prince* 87, 88, 94, 123
All-In African Conference, *1961* 211
Allan, Ann 81
Allan, John 81
Allan, Martha 81
Allan, Thomas 81
Allard, *Bp.* Jean Francois 78, 168, 179–80
Allen, *Dr* James, 194
Allison, A.T. 63
Allison, *Revd* James 66, 79, 166–7
Allison, Reg 253
amateur dramatics 104, 108, 224–5
Anderson, Robert 78–9
Anglican Church 167, 168, 169
Anglo-Boer War *1899–1902* 108, 116
Anglo-Zulu War *1879* 68, 87, 116
Anstie, Paul 122
apartheid 40–3, 209–11, 218–20, 224, 267
Apostoliese Geloof Sending Kerk 169
Arbuckle, *Mr* 75
archaeology 14–17
Archbell, *Revd* James 77, 81
Archbell Street 81
architectural conservation 262–4
architecture 48–52, 53–8, 266–7
Armitage, John 244
Army Nursing Service Reserve 182
Art in the Park *xxiv*
Arya Samaj Organizations 173
Ashdown 41, 74, 155
Ashworth, Val 244
Asiatic Land Tenure and Representation Act
    No.28 of 1946 39

Assembly of God Church 169
Association for Popularizing Maritzburg 90,
    128
Athlone 39
Augustinian Convent 180
Aurora Cricket Club 248, 249
Australopithecus 15
Ayliff, *Hon.* J. 98
Aylward, Alfred 204
Azanian People's Organization 211

B

Backhouse, Laurie 245
Baker, Gordon *252*, 253
Bale, Henry 99
Ballington, Kork 244, 245
Bambatha Rebellion *1906* 89, 109, 116–17
Baptist Church 81, 168, 169
Barker, *Lady* 68
barracks *35, 217*
Barret, *Fr.* Justin 180
Barter, Charles 32
Baylis, Leighton 79
Baylis, Louisa Martha 79
Baynes, Joseph 81, 92, 132, 133
Baynes, Richard 81
Beardmore, Isabel S. 216
Beatrice, *Sister* 180
beer halls 142–3
Belvidere Mill 122
Berg Street Native Recreation Ground 249
Berg Street swimming pool 247
Bergtheil, Jonas 60, 168
Berry, *Revd* W. 168
Besselaar, *Prof.* G. 207
Bestall, Darryl 244
Bews, *Prof.* J.W. 157
Bezzio, *Lt.* Luigi 112
Bhagwan Sri Sathya Sai Baba Centre 173
Bhele people 20
Biggs, Danny 253, *254*, 255, 256
Biggs, Tim 255
Binns, *Sir* Henry *98*
bird sanctuary 61
Bird, C.J. *87*
Bird, John 80
Bishop's College 77, 152
Bishop, Anna 230
Bisley Valley Conservation Area 5, 266
Black Horse Bar 105, *240*
Black Sash 200, 211, 216
Blackridge 3
De Bode 208
Boers *see* Voortrekkers
Boniface, Charles Etienne 121, 235
Booysen, Peter de Villiers 244
Boshoff, D.P. 206
Boshoff, Henri 100
Boshoff, Jacobus Nicolaas 81
Boshoff Street 81
Botanic Gardens 9, 17, 29, *59, 61*, 62–3, *239*
Bowditch, *Canon* 152
Bowen, Bert 244
Boys' Model School 154
Boys, *Lt.-Col.* Edmund French 77, 103
bricks and brickwork *30*, 50–57

British Army 102–9
British Ex-Serviceman's League 211
British settlers 29–31, 121–2
Brookes, *Dr* Edgar 200, 209, 211
Brooks, Thomas Warwick 151, 154
Brookside 247
Broome, Eleanor 151
Broome, Frank 100
Broome, John 100
Broome, William 100
Brown, Peter 200
Bruce, *Revd* John 168
Bruwer, Martha Maria 163
Buchanan, David Dale 79, 96, *202*, 202–3, 205
Buchanan Street 79
Buchanan Street baths 247
Buddhism 166, 175
building methods 52
Buller, *Gen. Sir* Redvers 108
Bulwer, *Lt.-Gov. Sir* Henry 87, 203
Burchell, Exton Mabbutt *98*, 100
Burchell, Frank Bruce *98*, 100
Burchell, Jonathan Mark *98*
Buree, Noel 253
Bush, *Prof.* S.F. 162
Bushmen *see* Khoisan
Buthelezi Commission 155, 267
Buthelezi, *Chief* M.G. 205, 210
Byrne settlers 94, 121
Byrne, Joseph 121

C

Calder, William 152
Callaway, Henry 167
Calpin, G.H. xxv, 204
Calvary Full Gospel Church 169
Cameron, W.M. 99
Campbell, Henry 99
Campbell, *Revd* William 77, *78*, 168
Camps Drift 39, 147, *194*, 195, 247
Cape Language Association 208
Cape Mounted Rifles (CMR) 102, 103, 105
Capital Towers building 53
Carbis, Peter 81
Carey, Hugh 200
Carter, J. Withers 239
Carter High School 154
Cathedral of the Holy Nativity 53, *53*, 57,
    169, *170*, 265
Catholic Church *see* Roman Catholic Church
Catterrall, Brent 244
cemeteries 176–177
Cetshwayo 105
Chamberlain, Joseph 88
Chapel Street *166, 167, 168, 193*
charismatic churches 169
Chase Valley Darkies 227
Chatterton Road sports grounds 247
Chetty, A.S. 211
Chetty, D.V. 211
Chiazzari, W.L. 161
Christadelphian Church 169
Christian Centre 169–70
Christian Endeavour Society 206
Christian Scientists 168
Christian Victor, *Prince* 95
Christian Young People's Association 206–7
Christie's tea room *129*, 239

Christy Minstrels 227
Chunu people 20
Church of England *see* Anglican Church
Church of the Vow *26*, 27, 28, *28*, 51, 163, 166, *206*
Church Street *xx*, 35, 41, *50, 51, 57, 65, 92, 241, 263*
Churchill, *Sir* Winston 63, 88
cinemas 113, 238–9
circuses 225
City and Port Hotel 240
City Council 82–3, 90, 152, 213, 214, 216, 218, *218*, 219–20, *220 see also* Town Council
City Guard 106
City Hall (first) *xx*, *47*, 49, 54, *54*, 93, 94
City Hall (present) *xx, xxii, 35*, 52, *54*, 56, *118, 251, 265*
City Sporting Club 115, 246
Claasen, George 252
Claasen, Wynand 252
Clancey, Phillip A. 161
Clapham, Vic 251, 253
Clarendon 39
Clark, R.D. 151, 152
Clark, *Sgt.* 107
Clark House *55*
Clarke, Billy 244
Clarke, Ernie 255
Clarke, Ted 244
climate 8–11
Cloete, Hendrik 96
Cloete, Henry 160
Co-ordinating Committee for the Development of the Pietermaritzburg Region 147
coat of arms 34
Colenso, *Bp.* John William 63, 79, 88, 97, 105, 107, 122, 167, 174, *174*, 200, 204
Collegians Basketball Club 244
Collegians Harriers Club 252
Colley, *Sir* George 87–8
Collins, William Millward 77
Colonial Buildings (first) *87, 106*
Colonial Buildings (present) 49, 56, *89*
colonial government 86–9, 93
Coloured Convention Movement 211
Coloured Sports Ground Association 247
Coloured Welfare League 216
Comins, *Miss* 75
commerce 127, 144–7
Commercial Road *57, 128, 266, 269*
Commercial Road Cemetery 176–7
Committee of Twelve 84
communications 125–8
Communist Party 209
Comrades Marathon 251–3, *251–3*
Comrades Marathon Association 252
Congregational Church 167–8, 169
Congress Alliance 211
Congress Movement 200, 211
Congress of the People 209, 211
Connaught, *Duke of* 157
Connor, Henry 98
constituencies 198
Convent of St. John the Divine 167
Cooper, Arnold 162
Cornell, Mark 84
Cornish, Tim 255, 256
COSATU 74, 221, 222
Council of Education 151
Country Club 246
Coxon, *Lt.* George Stacpole 77
Cragg, Tommy 238
Crown Hotel 77, 122, 240
Cullerne, Irene Augusta Violet 81
Cunynghame, *Sir* Arthur 114
Cussons, Sheila 236
Cygnet Theatre 224, 257

D

Dale, Darrel 252
Dare, John 123
Darvill Disposal Works 3, 5
Davis, Alfred 80
Davis, Peter 79, 80 *see also* P. Davis & Sons
Davis, Peter *jun.* 80 *see also* Peter Davis Infants' Home
Dawney, Robert 122
Day, Margaret R. 77
de Beer, *Mrs* F.D. 208
de Klerk, Mike 244
de Villiers, Henry 98
Deane, H.G. 244
Deane, John M. 162
Deane, W.A. 198
Deanery Lane 79
Defiance Campaign *1952* 211
Delvin, Herman 252
Denison, *Prof* R.B. 157
Dent, Edward 79
Department of Education and Training 155, 156
Department of National Education 155
Department of Speech and Drama (University of Natal) 225
depressions (economic) 124, 129
Deputation of Liberty 206
detentions 211, 222
Dhanilal, Sri Roopchand 173
Dhlomo, *Dr* O. 155, 156
Dingane 20, 21, 43
Dinuzulu 89, 99
District Court 96
Dittmar, Gisbert 244
Divine Life Society of South Africa 172
Dixon, E.R. 122
Dlanyawo people 18
Dorpspruit 11, 24
Douglas, *Lt.-Gen.* R.P. 105–7
Downes, C.B. 215
Drakensburg Bantu Administration Board 83, 250
Driver, Kate 182
du Plessis, Norman 245
Durban Girls' College 153
Durban Light Infantry 115
Durban Road prisoner of war camp 110, 111–13
Durrant, Geoffrey 200
Dutch Reformed Church *see also* Church of the Vow, *124*, 163, 166, 169, 206
Duzi Canoe Marathon 254–6, *254–6*
Dynamoes Basketball Club 244

E

Eaglestone, Gabriel 29
Ebenezer Chapel 79, *169*
Ebenezer Street 78, 79
Edendale xxiii, 33, 41, 66–9, *67*, 71, 74, 155, 167, 169, 219, 222
Edendale Football Association 250
Edendale Hospital 184, 189–92, *189–191*
Edendale Road Football Ground 250
Edendale Road Native Soccer Ground 249
Edendale Trust 66–7
Edmonds, John 255
Edmonds, *Mrs* 153
education 92
  black 155–6
  white 150–4, 180

Edward, *Prince of Wales* (later King Edward VIII) 95, 114–15, *117*, 146
Edwards, Brian 244
Eeufees Kerk 169
Eiselen, S.S.M. 83
Ekerold, Jon 244, 245
Ekukhanyeni 167
elections *197*, 198–200
Elizabeth, *Princess* (later Queen Elizabeth II) 95
employment 43, 72–73, 74 *see also* unemployment
Epidemic Hospital 193
Epworth High School 79, 153, *154*
Erasmus, F.C. 115
Erskine, *Maj.* David 97, 125
Erskine, Robert 116
Escombe, Harry 97, 99
Eugenie, *Empress* 88, 94
Evangelical Bible Seminary 169
Excelsior Cinema 238

F

Faculty of Agriculture (University of Natal) 158
fauna 32
Favell, Benjamin 79
Federal Theological Seminary 169
Feetham, Richard 100
Feinstein, Albert 244
Ferreira, Phillip 29, 81
Few, Edward 78
Few, Joseph 78
Finnemore, Catherine Augusta 81
Finnemore, Robert Isaac 81
firewalking ceremony 170–1
Fleming Street 78
Flesch, Julius 77
floods 11, 64
flora 29, 31, 32
Florey, Charles 77
Fodo kaNombewu 20, 21
Foley, William 254
Fordyce, Bruce 251, *253*
Forrester, J.M. 214
Fort Napier 86, 102–9, *102, 103*, 110
Fort Napier Hospital 188
Fowler, Val 245
Frangenheim, Eric 245
Fraser, Caroline 100
Fraser, *Col.* J. 162
Free Church of Scotland 168, 169
Freeman, John 78
French, F.M.H. 14, 15
Frere, *Sir* Bartle 87, 88, 125
Friendly Society 207
Froomberg, Sammy 105
Funamalungelo 69
Fuze people 21

G

Gallwey, *Sir* Michael 98, *98*, 99, 114
Game Protection Association 161
Gandhi, Mohandas Karamchand 99, *99*, 100, *196*, 201, 209, 211, 217, 268
Gardiner, *Capt.* Allen 20
geology 6–7
George V, *King* 94–5

George VI, *King* 95, 115
Georgetown 66
Georgetown High School 250
Gereformeerde Kerk van Suid-Afrika 169
German Lutheran Church 169
Gert Maritz School 154
Ghetto Act 39
Gibb, *Lt.* Charles 102, 103
Girdlestone, Errol 227
Girls' Collegiate School 80, 153, *153*, 214
Girls' Model Primary School 151
Gordon, Ruth *xxx*, xxxi
Government Clothing Factory 92
Government House 55, 88, *88*, 90
Government School 103
Gower, *Dr* Samuel 182
Grand Cinema 238
Grange 41
Green, *Revd* James 77, 79, 167, 174
Green, Morton 160
Green, Samuel 128
Greene, *Mr* 99
Greene, Thomas 103
Grey, Charles Lascelles 226–7, 230
Grey, *Sir* George 66, 86, 94, 182
Grey, *Bp.* Robert 167, 174
Grey's Hospital 123, 124, 182–5, *182–5*
Group Areas Act 41, 42, 45, 83, 169
Grové, A.P. 236
Grové, Henriette 236
Guest, Henry 115
Gujerati Vedic Society 172
Gumede, Archie 209, 211
Gumede, James 209
Gwala, Harry 209

H

H. Daniel and Co. 67
Habibia Soofie Mosque 178
Hackett, R.M. 79
Hackland, Richard 255
Haensel, Helmuth 112
Halberstadt, Johnny 252, *253*
Gall, Garda 238
Harding, Walter 96, 98
Hare Krishna movement 172
Harlequins Basketball Club 244
Harrison, Barry 244
Harrison, C.W. Francis xxv
Harward Boys' School 154
Harwin, John 79
Hathorn, Anthony 100
Hathorn, Kenneth 100
Hathorn, Roy 100
Hattersley, *Prof.* A.F. *xxviii*, xxix, xxxi, 37, 38, 185
Hay Paddock 147
Hay Paddock Transit Camp 110, 113
Hayes, Michael 179
Hayfields 33, 110, 147
Hayward, Frances 252
Hayward, Wally 253
Helen (Christian), *Princess* 95
Hely-Hutchinson, *Sir* Walter 87, 89
Hemuhemu, *Chief* 132
Henley Dam 255
Henwood, B.H. 198
Henwood, Paul 78
Herald Players 227, 257
Herman's Delight 252
Hershensohn, J.M.N.A. 208
Hesketh, Roy 80, 245
Hill, Ken 211

Hilton 43
Hilton College 115
Hindu Alliance 172
Hindu Prayer Circle 173
hinduism 170–3, 175
Hinton House School 80–1, 150
Hirst, Allan 147
Hodgkins, John 81
Hodgkins, Lancelot C. 81
Hodson, *Misses* 75
Holliday, J.D. 121
Holliday, Rupert 75
Holy Family Convent 153, 179, 180
Holy Name Chapel 180
Holy Name Sanatorium 180
Horn, Thomas 179
Horseshoe Hotel *241*
A hospital century 185
hospitals 105, 123, 124, 182–5, 188, 189–92
hotels 80, 240, 241
housing 42–3, 82, 83, 145, 267
hunting 31, 32, *32*
Hurley, *Abp.* Denis. 211
Hutton, Henry James Cooper 80
Hyslop, *Dr* J. 187

I

Imbali 33, 41, 42, 43, 74, 83, 155, 169, 219
Imbali Stadium 250
Imperial Hotel 239
Inchbold, Robert 100
Indian Penetration Commission 39
Indian settlers 35
Indian Sports Association 247
Indians, discrimination against 40, 127–8
Indumiso College of Education 152, 155, 156
Industrial and Commercial Workers' Union (ICU) 80, 209
industry 128, 144–7
influenza epidemic *1918* 193
informal sector 37, 73–4
Ingram, J. Forsyth xxi, *xxvi*, xxix
Inkatha 74, 209, 211, 221, 222
Iron Age 16–17
Iron Man Award 256
Irvine, Brian 244
Isaacs, James Henry 168
Isandlwana 87, 106
Isivimbo Minstrels 227
Islam 175, 178
Islamia Muslim Society 178
Isolation Hospital 158
ivory 32

J

Jackson, Fred 116
Jagger Commission *1915* 153
James, Neville 100
Jamieson, Craig 244
Jamieson, Mark 255
Jan Smuts Stadium 61, 247
Jana, Aia 163
Jansen, *Dr* E.G. 206, 207, *207*, 208
Jansen, Mabel 207
Jehovah's Witnesses 169
John & Salter's 79
Johnson, Ashley 252
Joint Management Centres 220
Jolivet, *Bp.* Charles Constant 168, 180

Jonckheere, W.F. 237
Jordaan, P.W. 163
Jordan, Thomas 111
Judaism 166, 168

K

Kambule, Elijah 68
Kambule, Job 66
Karkloof forests 29, 31
Keate, *Lt.-Gov.* Robert 87, 203
Kellenbach, H *196*
Kelly, Benjamin Swete 79
Kershaw Park 60, 256
Khoisan 16
kholwa 66–9, 125, 128, 132, 133
Killarney Terrace 79–80
Kitchener, *Lord* 114
Knoessen, Paul 245
Knoessen, Ricky 245
Kok, Adam 68
De Kondschapper 208
Kombis *see* minibus taxis
Het Kongres 206
Koornhof, *Dr* P. 248
Kotze, John 98
Kritzinger's mill 210
Kruger, Paul 63, 88
Kuper, Leo 211
KwaZulu Department of Education and Culture 155
KwaZulu Government 219
KwaZulu-Natal Indaba 222, 267
KwaZulu/Natal Planning Council 155

L

labour, black 80, 125, 133–4
Lady Enchantress 63
Laite, W.J. 144
Lakhi, M.E. 184
Langalibalele 87, 88, 97, 98, 116, 174, 203
Langalibalele Rebellion 68, 107
Late Stone Age 15
Law, Peter 63
Law Faculty (University of Natal) 100
Lawrence, *Dr* Reginald F. 161
le Roux, J.J. 207
Legislative Assembly 93
Legislative Assembly buildings 48, *93*
Legislative Council 93
Leighton Street 79
Liberal Democratic Association 200
Liberal Party 199, 200, 209, 211
libraries 156
Lidgett, John 78
Lincoln Meade 5
Lindley, *Revd* Daniel 28, 59, 150, 166
Lindsay, David 79
Lindsay, Robert 78, 79
Linpark School 244–5
Lloyd, *Capt.* Walter 77
Local Affairs Committees 219, 220
Loft Company 225
London, Edward 81, 150
London, Emily 81, 150
Longmarket Girls' School 11, 154, 265
Longmarket Street *25*, *27*
Loop Street *49*, 75, *76*, 77–81, *78*, *126*, *127*, *179*
Lorimer, *Mrs* E. 233
Lotus Park 61

Louis Napoleon, *Prince Imperial* 88, 94, 116
Lowe, *Miss* 153
Lugaju kaMatomela 21
Lugsdin, A.G. 238
Luthuli, Albert 211

M

Maas, *Miss* 153
Mabhida, Moses 209, 211
Macdonald, Elizabeth 78, 182
Macfarlane, *Maj.* G.J. 116
Machibise kaMlithwa (kaMlifa) 18
Mackenzie, Precious 245
Mackeurtan, Graham 100
Maclean, *Col.* 107
Maclean, Gordon 3
Macmillan, *Prof.* R.G. 162
Macrorie House 77–8
Macrorie, *Bp.* William Kenneth 78, 107, 152,
   167
Madlenya kaMahawule 21
Maharaj, S.B. 211
Majola, A.B. 209
malaria 194–5
Malherbe, *Prof.* E.G. 157–8, *158*, 212
Mandela, Nelson 211
Mann, *Dr* Robert James *150*, 151
Mantle, Errol 244
Maqaleni Football Ground 250
Maree, Paulus 163
Margaret Rose, *Princess* 95
Marian Centre 180
Marian Indian Government-Aided School 180
Marianny, Paul 254
Marist Brothers 180
Maritz, Gerrit 36
Maritzburg and District Bowling Association
   249
Maritzburg and District Native Football
   Association 249
Maritzburg Botanic Society 62, 81
Maritzburg College xxiii, *55*, 105, 115, 151,
   151, 152, 154, 244, 245, 250
Maritzburg Comrades' Athletic and Cycling
   Club 252
Maritzburg Croquet Club 246, 259
Maritzburg District Cricket Union 248
Maritzburg Cricket Union 248
Maritzburg East Bowling Club 246
Maritzburg Golf Club 246
Maritzburg High School 152
Maritzburg High School for Girls 153
Maritzburg Indian Sports Association 247
Maritzburg Lawn Tennis Association 246
Maritzburg Rifles 106, 118
Maritzburg Turf Club 103, 104
Maritzburg West Bowling Club 246
Marjorie Pope-Ellis Weaving School 82
Market Square *xx*, 62, *119*, 121, *124*, *130*
Marquard, Johan David 79, 81, 150
Marriamen Temple 170–1
Marriott, W.E. 63
Marsh, J.V. 247
Marwick, Sybil 184
Maryvale 180
Maryvale African Primary School 180
Mason's Mill 82, 147
Mason, Arthur 98
Mason, *Miss* 153
Masterton-Smith, Phil 253
May, *Princess* 94–5
Mayor's Gardens 61
Mayor's Unemployment Distress Fund 129
Mayr, *Fr.* Franz 180

McCallum, *Sir* Henry 160
McCarthy, Cuan *245*
McConkey, W.G. 215
McDonnell, *Capt.* John 168, 179
McGlew, Jackie 244, *245*
McKenzie, Leslie 245
McLean, Roy 244, *245*
McLeod, Catherine 77–8
McLeod, Edward 77–8
McLeod, Ellen 150
Mechanic's Institute 207
Meckler, Jackie 252
Medway, Basil 244
Meester, *Prof.* J.A. 162
Merchiston School 11
Merryweather's *124*, 144
Methley family 132, 133
Methodist Church 167, 168
Methuen, *Lord* 88
Methven, Cathcart 48
Metropolitan Methodist Church *166*, 167, *167*,
   168, *168*, 169
Metropolitan Open Space System (MOSS) 5
Michaelhouse 77, 153
Middle Stone Age 15
Midlands Hospital 188
migrant labour 134
Miles, John 236–7
military police 111
Miller, Agnes 75
Miller, Henry 75
Milne, Alexander 100
Milne, Alexander John 100
Milner, *Lord* Alfred 88, 89
minibus taxis 138
Miranda-Harper Company 227
missionaries 166, 167
Missionary Oblates of Mary Immaculate 179
Mitchell, *Lady* 153
Mitchell, *Lt.-Col.* C.B.H. 106
Mitchell, *Sir* Charles 94
Mitchell, G. 62
Mitchell, John 227
Mitchell, Sonny 254
Mkhondeni 147
Mkhondeni valley 3, 5
Mkungu, *Prince* 105
Mockler, John 105
Moll, Cornelius 121, 235
Montrose 3
Moolman, Jacobus Phillipus 163
Moore, Mary 153
Morcom, William 100
Mormon Church 169
Morris, Fatty 76
mosques *170*, *171*, 178
Moss, John 81
Moss, Mary 81
Motala, *Dr* Chota 211
motor racing 245, 260, *260*
Mountain Rise 17, 42
Mountain Rise Golf Club 246
Mpophomeni 71
Mpumuza people 21
Mpushini valley 3
Msimang, Selby 143, 200, *200*, 209, 211
Msunduze River 5, 7, 8, 11, 14, 15, 16, *61*, *64*,
   124, *194*, *242*, *245*
Muller, Catharina 150
Mungal, Suthie 211
Municipal Board of Commissioners 33
Municipal Building 57, *57*, 265
Murphy, *Fr.* Thomas 168, 179
music 226–9
Muslim Students' Association 178
Muslim Youth Movement 178
Muslims 35, 175, 178
Mzimba, *Chief* 132

N

Naicker, *Mr* 211
Naidoo, G.R. 211
Naidoo, S.R. 209–11
Napac 225, 227
Napac Dance Company 229
Napier, *Sir* George 102
Natal Bank 128
Natal Bird Club 3
Natal Brewery 128, 144
Natal Buddhist Society 175
Natal Carbineers 95, 106, 110, 114–18, *115*,
   116, *117*, *118*
Natal Carbineers Veterans Association 114
Natal Carbineers' Band 160
Natal College of Education 88, 154
Natal Convention *1961* 211
Natal Cricket Association 248
Natal Education Department 156
Natal Evangelical Protestant Ladies' School
   Association (Ltd) 153
Natal Fire and Life Assurance Company 124
Natal Government Railway 114, 139
Natal Indian Congress 209, 211
Natal Indian Organization 209
Natal Law Society 98, 99, 99–100, 100, 212
Natal Light Horse 117
Natal Museum xxiii, 14, 160–2, *160*, *162*
Natal Native Congress 69
Natal Parks Board 266
Natal Parliament 93, 105
Natal Philharmonic Orchestra 226
Natal Provincial Administration 84
Natal Provincial Council 93
Natal Rifle Association 106
Natal Society 122–3, 146, 160, 257–8
Natal Society Drama Group 224, 257
Natal Society Library *xx*, 58, 156, 258
Natal Spruit Camp 127
Natal Tanning Company 128
Natal Tanning Extract Company 145
Natal Training College 88, 152
Natal University College 127, 157, *157*, 158
Natal Witness 80, 87, 99, 114, 117, 202–4, 205,
   206, 235
Natal Witness Garden Show 64, 115
Natal Womens' Hockey Association 245
Natalia Building 53, 56, *57*, 93
Die Natalier 121, 202, 235
Die Natalse Afrikaner 208
Nathan, Albert 183
Nathan, *Sir* Mathew 63
Nathan Brothers building *264*
National Convention *1908* 89, 90, 153
National Council of Women 216
National Front Party 199
National Party 198, 200, 206, 218–9
National Security Management System 220
Native Administration Standing Committee
   214
Native Administration Act 97
Native High Court *96*, 97, 98–9, 100
Natives Sports Ground 247
Natives' Representative Council 209
nature conservation 3–5, 31, 32, 266
nature reserves 3, 5
Nederduitsch Hervormde Kerk 169
Need Fund 147
Neethling, Willem 88
Nel, Elsie Hendrina 163
Nel, *Mrs* Louis 150
Nel, Philip 244
New Asylum 186
New Republic Party 198, 199
Newton, Arthur 252
Ngidi, Joe 'Axe Killer' 245
Nhlangwini people 20

Nicholson brothers 132
Nicholson, Skonk 244
Nienaber, C.J.M. 237
Nienaber, *Prof.* G.S. 162, 207, 235
Njilo people 18, 21
Nobanda kaNgwane 21
Noel, Dempsey 211
Non-European Unity Movement 211
oNonhlevu 66, 68, 69
Northdale 33, 41
Northdale Hospital 191, *191,*
Northern Park 60
Nott, Tommy 75
Nqondo people 18
Nucleus 158–9
Nurses Home 183
Nxamalala people 21
Nyamvu people 18, 21

O

O'Brien, W.J. 198
O'Hara, Isobel 82
Odams, John 185
Old Apostolic Church 168
'Old Bailey' 99
Old Deanery Ladies' School *149*, 153
Olivier, *Miss* 150
Opperman, D.J. 235, *235*
Order of Court of 1932 100
Order of the Golden Age 239
Organization of Dutch and Afrikaans
    Language Friends in Natal 207
Oribi Airport 128
Oribi Government Village 110
Oribi Military Hospital 110–11, 158
Oribi Military Hospital Association 111
Ortmann, C. 27, 29, 120, 121
Otto, Piet 29
Our Lady of Health of Vailanganni Church
    180
Outspan No. 6 39
Overpark 78
Oxenham's Bakery 80
Oxlee, Keith 244

P

P. Davis & Sons 80, *122*
P.J. Jung & Co 77
Pachonik, Carl 245
Pagel's Circus 238
Palmer, Alfred 160
Palmer, John 122
Palmer, *Dr* Mabel 212
Park Ross, *Dr* 195
Park View 78–9
Parker, M.J. 'Nettie' 215
Parkinson, *Mrs* 75
Passive Resistance Campaign 196, 211
Passive Resistance Council 211
Paton, Alan xvii, 200, 211, 212, 237
Paton, Athol 76
Paton, Wallace 48
Peacock, Peter 255
Pearce, Ernie 255
Pegging Act 39
Pelham 3
Pellissier, *Revd Dr* G.M. 63, 163, 207, 208
Pennefather, Rory 255
Pentecostal Movement 169
Pentrich 40, 41
Petrie, *Prof.* Alexander 184
Pevsner, Nicolaus 51
Philharmonic Choir 226

Philharmonic Society *see* Pietermaritzburg
    Philharmonic Society
Philip, *Dr* John 202
Phillips, H.J. 252
Phillips, Henry Lushington 98
Pietermaritzburg, general views *xviii, 1, 2, 3,
    23, 25, 27, 31, 36, 38, 39, 42*
Pietermaritzburg Agricultural Society 122–3
Pietermaritzburg Boer Society 206
Pietermaritzburg Botanical and Horticultural
    Gardens Company 60
Pietermaritzburg Chamber of Industries 216
Pietermaritzburg Choral Society 226
Pietermaritzburg Closer Union Society *91*
Pietermaritzburg Collegiate Institute 152
Pietermaritzburg Debate and Literary Society
    206
Pietermaritzburg Girls' High School *148*, 151,
    154
Pietermaritzburg Government High School 81
Pietermaritzburg Government School 150
Pietermaritzburg Irregular Horse 117
Pietermaritzburg Philharmonic Society 224,
    226, 227, 230, *230*
Pietermaritzburg Society 53, 257
Pietermaritzburg Sports Association 246
Pietermaritzburg Turf Club *see* Scottsville
    Racecourse
Pietermaritzburg Vigilance Committee 207
Pietermaritzburg Yeomanry Corps 117
Pieterse, Coenraad Lukas 163
Pillay, K.R. 171
Pine, *Lt.-Gov. Sir* Benjamin 77, 86, 87, 88, 97,
    174, 202
Piper, Dave 252
Pistorius brothers 27, 29, 52
Pistorius, C.W. 120
Pitchers' British Hotel 241
Player, Ian 255, 256
Plessislaer 41
Plessislaer Technical College 155, 156
Plowman, *Sir* George T. 137, 153–4, 162
Polak, *Mrs* M. 196
political parties 198, 199
political protest 209–11, 212
political violence 74, 218, 221–2
pollution 10, 255
Poole's Fruiterers *51*, 265
Pope-Ellis, Graeme 255, *255*, 256
Pope-Ellis, *Mrs* 62
population 3, 43
Posselt, Christiane 84
Posselt, *Revd* Carl Wilhelm 84
Post Office *55*
Presbyterian Church *xx,* 7, 56, 78, 106, *165,*
    168, 169, *197*
press freedom 205
Prestwich, *Prof.* Mark 159, *203*, 204
Pretorius, A.W. 150
Pretorius, Andries 24, 25, 88, 163
Prince Imperial *see* Louis Napoleon, *Prince
    Imperial*
Prince of Wales Hotel 241
Pringle, *Dr* John A. 161
prisoners of war *108*, 110–12
Pritchard, *Revd* 152
Progressive Federal Party 198, 199
Progressive Party 200
Provincial Council 90, 93
Publicity House *47*
pubs 241–2

Q

quarries 29
Queen Alexandra's Imperial Military Nursing
    Service 182–3
Queen Elizabeth Park 61

R

R.G. Pilditch swimming pool 247
Raadzaal *xx,* 98, *124*
Rabie, J.S.M. 206
Radebe, Joshua 226, 257
Radha-Krishna Mandir Temple 172
railway station *107, 196, 201,* 201
railways 126, 127, 128, 135–7, 139–41
rainfall 8–9, 10
Raisethorpe 41, 169
Raisethorpe High School 250
Ramakrishna Centre of South Africa 172
Rambaram, Guru 173
Ramdeen, L.T. 211
Raw and Wilkinson 124
READ 156
Red Lion Tavern 240
Reddy, Kistappa 171
regiments (list) 109
Reid, Pamela 63, 215, *215*, 216, 233
Reid's Building 265
Reid's Cabinet Works 144
religion 166–75, 178
Repsold, H.A. 150
Republic of Natalia 18, 86
responsible government 93, 108
Retief Street area 24, 26, 40, 41
Retief, Piet 24, 26
Rhodes, Jonty 244
Richards, *Revd* John 166
Ricketts, Stanley 238
rickshaws *78*, 138
Ridley, Ralph Errington 203
Rinko Cinema 238
riots 83
Robbertse, I. 163
Robinson, *Brigade Surgeon* 187
Robinson, George 252
Robinson, *Sir* John 88
Roman Catholic Church *78*, 168, 169, 179–80
Rose, F. Horace 128
Rose Innes, James 98
Rousseau, Ina *235*, 235–236
Rowe, *Miss* 153
Rowlands, *Pastor* J.F. 169
Royal Agricultural Show xxiii, 146
Royal Agricultural Society 146
Royal Artillery 103
Royal Engineers 102, 103
Royal Garrison Regiment 108
Royal Inniskilling Dragoons 108
Royal Inniskilling Fusiliers 108
Royal Natal Carbineers 110
royal visit *1947* 76, 95, *95*
Royston, William 116
Rudolph, J.B. 163
Rump, *Mr and Mrs* 75
Russell, Eleanor Ethel Mariella 95, 145, 147,
    213–16, *213*
Russell, Robert 151, 152
Russell, W.A.D. 214
Russell High School 151
Russom, John 81
Russom, Susan 81

S

Saamwerk-Unie 207, 208
Saiva Sithanthasungum of South Africa 172
Salvation Army 168
Sanathan Ved Dharam Sabha 170
Sanathanists 170
Sanders, D. 251
sanitation 72, 194
Satyagraha Campaign *see* Passive Resistance
    Campaign

Saunders, James Renault 79–80
Schaffer, E.M. 187
Schmidt, Fred 255
schools 150–156 *see also* names of individual
  schools
Science Block (University of Natal) *55, 56*
Scott's Theatre *223*, 238
Scott, Daniel Burton 77
Scott, *Lt.-Gov.* John *86*, 87, 88, 105, 152
Scottsville 3, 14, 33, 39
Scottsville Golf Course 246
Scottsville Racecourse *258*
Second World War 110–13, 117
Sefton Parry Company 225
segregation 33–43
Seme, *Dr* 209
Senate Building *93*
Sendall, W.J. 88, 204
servants 80
service organizations 257
Settlers Park 60
Seventh-Day Adventists 168
Shaka kaSenzangakhona 20
shale *6, 7, 7, 111*, 112
Shankaranand, *Swami* 173
Shaw, *Mrs* 75
Shearer, *Col.* Oswald 111, 158, 198
Shepstone, Denis Gem 158
Shepstone, 'Offy' 98, 116
Shepstone, *Sir* Theophilus 60, 64, 77, 78, 81,
  86, 87, 96, 97, 116, 174
Shepstone Lane *35*, 78
Sim, T.R. 62
Sinathing 155
Singh, T. Ramkolowan 'Tommy' 217, *217*
Sisters of the Holy Family 153
Sisters of the Society of St. John the Divine 153
Siva Nyana Sabha 171–2
Slangspruit 43
Smit, Erasmus 24, 163, 166
Smith, Darryl 245
Smith, *Sir* Harry 86
Smith, Jesse 29
Smith, *Revd* John 168
Smith, *Maj.* Thomas Charlton 102
Smithwick, John 186
Smuts, *Gen.* Jan 63, 95
Smuts, Tobias 121
Smythe, Charles 88, 132–3, 152
Smythe, *Sgt.* Quentin 117–18
Smythe family 132, 133
Sobantu Community Council 84
Sobantu Village 11, 39, *39*, 40, 41, 42–3, 82–4,
  83, 155, 169, 214, 215, 219–20
soils 7–8
Soldiers' Club 113
Soobiah, Joe 209
South African Academy 207
South African Association of University
  Women 216
South African Council of Sport 248, 250
South African Cricket Board 248
South African Defence Force 110, 218
South African Liberal Association 200
South African Medical Corps 111
South African Native Congress 209
South African Party 206
South African Women's Auxiliary Services
  215
Spencer, Amelia 75
Spencer family 75–6
Spiritualist Church 168
sport 61, 108, 244–5, 246–7, 257
sports facilities 61, 246–7
Sri Sathya Sai Baba Centre 173
Sri Siva Soobramoniar Temple 170, *171*
Sri Vishnu Temple 170, *172*
St. Alphege's Church 169

St. Andrew's Church 167, 168
St. Anne's Diocesan College 77, 152–3
St. Anne's Hospital 168
St. Anthony's Church 180
St. Anthony's Primary Day School 180
St. Charles College 180, 244–5
St. Charles Grammar School 179, 180
St. David's Church 169
St. George, *Sir* Theophilus, 114
St. George's Garrison Church 105, 108
St. Joan of Arc Church 168, 180
St. John's Church 168, 169
St. John's Diocesan High School for Girls 153
St. Luke's Church 167, 169
St. Mark's Church 79, 167
St. Mary's Church (Anglican) 93, 167, 169
St. Mary's Church (Roman Catholic) 168, 169,
  170, 179
St. Mary's Diocesan College 152, 153
St. Peter's Cathedral 7, 29, 57, 167
St. Saviour's Cathedral 79, 167, 174, *174*
Stacey, Ruby 75
Stacey, Winnie 75
Stals, *Dr* A.J. 158
Standard Bank 128
Stanger, *Dr* William 63, 77, 86, 88, 123
Star and Garter Hotel *241*
state of emergency *1986* 211
Statham, Francis Reginald 204
Steel, *Lady* Barbara Joanna 214
Stevenson, *Dr* R.E. 183
Stewart-Dunkerley, *Lt.-Col.* 113
Stirling, John 244
Stock Exchange 126
Stodel, Jack 251
Stone Age 14–16
Stone, Ron 244
Stott, Clement Horner 79
Strachan, T.G. 198
Strathallan *20*, 56
Street-Wilson, William 49, 54
Sukuma High School 156
Sunni Muslims 178
Supreme Court 48, 96–8, 98–9, 99, 100, 123
Supreme Court building 56, 57, 93, *96*, 106,
  263, 265
Sutherland, *Dr* Peter 182
Sutton family 132, 133
Sutton, George 133
Swartkop forest 29
Swartkop location 21, 71, 131, 132 *see also*
  Vulindlela
Symons Centre *265*
synagogue 168

T

Tabligh Jamaat 178
Tarr, Brian 63
Tatham Art Gallery 231–4, 263
Tatham Memorial Ground 247, 250
Tatham, Ada 231
Tatham, F.S. 62
Tatham, Frederick 100
Tatlow, A.H. xxv
Templeton, Bob 255
Terry, Gwladys *215*, 216
Terry, Joseph 81
Terry Street 81
Thanet House School *149*, 153
theatre 225 *see also* amateur dramatics
Thembu people 20
Thetheleku, *Chief* 97, *130*, 132
Thomson, George 79
Thresh, George 239
Thresh, *Mrs* George, 231
Thuli paramountcy 18

Tidmarsh, *Mr* 62
timber 29–31
Tjale, Hosea *253*
Tocknell, Mike 255
Todd, Errol 244
Toerien, Pieter 225
Tomlinson, *Maj.* R.C. 117
Torch Committee 204
Town Council 54 *see also* City Council
Town End House 81
Town Hill Hospital 185, 186–8, *187*
Town Offices, 54, *54*
trade unions 74, 221
Trading and Occupation of Land (Transvaal
  and Natal) Restriction Act No.35 of *1943* 39
trails 5
trams 39, 138, 157
transport 39, 41, 41–2, 72, 120, 122, 123, 125,
  126, 127, 128, 135–41, 138, 267
trees 59–60, *60–61*, 61–2, 62, 63, *63*
Trekkers *see* Voortrekkers
Tricameral Parliament 93
Trust Bank Building 56
Tully, J. Collingwood 51, 157
Turnbull, John William 80
typhoid 193–4

U

Ukulinga Experimental Farm 158
Umgeni Rangers 117
Umgeni Waterfall Institution 188
Umgungundhlovu 44
Umhlatuzana Shelter 15
Umgeni Valley Nature Reserve 17
Umvoti Mounted Rifles 95, 115
Umsinduzi River, *see* Msunduze River
unemployment 129, 134, *134*, 145
Union *1910* 89, 90, 92, 109, 204
United Churches 169
United Democratic Front (UDF) 74, 209, 211,
  221, 222
United Party 198, 199
University Music Society 229
University Dramatic Society 224–5
University of Natal 156, 157–9, *158, 159*, 212,
  244, 253
University of South Africa 157
unrest *see* political violence
Uplands High School 153
Urban Areas Act *1923* 40
Urquhart, *Mrs* 76
Usherwood, Emma Jane 77

V

van der Bijl, Vincent 244
van Gijlswijk, *Abp.* 113
van Heerden, Izak 244
van Rensburg, Mike 244
Vanderplank, John 121
Veda Dharma Sabha 173
Vedalankar, *Pandit* Nardev 173
Vedanta Satsang Society 173
Vedic Mandir 173
vegetation 3, 29
Vermeulen, H.J. 237
Victoria, *Princess* 95
Victoria Bar 240
Victoria Bowling Club 246
Victoria Club *55*, 77, *95*, 123, 207, 258
Victoria suspension bridge 114, *124*
Vigilance Committee 92
vigilantes 211, 221, 222
Visagie, C. 121
Visagie's mill 77, *144*

Vishnu Temple 171
Volksraad 93, 102
Voortrekker Museum 28, 51, 156, 163–164, *164*
Voortrekker School 154
Die Voortrekker 208
Voortrekkers 3, 16, 21, 24–7, 29, 31–2, 33, 55, 59, 63, 64, 86, 102–3, 150, 163–4, *208*
Vorster, B. 208
Vorster, Piet 253, 256
Vulindlela *42*, 71–4, *72*, 219

W

Wadley Stadium 250
Walker, Arthur 96
Wanderers Basketball Club 244
Warren, *Dr* Ernest 160–1, 162
water supply 72, 103–4
Waterhouse, *Revd* S. 167
Waterloo Bar 105
Watson, William 107
Watt, Johanna Catherine 214
Webber, W.T. 198
Weight, Lindsay 253
Welch, J.W. 123, 125
Welch, Martha 184
Welfare (Sports) Association 247
Wembley 39, 43

Wesleyan Church 166
Wesleyan Missionary society 66, 166
Wesleyan-Methodist Church 153
West, *Revd* F.G. 168
West, *Lt.-Gov.* Martin 77, 86, 104, 202, 241
Westbury 81
Westgate 41, 43
Wheeler, *Mr* 76
Wheeler, Napoleon 60
Whitwell, *Lt.-Col.* Robert 231, 232
Williamson, Arthur Faure 100
Williamson, *Maj.* 77
Willowton 41, 42, 147
Wilson, John Dove 99, 100
Winder, George 77
Winston Churchill Theatre 257
Winterskloof 43
Witness Lane 80
Wolseley, Sir Garnet 87, 88, 107, 114, 203, 204
Women's Auxiliary Army Service 111
Women's Enfranchisement Association of the Union 214
Women's Enfranchisement league 214
Wood, *Sir* Evelyn 94
Wood, Medley 62
Wood, 'Timber' 254
Woodburn Stadium 250
Woodland Sports Centre 247
Woodlands 41
Woods, Sarah Ann 214
Woods, *Dr* W.J. 193

Woolpack Hotel 240
Wushe people 18
Wykeham School 153
Wylie Park 61

Y

Yardley, *Capt.* 107
Yenge kaNontshiza 21
Yengwa, M.B. 209
Yeomanry Corps 114
YMCA Building *46*
YMCA Comets 244
Yobeni people 18
York, *Duchess of* 88, 94
York, *Duke of* 88, 94
Young Men's Christian Association (YMCA) 207

Z

Zeederberg, J.C. 77, 80
Zeederberg brothers 120
Zizi people 20
Zulu people 18–20, 21
Zwide kaLanga 20